Inscribed Athenian Laws and Decrees
352/1–322/1 BC

Brill Studies in Greek and Roman Epigraphy

The titles published in this series are listed at brill.nl/bsgre

Inscribed Athenian Laws and Decrees 352/1–322/1 BC

Epigraphical Essays

By

Stephen Lambert

BRILL

LEIDEN • BOSTON
2012

Cover illustrations: (Front) Athenian Assembly decree of 346/5 BC honouring Dioskourides of Abdera and his brothers (*IG* II^3 1, 302, photo courtesy of the Epigraphical Museum, Athens) (Back) Dedication to Hephaistos by the Athenian Council of 343/2 BC and beginning of the Council's decree honouring Phanodemos of Thymaitadai as the best speaker in the Council in the ninth prytany (*IG* II^3 1, 306, photo courtesy of the Epigraphical Museum, Athens).

This book is printed on acid-free paper.

Library of Congress Cataloging-in-Publication Data

Lambert, S. D., 1960–
Inscribed Athenian laws and decrees 352/1–322/1 BC / epigraphical essays by Stephen Lambert.
p. cm. — (Brill's Studies in Greek and Roman Epigraphy)
Includes bibliographical references and index.
ISBN 978-90-04-20931-2 (hardback : alk. paper)
1. Law, Greek—Sources. 2. Law—Greece—Athens—Sources. 3. Law—Greece—Athens—History—To 1500. 4. Athens (Greece)—Politics and government. 5. Greece—Politics and government—To 146 B.C. I. Title.

KL4115.A75L36 2012
340.5'38—dc23

2011043461

ISSN 1876-2557
ISBN 978 90 04 20931 2 (hardback)
ISBN 978 90 04 22852 8 (e-book)

PRINTED BY DRUKKERIJ WILCO B.V. - AMERSFOORT, THE NETHERLANDS

CONTENTS

PART C

CHRONOLOGY

ACKNOWLEDGEMENTS

The publication of fascicule 2 of *IG* II³ 1 and this collection of associated prolegomena mark the end of the epigraphical phase of my work on the inscribed laws and decrees of Athens, 352/1–322/1 BC. Begun in 1999, the work was substantially complete by 2005. Since then obstacles various in shape and size have strewn the path, but now that the journey is done, I am less mindful of them than I am of the many debts of gratitude I owe to the individuals and institutions who have helped along the way.

First and foremost, when working on the third edition of a great epigraphical corpus, one is acutely aware that one's steps are guided by the kindly light shone by the labour of one's predecessors. Numerous scholars have made lasting contributions to the epigraphy of these 282 inscriptions in the 250 years since the first was published by P.M. Paciaudi in 1761 (see chapter 8); and that includes all whom I may mention from time to time in the following pages in disagreement. It is a pleasure to acknowledge here the pioneering work of the early Greek scholars, in particular Kyriakos Pittakis, Alexandros Rangabé and Stephanos A. Koumanoudes, the heroic labours of Johannes Kirchner, editor of the second edition of *IG* II, and the invaluable work of Benjamin Meritt and the team of epigraphists responsible for publishing the inscriptions from the Agora excavations. The contributions of two scholars of past generations, however, are outstanding in quality and quantity: Ulrich Köhler, editor of the first edition of *IG* II, and Adolf Wilhelm, who was responsible for much of the best work in the second edition. Both were brilliant scholars, but I rate Köhler's contribution more highly, for he achieved the greatest transformation in the quality of this corpus, introducing order and light, and was a particularly good judge of the point at which restoration of text not preserved on the stone ceases to be legitimate and helpful and becomes speculative and potentially misleading.

I gladly reiterate here my warm thanks to the many scholars of the present generation whose contributions are acknowledged in the individual papers collected in this volume. To these I add now three further grateful acknowledgements: to Emmanuel Vintiadis and Peter Liddel, who rendered invaluable assistance in the early years, particularly in researching older bibliography; to Klaus Hallof and Angelos Matthaiou for their important contributions in the later stages; for moral support to Ron Stroud, especially in the earlier stages, and, especially in the later stages, to Robin Osborne and above all to Peter Rhodes. It is also a pleasure to acknowledge here the tremendous value, for this project and for Attic epigraphy more broadly, of the contribution made by Stephen Tracy's pioneering work on epigraphical hands.

One of the principles underlying all good epigraphical corpus work is, where practicable, comprehensive autopsy of the stones, and this requires the collaboration of many museums. I have great pleasure in reiterating here the thanks expressed in the individual papers to all the museums I have visited in the course of this work, and their staffs, who have invariably been courteous, friendly and helpful. To these I add now my thanks to the staff of the British Museum for facilitating access in 2010 to inv. no. 773 (*IG* II^3 1, 395). Because of the number of inscriptions discovered in the Agora and the even larger number stored in the Epigraphical Museum at Athens, I owe special debts of thanks to John Camp and the staff of the Agora excavations, and above all to the staff of the Epigraphical Museum and its successive Directors, and most especially, since most of the work was done during his Directorship, to Charalambos Kritzas.

Excellent libraries are also indispensable to good epigraphy. For the most part the library work was done at the British School at Athens in 1999–2004, and I take this opportunity to thank successive Directors and staff, and Penny Wilson, the librarian, for their unstinting support. In the very last stages of the work, in 2009–2011, I was also privileged to enjoy, as Visiting Fellow of Utrecht University, the library and the other incomparable facilities of the Fondation Hardt, in Vandoeuvres, Geneva, and I am extremely grateful to Monica Brunner, Heidi del Lago and the other staff who make visits there so agreeable. These visits were facilitated by my happy collaboration with Josine Blok on her project on religion and citizenship in Athens, and I am grateful to her too for much support of many kinds.

Serious epigraphy is a fundamentally important business, but it is also a laborious one and, unlike my predecessor as British editor of an Attic IG, David Lewis, editor of *IG* I^3, I do not hold a University post in epigraphy. In these circumstances this work would not have been completed had I not been prepared to do a significant proportion of it in my own time and at my own expense. Nevertheless, it would also have been impossible without financial support. I gratefully acknowledge the contribution of the UK Arts and Humanities Research Board, who funded my work part-time (50%) between 1999 and 2004 on a project for which the grant-holder was John Davies (for whose patience over the long haul I am very grateful); and the Packard Humanities Institute, which also supported my work between 1999 and 2005. Some of the initial groundwork was laid at the University of Heidelberg, where I was privileged to enjoy a Humboldt Fellowship for parts of the two years 1999–2001, at the kind invitation of Angelos Chaniotis.

Finally I owe four debts of gratitude specific to this volume: to Adele Scafuro, for proposing it; to Benjamin Millis and Evelyn van 't Wout for expert help in compiling the indices; to the original publishers of the papers for permission to reprint them here: to Habelt-Verlag of Bonn for chapters I–XI and XIII; to the Canadian Institute in Greece for chapter XII; to the Greek Epigraphical Society for chapters XIV, XV and XVIII; to Nicholas Sekunda and the Institute of Archaeology, Gdańsk University, for chapter XVI; and to Éditions Ausonius of Bordeaux for chapter XVII; and to the Epigraphical Museum, Athens, for supplying from their archive the photographs reproduced on the cover.

PREFACE

As soon as I began work on the new edition of the inscribed laws and decrees of Athens, 352/1–322/1 BC (*IG* II^3 Part 1, fascicule 2) in 1999, it became clear to me that it would be desirable to publish a series of prolegomena. The pages of *IG*, with its tradition of extremely concise presentation of epigraphical texts, were not the place to describe, justify and explain in adequate depth and detail the epigraphical innovations, such as new readings and restorations, joins and datings, and the fresh interpretative ideas that I had to propose (some my own, some kindly communicated to me by colleagues); and it seemed proper to expose these innovations and ideas to open scrutiny before they became incorporated in a Corpus which ought ideally to reflect not so much the private opinions of any individual as a collective scholarly view.

The result was the 18 papers gathered in this volume. Originally published between 2000 and 2010 in the *Zeitschrift für Papyrologie und Epigraphik*, conference proceedings, commemorative volumes and Festschriften, they are arranged here into three parts. Part A is a connected series of five papers, a catalogue of the inscriptions arranged thematically, with bibliography, notes on some of the results of my work on individual texts and some discussion of historical context and physical features of the stones. Part B consists of papers reporting findings relating to inscriptions individually or in small groups. Some of these also treat inscriptions outside my Corpus fascicule; for example, one of the papers proposes new restorations of names in inscriptions both in my Corpus and outside it; another reports the results of a visit to the University Museum, Oxford Mississippi, where I studied not only the one inscription there that belongs in my Corpus, but also other Greek inscriptions in the collection. Though most of the papers in this Part are primarily epigraphical in focus, most also contain some discussion of historical context, and two of the later ones, on honorific decrees relating to the theatre and on inter-state treaties, are quite strongly historical in emphasis. Part C contains a single paper on the chronology of Athens in this period, a subject on which the prescripts of inscribed laws and decrees supply most of the evidence and which is in turn fundamental to the restoration of incompletely preserved prescripts.

My hope that the publication of prolegomena would stimulate further progress in the epigraphy of these texts has been realised. Select addenda and corrigenda to 2007 are at pp. 208–214, and I include at the end of this volume a note of the more important further improvements that have been achieved since 2007.

Some readers will consult this collection in pursuit of a reference in *IG* or elsewhere to one of the original papers, and to assist them an indication of the original page numbers has been embedded in the reprinted texts. (A vertical line marks the end of the original page-number printed in the margin alongside it.) Indices and concordances, including the new *IG* numbers, have been included to assist those searching for discussions of specific inscriptions. The opportunity of re-publication has been taken silently to correct some typographical errors in the original papers.

Photographs of inscriptions were included in the original papers only where no photograph had previously been published. That gap in the literature has now been filled, and a complete set of photographs is now readily accessible in the *IG* fascicule itself. It has therefore been decided not to reproduce the photographs once again in this volume.

English translations of the inscriptions are being made available on-line.

PART A

MAIN SERIES

CHAPTER ONE

ATHENIAN STATE LAWS AND DECREES 352/1–322/1 I DECREES HONOURING ATHENIANS*[1]

This is the first of a series of articles on categories of inscribed Athenian state laws and decrees, 352/1–322/1. They are intended

* This chapter was previously published in *Zeitschrift für Papyrologie und Epigraphik* 150 (2004), 85–120.

[1] I am very grateful to the following scholars for their help in the preparation of this article: Sean Byrne, Jaime Curbera, Malcolm Errington, Simone Follet, Christian Habicht, Klaus Hallof, Sally Humphreys, Charalambos Kritzas, Angelos Matthaiou, John Morgan, Robert Parker, Peter Rhodes, Ronald Stroud, Leslie Threatte and Stephen Tracy. I alone am responsible for remaining flaws. Charalambos Kritzas and John Camp kindly facilitated access to inscriptions in the Epigraphical Museum and the Agora. I thank Charalambos Kritzas also for supplying the photographs of inscriptions in the EM and Klaus Hallof for the images of the squeeze in the IG archives at the Berlin Academy reproduced at Fig. 8. Wherever possible, I have read every letter of every inscription at autopsy. I have also examined squeezes (principally those in Berlin, Oxford and Princeton), photographs and, where this seemed likely to be fruitful, early transcripts. Following the principles that have been adopted for *IG* II^3, where an inscription can not be dated precisely and the possible dates span the periods of more than one fascicle, it has normally been allocated according to the highest date in the range. Accordingly some decrees that might date to 352/1–322/1 are not included here and some inscriptions that are included might not date to within this period. Some very fragmentary items that might have honoured Athenians will be listed in *Ath. State* III. The following abbreviations are used:
Agora XV: B.D. Meritt and J.S. Traill edd., *The Athenian Agora. Vol. XV. Inscriptions: the Athenian Councillors* (Princeton, 1974);
Agora XVI: A.G. Woodhead ed., *The Athenian Agora. Vol. XVI. Inscriptions: the Decrees* (Princeton, 1997);
APF: J.K. Davies, *Athenian Propertied Families 600–300 BC* (Oxford, 1971);
Ath. State I–III: articles in the present series;
Develin, *AO*: R. Develin, *Athenian Officials 684–321 BC* (Cambridge, 1989);
Faraguna, *Atene*: M. Faraguna, *Atene nell' età di Alessandro* (Rome, 1992);
Gauthier, *Bienfaiteurs*: Ph. Gauthier, *Les cités grecques et leurs bienfaiteurs* (Paris, 1985);
Henry, *Honours*: A.S. Henry, *Honours and Privileges in Athenian Decrees* (Hildesheim, 1983);
Henry, *Prescripts*: A.S. Henry, *The Prescripts of Athenian Decrees* (Leiden, 1977);
Humphreys, *Strangeness*: S.C. Humphreys, *The Strangeness of Gods* (Oxford, 2004);
IOrop: B. Petrakos, Ἐπιγραφὲς τοῦ Ὠρώπου (Athens, 1997);
IRham: B. Petrakos, Ὁ δῆμος τοῦ Ῥαμνοῦντος. *Vol. II*, οἱ Ἐπιγραφές (Athens, 1999);
Knoepfler, *Eretria XI*: D. Knoepfler, *Eretria XI. Décrets érétriens de proxénie et citoyenneté* (Lausanne, 2001);
Lettered Attica: D. Jordan and J. Traill edd., *Lettered Attica. A Day of Attic Inscriptions, Proceedings of the Athens Symposium, 8 March 2000* (Publications of Canadian Institute at Athens, no. 3; 2003);

as prolegomena to *IG* II[3] fascicle 2[2] and have a threefold purpose:

(a) to make available photographs of inscriptions of which none has been published previously;
(b) to discuss new textual and occasionally contextual points more fully than is possible within the constraints of a concise corpus format;
85 (c) to facilitate historical research. |

Athens began regularly inscribing decrees honouring its own citizens in the 340s.[3] The few known cases from before this are exceptional. Earlier in the 4th century the city had awarded high honours to the generals Konon, Iphikrates, Chabrias and Timotheos.[4] None of the decrees survives, but at least in the case of Konon it seems that it was inscribed, for at XX 69 Demosthenes quotes from "the stele" (ἐν τῇ στήλῃ γέγραπται): "ἐπειδὴ Κόνων" φησὶν "ἠλευθέρωσε τοὺς Ἀθηναίων συμμάχους". The honours included *ateleia* and a bronze statue. At XX 70 he has the decrees for Konon read out (the texts are not preserved in the manuscripts). At XX 86 he has the decrees

---

LGPN II: M.J. Osborne and S.G. Byrne edd., *A Lexicon of Greek Personal Names. Vol. II. Attica* (Oxford, 1994);
Meritt, *Ath. Year*: B.D. Meritt, *The Athenian Year* (Berkeley, 1961);
Mikalson, *Calendar*: J.D. Mikalson, *The Sacred and Civil Calendar of the Athenian Year* (Princeton, 1975);
PAA: J.S. Traill ed., *Persons of Ancient Athens* (Toronto, 1994–);
Prakt. Wilhelm: A.P. Matthaiou ed., Ἀττικαὶ ἐπιγραφαί, Πρακτικὰ Συμποσίου εἰς μνήμην *Adolf Wilhelm* (Athens, 2004);
Pritchett-Neugebauer: W.K. Pritchett and O. Neugebauer, *The Calendars of Athens* (Cambridge Mass., 1947);
Rationes: S.D. Lambert, *Rationes Centesimarum* (Amsterdam, 1997);
Rhodes, *Boule*: P.J. Rhodes, *The Athenian Boule* (Oxford, 1972, rev. 1985);
RO: P.J. Rhodes and R. Osborne, *Greek Historical Inscriptions 404–323 BC* (Oxford, 2003);
Schwenk: C.J. Schwenk, *Athens in the Age of Alexander* (Chicago, 1985);
Threatte: L. Threatte, *The Grammar of Attic Inscriptions* (Berlin, I 1980, II 1996);
Tracy, *ADT*: S.V. Tracy, *Athenian Democracy in Transition* (Berkeley, 1995);
V.-Terzi: C. Veligianni-Terzi, *Wertbegriffe in den attischen Ehrendekreten der klassischen Zeit* (Stuttgart, 1997);
Whitehead, *Demes*: D. Whitehead, *The Demes of Attica* (Princeton, 1986).

[2] The fascicle will contain c. 250 texts.

[3] No. 18, passed in 346/5 and honouring a man who held office in 347/6, is the earliest dated example in the series. In general on the history of honorific practice in Athens and elsewhere in Greece see Gauthier, *Bienfaiteurs*; on Athens see recently also I. Kralli, *Archaiognosia* 10 (1999–2000), 133–62.

[4] On the award of the *megistai timai* in the 5th and early 4th centuries see Gauthier, *Bienfaiteurs*, 24–8 and 92–103; *RO* notes to 8 and 22.

for Chabrias read out, though he does not specify in this case that they were inscribed. The unusualness of these honours is confirmed by the epigraphical record, for of the over 250 extant decrees of the period 403–352 inscribed at the initiative of the state, there is not one the main purpose of which is to honour an Athenian.[5] *Agora* XVI 52, for Eukles, herald of the Council and People, supporter of democracy and freedom in 403, and for his son Philokles, appointed to the same office, is probably not an exception, since the decrees lack the customary clause providing for their inscription and were perhaps set up at private initiative and expense.[6]

From these cases, from other allusions in the orators[7] and from the evidence of inscribed dedications made by officials honoured by the Council and/or People,[8] it is clear that decrees honouring Athenians were not a wholly new phenomenon in the 340s; it was the regular

[5] Athenian envoys are quite commonly praised and invited to dinner (δεῖπνον, the term normally used for Athenians) in the *prytaneion* in decrees dealing with diplomatic matters (e.g. for envoys returning from Mytilene in 368/7, *IG* II² 107 = *RO* 31, 24–6) but they are not usually named and the honour is incidental to the decree's main purpose. Often it was patently part of the intention in such cases to enable the envoys to participate in the hospitality (ξένια, the term used for foreigners) offered to visiting foreign diplomats (at *IG* II² 107, 26–30, to the representatives of the Lesbian cities at the allied Council). It is also probably in a diplomatic context that one should understand the invitation to δεῖπνον in *IG* II² 70 of c. 390–378, extended to three Athenians who had apparently been made citizens of Phokis (cf. Develin, *AO* 229). The unusual *IG* II² 366 = Schwenk 80 (archon Kephisodoros), inscribed (perhaps at private initiative) in a crown on a base, may date to 366/5 rather than 323/2 (proposer with name only would be anomalous in 323/2, cf. Henry, *Prescripts*, 43). The honorand is also invited to δεῖπνον, so might be an Athenian, but might as easily be a naturalised foreigner (commonly recipients of invitations to δεῖπνον, e.g. *IG* II² 226, 26–8) or a foreigner exceptionally invited to δεῖπνον (as e.g. Lapyris of Kleonai, *IG* II² 365b, 9–11, of 323/2, cf. P.J. Rhodes, *ZPE* 72 (1984), 193–9). *IG* II² 171, honouring Artikleides (possibly an Athenian), is dated to before 353/2 in *IG* II² but may rather date to 335 or later (see *Ath. State* III). *IG* II² 143 (cf. *SEG* XXXIV 63) includes a list of Athenians honoured preceded by some highly fragmentary text. This appears to include wording reminiscent of a decree, perhaps a quotation from a decree, but though it was included in *IG* II² among the decrees, it might more appropriately be classified as a dedication.

[6] Support for the democracy in the crisis of 403 may have been a factor influencing the decision to inscribe in this case. The decree of Theozotides, which provided for the sons of citizens who had died fighting for democracy in 404–403, was also inscribed (*SEG* XXVIII 46). Though not explicitly an honorific decree in form, it was implicitly honorific in intention.

[7] E.g. Demosthenes' claim that he had frequently been crowned by the People (XVIII 83, 120, 222, 257).

[8] See for example the first thirty or so inscriptions in *Agora* XV. Council prytanies had been honoured since the 5th century, but the relevant decrees began to be inscribed regularly only after 307 (cf. *Agora* XV p. 2). No. 4 and, if it is genuine, no. 8 are apparent early forerunners. The series of dated dedications by other officials

inscribing of the decrees by the city that was new. It is tempting to ascribe the development in part to an increased inwardness of political focus consequent upon Athens' reduced international standing after Chaironeia. This may have been a contributing factor after 338, but it is notable that the series begins a decade earlier, when Athens was still fully and vigorously engaged on the international scene. Probably more significant was the developing culture of the written word in the activities of the polis, which reached its zenith in the Lykourgan period, epigraphically the most intensely documented in Athenian history as regards the number and variety of inscriptions produced by the polis and its organs and subgroups; and also in their preoccupation with administrative detail. The routine honouring of officials by
86 inscriptions was the product of an administrative culture which | was becoming increasingly epigraphic, but also in a wider sense more literate and more bureaucratically developed. Indeed it is perhaps significant in this regard that secretaries—officials concerned with the writing up of both epigraphic and other types of documents—feature prominently among the early honorands. Athenian political culture was also intensely timocratic, however, and it is arguably more surprising that decrees honouring Athenians had not been routinely inscribed before the 340s than that they began being inscribed then. The practice was perhaps facilitated by new legislation or at least new financial arrangements (crowns, sacrifices and inscriptions were a budgetary expense which required legal provision).[9] It may also be relevant that the tribes had long been inscribing decrees honouring Athenians (usually their own members) and this may have generated pressure for the polis to do the same.[10]

---

stating explicitly that they had been crowned by the Council and People begins in the 350s (e.g. *SEG* XXI 668, taxiarchs of 356/5; *IG* II^2 2821, δήμου συλλογῆς of 351/0).

[9] Note in this respect the early item in the series, no. 3, where the award of crowns required a retrospective amendment to the law to authorise the expenditure. Cf. M.H. Hansen, *GRBS* 20 (1979), 39–43.

[10] See e.g. *IG* II^2 1138–41. Honorific decrees of other subgroups of the polis, however, are rare before the middle of the fourth cent. Most of those inscribed by demes date to the second half of the century (see the list at Whitehead, *Demes*, 374–93). State decrees honouring Athenians seem often, perhaps normally, to have been awarded at the initiative of the honorand. Cf. Ath. Pol. XLVI 1 (on awards for the Council). In several cases this is implicit in the wording of the decrees, which may refer to the honorand's statement or report as the basis of the award (the earliest dated example is no. 20 of 337/6) or grant the official the right to seek honours on a later occasion (e.g. no. 5, 30–32). We can not infer from the absence of such wording in other cases that the honorand's initiative was lacking, since its inclusion may have been at the

All the decrees listed below honoured Athenians as holders of a state office or for analogous activities, never (at least explicitly) for any distinction they may have enjoyed as private citizens. In this period the honorands fall into three main (overlapping) categories: (A) councillors, Council officials and secretaries; (B) priests and other officials whose duties were primarily religious; and (C) those honoured for services in connection with the Amphiaraion in Oropos. Under (D) are grouped those whose office is unknown or who do not fall into any of the other categories. (E) and (F) are not self-standing state decrees and will not be in fascicle 2 of *IG* II^3, but are included here for completeness.[11]

The reference section of the table lists key bibliography since *IG* II^2. Other items relevant to the text can be traced via the references given or the notes. New points are set out in footnotes or in longer notes following the tables (indicated by a star against the number in column 1). "(ph.)" indicates a published photograph; in such cases I do not usually publish a new photograph here. Column 4 of the table gives the name of the honorand and the office held, where known. New readings or restorations of names and relevant new prosopographical information are set out in the notes. For the rest, data on the individuals can be traced via the bibliography given or via *LGPN*, *APF* and *PAA*. Only one man appears more than once as honorand, Phanodemos son of Diyllos of Thymaitadai, the Atthidographer (*FGH* 325), honorand of no. 1 decree 3, sole honorand of no. 16 and first honorand of no. 17. He was also proposer of no. 1, decree 2, of *IOrop* 296 honouring the god Amphiaraos (see introduction to section C) and was first on the list of contributors from outside the Council on no. 6 (l. 19). That he should be a figure who was (or was to become, cf. Humphreys, *Strangeness*, 102 n. 61) best known for his literary work adds a further dimension to the "literate" quality of this type of inscribed decree in its early phase. One also suspects that the character of his work as a specialist in cult placed him outside the political fray and made him an uncontroversial candidate for honours.[12] At any rate political anonymity

choice of the drafter. Some honours, however, were awarded as the result of a competition (explicitly for Phanodemos as a councillor at no. 1, decree 3). Cf. Gauthier, *Bienfaiteurs*, 112–120.

[11] An analysis of these categories and their development after 321 would be fruitful, but lies beyond the scope of this article.

[12] Cf. Jacoby, introduction to *FGH* 325, pp. 172–3. Phanodemos' cultic interests are apparent from his literary work, as well as the epigraphical record. The strong

is something Phanodemos shares with nearly all the honorands in the list below (the general Diotimos, perhaps honoured by no. 21, might be an exception, but the text is very fragmentary and the restoration of
87 his name uncertain). There were, | it seems, a few decrees granting high honours to prominent Athenian political figures of this period,[13] but they were either not inscribed, or the stones have not been found.

The final column of the table lists the honours awarded:[14] normally a crown; occasionally with additional provision for sacrifice, with or without a dedication (cf. note on no. 1). In every case where the decree is erected at the initiative of the state and the relevant information is preserved the crown was of gold.[15] Foliage (θαλλοῦ) crowns were awarded to some foreigners at this period, but no. 27 (restored) and no. 28 are the only such awards to Athenians. It is unlikely to be coincidental that in both cases the monuments were erected at the initiative of the honorands or of the relevant tribe (Kekropis). We may infer that, when foliage crowns were awarded to Athenians at this period, the relevant decrees were not usually inscribed.

At this period the price of gold crowns is usually (but not always) specified in the decree. For both citizens and non-citizens they were of 500 or 1,000 drachmas (cf. Henry, *Honours*, 24–5; other values provided for in no. 29, but that was not itself an honorific decree). It is a possible implication of the decrees listed below (especially no. 1) that the Council was only entitled to award 500 dr. crowns to Athenians and that 1,000 dr. crowns required an Assembly decree, but there is insufficient evidence to establish that this was a definite rule.

---

flavour of local patriotism in his Atthis (cf. Jacoby, p. 173) would also doubtless have recommended him as a candidate for honours. Apart from the Atthis, he wrote about the island Ikos and served with other prominent Athenians on a Pythais, probably in 326 (*Syll.*^{3} 296, with R. Parker, *Athenian Religion* [Oxford, 1996], 247). Phanodemos patently had much in common with Lykourgos, but there is no evidence directly linking the two men.

[13] E.g. Demades (Gauthier, *Bienfaiteurs*, 109–10; P. Brun, *L'orateur Démade* [Bordeaux, 2000], 78–83); Euboulos (Hyp. F104–106 Jensen, with Gauthier, 107). On the *megistai timai* in hellenistic Athens see also Kralli [n. 3].

[14] In general, Athenians could not be crowned for their tenure of office until they had rendered their accounts (*euthynai*) and this is reflected in the wording of decrees. See C. Veligianni, *Hellenika* 40 (1989), 239–56.

[15] In general on crown types see Henry, *Honours*, 22–42.

A. *Decrees honouring councillors, Council officials and secretaries*

	Date	Reference	Honorand	Honour	
1*	343/2[16]	*IG* II^{2} 223 + Add. p. 659. *Syll.*^{3} 227. *Agora* XV 34 (C only). Gauthier, *Bienfaiteurs*, 114–8. V.-Terzi, B5.	1. Council in office for its work at City Dionysia (B8–10) Council decrees: 2. provides inter alia for inscribing of 1 (B1–7) 3. honours Phanodemos son of Diyllos of Thymaitadai (councillor) (A4–16) 4. honours Eudoxos son of Theangelos of Sypalettos (in charge of Council administration) (B11–17) 5. same as 4 (C1–16)	1. 500 dr. c(rown) + 50 dr. for sacrifice 3. 500 dr. c (+ *probouleuma* proposing that Assembly awards 1,000 dr. c) 4. 500 dr. c (publicly funded) 5. 500 dr. c (privately funded by councillors)	
2*	337/6? pryt. 10	E. Schweigert, *Hesp.* 7 (1938), 292–4 no. 19 (ph.). Schwenk 9 (*SEG* XXXV 64). Tracy, *ADT* 78. V.-Terzi, B7.	An official in office, perhaps Chairestratos son of Ameinias of Acharnai, prytany secretary of 337/6	c |	88
3*	1. 336/5 pryt. 9 2. 336/5 pryt. 10 3. 335/4 pryt. 3 or 8	*IG* II^{2} 330 + 445. Schwenk 18. Develin, *AO* 364 (*SEG* XXXIX 81). Tracy, *ADT* 118. V.-Terzi, B8.	1. Council decree honouring Phyleus son of Pausanias of Oinoe (secretary of Council and People?, in office) (29–46) 2. Decree of Council and Assembly: honorand as decree 1 + associate secretaries?, in office (47–65)	1. [500 or 1,000 dr.][17] c 2. Phyleus: c syn[grammateis?]: 1,000 dr. c	

[16] Decree 1 was passed at the Assembly in the theatre after the City Dionysia (Elaphebolion = pryt. 8) 343/2. Decrees (2 and?) 3–5 were passed at or shortly after the end of 343/2.

[17] Currently restored as 1,000 dr., but in no. 1, decree 3, the Council awards a crown of 500 dr., and proposes that the Assembly award a crown of 1,000 dr., so it is possible that this Council-awarded crown was also of 500 dr. and separate from that awarded to Phyleus in decree 2.

Table (*cont.*)

	Date	Reference	Honorand	Honour
			3. honorand as decree 1, office completed (1–28)	3. [1,000 dr.?] c[18]
4*	c. 340–325[19]	J.S. Traill, *Hesp.* 47 (1978), 274–7 no. 5 (ph.) (*SEG* XXVIII 52). A.S. Henry, *ZPE* 110 (1996) 301–2. Tracy, *ADT* 78. V.-Terzi, B10. S.D. Lambert, in *Prakt. Wilhelm*, 327–41 nos. 4, 5, 16, 44.	Prytany treasurer (?) and *prytaneis* of Leontis (?)	[500 or 1000 dr.] c
5	c. 340–325[20] 2. pryt. 10	*IG* II^2 415. C. Veligianni, *Hellenika* 40 (1989), 249 n. 49. Tracy, *ADT* 84. V.-Terzi, B15.	1. End of a decree. Relationship to decree 2 obscure[21] 2. Decree of Council and Assembly honouring Kallikratides son of Kallikrates of Steiria (*anagrapheus*).	1. ? 2. 500 dr. c

[18] This is apparently confirmation, after his *euthynai*, of the crown provisionally awarded to Phyleus with no specified value in decree 2. 1,000 dr. would be in line with the crown(s) awarded to the *syn[grammateis?]* in decree 2. Cf. however the 500 dr. crown awarded the *anagrapheus* in no. 5.

[19] The date is inferred from hand (see Tracy) and prosopography (see Traill). 339/8 is excluded by *SEG* XVI 52, 4, 336/5 (?) by *Agora* XV 42, 335/4 by *Agora* XV 43, 332/1 by *IG* II^2 546 (see S.D. Lambert, *ZPE* 141 (2002), p. 118 l. 7), 328/7 by *Agora* XV 49, 14.

[20] Lettering: "Cutter of *IG* II^2 334", c. 345–c. 320 (Tracy). The year was ordinary (last pryt. had 34 or 35 days, ll. 8–9, cf. Ath. Pol. XLIII 2 with Rhodes). 335/4 is excluded by *Agora* XV 43, 229; 324/3 by *Agora* XV 53, 13–15. Since the officer responsible for inscribing the decrees was the prytany secretary (2–3) they should date to before 321/0, when the *anagrapheus* acquired that function (cf. A.S. Henry, *Hesp.* 71 (2002), 107–8).

[21] It is also obscure whether the invitation to the honorand in decree 2 to seek further honours from the Assembly (28–31) looks genuinely to the future or is a clause originally contained in the *probouleuma* which has remained embedded in the decree as passed by the Assembly (cf. no. 3, 45–6).

Table (*cont.*)

	Date	Reference	Honorand	Honour	
6*	328/7	B. Leonardos, *Arch. Eph.* 1917, 40–8 no. 92 (ph.). D.M. Lewis, *ABSA* 50 (1955), 34–6. *Agora* XV 49. J.S. Traill, *Hesp.* 47 (1978), 271. Schwenk 56. Tracy, *ADT* 92–3. V.-Terzi, B17. *IOrop* 299 (ph.)	Council dedication with list of contributors, both councillors and non-councillors, and Council decree honouring the councillors Euthykrates son of Drakontides of Aphidna, Philostratos son of Philinos of Acharnai and Chairestratos son of Chairedemos of Rhamnous	500 dr. c |	89
7*	326/5–324/3?	*IG* II^2 547. Schwenk 74. Tracy, *ADT* 114–5.	*proedroi?*[22]	?	
Uncertain					
8*	339/8 or 331/0[23]	*IG* II 221. J. Kirchner, *AM* 51 (1926), 157–8. E. Schweigert, *AJP* 61 (1940), 358. O. Masson, *Mus. Helv.* 50 (1993), 44–60 (especially 51–3).	A Council prytany	–	
9*	c. 350–340?	*IG* II^2 298. Tracy, *ADT* 70.	?	c ?	

[22] That the honorand(s) were Athenian official(s) is implied by l. 21, where they are praised conventionally for performing their duty as the laws require, o]ἱ νόμοι αὐ[τοῖς προστάττουσιν *vel sim.* That they were the *proedroi* is a possible implication of 17–18: - -] προε[δρ- - | - -] προγραμμ[α- -, since the πρόγραμμα, the agenda of the Council and Assembly, was a responsibility of these officials (Ath. Pol. XLIV 2). For a decree honouring προέδροι in the literary record see Hyp. *Phil.* 4, cf. Whitehead, *Hypereides* (Oxford, 2000), 54.

[23] If genuine, the decree was passed in the third month, Boedromion, and would presumably have honoured a prytany of the previous year, after its *euthynai*.

1. IG *II² 223*

B6–7. A. Wilhelm, *Wien. Stud.* 61–2 (1943–7), 162–6, proposed to restore Ἐλευθερέως, epithet of Dionysos, in the erasure at no. 10, 39–40, where the place of erection of the stele is specified, and in our text where the Council is praised because it καλῶς ἐπιμεμ̣[ελῆσθαι τῆς εὐκοσμίας τῆς περὶ] τὴν ἑορτὴν τοῦ Διονύσου το[ῦ--]. In no. 10 the conjecture arose from an error in the number of spaces indicated at the end of *IG* II² 410, 39 and is inconsistent with letter traces legible in the erasure.[24] The resulting absence of a parallel casts doubt on it in our text. I have suggested that no. 10, 39–40, read: ἐν τῶι θεάτρωι τοῦ Διονύσου [[τ̣[ῶι[25] ἐ]|μ [Πειραεῖ]]]. Here I suggest that we also have to do with specific locations. I restore περὶ τὴν ἑορτὴν τοῦ Διονύσου το[ῦ | ἐν ἄστει]. Cf. no. 11, 33, ὁ ἱερεὺς τοῦ Ἀσκληπιοῦ τοῦ ἐν ἄστ[ει; and *IG* II² 783, 6, ὁ ἱερεὺς τοῦ Διὸς τοῦ Σωτῆρος τοῦ ἐμ Πειραιεῖ. The intention in all four cases is to distinguish city and Piraeus cults of the same deity; and in our case the qualification also serves to distinguish the city Dionysia (Διονύσια τὰ ἐν ἄστει, cf. e.g. Dem. XXI 10, *IG* II² 851, 11–12 and 958, 29–30) from its rural counterpart.

B10. In the amount allocated for sacrifice to τοῖς δ[ό]ξασιν ἄριστα τῶν βουλευτῶν ἐπιμεμελῆσθαι τῆς εὐκοσ[μίας], in addition to the left vertical what is probably the left part of a pendent delta is just legible at autopsy, so 𐅄 (Γ *IG* II², "Ich erkenne…eine Zahl, vermutlich Γ mit einem eingeschriebenen Zeichen", A. Wilhelm, *Urkunden dramatischer Aufführungen* [Vienna, 1906], 234). Cf. no. 17, 37, 100 dr. for sacrifice and dedication for the ten *epimeletai* of the Amphiaraia; no. 11, 24, 30 dr. for sacrifice for the priest of Asklepios; no. 10, 36, one figure amount, probably 100 or 50 dr., for ten *hieropoioi* for sacrifice and a dedication.

B11. Certainty is impossible, but given the father's name in -κράτης and the very small deme (bouleutic quota 0–1, cf. J.S. Traill, *Demos and Trittys* [Toronto, 1986], 126) it is possible that the proposer of the first decree for Eudoxos, [- c. 6 -ω]ν Ἀντικράτους Παμβωτάδης bore the only name current in iv BC and attested in Pambotadai that will fit, Καλλιφῶν, and was an ancestor of *LGPN* II Καλλιφῶν 18, s. Σωκράτης
90 of Pambotadai, s. ii BC. |

[24] Cf. S.D. Lambert, in *Lettered Attica*, 57–67 [= this volume, 299–310].

[25] τ̣[οῦ is perhaps preferable.

2. SEG *XXXV 64*

Though it has been generally accepted, Schweigert's ingenious scheme of restoration of this fragmentary inscription to yield an honorific decree for the prytany secretary of 337/6, Χαιρέστρατος Ἀμεινίου Ἀχαρνεύς (cf. Schwenk, 4–14), while attractive at several points, is not wholly secure (cf. the critical remark of R. Flacelière, J. and L. Robert at *Bull. ép.* 1939 no. 59). There is no physical indication of line length (the left side is not preserved) and the scheme depends crucially on the recognition of κατ]ὰ πρυταν|[είαν in 7 as a reference to the honorand and of Ἀ̣μεινί- in 11[26] as his father's name. Schweigert restored:

ἕν]εκα, δεδ- stoich. 40
[όχθαι τῶι δήμωι ἐπαινέσαι Χαιρέστρατον] Ἀ̣μεινί-
[ου Ἀχαρνέα δικαιοσύνης ἕνεκα καὶ στεφαν]ῶ̣σαι αὐ-
[τὸν χρυσῶι στεφάνωι, ἐπειδὰν τὰς εὐθύνας] δῶι, δόξ-
[αντ' ἄρξαι τὴν ἀρχὴν δικαίως καὶ κατὰ τοὺς] νόμους

Ἀμεινίας was not a rare name (45 citizen cases in *LGPN* II) and it can not be ruled out that the honorand was another Athenian with this father's name. Moreover, as Schwenk points out, the restoration of the prescript works only if it is assumed that ἧι was omitted before the name of the secretary and his father's name after it:

δ]εκά-
[της πρυτανείας· Χαιρέστρατος Ἀχαρνεὺς ἐγρ]α̣μμά-
[τευεν·

Omission of ἧι before the secretary has been plausibly restored in two other decrees of this year (*IG* II^2 242 = Schwenk 10 and *IG* II^2 276 = Schwenk 12); and the secretary's father's name is occasionally omitted in prescripts at this period (cf. e.g. Schwenk 31, 7–8 = *IG* II^2 336B; Henry, *Honours*, 42–3).[27] Together, however, these two irregularities induce a measure of unease.

There are more serious problems at 8–10, where Schweigert prints:

[26] Enough of the mu is legible for the letter to be beyond doubt; of the alpha only the bottom of the right diagonal is preserved.

[27] Schweigert's date, 16 Skir. = 22nd of pryt. 10 is almost wholly restored, but is apparently the only one that would suit the remains of the prytany number in 1 (δ]εκά[της), the other calendrical data for this year and the posited line length. It is accepted by Pritchett-Neugebauer, 42; Meritt, *Ath. Year*, 77.

κατ]ὰ πρυταν-
[είαν ἐν παντὶ καιρῶι καλῶς καὶ φιλοτίμω]ς ἄρχει τ-
[ὴν ἀρχὴν αὐτοῦ καὶ ἡ βουλὴ ἐπηίνεσέ τε καὶ] ἐστεφά-
[νωσεν αὐτόν........15.......εὐνοίας ἕν]εκα

This is unsatisfactory. ἐν παντὶ καιρῶι is typically used in connection with services rendered on repeated, discrete, past occasions by foreign honorands, e.g. διετέλ[ει λέγων καὶ πρά]|[τ]των ἐν παντὶ καιρ[ῶι τὰ συμφέροντα]| [τῶι] δήμωι, *IG* II^2 498, 21. There is no parallel for its use in relation to an Athenian honorand at this period and it is unsuitable with a present indicative verb such as ἄρχει, describing a single continuous period of office. "Performed his office" is idiomatic English, but ἄρχει τὴν ἀρχὴν αὐτοῦ (or αὑτοῦ) is not in the idiom of Athenian decrees. Moreover while τε...καὶ is not uncommon, τε καὶ does not occur in any inscribed state decree of 352/1–322/1 and is very rare in such decrees at adjacent periods.[28] It is also far from sure that the
91 honorand was crowned by the Council: in the two other decrees | from this period certainly or probably honouring secretaries, the crowning was done by the prytanies (no. 5, 16; no. 3, 9 etc.).

Two suggestions for improvement are made by Veligianni-Terzi: ἀρετῆς τε καὶ δικαιοσύνης ἕν]εκα in l. 10 uses vocabulary better attested in this context, but is again unattractive on acount of τε καὶ. In fact the number of letters available for the restoration in 10 is indeterminable, since we do not know what was the ending of the verb, ἐστεφα|νω- in 9–10 (it might have been passive, cf. no. 3, 9). In 12–13 she suggests [καὶ χρυσῶι τε στεφάνωι στεφαν]ῶσαι αὐ[τὸν ἀπὸ XXXX δραχμῶν], but apart from the questionable insertion of τε, the inversion of the normal order, στεφανῶσαι...χρυσῶι στεφάνωι is unexampled in state decrees at this period,[29] and crowns were of 500 dr. or 1,000 dr., but not more (see above). The absence of price with a gold crown, while unusual, would not be unexampled (a partial list of cases at Henry, *Honours*, 25). θαλλοῦ στεφάνωι might be considered (cf. Henry, *Honours*, 39–40), but would be without parallel in this period in an Assembly decree for an Athenian (see above). At 15 fin.–16 in.

---

[28] The reason is perhaps that τε καὶ is inconsistent with the economy of expression which is normally a feature of decree language at this period. Cf. J.D. Denniston, *The Greek Particles* (Oxford, 1954), 512. The restored example at *Agora* XVI 94 fr. c + j is removed at *ZPE* 136 (2001), 67. There is an unrestored example from 319/8 at *SEG* XXI 310, 21.

[29] There is a restored example in a decree of the Paraloi at *SEG* XXXVII 102, 8.

-]εν τὸ ἀρ||[γύριον is perhaps possible, i.e. reference to the provision of money for the gold crown which occurs in other decrees in this list, e.g. no. 1 and no. 3 (cf. Henry, *Honours*, 36–8).

At 13–14 Schweigert restores:

ἐπειδὰν τὰς εὐθύνας] δῶι, δοξ-
[αντ' ἄρξαι τὴν ἀρχὴν δικαίως καὶ κατὰ τοὺς] νόμους

The precise wording can not be regarded as certain, but the general sense is likely to be correct, cf. no. 3, 32–5 (restored from 8, 22, 60–1):

ἐπ|ειδ]ὴ Φυλεὺς...
..... τὴν ἀρχὴν ἄρχει δικαίως καὶ κατὰ]
[τοὺς ν]όμους,[30]

and now also no. 4, 21–2, as restored by Parker:

ἐπειδὰν τὰς εὐθύνας δ]ῶι, δόξας
[δικαίως ἄρξαι·

See on no. 4 for other comparanda.

At 19–21 Schweigert restores:

ἀναγράψα]ι δὲ [τ]-
[όδε τὸ ψήφισμα τὸν γραμματέα τὸν κατὰ πρυταν]ε̣[ία]-
[ν ἐν στήληι λιθίνηι

but, like Schwenk, I am unable to confirm the epsilon in 20. Without it, there is insufficient basis for restoration.

3. IG *II² 330 + 445*

The main issue is the identification of the offices held by the honorands, apparently three (or four, see below) in number and all from the same deme, (Aiantid, cf. *Agora* XV 72, 204) Oinoe. Köhler suggested that they were a tribal contingent of the thirty συλλογεῖς τοῦ δήμου. Members of this board are attested performing duties as *hieropoioi* for Athena and for Zeus Olympios at the Olympieia (see Rhodes, *Boule*, 129–30; *IG* II² 1257 = Schwenk 77; 1496, 82–3 and 113–4) and Köhler restored our text at several points on the basis that they were being

---

[30] κατὰ τοὺς νόμους is formulaic and it seems unlikely that there is a direct connection with the famous anti-tyranny law, also passed in 337/6 (*RO* 79). Cf. B.D. Meritt, *Hesp.* 21 (1952), 357; V.-Terzi, 111 n. 332.

honoured for these duties. This, however, is problematic on a number of counts. Only Phyleus is said to have been elected, ἐπ|ε]ιδὴ Φυλεὺς χειροτ[ονηθεὶς...(5–6), tending to imply that he was the holder of a unitary office, not member of a board. Moreover the secondary honorands are not only from the same deme as him, they are also not required to render separate accounts (62, cf. 58). One obtains the clear impression that they are subordinates, not co-responsible members
92 of a | board.[31] Another problem is that there is no suggestion, in the wording justifying the honours, that the duties performed had been of a religious nature. This contrasts with the decrees for religious officials listed below (section B) and in particular with the other substantial extant decree honouring *hieropoioi* at this period, no. 10, where their work is described as follows:

ἐπε-
ιδὴ δὲ οἱ ἱεροποιοὶ οἱ αἱρεθέντες ὑπὸ τῆς βουλῆς καλῶς
καὶ φιλοτίμως ἐπεμελήθησαν τ[ῆ]ς παρασ[τάσ]εως τῶν ἱερέ-
ων καὶ τῶν θυσίων [.......... *traces 20* ....] τῶν ἡρ[ώ]ων καὶ
τἆλλα τὰ περὶ τήν |[........... *traces 22* ....] | Λ [.] ἐπιμε-
μέληνται δικαίως καί φι[λ]οτ[ίμ]ως, [ἐπαι]νέ[σ]αι τοὺς ἱεροπ-
οιοὺς κτλ.

In our case it would be especially odd to choose to call the "*syllogeis*" "*hieropoioi*", but not to refer in the decree to any religious functions.

Rhodes left the office open. What seems the correct solution has been suggested to me by Angelos Matthaiou per. ep., viz. that the principal honorand is the γραμματεὺς τῆι βουλῆι καὶ τῶι δήμωι. This official, not to be confused with the γραμματεὺς τῆς βουλῆς = γραμματεὺς κατὰ πρυτανείαν, is mentioned in *Agora* XV 12, 64–5 (400–350) and 36, 34–5 (343/2?) and may be identical with the γραμματεὺς τῶι δήμωι referred to in *Agora* XV 43, 228 (335/4). In *Agora* XV 32, 64 (after mid-iv) and 44, 45–8 (334/3) his title is γραμματεὺς τῆς βουλῆς καὶ τοῦ δήμου. His principal (or according to Ath. Pol. sole) function seems to have been to read out documents in the Council and the Assembly (Ath. Pol. LIV 5 with Rhodes p. 604; A.S. Henry, *Hesp.* 71 (2002), 93). Matthaiou's restorations, which suit excellently the space available and the context, are:

[31] Cf. Rhodes; Schwenk, who also points out that, even when they were functioning as *hieropoioi* the *syllogeis* were known as *syllogeis* (*IG* II[2] 1257 = Schwenk 77). Schwenk takes the honorands to be *hieropoioi* and not *syllogeis*, but her argument that they were not equal members of a board goes equally against their being *hieropoioi*.

(a) 6 Φυλεὺς χειροτ[ονηθεὶς γραμματεὺς τῆι τε βουλῆι κα]-
[ὶ] τῶι δήμωι
τῆι τε βουλῆι κα|ὶ Koe.

(b) 13 ἐ[παινέσαι τὸν γραμματέα τῆς βουλῆς καὶ τοῦ]
[δή]μου τὸν ἐπὶ Π[υθοδήλου ἄρχοντος

(c) 21 καὶ οἱ ἄλλοι οἱ καθιστάμε[νοι γραμματεῖς φιλοτιμῶντα]ι

This exceeds the normal line length by 1 letter, as, in the text of *IG* II[2], following Wilhelm, does the previous line.

(d) 33 χειροτονηθείς γραμματεὺ]-
[ς τῆι] βουλῆι καὶ τῶι δήμω[ι

(e) 51 περὶ ὧν Φυλε[ὺς λέγει ὁ γραμματεὺς τῆς βουλῆς]
κα[ὶ] τοῦ δ[ή]μου

The normal word-order in clauses like (e) is περὶ ὧν ὁ δεῖνα λέγει. Cf. however also *IG* II[2] 47, 23–4, περὶ ὧν ὁ ἱερεὺς λέγει ὁ το(ῦ) Ἀσκληπιο(ῦ) Εὐθύδημος and *IG* II[2] 127, 9, [ἐφ' οἷς Μονο]ύνιος λέγει ὁ ἀδελφὸ[ς ὁ Κετριπόριος].

The terms in which the honorand is praised also suit a secretary very well. Note in particular the similarity between the wording of this decree and nos. 2 and 5, which also certainly (5) or possibly (2) honoured secretaries at this period and which also refer to the crowning of the honorand by the prytanies (no. 5, 16; cf. 35–6 etc. of our decree), use the verb ἄρχει and the adverbs καλῶς and/or δικαίως (no. 5, 14–17; cf. | 8, 34 etc. of our decree) and mention that the honorand 93
had performed his office "according to the laws" (no. 2, 14; cf. 8, 34–5 etc. of our decree).

What, then, of the secondary honorands, surprisingly mentioned in preserved text in only one of the three decrees (47–65)? At 52 they are οἱ συν[-, restored hitherto as συν[άρχοντες. This suited the theory that they were fellow members of the board of *syllogeis*, but is less obviously appropriate to subordinate secretaries.[32] The term συγγραμματεύς ("co-" or "associate" secretary) is attested in classical

[32] It seems that we can rule out that our co-honorands were other state secretaries, e.g. the ἀναγραφεύς, the γραμμ. ἐπὶ τὰ ψηφίσματα and the ἀντιγραφεύς (cf. *Agora* XV 43, 229–231), for those officials held independent offices, were required to render independent accounts and one would not expect them all to come from the same deme. In *Agora* XV 43 the ἀναγραφεύς is from the same deme as the γραμμ. τῶι δήμωι, but the other secretaries are from different demes and, unsurprisingly, that seems to be the normal pattern.

Athens. At *IG* I^3 71, 8, a board is required [hελέσθαι καὶ γραμμα]τέα καὶ χσυ[γγραμματέα ἐχ σφῶν αὐτ]ῶν and in *IG* I^3 269 (of 443/2) and 270 (442/1) Σάτυρος Λευκονοεὺς χσυνεγραμ[μάτευε while on the same inscriptions, in 443/2, Σοφίας ἐγραμμάτευε and in 442/1 Χαλκιδεὺς Μελιτεὺς ἐγραμμάτευε.[33] ὑπογραμματεύς was also used. E.g. the unidentified board at *IG* II^2 2825 was served by both a γραμματεύς and a ὑπογραμματεύς. After 307 a single ὑπογραμματεύς appears in bouleutic texts and it is interesting that it is with the γραμματεὺς τῆς βουλῆς καί τοῦ δήμου that he is then associated (cf. *Agora* XV p. 15). Should we perhaps envisage a development from a 4th century arrangement under which the γραμματεὺς τῆς βουλῆς καὶ τοῦ δήμου was responsible for a pool of "associate secretaries" with whom he might be personally connected (and who might have assisted the other state secretaries as well as himself?) to a hellenistic system in which there was a single formal, professional, "undersecretary"? The absence of other fourth century evidence for state συγγραμματεῖς urges caution, as does another apparent anomaly. Line 52 currently reads:

> καὶ οἱ συν[άρχοντες ἱεροποιοὶ λέγουσιν Παυσ]-
> ανίας καὶ Χαρίδημος

This was never satisfactory, since συνάρχων, like ἄρχων, is normally used substantively, not adjectivally. συν[γραμματεῖς would dispose of this problem, but would tend to imply that the number of them was three rather than two,[34] i.e.

> συν[γραμματεῖς λέγουσι--$^{5\ or\ 6\ name}$--καὶ -$^{3\ or\ 4}$-]-
> ανίας καὶ Χαρίδημος

Similarly at 59–60 instead of:

> ἐπα]ινέσαι δὲ [καὶ τούς συνάρχοντας ἱεροποιοὺς Παυσανί]-
> [αν καὶ Χ]αρίδημον Ο[ἰ]να[ίους

we should have:

> ἐπα]ινέσαι δὲ [καὶ τοὺς συνγραμματέας-$^{5\ or\ 6\ name}$- -καὶ -$^{3\ or\ 4}$-ανί]-
> [αν καὶ Χ]αρίδημον Ο[ἰ]να[ίους

---

[33] Cf. Rhodes, *Boule* 139 with n. 3.

[34] Klaus Hallof points out per ep. that one might retain two by restoring σὺν [αὐτῶι γραμματεῖς, but it is difficult to find a parallel for such an expression in an Athenian decree of good period.

This is possible, but there is a consequential issue to be addressed in l. 61, where since the ed. princ., C.D. Tsuntas, *Arch. Eph.* 1885, 131–142, the restoration has been κα[ὶ στεφανῶσαι ἀμφοτέρους χρυσῶι στε|φάνωι ἀ]πὸ : X : δραχμῶν. ἀμφοτέρους is problematic. It might conceivably indicate a single crown awarded jointly to two honorands, but there is no parallel in the many hundreds of decrees of the Athenian state which award crowns (see Henry, *Honours*, 46–7).[35] The phrase invariably used for two honorands is | ἑκάτερον αὐτῶν, for more than two, 94
ἕκαστον αὐτῶν. ἑκάτερον αὐτῶν would exceed the space available by three letters and can probably be ruled out. ἕκαστον αὐτῶν, however, is also too long, albeit by two letters. This is not a decisive argument against it: restorations of other lines exceeding the normal length (by one letter) have been accepted elsewhere in the text, e.g. in l. 20.[36] On the other hand we can not be certain that ἕκαστον αὐτῶν is correct; and that confirms the advisability of a cautious approach to the restoration of lines 52 and 59–60.[37]

Wilhelm's restoration of one of the co-honorands in 52 and 59 as Παυσ]ανίας (*Hermes* 24 (1889), 136–9), to yield homonymy with the father of the principal honorand, while quite possible, is also not compelling. At this period family relationships are as, or more likely, to be manifest in shared name components than shared whole names;[38] and the name Λυσανίας is also attested in Aiantid Oinoe in iv BC

[35] There is a verbal parallel in a hellenistic decree from Rhamnous, *IRham* 17, 11, of 236 BC: αὐτοὺς ἀμφοτέρους Ῥαμνούσιοι καὶ Ἀθηναίων οἱ οἰ|κοῦντες τὸ φρούριον ἐστεφάνωσαν χρυσῶι στεφάνωι κατὰ τὸν νόμον. I have failed to find a parallel in non-Attic inscriptions, with the exception of *ID* 1521 (ii BC), which reads (12–14):

> δεδόχθαι ἐπαινέσαι τε | ἀμφοτέρους αὐτοὺς καὶ στεφανῶ|σαι ἑκάτερον αὐτῶν χρυσῶι στεφάνω<ι>

and at 19–21:

> καὶ καθ' ἑ|κάστην πόσιν στεφανοῦσθαι ἀμφοτέρους | ἐν τῶι κοινῶι μετὰ ἀναγορεύσεως·

[36] The stoichedon arrangement on this stone is on any account unusual. Two letters were added to each line in 29 ff., expanding the line length from stoich. 46 to stoich. 48. This was achieved not, as was normal in such cases, by a change in letter size or spacing, but by beginning (and presumably finishing) the text one letter into the margin on either side. This suggests that the stone widened significantly towards the bottom, though its fragmentary state makes this difficult to assess accurately.

[37] There are various ways that crowns could be arranged on an inscription and the number of them can not be inferred from the one that survives (cf. Schwenk, p. 100).

[38] Cf. M. Runes, *Wien. Stud.* 44 (1924/5), 173 and most recently Lambert, in *Prakt. Wilhelm*, 335–6 [= this volume, 329–30].

(e.g. *Agora* XV 59, 29; Φανίας only in Hippothontid, e.g. *IG* II^2 1926, 131).

The restoration of the calendrical elements of this text (1–3, 29–31, 47–9) has been regarded as settled since Köhler.[39] However, the date of the latest of the three decrees (ll. 1–3), the only one passed after the end of the honorand's term of office (and after the rendering of his accounts), is uncertain. Köhler restored 17th of pryt. 3. (ll. 1–3), which is the earliest possible date in the year (which was ordinary) consistent with the data. It may seem *prima facie* reasonable that such a decree would have been passed at the earliest opportunity, but the assumption is doubtful. Of decrees certainly honouring Athenians in this period, there is only one dated one which appears to have been passed after the end of an annual term of office, i.e. no. 18, of the 8th pryt. of the year following that in which the honorand had been elected to office. Most likely the term of the office in that case was annual (see note below on no. 18). No. 17, honouring the *epimeletai* of the Amphiaraia, was passed on 16th Pyanopsion = 33rd day of pryt. 3, but these *epimeletai* performed duties at a specific festival. It is not clear that they held office for an annual period.[40] No. 8, apparently honouring *prytaneis*, was passed in the second prytany, presumably of the year after that in which they had served; but the authenticity of this decree is in doubt. Examples are not difficult to find from other periods where there was a significant passage of time between the office held and the subsequent honorific decree. In 103/2, for example, the decree honouring the *parthenoi* who had worked on the *peplos* presented at the Panathenaia in the first month of the year, Hekatombaion, was not passed until the 7th prytany, 11th Gamelion (*IG* II^2 1034). Before all the fragments of that inscription were known, both Köhler and Foucart had assumed that the decree must have been passed at the earliest opporunity after the festival, i.e. in Hekatombaion or Metageitnion, an assumption which the discovery of a new fragment showed to be false (cf. S.D. Lambert, *ZPE* 142 (2003), 74). The clear implication is that caution is appropriate in restoring calendrical text in cases of this sort. In our case, other dates in this year are epigraphically and calendrically possible. If, like no. 18, the decree was passed in pryt. 8, the equation

[39] Cf. Pritchett-Neugebauer, 44; Meritt, *Ath. Year*, 79.
[40] Cf. C. Veligianni, *Hellenika* 40 (1989), 245.

17th day of 8th prytany ([ὀγδόης] in l. 1) = ἕνηι καὶ νέαι [Elaphebolion] would suit.[41] | 95

There have been attempts to restore the tribes in prytany, but in no case can this be determined on current evidence. Antiochis is now known to have held the tenth prytany in 335/4 (see *SEG* XXI 272), not the third (as restored at *IG* II² 331), so on any account Kirchner's restoration of it in l. 1 falls. Spacing at l. 29 would normally suggest Aegeis or Oineis, but given the possibility of reading πρυτανέας for the more common πρυτανείας (cf. Threatte I, 316–7; *IOrop* 296, 3), even that is not certain (though admittedly there are no comparable irregularites in this text, as preserved).

There is insufficient basis for identification of the decree proposers at 5, (Θεοδω[ρ..........22..........εἶπε) and 32 ('Αγασι[..........22..........εἶπε). At 5 Lolling suggested Θεόδω[ρος 'Αντιφάνου 'Αλωπεκῆθεν εἶπεν, a man attested as councillor in 334/3 (*Agora* XV 44, 56) and this was accepted into *IG* II². There is no reason, however, to make a link between a councillor in 334/3 and the proposer of a decree in 335/4; and the scope for possible restorations when only Θεοδω[ρ- is preserved is wide indeed. Kirchner's tentative restoration of 32 as 'Αγασί[ας Χαιριγένους 'Ικαριεὺς, attested at *IG* XII. 8. 100, 2, is similarly adventurous and runs up against the problem that, though our man was a councillor in 336/5, he does not appear among the Ikarians on the Council list probably of that year, *Agora* XV 42 (cf. Develin, *AO* 364 [*SEG* XXXIX 81]). Correctly, it is not accepted at *LGPN* II s.v. 'Αγασίας 4, cf. 10.[42]

There has been uncertainty about the reading and restoration of 64–5. Autopsy indicates clearly that the final preserved letter of 64 was delta, not the alpha read by some eds.[43] It seems therefore that

---

[41] There is no firmly attested calendar equation for 335/4 before 18th Skirophorion = 23rd of pryt. 10 (*SEG* XLVIII 101, cf. Meritt, *Ath. Year*, 80). That is a regular equation for an ordinary year. We have no means of assessing the sequence of full and hollow months earlier in the year, but the equation 17th day of 8th prytany = ἕνηι καὶ νέαι Elaphebolion would be consistent with its being day 266 of a regular ordinary year, i.e. (4 × 36 day prytanies) + (3 × 35 day prytanies) + 17 = 266th day; (5 full months × 30) + (4 hollow months × 29) = 266th day. For ἕνηι καὶ νέαι Elaphebolion as a meeting day of the Assembly cf. Mikalson, *Calendar*, 136.

[42] In fact, as Develin notes, the restoration 'Αγασί[ας is not quite certain. The rarer 'Αγασί[ων is also possible.

[43] One gains a better impression of this letter at autopsy than on the Berlin squeeze. Completely preserved, it is raised somewhat from the bottom of the stoichos as typically with deltas in this script. The triangle is too large in this script to be the upper

R. Schöll, *Sitzungsber. Akad. München* 1886, 114–5 n. 1, was right to restore δ[οῦναι here rather than ἀ[πολαβεῖν (Köhler). The recovery provision seems to come in the next line, where I read a probable iota (upper vertical with no adjoining stroke to the right of it) before the omicron and restore the inevitable ἀργύρ]ι̣ον (cf. 18, ὅπως δ' ἂν ὁ τ[α]μίας ἀπολάβ[ηι τὸ ἀργύριον). So:

[. . .⁵. . τὸν] δ[ὲ] ταμίαν δ[οῦναι -------------]
[. . .⁵. . ἀργύρ]ι̣ον ἀπο[λαβ ------------------]

For helpful discussion of the honorific language used in these decrees see Veligianni-Terzi. Her suggestion, τῶ[ν] λαγχαν[όντων] for το[ῖς] λαγχάν[ουσι] at 37, however, is contradicted by my reading of the TO at autopsy (not visible to Schwenk; the horizontal and a slight suggestion of the vertical of the tau and most of the O, i.e. upper section, are legible). Since the text does not correspond precisely with a known formula, the square brackets are better left empty.

4. SEG *XXVIII 52*

The text is inscribed on a block of grey marble of which the top, bottom and back, all smooth, are preserved. This suggested to H.A. Thompson ap. Traill that it belonged to the lintel or epistyle of a monument. Near the centre of the top is an iron dowel, indicating another course above (Thompson). The preserved face contains a decree of the Council honouring the treasurer (?), and a prytany list of Leontis. As the earliest certain extant example of an honorific state decree inscribed together with a prytany list (though cf. no. 8), the text is of considerable interest. Traill notes that "several other prytany or bouleutic inscriptions may have been composed of more than one block, but there is no parallel for the listing of councillors on a larger architectural composition as required here." Other relevant texts (e.g. a decree honouring the prytany Leontis) may have been inscribed on the block above and perhaps on one or other of the sides of the present block, which are not preserved (cf. no. 1).

---

section of alpha. The horizontal is nearly, but not quite at the bottom of the letter. Cf. the comment of Tracy, *ADT* 117, on the deltas of this cutter: "sometimes the crossbar is not placed exactly at the bottom, with the result that the letter can be mistaken for alpha".

The surviving text of the decree is very fragmentary and while there are formulaic passages which Traill (advised by Meritt) was able to restore convincingly, there are enough striking and unique features | 96
to urge caution elsewhere. The honorand, it appears, was treasurer (τα]μ̣ί̣αν, l. 1, the traces of the mu and iota are very slight); presumably of the prytany Leontis, but serving also as treasurer of the whole Council (cf. *Agora* XV p. 9). My text of the decree, which occupies column 1 of the inscribed face, is as follows:

[------ ἐπαινοῦσι τὸν τα?]μ̣ί̣αν Π- stoich. 27
[........[15].......Παιονί?]δ̣η̣ν ἀπο-
or Χολλεί?]
[φαίνοντες αὐτὸν ἄνδρα ἀγ]αθὸν εἶ-
[ναι........[16]........π]άντων ὧν
[..........[20]..........]εται καλ-
[ῶς.........[17]........ἄλ]λα βουλ-
[......[12]......λέγων καὶ π]ράττων
[.........[19].........τῶ]ι δ̣ή̣μωι
[.......[12]......ἐψήφισθαι ?] τῆι βου-
[λῆι τοὺς προέδρους ο]ἳ [ἂν λ]άχωσιν
[προεδρεύειν ἐν τῶι δή]μ[ωι] ε̣ἰ̣ς τὴν
[πρώτην ἐκκλησίαν χρ]η̣μ̣α̣τίσ[α]ι πε-
[ρὶ τούτων, γνώμην δὲ ξυν]β̣ά̣λλ[ε]σθα-
[ι τῆς βουλῆς εἰς τὸν δῆμον ὅ]τ[ι] δ̣οκ-
[εῖ τῆι βουλῆι ἐπαινέσαι Π..[4]..]ΝΑ̣
[.....[9]....Παιονίδην? ἀρετῆς ἕ]νε-
or Χολλείδην?
[κα καὶ δικαιοσύνης τῆς εἰς] τ̣ὴν β̣ο̣-
[υλήν.........[17]........χ]ρ̣υσεα
[......[11].....καὶ στεφανῶ]σαι αὐτ-
[ὸν χρυσῶι στεφάνωι ἀπὸ: .]: δραχμ-
[ῶν, ἐπειδὰν τὰς εὐθύνας δ]ῶι, δόξας
[δικαίως ἄρξαι· ἀναγράψα]ι̣ δὲ τόδε
[τὸ ψήφισμα τὸν γραμματέ]α τῶν πρυ-
[τάνεων......[11].....λι]θίνηι καὶ
[στῆσαι ἔμπροσθεν τοῦ] βουλευτηρ-
[ίου· εἰς δὲ τὴν ἀναγραφ]ὴν τῆς στήλ-
[ης δοῦναι τὸν ταμίαν το]ῦ δήμου: ΔΔΔ (the underlined pairs of letters occupy one stoichos)
[δραχμὰς ἐκ τῶν κατὰ ψηφίσματα] ἀναλισκομένων non-stoich.
[τῶι δήμωι, ὅπως ἂν φιλοτιμῶνται] καὶ οἱ ἄλλοι λέγειν
[καὶ πράττειν τὰ ἄριστα εἰδότ]ε̣ς ὅτι χ̣άριτας ἀξίας ἀπολήψονται
παρὰ [τῆς] β̣ο̣[υ]λ̣[ῆ]ς καὶ τοῦ [δήμου].

1–9. Traill printed:

[---- ἐπαινοῦσι τὸν τα]μίαν Π-
[...ωνα.....⁹....Παιονί?]δην ἀπο-
or Χολλεί?]
[δεικνύμενοι αὐτὸν φιλάγ]αθον εἶ-
[ναι καὶ ἐπιμεμελῆσθαι π]άντων ὧν
[αὐτῶι προσέταξαν οἱ φυλ]έται καλ-
[ῶς καὶ φιλοτίμως· τὰ δὲ ἄλλ]α βουλ-
[εύων διατελεῖ λέγων καὶ π]ράττων
97 [ἐν τῆι βουλῆι τὰ ἄριστα τῶ]ι δήμωι |
[τῶι Ἀθηναίων ᵛᵛ δεδόχθαι] τῆι βου-
[λῆι

L. 6 is one letter short. φιλάγαθος has a strongly hellenistic flavour and does not otherwise appear in bouleutic texts before i BC (e.g. κα]λῶς καὶ φιλαγά[θως, *Agora* XV 264, 5). Veligianni-Terzi's ἀπο|[φαίνοντες αὐτὸν ἄνδρα ἀγ]αθὸν is preferable. Similarly, I can find nothing in an Assembly decree very close to ἐπιμεμελῆσθαι π]άντων ὧν | [αὐτῶι προσέταξαν οἱ φυλ]έται in 4–5, and it is possible that]εται is from some other noun, or verb (e.g. φαίν]εται). [ἐν τῆι βουλῆι τὰ ἄριστα τῶ]ι δήμωι [τῶι Ἀθηναίων ᵛᵛ δεδόχθαι κτλ. at 8–9 is more plausible, though the vacat of two letters raises suspicion; ἐψήφισθαι would reduce it to one.

10–18 in. are as persuasively restored by Traill according to the normal formula (I print minor new readings from autopsy). χ]ρυσεα at 18 is very striking. Traill ventures γράψαι δὲ καὶ εἰκόνα χ]ρυσέα|[ν, rightly queried by J. and L. Robert, *Bull. ép.* 1979 no. 151. One expects στῆσαι for statues, which are very rare honours for Athenians (or indeed foreigners); a golden one would be unique in the epigraphical record (bronze is the usual material); and the provision, in prytany decrees, of painted portraits on gilded shields is not attested until after Sulla (see Henry, *Honours*, 294–303). A *painted* statue would be unique and unexpected. In the absence of parallels restoration is imprudent. We may have to do with an award of some sort, but if the honorand is treasurer, the reference might alternatively be to some action he has taken with respect to golden object(s).

In 20 Traill restores 1000 dr. as the value of the crown awarded, comparing no. 1; possible, but 500 dr. can not be ruled out (cf. above, Introduction).

Between the rendering-of-accounts formula and the inscription formula we have a short phrase beginning δοξας (21–22). Traill's δοξάσης τῆς βουλῆς is without parallel in an Attic inscription and does not yield satisfactory sense in context. The subject of δοξάσ- in this type of context ought to be the honorand. δόξας | [δικαίως ἄρξαι was suggested to me by Robert Parker.[44] Close parallels are no. 2, 13–14, as restored by Schweigert:

ἐπειδὰν τὰς εὐθύνας] δῶι, δόξ-
[αντ' ἄρξαι τὴν ἀρχὴν δικαίως καὶ κατὰ τοὺς] νόμους

SEG XLIII 26,15 (decree of Acharnai):

...καὶ τὰς εὐθύνα[ς] δέδωκεν, δ[ό]ξας δικαίως τεταμιευκέναι...

Cf. also no. 1, B5–6:

ἐπιγράψαι δὲ καὶ τὸ ψήφισ]μα καθ' ὃ ἐστεφανώθη ἡ βουλή |
[ὑπὸ τοῦ δήμου ἐν] τῆι ἐν Διονύσου ἐκκλησίαι δόξασα καλῶς ἐπιμεμ̣-
[ελῆσθαι τῆς εὐκοσμίας τῆς περὶ] τὴν ἑορτὴν...

no. 5, 28–30:

ἐπε[ι]δὰν τὰς εὐθύνας δῶι· ἐπε[ι]-
[δὴ δὲ κα]ὶ ὁ νόμος κε̣λ̣[εύε]ι, ἐὰν δόξει̣ [δι]-
[καίως ἄρ]ξ̣αι τ̣ή̣ν [ἀρχὴν,....

At 23–4 we encounter another oddity. Here there seems no obvious alternative to Traill's restoration τὸν γραμματέ]α τῶν πρυ||[τάνεων, but this is a unique way of describing the officer responsible for the inscription of a decree, usually known as the γραμματεὺς κατὰ πρυτανείαν (cf. A.S. Henry, *Hesp.* 71 (2002), 104, not noting this case). At 24 Traill restores ἐν τῆι στήληι λι]θ̣ίνηι, but the definite article would be surprising. One might suspect that a word other than stele was used for this monument, but the term occurs unrestored in l. 26. There seems to be no obvious solution (stoichedon irregularity?). φιλοτιμῶνται in 29 is Henry's correction of Traill's ἐφάμιλλοι ὦσι (cf. *IG* II² 509 vv. 7–11; later also suggested by Veligianni-Terzi). At the end of 30 Traill prints κα⟨ὶ⟩ πρυ[τάνεων], but the correct reading is καὶ τοῦ

[44] A similar idea was proposed to me independently by Angelos Matthaiou.

98 [δήμου.[45] | This, in turn, points to the deletion of τῶι δήμωι, restored by Traill after ἄριστα, a deletion which considerations of spacing also indicate (the kappa in 29 is aligned between the epsilon and sigma at the preserved beginning of 30).

6. *IOrop 299*

This monument of 328/7, set up by the Council at the Amphiaraion, is unusual in a number of ways. Physically it is unique among the decrees of this period in being inscribed not on the normal tall/narrow/thin stele, nor on the wider/shorter/thicker block which usually served as a dedication base, but on a block which was tall and narrow like a stele (H. 0.97, w. 0.26), but also relatively thick so that it could serve as a base for a dedication (th. 0.195 (top)–0.210 (bottom)); see the phots. in *Arch. Eph.* and *IOrop.* The "stele" has a thickened foot, with a moulding at the bottom that extends across the front and a little way (4–5 cm.) along each side. The crowning element is missing. It perhaps included a small statue of Amphiaraos (Petrakos).

The monument is also unique in that, while fully official (ἀνέθηκεν ἡ βουλὴ ἡ ἐπ' Εὐθυκρίτου ἄρχοντος, 1–2), it was paid for privately by less than five percent of the councillors in office that year (twenty-one are listed, plus treasurer and two secretaries), and they were joined by a group of ten Athenians from outside the Council. To the list of their names is appended a Council decree honouring the councillors who took the lead in the project and whose names are at the top of the list of councillor-donors. What factors determined the involvement of this group of men with this project? Two features are notable. Part of the purpose of the monument, as with the decrees listed in section C, was patently that of establishing symbolically the presence of the Athenian state at the Amphiaraion in the years immediately following the cession of Oropos to Athens, probably by Alexander in 335 (Knoepfler, *Eretria* XI, 367–89, esp. 372). The first feature, the prominence of the men listed, reflects the importance attached to the acquisition of

[45] Henry also detected that something was amiss in this line, but his reading of the end of the line, based only on Traill's printed photo, καὶ τῶ̣ν̣ [πρυτάνεων], is incorrect.

the shrine.[46] Lewis noted this in respect of the non-councillors, headed by three of the leading figures of the period, Phanodemos, Demades and Polyeuktos of Sphettos,[47] but the councillors too are more prominent than would be a random cross-section of the Council. Five of the twenty-one are from known liturgical and/or very prominent families, including two of the three honorands of the decree;[48] and all but three of the rest are well-known or at least probably or possibly attested elsewhere in person or by family.[49] | 99

The other detectable feature (not previously noticed) is regional. Several of the contributors have links, not only with the Amphiaraion, but with the surrounding region; and again this applies to both the councillors and the non-councillors. Phanodemos seems to have been the leading Athenian in matters connected with the Amphiaraion in these years (cf. the inscriptions at section C) and both he and

[46] Tracy, *ADT* 93 n. 24 notes that the inscription, cut in small and crowded lettering in a non-stoichedon style, is surprisingly unprepossessing. The number of orthographic irregularities is also greater than was normal on state inscriptions. The cutter is not known. Perhaps it was the work of a local mason. One wonders if it was the associated statue that drew so many distinguished contributors (was it in a precious metal?).

[47] Of the seven other contributors from outside the Council, the fifth listed was wealthy/prominent, Kephisophon of Cholargos (l. 23, *LGPN* II Κηφισοφῶν 26, see further below), as, if the demotic is correctly restored, was the seventh, Pheidippos of M[yrrhinous] (l. 37, *LGPN* II Φείδιππος 11, ? = 10, cf. *APF* p. 42). The sixth, Aristeides of Hermos, is the only one who is certainly not otherwise known, or from a known family. Of the last three (ll. 38–40) only parts of names are preserved, all fairly common and with no demotics. As Lewis noted, they can not be identified. The fourth is Εὐ[-$^{6-7}$- Κ]ολλυτε. Six letters are missing, or possibly seven if iota was included. Since it is the only name attested in Kollytos that will fit, Εὐ[φραῖος is possible, though the company would be distinguished for a family known hitherto only from two hellenistic funerary monuments (*IG* II^2 6501 and 6502).

[48] First honorand: *LGPN* II Φιλόστρατος 24. Cf. Φιλῖνος 32, Κλειππίδης 4, Φιλόστρατος 23, *APF* 14726. Second honorand: *LGPN* II Εὐθυκράτης 16, cf. 17 (and see below). Other councillors: *LGPN* II Εὐκράτης 39, *APF* 5758; *LGPN* II Εὐετίων 6, *APF* 5463; *LGPN* II Φιλοκράτης 50, cf. *APF* p. 276.

[49] References can be traced conveniently via *LGPN* II and *PAA*. On Chairestratos of Rhamnous, Oulias of Steiria, Kallisthenes of Trinemeia and Demetrios of Aphidna see below. *LGPN* II Φάλανθος 15 (l. 8) was probably related to Φάλανθος 13, 14, Μυρρίνη 27. *LGPN* II Ἔμπεδος 4 (l. 13) was probably related to Ἔμπεδος 2 and = or related to 3. *LGPN* II Θεοκρίνης 3 (l. 14) ? = the famous "sykophant" of Dem. LVIII etc. (cf. Θεοκρίνης 1, 2), as Petrakos and Traill saw (cf. *PAA* 508320). *LGPN* II Ἀμεινίας 16 (l. 25) = or related to Ἀμεινίας 15 (cf. *PAA* 123175). *LGPN* II Ἀντίδοτος 17 (l. 26) ? = 16 (cf. *PAA* 132725). *LGPN* II Θεόδωρος 196 (l. 27), ? = 195. *LGPN* II Λυσίθεος 13 (l. 30) (cf. 14, but heavily restored). The three unknowns are: Protokles of Kephisia (l. 16), Epigethes of Eroiadai and Nikandros of Marathon (ll. 28–9), respectively 13th, 19th and 20th on the list.

Demades had been honoured as *epimeletai* of the Amphiaraia the previous year (no. 17). The three leading contributors, who were also the honorands of the decree, were all from demes in north or northeast Attica (Acharnai, Aphidna and Rhamnous);[50] and one of them, Euthykrates of Aphidna, as Habicht has seen (*Untersuchungen zur politischen Geschichte Athens in hellenistischer Zeit* [Munich, 1979], 150), was ancestor of a *proxenos* of the Boeotian koinon in iii/ii BC, a fact attested by another inscription set up in the Amphiaraion (cf. *IOrop* 188). This family from the large and ancient deme of Aphidna, supposed to have been one of the twelve originally independent Ur-poleis of Attica,[51] seems to have had a definite northward-facing orientation. Oe was not, it seems, located in northern Attica,[52] but the involvement of Empedos of Oe (l. 13) in this group may have reflected comparable northern interests, for the same man (or a related homonym) was Athenian ambassador in connection with a treaty with Thessaly c. 360 (*IG* II^2 175, 2). In 332/1 another man from Aphidna on the list, Demetrios (l. 24), had proposed the decree from the Amphiaraion honouring Phanodemos for his legislative work for the festival Amphiaraia, no. 16 below. Finally, despite my hesitation at *Rationes*, 171, Oulias of Steiria, listed immediately after the three principal donors in l. 7, may with high probability be identified with (or as a relation of) the only other bearer of this name attested in Attica, the Oulias who bought property sold by the Melaineis in the Lykourgan public land sale programme (*Rationes*, F10B, 20), for, as I showed at *Rationes*, 196, this group was located in the northeastern border area of Attica.

The order in which the contributors are listed is also of interest. Leonardos, 42, noted that it is not, as usually on bouleutic monuments, tribally determined. There are two obvious possible criteria: size of contribution and seniority. The fact that the un- or not-well-knowns on both lists cluster toward the end might suggest the former;[53] but the inference is not certain since the quality of our prosopographical data

[50] The third honorand, Chairestratos of Rhamnous, was perhaps identical with the Chairestratos who was sculptor of Themis at Rhamnous. Cf. *IRham* 120. Note also the demotics of Nikandros of Marathon (l. 29) and the treasurer, Sotiades of Acharnai (l. 32).

[51] *FGH* 328 Philochoros F 94; cf. Whitehead, *Demes*, 11; *Rationes*, 193–4. Euthykrates probably bought property at Aphidna in the Lykourgan public land-sale programme, *Rationes*, 158, cf. 244, 288–9.

[52] *SEG* XLVIII 297.

[53] Cf. above nn. 47 and 49.

for 321–307, the period when young men in 328/7 could be expected to have made their greatest impact on the historical record, is generally less good than for the preceding democratic years. There is a cluster of men who were apparently just over sixty in 328/7 in ll. 10–14, but if age was the criterion it does not look as if it can have been precisely applied since, on the most likely prosopographical arrangements, a man who was in his sixtieth year (i.e. public arbitrator) in 329/8 is sandwiched between two men who were in their sixtieth years in 330/29.[54] Among the non-councillors there could be no objection to a hypothesis that the first three, Phanodemos, Demades and Polyeuktos of Sphettos were in order of seniority. Current scholarship places Demades' date of birth around the early 380s,[55] that of Polyeuktos in the second half of that decade.[56] We lack firm information with regard to Phanodemos, but since he was honoured by the Council in 343/2 it is quite plausible that he was then over fifty, i.e. born perhaps c. 395
and in his late 60s | at the time of this dedication.[57] On the other hand, 100
Phanodemos' pole position might be due to the leading role he played at the Amphiaraion after 335; and if (what is not sure) the fifth man on the list, Kephisophon of Cholargos at l. 23, was identical with the man of this name who was public arbitrator in 330/29,[58] he was probably older than both Demades and Polyeuktos.

The proposer of the decree on the stone is given as Καλλισθένης ΧΑΡΠΙΔΟΥ Τρινεμεὺς (l. 41, also, without father's name, one of the contributors at l. 11). Leonardos plausibly suggested Χαρ⟨ο⟩πίδου or Χαρ⟨μ⟩ίδου. Both names are well-attested in Attica (*LGPN* II pp. 477–8) and there are several instances on this stone where the cutter has wrongly inscribed a single letter, and one or two where he may have inadvertently omitted a letter (ΛΑΜΠΡΕΥ for ΛΑΜΠΤΡΕΥ at l. 9, cf. Threatte I, 579; perhaps also ΛΥΚΟΡΓΟΣ for ΛΥΚΟΥΡΓΟΣ at l. 10, as the stone does not otherwise show -o for -ου, which would be a

[54] *Diaitetai* in 330/29: Lykourgos of Melite (l. 10), *SEG* XXXVII 124.2; Theokrines of Hybadai (l. 14), *IG* II^2 2409, 44 (cf. Lewis, 32). *Diaitetes* in 329/8: Euetion of Sphettos (l. 12), *IG* II^2 1925, 16–17.

[55] P. Brun, *L'orateur Démade* (Bordeaux, 2000), 12 n. 5.

[56] A. Oikonomides, *AW* 22 (1991), 3–8; cf. Lewis, 35.

[57] Cf. Lewis, 35.

[58] *IG* II^2 2409, 68 (cf. Lewis, 33). Cf. *PAA* 569375, 569056 and 569380. A Kephisophon of Cholargos was last on the list of *epimeletai* of the Amphiaraia (no. 17, 329/8), for which a good case can otherwise be made that it is in order of seniority. That might suggest that he was a young man in 329/8 and tends to confirm that we should be cautious about identifying him with the public arbitrator of 330/29.

rarity in a state decree at this late date). J.S. Traill, *Hesp.* 47 (1978), 271, however, advised by Habicht, proposed Χαρ⟨μύλ⟩ου, on the basis of the known Χαρμύλος son of Kallisthenes of Trinemeia who was a lessee in the accounts of the Delian Ampictyony (*IG* II^2 1641, 17) and is also on the mid-iv BC bouleutic list published by Traill (cf. *LGPN* II s.v. Χαρμύλος 7).[59] This was noted but not accepted into his text by Petrakos in *IOrop.* Though there is no other case on the stone of corruption of a whole syllable, Habicht's suggestion is attractive. It can not, however, be ruled out that, as commonly at this period, we have to do with a family in which more than one name in Χαρ- occurred.[60]

The confusion of upsilon and iota which Habicht's correction entails suggests another. At 33–5 the current text is:

γραμματεύς
Σωκράτης Παιονίδ
Πυθόδηλος Ἁγνούσιο

Now in fact it is the second of these two men who is known to us as secretary of 328/7 (γραμματεὺς κατὰ πρυτανείαν, cf. A.S. Henry, *Hesp.* 71 (2002), 91–94; *LGPN* II s.v. Πυθόδηλος 9 and 10 are the same man). The rubric γραμματεύς in 33 clearly applies also to this man. Sokrates of Paionidai (for whom see *LGPN* II s.v. Σωκράτης 104) presumably held one of the other secretaryships (γραμματεὺς τῆι βουλῆι καὶ τῶι δήμωι?, cf. *Agora* XV 43, 228, also listing two secretaries). This suggests that the rubric should read γραμματε<ῖ>ς (as e.g. at *IG* II^2 2941, 1732, 7).

7. IG *II^2 547*

Progress may be made on the date, on which the key bibliography since *IG* II^2 has been:[61]

[59] The only other identifiable member of the family at present is Theoteles son of Kallisthenes of Trinemeia, councillor in 303/2 at *Agora* XV 62, 225.

[60] The phenomenon of shared name components in families is discussed most recently by me in *Prakt. Wilhelm*, 335–6 [= this volume, 329–30].

[61] It is not necessary to discuss in detail the restorations of the prescript proposed in *IG*$^{1-2}$. They entail significant epigraphical or calendrical irregularities and were superseded by the proposal of Dow, Meritt and Pritchett (see below). E.g. Kirchner assumed that δευτέραι μετ' ε|ἰκάδας could mean 22nd of a month. It has since become established that it designates 29th (or perhaps occasionally 28th) of a month. He also assumed that two of the first four prytanies had 35 rather than 36 days, which is inconsistent with Ath. Pol. XLIII 2.

B.D. Meritt, *Hesp.* 4, 1935, 536; W.K. Pritchett and B.D. Meritt, *The Chronology of Hellenistic Athens* (Cambridge Mass., 1940), 2–3 (*SEG* XXI 292); Pritchett-Neugebauer, 56; Meritt, *Ath. Year*, 105–6; S. Dow, *Hesp.* 32 (1963), 339–40, 351; Summary at Schwenk 74. M.H. Hansen, *GRBS* 23, 1982, 348 no. 81. Tracy, *ADT* 114.

The parameters are supplied by the hand, Tracy's "Cutter of *IG* II^2 337", whose known work dates to 337–323. Beyond that, the only significant information supplied by the very fragmentary remains of the | 101
prescript is that the secretary's demotic ends]ος. This would suit 335/4, 332/1, 328/7, 325/4 or 324/3. The demotics of the secretaries of 336/5, 331/0 and 326/5 are not known.[62] The date is unlikely, on current evidence, to be before 333/2, the year of the earliest decree naming the *symproedroi* (*IG* II^2 336B = Schwenk 31). Most probably, therefore, this decree dates to 332/1, 331/0, 328/7, 326/5, 325/4 or 324/3. The names of the archons and/or secretaries of the first three of these years can not be accommodated to the surviving text without assuming a significant irregularity. Any of the last three, however, is currently possible with no irregularity. Pritchett and Meritt, building on a suggestion of Dow (ap. Meritt 1935), restored 5th of pryt. 10 = 29th Thargelion 324/3, an equation suitable to a regular ordinary year. Hansen pointed out that 10th of pryt. 9 = 29th Mounichion 324/3 is also possible.

On current evidence for the year 326/5, the same two equations can be applied, mutatis mutandis, to that year, which was also ordinary, i.e.

[ἐπὶ Χρέμητος ἄρχοντος ἐπί τῆς Οἰν or Αἰγ]- stoich. 28
[ηίδος δεκάτης πρυτανεία]ς ἧ[ι Κηφι]-
[σοκλῆς.......^{13}......]ος ἐγ[ραμμά]-
[τευεν· Θαργηλιῶνος] δευτέρα[ι μετ' ε]-
[ἰκάδας, πέμπτηι τῆς] πρυτανε[ίας· ἐκ]-
[κλησία· τῶν προέδρων] ἐπεψή[φιζεν

or [ἐπί Χρέμητος ἄρχοντος ἐπὶ τῆς Αἰα]-
[ντίδος ἐνάτης πρυτανεία]ς ἧ[ι Κηφι]-
[σοκλῆς.......^{13}......]ος ἐγ[ραμμά]-

---

[62] The secretaries of this period are conveniently listed by Develin, *AO*. *IG* II^2 328 (= Schwenk 15) has been thought to show that the secretary of 336/5 had 19 letters, but the prescript of this decree can as easily be restored to the year 335/4. Νικόστρατος Λ[-, inscribed on the moulding of *IG* II^2 348 (= Schwenk 44), is more likely to be the honorand than the secretary of 331/0. On both these decrees see *Athenian State* III.

[τευεν· Μουνιχιῶνος] δευτέρα[ι μετ' ε]-
[ἰκάδας, δεκάτηι τῆς] πρυτανε[ίας· ἐκ]-
[κλησία· τῶν προέδρων] ἐπεψή[φιζεν

The known calendrical data for 326/5 are:

(a) Leontis probably held the sixth prytany. See *IG* II^2 800, as restored by S. Dow, *Hesp.* 32 (1963), 358–63 = Schwenk 64, which implies that the father's name + demotic of the secretary of this year had 15–16 letters, consistent with l. 3 of our text.
(b) 30th of [pryt. 7], Erechtheis = 8th [Elaphebolion], an equation suitable to a regular ordinary year (*IG* II^2 359 = Schwenk 63).
(c) Pandionis occupied the..^{4}..ης prytany (*SEG* XXXV 74).
(d) *IG* II^2 363 = Schwenk 67 is too fragmentary to yield firm information (might not date to 326/5).

The prescript can also be restored for the intercalary year, 325/4, i.e.

325/4 [ἐπ' Ἀντικλέους ἄρχοντος ἐπί τῆς Οἰ]- stoich. 28
[νηίδος τρίτης πρυτανεί]ας, ἧι [Ἀντι]-
[φῶν Κοροίβου Ἐλευσίνι]ος ἐγ[ραμμά]-
[τευε· Βοηδρομιῶνος] δευτέρα[ι μετ' ε]-
[ἰκάδας, δεκάτηι τῆς] πρυτανε̣[ίας· ἐκ]-
102 [κλησία· τῶν προέδρων] ἐπεψή[φιζεν |

There are two decrees of 325/4 which preserve calendrical information: *IG* II^2 360 = Schwenk 68 = *RO* 95; *IG* II^2 361 = Schwenk 69.

The known prytanies in 325/4 are Aegeis (5th, Schwenk 68) and Akamantis (10th, Schwenk 69).

If 325/4 began as a normal intercalary year, with two prytanies of 39 days, 10th of pryt. 3 was the 88th day (39 + 39 + 10). If one assumes that Hekatombaion and Boedromion were full and Metageitnion hollow, δευτέραι μετ' εἰκάδας (29th) Boedromion = 88th day (30 + 29 + 29). No datum is inconsistent with these assumptions, though it is clear that, by the time *IG* II^2 360 = Schwenk 68 was passed, on 34th of pryt. 5 = 11th [probably Posideon II (intercalated)] the prytany calendar and the festival calendar had become out of step by about 2 days.

8. IG *II 221*

The current text is:

339/8 [ἐπὶ Λυσιμαχίδου] ἄρχοντος ἐπὶ τῆς Ἀκαμα- stoich. 33
[ντίδος δευτέρας] πρυτανείας ἧι Φαῖδρος

[Χολλείδης ἐγραμ]μάτευεν· Βοηδρομιῶνος
[ὀγδόηι ἐπὶ δέκα τ]ῶν προέδρων ἐπεψήφιζε
[......^{12}......'Αρ]ιστίππου· ἔδοξεν τῆι βο-
[υλῆι καὶ τῶι δήμω]ι· ἐπειδὴ οἱ πρυτάνεις ο-
[ἱ--------------------]

The inscription was first published by Lenormant (*Rh. Mus.* 21 [1866], 363 no. 102) and, as often with inscriptions from this source, it is difficult to resolve satisfactorily the question of its authenticity (see in general O. Masson, *Mus. Helv.* 50 (1993), 44–60, this inscription, 52–3). Köhler included it in *IG* II, but registered scepticism. He noted that no prytany decree was known earlier than iii BC; that the omission of the proposer and of the demotic of the chairman would be highly unusual; and that the repetition of the article after οἱ πρυτάνεις would be unexpected. The inscription was excluded altogether from *IG* II^{2}. The subsequent discovery of a squeeze in Berlin, however, led Kirchner to republish it in 1926 as genuine, with a restoration of the prescript to the second prytany of the year 339/8. Subsequently an inscription discovered in 1937 and published by E. Schweigert, *Hesp.* 7 (1938), 291–2 no. 18 = *SEG* XVI 52, revealed that the demotic of the secretary of 339/8 was Χολλείδης. This suited the space available at l. 3 of our text, and Schweigert (1940) restored accordingly.

A photograph of the Berlin squeeze is at Fig. 8.[63] Clearly the inscription existed, but was it genuine or a forgery? As Stephen Tracy points out *per ep.*, the slight irregularities in the stoichedon layout might be an argument for authenticity: "the text…is…characteristic of what cutters do in practice, especially if they are working free hand without making a careful final layout. This is, I think, most often the way they worked. The vertical columns wander or maeander a bit and this "wandering" is caused in large part by iota which this inscriber always places at the left side or edge of the stoichos. This placement pulls over as it were the letter immediately to the right; omega in line 3 and zeta in line 4 are good examples. He also makes tau as though it were an iota so that the vertical is placed at the left side of the stoichos. When the crossbar is then added, the letter falls to the left (see the tau in l. 6). I find nothing amiss with the shapes of the letters, not even the omega.[64] Their somewhat thick appearance may be due to the hardness of the

[63] According to Lenormant in 1866 the inscription was in Toulouse "apud D. Montano". Enquiries in the Toulouse region have so far failed to trace the stone.

[64] This was in reply to my observation that the omega was unusually tall and thin.

squeeze paper... in any case stamps can not be used to incise letters.[65]
103 I also find the sort of | small inconsistencies that are characteristic of ancient cutters. [E.g.] the central horizontal of the epsilon is usually quite long and occasionally slants upwards a bit. It is once or twice shorter (l. 5)." As Tracy implies, the forms of the letters can in general be paralleled in the second half of the fourth century (see, for comparison, the phot. of *IG* II² 540 a at Fig. 9); and as the foremost present day authority on Attic letter cutters his opinion should be accorded considerable weight. However, the hand is unidentifiable and the general impression created by this squeeze makes me somewhat uneasy, an unease shared by Angelos Matthaiou. Apart from the omega, Matthaiou notes (personal communication) that the omicron is unusually large in proportion to other letters (suggestive almost of a 5th century hand) and that the shape of the kappa is somewhat odd. He is also struck by the unusual thickness of the letter strokes (c. 1.5–2.0 mm.). Another unsettling feature is the stoichedon grid, horiz. 0.0137 × vert. 0.0176. The vertical exceeds the horizontal stoichedon by over 25%. Of the c. 130 Athenian state laws and decrees which certainly date to 352/1–322/1 there are only three in which vertical stoich. exceeds horizontal by more than 10%. From the point of view of the script, we must conclude that, on present evidence, it is possible that this was the work of an ancient craftsman, but we can not rule out that it was a clever forgery made by a skilled 19th century mason. If he used a genuine ancient decree as an exemplar that might explain why the inscription in many respects looks authentic.

Some of the peculiar textual features noted by Köhler also continue to give cause for concern. The omission of a proposer, though very rare, can be paralleled at this period (Henry, *Prescripts*, 44), but the inclusion of the chairman's father's name, but no demotic, can not at any period (cf. Henry, *Prescripts*, 41). A prytany inscription in 339/8 would no longer be as surprising as it was in Köhler's time, since we now have no. 4, discovered in 1973 and dating to c. 340–325; but the inclusion of the definite article after οἱ πρυτάνεις continues to surprise (one expects ἐπειδὴ οἱ πρυτάνεις τῆς + tribe name, cf. *Agora*

[65] This was in reply to my observation that the unusually thick strokes of the letters gave the impression of being blocked in with a stamp or template rather than of incised strokes. One can not perhaps altogether exclude the possibility that the original was not a stone but some other hard medium which would take a template and a squeeze.

XV 69 ff.). It is notable that the demotic of the secretary of 339/8 suits the space available in l. 3 of our text, but there were many Athenian demotics with nine letters.

If the text is genuine there remains the question of the precise date. The form of the prescript, including three of the four dating elements (date in prytany is missing) suggests c. 340–330, when the full form with four dating elements was being established; and this is consistent with the general character of the lettering. Before 340 one would not expect both month and day in the month (the earliest Attic decree certainly containing both these elements is *IG* II^2 237 of 338/7). Apart from the intercalary year 339/8, however, there is one other year in the period 340–322/1 whose secretary is unknown and whose archon could be accommodated comfortably in l. 1, i.e. the ordinary year 331/0:

331/0 [ἐπ' 'Αριστοφάνους] ἄρχοντος ἐπὶ τῆς 'Ακαμα- stoich. 33
[ντίδος δευτέρας] πρυτανείας ἧι Φαῖδρος
[.....^{9}....ἐγραμ]μάτευεν· Βοηδρομιῶνος
[τρίτηι ἐπὶ δέκα· τ]ῶν προέδρων ἐπεψήφιζε
[......^{12}......'Αρ]ιστίππου· ἔδοξεν τῆι βο-
[υλῆι καὶ τῶι δήμω]ι· ἐπειδὴ οἱ πρυτάνεις ο-
[ἱ---------------------]

The only known prytany of 331/0 is the tenth, held by Kekropis (*IG* II^2 349 = Schwenk 45). It has been thought that the very fragmentary *IG* II^2 348 = Schwenk 44 shows that the secretary of this year was Ν̣ικόστρατος Λ-, whose name is inscribed on the moulding above the main text of the decree, but the dating of this inscription to 331/0 is no more than conjecture and I shall show in *Ath. State* III that Nikostratos may rather have been the honorand. 331/0 was an ordinary year (cf. Pritchett-Neugebauer, 49–50; Meritt, *Ath. Year*, 90–1). In a regular ordinary year in which Hekatombaion is full and Metageitnion is hollow and in which the first two prytanies have 36 days, 13th Boedromion = 72nd day (30+29+13) = [36th day of] pryt. 2 (36 + 36). 13th Boedromion saw the beginning of activities relating to the Mysteries, but was not itself a festival day (Mikalson, *Calendar*, 54).

If the year is 339/8, Kirchner's restoration is the only plausible one available, without assumption of irregularities or Assembly meetings on festival days. In a regular intercalary year in which the first two | 104
months are full and in which the first two prytanies have 39 days, 18th Boedromion = 78th day (30+30+18) = 39th day of pryt. 2 (39 + 39).

9. IG *II² 298*

Of this decree only the final words are preserved, instructing the secretary to inscribe the decree

ἐστή[ληι λ]-
[ιθίνηι] καὶ στησάτω πρόσθε τ-
[οῦ βουλ]ευτηρίου. *vac.*
vac. 0.275

The erection of decrees "in" or "in front of the Council chamber" was rare (cf. P. Liddel, *ZPE* 143 (2003), 88–9 table 4). At an earlier period it did not necessarily indicate that the decree was honorific, or, apparently, even that it related directly to the Council. For 5th century cases see cf. *IG* I³ Index p. 1071 s.v. βουλευτήριον. The only earlier 4th century case is *IG* II² 195. It is heavily restored, but apparently honoured a foreigner and referred to an earlier decree in this location. By our period, however, this place of erection was associated with decrees honouring councillors or Council officials. No. 4 was to be set up ἔμπροσθεν τοῦ] βουλευτηρ|[ίου (25–6); *IG* II² 487, a Council decree of 304/3 honouring Euchares son of Euchares of Konthyle, an official who inter alia had written up the laws, concludes with a clause to the same effect, ἀνα[γ]ράψαι... καὶ σ[τ]|ῆσαι ἔμπροσθεν [τ]οῦ βουλευτηρίου; and the early prytany decree *Agora* XV 58 was also set up ἔμπροσσθεν τοῦ] β̣ο̣υ̣λευτη[ρ]ίου (6).[66] It may well be, therefore, that *IG* II² 298 also honoured a councillor or Council official. The extensive vacat below the text would be suitable for a painted crown. There is discolouration which I have occasionally thought might be a remnant trace of the upper part of it. The parameters for the date are supplied by the hand, which is that of Tracy's "Cutter of *IG* II² 105", active 368–339. Since our earliest state decrees for councillors and council officials date to the 340s, it would be likely that the decree dates to the last decade of the Cutter's known career.

[66] The copy of the famous anti-tyranny law of 337/6 to be set up at the entrance to the Areopagos, ἐπὶ τῆς εἰσόδου τῆς εἰς Ἄρειον Πάγον τῆς εἰς τὸ βο|υλευτήριον εἰσιόντι is not relevant, since that is the "Council chamber" of the Areopagos, not of the Council of 500 (correctly understood by S.N. Koumanoudes, *Horos* 4 (1986), 157–8 and *RO* 79, p. 393). For a doubtful case of a citizenship decree set up ἐν τ]ῶι βουλευτηρίωι in iii BC see M. Osborne, *Naturalization in Athens* (Brussels, 1981), D85 (= *IG* II 328, from Lenormant).

B. *Decrees honouring holders of religious offices*

	Date	Reference	Honorand	Honour
10	c. 340–330[67]	*IG* II² 410. V.-Terzi, B14. S.D. Lambert in *Lettered Attica*, 57–67 (ph.) (summarised: *ZPE* 135 (2001), 52 no. 3). Humphreys, *Strangeness*, 111.	Meixigenes of Cholleidai, priest of Dionysos; Himeraios of Phaleron, priest of Poseidon Pelagios; Nikokles of Hagnous, priest of Zeus Soter; Pausiades of Phaleron, priest of Ammon; ten named *hieropoioi*.	500 dr. c + [50] or [100][68] dr. for sacrifice and dedication | 105
11	328/7 (pryt. 8)[69]	*IG* II² 354. R. O. Hubbe, *Hesp.* 28 (1959), 171–4 no. 2 (ph.). Schwenk 54. Tracy, *ADT* 106. V.-Terzi, B18.	Androkles son of Kleinias of Kerameis, priest of Asklepios (in office).	1. 1,000 dr. c + 30 dr. for sacrifice (1–31) 2. ? (32–44)

[67] I suggested 337. Faraguna, *Atene*, 223 n. 43 suggested 331/0 on the grounds that Phileas of Paionidai, one of the *hieropoioi* honoured by no. 10, was proposer of *IG* II² 348, honouring an actor at the City Dionysia of that year. However, there is no good reason for identifying these two men named Phileas and the date of *IG* II² 348 is quite uncertain. Cf. *Ath. State* III. Humphreys, *Strangeness*, suggests 334, on the eve of the departure of the Athenian naval contingent to join Alexander, but her claim that "prosopographical evidence supports a date in 335/4" rests on dubious assumptions, including: (a) that our elected *hieropoioi* were councillors (the bouleutic *hieropoioi* of Ath. Pol. LIV 6–7 were allotted); (b) that Phileas of Paionidai, councillor probably in 336/5 (*Agora* XV 42, 244) was not the son of Antigenes of this name who was one of our *hieropoioi*, but was the Phileas son of Antiphon (demotic not preserved) of *IG* II² 1251. The erasure of the place of erection of the stele, effectively moving its intended location from Piraeus to Athens, seems to me easier to explain in the aftermath of Chaironeia, when the Piraeus was briefly centre of attention as a safe haven.

[68] Cf. note on no. 1.

[69] A. Reusch, *Hermes* 15 (1880), 341, noted that, if epsilon is read at the end of l. 5, the day of the prytany can be restored either as 26th, ἕ|[κτηι καὶ εἰκοστ]ῆι, if the year was intercalary, or 19th (ἐ|[νάτηι καὶ δεκάτ]ηι), if the year was ordinary. The letter does indeed appear to be epsilon (thus read also by K. Maltezos, *Arch. Eph.* 1914, 190, Schwenk and independently of my reading by J. Morgan and Ch. Kritzas). The vertical and top horizontal are clear; the bottom horizontal is faint, but definite trace of it is legible at autopsy and on the Oxford squeeze, which also shows uncertain

Table (*cont.*)

	Date	Reference	Honorand	Honour
12	326/5	O. Palagia and K. Clinton, *Hesp.* 54 (1985), 137–9 (ph.) (*SEG* XXXV 74)	Priest (of Asklepios or Dionysos?)[70]	–
13*	325/4	*IG* II ^{2} 2838. W. Peek, *Kerameikos* III (1941), 13 no. 10.	Annual (κατ' ἐνιαυτόν) hieropoioi.[71]	c

trace of the spring of the central horizontal. The bottom horizontal does not have the character of a casual mark and, since it was read in 1914, can not be of recent origin. It is not clear on the Berlin squeeze, which explains the scepticism, based on that squeeze, of G. Klaffenbach, *Gnomon* 21 (1949), 135, who, with a number of other scholars (listed by Schwenk), inclined to gamma or pi (though all restorations that have been proposed for pi or gamma are epigraphically or calendrically anomalous. ἕνηι καὶ νέαι π[ροτέραι, restored here in *IG* II ^{2} following Wilhelm, is only attested in Skirophorion). Apparent on the Berlin squeeze is an abraded area under the right end of the top horizontal (kindly confirmed by Klaus Hallof, per ep.). This suggested pi to Klaffenbach, but the abrasion is a consequence of the chipping away of the stone at the edge. It does not imply that there was ever an inscribed stroke at this point. Though the other inscription crucial for determining the character of this year, *IG* II ^{2} 452, is also fragmentary and difficult to read, the weight of scholarly opinion, with which I agree, has favoured a reading of the prescript which yields an intercalary year (see especially S. Dow, *Hesp.* 32 (1963), 348–50; cf. C. Habicht, *Chiron* 19 (1989), 1–5; and see further *Ath. State* III). The equation ἕνηι καὶ νείαι Elaphebolion = 26th day of pryt. 8 is consistent with a regular intercalary year in which the first four prytanies had 39 days, the others 38 (cf. Ath. Pol. XLIII 2 with Rhodes), and in which six of the first ten months (including the intercalary month) were full and four were hollow.

[70] The fragment was probably found built into a modern house to the east of the theatre of Dionysos. This suggested to Clinton and Palagia that the honorand was priest of Asklepios at the Asklepieion west of the theatre (cf. no. 11). He might alternatively have been priest of Dionysos (cf. no. 10).

[71] Cf. Ath. Pol. LIV 6–7. I hope to publish a photograph of this inscription elsewhere.

	Date	Reference	Honorand	Honour
Uncertain				
14	c. 350–300[72]	B.D. Meritt, *Hesp.* 29 (1960), 1–2 no. 2 (ph.). M.H. Hansen, *GRBS* 25 (1984), 136 n. 33. *Agora* XVI 61.	Official performing religious functions?[73]	–

13. IG *II² 2838 (non vidi)*

Peek's interpretation requires amendment on two important points. First, on the right side of the inscribed face he reads οἱ συνάρχοντ̣ε̣ς̣ ἐ̣σ̣τ̣ε̣φ̣ά̣ν̣ωσαν, followed by a name in the accusative, Timokrates son of Philinos of Eleusis, who also appears (largely restored) as one of the ten *hieropoioi* listed to the left. It is clear from parallels that συνάρχοντ̣ε̣ς̣ in such a context designates a man's colleagues in office, i.e. in this case his fellow-*hieropoioi*, not, as Peek thought, other officials of the Council and People; and we may also infer that, whether or not it was inscribed somewhere on this stone, they had passed their own decree crowning Timokrates. Cf. *IG* II² 1251; 1257; 1317, 2; 1455 a 17–18; 2837. Second, Peek raised the possibility that -] τὸν βασιλέα καὶ (l. 20) referred to the Athenian archon, but rejected it in favour of the | 106
Macedonian king, Alexander. Reference to the Macedonian leader as "the king" in a decree of the classical Athenian democracy would be surprising. In *IG* II² 329 he is Ἀλέξανδρος, though the "friends of the king and Antipater" in *SEG* XLII 91 might admittedly be Alexander (or perhaps Philip Arrhidaios, cf. A. Bosworth, *CQ* 43 (1993), 420–7) and the difficulty would be less severe if Alexander's name was included before -] τὸν βασιλέα (cf. Bosworth, 420 with n. 7). In any case in a

---

[72] Tracy, per ep., from lettering. Mid-iv BC Meritt.

[73] So taken by Meritt, restoring a very fragmentary text. However, the prescript would be unusually truncated for an honorific state decree (cf. Hansen) and it is possible that this was a non-state decree or a dedication. Meritt prints the first preserved words as ἄρχον]τος ἐπὶ [τῆς-- | πρυτανείας, but Christian Habicht kindly confirms from the Princeton squeeze my suspicion that only the upper horizontal of the first letter can be read securely. χορη]γ̣ὸς ἐπὶ [-, cf. *IG* II² 1157, 2, or names, -ος Ἐπι-, might be considered.

decree honouring religious officials it would seem preferable to take the reference as to the archon who presided over Athenian religion (cf. Ath. Pol. XLVII 1).

C. *Decrees honouring Athenians for services connected with the Amphiaraion*

There are five extant Athenian state decrees from the Amphiaraion dating to the period immediately following the acquisition of Oropos by Athens (in 335? cf. Knoepfler, *Eretria* XI, 367–89).[74] One, passed on the same day as no. 16, honours the god Amphiaraos (*IG* VII 4252 = Schwenk 40 = *IOrop* 296 (ph.) = V.-Terzi, B12).[75] The other four all honour Athenians. One is no. 6, above; the others are listed below (cf. Tracy, *ADT* 92–3). Note also from Oropos the very fragmentary *IG* II^2 375 = Schwenk 89 = *IOrop* 300, of the tenth prytany of 322/1, the last extant decree of the classical democracy.

	Date	Reference	Honorand	Honour
15*	333/2 pryt. 1[76]	*IG* II^2 338. *Syll.*^{3} 281. Schwenk 28. R. Develin, *ZPE* 57 (1984), 135–6. C. Habicht, *ZPE* 77 (1989), 83–7. Tracy, *ADT* 84. V.-Terzi, B11. *IOrop* 295 (ph.). Humphreys, *Strangeness* 86, 98 with n. 50.	Pytheas son of Sosidemos of Alopeke (superintendent of water supply)	1,000 dr. c

[74] Also noteworthy in this connection is *IG* II^2 171 (cf. n. 5).

[75] This, the only Athenian decree crowning an immortal, will be discussed in a forthcoming paper by Adele Scafuro. It provides for proclamation of the crown by the herald of the people (on whom cf. *Agora* XVI 52). This occurs occasionally in decrees honouring foreigners at this period, not normally for Athenians (cf. Henry, *Honours*, 28–30; *IG* II^2 1629 = *RO* 100, 190–204).

[76] Pytheas was still in office (present tense, ἐπιμελεῖται in l. 13; use of a present tense in relation to an official who has completed his term of office would be unparalleled). The view of most scholars, with which I agree, is that this implies that Pytheas' term of office ran from Great Panathenaia 334/3 to Great Panathenaia 330/29 (see Ath. Pol. XLIII 1 with V.-Terzi, who gives references to earlier bibliography).

Table (*cont.*)

<table>
<tr><th></th><th>Date</th><th>Reference</th><th>Honorand</th><th>Honour</th><th></th></tr>
<tr><td>16</td><td>332/1 pryt. 9</td><td>IG VII 4253. Syll.^{3} 287. Schwenk 41. D. Knoepfler, in ed. M. Piérart, Aristote et Athènes (Paris, 1993), 279–302. Tracy, ADT 78. V.-Terzi, B13. IOrop 297 (ph.)</td><td>Phanodemos son of Diyllos of Thymaitadai, legislator (νενομοθέτηκεν) for the penteteric Amphiaraia (cf. n. 84)</td><td>1,000 dr. c</td><td></td></tr>
<tr><td>17</td><td>329/8 pryt. 3</td><td>IG VII 4254. Syll.^{3} 298. D.M. Lewis, ABSA 50 (1955), 27–36 no. 29. Schwenk 50. Knoepfler (as 16). V.-Terzi, B16. IOrop 298 (ph.)</td><td>10 epimeletai of the Amphiaraia: Phanodemos son of Diyllos of Thymaitadai; Lykourgos son of Lykophron of Boutadai; Demades son of Demeas of Paiania; Sophilos son of Aristoteles of Phyle; Thrasyleon son of Theophon of Acharnai; Epiteles son of Soinomos of Pergase; Nikeratos son of Nikias of Kydantidai; Epichares son of Agonochares of Paiania; Thymochares son of Phaidros of Sphettos; Kephisophon son of Lysiphon of Cholargos.</td><td>1,000 dr. c + 100 dr. for sacrifice and dedication |</td><td>107</td></tr>
</table>

15. IG *II*^{2} *338*

Habicht identified *SEG* XXXVII 159, c. mid-iv BC, inscribed Πυθέας Σωσιδήμου Ἀλωπεκῆθεν, as the funerary monument of the honorand of this decree (see also Μέντωρ 24 (1993), 4–5). The name Pytheas was not especially rare (33 citizen cases in *LGPN* II), but it is probable that Nikostratos and Pytheas sons of Archonides of Alopeke on the funerary monument of mid-iv BC, *IG* II^{2} 5573, were of the same family. Pytheas of A., councillor c. 330 (*Agora* XV 46, 53), was perhaps our honorand. As Habicht notes, he is less likely on chronological grounds to have been the son of Archonides. The only other family members attested hitherto are Nikostratos father of -]ρατος of A., councillor c. 321 (*Agora* XV 55, 34), and Sosidemos of A., councillor c. 150 (*Agora* XV 236, 16). Our knowledge of the family is expanded by another funerary monument, hitherto unpublished, recorded by Fourmont, whose manuscript I examined in Paris in 2003 (Parisinus Supplément grec 854, no. 258). It may be restored as follows:

> Ἀρχεδίκη Πυθέ[ου]
> Ἀλωπεκῆθε[ν]
> θυγάτηρ
> Ναυσικράτης
> [Ν]αυσικράτου[ς]
> [Θ]ορίκιος

This is the first attestation of the name Ἀρχεδίκη (or Ἀρχέδικος) in Alopeke (or Thorikos) (see *LGPN* II p. 68). Her father may have been the honorand of *IG* II^2 338 or the Pytheas son of Archonides of *IG* II^2 5573. Nausikrates son of N. of Thorikos will have been a relation (husband?) of Archedike. A Nausikrates of Thorikos, presumably a relation (father?) of our Nausikrates, is on the mid-iv funerary monument, *IG* II^2 6234, with a Boularchides of Thorikos. There might be a connection with the only other attested Athenian with the name Boularchides, father of Boulekles on the liturgical catalogue of c. 380, *IG* II^2 1929, 10 *(APF* 2914).

D. *Other office holders*

	Date	Reference	Honorand	Honour
18*	346/5 (pryt. 8).	*IG* II^2 215. R. Develin, *ZPE* 57 (1984), 135.	-doros son of Kalli-(held unknown office in 347/6)	c
19	344/3 or shortly after	*IG* II^2 221. D.M. Lewis, *ABSA* 49 (1954), 50. Tracy, *ADT* 70, 74.	-machos son of Diopeithes and others (held unknown office in 344/3)	?
20	337/6 (pryt. 10)	*IG* II^2 243 (= Schwenk 11) + A. Themos, *Horos* 14–16 (2000–2003), 51–1 (ph. fr. b, drawing both fr.).	Kalliteles son of Kalliphanes of Kydantidai[77] (honoured on last day of tenure of unknown office)	c

[77] Cf. *PAA* 562568 and 562845.

Table (*cont.*)

	Date	Reference	Honorand	Honour	
21	334/3? ([pryt. 9]?)[78]	*IG* II² 414a. E. Schweigert, *Hesp.* 9 (1940), 340–1 (ph.) (*SEG* XXI 276). Schwenk 25. Tracy, *ADT* 123 n. 2, 126–7.	[Diotimos?] (general?)[79]	– |	108
22	327/6 ([pryt. 9])[80]	B.D. Meritt, *Hesp.* 3 (1934), 3–4 no. 5 (ph.). Schwenk 59. *Agora* XVI 85.	*Epimeletai?*	–	
23*	paullo post 350	*IG* II² 2827.	officials connected with Dionysos/Dionysia?	c	
24	c. 340–320	B.D. Meritt, *Hesp.* 29 (1960), 51 no. 66 (ph.) (*SEG* XIX 55). *Agora* XVI 65. Tracy, *ADT* 101.	official(s)?[81]	c?	

[78] The year and prytany depend on the restoration of the chairman (ll. 7–8), Δ]|ημοκ[.......14.......as Δημοκράτης Παιανιεύς, chairman in the dated decrees, Schwenk 23 = *IG* II² 335 and 24 = *IG* II² 405. This is possible, but not certain since, to make the prescript fit the available space, the secretary's demotic has to be abbreviated arbitrarily to Φαλη(ρεὺς).

[79] The name is wholly restored and is dependent on the identification of this decree with the one mentioned by [Plut.] *Mor.* 844a, ἐψηφίσατο (sc. Λυκοῦργος) δὲ καὶ Διοτίμωι Διοπείθους Εὐωνυμεῖ τιμὰς ἐπὶ Κτησικλέους ἄρχοντος. This is attractive, but uncertain (cf. previous note). Diotimos led an expedition against pirates, under the terms of a decree proposed by Lykourgos in 335/4 (*IG* II² 1623, 276–85, cf. *APF* 4386; Faraguna, *Atene*, 238–9, 332).

[80] The main point of interest has been the restoration of the calendical expression at ll. 3–4, Μουνιχιῶνος [..4..|........15.......] ΔΕΙ//άτει μετ' εἰκά[δας (3–4), which can be articulated δ' ἐνάτει μετ' εἰκά[δας (Pritchett-Neugebauer, 53), or δεκάτει μετ' εἰκά[δας (B.D. Meritt, *TAPA* 95 (1964), 221–5, Schwenk; but unparalleled in Attica and withdrawn by Meritt, *Arch. Eph.* 1968, 107–8). There is no contemporary parallel for the expression of the date in the month in two different ways and any restoration is accordingly speculative. In *Agora* XVI Woodhead reviews proposed restorations (several of them based on incorrect readings) and prudently comments: "any supplement at this point will be unusual if not unique among calendric formulas and should not be hazarded in a definitive text". Cf. Henry, *Prescripts* 47–8. A possible interpretation of the other prescripts of this year (*IG* II² 356 = Schwenk 58 and 357 = Schwenk 57) is that the calendar was dislocated by the insertion/subtraction of (3?) intercalary days and it is perhaps possible that, as occurred occasionally at a later period (see *Agora* XVI p. 365), a distinction was being made between a κατὰ θεόν and a κατ' ἄρχοντα date, i.e. perhaps ἑβδό|μηι, κατ' ἄρχοντα δὲ] δεκάτει κτλ. A pre-second century parallel for such a formulation, however, is lacking.

[81] τὰς] εὐθύνας [- (3) is probably from the formulaic clause conferring crown(s) on Athenian official(s) subject to the rendering of accounts, ἐπειδὰν τὰς] εὐθύνας [δῶι or δῶσι.

Table (*cont.*)

		Date	Reference	Honorand	Honour
	25	334/3–314/3	B.D. Meritt, *Hesp.* 13 (1944), 243–6 no. 8 (ph.). *Agora* XVI 127. Tracy, *ADT* 124.	six officials and their "allotted secretary" (-]ν τὸν κληρ[ωτὸ|ν γραμματέα, 13–14)[82]	1,000 dr. c
109	26	c. 325–304[83]	*IG* II² 433 + E. Schweigert, *Hesp.* 7 (1938), 300–1 no. 24 (ph. fr. a) (*SEG* XVI 57). A.M. Woodward, *ABSA* 51 (1956), 6 no. VIII. V.-Terzi, B20.	[thesmo-?, nomo-?] thetai[84] (and their secretary?)	c |

[82] A secretary of this description has been restored at *Agora* XVI 194, 7 and 22, honouring *sitophylakes*. According to Ath. Pol. LI 3: ἦσαν δὲ καὶ σιτοφύλακες κληρωτοὶ ⟨ι̅⟩, πέντε μὲν εἰς Πειραιέα, πέντε δ' εἰς ἄστυ· νῦν δ' εἴκοσι μὲν εἰς ἄστυ, πεντεκαίδεκα δ' εἰς Πειραιέα. Meritt, followed by Woodhead in *Agora* XVI, suggested that our decree dated to the period of twelve tribes (shortly after 307/6) and honoured half the board of *sitophylakes*, assuming it to have had 12 members at that time. Tracy, however, has now dated the cutter of this inscription to the period of the ten tribes. Moreover, the boards served by allotted secretaries at *IG* II² 1710 and 1711 (the latter dating to c. 130, cf. S.V. Tracy, *Attic Letter Cutters of 229 to 86 BC* [Berkeley, 1990], 244) are not named and there is insufficient reason to suppose that any board associated with an allotted secretary were *sitophylakes* (see also *IG* II² 3579).

[83] Cf. Schweigert. Since the price of the crowns is given the decree should date to before c. 304, cf. Henry, *Honours*, 26. Since the officer responsible for inscribing the decree is the prytany secretary, it can not date to the oligarchy of 321–318 (A. Henry, *Hesp.* 71, 2002, 107–8). No decree was certainly erected at the initiative of the state in the period of Demetrios of Phaleron's rule, 317–307, cf. Lambert, *ABSA* 95 (2000), 488.

[84] Malcolm Errington notes per ep. that, while there is other evidence for the crowning of *thesmothetai* individually (e.g. *Agora* XVI 86 and 87, *IG* II² 2836 etc.) they were not usually honoured as a board and wonders if the honorands might rather have been *nomothetai*, restoring ἐνομο]θέτησαν in b2 for Schweigert's ἐθεσμο]θέτησαν. As he notes, τοὺ]ς θεσμοὺ[ς (a3) and κατὰ τὰ πά]τρια (a4) would be consistent with either restoration. Honours were occasionally awarded at this period for services in connection with the laws, e.g. the ἀναγραφεὺς τῶν νόμων in *IG* II² 487 of 304/3, and Phanodemos, who νενομοθέτηκεν for the penteteric Amphiaraia in no. 16; but Phanodemos was perhaps proposer of a law to the *nomothetai* (as implicitly Leptines at Dem. XX 96), not sole legislator in his own right. There is no other inscribed decree crowning the *nomothetai* themselves and the award of such an honour by the Assembly to the constitutionally superior body would perhaps be unexpected. It can not be ruled out, however, that the honorands of this decree ἐνομο]θέτησαν in the same sense as Phanodemos νενομοθέτηκεν, i.e. that they were two or more men who had been proposers of laws.

18. IG *II*^{2} *215*

Köhler (*IG* II. 5. 110c) restored the honorand as superintendent of the water supply, αἱρεθέ]|ντος ἐπ[ὶ] Θε[μιστοκλέους ἄρχον]|τος (347/6) ἐπι[μέλεσθαι τῶν κρηνῶν (10–12). However, Ath. Pol. XLIII 1 and no. 15 probably imply that the tenure of this office was from Great Panathenaia to Great Panathenaia and that does not suit our case, since 347/6 was not a Great Panathenaic Year. It is not impossible e.g. that there was a change in the tenure of this office between 347/6 and 333/2 (cf. Develin); but it is more likely that our honorand had held some other, annual, office (appointed by the Council or Assembly, cf. e.g. no. 10, 3; no. 17, 11 and 21).

Kirchner's restoration of the honorand as Κηφισο]|δώρο Καλλί[ο Ἁγνουσίου (9–10), a known individual (*LGPN* II s.v. Κηφισόδωρος 70), is no more than possible. -δωρος and Καλλι- are very common name components. Connections with known men could also be made by restoring Ἀπολλο]|δώρο Καλλί[ου Ἀθμονέως (cf. *SEG* XXIV 197, 22) or Κηφισο]|δώρο Καλλί[ου Θριασίου (IG II^2 6258).

23. IG *II*^{2} *2827*

Found on the Acropolis east of the Erechtheion, this is a fragmentary dedication to Dionysos (A3, 6) erected by men (presumably officials of some description) who had been crowned by the Council and People. Face A contains the dedication formula and a formula naming the priest, presumably of Dionysos. Face B is inscribed with what appears to be the decree by which the crown was awarded. In B I agree with the following readings and restorations, first made by Curbera:

B11: -ἀρε]τῆ[ς] ἕνεκ̣[α καὶ δικαιοσύνης τῆς εἰς τὴν βουλὴν καὶ τὸν δῆμον. Cf. no. 1, A4–5.
B13: ἀναγράψαι δὲ καὶ τόδε τὸ ψήφισμα ἐπὶ τ]ὸ̣ [ἀ]νάθη[μ]α τοὺς αἱρ[εθέντας ποήσασθαι τὸ ἀνάθημα. Cf. no. 1, A8.
B16: shown as vacant in previous eds., but in fact reads: ΣΑΙΣ *vac.*

In addition I note that, in the word printed δόξαντα at B14, the xi appears on the stone a clear Σ. I read -$^{c.\ 4-5}$-]ΗΙΤΑ̣ΔΟΣΑ̣ΝΤΑΠ[--, but can think of no obvious supplement.

A6 presents a conundrum. The current text reads:

[ἐπὶ] Ἀγαθάρχου Ἀστυκράτους ἐκ Κεραμέων ἱερέως πρῶτον.

πρῶτον is obscure. If Agatharchos was the first holder of this priesthood (i.e. if the priesthood was newly created) one would expect the adjective, πρώτου (cf. e.g. *IG* II^2 3562, 3809 and 4193). If Agatharchos was priest for the first time (highly unlikely to be specified in any case), one would expect τὸ πρῶτον, as commonly with iterated offices (e.g. *IG* II^2 3539 = *ABSA* 95 (2000), 501–2, E11, [τὸν ἐπὶ τοὺς ὁπλείτας] στρατηγὸν τὸ ἕβδο[μον]). One might consider "on first becoming priest", "at the beginning of (in the first year of?)" the priest's tenure of office, but I have not been able to trace an epigraphic parallel. It is perhaps preferable to assume that the sense was completed on the following line. This is possible as the first c. 20 letter spaces of that line (A7) are abraded such that they may have carried text which is no longer legible.

No. 1 honours the Council for its work in connection with the City Dionysia and individual councillors for their contribution to the work of the Council during their year in office. The parallel with no. 1 created by Curbera's new readings and restorations of B11 and 13 of *IG* II^2 2827 might imply that Agatharchos was priest of Dionysos on the south slope of the Acropolis and that our honorands had also performed services at the City Dionysia (cf. also no. 11).

E. *Inscriptions on which a decree of the Council is inscribed together with decree(s) of subgroup(s) of the polis*

		Date	Reference	Honorand	Honour
110	27	339/8	*IG* II^2 1155. V.-Terzi, B6. Tracy, *ADT* 99. Inscribed with decree of Kekropis.	Boularchos son of Aristoboulos of Phlya (taxiarch of Kekropis)	[foliage] c |
	28[85]	334/3	*IG* II^2 1156. V.-Terzi, B9. Inscribed with list of ephebes and decrees of Kekropis and demes Eleusis and Athmonon.	Ephebes and Adeistos son of Antimachos of Athmonon, sophronistes of Kekropis.	foliage c

[85] *IRham* 102 (333–324) appears to have been of similar type; cf. *SEG* XXXVIII 67; XXXIX 110 (probably later, see Stroud's note in *SEG*).

F. *Assembly decree relating to foundation of colony on Adriatic coast (incorporated in naval list)*

	Date	Reference	Honorand	Honour
29	325/4	*IG* II^2 1629, 190–204 and 258–63. Gauthier, *Bienfaiteurs*, 114. V.-Terzi, B19. *RO* 100.	1. trierarchs 2. provision for the Council and prytanies, when they have supervised the despatch, to be crowned by the People	1. 500 dr. c for first trierarch to bring ship in, 300 dr. c for second, 200 dr. c for third 2. 1,000 dr. c

Postscript. While this article was in press I realised that *IG* II^2 257 + 300 (cf. *SEG* XL 70) probably also honoured Athenian official(s). See *Ath. State* III. | 111

CHAPTER TWO

ATHENIAN STATE LAWS AND DECREES, 352/1–322/1: II RELIGIOUS REGULATIONS*

This is the second in a series of articles intended as prolegomena to fascicle 2 of *IG* II³.[1] It will be concerned primarily with religious regulations,[2] but I begin with a digression.

---

* This chapter was previously published in *Zeitschrift für Papyrologie und Epigraphik* 154 (2005), 125–159.

[1] On the purpose of the articles and for general abbreviations and acknowledgements see *Ath. State* I. For courteous access to stones I am again particularly indebted to Charalambos Kritzas at the Epigraphical Museum and to John Camp in the Athenian *Agora*; in respect of all the articles to the ephor for Attica and Piraeus, G. Steinhauer, to Kalliope Papangeli at Eleusis and to the other Greek authorities and staff in the *Agora*, the Epigraphical Museum, in the Piraeus and at the Amphiaraion; on this occasion also to Mrs. J. Stroszek at the Kerameikos and to the Greek authorities and staff there. In connection with this and other articles in the series Klaus Hallof and Jaime Curbera kindly facilitated access to squeezes and archives in Berlin, Charles Crowther in Oxford and Christian Habicht in Princeton. Photographs of stones in the Epigraphical Museum were kindly supplied by Charalambos Kritzas. Adele Scafuro spared generously of her time to help with the examination of *IG* II² 2838 and supplied the photograph at fig. 1. Jaime Curbera kindly supplied the copy of Wilhelm's transcript of *IG* II² 333 fr. f in the archive of the Berlin Academy reproduced at fig. 8. I am very grateful to Kevin Clinton for showing me drafts of two lemmata from his forthcoming corpus of Eleusinian inscriptions; to Sally Humphreys, Angelos Matthaiou and Robert Parker for reading an early draft; to Adele Scafuro for reading a final one. In addition to the abbreviations listed in *Ath. State* I the following are used:

Ath. State I: S.D. Lambert, Athenian State Laws and Decrees, 352/1–322/1. I. Decrees Honouring Athenians, *ZPE* 150 (2004) 85–120;

IEleus: Corpus of Inscriptions of Eleusis edited by K. Clinton (forthcoming);

Lambert, *Sacrificial Calendar*: S.D. Lambert, The Sacrificial Calendar of Athens, *ABSA* 97 (2002), 353–399;

Lawton: C.L. Lawton, *Attic Document Reliefs* (Oxford, 1995);

Lewis, *Sel. Papers*: P.J. Rhodes ed., *D.M. Lewis. Selected Papers in Greek and Near Eastern History* (Cambridge, 1997);

Loomis, *Wages: W.T. Loomis, Wages, Welfare Costs and Inflation in Classical Athens* (Ann Arbor, 1998);

LSCG: F. Sokolowski, *Lois sacrées des cités grecques* (Paris, 1969);

Osborne, *Nat.*: M.J. Osborne, *Naturalization in Athens* (Brussels, 1981–1983);

Parker, *Ath. Rel.*: R. Parker, *Athenian Religion. A History* (Oxford, 1996);

Rhodes, *Nomothesia*: P.J. Rhodes, Nomothesia in Classical Athens, *L'educazione giuridica* V (1987) II 5–26;

Rosivach, *Sacrifice*: V.J. Rosivach, *The System of Public Sacrifice in Fourth Century Athens* (Atlanta, 1994);

Stroud, *Grain Tax Law*: R.S. Stroud, The Athenian Grain Tax Law of 374/3 BC. *Hesp. Suppl.* 29 (1998).

[2] By "religious regulations" I mean laws and decrees of the polis the prime purpose of which is to regulate religious matters. I exclude decrees honouring holders

I. *Addenda to Ath. State I:*
(a) *Early inscribed decrees honouring Athenians*

As a rule, Athens did not inscribe decrees honouring its own citizens before the 340s. Two further exceptions should be added to those mentioned at *Ath. State* I, 86:

(i) along with *SEG* XXVIII 46 should have been mentioned *SEG* XXVIII 45, for the Athenians who captured Phyle in 403/2.
(ii) Lawton suggests that the relief she discusses on p. 125 no. 91 (ph.) is from an honorific decree for a priestess of Athena of the first quarter of the 4th century (no text preserved).

These cases are testimony to the exceptional position and status which, in different ways, were enjoyed by the honorands.

(b) *IG II^{2} 2838 and the physical form of inscribed decrees honouring Athenians*

I have now been able to examine *IG* II^{2} 2838 and can add a little to my remarks at *Ath. State* I, 106–7. My provisional revised text is as follows:[3] | 125

Fig. 1. Kerameikos Mus. I 5. Two joining fragments of a stele of white marble, top and right side preserved. South of Dipylon, east of Propylon of the Pompeion, 1929. H. 0.68, w. 0.77 (inscribed surface c. 0.65), th. 0.1. Letters: h. ll. 1–12 c. 0.01–0.011 (O 0.009, Y 0.012), l. 13 0.009, ll. 14–16 0.007, ll. 17–19 c. 0.005. Height of letters + interline (non-stoich.): c. 0.019. Stoich. ll. 17–19 (square?) c. 0.0105.

Edd. *IG* II^{2} 2838; W. Peek, *Kerameikos* III (1941), 13–16 no. 10.

Cf. *Ath. State* I no. 13.

---

of religious offices (for which see *Ath. State* I) and religious texts, such as sacrificial calendars, which are not explicitly laws passed by the *nomothetai* or decrees of the Athenian Council and/or Assembly.

[3] "Provisional" because, despite the generous help of Mrs. J. Stroszek and the Greek staff, a definitive account of this inscription must await its examination under better conditions as regards space and lighting than those which currently prevail in the storeroom of the Kerameikos.

325/4 [ἱεροποιοὶ] οἱ κατ' ἐνιαυτὸν οἱ ἐπ' Ἀντικλέους non-stoich.
ἄρχοντος ἀνέθεσαν *vac.*
[στεφανωθ]έντες ὑπὸ τῆς βουλῆς καὶ τοῦ δήμου ἀρετῆς ἕνεκα καὶ δικαιοσύνης·

[Πολύ]ευ̣κτος [-c. 5-]δίο Θη̣μακεύς[I] 13 οἱ συ̣νάρχοντ̣ε̣ς̣ ἐ̣σ̣τ̣ε̣φ̣ά̣νωσαν
[-c. 6 - λ]υκος ΚΛ[-c. 3-]ει[-c. 3]ου̣ Ικ[α]ριεύς[II]
[--c. 7-]ι̣ο̣ς̣ Κ̣[ρ]α̣τ̣ίο[υ] Κ̣[υ]δαθ̣η̣ν̣αιεύς[III]
[------------Λευκ]ο[νοε]ύς[IV] [Τ]ι̣μοκράτην
[------------]ος Κεφαλῆθεν[V] Φιλ̣ίνου
[------------]ου Π̣ερι̣θοί[δη]ς[VI] Ἐ̣λ̣ευσίνιον[VIII]
-----------------[VII]
[Τιμοκράτης Φιλίνου Ἐ]λ̣[ευσί]ν̣ι̣ο̣ς̣[VIII]
--------------------[IX]
--------------------[X]

[---------c. 43---------]ΟΣ[...] stoich. *painted crown(s)?*
[---------c. 43---------..]Λ̣[..]
[---------c. 43---------]ΤΗ̣Σ[.]Σ̣
[---------c. 43---------..]Ι̣[..]

c. 20 lines severely worn *vacat*

41 [--------------------c. 65--------------------σ]αν ἐν τῶι
[--------------------c. 63-------------------]σ̣α̣ν̣ δ' ἑαυτοῖ-
[ς -------------------c. 63---------- ------------]̣ ἐπαινέσαι
[--------------------c. 48-------ἕν]ε̣[κ]α̣ τ̣[ῆ]ς [πρὸς] τὸν βασιλέα καὶ
[--------------------c. 51------------προσέτ]αξεν αὐτοῖς ὁ δῆμος
[--------c. 26---------καὶ στεφανῶσαι αὐτοὺς χρυσῶι στε]φ̣άνωι, ἐπειδὰν τὰς εὐθύ-
[νας δῶσιν· ἀναγράψαι δὲ---------c. 34------------καὶ] στῆσαι ἐν τῶι ἱερῶι τ-
[---------------c. 42-----------δοῦ]ναι τὸν ταμίαν τοῦ δήμου τοῖς ἱερο-
[ποιοῖς-----------c. 45----------------]. Τ̣ΩΙ̣[..........18.........]

stone breaks away

I have retained all Peek's readings, many of which I was able to confirm at autopsy. I have also retained his restorations (due in some places to Kirchner and Klaffenbach), subject to pruning of the more speculative. I saw enough to justify removal of dots or square brackets here and there and traces consistent with Peek's restoration εὐνοίας (or some other quality) ἕνεκα τῆς πρὸς] in l. 44. As Peek saw, l. 49 may have read ἐκ τῶν κατὰ ψηφίσματα ἀναλισκομένω]ν̣ τῶι [δήμωι. Peek began his decree text in my line 41, suggesting that the space under the list of names to the left had perhaps been occupied by crowns. In fact, however, there are enough traces visible at autopsy[4] to show that

[4] As often with worn stones, the traces are visible primarily from discolouration. They do not appear on my squeeze.

this space was occupied by the beginning of the decree text, which ran for about 24 lines before the lines increased in length at l. 41. I have noted some tentative readings of letters towards the end of the first four lines. It should be possible to improve on the reading of this part of the text when the stone can be examined under optimum lighting conditions. There is a somewhat similar arrangement, i.e. a column of text with lines which lengthen towards the bottom under a list of names in another column, on *Ath. State* I no. 4. It is possible
that we have to do with two | separate short decrees, the upper one 126
passed by the *hieropoioi* in favour of Timokrates (for comparanda see *Ath. State* I 106); more likely that the whole text is that of the state's decree honouring the *hieropoioi.* The total number of letters would be comparable with the other extant decree honouring *hieropoioi* at this period, *Ath. State* I no. 10.[5] As Peek noted, the space immediately above the preserved end of l. 41 is vacant. Above that, under the name of Timokrates, the stone is worn. The space was perhaps occupied by painted crown(s).

The most notable feature of this inscription, however, is its physical form, which is unique among Athenian state laws and decrees of this period. Peek described it as a "stele" and that is correct insofar as, like other "stelai", it was inscribed on a block of stone which was relatively thin in proportion to its height and width. It differs from normal stelai, however, in several respects:

(a) most stelai were significantly higher than they were wide. This one is much wider than usual (normal ratio of thickness to width: 1:4.5; this stele: 1:8). It may have been somewhat wider than it was high, or about square. The original left side and bottom are not preserved, but, as Peek noted, from the text to be restored to the left the width can be calculated at about 0.80. If there was little or no text after l. 49 and no significant vacat at the bottom, the height will have been about 0.70.

(b) the back is not rough picked, like most stelai, nor smoothed to take an inscription, as occasionally occurs at this period (see below), but flattened, so that it could be placed flush against another surface behind it, perhaps a wall.

[5] Our decree: (24 × 48 = 1152) + (c. 10 × 73 = 730) = c. 1882 letters. *Ath. State* I no. 10: c. 47 × 45 = c. 2115 letters.

(c) there are two cuttings in the top for T-clamps to affix the "stele" to a structure behind.[6] It was not, it seems, a self-standing "stele", but rather an inscription affixed to a ?wall (at eye-level?). One might perhaps describe it as a "plaque". It was apparently located in a sanctuary (ll. 47–48).[7]

The physical character of the inscription is relevant to another aspect of its interpretation. Most state inscriptions honouring Athenians at this period were inscribed on normal self-standing stelai, but there are three others which have the character of a dedication, with appended decree(s). They are:

1. *Ath. State* I no. 1 (ph.) = *IG* II^2 223 (343/2). The five decrees are inscribed on three sides of an orthogonal base, with cuttings in the top to receive a statue. The dedicatory formula is: ἡ βουλὴ ἡ ἐπὶ Πυθοδότου [ἄρχοντο]ς ἀν[έ]θ[ηκεν] | Ἡφαίστωι στεφανωθεῖσ[α ὑπὸ] τοῦ δήμου | ἀρετῆς ἕνεκα καὶ δικαιοσύνης. This appears to reflect the provision made in the fragmentarily preserved decree II (Face B, ll. 3–4): ἀναθεῖναι τό τε ἄγα|[λμα----c. 9---τῶι Ἡφ]αίστωι καὶ τῆι Ἀθηνᾶι τῆι Ἡφαιστίαι. It is not clear why Athena Hephaistia is mentioned in the decree, but not in the dedicatory formula. Köhler suggested that it may have been because the statue depicted Hephaistos only (see also M. Walbank, *ZPE* 139 [2002], 62). In fact it is obscure why Hephaistos was the object of this dedication at all. There is no obvious connection between him and the subject matter of the decrees, the first two of which relate to the honouring of the Council for its work at the city Dionysia, while the last three honour contributions to the Council's work during the year. Phanodemos was the prime mover, proposer of decree II and honorand of decree III.[8] Humphreys, *Strangeness* 102

[6] One of these cuttings is located 0.25 from the preserved left side, at the break point of the two fragments, the other 0.04 from the right side. Length of cross-bar of T: c. 0.04. Depth: 0.03. The cuttings are of similar type to those used for clamping together the stelai of the sacrificial calendar of Athens in its Ionic phase. Cf. Lambert, *Sacrificial Calendar* (illustration and detailed description of cuttings at S. Dow, *Hesp.* 30 [1961], 58–73).

[7] The inscription was found south of the Dipylon, east of the Propylon of the Pompeion in 1929. Its findspot is unusual (one of only two published inscriptions of this period bearing state decrees found in the Kerameikos excavations), but it is unclear how far it may have wandered from its original location.

[8] Decree II, passed by the Council, apparently provided for setting up the dedication and for inscribing on it the decree of the Assembly honouring the Council for its

n. 61, thinks of the festival of Hephaistos, the Chalkeia, which was apparently discussed by Phanodemos in his published work (Harp. s.v. Χαλκεῖα· Φανόδημος δὲ οὐκ Ἀθηνᾶι φησιν ἄγεσθαι τὴν ἑορτὴν ἀλλ' Ἡφαίστωι, *FGH* 325 Phanodemos F 18), but there is no obvious connection | between the content of the decrees and that festival. More- 127
over the Chalkeia took place on the last day of Pyanopsion,[9] which will have fallen early in pryt. IV in 343/2 and 342/1. The decrees, on the other hand, appear to have been passed between the City Dionysia in pryt. VIII and around the end of the year. The answer may lie in the lost parts of decree II, the most fragmentarily preserved of all the decrees on this stone. It is perhaps conceivable that Phanodemos looked forward to the Chalkeia as a suitable occasion for the dedication following the Council's rendering of accounts after the end of its year in office, but this would be unparalleled and seems far-fetched. One wonders whether the dedication was set up in the Hephaisteion[10] and whether this was chosen simply as the major temple closest to the Council chamber.

2. *Ath. State* I no. 6 (ph.) = *IOrop* 299 (328/7). The Council decree is inscribed under the list of donors to the Council's dedication, uniquely on a base which has the form of a thickened stele. A small statue was perhaps affixed at the top. The introductory formula is: οἵδε ἐπέδοσαν εἰς τὸ ἀνάθημα ὃ ἀνέθηκεν | ἡ βουλὴ ἡ ἐπ' Εὐθυκρίτου ἄρχοντος. It was set up in the Amphiaraion in Oropos.

3. *Ath. State* I no. 23 = *IG* II² 2827 (shortly after c. 350). This was an orthogonal base, comparable in this respect to 1, inscribed on the front with the following dedicatory formula: -----|--- ΝΙ̱----[ἀ]ν̣ε̱θηκ̣α̣[ν.]---------Ι̱ΟΑ[-$^{c.\,4}$-]Σ̱[-$^{c.\,2}$-]Ε̱[--$^{c.\,7}$--]εις ἀνέθεσαν τ̣|[ῶι Διο]νύσ[ωι στεφανωθέντες ὑπὸ τῆς] βου[λῆ]ς καὶ τοῦ δήμου χρ̣υ̣|[σῶ]ι στε[φάνω]ι ἀ[ρετῆ]ς [ἕν]εκα καὶ δικαιοσύνης τῆς εἰς τὴ̣|[ν β]ο⟨υ⟩λὴν καὶ τὸν̣ δ̣ῆμον. *vac.* [ἐπὶ] Ἀγαθάρχου Ἀστυκράτους ἐκ Κεραμέων ἱερέως πρῶτον [--?]. The honorific decree was inscribed on the right side (the left side is not preserved). I suggested in *Ath. State* I that the dedication might

---

work at the City Dionysia in pryt. VIII (decree I). Decree III honours Phanodemos as best speaker in the Council in pryt. IX. It may be that decree II was proposed in pryt. IX and was one of Phanodemos' proposals recognised by decree III.

[9] Mikalson, *Calendar* 78. *IG* II² 353 = Schwenk 51, proposed by Demades, was passed at an Assembly on this day in 329/8.

[10] In that case it will have travelled somewhat to its findspot, in the foundations of the church of St. Demetrios τοῦ Κατηφόρη, east of the tower of the winds. Evidence for other inscriptions set up in the Hephaisteion is very slight. Cf. *IG* II² 2792.

have been set up by officials who had performed some function at the City Dionysia. If, as in decrees I and II of *Ath. State* I no. 1, they were councillors, -]εις ἀνέθεσαν might perhaps be πρυτάν]εις. Cf. *Ath. State* I no. 1, decrees IV and V: ἐπειδὴ Εὔδοξος Θεαγγ̣[έλου | Συπα]λήττιος καλῶς καὶ δικαίως ἐπεμελήθη τῆς διοικήσεως ὑπὸ τῆς βουλῆς {φ}ἐφ' ἧν εἰρέθη καὶ τῆς ἄλλης [εὐ|κοσμί]ας τῆς βουλῆς μετὰ τῶν πρυτάνεων τῶν ἀεὶ πρυτανευόντων. This base has been hollowed out and its top is not preserved; but it can be assumed that it was originally mounted by a statue, like *Ath. State* I no. 1. The base was found on the acropolis and, like the large majority of inscriptions found there, that was probably its original location.

Now in all three of these cases the dedication consists of two objects: the preserved inscription and the (lost) statue, for which the inscription served as a base. In our case it seems impossible that any object can have been affixed to the plaque: instead the plaque was apparently affixed to a structure. It seems that the object dedicated must either have been the structure itself, or an object, such as a statue, placed in close proximity, by or in the structure to which the plaque was affixed. In this respect the dedication perhaps had something in common with *Ath. State* I no. 4, though in that case the inscription was not affixed to a wall, it was itself apparently a wall-block, perhaps from the lintel or epistyle of a monument, apparently set up in front of the Council chamber (ll. 24–26).

At this period the inscribing of state decrees on dedications is a feature specific to decrees honouring Athenians.[11] As we know from clauses contained in four of the surviving decrees, one of the honours awarded an Athenian was, or might be, money for sacrifice and a
128 dedication.[12] There was most likely a | similar provision in our decree at l. 48, which, as Peek saw, can be restored from these parallel cases

[11] Foreigners might choose to dedicate the crown they were awarded and it might be inscribed appropriately (e.g. *IG* II^2 222 = RO 64, 33–39), but they were not awarded money specifically for a dedication.

[12] *Ath. State* I no. 1 decree I (Assembly): sacrifice (the dedication was provided for in decree II (Council)); no. 10: sacrifice and dedication; no. 11: sacrifice; no. 17: sacrifice and dedication. It is obscure why no. 11 lacks provision for a dedication (it might conceivably have been contained in decree II). It may not be coincidental that in all four cases the services had been of a religious character: for festival organisation (no. 1 decree I for the Council's work at the City Dionysia, no. 17 for *epimeletai* of the penteteric Amphiaraia, no. 11 for a priest of Asklepios) or performance of sacrifices (no. 10 for *hieropoioi*).

along the lines εἰς δὲ θυσίαν καὶ ἀνάθημα δοῦ]ναι τ̣ὸ̣ν τ̣α̣μίαν τοῦ δήμου τοῖς ἱερο||[ποιοῖς -. As pointed out in *Ath. State* I (p. 86 with n. 8), the practice of inscribing the dedications preceded the practice of inscribing the decrees.[13] When, in the 340s, it became common to inscribe the decrees, the option of inscribing them on the dedication itself rather than (like decrees for foreigners) on a self-standing stele naturally presented itself and was taken in some cases (a minority, it seems).[14] One might even inscribe the decree both on the dedication and on a separate stele (envisaged in *Ath. State* I no. 1, decree III).[15]

I conclude this brief discussion with a summary table setting out the physical form of decrees honouring Athenians at this period:

normal stele[16]	*Ath. State* I nos. 3, 5, 10, 11, 12, 15, 16, 17, 20, 25
dedication: base[17]	*Ath. State* I nos. 1, 6,[18] 23
dedication: plaque[19]	*Ath. State* I no. 13
block from lintel or epistyle of monument?[20]	*Ath. State* I no. 4
uncertain[21]	*Ath. State* I nos. 2, 7, 9,[22] 18, 19,[23] 21,[24] 22,[25] 24,[26] 26

[13] For dedications by *hieropoioi* without inscribed decree see e.g. *IG* II² 2832, II² 2859.

[14] Groups other than the Assembly and Council also began commonly inscribing decrees on dedications in around the 340s; see e.g. *Agora* XV 26 and 38.

[15] The evidence is insufficient to establish a progression from inscribing the decree on the dedication to inscribing it on a stele.

[16] All these inscriptions preserve original backs. Thickness is in the range: 0.06–0.155 m.

[17] Thicknesses are: no. 1, 0.75; no. 23, at least 0.33 (back not preserved); no. 6, 0.2.

[18] A base in the form of a thick stele.

[19] Thickness: 0.10.

[20] Thickness: 0.33.

[21] I include in this category all fragments which do not preserve an original back. It is primarily from the thickness of a fragment that one can determine whether it is from a stele or a base or wall block.

[22] It is possible that the back of this fragment is original. If so, it was a stele (thickness: 0.09).

[23] It is possible that the back of this fragment is original. If so, it was a stele (thickness: 0.11).

[24] It is possible that the back of this fragment is original. If so, it was a stele (thickness: 0.08).

[25] It is possible that the back of this fragment is original. If so, it was a stele (thickness: 0.105).

[26] Described by Meritt as a “block”. However, the back is not original, and the surviving thickness, 0.113, would be consistent with either a stele or a base.

II. *Religious regulations: a physical characteristic*

Physical features are also crucial to our understanding of the religious regulations of this period. A normal stele bearing a law or decree, as was noted above, had a rough-picked back. A few such stelai, in contrast, are opisthographic or have backs which are smoothed to take an inscription.[27] In this period, they are the following:

1. *IG* II^2 333 = *Ath. State* II (below) no. 6. Laws about cult objects. Smooth back (preserved only on fr. c + f). Set up on acropolis. Thickness: 0.16.
2. *SEG* XVI 55 = *Ath. State* II no. 8. About a Festival. Smooth back.
129 Found on north slope of acropolis. Thickness: 0.132. |
3. *SEG* XXXII 86 = *Ath. State* II no. 9. About a Festival. Smooth back. Found in Agora.[28] Thickness: 0.113 (top)—0.118 (bottom).
4. *IG* II^2 310 = *Ath. State* II no. 11. Lease of sacred land? Smooth back. Findspot unknown. Thickness: 0.15 (top)—0.155 (bottom).
5. *IG* II^2 244. See most recently M.B. Richardson in ed. P. Flensted-Jensen et al., *Polis and Politics* (Copenhagen, 2000), 601–615. Law and specifications for repair of walls. Smooth back. Found in Piraeus and probably originally set up there. Thickness: 0.125 (top)—0.13 (bottom).
6. *IG* II^2 236 = RO 76 = Schmitt, *Staatsverträge* III no. 403. Treaty establishing League of Corinth. Smooth back. Found on Acropolis (fr. a). Thickness: 0.132.
7. *IG* II^2 412. See M.H. Hansen, *C & M* 33 (1981–2), 119–23 (cf. *GRBS* 20 [1979], 32–35). Law fragment. Opisthographic.[29] Findspot unknown. Thickness: 0.078.

It should, of course, be borne in mind that original backs are not preserved on many fragments and in such cases we can not tell whether

[27] This type of smooth back can in principle be distinguished from the flattening which is designed to enable the back to fit flush against another surface, such as a wall (as e.g. *IG* II^2 2838, discussed above), though in practice, especially with small and/or worn fragments, the distinction can not always confidently be made.

[28] At this period very few state laws and decrees were set up in the area of the agora and most of the fragments found there belong to inscriptions originally set up on the acropolis.

[29] The opisthographic character of this fragment has not previously been noted. Only a few letters are legible on the "back" (no complete word).

or not they were smoothed or inscribed. In other cases it is difficult to make a judgement as to whether the back is original. This applies, for example, to *IG* II^2 334+ = RO 81 = *Ath. State* II no. 7, the two fragments of the law and decree on the Little Panathenaia. Their backs may be original at their thickest points,[30] but show signs of reworking, including mortar(?) adhering to the backs and sides.

Now the most notable feature of this group is that several of them are laws. *Ath. State* II no. 6 carries two laws. *IG* II^2 244 carries a law. From their subject matter *IG* II^2 412 and *Ath. State* II no. 9 can reasonably be identified as laws. Very few 4th century laws are preserved on stone.[31] It is not likely to be coincidental that laws figure so prominently among the few stelai from our period which are opisthographic or have smooth backs. On the other hand it is not the case that all laws were inscribed on stelai of this type. The recently published grain tax law, for example, has a rough-picked back (see Stroud, *Grain Tax Law* 1–2) as, from our period, does the law against tyranny (*SEG* XII 87 = RO 79). Nor can we quite assert that only laws had smooth backs. *IG* II^2 236 does not seem to be a law and it is questionable whether *Ath. State* II no. 11 is a law. *IG* II^2 236 has the same thickness as *Ath. State* II no. 8. As we shall see below (discussion of no. 8), the two stones are companions, most likely set up next to eachother. What, it seems, we can say is that, in contrast to normal decree stelai, the rough-picked backs of which were clearly not designed to be looked at, a back which was inscribed, or smoothed to take an inscription, was intended to be seen.[32] In principle the inscription should have been set up in a location where one could walk around it; and it seems that this mode of display was regarded as particularly appropriate for at least some laws. The reason for this is not entirely clear, but perhaps tradition had something to do with it. Solon's laws had been inscribed on objects

---

[30] The maximum preserved thickness of fr. a is 0.13; of fr. b, from lower down the stele, 0.135.

[31] Stroud, *Grain Tax Law* 15–16, counts nine, plus some possible cases, to which others might be added (e.g. RO p. xviii n. 7). There are about 800 inscribed state decrees of the 4th century.

[32] It might be tempting here to draw a distinction between the opisthographic stele and the smooth-backed stele, but caution is in order. On none of these inscriptions is the entire back preserved (in my view the top of *IG* II^2 244 has probably been cut down) and it can not be ruled out that they were inscribed on some part of the back which is not preserved. Nor can it be ruled out that some of these backs were painted rather than inscribed (there are extensive vacats at the tops of some normal decree stelai, most likely intended to take paintings).

inscribed on more than one side (axones) and some of the inscriptions which carried the laws produced by the revision process at the end of the 5th century were opisthographic, in particular, it seems, the Athe-
130 nian sacrificial calendar in its Attic phase (410–404).[33] |

III. *Religious regulations: general remarks*

It is convenient to subdivide the inscriptions in this category as follows:

A. on Eleusinian matters
B. on (non-Eleusinian) sacred land or property (statues, dedications etc.)
C. festival regulations
D. dubia.

In *Ath. State* I (see also section I a of this article) we saw that, with rare earlier exceptions, decrees honouring Athenians began to be inscribed in the 340s. The pattern of incidence of religious regulations is rather different. Looking backwards, categories A and B were well-established. They show several examples from the first half of the fourth century and their incidence can not be said to intensify in our period.[34] Inscribed festival regulations, however, are characteristic of the Lykourgan period and are almost unexampled in the earlier fourth century.[35] With decrees honouring Athenians we saw that the appearance of the genre in the 340s should be ascribed, at least to an extent,

---

[33] See most recently Lambert, *Sacrificial Calendar*. It is unclear whether the wall referred to in connection with the later phase of the revision of the laws (403–399) in the decree of Teisamenos cited by Andoc. Myst. 84, τοὺς δὲ κυρουμένους τῶν νόμων ἀναγράφειν εἰς τὸν τοῖχον, is relevant here. It is possible that this refers to temporary display of laws undergoing ratification. See P.J. Rhodes, *JHS* 111 (1991), 95–100; Rhodes, *Nomothesia*, 12.

[34] Eleusinian: *Agora* XVI 56 (367–348) regulates the Mysteries; *Agora* XVI 57 (400–350) on Eleusinian first fruits; *IG* II^2 140 (*SEG* XXX 62, XLV 56, L 43 and 141) (353/2) on Eleusinian first fruits. Sacred land, objects etc.: *IOrop* 290 (369/8) on repairs to Amphiaraion, spring there etc.; *IG* II^2 217 and 216 + 261 (*SEG* XIV 47) (365/4) on sacred objects on Acropolis (cf. below no. 6); *SEG* XXI 241 (*SEG* XLVI 122, cf. XLVII 29) (363/2) on listing of sacred gifts (Piraeus); *IG* II^2 47 (*SEG* XXI 233) (*SEG* XLVII 122) (c. 370–50, cf. Parker, *Ath. Rel.* 182, 184) on Asklepieion at Zea (apparently establishes sacrifices and provides money for construction of temple); *IG* II^2 120 (*SEG* XXXVII 74) (353/2) on chalkotheke.

[35] *IG* II^2 47, however, might arguably be assigned to this category, as well as *Agora* XVI 56.

to a change in inscribing practice. Such decrees had been passed before (we do not know with what frequency), but were regularly inscribed only from the 340s. The same issue arises in relation to the festival regulations of the Lykourgan period. Was it an especially busy one for festival regulation, or was it simply that more such regulations were being inscribed? The increased incidence of such inscriptions is certainly consonant with other indications that this was a period of intense interest and activity in the religious sphere.[36] However, a measure of caution is in order. The religious regulations on stone are, for the most part, laws. As already noted, the number of extant laws inscribed on stone in the fourth century is very small. The reasons for this (as with many aspects of fourth century Athenian law-making) are not yet well understood. It may not have been normal practice to inscribe laws; there may have been fewer laws than decrees; they may have been inscribed in places (or conceivably in a medium, such a bronze) such that they have perished or have not been found in such large numbers as decrees.[37] A combination of such factors seems likely to be relevant. We can not rule out that the incidence of extant laws at different times is in part a product of changes in such factors. In other words it may be that (as with decrees honouring Athenians) a higher proportion of all laws passed (or of laws with religious content) were inscribed at this period than previously;[38] or that there was a shift in the place (or medium) in which they were inscribed such that more have been found. Certainly it was not the case that there was no innovation by the state in the sphere of cult and sacrifice in the first half of the fourth century.[39]

So far as I know, no inscription in any of the categories A–D is extant from the period 321/0–301/0. This is not the place for a full consideration of the reasons for this, nor for examination of the incidence of religious regulation through the 3rd century and beyond. To
an extent the fall-off can be accounted for by | developments in legal 131

[36] Cf. Parker, *Ath. Rel.* 242–55.

[37] The large majority of 5th and 4th-century Athenian decrees were set up on the acropolis and have been found on or in close proximity to this well-researched site. If Richardson [above, section II] is right that laws tended to be set up in places appropriate to their content, they will have been more scattered and one would expect fewer of them to have been found.

[38] There is some support for this in that the majority of extant inscribed fourth century laws are of Lykourgan date.

[39] Note e.g. the cult of Peace, introduced in 375 (Parker, *Ath. Rel.* 229–30 and in general 218–42).

and epigraphic practice. Demetrios of Phaleron (317–307) undertook a complete revision of Athenian laws and there was apparently another revision after his fall from power.[40] Neither process seems to have produced inscriptions. Indeed the state seems to have ceased inscribing decrees altogether in the period of Demetrios of Phaleron's government. It is possible, however, that the epigraphic trend in the religious sphere also reflects broader historical developments. After 325, with the death of Lykourgos (and, we may assume, other leaders of his ilk, such as Phanodemos, around the same time), it is not implausible that there might have been a reaction against the intense activity in the religious sphere which had apparently characterised the period since Chaironeia; nor that, given the political, military and constitutional upheavals of these years, Council and Assembly might have been preoccupied with other matters.

IV. *Religious regulations: annotated list*[41]

A. *On Eleusinian matters*

No. 1 was set up in Eleusis and in the City Eleusinion (ll. 56–7). We possess the former copy. No. 2 is the only other state decree certainly dating to this period found in Eleusis and was doubtless also set up there.

	Date	Reference	Subject
1*	352/1	*IG* II^2 204 + Add. p. 659; D. Peppas-Delmousou, Ἀρχ. Δελτ. 30 B (1975) [1983], 7 (ph.); A. Scafuro, *Symposion* 14 (2003), 123–143; RO 58 (reflects some of the points made below); *IEleus* 144 (ph.).	Sacred Orgas
2	349/8	*IG* II^2 209; *IEleus* 78 (ph.); Lawton no. 34 (ph.).	Eleusinian cult?[42]

[40] *IG* II^2 487. Cf. Rhodes, *Nomothesia*, 20.

[41] As in *Ath. State* I the function of this list is not to discuss each decree in extenso, but to supply pointers to key epigraphical bibliography since *IG* II^2 and to present significant new textual (and occasionally contextual) points.

[42] Perhaps to be inferred from findspot and relief, the surviving portion of which depicts Demeter, seated and draped, facing to the left.

1. IG *II*^{2} *204* = *RO 58* = IEleus *144*
As Clinton notes, many letters read by earlier editors towards the left are no longer legible from the stone.

1 Only the final letter of the line is legible: Ị Lam., E previous eds. A vertical stroke is apparent in the centre of the stoichos (to the right of where one would expect the left vertical of E). There are some scratches to the right which have perhaps been taken to be from the horizontals of epsilon, but are in my view casual marks.

2–]. ΙΙ επ-. I confirm Clinton's reading of two verticals, most likely nu, before the epsilon. There is a nick at the bottom right of the previous stoichos, on the break of the stone, taken to be from a vertical (Clinton) or diagonal (*IG;* the Berlin squeeze appears to indicate diagonal). It is rather low and might alternatively be a casual mark. εἶπε]ν̣· ἐπ|[ειδὴ would seem possible.

7–12 The restoration of the beginnings of 7–12 in *IG* II^2 is doubtful as it assumes a process of dispute settlement (διαδικασία). Scafuro argues that what took place was rather determination of boundaries by investigation and unilateral decision. In 7 Matthaiou, per ep., persuasively suggests τοὺς δὲ αἱρεθέντας καθίζειν ἐν τῶι Ἐλευσ]ινίωι for *IG* II^2's δικάζειν ἐν τῶι Ἐλευσ]ινίωι (due to Foucart). Cf. *SEG* XII 87 = Schwenk 6 = *Agora* XVI 73, 14–15; Dem. XXIV 89, XXV 23 etc.

17 in. ΙΩΝ Foucart, ιΩΝ Lolling. τεμεν]ῶν Tsuntas, πατρ]ίων Foucart, ἁπάν]των Ziehen, ἁπάντ]ων *IG* II^2. The vertical stroke read by Foucart and Lolling is legible on the Berlin squeeze. Curbera reports that its position (0.006 from the left of the following omega) indicates that it is a right vertical (for a central | vertical one would expect 132
c. 0.01). This tends to confirm Tsuntas' restoration.

26 ἐ]νειργασμ[έ]να. *IG* II^2 and Clinton follow Foucart against Ziehen (ἐ]πειργασμένα) and Köhler and Dittenberger (μ]ὴ̣ εἰργασμένα). *IG* II^2 and Clinton are correct; all strokes of a definite nu remain visible.

30–1 γραμ|ματεὺς *IG* II^2. The last letter of 30 is certainly N (cf. Foucart and Köhler's majuscule). Cf. Threatte I, 595–7.

56–7. στ[ήλαιν λιθίναιν καὶ στῆσαι τὴν] μὲν Tsuntas. 55–6, read with 60–1 (especially ἑκατέραν), are most naturally taken to imply that both this decree and the decree of Philokrates were to be inscribed on the same stele, of which one copy was to be erected in Eleusis, the other at Athens in the Eleusinion. In the event there may have been two stelai in each location. The preserved dimensions of our stele are 1.29 h., 0.62 w. (original), 0.13 th. (original). Neither top nor, probably, bottom as preserved is original, though the bottom may be close to its original position and we may not be missing much more than the prescript from the top. On any account the height is considerable, both in relation to most ordinary decree-bearing stelai and to this stele's other dimensions. Compare Dow's norm for the relative proportions of the thickness, width and height of a decree stele: 1:4.5:9. Our stele, as preserved: 1:4.75:10. Unless Philokrates' decree was very short, it seems unlikely that its text was accommodated above our decree.[43] This sort of minor divergence from the precise provisions of the decree would not be surprising, even without the explicit clause in 84–6 enabling corrections.[44]

The dual, στήλαιν λιθίναιν, is possible in this context (5th cent. cases at Threatte II, 94), especially in a decree in which there is frequent use of the dual in other contexts (cf. 27 τοῖν θεοῖν, 23–24 καττιτέρω ἴσω καὶ ὁμοίω, etc.), but there appears to be no unequivocal case in a 4th century decree (that at *IG* II^2 17, 9 is restored), whereas the 4th century does show examples of the plural used for two (e.g. *IG* II^2 448, 26–7; *SEG* XII 87, 23 has ἐν στήλαις λιθίναις δυοῖν) and indeed the singular for two (*IG* II^2 125, 17–18, where two copies are probably envisaged; *SEG* XXVI 72, 44–7). One can not rule out, therefore, στήλαις λιθίναις καὶ στῆσαι τὴν μὲν κτλ. and (assuming an additional letter, not problematic in this text), στήληι λιθίνηι καὶ ἀναθεῖναι τὴν μὲν κτλ. Cf. on 61.

59–60......^{10}....<u>.]O</u>[..^{3}.] τὸν <u>ταμ</u>ίαν τοῦ δήμου το||[ῖς?----: - : δραχμάς]· Lam., δοῦναι δ' αὐτοῖς] τὸν ταμίαν τοῦ δήμου τὸ | [ἀργύριον τριάκοντα δραχμάς] *IG* II^2. (The underlined letters occupy 1 and 2 stoichoi respectively). Prices elsewhere (rather later) for an ἀρεστήριον, include 15 dr, *IG* II^2 839, 46; 20 dr., *IG* II^2 1537, 26. *IG* II^2's text is unconvincing, because (a) the restored wording at the beginning of 60 (due to Wilamowitz), awkwardly juxtaposing ἀργύριον and the

[43] The width of the stele increases markedly from top to bottom (0.605 at l. 28, 0.620 at l. 72). The width of the margin to the right of the text remains steady at 0.014–5 (the left margin can no longer be detected); but in line with the widening of the stele the horizontal stoichedon dimension increases from c. 0.0122 at the top to c. 0.0128 at the bottom.

[44] Compare the decree for Lapyris of Kleonai (*IG* II^2 365), required to be erected:

εἰς τὴν στήλη[ν τὴν ἐν ^{v}]
ἀκροπόλει ἐ[ν] ἧι γέγραπται Ἐχεν[βρότωι]
Κλεωναίωι τῶι προ⟨γό⟩νωι τῶι Λαπύ[ριος ^{v}]
ἡ προξενία.

What is apparently the earlier decree survives (*IG* II^2 63) and it is in fact on a separate stele.

amount, is not in line with the similar clauses in 61–65 (where numbers rather than words are used for the amount) or in general with parallels in comparable contexts;[45] (b) the restoration of the lacuna in 59 is undermined by my new reading (confirmed by Angelos Matthaiou) of O or Θ, aligned between the O and Y of δοῦναι in the following line. I have as yet been unable to find wholly convincing supplements. In 59 one might consider εἰς δὲ τοῦτο δ]ο̄[ναι (yielding 11 letters in space for 10, not problematic in this text; cf. 63 for the orthography, δο̄ναι). το- at 59 fin. is perhaps dative plural expressing the recipients. | 133

60–1 εἰς τὴν ἀναγραφ|φ[ὴν ταῖν στήλαιν : ΔΔ : δραχμὰς *IG* II^2. On the one hand the dual in this context, while possible, has no certain parallel in the 4th cent. (cf. on 56–7). On the other, the plural, τῶν στηλῶν, would tend to imply restoration of 40 dr. (: ΔΔΔΔ :) εἰς] ἑκ[α]-τέραν on grounds of spacing. Normal provision at this period was 20 or 30 dr. a stele (cf. Loomis, *Wages* 163–164), though 40 dr. can not perhaps be ruled out where two decrees were involved and where, in fact, four stelai may have been erected (cf. on 56–7). : ΔΔΔ : with stoichedon irregularity is also possible in this text, with either ταῖν στήλαιν or τῶν στηλῶν.

62 fin. I agree with Clinton that the letters inscribed were ΤΩΝ not the TON read by earlier eds.

63 τῶν αἱρεθ|έ[ντων εἰς Δελφοὺς ἑκάστωι : Δ :] δρ[α]χμὰς RO (Δ Foucart, ..^{3}. *IG* II$^{1 \text{ and } 2}$). Ten drachmas is possible for the travel expenses of those sent to Delphi, but, even if one figure is to be restored, parallels (for which see Loomis, *Wages* ch. 12; this case 212–3) are insufficient to rule out the other one-digit possibilities, i.e. ⊢, Γ or even 𐅄; and we can not be sure that one digit is needed since stoichedon irregularity is frequent in this part of the text. No. 13 raises the possibility ⊢⊢⊢.

66–71 It would seem that this section of text provided for the making of the *horoi*, under, it seems, a contract let by the *poletai* (in which context the Council was also referred to); that the *proedroi* were involved; that there were to be written specifications; and that the *horoi* were to be placed as directed by the commission. The *horoi* were to be funded by the treasurer from the People's fund for matters relating to decrees. In the absence of parallels it is very doubtful whether there is enough basis for restoration of specific wording, and none of

[45] E.g. *IG* II^2 223, B15, ἑλέσθαι πέντε ἄνδρας... οἵτινες ποήσονται τὸν στέφανον· τοὺς δὲ ταμί[ας δοῦναι τ]ὸ ἀργύριον ἐκ τῶν κατὰ ψηφίσματα ἀνα[λισκο]μένων...); 1202, 12: δοῦναι δὲ αὐτοῖς τὸ ἀργύριον τὸ εἰς τοὺς στεφάνους Ἡγησίλεω τὸν δήμαρχον κτλ.

the suggestions made hitherto is satisfactory (see e.g. the objections of Rhodes, *Boule* 27–8; others might be added; one uncertainty is the function of τε in 67. As Foucart saw, one would expect an answering καὶ in a decree text at this period). There seems little to be gained by further attempts.

74–86 My text, which does little more than add detail to Köhler's, is:

[οἵδε ἡιρέθησαν ἐπὶ τὴν ἱερὰν] ὀργά[δ]α ἀντὶ τῶν ἐκπεπτωκό[τ]-
[ων νέους ὅρους θεῖναι : ἐκ τῆς β]ο[υλῆ]ς : Ἀρκεφῶν : Ἀ̣λ̣α̣ι̣εύς *v*
[.. *nomen* ......29...... *demoticum* .... *nomen* ...]ης : Θριάσ̣ιος *vvvvvvv*
[.. *nomen* .....25.. *demot.* ... *nomen* .....:] Ἁγνούσιος *vac.*
[ἐξ ἰδιωτῶν : ... *nomen* ...16... *demot.* .]ιος [:] Ἱπποκράτης : ἐκ Κερ[α]-
[μέων : .. *nomen* .9. *demot.* .]ο̲ς̲ : [....]ε̲[.]ω̲[ν :] ἐκ [Κ]η̲δών : Ἐμμενίδης : Ε[..]*b*
[.......14... *nomen* . : Σ]ουν[ιεὺς : Ἀ]ριστείδης : Οἰῆθεν *vvv* [*vvv*]
[... *nomen* ..17.. *demot.* ..]ιος : Γλαύκων : Περιθοίδης : Φαῖδρος
[....7. *demot* .. : ἐπὶ τὸ μαν]τεῖον εἰς Δελφοὺς : ἐξ ἰδιωτῶν· *vvvvvv*
[... *nomen* .....16.... *demot.* ....]εύς : Εὐδίδακτος : Λαμπτρεύς· *vvvvvvv*
[ἐκ τῆς βουλῆς : ...6...]ος : Λαμπτρεύς : [τ]άδε ἐπαν[ο]ρθοῦται·
[ἐὰν δέ του προσδέηι τόδ]ε τὸ ψήφισμα, τὴν βουλὴν κυρίαν εἶνα-
[ι ψηφίζεσθαι ὅτι ἂν αὐτῆι δ]οκῆι ἄριστον εἶναι. *vac.*
vac. 0.245

75 I confirm from the stone Clinton's excellent new reading Ἀ̣λ̣α̣ι̣εύς (Λαμπ⟨τρ⟩εύς earlier eds.). One gains impressions of the left half of mu and of the right side of pi, but on closer examination it is apparent that these are caused by scratches.

79–86 Fr. b (EM 5136), lost at the time of II², but rediscovered and joined to fr. a by Peppas-Delmousou, contains the very end of 79, the last 3 stoichoi of 80 (surface not preserved), the last 3.5 stoichoi of 81, the last 5 (vacant) stoichoi of 82, the last 6 (vacant) stoichoi of 83, the last 7.5 stoichoi of 84, the last 9 stoichoi of 85 and the entire vacant end of 86. If the letters at the start of 79 are correctly read and articulated (nothing is now clearly legible from the stone before ΔΩΝ), the space available for name + punctuation + start of demotic at 79 in., is rather short and abbreviation of the demotic of Kerameis (at line end?) is possible. Köhler restored [Χαιρ]ε[φ]ῶν (not an attested name in Kedoi). There are other possibilities, e.g. [Διομ]έ[δ]ων; and I note
134 Ἱέρων of Kedoi at *Agora* XV 42, 15. |

79–80 Kirchner identified this man with the Ἐνμενίδης (sic) of Koile who was chairman in *IG* II² 208 (349/8), restoring ἐ[κ Κ]|[οίλης here, and this is accepted by *LGPN* II; but we now know that an Ἐμμενίδης of Hekale was councillor in 336/5 (*Agora* XV 42, 263) and Ἑ[κα|λῆθεν is accordingly equally possible.

84–86 ἐάν δέ του Lam. ἐάν τοῦ Foucart, ἐὰν δέ το Wilhelm in *IG* II². Wilhelm assumes -ο for -ου, possible in this text (cf. e.g. προέδρος in 67), to yield the correct number of letters in the line. However, since 86 in. seems to have contained an additional letter, it is not problematic to assume that 85 in. did also.

The extent of vacant stone beneath the text is 0.245 (0.12 *IG* II²). The difference is due to the re-addition of fr. b, which preserves a greater extent of vacat at the bottom.

B. *Sacred land or objects*

	Date	Reference	Subject
3*	c. 340–330[46]	*IG* II² 403; *Syll.*³ 264; *LSCG* 35; W. Bannier, *Ph. Woch.* 45 (1925), 463–64 (*SEG* III 85); A.M. Woodward, Ἀρχ. Ἐφ. 1937 A. 159–70 (especially 169–70); W.K. Pritchett, *Studies in Ancient Greek Topography* VIII (Amsterdam, 1992), 73–6; I. S. Mark *Hesp. Suppl.* 26 (1993) 113–4, 123–5 (*SEG* XLIV 39).	Repair of statue of Athena Nike
4	333/2	*IG* II² 337; Tracy, *ADT* 114; RO 91.	Permitting Kitians to found temple of Aphrodite
5*	mid-iv[47]	*IG* II² 295; Humphreys, *Strangeness* 119 n. 30.	Lease of sacred land?
6*	c. 335	*IG* II² 333 (ph. *a* ll. 4–12, J. Kirchner, *Imagines Inscriptionum Atticarum* [Berlin, 1935], pl. 29 no. 63); A.M. Woodward, *Hesp.* 25 (1956), 106; J. Tréheux, *BCH* 80 (1956), 462–79; Meritt, *Ath. Year,* 80; D.M. Lewis ap. N. Conomis ed., *Lycurgi in Leocratem* (1970), p. 21 (c+e f, ll. 20–21); T. Linders, *Studies in the Treasure Records of Artemis Brauronia* (Stockholm, 1972), 56 n. 36, 74–75; T. Eide, *Symb. Os.* 59 (1984), 21–8; Schwenk 21; Tracy, *ADT* 84.	Laws about cult objects

46 Cf. Mark; Tracy, *ADT* 11 n. 28; Humphreys, *Strangeness* 119 with n. 28.

47 "Litt. volg. med. s. iv" Kirchner. ἐς for εἰς (10, cf. 5) was unusual after 350 (Threatte I, 189).

3. IG *II*[2] *403*

This fragmentary and somewhat neglected decree is of considerable interest.[48] It is based on a report by a board elected to oversee the repair (ἐπὶ τὴν] ἐπισκευὴν) of a statue of Athena Nike which had originally been dedicated from the spoils of campaigns in western Greece during the Peloponnesian War. The substance of the decree is only fragmentarily preserved, but appears inter alia to have provided for a propitiatory sacrifice (ἀρεστήριον, 19) and to have praised the sculptor responsible for the repair (30–4).

Fr. b is very difficult to read. It has not previously been worked over as thoroughly as fr. a and has yielded some new readings, the most significant of which is at 23–25, where I read (autopsy and Oxford
135 squeeze): |

ἐπειδ[ὴ] ὁ ἀ[νδ]ρι̣αν[τ]ο̣π[οι]ὸ-
[ς.....9....]ν ὑψηλό[τ]ε̣[ρ]ο[ν π]ο̣ι[η]σ̣α[..3.]
[.....10.....]Ε̣Τ̣Α̣Ν

That the ἀνδριαντοποιός,[49] praised in 30, was also lurking in 23 was seen by Bannier[50] and is confirmed by my new readings. The words in 24, however, are entirely new[51] and indicate the nature of the work that had been carried out: the statue had been made higher (most probably, it seems, by raising the base).[52] This is not the place for an explora-

[48] It received some attention in early collections (e.g. E.L. Hicks and G.F. Hill, *A Manual of Greek Historical Inscriptions* [Oxford, 1901] no. 147), mainly as a sort of footnote to Thucydides (cf. n. 54), but its significance as evidence for the mentality of the 330s (a subject that can not be pursued at length here) has not been recognised.

[49] Usually this signifies a sculptor of human figures, but here a worker in metal seems to be meant, as opposed to a sculptor in stone, as also at Arist. *EN* 1141a 10–11.

[50] Also by Wilhelm in his transcript of this inscription preserved in the *IG* archive in Berlin.

[51] *IG* II[2] prints only: .....10.....]N[.]YH/[....7...]/[...]AΛ[.. | ....10.....]EIAN?. In ΥΨΗΛΟ the omicron is read from the Oxford squeeze. The stone has now eroded away at this point. Of the epsilon there is trace of the left vertical. The second omicron is fully visible, though damaged in its upper part. In π]ο̣ι[η]σ̣α[the iota and alpha are clearly legible in full. The omicron is damaged and somewhat distorted in shape, as commonly on this stone. The sigma is damaged and abraded, but the top and apparently more markedly sloping bottom bars are visible. As Matthaiou suggests per ep. we might restore [τό τε βάθρο]ν ὑψηλό[τ]ε̣[ρ]ο[ν π]ο̣ι[ή]σ̣α[ς vel sim. Cf. *IG* I[3] 472, 157; II[2] 1388 B 65.

[52] For advice on this point I am most grateful to Antonio Corso, who informs me that a fashion for higher statue bases seems to have developed in the late 4th century. It would be tempting to interpret τρε?]ῖς πόδ[ας (Kirchner's tentative reading) in 32 as alluding to the height by which the statue was raised. However, while the reading is difficult, I was inclined at autopsy marginally to prefer Lolling/Köhler's τ̣ῆς πόλ̣ε̣[ω]ς̣

tion of the art-historical implications. The symbolic implications of restoring and "raising" an Athena Nike are clear enough. The proposer was an unidentifiable man from Lakiadai, not Lykourgos, but both the decree and the action it commemorates are markedly "Lykourgan" in character: in the way that they look back self-consciously to a glorious episode of the Peloponnesian War, when the power and prestige of Athens was at its height;[53] in the concise, but slightly pedantic, way that the original circumstances of the capture of the booty from which the statue was made are detailed;[54] and particularly in that the whole episode is reminiscent of one of the statesman's famous achievements: the replacement of the fifth-century golden *Nikai* which had been melted down for coin in the later stages of the Peloponnesian War (c. 406/5, [Plut.] *X Orat.* 852b, cf. Paus. I 29, 16; for the accounts of this, dating to 334/3 or later, see below on no. 6; Woodward). It is improbable that the repair of this *Nike* was distant in time from that event; it might perhaps have been a prelude to it. One suspects a date after Chaironeia, though neither hand nor other internal evidence (the prescript is largely lost) rule out a slightly earlier date. On any account the decree should be brought into connection with the striking quantity of epigraphical evidence for Athenian diplomacy with Akarnania in this period. The spoils from which the statue was made were inter alia ἀπ'] Ἀν|[ακτοριῶν (11–12), where Athens had waged a successful campaign with her Akarnanian allies in late summer 425 (Th. IV 49). Compare the well-known decree of 338/7 honouring Akarnanian exiles who had fought with Athens at Chaironeia (*IG* II² 237 = RO 77) and the decree of 337/6 honouring the Akarnanian doctor Euenor[55] (*IG* II² 242+373; M.B. Walbank, *ZPE* 86 [1991], 199–202; *SEG* XL 74, cf. XLI 44; Veligianni-Terzi, *Wertbegriffe* 100–101 A165). See also *IG*

(*IG* II 5, 513e). The Λ sports what looks like the left end of a bottom horizontal, but this is perhaps a casual mark, or possibly a cutting error. There is insufficient basis for Kirchner's identification (at *Syll.*³ 264), following H. Pomtow (see *Jhb.* 37 [1922], 83), of the ἀνδριαντοποιός as Menekrates. See Colin ad *FD* III 4, 3; Pritchett n. 91.

[53] Lyk. 1, for example, is full of such nostalgic antiquarianism with respect to Athens' 5th century past. Cf. Lyk. fr. 9.2 Con. This tendency is of course manifest in other actions of Lykourgos (e.g. the establishment of the tragic canon) and in the activities of others, such as Phanodemos, who had comparable interests. This was the period when 5th-century Athens began to weigh heavily on the Western Mind.

[54] The events are narrated at Th. III 85, 106–112, 114; IV 2–3, 46, 49.

[55] The relevant part of the text (ll. 8–15) is largely illegible, but it is an attractive speculation that the decree was occasioned by services rendered by Euenor to soldiers wounded at Chaironeia, just as the date of the second decree (322/1) suggests services during the Lamian War.

II^2 266; 267; *Agora* XVI 66?; *IG* II^2 208 = Bengtson, *Staatsverträge* II
136 no. 325. |

5. IG *II^2 295*

The lettering is non-stoich. The right side of the stone is preserved, with space for c. 7 letters to the right of the last letter in 1 (which reads HP, not NI). The text places obligations on the *basileus* (note the imperatives in 9, -]τω ὁ βασιλε[ὺς[56]—, and in 11, where the correct reading is -]σθω ὁ βασ[ιλε|ὺς)[57] and is therefore a state decree, probably a lease of sacred land (a temenos and sanctuary?). Cf. *Agora* XIX 154–155. Such leases were a responsibility of the *basileus,* Ath. Pol. XLVII 4; cf. e.g. *IG* I^3 84; in our period, above no. 1, 25. The findspot in the suburbs of Athens (near the children's hospital, Ampelokipi, Alexandras St.) is very unusual. It may be a pierre errante from the acropolis, but it may also be that the inscription was set up on the land to which it related (as not infrequently with leases, cf. e.g. *Phratries* T5). For sacred properties leased at this period cf. *Agora* XIX L6.

6. IG *II^2 333*

Fr. a + b contain parts of two laws:

Law 1. fr a + b, 1–12. Not enough survives to yield continuous sense, but the law seems to have related to dedications and movement of objects (including processional vessels?, πομπέα, 2) on or down from the acropolis. Penalties for breaches are imposed on public slaves.

Law 2. fr. a+b, 13–19. Proposed by Lykourgos and dated to 6 Skirophorion (year not preserved, see below). Unless, uneconomically, we posit a third law, this ought to be the law πε]ρὶ τῆς ἐξετάσεως τῶ[ν—referred to in law 1(11). An *exetasis* (more usually, *exetasmos*) was a special or one-off examination of dedications and other valuable objects in a temple.[58] Only a few words are preserved. Reference to "silver amphoras and baskets and other things..".

fr. c+e and f contains the most substantial block of text. Since they do not deal explicitly with *exetasis* they might have belonged to law

---

[56] Matthaiou per ep. suggests e.g. ἀπομισθωσά]τω, cf. *IG* I^3 84, 7, or ὁρισά]τω, cf. *IG* I^3 78, 54.

[57] Matthaiou per ep. suggests e.g. εὐθυνέ]σθω, cf. *IG* I^3 84, 18–20.

[58] Cf. Tréheux, 471–4; S. B. Aleshire, *The Athenian Asklepieion* (Amsterdam, 1989), 105.

1; but they would not have been entirely out of place in a law on that subject and we can not rule out that they belonged rather to law 2 (or conceivably to a hypothetical law 3).

1–10 Very fragmentary. Reference inter alia to advance loans and processional vessels.

11–23 Arrangements for the provision of adornment or cult equipment (κόσμος, singular or plural, apparently indiscriminately) for various named deities from named sources of funding by specified officials (including, at end, reference to τὸ ἀργύριον [τ]ὸ ἐκ τοῦ δερματικοῦ γ̣[ιγνόμενον).

24–32 Provision to consult the god about whether the cult equipment (κόσμος) of Artemis Brauronia and of Demeter and Kore (and other deities, 31) should be enhanced or left as it is. In this context reference is made to the small items which are not included in the *paradosis,* i.e. the periodic transfer of responsibility from a board of treasurers to their successors, the point perhaps being whether these items are to be melted down for the enhancement of the κόσμος. Text breaks off before end of this section.

fr. d. Small fragment preserving a few words only; location in relation to other fragments unknown. The fragment joins the unpublished fr. g (cf. Schwenk), which adds little of significance (there is a squeeze in Oxford).

Remarkably little work has been done on the explication of these important Lykourgan laws. A full study, however, would take us beyond the scope of this article and I confine myself for the time being to two points of immediate concern: (I) the date, (II) the text of fr. c + e and f.

I. Date

The current text of the end of law 1 and the beginning of law 2 is: | 137

11 τὸν δὲ νόμον τόνδε καὶ τ[ὸν πε]ρὶ τῆς ἐξετ̣άσεως τ̣ῶ[ν------]
[-- ἐν στήληι λιθίν]ει καὶ στῆσαι ἐν ἀκροπόληι· ε[ἰ̣ς] δὲ τὴν ἀν̣αγραφὴν μερί[σαι------]

vacat 0.04

335/4 [ἐπὶ Εὐαινέτου ἄρχοντος ἐπὶ τῆς Ἀντιοχίδος δεκά]της· Σκιροφορ[ιῶνος ἕκ]τηι ἱσταμένου· νομο[θετῶν ἕδρα·]·
[τῶν προέδρων ἐπεψήφιζεν.......[14].......Λυκοῦρ]γος Λυκόφρ[ονος Βου]τάδης εἶπε[ν]·

Suppl. Köhler || 11 fin. τῶ[ν ἱερῶν χρημάτων? J. Tréheux, *BCH* 80 (1956), 469 || 13 in. R. Schöll, *Sitzungsber. Akad. München,* 1886, 120, Ἀντιοχίδος add. Meritt, *Ath. Year* 80 || 13 fin. dub. Foucart, *Journ. des Savants* 1902, 186 (νομο[θέται Schöll) || 14 in. Schöll.

If, as is likely, the line length was the same as fr. c+e and f there will have been 82 letters per line. However, neither left nor right side is preserved on fr. a+b, and the distribution of letters to either side of the preserved text is uncertain. Considerations of spacing are of no help, therefore, in restoring the beginning of l. 13.

There are in fact two questions, which it is well to keep separate:

(i) what was the date of these laws?[59]

Traditionally, following Köhler and Schöll, they have been dated to 335/4 and the archon of that year has been restored in 13. However, the only information provided directly by the text is that law 2 was passed on 6 Skirophorion, the last month, of an unknown year. The other chronological indicators are as follows:

(a) the hand is that of Tracy's "Cutter of *IG* II^2 334", whose dated work falls within the period c. 345–320.

(b) it is a reasonable assumption that both laws postdate the beginning of Lykourgos' first quadrennium "ἐπὶ τῇ διοικήσει τῶν χρημάτων" (Hyp. fr. 118, cf. the new reading at c+e and f, 9), earlier placed in 338, but now more commonly in 336/5 (Lewis, *Sel. Papers* 221–9; Faraguna, *Atene* 197–205).

(c) the laws stand in some relationship to the accounts, (1) *IG* II^2 1496 + *Hesp.* 9 (1940), 328–30 no. 37 + *IG* II^2 413[60] and (2) *IG* II^2 1493 + 1494 + 1495 + 1497 + *Hesp.* 6 (1937), 456–7 no. 6 (on which see most recently Lewis, *Sel. Papers* 226–7). Lewis was proposing to show that the obverse of (1) was concerned entirely with the *dermatikon* receipts (i.e. from sales of skins of sacrificial animals), "the reverse with their products, the *kosmos kanephorikos* of [Plut.] *X Orat* 852b".[61] Now our text is also concerned with *kosmos* and the *dermatikon* is mentioned at c+e and f, 23. Moreover, the cults whose *kosmos* is to be funded under c+e and f correspond closely with those listed in

---

[59] I assume in the following that there were only two.

[60] See the Endnote to this item.

[61] The study promised at 226 n. 38 has not appeared. [Plut.] ascribes to Lykourgos the provision of *kosmos* for the goddess, solid gold *Nikai*, gold and silver processional vessels and gold *kosmos* for a hundred *kanephoroi*.

the *dermatikon* accounts. The connection between our text and these accounts, however, is somewhat oblique. The (*kosmos?*) *kanephorikos* is *mentioned* c+e, 10, but, while possible, it is not immediately obvious that the *kosmos provided for* in c+e and f is this same *kosmos kanephorikos*. Moreover, it is to be funded, directly at least,[62] from various sources, including one designated by the general term, "sacred fund" (ἐκ τῶν ἱερῶν χρημάτων) and the first fruits of *temene,* not (the mention in 23 aside) the *dermatikon.* As far as chronological implications are concerned, the earliest securely dated entry on (1) is the beginning of the *dermatikon* account at 1496A, 68, which belongs to Posideon 334/3, and which continued until at least the ninth month of 331/0. Since it refers to the *dermatikon,* the law to which c+e and f belong is unlikely, therefore, to date very much earlier than Posideon 334/3. It is possible that c+e and f anticipated the operation of the *dermatikon* system apparent in the accounts, but the reference to it at l. 23 might be to a system already in operation. In other words we can not rule out that c+e and f postdate Posideon 334/3. Linders, 75 n. 60, raises the possibility that in *IG* II² 1496B, 200ff., where there is reference to gold taken from the acropolis and melted down | and to additional 138
gold which the treasurers have bought, there is evidence of the putting into effect of the combination of small items to make larger ones at c+e and f, 25 ff., but the link is not sure and this face of the accounts is in any case not dated (though it seems likely enough that it relates to a comparable period to Face A).

As far as (2) is concerned, *IG* II² 1493, which appears to record the making of the golden *Nikai* and processional vessels, has traditionally been dated, following Köhler, to 334/3; but the year is wholly restored and is doubtful;[63] Lewis noted that 1497 recorded operations covering 327/6; and again the connection with our text seems oblique. It is possible that our laws provided for the making of *Nikai* and processional vessels in lost or fragmentary sections, but no clauses to that effect are preserved and it is also possible that the matter was dealt with in other legislation.

(d) there is a further chronological indicator in the mention of Amphiaraos in 21, for Knoepfler has argued persuasively that Oropos

[62] It is apparent from c+e and f, 7–10 that the financial arrangements might have been complex.

[63] Cf. Lewis, 227; Osborne, *Nat.* I, 76; F. Mitchel, *TAPA* 93 (1962), 227–9; *AJA* 70 (1966), 66.

and the Amphiaraion, earlier thought to have been acquired by Athens immediately after Chaironeia, were transferred only in 335 *(Eretria* XI, 367–89). While not absolutely certain (for Athens' interest in the cult at Oropos pre-dated 335 and it can not be ruled out that there were other Attic cults of Amphiaraos at this date, cf. Parker, *Ath. Rel.* 148–9), it does indeed seem likely that our A. is the one worshipped at the Ampiaraion (thus also L. Robert, *Hell.* 11–12 (1960), 195 n. 4; A. Petropoulou, *GRBS* 22 (1981), 61). If Knoepfler is correct, therefore, our text is unlikely to date earlier than 335; but it might be somewhat later. The earliest securely dated evidence from the Amphiaraion of Athens' control of the shrine is the decree for Pytheas of Alopeke, of the first prytany of 333/2 (*IG* II^2 338 = *Ath. State* I no. 15); and the decree honouring Phanodemos for his legislation for the Great Amphiaraia dates to 332/1 (*IOrop* 297 = *Ath. State* I no. 16).

(e) We can not, it seems, do much with the reference to a quadrennial period, τετραετίαι (14 and 17). This may have been the Panathenaic quadrennium, 334/3–330/29 (cf. the *dermatikon* accounts on *IG* II^2 1496A, which begin in the Great Panathenaic year, 334/3, Köhler, Dittenberger at *Syll.*^{3} 1029 n. 1, but see also Lewis, 226), but the quadrennium of the office ἐπὶ τῇ διοικήσει (note the new reading at f 8, below), on Lewis' view 336–332, 332–328 etc., is also possible, or even (remotely) quadrennial cycles of the relevant cults (though the use of multiple cycles in a single law would perhaps be unexpected).[64] In any case, while the assumption is perhaps most comfortable, it is not certain that the law must have been passed just before the beginning of the quadrennium. The text speaks rather of "each year in the quadrennium"; it is annual periods that are at issue, within an overall quadrennial structure.

I conclude that, on present evidence:

(a) the law to which c + e and f belongs might date to late 336/5. 335/4 is more comfortable. 334/3 or a slightly later date can not be ruled out;
(b) if c + e and f were part of law 2, law 2 would date as (a), if part of law 1, law 1 would date as (a).
(c) since law 1 provides for the inscription both of itself and law 2 it can not pre-date law 2; either the two laws have the same date or,

[64] For timing by quadrennial period cf. *IG* II^2 463 + *Agora* XVI 109.

more likely since law 2 is explicitly dated, law 1 postdates law 2. If c + e and f were part of law 1, therefore, little could be said about the date of law 2 except that it was probably somewhat earlier (most comfortably perhaps from Skirophorion of the year before law 1, but this is uncertain). Conversely, if c + e and f were part of law 2, little could be said about law 1, except that it was probably somewhat later.

(ii) what text should be restored in a + b, 13?
We possess very few inscribed prescripts of laws. Moreover, this inscription is on any account unique, for it is the only one on which two laws are inscribed consecutively. Where decrees are inscribed consecutively, the second (and any subsequent) ones may be given an
archon date, but this is not invariably the | case. For example, archons 139
are inscribed at the beginning of all three decrees of *IG* II^2 330 = *Ath. State* I no. 3, the first dating to 335/4, the subsequent two to the previous year. No archon is given, however, at the beginning of the second surviving decree of *IG* II^2 415 = *Ath. State* I no. 5, of c. 330, which begins with the lunar and prytany dates. On *IG* II^2 354 = *Ath. State* I no. 11, of 328/7, the second decree appears to have been proposed at the same Assembly as the first and is not separately dated, beginning with the proposer. The general rule seems to have been that, if the year of decrees inscribed on the same stone is different, archons will be named; if the decrees are from the same year, the archon may, but is not necessarily, included for each one. There are exceptions, however. *IG* II^2 360 = RO 95 contains several decrees dating to different years, of which only the first one inscribed is dated at all, the others beginning with the proposer's details only. On *IG* II^2 336 = Osborne, *Nat.* D23 (on which see *Ath. State* III), the second decree (as I believe it to be), though from a different year from the first, is dated by secretary only, with no mention of the archon. The analogy of decree practice, therefore, would suggest that it is uncertain whether law 2 began with an archon date. In particular, if law 1 was passed on the same day as law 2, or later the same year (i.e. in the remaining days of Skirophorion), there would be a strong possibility that there was no archon specified at the beginning of law 2. If law 1 was passed in the subsequent year it is more likely that there was an archon date at the head of law 2, but not certain. Uncertainty is increased by the fact that the form of law prescripts varies considerably and is sometimes much briefer than that used in decrees (see the nine inscribed Athenian laws at Stroud, *Grain*

Tax Law 15–16. At least one of these, *IG* II² 140, lacks an archon date in the prescript).

I agree with earlier editors that, in context, and since we are in the last month of the year,]της is likely to be the word δεκά]της (omission of the word πρυτανείας is unusual, but not unparalleled, cf. e.g. *IG* II² 224 of 343/2. Foucart compared the laws at Dem. XXIV 39, 71).

There is no parallel, among surviving inscribed laws, for the wording restored by Foucart at the end of 13. There is, however, now a likely parallel in the most recently published inscribed law, which reads, *Grain Tax Law* 3–4: νόμος περὶ τῆς δωδεκάτης τοῦ σίτου. I suggest that our text read: νόμο[ς περὶ τῆς ἐξετάσεως τών --.

It is possible that the chairman was named between this clause and the name of the proposer; but this is far from certain. As already noted, law prescripts adhere to no fixed pattern and are often abbreviated. In the grain tax law, for example, the title of the law is followed directly by the name of the proposer. My text of the beginning of law 2 is accordingly:

c. 335 *II* --- ἐπὶ τῆς - ίδος δεκά]της· Σκιροφορ[ιῶνος ἕκ]τηι ἱσταμένου·
νόμο[ς περὶ τῆς ἐξετάσεως τῶν --
--.........¹⁷........Λυκοῦρ]γος Λυκόφρ[ονος Βου]τάδης εἶπε[ν]·
ὅπως ἂṿ----------

II. Text of c+e and f

The main textual problem with these fragments concerns fr. f. It was first published by Kirchner in *IG* II² on the basis of a transcript of Wilhelm, but the published text was flawed. Schwenk disentangled some of the problems of alignment with c+e and made some valuable new readings; but there is considerable scope for further improvement, of both readings and restorations. Fr. f is fairly severely abraded, such that careful autopsy is essential. Wilhelm's transcript is preserved in the archives of the Berlin Academy and is reproduced at Fig. 8. It includes letters and letter-strokes that were not eventually included in the *IG* II² text. Some of them turn out to be correct readings. My revised text is below. I restrict comment to the more significant new points, or those requiring explanation. Underlined letters are no longer legible. Double underlining = 2 letters in one stoichos (ll. 10, 27), 4 letters in 3 stoichoi and 9 letters in 7 stoichoi (l. 22), 2 letters in 3
140 stoichoi (l. 26). |

fr. c. [..........[23]..........]I[--
[..........[22]..........]_I[--
[..........[22]..........]ΛI[...[5]..]ΩΚΟΣ[--
[..........[22]..........]ΛΚ[.].ΑΓΕΙΤΟΥ[-- (before A a bottom horizontal, as of Δ)
[..........[21]..........]ἐπειδὴ δ' ἐκ τοῦ [..............[32]..............]ΛΙ[.......[15].......] fr. f stoich. 82
[.......[14].......τὰ περιό?]ντα τούτων τῶν χρη[μάτων..........[24]..........]ε καν[.......[13].......]
[........[18]........πρ]οδεδανεισμένα εξα[............[26]............πο]μπέα[.]Α[......[12]......]
[........[20]........]ια τὰ μεγάλα μερίζεσθ[αι.........[20].........πο]μπείων ΕΝΔΕ[.....[10].....]
[.......[15].......ἀπαλ?]λακτικὸν εἰς τὰ προδεδ[ανεισμένα.......[16].......] ἐκ τῆς διοική[σεως..[4]..]
[......[13]......κόσμο?]ν τὸν κανηφορικὸν ὅπως ἂ[ν..........[25]..........]ος καὶ ταμιευ. [....[7]...]
[........[17]........]αι πεντήκοντα αἰγίδ[α]ς κα[..........[22]..........τῶι Δι]ὶ τῶι Σωτῆρι κα[ὶ τῆι Ἀ]-
[θηνᾶι τῆι Σωτείραι π]έντε τοῦ ἐνιαυτοῦ ἑκάστο[υ............[27]............] καὶ τοῦ ταμίου [..[4]..]
[. τῶν ἱερῶν χρημάτ?]ων τοῦ Διὸς τοῦ Σωτῆρος· πο[ήσασθαι δὲ καὶ τοῖν θεοῖν : : κόσμον] τοῦ ἐνιαυτοῦ ἑκάσ[το]-
[υ ἐν τῆι τετραετί]αι τοὺς αὐτοὺς μετὰ τῶν ἐπι[στατῶν......[14]......τῶν ἱερῶ]ν χρημάτων τοῖν θεοῖν· [π]-
[οήσασθαι δὲ κα]ὶ τῶι Διὶ τῶι Ὀλυμπίωι : : κόσμ[ους τοῦ ἐνιαυτοῦ ἑκάστου τοὺς αὐ]τοὺς μετὰ τῶν τοῦ..μ .[.]
[.....[9]....κα]ὶ τοῦ ταμίου τοῦ δήμου ἐκ τῶν ἱ[ερῶν χρημάτων..[4]..ποήσασθαι δὲ] καὶ τῶ[ι] Διονύσωι κόσμον
[ἑκάστου το]ῦ ἐνιαυτοῦ ἐν τῆι τετραετίαι ἐκ [τῶν ἱερῶν χρημάτων· ποήσασθαι δὲ] καὶ τῆι Ἀθηνᾶι τῆι Ἰτωνί-
[αι : : : κόσ]μους ἐκ τῆς ἀπαρχῆς τῆς ἀπό τῶν τε[μενῶν..........[22]..........]σθαι δὲ τοῦτο τὸ τέλος ἐ.
fr. c + e [...[6]...π]οήσασθαι δὲ καὶ τῆι Ἀγαθῆι Τύχηι κ[όσμον τοὺ]ς [ταμίας τῶν ἱερῶν χρημά]των τῆς Ἀγαθῆς Τύχης με-
[τὰ τῶν ἐπι]στατῶν τοῦ ἱεροῦ τῆς Ἀγαθῆς Τύχης· πο[ήσασ]θα[ι δὲ...[5]..τῆι Ἀρτέμιδι] τῆι Μουνιχίαι καὶ το[ῖς]
[δώδεκα θε]οῖς καὶ τῶι Ἀμφιαράωι καὶ τῶ[ι] Ἀσκληπιῶ[ι] κεκ[...........[25]...........]ο. ου · ἐπιγρά[ψαι]
[δὲ ἐπὶ τὸν κ]όσμον ἕκαστον ὅτου ἂν ἧι τῶν θεῶν ἱερὸς καὶ τὸ στ[αθμὸν.........[19].........]ΟΥΤΟΥ ποιου[..[3].]
[...[6]...]ιοις τῶν θεῶν τὸ ἀργύριον [τ]ὸ ἐκ τοῦ δερματικοῦ γ[ιγνόμενον......[12]......]I[της· περὶ δὲ [..[4]..]
[...[6]...] τῶν ἱερῶν τῆς Ἀρτέμιδο[ς τ]ῆς Βραυρωνίας καὶ τῶν [..........[20]........]. Ε . [.]ους καὶ ἐπε[ρέσθ]-
[αι τὸν θ]εόν, εἰ λῶον καὶ ἄμεινον [τ]ῶι δήμωι τῶι Ἀθηναίων π[οησαμένωι τοὺς κόσμους ἱ]ε[ρ]οὺς τῆι Ἀρτέ[μιδι]
[μείζου]ς καὶ καλλίους ἢ ἐῶντι ὥσπερ νῦν ἔχει· ἐπερέσθαι [δὲ καὶ.........[20].........]. ου δὲ κε[..[4]..]
[..τὰ κα]τὰ μικρὰ [ἱ]στάμενα καὶ ὅσα μὴ ἐμ παραδόσει ἐστί[ν..[3].εἰ λῶον καὶ ἄμεινον ποησαμέν]ωι τῶι δή[μωι τ]-
[οὺς κό]σμους ἱεροὺς τῆι Δήμητρ[ι] καὶ τῆι Κόρηι μείζο[υς καὶ καλλίους .[2]. ἢ ἐῶντι ὥσπερ νῦν ἔ]χει· ἐπερ[έσθ]-
[αι δὲ καὶ π]ερὶ τῶν ἐν τοῖς ἄλλο[ι]ς ἱεροῖς τῶν κατὰ μι[κρὰ ἱσταμένων..........[22]..........ἀ]ργυρι[.]
[....[8]....]Ο[.]ΤΟΙ[..]ΟΝ[..[3].] . [..[4]..]τα κατὰ ταυτὰ τὸν Λ[................[37]................] κόσμο-
[......[12]......]ου[......[11].....μ]ε[ί]ζους καὶ κ[αλλίους ἢ ἐῶντι ὥσπερ νῦν ἔχει·.......[15].......τ]ῶν ἱερ-
[ῶν χρημάτων?..........[22]..........]ΣΙΩΙ[.....................[46].....................]
[...............[33]...............]Ο[--------------------------------- |

141

6 τὰ παρό]ντα *IG* II^2, but Köhler's τὰ περιό]ντα is more likely. Cf. *IG* II^2 1202 (decee of Aixone), 10–12: ..τὸ δὲ ἀργύριον εἶναι τὸ εἰς τοὺς στεφάνους| ἐκ τῆς διοικήσεως ἐκ τῶν περιόντων χρημάτων | τῶν ἐπὶ Θεοφράστου ἄρχοντος.

8 Παναθήνα]ια Köhler, or e.g. Μυστήρ]ια, Ἐλευσίν]ια? Lam. Since the later part of this text deals with a variety of deities, not including Athena, and since processional vessels etc. were features of festival processions generally, it is not certain that the "Great" festival here referred to was the Panathenaia (on quadrennial festivals cf. Ath. Pol. LIV 7).

πο]μπείω̣ν̣ ENΔE[- Lam.,]λ̣ε̣ι ὅ[θ]ε̣ν δὲ Schwenk. πο]μπεῖο̣ν̣ is a possible reading, but there is a definite thickening of the incised curve towards the bottom, both to right and left, suggesting the tails of omega.

9 in. ἀπαλ]λακτικὸν? Lam.]λακτικὸν previous eds. cf. *LSJ* s.v. ἀπαλλάσσω A4, discharge a debt. I take the sense to be that something is to be in redemption of, or exchange for, money loaned in advance (see further next note).

9 fin.] ἐκ τῆς̣ διοική̣[σεως Lam. ἐκ τῆς .IOỊ| Π̣ Schwenk. The small delta is very worn but completely visible under good lighting at autopsy. Cf. again the deme text, *IG* II^2 1202 (quoted above, note on l. 6) and note that Lykourgos was ταχθεὶς δὲ ἐπὶ τῇ διοικήσει τῶν χρημάτων (Hyp. fr. 118, cf. Faraguna, *Atene* 197–9). On διοίκησις as fund cf. Stroud, *Grain Tax Law* ll. 59–61 with p. 81; Ath. Pol. XLIII 1.

10 .]ος καὶ ταμιευ. [. Lam.]ο̣ν καὶ ταμιευ[Schwenk. The sigma after the omicron is certain. After the upsilon uncertain trace of the extreme lower left corner of sigma.

11–12 in. τῶι Δι]ὶ τῶι Σωτηρὶ κα[ὶ τῆι Ἀ|θηνᾶι τῆι Σωτείραι π]έντε Lam. τῶι Δι]ὶ τῶι Σωτηρ[ὶ] I: [...^{5}.. | -^{16}- π]έντε Schwenk. T[..]I[.]ΩT[.] P Wilh. transcript. Wilhelm's readings are accurate as far as they go, except that his first T is I. Note that this is one of several points where he is more accurate than the text in *IG* II^2, which erroneously reads T[..]I[.]Ω[.]P. I confirm Schwenk's important new reading of Zeus Soter here; but her I: is in fact kappa (vertical and upper diagonal clear) and is followed by / from which flows the restoration of Zeus Soter's usual cultic consort, Athena Soteira, who suits the space exactly.

12 fin.] καὶ τοῦ ταμ̣ίου [Lam.]ο :̣ καὶ τούτων τ̣ου̣[Schwenk,] : ΚΑΙΤΟΥΤ̣[..]Ι̣[Wilh. transcript.

13 in. Lam. cf. 14 fin. 16 med. 17 med. 19 fin. The five xs (possibly, but not necessarily aegises) for Zeus S. and Athena S. are to be provided by y (official(s)) with the z (official(s)) and the treasurer. The pattern is as 15–16. It is unclear, however, whether τῶν ἱερῶν χρημάτ?]-ων is a designation of the source of the funding (as 16–17) or part of the treasurer's title (as 19).

13 med. – 15 med. Lam. The restorations adopt elements from the formulaic wording of later lines and seem inevitable. The "two gods" are the two goddesses, Demeter and Kore (thus also e.g. at no. 4, 27–8). 14 med. should probably restored, Ἐλευσινόθεν ἐκ (13 letters) or καὶ τῶν ταμιῶν ἐκ. Cf. *IG* II^2 1672, 37, λόγος ἐπιστατῶν Ἐλευσινόθεν καὶ ταμιῶν τοῖν θεοῖν.

15 fin. – 16 in. μετὰ τῶν τοῦ..μ .[.ǀ.....^{9}....κα]ὶ τοῦ ταμίου Lam. [τε]μ̣έ[νǀους...^{5}..μετ]ὰ Wilh. in *IG* II^2 followed by Schwenk. The first surviving letter of 16 is not the right diagonal of Λ but a slightly backward leaning iota in the centre of the stoichos. So again the responsible officials are the x with the y and the z. This leaves the way open to restore τε]μέ[νǀους ταμιῶν, but I am not sure that [τε]μ̣έ̣[νǀους is correct. Before the mu one gains the impression Λ̣//ǀ, it being equally possible that the vertical stroke is iota or a right vertical. What is read as the bottom left corner of epsilon after the mu might alternatively be part of O. Note also that Wilh. (transcript) apparently originally read an omicron before the mu.

16 med. The restoration is Wilhelm's and seems secure. ..^{4}..probably does not represent a missing word, but a stoichedon irregularity, interpunct, ποι- for πο- (cf. 7 fin and 8 fin.) or a combination of these.

17 fin.–18 in. ποήσασθαι δὲ] καὶ τ̣ῆ̣ι Ἀθηνᾶι τῆι ’Ι̣τωνί̣ǀ[αι : : : κόσ]μους Lam.]σαι τ̣ῆ̣ι Ἀθηνᾶι τῆι ’Ι̣τωνῆ̣ǀ[ι τοὺς κόσ]μ̣ους Schwenk (restoring as *IG* II^2). The article with κόσ]μ̣ους is out of place here; and my reading of a single damaged vertical at the end of 17 (note that Wilh.'s transcript also shows a single central vertical) confirms the expectation that this epithet of Athena should be adjectival, as at *IG* I^3 | 142
383, 151. For the interpuncts after the name of the deity cf. 15. There may also or alternatively have been a stoichedon irregularity (e.g. [αι : : in 5 spaces).

18 fin.]σ̣θ̣α̣ι δὲ τοῦτ̣ο τὸ τέλος̣ ἐ. Lam. ονια . τοῦτο τὸ τέλος ἐμ̣ Schwenk. The final stroke slopes slightly, but could be a vertical in this script. At the start, if not ποήσασθαι then probably some other aorist middle infinitive.

20–21 π̣ο[ήσασ]θα[ι δὲ κόσμον τῆι Ἀρτέμιδι] τ̣ῆ̣ι̣ Μουνιχίαι καὶ το[ῖς | δώδεκα θε]οῖς Lewis. I confirm Lewis' new reading and restoration of Artemis Mounichia and the twelve gods here (missed by Schwenk and A. Petropoulou, *GRBS* 22 (1981), 61 = *SEG* XXXI 78). κόσμον is one letter too long, however. That is not impossible in this text, but one expects καὶ (and postponement of κόσμον) in this text. So perhaps e.g. π̣ο[ήσασ]θα[ι δὲ καὶ : : τῆι Ἀρτέμιδι].

21 fin. ΟΣ̣ΟΥ Schwenk, ΟΙΟΥ previous eds. I can not confirm either reading. Perhaps: Ο̣Υ̣[..³.]Ο.ΟΥ. Note that Wilhelm's transcript has Ο̣Υ[.]ΙΟΙΟΥΕΠΙΓΡΑ.

22 ὅτου ἂν ἦι τῶ̣ν θεῶν ἱερὸς καὶ τὸ στ[αθμὸν..........[19].........] ΟΥΤΟΥ ποιου̣[..³.] Lam. καὶ τὸ στ̣[όλισμα ἕκαστον? --]ο̣υτο ὑπὸ τ̣οῦ [δήμ|ου Schwenk. The requirement is for the objects to be inscribed with deity, weight and maker, as commonly in inventories, e.g. *IG* II² 1474B, 14–17, πίν]αξ ἀργυροῦ[ς], ἐ[φ' ὧι] ἐπιγέγρ[άπτα]ι ἱερὸς Ἀθηνᾶς Π[ολι]άδος· Νικ[οκράτη]ς ἐποίησεν ἐπὶ Ἀρχίππου Ῥ[αμ]νουσίου ἄρχοντος : σταθμὸν : Χ[.]ΗΗΗΔ. Similarly 1492 *passim*.

23 in.]ι|ο̣|ς Lam.]ι̣ο[ι]ς Schwenk. I detect the lower section of a central vertical in first place and faint and slightly unsure trace of the bottom of a vertical in third place. The gamma after δερματικοῦ could be pi.

24 med. τῶν̣ [Lam. τῶι Schwenk. The vertical is to the left of the stoichos and there is faint trace of the spring of the rather low-slung diagonal, as typically on nus in this script.

fin. Before the E, upper and lower diagonals as of the extreme strokes of sigma, or possibly kappa or (less likely) chi. After the E, bottoms of verticals or diagonals at the extreme left and right of the stocihos followed by the bottom of a vertical or diagonal at extreme left of stoichos.

26 My reading is slightly tentative. Before the omicron upper round as of rho. The diagonals of the kappa are very faint. After the epsilon the left and centre of the stoichos (surface preserved) is vacant; there is apparent trace of a lower vertical at the right edge of the stoichos - i.e. perhaps another stoich. irregularity.

27 εἰ λῶον καὶ ἄμεινον τῶι ποησαμέν]ωι Schwenk, εἰ λῶιον καὶ ἄμεινον ποιησαμέν]ωι *IG* II². Schwenk's added article would be surprising. Probably there was an interpunct, addition of iotas (*IG* II²) and/or stoich. irregularity.

28 The space in mid-line is perhaps to be accounted for by a stoichedon irregularity, interpunct vel. sim.

30 fin. The kappa gives the impression of epsilon. Of the omicron what appears to be the lower part is visible.

Endnote to no. 6

IG II² 413 has been incorrectly classified in the Corpus as decree. Rather, it is from the top of a stele bearing opisthographic accounts of the Lykourgan period. I confirm that, as suggested by D.M. Lewis, in ed. D. Knoepfler, *Comptes et inventaires…Jacques Tréheux* (Neuchatel, 1988), 297 (cf. *Sel. Papers* 226), it goes with *IG* II² 1496 + *Hesp.* 9 (1940), 328–30 no. 37. Marble type, script and thickness are compatible. Pending a full re-edition of these accounts, I print photographs (figs. 9–10) and offer some observations on the text in *IG* II²:

Face A: l. h. 0.004–0.005, stoich. horiz. c. 0.0085, vert. c. 0.0089. Vacant space above l. 1: 0.034. *IG* II² incorrectly gives the impression that the letters in l. 1 are larger than ll. 2ff. Read at A1,]ΥΤΩΝ, 6 perhaps στεφανω]θ̣έντες ὑ[πὸ (cf. 1496A *passim*), 7 after Ki. ἐ]κ Κολων̣[οῦ, 8 Τ̣ΗΣΓ.

Face B is in much larger letters (0.009–0.011), patently a heading. Both *IG* editions record that it is also stoichedon, incorrectly. Line spacing is 0.021. No margin preserved: | 143

---] Λυκοῦ[ργ---
---]ΟΡ[.]Ε̣[---
- Ἀθ]ηναί[ων ---
---]ΡΓ[.]Τ[---

4. εὐε]ργ[ε]τ[-? cf. Hiller in *IG* II²; e.g. Γα]ργ[ή]τ[τι- (from name of an official?)? Lam.

C. *Festival regulations*

The institution of a new festival or the introduction of new elements into an existing one normally required a law, rather than a decree, for such measures affected a fundamental aspect of the Athenian constitution, i.e. the city's sacrificial calendar, a central component of the laws of Solon and in the revision of Athenian law effected by Nikomachos' commission at the end of the fifth century (cf. Lambert, *Sacrificial Calendar*).[65] Only one of the inscriptions in this section is well enough preserved for it to be securely identified from explicit content as a law, no. 7, which introduced enhancements to the Little Panathenaia (albeit that the detailed arrangements for implementing the law are contained in an appended decree).[66] However, we also know that new arrangements for the penteteric Amphiaraia were made at this period by means of a law.[67] From their subject matter no. 8, no. 9 and no. 10 are accordingly also candidates for identification as laws.[68] As we saw above, there was a tendency for some laws (but very few decrees) to be inscribed on stelai which were opisthographic or had smooth backs. This is consistent with the identification of no. 9 as a law. As we shall see, the explanation of the smooth back of no. 8 may be slightly different. The absence of a smooth back on no. 10 tends to confirm that we are right to hesitate to identify it as a state law (see below).

		Date	Reference	Subject
144	7*	c. 335–330	*IG* II^2 334 (+ Add. p. 659) + D.M. Lewis, *Hesp.* 28 (1959), 239–47 (*SEG* XVIII 13) (ph., a); L. Robert, *Hellenica* 11/12 (1960), 189–203; M.H. Hansen, *GRBS* 20 (1979), 33 no. 9; Schwenk 17; M. Langdon, *Hesp.* 56 (1987), 56–8;	Law and decree raising funds for sacrifices at Little Panathenaia by leasing the "Nea" |

[65] There is much to be said for the view that, in the fourth century, whether a law or decree was needed for a particular measure was determined primarily by whether the measure would affect an existing law and that, in turn, was determined by historical accidence, including decisions made by Solon about what to include in his legal code and decisions made at the end of the 5th century about what to include in the revised code (cf. Rhodes, *Nomothesia*, 14–15). While it was possible to draw an abstract distinction between law as something permanent and general and decrees as specific or of particular application (Rhodes, *Nomothesia*, 14 with n. 48), like Rhodes, I am unconvinced by the argument of M.H. Hansen, *GRBS* 19 (1978), 315–30 and 20 (1979), 27–53 that this was applied systematically in practice. This is not, however, the place to pursue this matter in detail. A thoroughgoing treatment of Athenian laws and lawmaking in the fourth century is much needed.

[66] The reason for that is unclear. Perhaps the Assembly was commissioned to act by the *nomothetai* (a different view at Hansen, *GRBS* 20 [1979], 35).

[67] See Schwenk 41 = *Ath. State* I no. 16.

[68] In addition to no. 7 Hansen, *GRBS* 20 (1979), 32–35, suggests that no. 8 and no. 10 might have been laws.

Table (*cont.*)

	Date	Reference	Subject
		O. Hansen, *Eranos* 87 (1989), 70–2; P. Gauthier, *Bull. ép.* 1988, 349; *Agora* XIX L7; XVI 75 (ph., a); Tracy, *ADT* 11 n. 25, 84; P. Brulé, *Kernos* 9 (1996), 37–63 (*SEG* XLVIII 103); RO 81 (reflects some of points made below); J.D. Sosin, *ZPE* 138 (2002), 123–5;[69] Humphreys, *Strangeness* 93, 112. [back not preserved]	
8*	c. 335–330	E. Schweigert, *Hesp.* 7 (1938) 294–6 (ph.) (*SEG* XVI 55); P. Roussel, *Rev. Arch.* 18 (1941), 215–6; A.M. Woodward, *ABSA* 51 (1956), 3–5 no. 6; J. and L. Robert, *Bull. ép.* 1959, 130; L. Robert, Ἀρχ. Ἐφ. 1977 [1979], 211–6; M.H. Hansen, *GRBS* 20 (1979), 33 no. 5; Tracy, *ADT* 11 n. 25, 78; Faraguna, *Atene* 359–60; J. Sosin, *Mus. Helv.* 61 (2004), 2–8; Humphreys, *Strangeness* 113–4 [back smooth]	About a festival
9*	c. 335–330	M.B. Walbank, *Hesp. Suppl.* 19 (1982), 173–82 (ph.) (*SEG* XXXII 86); O. Hansen, *Mnemosyne* 38 (1985) 389–90 (*SEG* XXXV 73); Tracy, *ADT* 11 n. 25, 92 n. 21; Humphreys, *Strangeness* 90 n. 33, 117. [back smooth]	About a festival

[69] An ingenious attempt to address the discrepancy between the two talents income from the Nea apparently envisaged in the law (16–22) and the 41 minai actual rental income mentioned in the decree (41–2) by supposing that the rental income was designed to accrue to form a capital sum and it was from the income from this accrued capital that the festival was to be funded. Doubts arise inter alia from lack of contemporary or Attic parallel for such an arrangement (Sosin cites one parallel, B. Laum, *Stiftungen…Antike* [Leipzig, 1914] no. 1, from hellenistic Kerkyra); and when the 41 minai to be expended on the sacrifices are described as ἐκ τῆς μ]ισθώσεως τῆς Νέας (42) one naturally infers that the rental income is to be directly applied. Moreover, the key section of the relevant text (ll. 16–22) is insuffιcently preserved, in the absence of parallels, to support any specific restoration or interpretation (for other suggestions see Lewis; Sokolowski). P. Gauthier, *Bull. ép.* 2003, 247 is also sceptical.

Table (*cont.*)

	Date	Reference	Subject
10	c. 330[70]	B.D. Meritt, *Hesp.* 37 (1968), 267–8 no. 3 (ph.); *LSCG* 179 (*SEG* XXV 82); M.H. Hansen, *GRBS* 20 (1979), 33 no. 6; Tracy, *ADT* 11 n. 25, 107, 115; *Agora* XVI 67; Humphreys, *Strangeness* 119 n. 30. [back rough picked]	About Dipolieia?[71]

7. IG *II² 334 +*

Date

The cutter of this inscription was active c. 345–c. 320 (Tracy, *ADT* 82), consistent with the identification of the proposer as Aristonikos of Marathon, who was active in the Lykourgan period and was killed after the Lamian War;[72] and the "Lykourgan" character of the measure might suggest a date c. 336–30 (cf. on no. 6). The space available for the name of the archon in a 2 is a constraint, but not a very helpful one, since this line was not inscribed stoichedon (the letters are more widely spaced than the text below) and the left side of the inscribed surface is not preserved. The surviving letters in this line are evenly spaced, but it is never certain, in this sort of case, that the spacing was at precisely the same intervals in the lost part of the line. This makes any calculations tricky and necessarily tentative. Mine suggest that, within the period 343/2–325/4 (a little wider than the range considered by Lewis), if there was no crowding of letters at the beginning of the line, only 339/8 and 329/8, when ἐπὶ+archon name occupied 15 letters, can fairly safely be ruled out on grounds of spacing (these dates were not considered by Lewis). 331/0 and 330/29, when the archons began Ἀ- and ἐπ(ὶ)+archon's name therefore occupied 14 or

[70] Lettering: "Cutter of *IG* II² 354", 337–324, (Tracy). As Tracy notes, ADT 11 n. 25, this fragmentary text should perhaps be classified with other festival regulations of the Lykourgan period. It is uncertain, however, whether it is a law, decree or sacrificial calendar, or whether it is a state text or an inscription of a deme, *genos* vel sim. For *gene* with responsibilities at the Dipolieia see Parker, *Ath. Rel.* 300. There was also a group called the Dipoliastai, *ibid.* 334; Lambert, *Rationes* 197. Most of Sokolowski's restorations should be stripped out.

[71] To the bibliography on this festival mentioned by the previous eds. add IK 26 *Kyzikos* II (Miletupolis) 1, 7 with C. Habicht, *EA* 31 (1999), 26–29 (*SEG* XLIX 1764); Lambert, *Sacrificial Calendar* F1B col. 2 with p. 386.

[72] *IG* II² 1623, 280–3 (cf. 1631, 169; 1632, 190); PCG Alexis F130–131; Lucian, *Dem. Enc.* 31. ?Son of *LGPN* II Ἀριστοτέλης 33 Μαρα., proposer of *IG* II² 43 = RO 22.

15 letters ("too long to come into consideration" Lewis, who apparently overlooked the possibility of ἐπ' for ἐπὶ), and 334/3 and 333/2, when ἐπὶ+archon name occupied 14 letters ("a little too long" Lewis), are in my judgement just possible, if only marginally. Beyond that, the date is controlled by one's view on the identification of the Nea, on which conclusive evidence or arguments are lacking. If Robert is right to identify it as territory in Oropos acquired by Athens after Chaironeia, a date shortly after 335 is likely.[73] In that case 335/4 (with 336/5, one of the two dates for this decree favoured by Lewis) will suit most comfortably the spacing constraints | for the archon's name. The (ill- 145
founded) theory of O. Hansen, that the *Nea* was the island Halonnesos, south of Lemnos, would indicate a date c. 340, when Hansen supposes that the island was briefly controlled by Athens. Langdon's theory that the *Nea* was a now sunken island off Lemnos implies no specific date. Fragmentary accounts of sales of hides from sacrifices at the (Little) Panathenaia of 333/2 and 332/1 survive (*IG* II^2 1496, 98–99 and 129; discussed recently by Rosivach, *Sacrifice* 104), but it is not clear whether these post- or pre-date our text. In the law the lease has yet to be drawn up, while in the decree the income from it is known. This suggests some passage of time between the two.

Great and Little Panathenaia and the *hieropoioi*

From the sense of the term, one could not rule out that Παναθήναια τὰ μικρά might have meant, at least in unofficial parlance, "the Panathenaia in years in which the Great Panathenaia was not celebrated", while Π. τὰ κατ' ἐνιαυτὸν was the more formal term referring to those elements of the Panathenaia which occurred every year (to which, in Great Panathenaic years, other elements were added). But other evidence (Harp. p. 234, 11 Dind., Lys. XXI 2, Menander F 384 K–A) is unclear on the point; and it does seem that on this inscription the terms are used synonymously, for it is not very plausible that the revenue from the *Nea* provided for in the law was to be drawn on only three years in four; and at b 16ff., where the specific application of that revenue is specified, we are in the midst of a decree explicitly dealing with things taking place every year (b 3, 5, 33). It would seem to follow that the little or yearly Panathenaia took place even in great Panathenaic years. This corresponds with the system implicit in the Attic

[73] For this date, Knoepfler, *Eretria* XI, 367–89.

sacrificial calendars (clear especially from the Athenian state calendar and the calendar of the Tetrapolis), in which events are distinguished as between annual, biennial, quadrennial etc. There does not seem to have been a concept of a sacrifice or festival taking place e.g. three years in four. See most recently, S.D. Lambert, *ZPE* 130 (2000), 43–70 (Tetrapolis); *Sacrificial Calendar* (polis). -] κατ' ἐνιαυτὸν in b 3 might refer to the Παναθήναια τὰ κατ' ἐνιαυτὸν (cf. 57; thus e.g. Dittenberger, *Syll.*³ 271; [J. von Prott and] L. Ziehen, *Leges Graecorum Sacrae* II fasc. 1 [Leipzig, 1906] no. 29) or, if the *hieropoioi* of this decree are to be identified with the ἱεροποιοὺς κατ' ἐνιαυτὸν καλουμένους, discussed by Ath. Pol. LIV 7, to them. According to Ath. Pol. these *hieropoioi* θυσίας τέ τινας θύουσι [καὶ τ]ὰς πεντετηρίδας ἁπάσας διοικοῦσιν πλὴν Παναθηναίων. Pace Ziehen and Rhodes ad loc., since our decree deals not with the penteteric festival (whose specific officials were the *athlothetai*), but the annual one, identification would not entail inconsistency with this passage. Nor, once it is recognised that the annual Panathenaic sacrifices took place also in Great Panathenaic years, would there be inconsistency with the evidence of *IG* I³ 375, 6–7 that the *hieropoioi* κατ' ἐνιαυτὸν received 5,114 dr. from the treasurers of Athena for a hekatomb at the Panathenaia in a Great Panathenaic year (410/9; the *athlothetai* received the much larger sum, 31,000 dr., on the same occasion). The circumlocution of 56–57, τοὺς δὲ ἱεροποιοὺς τοὺς διοι[κοῦντας τ]ὰ Π. τὰ κατ' ἐνιαυτὸν is a little curious; but I am inclined, following Rosivach, *Sacrifice* 110 n. 13, to take it as emphasis, on transition to a new subject, the *pannychis,* of precisely which *hieropoioi* are meant, "the *hieropoioi* managing the annual Panathenaia" (i.e. to distinguish them from other boards of *hieropoioi*). I doubt, therefore, that there is sufficient reason to posit a separate board of ἱεροποιοὶ εἰς τὰ Παναθήναια,[74] and would identify the *hieropoioi* of our decree with the *hieropoioi* κατ' ἐνιαυτὸν mentioned by Ath. Pol. and *IG* I³ 375. As noted above, receipts in respect of sale of hides from sacrifices at the Panathenaia by the same officials are recorded in the contemporary *IG* II² 1496, 98–99, and 129 (παρὰ ἱεροποιῶν, under 333/2 and 332/1, neither Great Panathenaic Years).

[74] Admittedly, with Rangabé, one might restore precisely this wording at b8, τῶν ἱεροποιῶν εἰς [......12......, but at this point I am inclined to accept the now established restoration (Köhler's): εις [τὸν αεὶ χρόνον.

Restoration of b 3–4

The current restoration of b 2–6 is:

ὅπως ἂν --------εὐ]σ[εβ]ῶς κα-
[ὶ..............[29]..............]κατ' ἐνιαυτὸν κ- | 146
[αὶ πέμπηται ἡ πομπὴ π]αρεσκε̣[υασμ]ένη ὡς ἄριστα τῆι Ἀ-
[θηνᾶι καθ' ἕκαστο]ν τὸν ἐνιαυτὸν ὑπὲ̣ρ τοῦ δήμου τοῦ Ἀ-
[θηναίων, καὶ τἆλ]λα ὅσα δεῖ διοικῆται περὶ τὴν ἑορτὴ-
[ν τὴν ἀγομένην τ]ῆι θεῶι καλῶς...

πέμπηται was suggested by B. Haussoullier *Rev. crit.* 50 (1900) 25 (l. 28), (τελεσθῆι Köhler). The Parthenon frieze looms perhaps larger in the minds of modern writers than it did in those of fourth century Athenians. The procession in fact features scarcely at all in the body of the decree as preserved; there are only brief references in b 19 and 34–6. The focus is on the sacrifices; and the phrase ὑπὲρ τοῦ δήμου τοῦ Ἀθηναίων is more suitable in reference to sacrifices than to a procession. With Rangabé one expects mention of the sacrifices in b 3–4, effectively introducing the main body of the decree, b 8–28. The tail of the decree, dealing with other matters, including the procession, is covered by the next introductory clause, b 6–7, τἄλ]λα...περὶ τὴν ἑορτὴ[ν. Rangabé's own suggestion, κα[ὶ τετέλεσται ἡ θυσία ἡ νενομισμέ]νη can not, in its detail, be right. γίγνομαι + past participle is a rarer construction in Greek inscriptions than "become" or "come to be" + past participle in English (cf. Th. III 68; *FD* III 4, 37, B 19), but one might nevertheless consider κ[αὶ γίγνηται ἡ θυσία π]α̣ρ̣εσκευ[ασμ]ε̣νη ὡς ἄριστα or perhaps ὅπως ἄν...ἡ θυσία γιγνήται...] κατ' ἐνιαυτὸν κ[α λῶς......[12]......π]αρεσκευ[ασμ]ε̣νη κτλ. Cf. *SEG* XXVIII 103, 5: ὅπως ἄν ἡ θυσία γίγνηται ὡς καλ|λίστη. *IG* II[2] 47, 27: καὶ ἡ ἄλλη θυσία γίγνηται ὑπὲρ τοῦ δήμου τοῦ Ἀθηναίων. For the singular, θυσία, cf. a 5 of our inscription.

8. SEG *XVI 55*

The date of this inscription is "Lykourgan", as was recognised by the first editor, Schweigert. The lettering is in a style characteristic of the period 345–320 (Tracy, *ADT* 78) and the content is of a piece with the other enhancements of the festival programme instituted at this time (cf. the other measures listed in this section; Tracy, 11 with n. 25; Parker, *Ath. Rel.* 230 n. 46; 246).

Schweigert was also right to bring the inscription into connection with the peace of Corinth. ---τ]ὴν στήλην τὴν περὶ τῆς εἰρ|[ήνης at the beginning of our text (ll. 3–4) is apparently a reference to the inscription recording that peace, *IG* II^2 236 = RO 76.[75] Both inscriptions have precisely the same thickness (0.132) and the same unusual working of the back: completely smooth, as if to receive another text (cf. section II above). Furthermore, the letter heights (0.004–0.005) and stoichedon grid dimensions (c. 0.0085 square) are precisely the same; and both stones are of grey marble. It seems fairly clear that our text was intended to complement *IG* II^2 236 physically as well as in content; perhaps the two stones were set up next to one another.[76]

Given the slight remains of the text and the absence of other direct evidence, no attempt to identify the festival is likely to be wholly compelling. However, the arguments raised by Roussel and Robert against the Panathenaia and the Eleusinia (possibilities raised by Schweigert and Woodward respectively) seem persuasive; and given the circumstances, their suggestion that we have to do with the cult of Peace has attractions. A sacrifice to Peace was instituted in 375 (Parker, *Ath. Rel.* 229–30), so our measure would have represented an enhancement to include new competitive elements (thus Faraguna). Sosin observes that the immediate aftermath of the Peace of Corinth is unlikely to have been regarded as an occasion for celebration and suggests a dating after the sack of Thebes and the favourable settlement with Alexander in 335 (cf. Knoepfler, *Eretria* XI, 367–89). Except for entries in the
147 *dermatikon* accounts from the later | 330s, however,[77] an Athenian cult or festival of Peace appears to have left no subsequent mark on the historical record.

Humphreys is also inclined to posit a gap between the Peace of Corinth and this measure, suggesting that it was part of Phanodemos'

---

[75] If the reference had been to the cult of the goddess Peace, or to a sacrifice or festival of Peace, one would have expected different language, i.e. τὴν στήλην τὴν περὶ τῆς θυσίας τῆι Εἰρήνηι vel sim. (cf. e.g. ὅπως ἄν τῆι] Ἀθηνᾶι ἡ θυσία ὡς καλλίστ[η ἦι no. 7, 5).

[76] I take this opportunity to note that the fragmentary *IG* II^2 329 (cf. RO p. 379), which records an agreement with Alexander the Great on military matters, was set up in Pydna as well as at Athens, and in some sense may belong in a series with *IG* II^2 236, also displays physical similarities to it. The lettering is very similar and the stoichedon dimensions are the same; but *IG* II^2 329 is in white marble and its surviving thickness (0.148, original back not preserved) is greater than on 236 and our inscription.

[77] *IG* II^2 1496A, 95, under 333/2, skin-yield 874 dr.; 127–8, under 332/1, specified as receipt from the generals, 710 ½ dr. The receipts are substantial; towards the upper end of those recorded in these accounts; but we can not tell if they reflect recent enhancement.

law for the Great Amphiaraia (cf. *IOrop* 297 = *Ath. State* I no. 16; *IOrop* 298 = *Ath. State* I no. 17). No. 9, below, is also a candidate for identification as this law.

A further possibility is that this was not a specifically Athenian festival, but an international one established by the Macedonians. The Peace of Corinth itself was a multilateral agreement, not specifically an Athenian-Macedonian one, and the same may have been the case with the related *IG* II^2 329 (above n. 76), required to be set up in Pydna. Diod. XVI 91, 4–92 describes a festival in the wake of the Peace of Corinth at Aegeae in Macedonia, said to have included musical competitions (cf. l. 5 of our inscription), albeit presented there as a celebration of the wedding of Cleopatra, not a recurring event.

The severely abbreviated prescript of our text, which did not certainly include any element except the secretary, would be very unusual in a decree. It would be less surprising in a law. The prescripts of laws do not accord to a fixed pattern and can be very brief (see the list of inscribed laws at R. Stroud, *Hesp. Suppl.* 29 [1998], 16; for the secretary in a law prescript see e.g. *Agora* XVI 73, 2–3 (337/6); cf. *IG* II^2 140, 31–2). As we saw above, the subject matter of the text and the smooth back would also be consistent with a law. Hansen's identification of this measure as a law is accordingly attractive. However in this case the abbreviation of the prescript may be due to this inscription's being not a self-standing measure, but an associate of *IG* II^2 236, and the smooth back of 236 may be due to its associate's being a law.

The text is not formulaic, the line length can not be determined, and aside from obvious completions of words, none of the proposed restorations is compelling. Matthaiou per ep. notes that, in l. 9, where Woodward thought of an announcement of the festival as far as Thermopylai, Robert tentatively suggested τὰς πρὸς τῶι Κεραμεικῶ]ι πύλας (taken as continuing the sense of l. 8, τὴν πανήγυριν περι[ὶ -), and Humphreys thinks of the town gates of Oropos, one might consider τὰς ἐν Κορίνθω]ι πύλας. Cf. *LSJ*^{9} πύλη II 2. In l. 12 Robert takes δέκα as the number of days duration of the inviolability of those coming to the festival (specifically θεωροί of states? Matthaiou, cf. Th. IV 118, 6), restoring [ἡμερῶ]ν̣ δέκα μὲν ἰοῦ[σιν] (cf. *IG* XII 7, 24, l. 9, ἐπέδωκεν τοῖς [ἰ]ο[ῦ]σιν εἰς τὴν ἑορτὴν, cf. 22), but the first surviving letter is certainly iota, not nu. One would not expect ἰθυ[- in an Attic text (unless a name), but if this originated as a Corinthian league document not drafted in Attic, ten might be a number of persons to be elected, ἑλέσθα]ι δέκα μὲν ἰ⟨θ⟩υ[- (e.g. ἰθυδίκους, theta at the end of

l. 6 also lacks central dot). This type of provision is common (e.g. no. 1, 5; no. 7 b 36–7).

9. SEG *XXXII 86*

The hand is Tracy's "Cutter of *IG* II² 244", 340/39–c. 320 (Tracy, *ADT* 101), indicating that, like the other measures of this section, this is a festival regulation of the Lykourgan period.

As Walbank notes, the stone is deceptively difficult to read. A number of improved readings have proved possible, though none, so far as I can see, supplies a definite key to this tantalising text. At 33, I read Λ̣ΠΗΛ̣ΙΟ̣ΙΣ ἐν τ̣ῶι Λ- (Ι̣Π̣ΗΛ̣Ι̣[.] δ̣ὲ̣ ἐν τ̣ῶι Ἀ̣[μφιαράωι Wal.). The first Λ is damaged and rather high and I should not put much weight on it. The second Λ is probably lambda, though delta could not be ruled out. The omicron is very damaged, but legible practically in its entirety. One might think of κ]α̣πηλίο̣ις, albeit that καπήλιον for καπήλειον is otherwise attested in iv BC Attic only in curse tablets (Threatte I, 165, cf. D.R. Jordan, *GRBS* 26 (1985), 164 no. 43). καπήλεια are attested at the Amphiaraion by *IOrop* 290, 18 (at the Samian Heraion by *IG* XII 6, 169).

In 34, where Walbank prints]NNẸẠN[and Stroud suggested [τὴ]ν Νέ̣αν (*SEG* XXXII 86, cf. above no. 7), I could be fairly confident only of]Ṇ[..]N *traces*. At 40 I read with some confidence from the stone,] χον τὸ βῆμα ποιεῖσθαι τῶι [-----] (Σ̣HMA? Wal., who noted that Β̣HMA

148 was an alternative possibility). | Matthaiou per ep. raises the attractive possibility τῶι [τρίποδι, cf. *IG* II² 1665, 3–4: ἐγ Κυνοσάργει τῶι τρίποδι ἑκάστωι βῆμα ποι|ῆσαι. In 45, where Walbank has]𐅄Δ̣Δ̣Δ ἀπὸ πέντε ιν[I read with fair certainty - τρί?]π̣ο̣δα ἀποπένπ̣ειν [(N for M in this verb also e.g. at *IG* II² 1283, 6–7). Articulated thus one might perhaps envisage a restriction on the movement of the tripod awarded to the victor, consistent with the construction of a tripod base in 40. As Matthaiou notes, however, τρί]π̣ο̣δα· ἀποπένπ̣ειν [δὲ is also possible. Cf. Ἀθηνῆθεν in the following line.

As with no. 8, given the fragmentary state of the text, the festival can not be determined with certainty (as Tracy notes) and I have no new theory. Walbank's suggestion, the Amphiaraia (also a candidate for no. 8), remains a strong possibility. τὸν ἱππόδρομο[ν (14) squares with mention of hippic events at the Great Amphiaraia at *IOrop* 298 = *Ath. State* I no. 17, 17; and τῶν] στα̣θέντων [ἐ]π[ὶ] εὐταξία̣[ν (or better, as Matthaiou points out, κατα]σταθέντων, cf. *IG* II² 949, 31; 1245,

2 etc.) accords with the reference to εὐταξία at the great Amphiaraia at *IOrop* 298, 44–5 (τῶι αἱρεlθέντι ἐπὶ τὴν εὐταξίαν).[78] The Bendideia, tentatively raised as an alternative by Walbank is supported by O. Hansen, but based on an unacceptable restoration, cf. Parker, *Ath. Rel.* 246 n. 100. Humphreys suggests the Epitaphia. This suits the references to the polemarch in ll. 19 and 32 since Ath. Pol. LVIII 1 identifies the ἀγῶνα τὸν ἐπιτάφιον ⟨ἐπὶ⟩ τοῖς τετελευτηκόσιν ἐν τῶι πολέμωι as a responsibility of that archon, but the polemarch might also have had a role in the Great Amphiaraia and there appears to be no other evidence that the Epitaphia was enhanced or re-organised in the Lykourgan period.

D. *Dubia*

	Date	Reference	Subject
11	c. 340–320[79]	*IG* II² 310; Tracy, *ADT* 11 n. 28, 98; Humphreys, *Strangeness* 119 n. 30.	Regulation of a temenos?[80] [back smooth]
12*	c. 340–325[81]	*IG* II² 326.	Decree relating to Artemis
13*	mid-iv?[82]	*IG* II² 260.	Fragment relating to pythaistai

[78] Pace Humphreys, 115–6, I doubt that this is a (highly abbreviated and obscure) reference to an (otherwise unattested) official in charge of the *eutaxia* competition for ephebes, but to an official responsible for maintenance of good order at the festival, as *SEG* XXXIII 115, 28. Such responsibilities are commonly mentioned in decrees, e.g. *IG* II² 223 = *Ath. State* I no. 1, B6; *IG* II² 354 = *Ath. State* I no. 11, 16 (for the comparable εὐκοσμία).

[79] Work of Tracy's "Cutter of *IG* II² 244", c. 340–320.

[80] As Hiller noted ap. *IG* II², "similis argumenti lex atque t. 295 [above no. 5]"; but this scrap is even less informative than that text; its findspot is not known and there is no positive indication that it was set up by the state rather than a priest or a group such as a deme, phratry, genos etc. The left side is preserved, with probably two letters to the left of the delta in 4, rather than the three shown by *IG* II². There are 11 lines of traces above the first printed line in *IG* II², but they yield no complete word. Tracy suggests a connection with the Lykourgan policy of refurbishment of sanctuaries apparent also in no. 3 and no. 6. Cf. *Agora* XIX L6. On the smooth back cf. section II, above.

[81] "Litt. volg. med. s. IV" and "ante 336/5" (Kirchner, the latter designation somewhat arbitrary). The -ει orthography for the ending of the feminine dative singular (l. 2) is not common before 340–330 (Threatte I, 369, 377–8).

[82] "Litt. volg. med. s. IV" and "ante 336/5" (Kirchner, cf. previous note).

12. IG *II² 326*

Acropolis. As well as the left side, the back is original (th. 0.08 finished side, c. 0.10 including rough back). My text is:

[...⁶...]Δ[---------ἐν στήλε]-   stoich.
[ι λι]θίνει καὶ στῆ[σαι -------τῆ]-
[ς Ἀρ]τέμιδος. *vac.*
vac. ἐπὶ ἱερέως Μ[--]
vac. 0.20

Readings as Wilhelm except 1 Δ Lam. Suppl. Wilhelm (see further
149 below). |

What cult of Artemis is this? Though inscriptions from elsewhere occasionally found their way up to the Acropolis, the findspot would normally suggest an acropolis cult. Artemis Brauronia was a rather feminine deity, served not by a priest, but at Brauron at least by a priestess (Dem. LIV 25 and *Hypoth.*; Din. II 12; Hyp. F 199J). One might think rather of the other Artemis apparently on the Acropolis, A. Epipyrgidia, for whom a priest (supplied by the genos Kerykes) is attested, albeit at a late date, by *SEG* XXX 93, 9–11 and *IG* II² 5050 = M. Maass, *Die Prohedrie des Dionysostheaters* (Munich, 1972), 122: πυρφόρος καὶ ἱερεὺς τῶν Χαρίτων καὶ τῆς Ἀρτέμιδος τῆς Ἐπιπυργιδίας (cf. K. Clinton, *The Sacred Officials of the Eleusinian Mysteries* [Philadelphia, 1974], 94–5).

While the Acropolis was the most common location for Athenian state decrees, more closely defined *Standorte* on the Acropolis are rare and this one would be unique (cf. P. Liddel, *ZPE* 143 [2003], 81 with table 3). In detail, however, Wilhelm's στῆ[σαι ἐν τῶι ἱερῶι τῆ|ς Ἀρ]τέμιδος (yielding a stoich. 29 line) is not compelling. Other possibilities are raised by *SEG* XXV 108, 20, στῆσαι ἐν ἀγορᾶι παρὰ τὸμ βωμὸν (for Artemis Boulaia); and the A. Epipyrgidia texts raise the possibility...τῶν Χαρίτων καὶ τῆς Ἀρ]τέμιδος.

There seems to be no clear parallel among state decrees for subscription of a priest immediately below the decree text. Superscription: *IG* II² 659 (state decree relating to Aphrodite Pandemos). Subscription following crowns in a state decre: probably at *IG* II² 304+ 604 = Schwenk 14 (date, 321–302, see Tracy, *ADT* 153), honouring two men and set up in the Asklepieion. So this may or may not be an inscription of the polis. Other possibilities are the *genos* Kerykes or a group of *thiasotai* using the same shrine (cf. II^2 1297–8; 788, Artemis Kalliste).[83]

13. IG *II^2 260*

The right side is preserved. Place and time of discovery not recorded (once no. 3802 in the collection of the Greek Archaeological Society in the National Museum). My text (autopsy and Oxford and Berlin squeezes) is:

c. mid-iv? ---------------- non-stoich.
[-----πυθ]α̣ι̣στ̣αῖς 𐅄Δ[-?]
[------] ἐφό̇δ̇ια̇ *vv* 𐅂𐅂𐅂 *v*
vacat 0.068

1 πυθ]α̣ι̣στ̣αῖς Lam. (δημ]οσίαις Kirchner)

While it is possible to see from the stone and the Berlin squeeze how Kirchner came to read δημ]οσίαις, that reading is incorrect. The surface is broken such that only the lower parts of letters are preserved. From a combination of autopsy and squeezes I read: bottom end of right diagonal followed by lower end of vertical. These two strokes are close together and in combination can give an impression of the bottom of O. Followed by: lower half of sigma, lower section of vertical (badly damaged). The width of this vertical and the relatively wide expanse of vacant stone to the left and right of it suggest that the inscribed letter was tau. This, together with mention of travel expenses in l. 2, suggests the restoration πυθ]α̣ι̣στ̣αῖς.

Kirchner suggested that the fragment might have been from the bottom of a decree. Doubtless he was thinking about payments made commonly to ambassadors and occasionally others travelling on state business (e.g. no. 1, above); but there seems to be no example of these being appended to a decree and the low amount would also be unexpected (usually 20 or 30 dr.). There is too little text to enable this

[83] I take this opportunity to note that the lost *IG* II^2 4594, which reads ἐπ]ὶ Φρυνίχου ἄρχον[τος (337/6) --]| Ἀρτέμιδος τῆς [---] | τὴν στοά[ν --- is probably correctly classified in *IG* II^2 as a dedication. D. Peppas-Delmousou in: ed. D. Knoepfler, *Comptes et inventaires…Jacques Tréheux* (Neuchatel, 1988), 331 n. 31 (*SEG* XXXVII 78), raised the possibility that it might rather have been "un décret pour la construction (ou la réparation) d'une στοὰ Ἀρτέμιδος τῆς -", but if so, one would have expected ll. 2–3 to be occupied with the prescript. Dedications were not uncommonly dated by archon, cf. *IG* II^2 2818, 2822, 2824 etc.

150 inscription | to be securely classified, but it is notable that the numbers
are aligned in what is in effect a separate column. This gives the impres-
sion that the fragment belongs to an account-type document, most
likely perhaps a sacrificial calendar. For reference to the pythaistai in
sacrificial calendars cf. Lambert, *Sacrificial Calendar* F1A, 26–30 and
F6 (state calendar); *SEG* XXI 541 *passim* (Erchia calendar). It is obscure
whether there is any connection with the well-known Pythaides of 355
151 or 326 (cf. *Syll.*[3] 296; Parker, *Ath. Rel.* 247). |

CHAPTER THREE

ATHENIAN STATE LAWS AND DECREES, 352/1–322/1: III DECREES HONOURING FOREIGNERS A. CITIZENSHIP, PROXENY AND EUERGESY*

This is the third in a series of articles intended as prolegomena to fascicle 2 of *IG* II³. It covers the most numerous category, decrees honouring foreigners, and is divided for convenience into two parts: A, decrees awarding citizenship, proxeny and euergesy; B, decrees which preserve no such award.

The greatest privilege that Athens regularly awarded foreigners was the Athenian citizenship. This is apparent from its relative infrequency, the relative prominence of the honorands, from decrees which awarded what were in effect components of citizenship, enktesis and isoteleia, as privileges in their own right, and from the fact that men awarded other honours sometimes progressed to the citizenship (e.g.

* This chapter was previously published in *Zeitschrift für Papyrologie und Epigraphik* 158 (2006), 115–158. On the purpose of the articles and for acknowledgements applicable to the whole series see *Ath. State* I–II. I am grateful once more to Klaus Hallof of *Inscriptiones Graecae* for supplying the transcript of Pittakis, to Stephen Tracy for advice on hands, to Elaine Matthews for advice about names in volumes of *LGPN* in preparation, to Henry Kim for advice on numismatic matters, to John Morgan for sharing his views on calendrical questions, to Mary Richardson for information about *SEG* LII in advance of publication, to Angelos Matthaiou for reading an early draft. Other specific debts are noted in the footnotes. I am particularly grateful to Malcolm Errington, Klaus Hallof and Jaime Curbera, whose comments on my draft lemmata for *IG* have indirectly helped eliminate errors from this article. Any that remain are my responsibility alone. In addition to the abbreviations listed in *Ath. State* I and II, the following are used:

Ath. State II: S.D. Lambert, Athenian State Laws and Decrees, 352/1–322/1: II Religious Regulations, *ZPE* 154 (2005), 125–59;

Bielman: A. Bielman, *Retour à la liberté. Libération et sauvetage des prisonniers en Grèce ancienne* (Paris, 1994);

Brun, *Démade*: P. Brun, *L'orateur Démade* (Bordeaux, 2000);

Culasso, *Prossenie*: E. Culasso-Gastaldi, *Le prossenie ateniesi del IV secolo a.C. gli honorati asiatici* (Alessandria, 2004);

Dittmar: A.M. Dittmar, *De Atheniensium more exteros coronis publice ornandi quaestiones epigraphicae* (Leipzig, 1891);

Dreher, *Hegemon*: M. Dreher, *Hegemon und Symmachoi. Untersuchungen zum zweiten athenischen Seebund* (Berlin, 1995);

no. 34). When awarded to foreigners resident in their own cities it was largely honorific, though in such cases it could be given practical effect if the honorands sought refuge in Athens as exiles, a not infrequent
115 occurrence | in the unsettled political conditions of the 340s and 330s (nos. 4, 5, 8, cf. 12, 97).[1] The other major award was proxeny (usually, but not always, combined with designation as "benefactor"), which in principle placed an obligation on the honorand to defend Athenian interests in his home city, though like citizenship, the intention was sometimes more symbolic than practical.[2] Citizenship, proxeny and euergesy and the various lesser privileges are noted in the right

---

Ghiron-Bistagne, *Acteurs*: P. Ghiron-Bistagne, *Recherches sur les acteurs dans la Grèce antique* (Paris, 1976);
Hansen-Nielsen, *Inventory*: M.H. Hansen and T.H. Nielsen, *An Inventory of Archaic and Classical Poleis* (Oxford, 2004);
Lambrechts: A. Lambrechts, *Texst en Uitzicht van de Atheense Proxeniedecreten tot 323 v. C.* (Brussels, 1958);
Pečírka, *Enktesis*: J. Pečírka, *The Formula for the Grant of Enktesis in Attic Inscriptions* (Prague, 1966);
Polis and Theatre: S.D. Lambert, Polis and Theatre in Lykourgan Athens: the Honorific Decrees. Forthcoming in volume in memory of Michael Jameson [= this volume, chapter 15];
Pouilloux, *Choix*: J. Pouilloux, *Choix d'inscriptions grecques*^{2} (Paris, 2003);
Tod II: M.N. Tod, *A Selection of Greek Historical Inscriptions. Vol. II. From 403 to 323 BC* (Oxford, 1948);
Veligianni: C. Veligianni-Terzi, *Wertbegriffe in den attischen Ehrendekreten der klassischen Zeit* (Stuttgart, 1997);
Whitehead, *Metic*: D. Whitehead, *The Ideology of the Athenian Metic. PCPhS* Suppl. IV (1977).
In the tables:
(K)—date determined principally by letter forms (Kirchner in *IG* II^2)
(T)—date determined principally by letter forms (Tracy in ADT)
ateleia = tax exemption
c = crown
dinner = invitation to dinner in the prytaneion on a single occasion (usually for Athenians, occasionally foreigners)
enk. = enktesis, the right to own landed property in Attica
eu. = euergesy, official designation as benefactor (usually, but not always, associated with proxeny)
hosp. = invitation to hospitality in the prytaneion on a single occasion (for foreigners)
isot. = isoteleia (equality of taxation with Athenians)
nat. = citizenship
pr. = proxeny
pref. access = right of preferential access to the Council/Assembly
prot. = clause requiring Council, generals or other officials to protect the honorand.

[1] Osborne, *Nat.* remains the standard treatment.

[2] E.g. no. 44, which may have been awarded after the destruction of the honorand's home city, Tyre. There is no full up-to-date treatment of the Athenian proxeny. Recent

hand column of the tables below. In addition crowns were frequently awarded. For foreigners they were usually of "gold" or "foliage" ("ivy" in no. 40). The value of gold crowns, sometimes, but not always, specified in the decree, was normally 1,000 drachmas.[3] The gold crown was more prestigious. Crowns accompanying citizenship awards, for example, are always gold, never foliage at this period. Proxenies were sometimes accompanied by foliage crowns. Provision is usually for a single crown, but in no. 3 the award is to be repeated at every Great Panathenaia. Unlike Athenians, foreigners were never awarded money for a dedication and sacrifice, but they might choose to dedicate their crowns on the acropolis (no. 3, 33–9, and note the many crowns listed in the inventories of the treasurers of Athena).[4] All the standard honours awarded by Athens are analysed from a linguistic point of view by Henry, *Honours*. This is not the place for a (much needed) historical analysis, but I take the opportunity to note three points, two methodological, one substantive.

First, inscriptions are documents which supply fundamental historical data; but they are also physical monuments deliberately placed in particular locations (usually, in the case of state decrees at this period, the Athenian acropolis). It is easy to fall into conceiving of the honours and privileges awarded as belonging in a separate category from the inscription which recorded them; but unlike the record of a decree in a public archive, an inscription did not merely "record" honours, it commemorated them and *qua* monument it was itself honorific in intention, no less than other tangible honours (like crowns)[5] and intangible privileges (like citizenship). It is this commemorative, monumental aspect of inscriptions which explains why honorific decrees account for such a high proportion of all decrees inscribed. The inscribing of the decree was not a necessary element in the suite of honours, but it was a desirable one from the honorand's point of view. This may be illustrated by the first decree inscribed on no. 66, passed in 344/3

discussions are, for Athens, Culasso, *Prossenie* 11–34; for Greece as a whole, Hansen-Nielsen, *Inventory* 98–102.

[3] On 500 dr. crowns see n. 75.

[4] E.g. there is an echo of the award in no. 3 at *IG* II^2 1485, 21–4 and 1486, 14–16 with S.M. Burstein, *ZPE* 31 (1978), 181–5.

[5] Or bronze statues, which were occasionally awarded, though none in an extant inscribed decree at this period (Athenians: e.g. Demades, Din. *Against Demosthenes* 101, cf. Brun, *Démade* 78–83; foreigners: e.g. *IG* II^2 450 = Osborne, *Nat.* D42 = Lambert, *ABSA* 95, 2000, 486–9, E1, of 314/3).

in response to an embassy from the city of Pellana in Achaia. Its sole purpose is to provide for the inscribing of a decree which Athens had voted in honour of Pellana the previous year:

> —son of Oinobios of Rhamnous proposed: concerning the report of the ambassadors of the Pellanians, the People shall resolve that the secretary of the Council shall inscribe the decree which Aristo- proposed [last year] about the Pellanians on a stone stele and stand it on the acropolis and the treasurer of the People shall pay 30 (?) drachmas for inscribing it from the People's fund for expenditure on decrees, so that the city of the Pellanians shall continue always to be friendly and well-disposed towards the Athenian People, as in previous times; and to praise the ambassadors of the Pellanians and invite them to hospitality in the *prytaneion* tomorrow. [Decree of 345/4, proposed by Aristo- in honour of the Pellanians, follows].

My second point is also well illustrated by the decree just cited. Honorific decrees not only recognised past benefactions, they were intended to influence future behaviour. Another example is no. 105, 3–7 (late 320s), which begins:

> In order that as many as possible of the friends of the king and of Antipater, having been honoured by the Athenian People, may benefit the
> 116 city of Athens.... |

An honorific decree aspired to influence the behaviour not only of honorands, but also of others, who, after c. 350, are often explicitly encouraged to emulate the honorands in order to attract similar honours for themselves.[6] In other words, honorific decrees were monumentalised diplomacy; and the study of them as a group over time has the potential to cast a powerful light on the changing priorities of Athenian foreign policy.

This is not the place to undertake such a study in detail. For most purposes a longer time span will be needed than the thirty-one years covered by this paper. One point, however, is clear enough from the decrees collected here: the marked shift in Athenian foreign policy after her defeat at the battle of Chaironeia in 338/7. To summarise: three broad themes or directions of diplomatic activity are especially prominent. The strongest, implicitly or explicitly, is relations with Macedon.

[6] These "hortatory intention" clauses are discussed from a linguistic point of view by A.S. Henry, *ZPE* 112 (1996), 105–19. In tandem with the appearance of such clauses, *philotimia* becomes a value which is explicitly recognised and encouraged in honorific decrees. Cf. RO pp. 232–3.

Before Chaironeia and again briefly after Alexander's death in 323 the diplomacy is concerned with alliance building against Macedon and support of Macedon's opponents. Between 337 and 323, and again after the defeat of the unsuccessful rebellion of 323–322, it is aimed at securing good relations with the newly dominant power and persons of influence there. Both before Chaironeia and for a few years after, and again after the Lamian War, it is concerned with providing for opponents of Macedon who, in consequence of their opposition, are in exile at Athens from their home cities. The second clear objective is the securing of the grain supply (decrees marked [G] in the tables). This, of course, was a perennial concern, detectable for sure in decrees predating Chaironeia (e.g. no. 2, no. 3, no. 73); but the systematic honouring of grain traders was a new policy after Chaironeia, a product of Athens' sudden loss of international power and influence following the defeat and the consequent dissolution of the Second Athenian League, and a response to increased vulnerability to the acute supply problems of the 30s and 20s.[7] The third most common preoccupation is with the theatre (decrees marked [Theat.]). In a world in which cities competed ever more vigorously for the attention of theatrical benefactors and celebrities, Athens deployed the honorific decree to recognise and encourage those who contributed to the maintenance of her status as the greatest theatrical city of Greece. Like decrees honouring grain traders, theatrical decrees are a particular feature of the post-Chaironeia period. I discuss them in more detail in *Polis and Theatre*.[8]

The standard physical form of an inscribed state law or decree in this period was the stele with rough-picked back. In *Ath. State* II I observed that the inscriptions listed in *Ath. State* I (honouring Athenians) and II (religious regulations) exhibit two variations from this norm. A few have smooth backs or are opisthographic, mostly laws. Since a fairly high proportion of laws at this period dealt with religious matters, this is mainly a feature of religious regulations. When the state honoured Athenians, one of the honours awarded might be money for a (sacrifice and) dedication. The practice of inscribing the dedications (usually with a brief dedicatory formula) pre-dates the practice

[7] On these problems see RO 95–96 with notes.

[8] This brief sketch of Athenian diplomatic activity as documented by the honorific decrees may be complemented by that which emerges from the smaller number of inscribed treaties and other diplomatic decrees of this period which were not honorific. On these see *Ath. State* IV.

of inscribing the decrees providing for them. When the state began regularly inscribing the decrees in the 340s they were either inscribed on the dedication or (like decrees honouring foreigners, a long established genre) on normal stelai. Dedications inscribed with honorific decrees include statue bases (in no case does the statue survive) and blocks from more complex monuments. As already noted, decrees honouring foreigners made no provision for separate dedications and, so far as we can tell,[9] with one or two exceptions (see below), at this period all the inscriptions bearing such decrees were stelai of the
117 normal type. |

The format of the stele is so familiar to epigraphists that they generally take it for granted.[10] The substantial group of 163 examples in *Ath. State* III provides us with an opportunity to note some of its features. The normal stele was substantially higher than it was wide and substantially wider than it was thick. The three fully (or almost fully) preserved examples in the group nicely span the normal range. No. 3, for the rulers of the Bosporos, is a large stele, 2.17 m. high, 0.55 wide (0.64 including the moulding below the relief) and 0.165 thick. No. 43, for Herakleides of Salamis, is a fairly average stele, 0.97 high, 0.37–0.40 wide and 0.08–0.11 thick (as commonly, width and thickness increase slightly towards the bottom). No. 70, for the Elaiousians, is a small stele, 0.51 high as preserved (most of the upper moulding is missing), 0.29–0.31 wide and 0.055–0.073 thick.

The sides of a stele were finished flat, but the back was normally left rough-picked, generally such that it protruded back beyond the back edge of the finished side. The surviving back of a stele is therefore usually very uneven and published (maximum) thickness measurements are generally more or less approximate. Since it has definite front and back edges, the thickness of the finished side can often be measured more precisely. In this group of inscriptions it is up to 4 cm. less than the full thickness of the stele. Including the rough-picked back, original thicknesses of most of the stelai are in the range 0.07–0.2 m. Two have maximum thicknesses less than 0.07: no. 64, honouring Dioskourides of Abdera and his brothers (0.065); and no. 11, for

[9] Where fragments do not preserve original tops, sides and, particularly, backs, it can be impossible to determine to what type of monument they belonged.

[10] On the origin of this format see J.K. Davies in: edd. P. Bienkowski et al., *Writing and Ancient Near Eastern Society. Papers in honour of Alan R. Millard* (New York, 2005), 283–300.

T- son of [Mo?]schos of Plataia (0.057). Four are thicker than 0.2 m. No. 4, for Arybbas of Molossia, the most massive of all Athenian honorific decree stelai, thickens from 0.215 to 0.26 at the bottom. The combined height of the two surviving parts is 2.83 m. (original height will have been greater). Only the crowning relief and a small patch of the text survives of no. 18, for a man from Kroton, but the thickness, 0.23, suggests that it too will have been a substantial monument. No. 42 for Eudemos of Plataia was also unusually thick. Surviving thickness is 0.218–0.24, but the back was reworked in the first century BC when *IG* II^2 4233 (honouring a daughter of L. Licinius Lucullus) was inscribed on it and we can not now be certain how much the stele (if indeed it was originally an ordinary stele) was thinned at that time. By far the thickest monument bearing a decree honouring a foreigner at this period, however, is no. 96, for a son of -emos of Plataia (perhaps related to Eudemos). Its preserved thickness (not perhaps original) is 0.35. It has a crowning relief in the manner of a normal stele, but its thickness and other features suggest that it perhaps belonged to a different type of monument.[11]

Twenty-one of this group of stelai preserve original right and left sides. Their width is normally in the range 0.3–0.5 m. The exceptions are stelai already mentioned: exceptionally wide are no. 3 (up to 0.64), no. 4 (up to 0.65) and no. 18 (0.54); exceptionally narrow no. 64 (0.29) and no. 70 (0.283–0.317).

None of the bases in which the decree stelai of this period were originally set survives and one can rarely be confident that we possess the original bottom. The top of the stele is normally finished in one of three ways: with a simple flat-topped moulding (e.g. no. 69, no. 32, no. 43), a pedimental moulding (e.g. no. 23, no. 118, no. 59) or, more extravagantly, a sculpted relief panel, typically representing the honorands, sometimes in the presence of Athena, who may be crowning them, sometimes in the presence of other divine figures, who may represent the honorand's home city (see the detailed study of Lawton).[12] Variations on the norm occur. For example, relief sculpture is normally at the top of the stele, but on no. 4 there is also a panel of relief under the decree text. Crowns representing those awarded to

[11] Michael Walbank (personal communication) suggests a doorway. I discuss these two decrees for Plataians in *Polis and Theatre*.

[12] State decrees honouring Athenians were not, it seems, usually decorated with relief. Cf. *Ath. State* I and IIIB (final section).

the honorand(s) are inscribed at this period usually below the decree text, but they are occasionally above it (e.g. no. 54, no. 80) and on no. 4 the crowns represent not those awarded in the decree, but previous
118 victories in Panhellenic festivals. |

The use of paint on Attic decree stelai has been a poorly researched topic, in part because it very rarely survives (where it does so at this period, it is red). It was used in two ways, to highlight letters (see e.g. the note on no. 43)[13] and for decoration. So far as we can tell, painted decoration seems to have taken three forms: it could substitute for relief sculpture or for inscribed crowns and it could supply frames or borders. There are two striking examples among the decrees of this set. No. 59 honoured some Akarnanians from Astakos. Just inside the edge of the crowning pediment is a painted red band. Apart from the heading naming the honorands and the invocation, θεοί, the pediment is now otherwise vacant as is the extensive patch of stele below it. We may assume that there was further painted decoration that does not survive. The top of no. 64, for Dioskourides of Abdera and his brothers, does not have a flat or pedimental moulding or relief sculpture. Instead it has a substantial akroterion which is now vacant, but we can tell that it originally contained a painting, because names labelling figures in the painting are inscribed underneath it: "Abderos", "Athena" and "Dioskourides son of Dionysodoros". It seems that the painting showed the same type of scene that is commonly represented in relief: the honorand being crowned by Athena, with the hero of his home city, Abdera, standing by.[14] As noted in *Ath. State* I, some of the decrees honouring Athenians at this period seem to have been decorated with painted crowns (occasionally one can perhaps detect a slight remnant trace). Where there is both relief sculpture and an extent of uninscribed stone we may surmise that the vacant surface was originally painted in a fashion which complemented the relief sculpture, perhaps with crown(s). A good example is no. 3, which is topped by a splendid relief depicting the honorands, the rulers of the Bosporan kingdom, enthroned, and their brother standing by. Their names are inscribed under the relief, but between the names and the beginning of the decree text proper is an extensive vacat of 0.275 m.

---

[13] Occasionally perhaps also to fill in parts of letters that were left uninscribed, though such missing strokes are not generally an issue with state laws and decrees at this period.

[14] Cf. S.N. Koumanoudes, *Horos* 4 (1986), 11–18.

The decree uniquely awards the two leading honorands, Spartokos and Pairisades, crowns at every Great Panathenaia, in addition to a single crown for their brother, Apollonios. There are no inscribed crowns, nor does the relief depict a crowning scene. The vacant patch of the stele was most likely filled with a painting, perhaps depicting crowns or a crowning.

A final feature of inscribed stelai at this period is noteworthy. Every stele is different. Indeed the range of variations is remarkable, whether in dimensions (e.g. of the twenty-one preserving original width, no two are identically wide), in the design of relief, mouldings and other decoration or in other features. Sameness was avoided, individuality emphasised. One suspects a desire to maximise distinctiveness in the vast mass of stelai on the acropolis. | 119

Citizenship Decrees[15]

	Date	Reference	Honorand	Honour
1*	mid-iv	*IG* II^2 251; Osborne, *Nat.* D19.	[.]υ[.]εου in genitive	nat. [+ dinner?]
2*	349/8?	*IG* II^2 207; H.W. Parke, *Proc. Royal Irish Academy* 43 (1935/7), 367–78; H. Bengtson, *Die Staatsverträge des Altertums* II (1962) no. 324; M.J. Osborne, *ABSA* 66 (1971), 297–321; P. Gauthier, *Symbola* (1972), 82–3, 168–9 no. XIII; Osborne, *Nat.* D12; R.A. Moysey, *ZPE* 69 (1987), 93–100; R. Develin, *ZPE* 73 (1988), 75–81; M.H. Hansen, *The Athenian Ekklesia* II (1988), 67; M.B. Walbank, *ZPE* 73 (1988), 83–5; M. Weiskopf, *The So-Called "Great Satraps Revolt", 366–360BC* (*Hist. Einzelschr.* 63, 1989); R.A. Moysey, *REA* 91 (1989), 123–5; D.H. Kelly, *ZPE* 83 (1990), 96–109; J. Tréheux, *Bull. ép.* 1990, 390, 391; 1991, 231; W.K. Pritchett, *The Greek State at War V* (1991),	1. Orontes (satrap or former satrap of Mysia) [G] 2. Envoys (from Orontes? Athenian?)	1. nat. + 1000 dr. gold c (also deals with other matters, including symbola agreement[16] and supply of grain for troops on campaign) 2. Foliage c

15 I should perhaps emphasise that the notes to the tables (inscriptions marked * are accompanied by longer endnotes) are mostly intended to supplement and not to summarise or repeat points made in earlier bibliography.

16 It is perhaps in this context that the thesmothetai are mentioned (l. 11). Cf. Ath. Pol. LIX 6 with Rhodes; Gauthier, *Symbola* 187–90; Develin, 78.

Table (*cont.*)

		Date	Reference	Honorand	Honour
			495–7 (*SEG* XLI 43); Tracy, *ADT* 69 note 2; Veligianni, A86; P. Debord, *L'Asie Mineure au IVe siècle* (1999), 151–2, 350–2.		
	3	347/6	*IG* II^2 212; *Syll.*^{3} 206; Osborne, *Nat.* T21; Lawton no. 35 (ph.); Veligianni, A110; Pouilloux, *Choix* 9; RO 64.	1. Spartokos and 2. Pairisades, sons of Leukon (rulers of the Bosporan kingdom) 3. Envoys from the Bosporan kingdom, Sosis and Theodosios 4. Apollonios, son of Leukon (brother of 1 and 2) [G]	1. and 2. Confirmation of grants to ancestors (nat. + ateleia, Dem. XX 29–40. XXXIV 36) + 1000 dr. gold c at every Great Panathenaia + grant of specific requests, including supply of Athenian ships' officers. 3. hosp. 4. c (once only)
120	4	342?	*IG* II^2 226 + Add. p. 659; *Syll.*^{3} 228; Osborne, *Nat.* D14; Lawton no. 122 (ph.); RO 70 (ph.).	Arybbas (former king) of Molossia[17]	nat. (confirmation of grant to ancestors) + prot. + pref. access + dinner (+ hosp. for those with him) + anyone who kills him to be treated as killer of Athenian + to be returned to power |
	5	338/7	*IG* II^2 237 + Add. p. 659; *Syll.*^{3} 259; Pečírka, *Enktesis* 49–51; Osborne, *Nat.* D16; Schwenk 1; Veligianni, A122; RO 77.	1. Phormio and Karphinas of Akarnania 2. Other Akarnanian exiles	1. gold c + nat. (confirmation of grant to ancestors) 2. pending their return home, enk. + ateleia of metic tax + equality with Athenians in legal procedure and in payment of eisphorai + prot.

[17] On the family see RO. The heading has been restored [Ἀ]ρ[ύββου] (as Osborne notes, nom., cf. no. 97, or dative, cf. no. 3, is also possible). It is likely that father's name and/or ethnic were included (as e.g. no. 97 and no. 3). They are occasionally omitted in headings at this period, but only, it seems, when names are functioning as labels under or over a relief (e.g. no. 138) and/or when multiple names have to be fitted into a single line on a moulding (e.g. no. 30). Neither applies in this case.

Table (*cont.*)

	Date	Reference	Honorand	Honour
6[18]	334/3[19]	*IG* II^2 405 + O. Broneer, *Hesp.* 4 (1935), 169–70 no. 32 (ph.); Osborne, *Nat.* D21 (ph.); Schwenk 24; M.B. Walbank, *ABSA* 85 (1990), 443 no. 14 (*SEG* XL 76); W. Heckel *ZPE* 87 (1991), 39–41 (*SEG* XLI 45); Tracy, *ADT* 8 n. 4, 122, 126–7; Veligianni, A143; Brun, *Démade* 92, 177 no. 6.	Amyntor son of Demetrios[20]	nat.
7	1. 334/3 2. 333/2[21]	*IG* II^2 336 + Add. p. 659; A. Wilhelm, *AM* 39 (1914), 266–9; *Attische Urkunden* V (1942), 103–7 no. 45; J. Pouilloux, *Recherches sur l'histoire et les cultes de Thasos* I (1954) pl. 47, 2, 3 (ph.); S. Dow, *Hesp.* 32 (1963) 341–2; Osborne, *Nat.* D17, D23; P. Gauthier, *REG* 99 (1986), 123–1 (*SEG* XXXVI 153); Schwenk 31; Lawton no. 41 (ph.); Tracy, *ADT* 98; Veligianni, A142. | 121	1. Archippos of Thasos (cf. *IG* II^2 24 and 25 = Osborne, *Nat.* D9) 2. Relations/ associates of Archippos?	1. 1000 dr. gold c + nat. + dinner 2. ?

[18] Walbank's association of the two fragments is persuasive but his alignment is not quite correct. The text at the join of the fragments should read:

21 τὸν δέ γραμ-
[ματέα τὸν κατὰ πρυ]τ̣[ανὲ]-
[ί]αν [ἀναγράψαι τόδε τὸ ψ]-
[ή]φισ[μα κτλ.

[19] On the calendar equation see *Ath. State* IV.

[20] Demetrios is a common name and Amyntor not a rare one (18 cases in *LGPN* I–IIIB, 16 in *LGPN* IV) and as Osborne noted, it is uncertain if this was the Amyntor who was father of Hephaistion, friend of Alexander (cf. Heckel).

[21] There has been debate about the sequence of the decrees on the two fragments (see most recently Gauthier). On the most economic view, which I follow, the beginning of *b* was from the end of the citizenship decree for Archippos begun on *a* (decree 1, dated by the secretary of 334/3). As Wilhelm first suggested (1914) and Dow confirmed from his reading of the secretary of 333/2, the following decree (decree 2, *b* 5 ff.) dates one year later than decree 1 and apparently honoured relations or associates of Archippos. The prescript of decree 2 omits the archon. This is unusual but, as with many aspects of Athenian prescripts, it is better to think in terms of normal practice to which there were occasional exceptions than of absolute rules. Cf. no. 43, a sequence of texts from different years, only the first of which is headed by an archon date. Note also that the prescript of decree 1, as preserved, is also headed with a secretary and did not certainly include an archon (one has been restored on the moulding above the text, but that is conjectural; there is no unrestored parallel at this period, cf. n. 42). The alternative is to assume that the archon of 333/2 was named at the head of a third decree, subsequent to decree 1 and prior to "decree 2", of which the words at the beginning of *b* are the conclusion. That, however, would imply that Archippos was the subject of two decrees dealing with his naturalization within the space of a few months, which is unparalleled and seems implausible.

Table (*cont.*)

	Date	Reference	Honorand	Honour
8	c. 334	*IG* II² 222; *Syll.*³ 226; *ID* 88; Osborne, *Nat.* D22; Veligianni, A141; Ch. Kritzas in: L. Parlama and N. Stambolides edd., *The City Beneath the City* (2000), 139–40 (*SEG* L 178).	1. Peisitheides son of Peisitheides of Delos 2. (Two?) others?[22]	1. nat. + anyone who kills him to be an enemy of Athens + 1 dr. a day subsistence + c? 2. c?
9	c. 334–321?	*IG* II² 297; Osborne, *Nat.* D27.	–	nat.
10	c. 330–320?	*IG* II² 301; Osborne, *Nat.* D28.	–	nat.
11	c. 325–322/1	B.D. Meritt, *Hesp.* 13 (1944), 231–3 no. 5 (ph.); Osborne, *Nat.* D26; Veligianni, A166; *Agora* XVI 96; Brun, *Démade* 48–50, 124–6.	T- son of [Mo?]-schos[23] of Plataia	nat.
12	323/2	*IG* II² 575; A. Wilhelm, *AM* 39 (1914), 260–2 no. 4; Osborne, *Nat.* D41.	[1. Euphron son of Adeas of Sikyon][24] [2. People of Sikyon]	1. [previous awards confirmed +] nat. [2. 1000 dr. gold c]

[22] There are three crowns under the text, the one on the left only partially preserved and apparently squeezed into a narrow space (see Osborne). The arrangement is not symmetrical. In the two fully preserved crowns ὁ δῆμος is inscribed. In the crown to the right, but not the middle crown, there is space between this word and the top of the crown. In that space, towards the left, there appears on the stone an inscribed vertical stroke followed by vacant space. Perhaps the cutter started to inscribe the name of the honorand (Πεισιθείδην ?), but stopped when he realised that it could not be fitted in. There is no case in this period of crowns being inscribed on a decree which did not crown the honorand(s) and the number of crowns depicted usually reflects the number awarded in the decree. Either we have to do with multiple crowns awarded to the same individual (the one on the left might conceivably have been awarded by the Council, cf. no. 43) or, in addition to Peisitheides, one or two others (family or associates) were also crowned in the lost part of the decree. καὶ τοὺς συν[- (l. 5) might refer to them (Osborne thinks rather of συν[έδρους, i.e. a reference back to the period of the Second Athenian League).

[23] Meritt suggested that this man was ancestor of Μόσχος Ἀπολλωνίου Πλατ., ephebe 39/8 BC, *IG* II² 1043 I 124.

[24] As Osborne noted, this seems to be a fragment of the decree honouring Euphron which was destroyed in the aftermath of the Lamian War and reinscribed under the restored democracy in 318/7 as *IG* II² 448 decree 1 (ll. 1–35). Cf. Osborne, *Nat.* D38; Schwenk 83; Lawton no. 54; Veligianni, A163; G. Oliver in: *Lettered Attica* 94–110 (ph.). Oliver's new reading of the second part of the inscribing clause of the reinscribed decree (p. 103) runs: τὴν δ'] | ἑτέραν ἐν ἀγορᾶι παρ[ὰ] τ[ὸ]ν τοῦ Δ[ιὸς τοῦ Σωτῆρος· εἰς] | δὲ τὴν ἀναγραφὴν κτλ. (*IG* II² 448, 28–30). He supplies the following parallels: *IG* II² 1672 A 169, ἐν τῶι τοῦ Πλούτωνος, cf. 177; Lyk. I 137, τὴν εἰκόνα… τὴν ἐν τῷ τοῦ Διὸς τοῦ Σωτῆρος ἀνακειμένην. He suggests that ἱερόν might be understood in these cases, βωμός in ours (but gives no parallel for omission of a masculine

Table (*cont.*)

Uncertain

<table>
<tr><th></th><th>Date</th><th>Reference</th><th>Honorand</th><th>Honour</th><th></th></tr>
<tr><td>13[25]</td><td>1. 332/1
2. 323/2[26]</td><td>IG II^2 368; M.B. Walbank, ZPE 48 (1982), 264–6 (SEG XXXII 92); Schwenk 82; Veligianni, A161; Culasso, Prossenie 285–93 (ph.).</td><td>Theophantos [see note on no. 41]</td><td>1. pr/eu.
2. nat.? [see note on no. 41] |</td><td>122</td></tr>
</table>

1. IG *II^2 251 = Osborne,* Nat. *D19*

The inscription consists of three small fragments associated by Wilhelm. Fr. a + c, now physically joined in the EM, preserve the original left side, fr. *b* the right side. In *ZPE* 10 (1973), 273–4, Osborne argued that c should be dissociated from the others. In 1981 (*Nat.* D19) he tentatively defended the same opinion. It seems that Wilhelm was right. As Osborne observed at *Nat.* D19, a and c have been reworked together in an unusual way to form slates or tiles which have the same thickness and identically worked sloping backs (both 0.032 m. thick

substantive). The relevant part of *IG* II^2 575, ll. 1–2, reads: ΕΑΝΛΙ-Ι-ΡΟΣ. From my examination of the Berlin and Princeton squeezes I agree with Osborne that rho is a possible reading of the initial E and with the P (faint but fully visible) at the beginning of l. 2. Oliver notes (personal communication) that his new text of 448 suits these readings, i.e.

[.....⁹.... ἑτέ]ραν δ' ἐ[ν ἀγορᾶι παρά τὸν τοῦ]
[Διὸς τοῦ Σωτῆ]ρος· εἰς [δὲ τὴν ἀναγραφὴν κτλ.

[25] I agree in essentials with Culasso's text. There is not enough to enable full restoration of the calendar equation in decree 2 (323/2, pryt. 5). δευτέραι ἐπὶ δέκα and δευτέρου (of a month, not in *IG* II^2 917, cf. *Agora* XV 128) would be unattested variants in Attic inscriptions for δωδεκάτηι and ἐμβολίμου and should therefore be avoided in restorations. Though it would be unique in unrestored prescripts before 321, an Assembly on an intercalary day is possible (cf. *IG* II^2 358 with Tracy, *ADT* 152, *IG* II^2 458 etc.) and the equation Posid. 2 + 1 = pryt. V 8 would yield an ordinary year in which there was an irregularity of about 2 days, consistent with the equation restored in *IG* II^2 448 decree I. Ποσι|δεῶνος] δευτ[έραι ἱσταμένου ἐμβολίμωι, ὀ|γδόει τῆ]ς πρ[υτανείας (Meritt, *Ath. Year* 107–8, cf. 86) is accordingly a possible restoration of ll. 21–3. As for ll. 23–4, if *IG* II^2 448, 4 is correctly restored to yield an ἐκκλησία κυρία on 22nd of this prytany (cf. Schwenk 83), ἐκκλησία κυρία should not also be restored here (cf. Ath. Pol. XLIII 2). ἐκκλησία ἐν τῶι θεάτρωι (Pritchett-Neugebauer 59, M.H. Hansen, *GRBS* 23, 1982, 338 n. 19) would be anomalous at this date. There are accordingly attractions in following Meritt with τῶν προέδρων ἐπεψ|ήφιζεν .]Ω.

[26] This is probably a reinscription (in 318/7?) of decrees honouring Theophantos which were destroyed after the Lamian War (cf. no. 12). See further below, note on no. 41.

at the original sides, thinning to less than 0.01 at the inside edge). Moreover there is identical pitting of the left side of the two fragments and a depression on the back of one which appears to run across onto the other. As Osborne acknowledged in 1981, the textual arguments he adduced in 1973 against association are answerable. I shall not go over them again here. The argument to which, in 1981, he was still inclined to give weight was that the final clause "apparently concerning an invitation to a meal in the *prytaneion*, can not be restored at all satisfactorily. It is not possible to restore δεῖπνον, which is appropriate in the case of a newly enfranchised citizen, without considerable violence to the stoichedon order, and even ξένια can only be restored by hypothesizing a strangely worded formula, viz.

[καλέσαι δὲ καὶ αὐτὸ]-
ν ἐ[πὶ ξένια ἐς αὔριον ἐς τ]-
ὸ [πρυτανεῖον------]."

I agree with Osborne about the wording of Kirchner's restoration. καλέσαι δὲ αὐτὸν καὶ ἐπὶ ξένια is a common formulation, but at this period one would not expect καὶ before a pronoun object (cf. Henry, *Honours* 262–3) or reversal of the normal word order, είς τὸ πρυτανεῖον εἰς αὔριον (cf. Henry, 267). There are, however, alternatives. For example the invitation clause might have been preceded by ἐπαινέσαι and the honorand named. Compare no. 23, 34–6, convincingly restored:

ἐπα[ινέσαι δὲ Θεογένη]-
[ν κ]αὶ [κα]λέ[σ]α[ι] ἐ[πὶ ξένια εἰς τὸ πρυτ]-
[ανεῖον εἰς αὔριον].

We know from ll. 7–8 that the honorand's name in the genitive was [.]υ[.]|εου. Αὐτέου, Λυκέου and Πυθέου, suggested by Wilhelm, are among the possibilities. N in 11 might therefore be the last letter of his name in the accusative, e.g.

[ἐπαινέσαι δὲ Πυθέα]-
ν Ε[...^{5}. . καὶ καλέσαι αὐτ]-
ὸ[ν - - - -

E in 11 would be the initial letter of his father's name (as no. 34, 27) or ethnic (as no. 34, 4). Cf. e.g. no. 107 = *IG* II^2 365 fr. b, 9–11: ἐπαινέσαι δὲ Λάπυριν Καλλί[ου Κλεωναῖ]|ον τὸν πρόξενον καὶ καλέσαι α[ὐτὸν ἐπὶ δ]|εῖπνον εἰς τὸ πρυτανεῖον εἰς [αὔριον].

2. IG *II^2 207 = Osborne*, Nat. *D12*

Fr. a of this decree is lost and has been known hitherto only from K. Pittakis, *L'ancienne Athènes* (Athens, 1835), 500–1 and A.R. Rangabé, *Antiquités Helléniques* II (Athens, 1855) no. 397. These two versions differ significantly, most notably as regards the date in line 11, where Pittakis prints ἐπὶ Νικομάχου ἄρχοντος | (341/0), 123
Rangabé ENIKAMMAXOY, which he interpreted ἐπὶ Κα<λλι>μάχου (349/8). The first two editions of *IG* privileged Rangabé over Pittakis, but this was called into question by Osborne, who pointed out that it was unclear what sound basis there could be for the reading of Rangabé, who himself states that he had not examined the stone: "le marbre, que M. Pittaki avait copié en 1820, s'est perdu depuis, et il m'a été impossible de rectifier sa copie". Osborne might have given more weight, however, to the statement of Köhler, who, referring to Rangabé, remarks "eiusdem (scil. Pitt.) ex schedis adcuratius titulum expressit". Köhler's comment implies that there was another version of *a* in Pittakis' papers, on the basis of which he, Köhler, believed that Rangabé had produced a more accurate version of the text than that in *L'ancienne Athènes.* In response to my request, Klaus Hallof kindly identified such a transcript among the papers of Pittakis at the Berlin Academy. It is reproduced at fig. 3. The text it contains represents a sort of mid-point between Pittakis' and Rangabé's published texts. It was this transcript (or possibly another, slightly different, copy of it, see below) that was patently the basis for Rangabé's text. Although the transcript appears to represent Pittakis' later thoughts, it will be apparent from the notes below that it is not automatically to be preferred to his earlier version. In the following text of *a* I therefore maintain Osborne's principle of giving preference to Pitt.'s earlier text, other things being equal (in the notes Pitt. 1 = *L'ancienne Athènes*, Pitt. 2 = Berlin Academy archive copy).

a ἔδοξε τῶι δήμωι· Πανδιονὶς <ἐ>πρυτάνευ[ε·-----------ἐγραμμάτευε· - -]
non-stoich.?
Φλυεὺς ἐπεστάτει· Πολυκράτης Πολυκράτους [--- εἶπεν· περὶ ὧν------οἱ]
πρέσβεις οἵ τε Ἀθηναί<ω>ν καὶ οἱ παρὰ <Ὀ>ρόν[του ἥκοντες----------]
[-] τῆι Ἀθηναί<ω>ν ΠΟΙΕΙΝΤΟΝΔΗΜΟΝΛΕΓΕΤΑΙ------------------

[-] ἀνὴρ ἀγαθὸς περὶ τὸν δῆμον [-----------------------------κα]-
[ὶ ν]<ῦ>ν καὶ ἐν τῶι ἔμπροσθεν χρόνωι, εἶναι Ὀρό[ντην Ἀθηναῖον - - δοῦναι τὴν]
ψῆφον περὶ αὐτοῦ τοὺς πρυτάνεις ἐν τῆι [πρώτηι ἐκκλησίαι - - στεφανῶσαι αὐ]-
τὸν χρυσῶι στεφάνωι ἀπὸ χιλίων δραχμῶν ΟΡ - - ΜΑ----------------
τοῦ στεφάνου· βουλεύσασθαι ΠΝΑ-- ὁπόθε[ν---------------------]
πάντα ΜΙΝΗΙΗΦ --- Ὀρόντου πρὸς το - - ΟΠΟ - - χων οἱ φ[----------το]-
[ὺς θε]σμοθέτας τοὺς ἐπὶ [*see below*] ἄρχοντος - - βουλευον- - ΛΧΟΛΙΟ----
Ἀθηναίων ἢ τῶν συμμάχων μὴ ΛΙΠΟΜΕΝ-----ΩΝΤΟΥΑΡΧΙ---------
δήμου τοὺς μὲν Ἀθηναίους δί[κα]ς <δ>ιδ<ό>ναι ἐν τοῖς συμβόλ[οις-------]
ΤΙΘΕΙΣΙΝ ἐκ τῆς Ὀρόντου ἀρχῆς ΕΤ[----------] συμμ<α>χ-----------
ἐξεῖναι τῶι ἐγκ<λ>ήματι ΩΙΛΛΟΕΠ--------ΑΝ-------------------
[-]υσιν· τὴν δὲ βουλὴν τὴν ----------------------------------
[-] καὶ τῶι δήμωι --

1 in. ΓΕΔΟΞΕ Pitt. 2 appears to be a slip.

1 fin. ΠΡΥΤΑΝΕΥΟΥΣΗΣ Pitt. 1, whence Osborne 1971, 302 tentatively suggested <ἐ>πρυτάνευ<ε>· Ὀ<ν>ήσ[ιππος Σμικύθο Ἀραφήνιος ἐγραμμάτευε (341/0). ΠΡΥΤΑΝΕ[- Ran., whence A. Wilhelm, *Hermes* 23 (1888), 473 suggested <ἐ>πρυτάνε[υε· Διεύχης Δημάρχου Φρεάρριος ἐγραμμάτευε (349/8). Pitt. 2 agrees with Pitt. 1.

2 Πολυκράτης Πολυκράτους Pitt. 1. ΠΟΛΥΚΡΑΤΟΥΣΠΟΛΥ[Ran., whence Köhler suggested Πολυκράτης Πολυ[εύκτου Φηγαιεὺς, cf. *LGPN* II Πολυκράτης 45–46 (but see Osborne 1971, 303 n. 31). Pitt. 2 agrees with Pitt. 1. ἀπαγγέλουσιν been restored after περὶ ὧν. λέγουσι is also possible (e.g. *IG* II^2 213, 6).

3 fin. ΠΑΡΑΘΡΟΝ Pitt. 1, παρὰ <Ὀ>ρόν[του ἥκοντες Ran. Pitt. 2 adds the variant ΒΑΡΑΘΡΟΝ, wisely ignored by Ran. (if indeed it was in his copy of Pitt.'s transcript).

4–5 ΤΗΙΑΘΗΝΑΙΟΝΠΟΙΕΙΝΤΟΝΔΗΜΟΝΛΕΓΕΤΑΙ | ΑΝΗΡΑΓΑΘΟΣΠΕΡΙΤΟΝΔΗΜΟΝΓΕΝΕΣΘΑΙ Pitt. 1, ΗΙΑΘΗΝΑΙΩΝΠΟΙΕΙΝΤΟΝΔΗΜΟΝΛΕΓΕ | ΑΝΗΡΑΓΑΘΟΣΠΕΡΙΤΟΝΔΗΜΟΝΓΕ Ran. Pitt. 2 has merely: ΗΙΑΘΗΝΑΙΩΝΠΟΙΕΙΝΤΟΝΔΗΜΟΝΓΕΝΕΣΘΑΙ. From this it
124 appears that Rangabé was either | working from a different copy of Pitt. 2 which contained the missing line, or that he was controlling Pitt. 2 against Pitt. 1. Pitt. 2's omission looks erroneous (ΓΕ, saut du même au même). Cf. l. 14.

3–4 in. τῆι πόλει τ]ῆι Ran., τῶι δήμωι καὶ τῆι βουλῆι] τῆι Osb., med. λέγ[οντες Ran.

4 fin. ἐπαινέσαι αὐτὸν (Ὀρόντην Osb.) ὅτι ἐστὶν] Dittmar, 174.

5 fin. <ἐ>γένε<το> ? Osb. 1971, 299 n. 17, cf. *IG* II^{2} 133, 10; [τὸν Ἀθηναίων καὶ πρόθυμος ποιεῖν ἀγαθὸν ὅτι ἂν δύνηται Dittmar, Osb. 1981.

6 in. [..]ΑΙΚΑΙ Pitt. 1,]ΝΚΑΙ Pitt. 2 and Ran.

6 med. ΧΡΟΝΩΙΕΙΝΑΙ Pitt. 1, ΧΡΟΝΩΝΩΙΕΙΝΑΙ Ran., whence <κα>ὶ εἶναι Dittmar, Osb. Pitt 2 has ΧΡΟΝΩΙΩΙΕΙΝΑΙ, tending to suggest that the second ΩΙ in that transcript and the ΩΙ in Ran.'s derivative text is dittography. fin. καὶ ἐκγόνους αὐτοῦ, δοῦναι δὲ τὴν] Dittmar.

Between lines 6 and 7 Osborne suggested a line was omitted: καὶ γρά]|<ψασθαι αὐτὸν φυλῆς καὶ δήμου καὶ φρατρίας ἥστινος ἂν βούληται εἶναι· δοῦναι δὲ καὶ τὴν>. Pitt. 2 does not bear directly on this, though its treatment of ll. 4–5 and 14 shows such an omission was not impossible.

7 fin. ἐν τῆι ἐκκλησίαι Pitt. 1, ΕΝΤΗΙ[-]ΝΚΤ Ran., whence Köhler suggested ἐν τῆι [πρώτηι ἐκκλησίαι, including πρώτηι according to the normal formula. Dittmar expanded to [πρώτηι ἐκκλησίαι τῶι δήμωι· καὶ στεφανῶσαι. Pitt 2 has ΕΝΤΗΙ- -ΝΚ, with ἐκκλησίαι noted above the line as restored, suggesting that ἐκκλησίαι in Pitt. 1 should have been in square brackets. ΝΚ might have been ΕΚ or ΚΚ from ἐκκλησίαι.

8 fin. ΟΡ- -ΜΑ Pitt. 1, ΟΡ[-]ΝΟΜΑ Ran., ΟΡ- -ΗϹΜΑ Pitt. 2.

9 ΤΟΥΣΣΤΕΦΑΝΟΥΣ Pitt. 1 and 2 and Ran.

10 ΜΙΝΗΙΗΦ Pitt. 1, ΜΙΝΗΙΗΦΟ Ran., ΜΙΝΗΙΗ̣ΦΕ Pitt. 2.

11 in. [ΘΕ]ΣΜΟΘΕΤΑΣ Pitt. 1, ΣΜΘΕΤΑΣ Pitt. 2 and Ran. appears to be haplography.

11 med. ἐπὶ Νικομάχου (341/0) Pitt. 1, ΕΝΙΚΑΜΜΑΧΟΥ Ran., whence he suggested Κα<λλι>μάχου (349/8); Νικο<φήμ>ου (361/0) dub. Osb. 1971, <Τιμοκράτ>ου (364/3) dub. Osb., *Nat.* 76. Pitt. 2 has ΕΠΙΚΑΜΜΑΡΧΟΥ. Since the only person to have seen the stone, Pittakis, recorded two different readings at different times, we can not be certain what was the correct text. The only specific new possibility suggested by Pitt. 2 is ἐπὶ Κλεάρχου ἄρχοντος, the archon of 302/1, but this seems impossible in light of the old-style elements in the prescript of *a* (see below) and the Athenian generals mentioned in *bcd*. See further below.

11 fin. ΒΟΥΛΕΥΟΝ-ΛΧΟΛΙΟ Pitt. 1, ΒΟΥΛΕΥΟΝΑΧΟΔΙΟ Ran., ΒΟΥΛΕΥΟΝ^ΛΧΟΔ Pitt. 2.

12 med. ΛΙΠΟΜΕΝ Pitt. 1, ΛΕΙΠΟΜΕΝΑΙΕΥ̣Ν Pitt. 2. Ran., followed by *IG*, prints a sequence similar to Pitt. 2.

12 fin. ΩΝΤΟΥΑΡΧΙ Pitt. 1, 2 and Ran., whence Köhler suggested Ὀρό]ντου ἀρχ[-

13 med. ΔΙ-ΣΑΙΔΟΥΝΑΙ Pitt. 1, whence δί[κα]ς δοῦναι Osb., ΔΙΚΑΣΑΙΔΟΥΝΑΙ, whence δίκας <δ>ιδ<ό>ναι Ran. (followed by Köhler), ΔΙΙ\^ΣΑΙΔΟΝΑΙ Pitt. 2. The present tense, διδόναι, is closer to Pitt. 2 (and arguably to Pitt. 1) than the aorist, δοῦναι, and is preferable for what would seem to be envisaged as a repeated action under the new σύμβολα arrangements.

14 in. ΤΙΘΕΙΣΙΝ Pitt. 1, whence ΤΙΘ εἰσὶν Osb.,]ΚΕΙΣΙΝ Ran., whence Κ εἰσὶν Köhler. This line is omitted altogether by Pitt. 2, perhaps in error (cf. l. 5). med. ΕΤ[Pitt. 1, ΕΤΛΠΑΙ Ran., fin. ΣΥΜΜΛΧ Pitt. 1,]ΜΜΑΧΑ[Ran. Ran.'s variants seem gratuitous and again raise the possibility that he was working from a different version of Pitt. 2 which included this line.

15 in. ΕΞΕΙΝΑΙΤΩΙΕΓΚΝΗΜΑΤΙ Pitt. 1,]ΣΕΙΝΑΙΤΩΙΕΓΚΛΗΜΑΤΙ Ran., ΙΕΙΕΙΝΑΙΕΓΚΝΗΜΑΤΙ Pitt. 2. Pitt. 2, which appears erroneously to omit the article before ἐγκ<λ>ήματι, does not weigh decisively on the question, whether the verb was εἶναι (thus Köhler, after Ran.) or ἐξεῖναι (Osb., following Pitt. 1). fin. ΩΙΛΛΟΕΠ - - ΑΝ Pitt. 1, ΩΙΑΛCΕΠ- -ΝΑ Ran., Pitt. 2 has the same as Ran., except that it agrees with Pitt. 1 in - ΑΝ for Ran.'s - ΝΑ.

The main subject of debate has been the date (traditionally 349/8, *IG*$^{1-2}$, Moysey, Pritchett; 341/0 or shortly after, Hansen, Kelly, cf. Develin,
125 Faraguna, *Atene* 188; late 360s, Osborne, Weiskopf). I agree | with Hansen, *Ath. Ekkl.*, cf. *GRBS* 25 (1984), 134 n. 31, that the strongest argument in relation to *a* is the form of the prescript. Pitt. 1, Pitt. 2 and Ran. agree that the proposer had a father's name (and a demotic may be restored), a firm indicator of a date after 354/3 (cf. Henry, *Prescripts* 32), while ἐπεστάτει (l. 2) in place of τῶν προέδρων ἐπεψήφιζεν is rare after the early 340s (latest unrestored cases: no. 3 and *IG* II^2 213, 347/6; restored in *IG* II^2 225, 343/2).[27] Given the differences in readings, the archon's name in l. 11 is a much weaker indicator, but the discovery of Pitt. 2 counteracts Osborne's argument that Rangabé's Κα<λλι>μάχου

[27] Some adjustment is necessary to the examples given by Hansen. ἐπεστάτει is tentatively restored in *IG* II^2 227, dated 342/1 in *IG* II^2, but lettering and formulae would be consistent with a date before the introduction of annual secretaries in the 360s. *IG* II^2 217 dates not to 346/5 but 365/4 (*SEG* XIV 47) and 218, which does date to 346/5, has τῶν προέδρων ἐπεψήφιζεν. The effect is to weaken the case for a date as late as 341/0.

(349/8) appeared to be wholly groundless. Do *bcd* belong to the same decree as *a*? As Kirchner noted, this can not be demonstrated conclusively given that *a* is lost, but, *pace* Osborne (*Nat.* I p. 52), it seems likely.[28] That the fragments are from the same *inscription* is strongly indicated by common subject matter and the fact that *a* appears to have been inscribed, like *bcd*, non-stoichedon (indicated by syllabification at most line-ends), a feature of no more than a handful of state decrees at this period.[29] As Osborne points out, it would still be possible that the texts are from different decrees on the same stone, but there is an argument against this in that the subject matter of the end of *a* is a σύμβολα agreement with Orontes (cf. n. 16), and this same subject matter comes up at the beginning of *bcd*, where we read καὶ τὰ σύμβολα δειχθῆι (l. 6). Parke, followed by Osborne, takes the latter to be a sort of "tessera hospitalis", which the Athenian envoys are to show to Orontes to establish their rights to take delivery of the grain, and distinct from the convention on dispute settlement which is the subject of *a*. σύμβολα, however, are mentioned very rarely in Athenian state decrees of this period[30] and I agree with Gauthier that the σύμβολα in *a* and *bcd* are more likely to be the same. In his view, *a* refers to a σύμβολα agreement which will have been made a short time before our decree was passed and *b* "laisse supposer que la convention, ratifiée à Athènes en présence des ambassadeurs d' Orontes, doit être présentée ensuite à ce dernier par des ambassadeurs athéniens". Moreover, as Moysey points out (95), it is attractive to identify the Athenian envoys whose report, along with that of the envoys from Orontes, is the basis of the decree at *a* 2, with the envoys who are praised in *bcd* 25–7.[31] There is an independent argument for dating *bcd* to the 340s in the generals mentioned. All four of them, Chares (*LGPN* II Χάρης 17,

[28] Osborne's main argument is that it is difficult to see how the specific arrangements for generals to collect grain from Orontes in *bcd* could be dealt with in the same decree as *a*. It is clear, however, from the last lines of *a* that the decree to which *a* belonged went on from the granting of citizenship to Orontes to other aspects of relations with him, and the arrangements in *bcd* might have flowed on quite naturally.

[29] Despite the text printed by *IG* II^2 and the more adventurous reconstruction of *bcd* by Parke, no line can be restored with sufficient confidence to yield a firm line length. The approximate length, however, is indicated by ll. 1–2 and Parke's text of *bcd* (adopted in revised form by Osborne, *Nat.* vol. 2, pp. 62–3) at least shows that line lengths may have been comparable.

[30] The only other certain reference is at *IG* II^2 208 (of 349/8; one wonders if the date is coincidental).

[31] *a* was passed in the prytany of Pandionis. In 349/8 (apparently an intercalary year, cf. *ASAAtene* 3–5, 1941–3, 81–2) Pandionis held the ninth prytany (no. 23), which would have included parts of Mounichion and Thargelion (the latter month

APF 15292), Charidemos (*APF* 15380), Phokion (*LGPN* II Φωκίων 2) and Proxenos (*LGPN* II Πρόξενος 20, *APF* 12270) are known to have been active in this decade. Charidemos, on the other hand, is unlikely to have been mentioned in a list of Athenian generals[32] before he became an Athenian citizen, probably c. 357;[33] and it has been argued that Phokion's career as a general began only after 350.[34] As Moysey notes (96–7), it is an argument in favour of 349/8 that all three of the group mentioned together in the decree, Chares, Charidemos and Phokion, are known to have been generals that year, Chares and
126 Charidemos commanding expeditions to Olynthos | (*FGrHist* 328 Philochoros F49–51), Phokion Athenian forces in Euboea (Plut. *Phok.* 12–13).[35] The only significant argument for dating these fragments to before the 340s is that they mention Orontes, since on the usual view this was the "satrap of Mysia" at the time of the Great Satrap Revolt in 362/1 (Diod. XV 90–1), who, in Osborne's view, should have been dead before the 340s. As others have noted in response to Osborne, however, this is not an insuperable problem. It is possible that the Orontes of the satrap revolt was a different man from the Orontas/es who was satrap of Armenia in 401 (Xen. *Anab.* III 5, 17, cf. IV 3, 4) and/or the Orontes who was commander of Persian forces in Cyprian War of the 380s (Diod. XV 8–11; Trogus, *Prol.* X) and that he was still alive in the early 40s. The key text relating to his death is M. Frankel, *I. Pergamon* 613a = *OGIS* 264, 4–9, ἀποστὰς ἀπὸ Ἀρταξέρξου... ἐκράτησεν τῶν Περγαμηνῶν καὶ μετώικισεν αὐτοὺς... εἶτα... τὴν πόλιν ἐπιτρέψας Ἀρταξέρξηι ἀπέθανεν. Osborne infers that he died shortly after the revolt,[36] but, as Pritchett points out (cf. Debord, 350 n. 364), the text might alternatively be taken to imply that he controlled Pergamon, if

mentioned in *b* 9), in 341/0 (also an intercalary year, cf. no. 54) the seventh pryt. (*IG* II² 228), which would have preceded somewhat the month Thargelion. Cf. Develin, 80.

[32] Χάρητος καὶ Χαριδήμου καὶ Φωκίωνος, l. 12; Χ[άρητος καὶ Χ]αριδήμου καὶ Φωκίωνος, l. 14.

[33] Thus most scholars, including Davies, *APF* 15380. Osborne's attempt to date Charidemos' citizenship back to the 360s (see *Nat.* T51) has not been found persuasive. Cf. Moysey, 98, Hansen, *Ath. Ekkl.* II 69; Kelly; Pritchett, 496; Debord, 351.

[34] By C. Bearzot, *Focione tra storia e transfigurazione ideale* (1985), 79, 94–5. Cf. Debord, 351.

[35] It is consistent with their operating in the same sphere of campaign that Chares and Charidemos are mentioned together three times (ll. 12, 14 and 21), on the last occasion separately from Phokion.

[36] M.J. Osborne, *Hist.* 22 (1973), 515–51, especially 519, 543–51, cf. *Nat.* II pp. 61–80.

not the whole of "Mysia", for a significant time after it. Alternatively the Orontes of our decree might be the Orontes who was satrap of Armenia in 331 (Arrian, *Anab.* III 8, 5; probably still in 317, Diod. XIX 23, 3, unless that was yet another man of the same name), who might be assumed to have succeeded his (father or grandfather?) as satrap of Mysia before moving to Armenia (suggested by Moysey, 97).

Other technical arguments, though not decisive as to date, pull towards the 40s.[37] Walbank's suggestion that the hand is the same as on *IG* II^2 138 and 143 has been contradicted by Tracy, *ADT*. The script, non-stoichedon with tightly spaced lettering and wide interlines, unusual at this period on any account, foreshadows hellenistic style. *IG* II^2 223 = *Ath. State* I no. 1 (ph.), of 343/2, is comparable. The orthography shows none of the features, such as -ο for -ου, which are characteristic of the earlier 4th century, but become progressively more unusual in the 40s and 30s.

I conclude that, while certainty is impossible, on current evidence both *a* and *bcd* are most comfortably allocated to the same decree of the 340s, and that the traditional date of 349/8 remains the most likely.

Proxeny/Euergesy

	Date	Reference	Honorand	Honour	
14	351/0?[38]	*IG* II^2 205 + Add. p. 659; D.M. Lewis, *ABSA* 49 (1954), 50 (*SEG* XIV 15); Lambrechts no. 104; Culasso, *Prossenie* 137–45 no. 7 (ph.).	Demokrates son of Euboulos of Lampsakos[39]	pr/eu.	
15	mid-iv? (K)	*IG* II^2 290; Lambrechts no. 125; Veligianni, A136.	[singular]	hosp. + pr/eu. |	127

[37] The mention of the stratiotic fund (*bcd* l. 11) is not a significant chronological indicator. It is attested for the first time in 374/3 (Stroud, *Grain Tax Law* = RO 26, 54–5).

[38] If Kirchner's attractive ἐπ[ὶ Θεέλλου ἄ|ρ]χοντος is accepted. The archon flows from the restoration of the secretary in 4–5 as Χρέμης Φ[ιλοιτίο Ἰων|ί]δης^{II}, a man apparently attested as councillor at *Agora* XV 36, 7. 351/0 is the only suitable vacant year for a secretary from tribe II. However, it can not be ruled out that the secretary was rather Εἰρεσ|ί]δης^{V} and the archon Θεοφίλο (348/7).

[39] Previous eds. have read the father's name as [Ε]ὐβο[ίο]υ (Εὐβοίου Culasso). Correct is Εὐβόλο̣υ. The upper section of the left and the whole of the right diagonal of the Λ are legible. Typically of this cutter, the right diagonal is not far from vertical (giving the impression of iota), the left diagonal more oblique.

Table (*cont.*)

	Date	Reference	Honorand	Honour
16	mid-iv? (K)	*IG* II² 288; Lambrechts no. 124.	[plural]	pr/eu. + isot.?[40] + prot. + hosp.
17	mid-iv? (K)	*IG* II² 267; Lambrechts no. 117.	-tros (and possibly another). Perhaps from Ak[arnania], Ak[anthos] or Ak[ragas][41]	pr(/eu.?)
18	c. 350[42]	*IG* II² 406; Lambrechts no. 133; Lawton no. 132 (ph.); E. Culasso-Gastaldi, in: D. Ambaglio ed., Συγγραφή (Como, 2002), 108–9 no. 2 (ph.).	From Kroton[43]	pr/eu.
19*	c. 350–340	*IG* II² 284 + Add. p. 659; *Syll.*³ 263; Tod II 170; Lambrechts no. 110; Bielman, *Retour* 15–18 no. 5 (ph. *a*, ph. squeeze of *b*); Veligianni, A112.	Kleomis son of Apollodoros (ruler) of Methymna[44]	pr/eu.

[40] [ἰσοτέλειαν Ἀθήνησι] (l. 7) is Köhler's plausible but unparalleled restoration. [ἀτέλειαν Ἀθήνησιν ᵛ] can be paralleled for *proxenoi* (e.g. *IG* I³ 227 II 21–22) as can [ἔγκτησιν Ἀθήνησιν ᵛ] (no. 51, 10, for ἔγκτησις with no reference to land or house cf. no. 37, 17), but there is no other stoichedon irregularity in this text. καθάπερ τοῖς ἄλλοις προξένοις (ll. 5–6) may express a limitation on the award (Henry, *Honours* 257 n. 62, 252 n. 15).

[41] After προξενία in 1 is a vertical stroke. The possible restorations are: προξενία κ[αὶ εὐεργεσία -]ǀτρωι Ἀκ- (cf. e.g. no. 14) or προξενία I[name καὶ -]τρωι Ἀκ-. There is a wisp of relief sculpture preserved in the tympanum of the crowning pediment (not noted by Lawton).

[42] "Third quarter of 4th cent." (Lawton). A date at the upper end of this range is suggested by the hand ("aetas Philippica" Köhler) and the placing of the archon in a heading separate from the main body of the text, the latest certain case of which is *IG* II² 129 of 356/5. Cf. Henry, *Prescripts* 23 n. 13; M.B. Walbank, *ABSA* 85 (1990), 437–8 no. 4 (*SEG* XL 66).

[43] I read (3–4):
[προξενία καὶ εὐ]εργεσ[ία]
[---ᶜ· ²⁰---] Κροτω[νιάτηι]
As Culasso notes, the ethnic should be in the dative, not genitive (*IG*¹⁻²). She raises the possibility of plural honorands, Κροτω[νιάταις], but unless the letters were severely crowded towards the end of the line, this is unlikely on grounds of spacing. The relief of Athena and a bearded figure leaning on a staff (Asklepios?), with a snake coiled between them, perhaps alludes to the medical reputation of Kroton (Hdt. III 131), or the honorand may have been a doctor (cf. no. 34).

[44] Cf. Isoc. *Epist.* VII 8–9 (Κλέομμις); *FGrHist* 115 Theopompos F227 Κλεομένης). On the different forms of the name see Dittenberger; R. Merkelbach, *ZPE* 22 (1976), 68; O. Masson, *BSL* 81 (1986), 223; A. Morpurgo-Davies, in: S. Hornblower, E. Matthews edd., *Greek Personal Names: Their Value as Evidence* (2001), 18.

'able (*cont.*)

	Date	Reference	Honorand	Honour	
:0	c. 350–335?[45]	G.E. Malouchou, *Horos* 14–16 (2000–2003), 55–8 no. 1 (ph.) (*SEG* LI 71).	–	pr/eu.[46] |	128
.1	c. 350–300? (K)[47]	*IG* II² 581.	–	pr(/eu?)[48] + prot. + c?	
:2	c. 350–300?[49]	*IG* II² 579.	–	pr/eu. + pref. access + prot.	
:3	349/8	*IG* II² 206; Lambrechts no. 109; Pečírka, *Enktesis* 46 (*SEG* XXIV 87); Veligianni, A109. (Fr. *b* is lost).	Theogenes son of Xenokles of Naukratis	pr/eu. + enk. + prot. + hosp.	

[45] Stephen Tracy advises per ep. that, based on the letter forms, he thinks a date earlier than 335 probable. He regards the general style as fairly close to that of his "Cutter of EM 12807" (334/3–314/3), but points out features of the mu, eta, pi and nu that are not characteristic of that cutter.

[46] The erection clause (ll. 8–9) runs στῆσαι ἐ[ν ἀκροπόλει ἐ]|πὶ τῆς Κεκρο[π.....⁹....]. There is no parallel to support restoration. Malouchou attractively suggests that we have to do with the (entrance to?) the Kekropion or perhaps some other "Kekropian" location. Matthaiou per ep. tentatively raises the possibility, ἐ]|πὶ τῆς Κεκρο[πίδος φυλῆς (scil. πρυτανείας), i.e. that the stele was to be set up in (sc. before the end of) the prytany of Kekropis. Cf. the common specification in inscribing clauses before 349, στῆσαι ἐν ἀκροπόλει δέκα ἡμερῶν (e.g. no. 24, 20). Omission of the word πρυτανείας is not uncommon in dating, e.g. *IG* II² 218, 4, but inclusion of the word φυλῆς would perhaps be unexpected. It is possible that the decree was connected in some way with the tribe Kekropis (cf. e.g. *IG* II² 1156, 35) or with the genos Amynandridai, which was responsible for the cult of Kekrops (*IG* II² 2338). However, this can not be a decree of either group as neither tribes nor gene could award the Athenian proxeny (ll. 1–4) or instruct the secretary of the Council (ll. 6–7) to erect their decrees. If there was an accompanying decree of a tribe or genos, one would expect the tribe or genos, not the state, to have provided for erection of the decrees (as e.g. *IG* II² 1155–6).

[47] "Litt. volg. s. iv" and "fin. s. iv" (Kirchner). There is very little to go on.

[48] προξεν- (l. 4), perhaps part of the inscribing clause (καὶ στῆσα[ι l. 5), justifies Kirchner's identification of this as a proxeny decree. In l. 2 I read THNTO for Kirchner's THNΠO. This suggests the following formulaic restoration for a 32 letter line: πρόξενον καὶ ευε|ργέ]την το[ῦ δήμου τοῦ Ἀθηναίων καὶ αὐτὸ|ν κ]αὶ ἐκγ[όνους. I have not, however, yet been able to find satisfactory 32-letter restorations of the rest of this inscription.

[49] The hortatory intention clause (ll. 16–18) indicates a date after c. 350, cf. A.S. Henry, *ZPE* 112 (1996), 107, the "preferential access" clause a date before c. 300, cf. Henry, *Honours* 191–9. "Litt. volg. s. iv" and "fin. s. iv" (Kirchner).

Table (*cont.*)

		Date	Reference	Honorand	Honour
	24	348?[50]	*IG* II^2 149; Lambrechts no. 84; D. Knoepfler in: edd. E. Frézouls and A. Jacquemin, *Les relations internationales* (1995), 324–31; Dreher, *Hegemon* 180–97 (ph.) (*SEG* XLVI 124); Veligianni, A114.	1. Ampheritos, Herakleiodoros[51] (and one or two others?) from Euboea (Hestiaia?). 2. Athenian and allied envoys	1. pr/eu. 2. dinner + supply of weapon tips
	25	c. 345–320 (T)	B.D. Meritt, *Hesp.* 30 (1961), 257 no. 58 (ph.) (*SEG* XXI 348); *Agora* XVI 145; Tracy, *ADT* 78.	–	pr/eu.[52]
129	26	c. 345–320 (T)	*IG* II^2 285 + 414 fr. d;[53] Lambrechts no. 121; Pečírka, *Enktesis* 54–6 (*SEG* XXIV 89); Tracy, *ADT* 77, 123 n. 2; Veligianni, A108; Culasso, *Prossenie* 157–64 no. 9 with pp. 279–82 (ph.).	- son of -ron of Phaselis	pr/eu. + enk. |

[50] This date, in the aftermath of Hegesileos' intervention in Euboea, is well argued for by Dreher (after O. Picard, *Chalcis et la confédération eubéene* [Athens, 1979], 239–40). Angelos Matthaiou and Stephen Tracy confirm per ep. my impression that the hand argues against a date as early as 375 (Knoepfler). Cf. Köhler's date, c. 356–352; M.B. Walbank, *AHB* 1989, 122. Knoepfler and Dreher are perhaps right to reject 343/2 (G. Cawkwell, *CQ* 56, 1963, 211–2 n. 7) and 341/0 (P. Brunt, *CQ* 63, 1969, 260, cf. Cawkwell, *Phoenix* 32, 1978, 67 n. 37). Inter alia the latest occurrence of δέκα ἡμερῶν in an inscribing clause (l. 20) is at no. 23, 31 of 349/8.

[51] Perhaps identical with or related to the Herakleiodoros who established a democracy at Oreos/Hestiaia, c. 376?, Arist. *Pol.* 1303a 19, cf. Knoepfler, 320.

[52] Ll. 4–7 may be read and restored:

εἶν[αι δὲ] stoich. 24
[πρόξενον καὶ εὐ]εργέτην [τοῦ δ]-
[ήμου τοῦ Ἀθηναίω]ν̣ αὐ[τ]ὸ[ν καὶ ἐ]-
[κγόνους

Cf. no. 37, 13–16.

[53] *IG* II^2 414d is a non-joining fragment associated with *IG* II^2 285 by E. Schweigert, *Hesp.* 8 (1939), 27 n. 1; *Hesp.* 9 (1940), 339. This was tentatively accepted by Pečírka and Tracy, but is doubted by Culasso. Certainty is impossible, but the fine differences in the lettering identified by Culasso are within the range of what might be expected of a single cutter and, apart from identical line lengths, at autopsy the association seemed to me persuasive on physical grounds. In particular the left side on *a* and the right side on *b* are worked in identical fashion. In both cases the thickness of the finished side is 0.08, with the rough working of the back taking overall thickness to 0.1 on the upper fragment, 0.11 on the lower. Consistently with the fragments' belonging to the same inscription, the vertical stoichedon is the same on both (0.0165) and the horizontal stoichedon increases a little from top to bottom (I measure it at 0.0172 at *a* l. 6, 0.0176 at *a* l. 13, 0.018 in *b*).

Table (*cont.*)

	Date	Reference	Honorand	Honour
27	c. 345–320?[54]	*IG* II^2 357; Lambrechts no. 137; M.H. Hansen, *GRBS* 23 (1982), 344 no. 46; Schwenk 57; J. Dillery, *CQ* 52 (2002), 466.	An [Ere]trian[55]	pr.[56]
28	c. 340–320?[57]	B.D. Meritt, *Hesp.* 30 (1961), 208–10 no. 3 (ph.) (*SEG* XXI 340); *Agora* XVI 66.	-machos son of -krates of Al- or Hal-[58]	pr. + prot.
29	340/39?[59]	*IG* II^2 235; Lambrechts no. 112; Tracy, *ADT* 77; Veligianni, A120.	Apelles son of Zopyros of Byzantium[60]	pr/eu. + prot.
30	340/39	*IG* II^2 231+ J.H. Oliver, *AJA* 40 (1936), 464 (ph.); Lambrechts no. 111 (ph.); Lawton no. 36 (ph.); O. Cavalier, *Silence et Fureur* (1996), 139–41 (ph.) (*SEG* XLVII 124); Lambert, *ZPE* 137 (2001), 55–68 (ph.) and 141 (2002), 121 n. 11; P. Gauthier, *Bull. ép.* 2002, 169 (*SEG* LI 75).	Phokinos, Nikandros and Dexi- (of Megara?)	c + pr. + prot. + hosp.

[54] There are few letters to go on, but the style appears to me close to Tracy's "litt. volg.", 345–320 (pp. 76–81). The very fragmentary prescript has been allocated to 327/6, based on the identification of -τοκλῆς (l. 5) as the secretary of that year, Αὐτοκλῆς Αὐτίου Ἀχαρνεύς. This, however, causes severe problems with the restoration of the rest of the prescript and is far from certain. Note that in the years between 350 and 322/1 there are seven secretaries whose names are not known: 350/49, 348/7? (cf. n. 38), 344/3, 342/1 (cf. n. 27), 339/8 (cf. no. 134a), 336/5 (cf. note to no. 84), 331/0 (cf. no. 78).

[55] Knoepfler, *Eretria* XI 316, speculates that the honorand may have exported cereals to Athens. A politico-military context seems no less possible. Cf. *IG* II^2 125 = RO 69; *IG* II^2 230 with *SEG* XLVI 119.

[56] The stone in l. 2 reads ΠΡΟΕΕΝΙΑ, an obvious error for ΠΡΟΞΕΝΙΑ.

[57] -ει for -ηι in τεῖ βουλεῖ (l. 6) tends to indicate a date after c. 340–330 (Threatte I 378). -ει- for -ε- as in γραμματεία (l. 14) was common c. 360–320 (Threatte I 147, 152). On the lettering see Tracy, *ADT* 115.

[58] [..⁴..]μαχος (l. 3) [..⁴..κ]ράτους Αλ[...⁶...] (l. 7), probably not κ]ράτου Σαλ[- as this gen. in -ου would be unexpected at this early date, cf. Threatte II 154–62. Meritt observed that at Diod. XVIII 11 the Alyzaioi from Akarnania (cf. no. 5, no. 34 etc.) are restored among Athens' allies against Macedon in 323.

[59] The lettering is Tracy's "litt. volg.", c. 345–320. Köhler suggested that the context was the siege of Byzantium, 340/39. Note the wording about the honorands' cooperation with generals sent from Athens at ll. 11–15.

[60] It is uncertain whether there is a connection with the Apelles of Byzantium who was a mercenary commander in Alexandria and father of Aristophanes of Byzantium the grammarian (Heichelheim, *RE* Suppl. 5, 1931, col. 43; W. Peremann and E. van't Dack, *Prosop. Ptolem.* 2151; cf. T.B. Mitford, *ABSA* 56 (1961), 10 no. 20). The names

Table (*cont.*)

		Date	Reference	Honorand	Honour
	31	c. 340? (T)[61]	*IG* II^{2} 416 fr. a; Lambrechts no. 136; M.B. Walbank ap. A.S. Henry, *JHS* 97 (1977), 157–8; Tracy, *ADT* 123.	Praxias [of] D[elphi?]	pr.
130	32	338/7	A. Wilhelm, *Öst. Jh.* 10 (1907), 32 (ph.); *IG* II^{2} 238; D. Peppas-Delmousou, *Arch. Delt.* 33 (1978) B1 [1985], 5 (ph. *bc*) (*SEG* XXXV 61); Schwenk 2; Tracy, *ADT* 72 n. 6, 77; Veligianni, A123.	Drakontides son of Amphoteros and Hegesias son of Stes- of Andros[62]	foliage c + pr/ eu. + pref. access + hosp. |
	33	337/6[63]	*IG* II^{2} 240; *Syll.*^{3} 262; Lambrechts no. 126; Tod II 181; A.J. Heisserer, *ZPE* 41 (1981), 216–8 (*SEG* XXXI 77); Schwenk 7; Tracy, *ADT* 77; Veligianni, A124; Brun, *Démade* 64–9, 177 no. 3.	– son of Andromenes of-[64]	pr/eu. + prot.

Apelles and Zopyros also occur in an Athenian family of the deme Erchia in i–ii AD, *LGPN* II Ἀπελλῆς 16–20, Ζώπυρος 40. Given the distance in time and that both names are fairly common, this may be coincidental, though it is not implausible that the honorand of *IG* II^{2} 235 might eventually have taken refuge in Athens and been awarded citizenship there (cf. no. 5, no. 34 etc.).

[61] Tracy, per ep. "Volg. med. s. iv" Kirchner.

[62] Wilhelm restored our Hegesias' father as Στησι|[αγόρ]ου (fr. b+c, 9–10) but there are other possibilities, including Στησι|[άνδρ]ου. Cf. *LGPN* I 412; *CID* II 22. The allusion to the honorands' military courage (ἀνδραγαθία, cf. L. Robert, *Arch. Eph.* 1969, 50–1, Tracy, *ADT* 72 n. 6), suggests that, like no. 5, passed in the same year, probably in the same prytany and possibly at the same Assembly, their services had been rendered in the context of the battle of Chaironeia. Athens sought help from Andros (and Keos, Troizen and Epidauros) after the battle (Lyk. I 42).

[63] Apparently shortly before news of Philip II's death reached Athens, cf. J.R. *Ellis, Philip II and Macedonian Imperialism* (1976), 306 n. 53.

[64] With Velsen, Wilhelm and Heisserer I read the father's name (l. 10) of this man who "looked after Athenians visiting Philip" (ll. 12–13) as Andromenes. His own name has never been got out. Prolonged examination of the stone on several occasions has yielded ἐπ[ειδὴ εὔ|νου]ς [ἐ]στ̣[ὶν] Δῖος Ἀνδρομένο̣[…^{5}..] | [πρ]ὸ̣ς̣ [τὸ]ν δῆμον τὸν Ἀθηναί[ων, though Δῖος is highly uncertain. The ethnic perhaps had four letters (Heisserer suggests Χῖος or Κρής) and there was either an additional letter in the line or the father's name was shortened to -μένου (cf. Threatte II 154–9) to avoid breaking the honorand's name at line-end. There is a comparable line-end irregularity after a name in l. 6 (vacat after chairman so that following proposer's name is not broken and occupies a line to itself).

Table (*cont.*)

	Date	Reference	Honorand	Honour	
34	1. 337/6 2. 322/1[65]	*IG* II² 242 (= Schwenk 10) + *IG* II² 373 (= Schwenk 88); Pečírka, *Enktesis* 72–4; Henry, *Honours* 214–5; M.B. Walbank, *ZPE* 86 (1991), 199–202 (*SEG* XL 74, cf. XLI 44); Lawton no. 39 (ph.); Tracy, *ADT* 98; Veligianni, A165.	Euenor son of Euepios of Argos in Akarnania (a doctor, Athen. II 46d, later awarded citizenship, *IG* II² 374 = Osborne, *Nat.* D50)	1. pr/eu. 2. foliage c + enk.[66] + prot.	
35	c. 337–324 (T)	*IG* II² 426; Lambrechts no. 129; Pečírka, *Enktesis* 77–8 (*SEG* XXIV 97); Tracy, *ADT* 106.	–	pr/eu. + enk. + prot. + pref. access + hosp. + c	
36	c. 337–324 (T)	A. Wilhelm, *Attische Urkunden* I (1911), 48 (ph.); *IG* II² 339b; Pritchett-Neugebauer, 48 n. 27 (*SEG* XVI 54); Lambrechts no. 130; Tracy, *ADT* 106. Cf. Schwenk 29.	Lyko- son of -kleides of Pydna[67]	pr/eu. |	131

[65] The dates raise the possibility that decree 1 recognised services performed by Euenor at Chaironeia (Veligianni-Terzi suggests that he may have been among the Akarnanians who accompanied Phormio and Karphinas to Athens after the battle, cf. no. 5), decree 2 services during the Lamian War. The (fully preserved) calendar equation in decree 2, 2 Tharg. = pryt. IX 23, is consistent with an intercalary year in which there was an irregularity of about 4 days. This should perhaps be accepted as an instance of intercalation/subtraction of days in the festival calendar (cf. W.K. Pritchett, *CSCA* 9, 1976, 187–8) rather than amended away (cf. Pritchett-Neugebauer 60; Meritt, *Ath. Year* 111–2; M.H. Hansen, *GRBS* 23, 1982, 345 no. 57). A similar phenomenon is observable in other years at this period, e.g. 325/4, also an intercalary year (see *IG* II² 361 = Schwenk 69; no. 43). I doubt that meetings on 2nd of the month were normally avoided as a so-called monthly festival day (cf. Mikalson, *Calendar* 15–6). Though some days might be considered unsuitable for business (such as the veiling of the image on 25 Thargelion in connection with the Plynteria, Xen., *Hell.* I 4, 12), Athens does not seem generally to have observed a rigid distinction between holidays and business days (other Assemblies are attested at this period on minor festival days) and may normally have avoided Assemblies during major festivals such as the Panathenaia largely for the pragmatic reason that citizens could not participate in an Assembly and attend a festival at the same time. Our slight evidence for 2nd of the month as day of the ἀγαθὸς δαίμων (listed by Mikalson) does not suggest that it was celebrated as a major state festival in classical Athens and it may be coincidental that there is no other Assembly firmly attested on this day.

[66] The grant is uniquely qualified by the phrase ἀπέχοντι τῶν [κ]οι[νῶν καὶ τῶν ἱερῶ]ν (ll. 45–6). This perhaps expresses more fully the effect of the qualification κατὰ τὸν νόμον, which occurs for the first time in the enktesis formula in no. 43, 20, of 325/4. A law restricting the capacity of enktesis grantees to acquire communal and sacred land would not have been out of place in the "Lykourgan" policy programme.

[67] Restored by Wilhelm (followed by *IG* II²) as Λύκο[ς Ἀριστ|οκ]λείδου Πυτ̣ν[αῖ]-ος (ll. 2–3), noting an uncertain connection with the Lykos who was general of

Table (*cont.*)

	Date	Reference	Honorand	Honour
37	c. 337–325[68]	J. Camp, *Hesp.* 43 (1974) 322–1 no. 3 (ph.); Tracy, *ADT* 33–1, 107; Veligianni, A160; E. Culasso-Gastaldi in: D. Ambaglio ed., Συγγραφή (2002), 109–17 no. 3 (ph.).	Sopatros son of Philistion of Akragas [G]	pr/eu. + enk. + hosp. + seat at City Dionysia[69]
38	333/2[70]	*IG* II² 339a; Lambrechts no. 131 (ph.); Schwenk 29; Lawton no. 42 (ph.); Tracy, *ADT* 106, 110 (*SEG* XLV 73).	Ar- (of Chios, implied by relief, cf. D.M. Lewis, *ABSA* 50, 1955, 27)	pr.

Lysimachos (Polyain. V 19). This, however, was based on the assumption that a short name was needed to suit *IG* II² 339a, 1. Now that 339a = no. 38 has been shown not to belong to the same stele as 339b (Pritchett-Neugebauer, cf. Schwenk), that constraint does not apply. At autopsy traces consistent with the kappa of the father's name and with all the letters of the ethnic (for the orthography cf. Threatte I 561) are legible. Among names attested at this period and region Λυκό[φρων Ἡρ|α]κλείδου and Λυκο[ῦργος Ε|ὐ]κλείδου are among the possibilities. (I am grateful to Elaine Matthews for advice in advance of the appearance of *LGPN* IV).

[68] Cut by a mason who operated 337–324 (Tracy). The proposer is Lykourgos, who died 325/4. The honorand had ensured that Athens was abundantly supplied with grain (ll. 8–11). The inscription has been linked with the grain shortages of the years 331–320. Tracy, 34 notes that it might alternatively relate to the crisis of 335. However, there is no explicit reference to any crisis in the decree and anxiety about grain supplies was a general feature of the post-Chaironeia period, an anxiety which, as Lykourgos himself makes clear, began in the aftermath of the defeat (Lyk. I 18, 42, cf. Dem. XVIII 171, 248). Moreover, as no. 43 clearly shows, honours for this type of service could be delayed until several years after the services rendered. These considerations caution against overly specific dating of this and some other decrees of this period honouring grain traders.

[69] The earliest extant award of a seat for a single festival (Henry, *Honours* 292–3), appropriately proposed by a politician with strong theatrical interests.

[70] The prescript has attracted interest in relation to the question of which day was omitted in a hollow month, but it is not decisive. The prytany was the second, the month Metageitnion. Possible restorations (ll. 6–7) include: (a) ἕκτ[ηι φθίνοντος, πέμ|πτηι κα]ὶ δε[κάτηι τῆς πρυτανείας (H. Usener, *Rh. Mus.* 34, 1879, 391–2), which is consistent with a regular intercalary year in which a day before ἕκτη φθίνοντος was omitted in a hollow Metageitnion (following a full Hekatombaion, cf. *IG* II² 338 = *Ath. State* I no. 15). This is perhaps the most comfortable solution, but also possible are: (b) ἕκτ[ηι φθίνοντος, ἑβδ|όμηι κα]ὶ δε[κάτηι] (Pritchett, *CSCA* 9, 1976, 188–91), consistent with omission of δεύτερα φθίνοντος in a hollow Metageitnion and insertion of an intercalary day earlier in the month; (c) ἕκτ[ηι μετ' εἰκάδας, ᵛἕ|κτηι κα]ὶ δε[κάτηι (Pritchett-Neugebauer, 46–8, cf. Pritchett, *Ancient Athenian Cals. on Stone* [1963], 276–7 (ph.)) or in place of the *vacat* ἕκ|κτηι (J. Morgan, personal communication, cf. Threatte I 531), consistent with omission of δεύτερα φθίνοντος in a hollow Metageitnion and no calendrical irregularity. Cf. Meritt, *Hesp.* 4 (1935), 532; *Ath. Year* 48–50 (ph.); *AJP* 95 (1974), 272–7; *Mnem.* 30 (1977), 229–30. For Pritchett's view see most recently his *Athenian Calendars and Ekklesias* (2001), 48, 59–61, 123–4.

Table (*cont.*)

	Date	Reference	Honorand	Honour
39*	332/1	E. Schweigert, *Hesp.* 8 (1939), 26–7 no. 6 (ph.); Lambrechts no. 132; Schwenk 39 (*SEG* XXXV 71); *Agora* XVI 79; Tracy, *ADT* 107, 110–1; Lambert, *Polis and Theatre.*	– son of Onoma-of – (actor?) [Theat.]	gold c + pr/eu.
40	332/1[71]	*IG* II^2 347; D.M. Lewis, *ABSA* 49 (1954), 37; Lambrechts no. 135; W.K. Pritchett, *CSCA* 5 (1972), 176; Schwenk 38; M.H. Hansen, *The Athenian Ekklesia* II (1988), 67; Lawton no. 45 (ph.); Tracy, *ADT* 12 n. 35, 110–1, 114; D. Whitehead, *C&M* 44 (1993), 69 n. 118 (*SEG* XLIX 101); Veligianni, A147; Lambert, *ZPE* 141 (2002), 117–8 n. 5 (*SEG* LII 94) and *Polis and Theatre* (ph.). |	Amphis son of Di- of Andros (dramatic poet, *PCG* II 213–35) [Theat.]	ivy c[72] + pr/eu. 132
41*	332/1	*IG* II^2 344; Lambrechts no. 134; M.B. Walbank, *ZPE* 48 (1982), 264–6 (*SEG* XXXII 92); Schwenk 33; Veligianni, A144; Culasso, *Prossenie* 289–93 (ph.).	[Theophantos? Original version of no. 13, decree 1?]	pr/eu.
42	330/29	*IG* II^2 351 + 624 (Add. p. 660); *Syll.*^{3} 288; Pečírka, *Enktesis* 68–70; Pouilloux, *Choix* 6; W.K. Pritchett, *CSCA* 9 (1976), 187; M.H. Hansen, *GRBS* 23 (1982), 344 no. 41; Schwenk 48; Veligianni, A153; I. Worthington, *ZPE* 137 (2001), 109–12 (*SEG* LI 82); J. Dillery, *CQ* 32 (2002), 462–70 (*SEG* LII 97); RO 94; Lambert, *Polis and Theatre* (ph.).	Eudemos son of Philourgos of Plataia[73] [Theat.]	foliage c + eu.[74] + enk. + military service and eisphora as an Athenian
43*	1–3 (ll. 46–65, 28–45) 330/29–328/7	*IG* II^2 360 + Add. p. 660; *Syll.*^{3} 304; Lambrechts no. 138 (ph.); Pečírka, *Enktesis* 70–2; Schwenk 68; Veligianni, A157; RO 95; Culasso, *Prossenie* 165–82 no. 10 (ph).	Herakleides son of Charikleides of (sc. Cypriot) Salamis [G]	1. Assembly decree commissioning a probouleuma (= 2)

[71] At the Assembly ἐν Διονύσου, same day as no. 39. See note thereto.

[72] Earliest attested award of a crown of this characteristically Dionysian type. Cf. Henry, *Honours* 40.

[73] Perhaps related to the honorand of *IG* II^2 345 = Schwenk 36 = no. 96.

[74] Unusually not associated with proxeny. Cf. Gauthier, *Bienfaiteurs* 23.

Table (*cont.*)

		Date	Reference	Honorand	Honour
		4–5 (ll. 66–79, 1–27) 325/4	1–3 recognise honorand's services in 330/29, 4–5 services in 330/29 and 328/7.		2. (probouleuma to 3) 500 dr. gold c[75] 3. (Assembly's decree) gold c + envoy to treat with Dionysos, ruler of Herakleia Pontika, about return of sails 4. (probouleuma to 5) 500 dr. gold c 5. gold c + pr/eu. + enk. + military service and eisphora as Athenian
133	44[76]	After c. 330[77]	*IG* II^2 342 + R. Stroud, *Hesp.* 40 (1971), 181 no. 29 (ph.); Lambrechts no. 139; Pečírka, *Enktesis* 61–3; M.B. Walbank, *ZPE* 59 (1985), 107–11 (*SEG* XXXV 70); Tracy, *ADT* 33; Veligianni, A159; Lambert, *ZPE* 140 (2002), 76 with n. 9 (*SEG* LII 93); Culasso, *Prossenie* 193–203 no. 12 (ph.).	Apses son of Hieron and Hieron son of Apses of Tyre[78] [G]	gold c + pr/eu. + enk. |

[75] The two 500 dr. crowns on this inscription are the only certain cases of such awards at this period in state decrees honouring foreigners. It is probably significant that they are both in *probouleumata* rather than Assembly decrees, confirming the impression given by decrees honouring Athenians that crowns of this value were typically awarded by the Council and perhaps that only the Assembly was entitled to award 1,000 dr. crowns (cf. *Ath. State* I 88). Two further cases, in very fragmentary decrees, will be noted in Part B.

[76] I agree in essentials with Culasso's text, except that the first legible letter in 1 is a certain alpha (thus also Stroud, *Hesp.* 1971), ruling out the restoration, Ἰτα]λία̣ι̣ [. After the alpha I read: central vertical (top not preserved, T possible); Λ̣ (Α̣ Stroud) or perhaps Κ̣; uncertain trace of the bottom of a central vertical.

[77] κατὰ τόν νόμον in the enktesis formula (l. 14) is absent in no. 42 of 330/29, present for the first time in no. 43 decree 5, of 325/4. The decree may therefore postdate the destruction of Tyre by Alexander in 332, after which many Tyrians moved to Carthage (mentioned l. 2), Diod. XVII 41, 1–2; 46, 3–4 (thus Culasso).

[78] Apparently Phoenicians referred to by Hellenized names. Cf. below, note on no. 43.

Table (*cont.*)

	Date	Reference	Honorand	Honour
45[79]	c. 330–322/1?[80]	*IG* II^2 425; Lambrechts no. 128 (cf. 163); Pečírka, *Enktesis* 77; Veligianni, A158.	– os son of Thyion[81] of –	1000 dr. gold c + pr/eu. + enk.
46	c. 329–322[82]	A.G. Woodhead, *Hesp.* 29 (1960), 81–2 no. 157 (ph.) (*SEG* XVIII 18) + *IG* II^2 564; Pečírka, *Enktesis* 89–91 (ph.); *Agora* XVI 111; Tracy, *ADT* 77; E. Culasso-Gastaldi, *ZPE* 144 (2003), 111–22; Culasso, *Prossenie* 205–22 no. 13 (ph.).	1. Ph-[83] son of Admetos of Priene 2. Envoys from Priene	1. 1000 dr. gold c + pr/eu. + pref. access + enk. + prot. 2. hosp.
47	After c. 329[84]	*IG* II^2 422; Pečírka, *Enktesis* 75–6 (*SEG* XXIV 108); Henry, *Honours* 138 with n. 144; Veligianni, A169.	P- son of Dioph- of Hestiaia[85]	[gold or foliage] c + pr/eu. + enk.

[79] The association with *IG* II^2 293 proposed by M.B. Walbank, *ZPE* 69 (1987), 265–8 was withdrawn by him ap. *SEG* XXXVII 70 and at *AHB* 3 (1989), 52–3 (*SEG* XXXIX 69).

[80] The criteria are: hand c. 350–325 (D.M. Lewis ap. Pečírka, post-336/5 Köhler, Kirchner); inclusion of hortatory intention clause, post-c. 350 (cf. n. 49); κατὰ τὸν νόμον in the enktesis clause, post c. 330–325 (cf. n. 77); inscribing officer prytany secretary not ἀναγραφεύς, pre-oligarchy of 321/0–318.

[81] In *LGPN* I–IV the name is attested in Samos, Achaia, Akarnania and Boeotia.

[82] κατὰ τὸν νόμον in the enktesis formula perhaps indicates a date after c. 329–325 (cf. n. 77). The reference to the Council of the Athenian cleruchy on Samos shows that the decree predates the end of the cleruchy in 322.

[83] Φ[-$^{c.\ 5}$–]ην[..] in accusative. Perhaps a relation of Admetos, ναοποιός at I. Priene 3 = Syll.^{3} 282, 24.

[84] κατὰ τὸν νόμον in the enktesis formula perhaps indicates a date after c. 329–325 (cf. n. 77). Nothing can be inferred from the presence or absence of καὶ συμπρόεδροι in the prescript. It is not restored in the current text, but if the chairman had a short name + demotic (11 letters), it would be possible to restore it at the end of l. 2. καὶ συμπρόεδροι probably occurs for the first time in no. 56 of 328/7, but is not normal before 321/0.

[85] Π[...^{6}...Διοφ. |..^{4}..Ἑσ]τιαιᾶ (ll. 8–9, cf. 7 for father; the right end of a top horizontal is legible before the first I of the ethnic). Father's name: Διόφ[αντος or Διοφ[άνης (Wilhelm). The conventional restoration has been Ἱστ]ιαιᾶ, but with both the ethnic (from the city Hestiaia in Euboea) and the Attic demotic (from the deme Hestiaia) the initial letter in Attic inscriptions is normally E (Threatte I 143 and 282). Pečírka noted that the ethnic is not absolutely certain. The only other serious possibility in an Athenian context, however, would seem to be Αἰ]γιαιᾶ, apparently attested as an ethnic on the funerary monument of c. 400, *IG* II^2 7946, ΑΙΓΙΑΙΕΥΣ. Jaime Curbera confirms per ep. that the Berlin squeeze leaves no doubt as to the reading. No such ethnic, however, seems to be otherwise attested (cf. Hansen-Nielsen, *Inventory* p. 1276) and Sean Byrne per ep. plausibly suspects a cutter's error for the Athenian demotic ΑΙΓΙΛΙΕΥΣ.

Table (*cont.*)

		Date	Reference	Honorand	Honour
	48	c. 325?[86]	*IG* II^2 184; Lambrechts no. 101; Pečírka, *Enktesis* 43–5 (ph.) (*SEG* XXIV 92).	–	[1000?][87] dr. gold c + pr/eu. + enk. + prot.
134	49	c. 325–300[88]	*IG* II^2 419 + M.B. Walbank, *Hesp. Suppl.* forthcoming; Lambrechts no. 127 (ph.); Lawton no. 158 (ph.); Culasso, *Prossenie* 255–62 no. 16 (ph.).	Sostratos of Herakleia[89]	pr. |
	50[90]	323/2?[91]	*IG* II^2 343 + Add. p. 659; Lambrechts no. 140; Pečírka, *Enktesis* 63–7 (*SEG* XXIV 103); Schwenk 84; Tracy, *ADT* 33; Veligianni, A162; Lambert, *ZPE* 140 (2002), 79 n. 20 (*SEG* LII 98); Culasso, *Prossenie* 183–92 no. 11 (ph.).	Apollonides son of Demetrios of Sidon[92] [G?]	1000 dr. gold c + pr/eu. + enk.
	51	322/1	*IG* II^2 308 + 371 (*SEG* III 82);[93] Wilhelm, *Attische Urkunden* V (1942), 159–60 no. 60; Pečírka, *Enktesis* 58–9 (ph.) (*SEG* XXIV 91); Schwenk 86; Tracy, *ADT* 77.		pr/eu. + enk.

[86] C. 350–325 Pečírka. Enktesis κατὰ τὸν νόμον perhaps suggests a date after c. 329–325 (see n. 77), -ει for -ηι (l. 9) after c. 340–330 (cf. Threatte I 378).

[87] Cf. n. 75.

[88] See Lawton.

[89] Cf. Σωστρα-, W. Ameling, *I. Heracl. Pont.* 161. It is unclear whether there is any connection with the Σώστρατος Ἡρακλεώτης in the mercenary catalogue of c. 300, *IG* II^2 1956, 155. Culasso (259–262) notes that, while it is impossible to rule out that this man was from one of the many other Greek cities named Herakleia (cf. Hansen-Nielsen, *Inventory* p. 1280), the evidence for strong political and commercial relations between Herakleia Pontika and Athens in the 5th and 4th cent. BC, especially in relation to the grain trade (e.g. in our list no. 43), and the slight evidence for relations with other cities of this name, creates an assumption that Herakleots honoured by Athens were from Herakleia Pontika. In this case we (unusually) have evidence for *proxenoi* on both sides of the diplomatic relationship. Kallippos, *proxenos* of the (Pontic) Herakleots at Athens, was prosecutor of the case in which [Dem.] LII is the defence (sect. 5).

[90] In 2002 I hesitantly raised the possibility that the proposer was [Πολυκ]λ̣ῆς Πο[λυκράτους] | Ἀναγυράσιο[ς (cf. *LGPN* II Πολυκλῆς 15). On Schweigert's restoration of the chairman (next note), the restoration of this name suits the space available. The father's name is one letter too long, but about half of the lines of this inscription have stoichedon irregularities, apparently motivated mostly by a desire to avoid breaking syllables or (in l. 7 and ex hypothesi in this line) names. Culasso suggests rather -ης Ἰσ[οκράτους (cf. *Agora* XV 42, 26), but I doubt the reading.

[91] Though not certain, Schweigert's suggestion that this decree was passed on the same day as *IG* II^2 448 decree I (same chairman's name, Ἐπαμείνων), is attractive.

[92] Probably a Phoenician referred to by a Greek name. Cf. below note on no. 43.

[93] Pečírka doubted Wilhelm's association. Absolute certainty is not possible in the case of two small non-joining fragments such as these, but the very slight differences

Uncertain

	Date	Reference	Honorand	Honour	
52	352/1?	*IG* II^2 272 + 274;[94] M.B. Walbank, *Hesp.* 54 (1985), 312–3 no. 2 fr. a (ph.) and *Hesp.* 58 (1989), 75–8 no. 4 fr. d; *Agora* XVI 45 fr. d; C. Veligianni, *Klio* 76 (1994), 185–91 (*SEG* LI 70); Tracy, *ADT* 70, 71–3 (*SEG* XLV 59); Veligianni, A106.	(Plural) from Sestos	pr.?[95] + prot. + dinner[96] |	135
53	c. 350–325?[97]	*IG* II^2 286 + 625; M.B. Walbank, *ABSA* 85 (1990), 442 no. 11 (*SEG* XL 72); Knoepfler, *Eretria* XI 56–8 with n. 193.	(Phthiotic?) Achaians[98]	pr/eu.? + ateleia[99] + asylia[100]	

(c. 1 mm.) which Pečírka notes in letter and stoichedon grid dimensions are not persuasive against Wilhelm's judgement, based on compatibility of marble, lettering style, line length and subject matter. With fairly large and well spaced lettering differences of this order in both letter-heights and stoichedon grid are within the normal range of variability on a single inscription. Moreover, apparently fine measurements can be misleading when based on small fragments preserving only a few letters. (Pečírka's measurements for the grid are: fr. a 0.0172 horiz., 0.175 vert.; fr. *b* 0.016 horiz., 0.016 vert. Mine are: fr. a 0.017 horiz., 0.0175 vert.; fr. *b* 0.016–0.019 horiz., 0.0165–0.0168 vert.).

[94] I find Tracy's association of these fragments persuasive. The marble looks compatible and over four lines the text duly flows from one fragment to the other in stoich. 33. The vertical space between adjacent lines varies considerably. This is observable internally on 274 and is consistent with the fact that vertical spacing on 272 appears at first sight tighter than on 274. In l. 5 Tracy restores βoλ]ῆς in place of βουλ]ῆς to suit the line length. At autopsy I tentatively detected the bottom strokes of the Λ preceded by what could be interpreted as the bottom of a vertical, consistent with βo] υλῆς in the same stoichos as another mark which might be the bottom segment of an Ọ, consistent with β]ọλῆς. However, these uncertain marks are in the area of damage as the stone breaks away above and to the left and should be discounted.

[95] As Tracy notes, -]oξε[ν (l. 2) might be πρ]oξε[ν or (more likely?, cf. next note) a name such as Philoxenos.

[96] Invitations to dinner rather than hospitality normally indicate that the honorands were Athenian citizens (exceptions: P.J. Rhodes, *ZPE* 57, 1984, 193–9, cf. M. Osborne, *ZPE* 41, 1981, 154–5). Here they were perhaps cleruchs, cf. Veligianni 1994, 122.

[97] "Litt. volg. med. s. IV" (Kirchner). Cf. Walbank.

[98] Walbank compares *IG* I^3 174.

[99] In what would be a unique grant in an Athenian decree this is described as ἀτέλεια πάντων (cf. Henry, *Honours* 245–6). This perhaps means not πάντων τελῶν, which would place the honorand in a more advantageous position than a citizen, but πάντων χρημάτων, i.e. freedom from export and import duties for honorands who were perhaps non-resident traders. Cf. RO 8 (= *IK Erythrai und Klazomenai* 6) 8–11, decree of Erythrai honouring Konon, 394: καὶ ἀτέλειαν πάντων χρημάτων καὶ ἐσαγωγῆς καὶ ἐξαγωγῆς καὶ πολέμου καὶ εἰρήνης.

[100] ἀσυλίαν καὶ αἰ[ὑτοῖς καὶ χ]ρήμασιν καὶ[ὶ πολέμου ὄ]ντος καὶ εἰ[ρήνης. I construe καὶ αἰ[ὑτοῖς καὶ χ]ρήμασιν with the asylia grant only, not also with the preceding

Table (*cont.*)

	Date	Reference	Honorand	Honour
54	341/0	*IG* II^2 229 + Add. p. 659; Veligianni, A116.	Theoklos of Corinth[101]	foliage c + pr.?[102]
55	337/6	*IG* II^2 239; Tod II 180; Osborne, *Nat.* T70, T71; M.H. Hansen, *GRBS* 23 (1982), 342 no. 21 (*SEG* XXXII 78); Schwenk 4; Lawton no. 37 (ph.); Brun, *Démade* 65, 177 no. 1.	Alkimachos[103]	pr.?
56*	328/7?	*IG* II^2 399 + Add. p. 660. See note below for bibliography.	Eurylochos (son of Akesandros) of Kydonia[104]	pr.?[105]

grant of ateleia. An explicit grant of asylia is also very unusual in Athenian decrees (cf. Henry, *Honours* 255 n. 40; Knoepfler; but note the immunity granted by *IG* I^3 174). Given the apparently un-Athenian character of this decree, there is perhaps a possibility that, as suggested by H. Francotte, *Les Finances des Cités Grecques* (1909), 292, it was a proxeny awarded an Athenian by a foreign state (cf. Knoepfler), though at this period one would not normally expect such a decree to be erected on the Athenian acropolis (there is no parallel among the Decreta…Civitatum Exterarum at *IG* II^2 1126–37). It was not impossible for the words of a foreign decree to be contained within an Athenian one (cf. *IG* II^2 1128 = RO 40, not honorific however). Cf. *SEG* LII 135.

[101] Previous eds. read the name as Θέο[..]ος. However, there is a kappa after the omicron in l. 11 (vertical and the right ends of the diagonals visible), which yields the restorations Θέοκλ]ος ὁ Κ[ο]ρίνθιος in l. 8 and Θέοκ[λον] in 11. The decree perhaps belonged in the context of alliance-building against Philip. Cf. J.B. Salmon, *Wealthy Corinth* (1984), 383.

[102] The award is not preserved. Veligianni-Terzi notes that it is suggested by ll. 7–9, which apparently praised the honorand for looking after Athenians in Corinth, a characteristic qualification for proxeny. This is attractive, but not certain. Cf. no. 3, 49–53.

[103] Ἀλκιμα[χ - up to 11–12-] (l. 2). Perhaps the Alkimachos referred to by Harp. s.v. Ἀλκίμαχος (Hyp. F 77 Jensen, κατὰ Δημάδου), Ἀλκίμαχον καὶ Ἀντίπατρον Ἀθηναίους καὶ προξένους ἐποιησάμεθα. He may well have been Ἀλκίμαχος Ἀγαθοκλέους Πελλαῖος, general and envoy of Philip and Alexander (Arrian, *Anab.* I 18, 1; VI 28, 4; cf. *IG* XII 5, 1001; A. Wilhelm, *Öst. Jh.* 11, 1908, 91; Osborne). It can not be ruled out, however, that our honorand was identical with or the father of Ἀλκίμαχος Ἀλκιμάχου Ἀπολλωνιάτης, made an Athenian citizen in 333/2 (*IG* II^2 391 = Osborne, *Nat.* D37).

[104] It is uncertain whether there is a family connection with *LGPN* I Εὐρύλοχος 1, Cretan commander in 217 (Polyb. V 79, 10), cf. Ἀκέσανδρος 2–3.

[105] May be implicit in the terms in which the honorand is praised (e.g. χρήσιμος ὢν καὶ κοινεῖ καὶ ἰδίαι τοῖς ἀφικνουμένοις Ἀθηναίων, ll. 12–14) that either he or his ancestors (cf. ll. 8–9, εὐεργέτησαν) were awarded proxeny (Veligianni, A154). See, however, n. 102.

19. IG *II*[2] *284*

The end of the text in *IG* II[2] runs:

a καὶ εἶναι *b*
[αὐτὸν πρό]ξενον [κ]αὶ εὐεργέτην αὐτ-
[ὸν καὶ ἐκγόν]ου[ς τοῦ δή]μου τοῦ Ἀθην-
[αίων].
vacat 0.02 | 136

Fr. a is now in the Metropolitan Museum, New York (accession number 26.60.4, cf. C. Alexander, *Bull. Metr. Mus.* 21, 1926, 176–8), where I examined it in 2003 (new photo at fig. 16).

After the end of the decree as printed by *IG* II[2] both Rangabé 497 and Köhler (*IG* II 141, from his own transcript) printed a letter A, Rangabé in stoichos 12 of l. 16, Köhler in stoichos 13 one line lower down. Fr. a preserves vacant stone in stoichoi 11–12 of l. 16; and there is vacant stone extending 0.011 below the bottom of l. 15 on fr. a, 0.015 below the bottom of l. 15 on fr. b. Stoich. is 0.009 square. In other words there was a vacant line after l. 16. After that the stone now breaks off. It is notable, however, that the current height of the fragment, 0.155 m., is 0.015 less than that recorded by Velsen, 0.17.[106] Probably the alpha was genuinely legible in the 19th century, but has subsequently been lost in consequence of damage to the bottom of the stone, damage which reduced its height by 0.015 m. As Köhler saw, the letter is most likely from a second decree. This was perhaps a rider to the first decree, which is probouleumatic (ll. 3–4) and unusually laconic, awarding no honour except proxeny and euergesy and including no inscribing clause.[107] The letter A might be from a dating formula or, if the rider was passed at the same Assembly, more likely from the nomenclature of the proposer (as e.g. *IG* II[2] 232, 18–19). Incorporating a minor new reading from autopsy, the text should run:

a καὶ εἶναι *b*
[αὐτὸν πρό]ξενον [κ]αὶ εὐεργέτην αὐτ-
[ὸν καὶ ἐκγό]ν̣ους [τοῦ δή]μου τοῦ Ἀθην-
[αίων]. *vac.*
vac. 1 line
II [......[12]......]Α[- εἶπεν· τὰ μὲν ἄλλα καθάπερ τῆι βουλῆι ?

[106] Sometimes this type of discrepancy in the record can be accounted for by a difference between overall height and height of inscribed surface, but this does not apply in this case.
[107] For a rider providing for inscription cf. *IG* II[2] 232.

39. Agora *XVI 79*

After the City Dionysia the Athenians held a special Assembly in the theatre of Dionysos dedicated to matters arising from the festival.[108] Four decrees passed at this meeting on 19 Elaphebolion 332/1 are extant (no. 39, no. 40, no. 95 and no. 96 = Schwenk 36–39). In no. 39 and no. 96 the Assembly is explicity designated ἐκκλησία ἐν Διονύσου, the first occurrence of this phrase in a decree prescript. The honorand of no. 40 is Amphis of Andros, apparently the poet of that name. No. 95 and no. 96 (see Part B) are too fragmentary for the services rendered by the honorands to be clear from the text. In no. 78 = *IG* II^2 348 of 337–323, also apparently passed at the special Assembly, the honorand is explicitly referred to as an actor (ἐπειδὴ Π[- -]| ὁ ὑποκρ[ιτὴς). No. 75 = *IG* II^2 429 was also for an actor. I suggest that no. 39 likewise honoured an actor and would restore:

ἐπειδὴ.....9.... ὁ ὑ]-
[ποκ]ριτὴς [..........21..........]
[..3.]ε προα[..........21..........]
[...] τῶι Δ[.........19........, δεδ]-
[όχθαι] τῶ[ι δήμωι ἐπαινέσαι....7...]
[.]ν Ὀν[ο]μα[......13......καὶ στεφαν]-
137 [ῶ]σαι χρυσ[ῶι στεφάνωι· |

In ll. 9–10 Schweigert, advised by Meritt, suggested ὁ Ἀ|βδη]ρίτης (for the style cf. no. 23, 8–9: ἐπειδὴ Θεογένης ὁ Ναυκρατίτης ἀνὴρ ἀγαθός ἐστιν). ὁ ὑ|ποκ]ριτὴς would imply that the honorand was introduced here by name only. Full identification, with father's name and ethnic, would follow in the formal praising-and-crowning clause in ll. 13–14. For this type of arrangement cf. no. 42: (11)...εἶπεν· ἐπειδὴ [Εὔδημ]ος (name only) πρότερόν...(21) ἐπαινέσαι Εὔδημον Φιλούργου Πλαταιέα (full identification). For name + descriptive term cf. e.g. *IG* II^2 502, 13,...εἶπεν· περὶ ὧν Ἀντ]ιφάτης ὁ δημό[σ]ιος ἔδοξεν...; *IG* II^2 713 + Add. p. 666, 11–13, as restored by Wilhelm: ἐπειδὴ

[108] The key item of literary evidence for this Assembly is Dem. XXI 8–10 (delivered 347/6), where two laws are cited, providing for the bringing at it of formal legal complaints (*probolai*) for offences committed during the festival. The scheduling of Assemblies in Elaphebolion 346 seems to confirm that at this period the special Assembly was not normally available for discussion of ordinary political matters or for honours for foreigners not related to the Dionysia ("always for business arising out of the festival", D.M. Lewis, *ABSA* 50, 1955, 25–6; RO 64 [= no. 3, above] with note, pp. 322–3). I discuss this Assembly further in *Polis and Theatre*.

Ἀρί|στ]ων Ἐχθατίου Θη[βαῖος αὐλητὴς διατε|λε]ῖ τοὺς ἀγῶνα[ς...; see also no. 107 = *IG* II[2] 365, 7–9. In this case our honorand's name will be.....[9]....(l. 9, ll. 13–14 in accusative), his father's name Ὀν[ο]μα[- (l. 14, Ὀν[ο]μά[ρχου, Schweigert, or e.g. Ὀν[ο]μα[κλέους), followed by his ethnic. Ll. 11 and 12 do no more than tantalise. 11 might contain a reference to the προα[γών of the City Dionysia (which took place on 8 Elaphebolion, Aeschin. III 66–67 with scholia), or e.g. προα[ιρούμενος (used of the actions of an honorand giving preference to Athens, e.g. no. 85 = *IG* II[2] 283, 4), or a temporal expression, πρὸ Ἀ[- (cf. no. 42, 18–20, ταῦτα πέπομφεν ἅπαντα πρὸ Παναθηναίων). L. 12 was restored by Schweigert, τῶι δ[ήμωι. One might think alternatively of τῶι Δ[ιονυσίων, cf. no. 101 = *IG* II[2] 551, 3–4, διατελεῖ περ-[ὶ τὸν ἀγῶνα τὸν Δι]ονυσίων φιλοτιμο[-.

13. IG *II[2] 368 and* 41. IG *II[2] 344*

Important recent discussions, through which earlier bibliography can be traced, are those of Walbank, Schwenk 33 and 82 and Culasso, pp. 289–93 (with ph. of both inscriptions).

Though the honorand's name is not preserved on no. 41, its preserved text (which is not blandly formulaic) is identical to no. 13 decree 1, a proxeny decree for Theophantos of 332/1, inscribed together with a decree of 323/2 honouring the same man. Dittmar, 80–2, accordingly argued persuasively that no. 41 was the original version of no. 13 decree 1. Walbank, however, made the important observation that the left side of no. 41 is preserved. This necessitated a realignment of the text and effectively changed the number of letter-spaces available for the name, father's name and ethnic of the honorand such that it no longer corresponded with no. 13, 9–10. Walbank inferred that, "the honorand is therefore not the same man as the honorand of no. 13", and in this he was followed by Schwenk and Veligianni. The inference, however, is questionable. Since Dittmar everyone has proceeded on the assumption that, if it was the original of the first decree on no. 13, no. 41 must have started with the words at the beginning of no. 13, [προξενία Θε]οφάντ[......[11].....]. However, it was quite normal on proxenies for this sort of heading not to be part of the text proper, but to be separated off at the top, sometimes immediately above the text, sometimes on a moulding over or under a relief, quite often in larger lettering. If we consider only the dated proxenies of 338/7–322/1 included in Schwenk's collection, in only one case does such a heading form part of the body of the text, Schwenk 57 = *IG* II^2 357 = no. 27. In four cases where the honorand is certainly (Schwenk 2 = *IG* II^2 238 = no. 32; Schwenk 29 = *IG* II^2 339a = no. 38) or possibly (Schwenk 4 = *IG* II^2 239 = no. 55; Schwenk 63 = *IG* II^2 359 = no. 104) awarded a proxeny, the heading including the honorand's name is separated off at the top and the text proper starts at the left margin, ἐπὶ – ἄρχοντος. If we assume that the heading on no. 41 was separated off in this manner and that the rest of the text contained the same number of vacats as in the reinscribed version, it is notable that the text of no. 13, 1–10, fits exactly Walbank's newly identified left edge of no. 41. Seen in this light, the identification of the left edge of no. 41 would seem to strengthen Dittmar's theory rather than weakening it.

There is no reason to suppose that there was more than one decree on no. 41. However, no. 13 is a reinscription, containing at least the decree of 332/1 and another decree for Theophantos of the fifth prytany of 323/2, both inscribed in the same hand.[109] Earlier editors assumed that no. 13 was erected at the time that the second decree on it was passed, i.e. 323/2. Schwenk observed, however, that that would tend to imply that the original decree of 332/1 had been destroyed at
138 some time before 323/2 and there is | no known circumstance in this period which would account for such an action. As she noted, it is more attractive to suppose that our case parallels that of Euphron of Sikyon, who was also awarded honours in the fifth prytany of 323/2 and whose decree passed then was destroyed in the aftermath of the Lamian War and re-inscribed together with a further honorific decree during the short-lived democracy of 318/7 (*IG* II^2 448 = Schwenk 83; the original version of the decree of 323/2 for Euphron is apparently no. 12).

No. 13, therefore, was perhaps inscribed in 318/7. The decree of 332/1 awarded proxeny. The next rung on the "honours ladder" was the citizenship, the honour awarded to Euphron in 323/2. As Schwenk noted, it is plausible that Theophantos was awarded the same honour in 323/2. Theophantos' patron for the proxeny was Polyeuktos of Sphettos. If this patronage carried through to the citizenship award (the name of the proposer of the decree of 323/2 is not preserved),

[109] In this way the inscription differs from no. 34, on which the decree of 322/1 was added in a different hand from that of 337/6.

Theophantos would naturally have become a member of the deme Sphettos. Though not rare, the name Theophantos was not especially common (borne by 13 Athenians in *LGPN* II). Our honorand might therefore have been father of the Lysimachos son of Theophantos of Sphettos who was councillor in 281/0, *LGPN* II Θεόφαντος 13 (*Agora* XV 72, 18).[110] We can only speculate on the specific circumstances of the 323/2 decree. The honorand's ethnic is not preserved. However, it seems that Polyeuktos was occupied in late 323 drumming up support for the allied cause in the Peloponnese (Plut. *Mor.* 846 c–d). It is not out of the question that this decree belongs in the same context and that Theophantos, like Euphron, was the citizen of a Peloponnesian city. It is interesting, though it may only be a coincidence, that the only Peloponnesian city in which the name Theophantos is attested is Sikyon (*LGPN* IIIA p. 206), the same city as Euphron's, and that Σικυωνίωι would suit the space available at no. 13, 1.

The top of no. 13 does not survive and we can not be certain that the proxeny of 332/1 was the first decree inscribed on it.[111] *SEG* XVI 52 = no. 134a is a decree based on a proposal of (possibly honouring, though that is not certain)[112] a Theophantos in 339/8. With no father's name, ethnic or other identifier, we can not tell whether this Theophantos was identical with our honorand.

43. IG *II² 360 = RO 95*

I do not intend to embark on extensive discussion of this remarkable inscription honouring the trader Herakleides son of Charikleides of (sc. Cypriot) Salamis, but point out some features of it that have not been fully recognised.

The latest of the five decrees, the one which awards most of the substantive honours and provides for the inscribing of "the other praises that there have been for him", is inscribed first. As Köhler saw and Culasso also notes (171–2), the "earlier praises" had patently not

[110] Our Theophantos' father's name began Λ- or Α-.

[111] Just enough stone is preserved above l. 1 to show that there was probably no text after stoichos 11 of a previous line. However, the end of a previous decree might not have extended this far in the line. Cf. l. 18, where the last line of the decree occupies only the first three stoichoi and is followed by a vacat.

[112] For a decree based on a proposal by a foreigner and also honouring him cf. *IG* II² 109 = Osborne, *Nat.* D 11 (made a citizen in the rider, fr. b).

previously been inscribed and were most likely obtained from copies in the Athenian state archive. The order of the four earlier decrees on the stone (5 * 3 1 * 2 4) is a little puzzling to the modern eye, but is clarified by the paragraphoi (correctly shown only in RO's text), inscribed at the points marked *, for 3 and 1 are the Assembly decrees, 2 and 4 the Council decrees. 2 and 4 are in chronological order, 3 and 1 strictly in reverse chronological order, but 1 is no more than the commissioning decree which eventually produced 3. In other words 3 and 1 are part of a single decree-making process. It seems quite likely that these features of the organisation of the decrees on the stone, in particular the division between Council decrees and Assembly decrees, reflect the organisation of the state archive. Indeed the paragraphoi themselves perhaps have an archival (or at least "documentary") flavour. They occur in only one other inscribed law or dercee of this period: *IG* II^2 244 after line 46, where a paragraphos separates off the text of a law
139 about the repair of walls from the detailed | specifications of the work to be done at Mounichia, [σ]υγγραφαὶ τοῦ τείχους τοῦ Μουνιχ[ί]ασι. In both this inscription and our no. 43 the paragraphoi mark off texts of different types, texts that have perhaps been obtained from different documentary or archival sources.[113]

Herakleides and Charikleides were common Greek names, but Herakleides was also a common metonym for a Phoenician theophoric Melqart-name (P.M. Fraser, *ABSA* 65, 1970, 31–6) and it is possible that he was a trader (ἔμπορος, l. 11), wholly or partly of Phoenician ethnicity (mixed marriages: Isoc. IX 50). In 333/2 the state granted religious privileges to men from Kition on Cyprus, doubtless Phoenicians wholly or in part (*IG* II^2 337 = RO 91 = *Ath. State* II no. 4; cf. Parker, *Ath. Rel.* 160–1 n. 29). Apses son of Hieron and Hieron son of Apses of Tyre, traders honoured by no. 44 (note the references to the Phoenician colony, Carthage, l. 2, and Italy, l. 4), apparently shortly after the destruction of the city by Alexander in 332, were patently Phoenicians, cf. O. Masson, *BCH* 92 (1968), 398–9; M.B. Walbank, *ZPE* 59 (1985), 108 n. 4; Culasso, *Prossenie* 197. Most likely Apollonides (Greek rendering of a Phoenician theophoric Mikl- name, cf. *ZPE* 140, 2002, 76 note 9, P.M. Fraser, *ABSA* 65, 1970, 34), son of Demetrios (in a Phoenician context cf. O. Masson, *BCH* 93, 1969, 698) of Sidon, a trader honoured by no. 50, perhaps in 323/2, was also a

[113] For paragraphoi in a different context cf. Lambert, *Sacrificial Calendar* 395–6.

Phoenician. *IG* II^2 283, of ca. 350–330 (perhaps 337), also honoured a trader from Salamis, perhaps also a Phoenician (Lambert, *ZPE* 140 [2002], 75–6).[114] See now also Culasso, *Prossenie* 181–2.

As with most decree stelai, the sides (i.e. the left and right lateral surfaces) are finished flat and the back is rough picked such that it extends the thickness of the stele beyond the back edge of the finished sides. In this case the maximum thickness of the stone, including the rough picked back, is 0.112 m., whereas the maximum thickness of the finished sides is 0.095. Unusually, however, the finished left side (0.082, thickening lower down to 0.095) is considerably thicker than the right side (0.07, thickening to 0.077). The stele also widens towards the bottom (from 0.37 m. to 0.40 m.). The stoichedon grid, however, remains steady at 0.0092 throughout and, as Dow observed (*AJA* 66, 1962, 363), the net effect is to cause the width of the margins on either side of the text to increase towards the bottom. From l. 65, however, the stoich. 39 arrangement of the text collapses and ll. 65–80 are inscribed non-stoichedon with lines running over into the right margin. In ll. 79–80 the left margin is severely abraded and it can not be ruled out that the text also ran over into the left margin in these two lines. The surface is also abraded immediately after the final sigma in l. 80, though the end of the line is certainly vacant. In l. 71 there are clear traces of red paint in XXX (= 3000), the number of drachmas which the honorand donated for grain purchase. It is highly unlikely that it is only by coincidence that paint remains in this place. In other words it is unlikely that all the letters of the inscription were originally picked out in red. The number was perhaps picked out to emphasise the honorand's generosity. The careful corrections of inscribing errors by erasure and reinscription have been noted by previous editors. Note also the unusual abbreviation of the demotics of secretary (l. 3) and chairman (l. 5), in both cases Ἐλευσί(νιος). The second may supply the rationale, for the effect is to give the proposer a line to himself, a not uncommon feature noted by Henry, *Prescripts* 64 note 59. In l. 77 Dittenberger restored ὅπως ἂν καὶ οἱ ἄλλοι ἐθέλωσι [ἑτοίμ]ω[ς εὐεργετεῖν], but I can not confirm the omega and the word ἑτοίμως

[114] This does not purport to be a full catalogue of epigraphical evidence for Athenian-Phoenician relations at this period. See also e.g. *IG* II^2 2496 with *SEG* LII 101.

sits somewhat uneasily in Attic decree language at this period. A PHI search reveals no certain instance of it before ii BC (*IG* II^2 956, 24; 958, 20, cf. *IG* I^3 75, 14). At 79 fin. perhaps πάσα̣ι̣ς (πάσ[α]ς Köhler).

56 = IG *II^2 399*

The significant bibliography since *IG* II^2 has been: Moretti, *ISE* 2; D.S. Potter, *ABSA* 79 (1984), 229–35; C. Habicht, *Chiron* 19 (1989), 1–5; P. Gauthier, *Bull. ép.* 1987, 248; E. Badian, *ZPE* 79 (1989), 59–64; J. Tréheux, *Bull. ép.* 1990, 394; Bielman no. 6; Veligianni, A154. See also Brun, *Démade* 89 n. 24, 149, 177 no. 9. |

140 The stone is lost and all texts of it derive ultimately from a transcript of Fourmont. Two edited versions of the transcript have formed the basis of all current texts, that of D. Raoul-Rochette, *Antiquités grecques du Bosphore cimmerien* (Paris, 1822), 175–7 and that of Boeckh at *CIG* 96, based on Bekker's transcript of Fourmont. These two versions differ in several details. Fourmont's original transcript is reproduced at Fig. 36. My text, based on that transcript, is:

328/7	[ἐπὶ Εὐθυκρίτου ἄρχοντος, ἐπὶ τῆς]	25½	non-stoich.
	[Ἐρεχθεῖδος ἕκτης πρυτανείας ἧι]	25½	
	[Πυθόδηλος Πυθοδήλου Ἁγνούσιος]	26½	
	[ἐγραμμάτευε· Γαμηλιῶνος ὀγδόει]	26	
	[ἐπὶ] δέκ[α, μιᾶι καὶ τριακοστεῖ τῆς]	24	
	πρυτανεία[ς· τῶν προέδρων ἐπεψή]-	25½	
	φι̣ζεν Πάμφιλος Φυ̣[λάσιος καὶ συμ]-	24½	
	πρ̣όεδροι· Δημάδης Δ̣η[μέου Παιαν(ιεὺς)]	(25)	
	εἶπεν· ἐπειδὴ πρότερό[ν τε οἱ πρό]-	24½	
	γονοι οἱ Εὐρυλόχου, κα[ὶ ὁ πατὴρ]	23½	
	Ἀκέσανδρος, φίλοι ὄντε[ς καὶ εὔνοι]	26	
	τῆι πόλει, πολλὰ καὶ μεγάλ[α εὐεργέ]-	26½	
	τησαν τὸν δῆμον τὸν Ἀθ[ηναίων],	23½	
	καὶ νῦν Εὐρύλοχος πατ[ρικὴν ἔ]-	23½	
	χων εὔνοιαν πρὸς τὸν δῆ[μον τὸν]	24½	
	Ἀθηναίων διατελεῖ χρή̣[σιμος ὢν]	24	
	καὶ κοινεῖ καὶ ἰδίαι τοῖς ἀ[φικνου]-	23½	
	μένοις Ἀθηναίων εἰς Κυδ̣[ωνίαν]	23	
	καὶ πολλοὺς Ἀθηναίων λ[υτρωσά]-	24	
	μενος ἐκ Κρήτης ἀπέστ[ειλε τοῖς]	25	
	αὐτοῦ ἀναλώμασιν καὶ [αἴτιος ἐ]-	23	
	γένετο τοῦ σω̣θῆναι ἐκ [-----]		
	[--]ν εἰς τὴν ἰδίαν, συν̣[-----]		

The text was non-stoichedon with syllabification at line-ends, or just possibly, despite the impression conveyed by Fourmont's transcript, stoichedon with variable line length to accommodate syllabification (cf. no. 42). The length of lines, counting iota as a half letter, was between 23 and 26½ letters. The basic restorations were made by Raoul-Rochette, Boeckh and Köhler. I note below significant divergences from Köhler's text.

1–7. The restoration of the prescript is developed from Habicht's persuasive suggestion, based on the name and initial letters of the demotic of the chairman in l. 7, that this decree was passed on the same day as *IG* II^{2} 452 = no. 146.[115] Since a little progress can also be made with the prescript of that text, I print a revised version of it below, noting the significant divergences from the most recent text, that of Schwenk no. 53:[116]

328/7 [ἐπὶ Εὐθυκρί]του ἄρχοντος̣ non-stoich.
[ἐπὶ τῆς Ἐρεχθεῖδ]ος^{I} ἕκτης πρυτ̣ανε[ίας ἧι Πυ^{v}]- stoich. 36 | 141
[θόδηλος Πυθοδήλ]ου Ἁγνούσιο̣ς [ἐ]γ̣ρ̣[αμμάτευε]·
[Γαμηλιῶνος ὀγδό]ει ἐπὶ δέκα̣, μ̣ι[ᾶ]ι̣ κ̣[αὶ τριακο]-
[στεῖ τῆς πρυτανε]ίας· ἐκκλη[σία κυρία· τῶν προ]-
[έδρων ἐπεψήφιζε]ν Πάμφιλο̣ς Φυ̣λ̣[άσιος·^{VI} συμπρ]-
[οέδροι.....^{9}....] Ἁλαιεύς^{II}, Θ[.......^{13}......^{III}]
[......^{12}......Χολλ]είδης^{IV}, Α[.......^{14}.......^{V}]
[.......^{14}.......Μ]ελιτεύς^{VII}, Γ̣[......^{13}.......^{VIII}]
[......^{12}......Οἰν]αῖος^{IX}, Βοῦλ[ις Θοραιεύς^{X} *vvv*]
[Λυκοῦργος Λυκόφρο]νος Βουτά̣[δης εἶπεν·

Careful observation of the spacing of surviving letters[117] enables one to see that what is printed by Schwenk as the first letter of lines 3ff. (Y in

[115] The only difficulty of substance is that, as pointed out by Badian, the phrase καὶ συμπρόεδροι is not otherwise found in Athenian decree prescripts before the oligarchic regime of the years from 321/0 (e.g. *IG* II^{2} 545 + 2406, *IG* II^{2} 448, 39). However, a few Athenian inscriptions with συμπρόεδροι followed by a list of names are now known to date to before 321/0 (the earliest case is no. 7 decree II, of 333/2) and *symproedroi* are listed on some inscriptions from Athenian cleruchies as early as the 340s (e.g. *IG* XII 6, 261, 10, Samos; a decree of the Athenian cleruchs on Lemnos perhaps dating to 349/8 (archon Kallimachos) includes the phrase καὶ συμπρόεδροι, *ASAAtene* 3–5 [1941–3], 81–2) [but see p. 211].

[116] John Morgan, in an unpublished paper of July 2003, which he has kindly shown me, independently arrived at substantially the same text of *IG* II^{2} 452.

[117] Neither side is preserved. The letters in the name of the archon are more spread out than those below. The crucial observation is that the ten letters to the right of the tau of the archon's name occupy the same space as 14 letters to right of the same point in lines below. Since there are also ten letters to the left of this point in l. 1, there should also be 14 letters to the left below. This is confirmed by l. 11, where it yields a proposer's name starting at the left margin, a common arrangement.

3, E in 4 etc.) belongs in fact to the end of the previous line. This gains confirmation from the fact that, in the resulting text, it becomes apparent that some attention has been given to syllabification at line-ends. It is the urge to syllabify and in particular to avoid breaking names and to highlight the name of the proposer (11), that accounts for the spacing irregularities at line-ends. Other new or significant points are:

2. The tribe has hitherto been restored as Ἀκαμαντίδ]ος^V. However, if we assume that, as usual, the *symproedroi* were listed in tribal order, the new restoration of the chairman's demotic, Φυ̣λ̣[άσιος^VI in 6, leaves Erechtheis^I as the only possibility, since all the other tribes are accounted for by the chairman and *symproedroi*. Ἐρεχθεῖδ]ος, one letter shorter than Ἀκαμαντίδ]ος, is also preferable on grounds of spacing.

4. in. ὀγδό]ει. ἐνάτ]ει is a possible alternative, entailing merely a slightly different assumption about the sequence of full and hollow months at the beginning of the year (4 hollow + 3 full rather than 3 hollow + 4 full).

4. fin. μ̣ι[ᾶ]ι̣ κ̣[αὶ τριακο|στεῖ. Thus also Schwenk. The argument about the reading of this line was swung heavily in favour of this reading by S. Dow, *Hesp.* 32 (1963), 348–50. I agree from autopsy that it is the best reading. It is also consistent with the best reading of *IG* II^2 354 (see *Ath. State* I no. 11 with n. 69).

6. Πάμφιλο̣ς̣ Φυ̣λ̣[άσιος·^VI. Earlier texts had the deme as Φ[ηγούσιος, but Habicht, p. 4, read from the Princeton squeeze Φι̣λ̣[αίδης^II or Φυ̣λ̣[άσιος^VI. Φι̣λ̣[αίδης^II can be ruled out, since there is a *proedros* from tribe II (Halai) listed in l. 7.

6–7. [συμπρ|οέδροι]. As in other lines it is possible that there was a stoichedon irregularity at line-end to achieve syllabification, e.g. [συμπρο|έδροι].

It will be seen that, as revised, the prescript of this inscription can be transferred very comfortably to no. 56, with line breaks falling very conveniently so as to avoid word-breaks at line ends. Boeckh and

[118] It is true that there is slightly more space at the beginning of this line indicated in the upside-down version in ink at the bottom of Fourmont's transcript, a version which he abandoned after copying only a few letters. I note that, aligned above the T of ΠΡΥΤΑΝΕΙΑ in this abandoned version, in the line before ΔΕΚ, there is a Δ faintly drawn in pencil. This perhaps represents another false beginning of the text (of which the first word is ΔΕΚΑ).

Köhler printed ΟΣ[..]ΔΕΚ at the beginning of 5, but the letters ΟΣ seem to be a false transcription. They are not in Fourmont's original (and were not included by Raoul-Rochette). The space before ΔΕΚ in Fourmont's transcript is suitable for the three letters ΕΠΙ (cf. the space occupied by ΕΙΠ at the beginning of 6).[118] Fourmont shows the demotic in 7 as ΦΙ, but one may assume that the stroke after the phi fell on the break of the stone and in these circumstances it is very plausible that he might have mistaken the vertical of an upsilon for an iota. | 142

10. κα[ὶ ὁ πατὴρ]. Raoul-Rochette showed Κ[as legible, Boeckh ΚΙ[. There is indeed a stroke after the kappa, but it is clearly the lower section of a diagonal, admirably confirming Veligianni's suggestion, κ[αὶ ὁ πατὴρ].

17. [ἀφικνου]μένοις Köhler. The lower section of the initial diagonal is apparent on Fourmont's transcript.

18. ἀναλ<ώ>μασιν. Fourmont has ΑΝΑΛΟΜΑΣΙΝ. Ο for Ω, while not impossible, would be very unusual in a state decree at this period. Threatte I 225 notes this case among "doubtful examples". Ο and Ω can be very close in hands of this period, especially if the letter is damaged towards the bottom. If this is an error in Fourmont's transcript, it is the only significant one. In general he seems to have been accurate.

20–21. ἑ|αυτου is possible, as Boeckh noted.

22–23. ἐκ̣ [τῶν πολεμίω]ν Boeckh, ληιστῶ]ν Moretti, Badian, μεγάλων or πολλῶν κινδύνω]ν Bielman. Discussed by Bielman. There is no precise parallel in an Athenian decree and the exact number of letters can not be determined. | 143

CHAPTER FOUR

ATHENIAN STATE LAWS AND DECREES, 352/1–322/1: III DECREES HONOURING FOREIGNERS B. OTHER AWARDS*

Part A of this article (*ZPE* 158, 2006, 115–158) listed the inscribed decrees of 352/1–322/1 which awarded citizenship, proxeny and euergesy. Part B lists the remaining decrees which honoured foreigners (section A) and decrees which may have honoured Athenians or foreigners (section B).

A. *Decrees honouring foreigners, where no award of citizenship or proxeny/euergesy is preserved*[1]

	Date	Reference	Honorand	Honour
57	mid-iv ? (K)	*IG* II² 303.	AGLAOKLE-?[2]	–
58	mid-iv ? (K)	*IG* II² 254.	Exiles	prot. + hosp.
59	mid-iv ? (K)	*IG* II² 266.	Akarnanians from Astakos, descendants of-[3]	
60	mid-iv ? (K)	*IG* II² 271. Veligianni, A130.	Name or father's name in -gesi-?[4]	–[5]

* This chapter was previously published in *Zeitschrift für Papyrologie und Epigraphik* 159 (2007), 101–154.

[1] I omit from this list *IG* II² 268, honouring one or more men from Emporion. Tracy advises per ep. that the hand is probably his "cutter of *IG* II² 1262", c. 320–290 (*ADT* 136, *Athens and Macedon* [2003], 38).

[2] The father of the honorand(s), perhaps named in l. 7, was not Ἀγαθοκλέ[ους (*IG* II²). The Berlin squeeze reads ΑΓΛΑΟΚΛΕ, perhaps Ἀγλαοκλέ[ους or [ιδους. For the name cf. Ἀγλωκλῆς from Thera or Thebes in Boeotia, iii BC, *LGPN* I p. 12, and Ἀγλωκλείδης from Karthaia on Keos, iv/iii BC, *IG* XII 5, 544 (uncontracted form e.g. *LGPN* I Ἀγλαοκρέων, Tenedos, iv BC).

[3] The preserved heading is [--up to c. 13--ἐκγ]όνοις Ἀκα⟨ρ⟩νᾶσι ἐξ Ἀσ[τακοῦ] (ΓΝΑΣΙ stone).

[4] *IG* II² prints Κ]τησι[κράτην (l. 5) but the correct reading is ΓΗΣΙ, indicating a name Ἡ]γησι[- or Α]γησι[-.

[5] Kirchner tentatively restored προξ]έν[ους (l. 7).

Table (*cont.*)

<table>
<tr><th></th><th>Date</th><th>Reference</th><th>Honorand</th><th>Honour</th><th></th></tr>
<tr><td>61</td><td>mid-iv ? (K)</td><td>IG II^2 211; Tod II 166; Osborne, Nat. X 12 (vol. iii–iv, pp. 125–6).</td><td>Exiles?[6]</td><td>ateleia of the metic tax?[7]</td><td></td></tr>
<tr><td>62</td><td>mid-iv (T)[8]</td><td>IG II^2 275; Veligianni, A132.</td><td>– son of Aristoteles –?[9]</td><td>prot. |</td><td>101</td></tr>
<tr><td>63</td><td>After c. 350[10]</td><td>O. Broneer, Hesp. 2 (1933), 395–6 no. 15 (ph.); E. Schweigert, Hesp. 7 (1938), 289–91 no. 17 (ph.) (SEG XVI 51); A.M. Woodward, ABSA 51 (1956), 1–2; Veligianni, A121.[11]</td><td>A man (Byzantine?) assisting Athenians in the Hellespont</td><td>–</td><td></td></tr>
</table>

[6] The basis is no more than ἐκκπεπ- (ἐκκπεπ[ολιόρκηνται Wilh. in *IG*^{2}) in l. 3 and]ορ[.]ηθεν- (ἐκπολι]ορ[κ]ηθέν[τες ὑπὸ Φιλίππου Wilh.) in l. 14. In a bravura display of creative restoration, Wilhelm, *CRAI* 1900, 524–32, followed tentatively by Kirchner, reconstructed this very fragmentary decree, which preserves no place name or ethnic, to yield a fully restored 16-line text providing for the reception at Athens of exiled Olynthians following the capture of their city by Philip in 348 (later, following a suggestion of Beloch, he changed their identity to exiles from Methone in 354, *Wien. Stud.* 58, 1940, 74–5). See the telling criticisms of Wilamowitz, *Hermes* 37 (1902), 310–12 ("scheint mir das Spiel solcher Ergänzungen zwar sehr gut, damit man *in corpore vili* das Handwerk lernt; weiter hat es keinen Zweck; man kann ja nur hinlesen, was man so schon weiss"). The line length can not be established and the decree can not be dated other than approximately by letter forms to around the middle of the 4th century. At this period not a few cities were besieged and, as the decrees in this list illustrate, many exiles took refuge in Athens and were granted rights there.

[7] [ἀτέλειαν] τοῦ μετοικ[ίου (l. 5);]ων τὴν ἀτέλ[ειαν (l. 9).

[8] Tracy, per ep., kindly informs me that the cutter is the same as *IG* II^2 125 = RO 69, which probably dates to 348 or 343.

[9] The decree confirms honours previously granted the honorand by Athens and the Athenians in the Chersonese, and the generals in office and the [archons] in the Chersonese (cf. no. 64, 19) are now to take care of him. He might be Ἀριστοτ[έλο]υς Ο[- in l. 2. There is no city in Ο- (or Θ-) listed in the Thracian Chersonese by Hansen–Nielsen, *Inventory* pp. 900–11. At this period and region one might think of Olynthos (for the name there cf. *SEG* XXXVIII 637, 8), but there are many possibilities. The definite article can not be ruled out. Cf. Λάπυρις ὁ πρόξενος, no. 107 passim.

[10] The "hortatory intention" clause in ll. 2–5 implies a date after c. 350, cf. A.S. Henry, *ZPE* 112 (1996), 106–8. Many of the proposed restorations are unconvincing. If ll. 9–11 are read, after Broneer, Βυ]|ζαντίωι πο[λιορκουμεν-|-τά] συνφέροντ[α the context will be the siege of Byzantium by Philip in 340/39. πο[λλάκις-|-τά] συνφέροντ[α or πο[ιών-|-τά] συνφέροντ[α are no less possible, however (cf. *IG* II^2 277, 4–5; *SEG* XXXVII 86, 12) and the honours may have been more generally for assistance rendered to Athenians in the Hellespont (Ἀθη[ναίων τῶν ἀφικνουμένων ε]|ίς Ἑλλήσπο[ντον, ll. 12–13, as persuasively restored by Veligianni, cf. οἱ [π]λ̣έον[τες.... ....16........Ἑλλή]|σπο[ντ-, ll. 17–18).

[11] Fr. a + b, 1–5, are most comfortably restored with a 30 letter line (the 31 letter restorations proposed for lines 8 ff. are not persuasive). Though the marble, lettering

Table (*cont.*)

	Date	Reference	Honorand	Honour
64	346/5[12]	*IG* II^2 218; *Syll.*^{3} 207; Pečírka, *Enktesis* 95 n. 4; Rhodes, *Boule* 73 n. 1; Gauthier, *Bienfaiteurs* 188; Henry, *Honours* 258–9 nn. 69 and 71; S.N. Koumanoudes, *Horos* 4 (1986), 11–18 (ph. upper part); Veligianni, A111.	1. Dioskourides son of Dionysodoros of Abdera and his brothers, 2. Charmes and 3. Anaxipolis[13]	1–3. prot. + permission to reside at Athens pending return to Abdera[14] + privilege relating to eisphora. 1. hosp.
65	345/4[15]	*IG* II^2 219; E. Schweigert, *Hesp.* 8 (1939), 172–3 (ph.); M.H. Hansen, *GRBS* 23 (1982), 342 no. 11 (*SEG* XXXII 76).	[The] Ela[iousians?][16]	–

style and stoichedon grid are compatible, fr. c, containing a formulaic inscribing clause, is restored more easily with 31 letters. Its association with fr. a and b is accordingly doubtful. An increase in line length on the same inscription is not impossible, but in that case one would expect a tightening of the stoichedon grid and/or change in letter size. No change in stoichedon grid or letter size is observable on fr. c. Unusually in a stoichedon inscription at this period, on *IG* II^2 330+445 an increase in line length is achieved by expansion of the line of text into the margin (cf. *Ath. State* I p. 95 n. 36). That is unlikely in our case, where the letters are larger and more widely spaced and there is almost no margin to the left of the text on fr. a + b (which preserve the original left side). Fragments cut in the same hand and stoichedon grid may of course belong to different inscriptions (an example at *ZPE* 136, 2001, 65–70 = no. 106).

[12] Read τεῖ in l. 9 (start) and Διοσκουρίδει in l. 29, early examples of -ει for -ηι, cf. Threatte I 377–8.

[13] In l. 14 I read at autopsy ἐπε[ιδὴ εὐ]εργέται [ἦσαν τô | δή]μο τοῦ Ἀθηναίων. Cf. *IG* II^2 110, 22; 181, 4. The honorands may stand in some relation to the Χάρμος (?, the legend is ΕΠΙ ΧΑΡΜΟ) and Ἀναξίπολις who were mint-magistrates on Abderan coins at this period. See J.M.F. May, *The Coinage of Abdera* (London, 1966), Period VIII, Group CXXVI; Period IX, Group CXXIX. On the dating of the coins see M.J. Price, *Coin Hoards* VII (*RNSoc.* 1985) no. 50 with pp. 42–4; K. Chrysanthaki, *REG* 114 (2001), 398–400. Abdera was a member of the Second Athenian League (*IG* II^2 43 = RO 22, 99). In 345 the city may recently have aligned with Philip, obliging our honorands to go into exile. Cf. L. Bliquez, *Eranos* 79 (1981), 65–79 (*SEG* XXXI 74); Chrysanthaki, 397–404.

[14] Cf. no. 5.

[15] Pryt. 8. The date in prytany (ll. 5–6) is restored with 15 letters as ἕκτηι καὶ δεκάτηι (Schweigert) or μιᾶι καὶ εἰκοστῆι (Hansen), but up to 16 letters is possible (reading Οἴο [ἐγραμμάτευε earlier in l. 5) and there are accordingly several other possibilities.

[16] The heading is ΕΛ/[-max. 7–8-]. Ἐλα[ιο(υ)σίων] (Schweigert) is attractive. Note the crowning of Athens by the Elaiousians the previous year (*IG* II^2 1443, 93–5) and the other Athenian decrees honouring them, *Agora* XVI 53 and no. 70. A personal name in ΕΛ/[-] (A. Wilhelm, *Anz. Ak. Wien* 84, 1947, 194) is less likely since there is insufficient room for the expected father's name and/or ethnic (cf. no. 4 with note).

Table (*cont.*)

	Date	Reference	Honorand	Honour	
66	1. 345/4 2. 344/3?	*IG* II^2 220; A.D. Rizakis, *Achaie* I (1995), 345–6 no. 615; Veligianni, A113.[17]	1. City of the Pellanians (sc. in Achaia) 2. Pellanian envoys	1. – (345/4) 2. hosp. (344/3) |	102
67	345–338[18]	*IG* II^2 232; Tracy, *ADT* 84, 90–1, 167 n. 2.	1. City of Tenedos 2. Aratos of Tenedos (cf. no. 72) 3. [Megatimos?], Kallistotimos and—, sons of [Meg?]atimos, brothers of Aratos 4. Envoy from Tenedos	1. 2. 3. each a [foliage] c 4. hosp.	
68	c. 345–320[19]	*IG* II^2 435.[20]	Exiles	prot. + hosp.	
69	343/2	*IG* II^2 224; Tracy, *ADT* 83.	Kephallenians or Lampsakenes?[21]	–	

[17] The original left side is preserved on fr. b. The letter printed in *IG* II^2 at the end of every line should be shifted to the beginning of the next one. In l. 1 read [.....^{10}.... .ἐγραμμάτευ]εν· [..^{4}..]. In l. 23 read [ἐπὶ E]ὐβούλο[υ not [ἐπ’. In l. 7, as Köhler noted, the last preserved letter (of the name of the proposer of decree I) may be O or Ω and the name should be left unrestored. In 27ff. (prescript of decree 1) read:

[τῶ]ν προέδ[ρων ἐπεψήφιζεν..]
[...^{5}..]ης Εἰτ[εαῖος· Ἀριστ O...^{5}..]
[...^{5}..]τονίκ[ου--είπεν---].

[18] The date is between c. 345 (hand, Tracy) and c. 338 (Second Athenian League implied ll. 6–7), but the precise relationship of this decree to no. 72 is obscure (cf. RO p. 361).

[19] Tracy kindly confirms per ep. that the hand meets the criteria of his “litt. volg.”, 345–320 (*ADT* 76–81).

[20] The end of the text is as follows:

16 [........^{18}........]. ονος E[..........^{21}.........]
[..........^{19}........] *vac.* 0.015
[------$^{c.\ 23}$------]Σ . [----------]

Kirchner printed nothing after l. 16, but in l. 18 are remains of a sigma (about stoichos 24, but the alignment with the text above is not precise), followed by a vertical stroke (noted correctly by Köhler). This might be e.g. from the beginning of the supplementary decree of the Council envisaged in ll. 7–9. The first letter trace in l. 16 is two upper verticals, as of N. Perhaps name(s), e.g. Ἐπαμεί]ṿονος E- (cf. *IG* II^2 204, 74–86).

[21] The body of the decree (l. 7) begins...^{6}...]ηνω̣ν ὁπόσοι ἂ[ν]. This may be restored either Κεφαλλ]ήνων (Wilhelm in *IG* II^2, cf. *Agora* XVI 46 with note) or Λαμψακ]ηνῶν (cf. no. 14; for the circumstances in Lampsakos at this time see P. Frisch, *Die Inschriften von Lampsakos, IK* 6, pp. 126–7). The very few surviving words suggest an honorific decree (thus *IG* II^2) rather than a treaty.

Table (*cont.*)

		Date	Reference	Honorand	Honour
	70	341/0	*IG* II^2 228; *Syll.*^{3} 255; Osborne, *Nat.* D15; Tracy, *ADT* 83; RO 71; Phot.: Kirchner, *Imagines* 29.	The Elaiousians	prot. + dinner
	71	340/39?	*IG* II^2 234; Veligianni, A119.	Chians?[22]	–
	72	340/39	*IG* II^2 233; Tracy, *ADT* 74 n. 12, 84, 91, 167 n. 2; Dreher, *Hegemon* 44–5; Veligianni, A118; RO 72.	1. People of Tenedos 2. Aratos of Tenedos, representative of Tenedos on allied Council 3. – Cf. no. 67	1. 1000 dr. gold c 2. [foliage] c 3. – Also makes arrangements to recompense Tenedos for assistance, perhaps at siege of Byzantium.
103	73*	c. 340	*IG* II^2 543.	An allied city [G?]	[1000?][23] dr. gold c |
	74	c. 340–320[24]	*IG* II^2 421; Develin, *AO* 419; Veligianni, A168.	[..]kles son of Sotairos of Amphipolis	–
	75	c. 340–320[25] (T)	*IG* II^2 429; Ghiron-Bistagne, *Acteurs* 80–1, 147 (ph.) (*SEG* XXVI 77); Tracy, *ADT* 98; Veligianni, A172; Lambert, *Polis and Theatre* (ph.).	An actor [Theat.]	–

[22] Chians are mentioned in l. 6 in the context of a siege, perhaps that of Byzantium (at which they assisted, cf. Diod. XVI 77.2).

[23] See footnote to no. 43.

[24] ἐκκλησία begins to appear in prescripts in 340–335 (earliest case, if the restoration is correct, is now *IG* II^2 451, re-dated by Tracy, *ADT* 73–4, to 340/39). The absence of *symproedroi* in the prescript is consistent with a date before 318/7. The proposer, Demophilos son of Demophilos of Acharnai, was active in the 320s (*APF* 3675).

[25] The prescript does not survive, but the subject matter indicates that the decree may have been passed at the Assembly after the City Dionysia (cf. note on no. 39).

Table (*cont.*)

	Date	Reference	Honorand	Honour
76	c. 340–300?[26]	*IG* II² 423; Tracy, *ADT* 34; A.S. Henry, *ZPE* 112 (1996), 107 (*SEG* XLVI 2); Veligianni, A170; Culasso, *Prossenie* 297.	Philomelos [G?][27]	–
77	c. 340–320 (337/6?)[28]	*IG* II² 276; E. Schweigert, *Hesp.* 9 (1940), 342; Schwenk 12; Tracy, *ADT* 98; Veligianni, A115.	Asklepiodoros son of [Po]ly-[29]	foliage c + hosp. + isot.[30] +?
78[31]	337–323 (T)	*IG* II² 348; Ghiron-Bistagne, *Acteurs* 79 (ph.) (*SEG* XXVI 76); Schwenk 44; Tracy, *ADT* 12 n. 35, 114; Veligianni, A148; Lambert, *Polis and Theatre* (ph.).	An actor [Theat.]	–

[26] In l. 11 the orthography is apparently ΒΟΥΛΕΙ not ΒΟΥΛΗΙ (the right side of the letter is damaged, possibly deliberately erased). This -ει for -ηι normally indicates a date after c. 340–330 (Threatte I 378). The inclusion of a "hortatory intention" clause indicates the 340s or later (cf. n. 10). In Kirchner's tentative text the honorand rendered financial assistance at a time of grain crisis, ἐν τ[ῆι σιτοδ]εία̣ι προεδάνεισ]ε χρήματα, but as Tracy notes, the restoration is not certain (e.g. ἐν τ[ῶι πρόσθ]εν χρόνωι or τ[ῶι πολέμωι are equally possible).

[27] Explicit praise for financial services indicate that he was a foreigner.

[28] Work of Tracy's "cutter of *IG* II² 244", 340/39–ca. 320. Schweigert restored the prescript to the same day as *IG* II² 243 = *Ath. State* I no. 20 on the basis that the chairman in that decree can also be restored in ours, viz. τῶν προέδρων ἐπε]ψήφιζε]ν [Εὐθυ] κράτη[ς Ἀφιδναῖος -] (ll. 5–6 Schwenk, whose text improves slightly on Schweigert's). This is attractive, but uncertain since (a) -κρατης is a very common name component, (b) to suit the stoichedon Schwenk is required to posit omission of ἧι before the secretary, of the secretary's father's name and of ephelkystic nu on ἐγραμμάτευε. None of these three irregularities is impossible, but together they induce some unease. Cf. *Ath. State* I p. 91.

[29] Honoured because he had turned in a good performance "fighting the enemy, sailing on the trireme of Chares of Aixone" (*LGPN* II Χάρης 16). If the date is 337/6 this probably refers to the recent war with Philip. In any case it seems that the occasion was distinct from the syntrierarchy on *Amphitrite* which Chares held between 356 and 346/5 (*IG* II² 1622, 751).

[30] The name is common, but the honour is not and the grant applies also to his descendants. As Wilhelm noted, Φίλων Ἀσκληπιοδώρου ἰσοτελής on the funerary monument *IG* II² 7879, may well be his son. Cf. Whitehead, *Metic* 11–13, 29–30.

[31] Most of the current restorations should be stripped out. The year can not be determined. The identity of Nikostratos, named on the moulding, is uncertain. At

Table (*cont.*)

		Date	Reference	Honorand	Honour
	79	337–323 (T)	*IG* II² 434; Tracy, *ADT* 114.	Arch-	hosp.
104	80	c. 337–320[32]	*IG* II² 312; Lawton no. 118 (ph.).	– [G]	c |
	81*	c. 337–326 (333/2?, see note)	*IG* II² 408; A. Wilhelm, *Praktika Akad. Ath.* 4 (1936), 22 and *Attische Urkunden* V (1942), 152–4 no. 56; Davies, *APF* 164; Tracy, *ADT* 33–4; Veligianni, A150; Culasso, *Prossenie* 297; R. Descat in: B. Marin and C. Virlouvet eds., *Nourrir les cités de Méditerranée* (Paris, 2004), 589–612 (non vidi).[33]	Mnemon and Kallias of Herakleia [G]	[gold or foliage] c
	82*	c. 337–320? (see note)	*IG* II² 409; Wilhelm, *Attische Urkunden* V (1942), 150–2 no. 55; Tracy, *ADT* 34; Veligianni, A151; Culasso, *Prossenie* 297; cf. footnote to no. 81.	Potamos (and another?), Milesians? [G]	–

this period parallels would suggest the honorand, but he may be the secretary (though no secretary of this name is otherwise attested at this period and the parallel, *SEG* XVI 55, is sui generis, cf. *Ath. State* II no. 8) or even (though this would be wholly unparalleled) chairman. If secretary, the available years between 337 and 323 (period indicated by the cutter) are 336/5 or 331/0. The decree proper begins ἐπειδὴ Π-. After the pi Wilhelm detected trace consistent with epsilon. My repeated examination of the stone and squeezes confirms that there is what may be the upper segment of a left vertical. To the right of this the stone is broken and I was unable to read anything with confidence. Π- may accordingly be the honorand, but e.g. πρ[ότερόν τε (as e.g. no. 96, 11) can not, it seems, be ruled out. Discussed more fully in *Polis and Theatre*.

32 The relief of a prow of a ship, with projecting stalks of grain, indicates that the decree honoured (two?, from number of crowns) men for the import of grain. It probably belongs in the same context as the other decrees of this type from this period, which all date ca. 337–320 (the earliest is perhaps no. 85). Cf. Tracy, *ADT* 33 n. 18. The right crown is inscribed ἡ βουλή, ὁ δῆμος. Though it is possible to see how Kirchner read ΒΟΥΛΕ, that would be anomalous orthography at this period and autopsy suggests that the final letter was in fact H.

33 Alain Bresson kindly informs me of a forthcoming volume of essays on the Black Sea region in which he will discuss this inscription and no. 82.

'able (*cont.*)

	Date	Reference	Honorand	Honour	
.3	c. 337–320?[34]	E. Schweigert, *Hesp.* 9 (1940), 332–3 no. 39 (ph.); *Agora* XVI 82; Tracy, *ADT* 33–4; Veligianni, A149.	Pandios of Herakleia?[35] [G]	–	
.4*	337–318 (331/0? see note)	*IG* II^2 363 (= Schwenk 67) + G. Malouchou, Ηόρος 14–16 (2000–2003), 58–9 no. 2 (*SEG* LI 72); B.D. Meritt, *Hesp.* 10 (1941). 48–9 no. 11 (ph.); Tracy, *ADT* 31; Culasso, *Prossenie* 297.	Dionysios [G]	c + military service and payment of eisphora as an Athenian	
.5	After 337?[36]	*IG* II^2 283; Bielman, *Retour* no. 4 (ph. of squeeze); Veligianni, A135; M.B. Walbank, *ZPE* 139 (2002), 61–5 no. 5; Lambert, *ZPE* 140 (2002), 73–9 (ph.); P. Gauthier, *Bull. ép.* 2003, 245 (*SEG* LII 91); Culasso, *Prossenie* 297.	Ph- son of – of (sc. Cypriot) Salamis [G][37]	[foliage or gold] c |	105

[34] The text is very fragmentary and the restorations of Schweigert and Woodhead are somewhat speculative in places. In particular in ll. 6–14 one can not be confident of more than obvious completions of words (in ll. 11–12 I read]εν ὁ στρ|[ατηγὸς, cf. the reference to an Athenian general in no. 81). However, σιτηγῶ|[ν̣ (ll. 7–8) in combination with the honorand's ethnic (apparently Ἡρα- in l. 16) tend to confirm the identification of the honorand as a grain trader (cf. e.g. no. 81). If so, the decree probably belongs in a group with the others of this period honouring grain traders. Like others that do not mention specific crises, it should be dated c. 337–320 (cf. *Ath. State* IIIA n. 68).

[35] Doubtless Herakleia Pontika (cf. no. 49 with note). The honorand's name is distinctively Attic (*LGPN* II p. 358; Elaine Matthews kindly confirms per ep. that there is no other known non-Attic case), suggesting a family or other close connection with Athens (cf. Phormio of Akarnania, one of the honorands of no. 5 = RO 77, probably named for the Athenian general of the Peloponnesian War. See RO's note).

[36] In 2002 I noted that the style of the lettering was similar to *IG* II^2 208 (349/8). Tracy per ep., however, advises that the cutter does not appear to be the same. The decree belongs in a group with others of this period honouring grain traders, all of which, where they can be accurately dated, were passed after the battle of Chaironeia.

[37] ἐσιτ]ήγησεν ἐξ Αἰγύπτου (l. 2). The restoration (Köhler's after Rangabé, universally accepted hitherto) is questioned by Humphreys, *Strangeness* 127 n. 50, who comments that "the context seems to be military rather than economic" (but note εὐωνοτέρων, l. 3) "and Egypt produced e.g. ropes as well as grain". However, while σιτηγέω is well attested in justification clauses for honours at this period (e.g. no. 83, 7; no. 43, 6; *IG* II^2 407, 4), it is difficult to see any other verb that would suit the context (ἐστρατ]ήγησεν, ἐξ Αἰγύπτου τ- does not seem likely). Moreover, while grain

Table (*cont.*)

	Date	Reference	Honorand	Honour
86*	336/5 or 335/4	*IG* II² 328; M.H. Hansen, *GRBS* 23 (1982), 343 no. 24 (*SEG* XXXII 79); Schwenk 15.	– son of Eupor- ?[38]	–
87	335/4	S.V. Tracy, *Hesp.* 67 (1998), 219–21 (ph.) (*SEG* XLVIII 101, cf. *SEG* XXI 272; Schwenk p. 128; Tracy, *ADT* 87).	Nikostratos	–
88	334/3–321[39]	*IG* II² 416b; A.S. Henry, *JHS* 97 (1977), 157–8; M. Walbank, *ABSA* 85 (1990), 444 no. 16; Tracy, *ADT* 16 n. 61, 34, 123, 127–8 (*SEG* XLV 77); Veligianni, A152.	-das of Kos [G]	–
89	334/3–314/3 (T)	*IG* II² 292; Tracy, *ADT* 122; Lambert, *ZPE* 136 (2001), 68 no. 3 (ph.) (*SEG* LI 85).	–	prot. + c
90	334/3–314/3 (T)[40]	*IG* II² 430; Tracy, *ADT* 128 (*SEG* XLV 71); Veligianni, A173.	A Pharsalian (or the Pharsalian People)[41]	–
91	334/3–314/3 (T)	*IG* II² 264; D.M. Lewis ap. Develin, *AO* 354; A.S. Henry, *ZPE* 78 (1989), 266–7; Tracy, *ADT* 122, 126 (*SEG* XLV 66); Veligianni, A127.	1. Iatrokles 2. Envoy from Iatrokles	1. – 2. hosp. + prot. in transit?

is commonly referred to (cf. no. 43 for allusion to low price), no other commodity is mentioned in the justification clause of an honorific decree at this period.

[38] [...5..]ς Εὐπορ[- (l. 16). No known Athenian male was named Εὐπορ- before c. i BC (*LGPN* II pp. 181–2), so he was almost certainly a foreigner (cf. *LGPN* I 183, IIIA 173, IIIB 164).

[39] "Cutter of EM 12807", 334/3–314/3 (Tracy, *ADT* 123). ὁ δῆμος ὁ ἐν Σάμωι (l. 3) is among those who have reported favourably on the honorand, indicating a date before the end of the Athenian cleruchy on Samos in 321 (cf. no. 46).

[40] The stone is lost and the primary source is now the Princeton squeeze. I am grateful to Christian Habicht for advice and for enabling me to examine it. The inscription should be added to the group of fragments cut by Tracy's Cutter of EM 12807, with letter heights c. 0.007–0.008 and square or roughly square stoichedon grid c. 0.016–0.018, which I discussed at *ZPE* 136 (2001), 65–70. As Tracy points out, Thessaly was a staunch ally of Athens during the Lamian War and it is possible that, like another fragment in this group (no. 106), this decree dates to that period.

[41] Φ]αρσαλι[-|- ε]ὔνους τῶ[ι δήμωι ll. 2–3. For the posssibility that the honorand was the Pharsalian People cf. no. 66, 15–18: ὅπως ἂν ἡ πόλις | τῶν Π]ελλα[νέων διατελῆι ἀεὶ φίλ|η οὖ]σα καὶ ε[ὔνους τῶι δήμωι τῶι Ἀ|θην]αίων.

Table (*cont.*)

	Date	Reference	Honorand	Honour	
2	334/3–314/3 (T)	*IG* II^2 414 fr. c; E. Schweigert, *Hesp.* 8 (1939), 27–30 no. 7 (ph.); *Hesp.* 9 (1940), 335–9 no. 42 fr. cj (ph.); as no. 106; Lambert, *ZPE* 136 (2001), 65–70 no. 2 (*SEG* LI 84); Culasso, *Prossenie* 297–8.	– and Astym- [and – and?] Polysthenes [and –] from the Bosporan kingdom[42] [G?]	[gold or foliage] c	
3	334/3–314/3 (T)	E. Schweigert, *Hesp.* 9 (1940), 335–9 no. 42 fr. h (ph.); as no. 106; Lambert, *ZPE* 136 (2001), 69 no. 4c (*SEG* LI 88).	–	prot.	
4	332/1?	*IG* II^2 546; Lawton no. 151 (ph.); Lambert, *ZPE* 141 (2002), 117–22 (ph.) (*SEG* LII 95).	Two? men	– |	106
5	1. ? 2. 332/1	*IG* II^2 346; Henry, *Honours* 263; Schwenk 37; Tracy, *ADT* 8 n. 4, 77, 110–1; Veligianni, A146; Brun, *Démade* 177 no. 7; Lambert, *Polis and Theatre* (ph.).	2. -os son of Aristeides[43] [Theat.]	–	
6[44]	332/1	*IG* II^2 345 + Add. p. 659; Schwenk 36; Tracy, *ADT* 8 n. 4, 84, 110–1; Lawton no. 44 (ph.); Lambert, *Polis and Theatre* (ph.).	– son of Eud?]emos of Plataia [Theat.]	–	
7	331/0	*IG* II^2 349 + Add. p. 659; Tod II 193; Davies, *APF* 15292, pp. 249–50, 430–1; Osborne, *Nat.* T66; Schwenk 45; Lawton no. 46 (ph.); Z.H. Archibald, *The Odrysian Kingdom* (Oxford, 1998), 218–22, 307–16. Cf. *SEG* LI 81.	Rheboulas son of Seuthes, brother of Kotys, of Angele[45]	–	

[42] Envoys? Cf. no. 3, 49–51.

[43] The honorand of this decree, proposed by Demades and passed on the same day as three others at the Assembly after the City Dionysia in 332/1, had perhaps rendered service to Athenian drama (cf. note on no. 39; *Polis and Theatre*).

[44] I argue in *Polis and Theatre* that the decree stands in close relationship to no. 42, for Eudemos of Plataia, also proposed by Lykourgos. It was passed at the same Assembly after the City Dionysia in 332/1 as three others (cf. note on no. 39 above) and the honorand's services probably related to the festival in some way (rebuilding of the theatre? cf. no. 42).

[45] Ῥηβούλας [: Σεύθου :] ὑός, Κότυος ἀδελφός, Ἀνγελ[ῆθεν]. The honorand, not otherwise attested in person, was apparently a member of the royal house of the

Table (*cont.*)

		Date	Reference	Honorand	Honour
	98	c. 330	A.J. Heisserer and R.A. Moysey, *Hesp.* 55 (1986), 177–82 (ph.) (*SEG* XXXVI 149); P. Gauthier, *Bull. ép.* 1988, 370; Tracy, *ADT* 10 n. 18, 87; Lambert, *ZPE* 148 (2004), 184–6 no. 4 and *Polis and Theatre.*	– [Theat.]	Privilege in relation to import/ export? + ateleia of metic tax ? + prot.
107	99	c. 330–320 (323–2?)[46]	*IG* II² 549 + 306; D.M. Lewis, *ABSA* 49 (1954), 50; Tracy, *ADT* 36 n. 2, 98, 99, 103 (*SEG* XLV 69).	1. [Kythnian][47] People 2. Kyth[nians] coming to Athens 3. General(s) or person(s?) standing in relation to general(s)[48]	1. [1000?][49] dr. gold c 2. pref. access[50] 3. c |

Odrysian kingdom of Thrace, enfranchised at Athens in the deme Angele. The inclusion of the demotic is very unusual for a foreign honorand and may suggest that he was resident in Athens in exile, perhaps occasioned by the assassination of his brother Kotys I (king c. 383–359 and also an Athenian citizen, Dem. XXIII 118) or the alignment of Thrace with Macedon in the late 340s, cf. Osborne. Citizenship had perhaps been awarded under the patronage of Chares of Angele (Davies, cf. Dem. XXIII 173). The inscribing of the father's name in an erasure and the first interpunct have not previously been detected. One suspects a scribal error caused by the unusual nomenclature, that the erroneously inscribed letters had occupied eight spaces and that the interpuncts included with Σεύθου are mere space fillers. In l. 10 read perhaps the common formula π]ερὶ ὧν ὁ δῆμος προ[σέταξεν τῆι βουλῆι. The absence of the secretary from the prescript may imply that the decree was erected at private initiative and expense (Henry, *Prescripts* 44).

[46] I confirm from autopsy Tracy's tentative association of the two fragments. Inter alia the working of the original left side on both is the same, with a distinctive, slightly uneven, back edge to the finished side. The working of the rough-picked back is also distinctive, protruding back slightly, but not very much, beyond the finished side. The vacant stone at the left margin is the same, c. 0.005. This is a work of Tracy's "cutter of *IG* II² 244", 340/39–320. The assignment of 50 drachmas for the inscribing costs indicates a date after c. 330 (Loomis, *Wages* 163–4). It seems, therefore, that the decree should no longer be associated with the Athenian liberation of Kythnos from the pirate Glauketes in 315/4 (*IG* II² 682, 9–13, cf. Köhler, L. Robert, *Rev. Num.* 1977, 23–4 with n. 89). The context may be the Lamian war. Except for the Lamian War period there are no decrees honouring whole cities (or bilateral treaties, cf. *Ath. State* IV) dating from the late 330s and 320s.

[47] The alternative, Kyth[era], would entail stoichedon irregularities in ll. 6 and 10 (and 13?). The multiple articles in the restoration at l. 6, however, τ]ὸν δῆμον [τὸν τῶν Κυθνίω|ν are unusual. Normal Athenian decree usage is τὸν δῆμον τὸν + ethnic (e.g. no. 23, 9–10), more rarely τὸν δῆμον τῶν + ethnic (e.g. no. 72, 7). τὸν δῆμον τὸν τῶν + ethnic is very rare, though it occurs apparently at *IG* II² 34, 12 and 35, 9.

[48] The relevant text was somewhat overconfidently restored in *IG* II². It reads:

Table (*cont.*)

	Date	Reference	Honorand	Honour
100	329/8[51]	*IG* II² 353; Schwenk 51; Brun, *Démade* 92–3 with n. 46, 177 no. 8.	– son of -oiros[52] of Larisa	–

ἐπ]-
αινέσαι δέ [.......¹⁴......]
ῳ̣ν στρατη[γ.......¹⁴......]
ΑΡΜΕΝΟΝ[.......¹³......καὶ]
[σ]τεφαν[ῶσαι-----------]

Kirchner's [καὶ τὸν τῶν Κυθνί]|ων στρατη[γὸν is possible, but uncertain. In l. 15 he thinks of Π]|αρμένον[τος, i.e. the general's father's name. We might alternatively have to do with the name Ἄρμενος (*IG* II² 4595, *LGPN* IIIA 71, IIIB 65 etc.). The Kythnians had a board of five generals (Hansen–Nielsen, *Inventory* p. 756).

[49] See footnote to no. 43

[50] Since Köhler the accepted reading (l. 9) of the recipients of this award has been τοῖς [ἥκουσι παρὰ τοῦ δή|μ]ου τοῦ Κυθ[νίων. Envoys and others are indeed commonly referred to as ἥκοντες παρὰ their city (e.g. no. 3, 10), but preferential access, as a long term privilege, was not normally granted to them. They would rather be brought before the Council or Assembly specifically in connection with their mission, for which the formula is προσαγαγεῖν πρὸς τὸν δῆμον (cf. Henry, *Honours* 191). Moreover, [ἥκουσι in our text exceeds the normal line length by one letter (there is no other demonstrable breach of stoichedon in this text) and is inconsistent with the traces of the first surviving letter, which appears to be an iota (I confirm Köhler's reading of an upper vertical in the centre of the stoichos. Unless there is an irregularity this is not consistent with eta in this hand). I suggest τοῖς ἰ[οῦσι παρὰ τοῦ δή|μ]ου τοῦ Κυθ[νίων. Cf. L. Robert's suggestion for *SEG* XVI 55 = *Ath. State* II no. 8, 12 (for persons attending a festival), δέκα μὲν ἰοῦ[σιν], not a certain restoration there (cf. *Ath. State* II p. 148), but nonetheless well paralleled in non-Attic inscriptions, as Robert points out (e.g. *IG* XII 7, 24 l 9, ἐπέδωκεν τοῖς [ἰ]ο[ῦ]σιν εἰς τὴν ἑορτὴν, cf. 22). The intention is to grant preferential access to Kythnians who may come to Athens in the future. παρὰ τοῦ δήμου τοῦ Κυθνίων may be intended to limit this to those on public business, though this is not entirely clear. For a perhaps even more openly worded grant cf. no. 110.

[51] The restoration of the calendrical elements, yielding an Assembly on the day of the Chalkeia, is sound, and I have nothing to add to previous discussions. Assemblies on minor festival days are not uncommon at this period (cf. *Ath. State* IIIA n. 65). The chairman's name is read as [...]ππος Ὤαθ[εν] by Schwenk. However, a sigma is reported in the second stoichos of the line by some early eds., including Köhler, and is still visible at autopsy. I detect the lower two strokes and, more faintly, the top one. This, however, presents a puzzle, because there is no name in *LGPN* II (or any other published volume of *LGPN*) in [.]σ[ι]ππος. If the sigma is not an illusion (and I judge that unlikely), it seems that we must assume crowding at the end of the previous line or (though this is uncommon) at the beginning of l. 8. There is severely damaged and uncertain trace of what might be a lambda slightly to the left of the normal first stoichos (clearest lower left), raising the possibility Λ̣[ύ]σ[ι]ππος.

[52] The father's name of the honorand has been restored (by Hiller in *IG* II²) as Χ]-οίρου (Velsen, *IG* II 178 read ΚΟΙΡΟΥ, the K lacking lower diagonal, but the letter was not confirmed by Köhler and no inscribed trace in this position was noted by Schwenk

Table (*cont.*)

		Date	Reference	Honorand	Honour
108	101	c. 329–317[53]	*IG* II^2 551; Pečírka, *Enktesis* 84–5 (*SEG* XXIV 109); Henry, *Honours* 246 with n. 51; Lambert, *Polis and Theatre* (ph.).	Nikostratos (son of?) Ke-[54] [Theat.]	c + isot.? + enk.
	102	327/6	*IG* II^2 113 (Schwenk 60) + E. Schweigert, *Hesp.* 7 (1938), 296–7 no. 21 (ph.); A. Wilhelm, *Attische Urkunden* V (1942) 154–6 no. 57; M.B. Walbank, *ZPE* 76 (1989), 257–61 (*SEG* XXXIX 91); Tracy, *ADT* 106.	– son of -odemos of – and Phanostratos [son of -odemos] of –[55] (brothers)	c + isot.

---

or myself at autopsy). This would be the only attestation of this name in Thessaly, or in the whole area of central Greece covered by *LGPN* IIIB (see p. 444; it is attested on Euboea [Chalkis] and Thasos, see *LGPN* I p. 486). Εὐμ]οίρου is a possible alternative, attested in Boeotia (*LGPN* IIIB p. 160) and Euboea (Eretria, *LGPN* I p. 180).

[53] The honorand is awarded ἔγκτ]ησιν κατ[ὰ τὸν νόμον (ll. 11–12. Sic legi. I agree with Pečírka that the lower right vertical of the H is visible at autopsy. The iota is displaced to the left in its stoichos, like the final iota in l. 11). This probably indicates a date after c. 329 (cf. *Ath. State* IIIA n. 77). Since the decree recognises services to the *choregoi* it should pre-date the abolition of the *choregia* by Demetrios of Phaleron. The inscribing officer was apparently the prytany secretary (12–14), ruling out a date during the oligarchy of 321–18, when that function was performed by the *anagrapheus* (cf. A.S. Henry, *Hesp.* 71, 2002, 107–8, 104 n. 66). There is no extant decree of the period of Demetrios of Phaleron (317–307) which was certainly erected at public initiative and expense (cf. *ABSA* 95, 2000, 488), a fact which argues against a date in that period for this decree (and a number of others in this list). A date during the brief democracy of 318/7, however, is possible. Given the subject matter it was perhaps passed at the special Assembly after the City Dionysia (cf. note on no. 39).

[54] Νικόστρατον Κη[.......13......ι.]την (τὸν αὐλη]τήν [cf. *IG* II^2 713 Add. p. 666] or ὑποκρι]τήν [cf. note on *Ath. State* IIIA no. 39] or ethnic, Wilhelm). The name is common. Poets: *IG* II^2 3094. *PCG* VII p. 93 Nicostratus II. Actors: no. 78?; *IG* II^2 2318, 332; 2320, 32 (I.E. Stephanis, Διονυσιακοὶ Τεχνῖται [1988], 1863). There is no obvious connection with the Nikostratos honoured by no. 87. The decree cites the honorand's continuing services (a) to the *agon* of the Dionysia, (b) in respect of his own profession or responsibility (τὴν αὐτοῦ ἐπιμέλειαν), or perhaps rather, as Peter Wilson and Angelos Matthaiou suggest to me, in respect of his responsibility for it, sc. the *agon* (τὴν αὐτοῦ ἐπιμέλειαν) and (c) to the *choregoi*:

καὶ τοῖς χορη]- stoich. 29
[γο]ῖς τοῖς αἰεὶ χορηγο[ῦσιν προθύμως]
[ὑ]πηρετῶν τὰ περὶ τοὺ[ς...6..., ἐπαινέ]-
[σαι

Y, the last letter of l. 7, is placed to the left of its stoichos, indicating that there was probably an additional letter in this line, as in ll. 5 and 6. I suggest χορούς (θεούς Koumanoudes, αὐλούς Wilhelm). He was perhaps a metic (Whitehead, *Metic* 29–30).

Table (*cont.*)

	Date	Reference	Honorand	Honour	
103	327/6	*IG* II^2 356 + Add. p. 660; Tod II 199; Schwenk 58; Veligianni, A155; RO 98.	Memnon of Rhodes[56]	gold c	
104	326/5	P. Kabbadias, *Arch. Eph.* 1898, 7 no. 2 with pl. 1 (ph.); *IG* II^2 359; Schwenk 63; Tracy, *ADT* 106.	Asty- (name or ethnic)[57]	–	
105	c. 324–322/1	A. Wilhelm, *Öst. Jh.* 11 (1908), 89–92 no. 5 (ph.); *IG* II^2 402 (+ Add. p. 660) + S. Tracy, *Hesp.* 62 (1993), 249–51 (ph.) (*SEG* XLII 91); C. Habicht, *Hesp.* 62 (1993), 253–6; P. Gauthier, *Bull. Ép.* 1994, 289; E. Badian, *ZPE* 100 (1994), 389–90; A. Bosworth, *CQ* 43 (1993), 420–7; Tracy, *ADT* 98.	Friend(s?) of the king (Alexander after c. 324? Philip Arrhidaios in autumn 322/1?) and Antipater[58]	–	
106	323/2	*IG* II^2 369; E. Schweigert, *Hesp.* 8 (1939), 27–30 no. 7 (ph.); *Hesp.* 9 (1940), 335–9 no. 42 fr. abid (ph.) (*SEG* XXI 298); Osborne, *Nat.* D25; Schwenk 85; *Agora* XVI 94; Lawton no. 50; Tracy, *ADT* 122, 127; Veligianni, A161; Lambert, *ZPE* 136 (2001), 65–70 no. 1 (*SEG* LI 83).	– son of Demetrios	[gold or foliage] c	
107	323/2[59]	*IG* II^2 365; M.B. Walbank in: *Classical Contributions. Studies… McGregor* (1981) 171–5 (*SEG* XXX 66); M. Piérart, *BCH* 106 (1981), 129–30; S.G. Miller, *Hesp.* Suppl. 20 (1982), 100–8; Schwenk 79; M. Piérart and G. Touchais, *Argos* (1996), 62–4.	Lapyris son of Kallias of Kleonai	dinner |	109

[55] For the father's name and ethnic Walbank suggested e.g. Κλεοδήμου Τήνιον.

[56] Member of a distinguished family. See RO.

[57] The first preserved line is a heading, [Ἀ]στυ-. The top of the stone is not preserved and it is possible that another line preceded it.

[58] Cf. *IG* II^2 401, currently dated to 320 (Tracy, *ADT* 134).

[59] 11 Hekatombaion 323. The date is between the death of Alexander (10 June 323) and the Nemean Games (probably in the next month, Metageitnion, cf. Lambert,

Table (*cont.*)

	Date	Reference	Honorand	Honour
108	322/1 or shortly after	*IG* II² 377; Schwenk 91; Veligianni, A164.	-	
109	c. 350–300?[60]	*IG* II² 270; Veligianni, A129; M. B. Walbank, *ZPE* 139 (2002), 63-4 (SEG LII 99); Culasso, *Prossenie* 298.	Lampyri[-[61] (l. 11) might be the honorand or his father	
110	c. 350–300?[62]	*IG* II² 660 decree 1; Pečírka, *Enktesis* 93–5; Henry, *Honours* 259–60; Veligianni, A175.	1. Tenian People 2. Tenians living at Athens 3. Two Tenian envoys or leaders[63] 4. Tenians[64]	1. 1000 dr. gold c 2. isot.[65] 3. foliage c 4. pref. access + prot. |

110

ZPE 139, 2002, 72–4). The decree was based on a report of the head of the Athenian delegation to the upcoming Games and Lapyris of Kleonai (the city traditionally responsible for the Games, cf. Piérart 1981, P. Perlman, *City and Sanctuary in Anc. Greece* [2000] [*SEG* L 343]), who was Athenian *proxenos* there. The body of the text is unfortunately extremely fragmentary (some minor new readings will be included in the text for *IG*, including στρατ|η]γοίς? ll. 30–1), but it apparently established arrangements for disbursements. πο]|λεμ[ι]οιΣ[in ll. 24–5 seems consonant with suspicions that this may have been a diplomatic initiative preparatory to the Lamian War (cf. Miller, C.J. Schwenk, *AJA* 90, 1986, 211). M. Piérart and J.-P. Thalmann, *BCH* Suppl. 6 (1980), 266–7 (cf. P. Charneux, *Bull. ép.* 1987, 605) raise the possibility of restoring Lapyris (ll. 41–2) as Λάπυριν Καλλί[ου Ἀργεί νν]|ον, but if the father's name is correctly restored, one would in that case have expected the whole ethnic to have been accommodated in l. 41. Κλεωναῖ]|ον suits the 32 letter stoichedon and is the ethnic borne by Lapyris' ancestor Echembrotos on the original award of proxeny, *IG* II² 63, and in l. 48 of our text. Whatever the political situation of Kleonai vis-à-vis Argos at this period, it would have been natural for Lapyris, *proxenos* at Kleonai (not Argos) by virtue of the grant to his ancestor, to have been Κλεωναῖος in this decree.

[60] Walbank wished to restore ἀναγρ]αφε[- in l. 1 and to date the decree to the period of the oligarchic *anagrapheis*, 321/0–318/7. At autopsy, however, the letter before the phi seemed to me N or more likely M. In general the text in *IG* II² is over-restored. The right side of the stone is not preserved, formulae are not identifiable from the surviving text and the line length can not be determined. τῆς ἐλευθερία]ς τῶν Ἑλλ[ήνων, ll. 6–7, might be a reference to the Lamian War, but e.g. στρατευομένου]ς τῶν Ἑλλ[ήνων is no less likely (cf. no. 103, 32).

[61] Λάμπυρις (*LGPN* I p. 282), Λαμπυρίδας or -ίων (*LGPN* IIIA p. 268, *FRA* 3207).

[62] G. Reger, *CQ* 42 (1992), 365–83, suggests c. 306, which is possible, but uncertain. The grant of *isoteleia* is renewed in decree 2, of 281/0 (archon Ourias), inscribed below decree 1. In relation to Tenos see also R. Stroud, *Hesp.* 40 (1971), 187–9 no. 34 (cf. *Ath. State* IV).

[63] The text should read:

[---------ἐπαινέσαι---]
[---------------καὶ στ]-
fr. b [εφανῶσ]αι θαλλοῦ στε[φάνωι ἑκάτερ]-
ο[ν, ὅτι] εἰσὶν ἄνδρες ἀγ[αθοὶ περὶ τό]-
ν δῆμον τὸν Ἀθηναίων

Table (*cont.*)

	Date	Reference	Honorand	Honour
11	c. 350–300?[66]	*IG* II^2 446.	[Eu]patas[67]	c
12	c. 350–300?[68]	*IG* II^2 424.	-anax son of Apol-, – son of –, Apollas son of Apol-, – son of Akamas, Ant- son of –, Apollodoros son of O-[69]	c

Kirchner restored the honorands here as envoys (πρέσβεις). They may alternatively have been named Tenian leaders (cf. the decrees awarding honours to the city of Tenedos and named leaders no. 67 and no. 72, 27–30). The number of lines to be restored between fr. a and b is uncertain.

[64] ε[ἶναι δὲ Τηνί]|οις πρόσοδον…(*b* 5–6). This is a remarkably vague and general grant of preferential access, almost unexampled in decrees certainly dating 352/1–322/1 (no. 99 supplies the closest parallel).

[65] The text should read:

fr. a εἶναι δὲ καὶ]
ἰσοτέλε[ιαν Τηνίων τοῖς οἰκοῦσιν]
Ἀθήνησ[ι..........^{21}..........]
.ΤΕ[............^{25}............]

IG^2 read ^Τ¯ in 8, restored στρ]ατε[υομένοις (Kirchner), or καὶ στρατεύεσθαι τὰς στρ]|ατε[ίας Henry. This seems to fit very conveniently, but Pečírka noted that the third letter of the line is not certain ("the upper cross-bar seems clear, but the spot is badly damaged"). Moreover, while it is possible that there has been damage to the first stoichos since Köhler, neither Graham Oliver nor I were able to confirm at autopsy that the first letter is alpha. What appears to be the upper section of E is apparent (neither Berlin nor Oxford squeezes show a clear letter trace at this point), raising the possibilities δ]ὲ τε[λ- or δι]ετε[λ-.

[66] Cf. "litt. volg. s. iv" and "post a. 336/5" (Kirchner).

[67] The name is [-$^{2-3}$-]ΠΑΤΑΝ. Εὐπάτας is the only attested name that will fit (Peloponnese, *LGPN* IIIA p. 172). The form suggests an honorand from a state which used the Doric dialect (cf. no. 112).

[68] Cf. "litt. volg. s. IV" and "post a. 336/5" Kirchner.

[69] The correct reading of ll. 3–8 is:

[..^{3}.|ΟΛΙ ΑΜΦ[.........^{20}..........]
[.ἀνα]κτα Ἀπολ[.........^{18}.........]
[..^{3}.], Ἀπόλλαν Ἀπο[λ.......^{15}........]
[..] Ἀκάμαντος, Ἀντ[........^{15}......]
[..] Ἀπολλόδωρον Ο[....^{7}...καὶ στεφα]-
[νῶ]σαι ἕκαστον αὐτ[ῶν

Ἀπολλόδωρος is ubiquitous, but Ἀπολλᾶς and Ἀκάμας suggest honorands of Peloponnesian, West or North Greek origin (cf. *LGPN* IIIA p. 21, p. 49; IV p. 12, p. 34; the cases in the *LGPN* I region are hellenistic), the recurrence of Apol- names members of a single family.

73. IG *II² 543*

My text is:

c. 340 vel paullo post

[-c. 9-]ωκρ̣[ατ-----------------------------Ἐλευ]- non-stoich.
σίνιος εἶπεν· ἐπ̣[ειδή--------------------------τῶ]-
ι δήμωι τῶι Ἀθ̣η[ναίων--------------------------]
τωι πρὸς τὸν δῆ[μον---------------------------ἤγ]-
αγον εἰς τὸ ἐνπ̣[όριον--------------------------ἐψ]-
ηφίσαντο [Μ]οιροκ̣[λ-----------------------------]
υν καὶ ἀφείλοντο τὸ π[----------------------------]-
ς τὸν Πειρ̣αεᾱ̣ διατ[------------------δεδόχθαι τῶι δ]-
ήμωι ἐπαι̣νέσ̣αι [-- καὶ στεφανῶσαι - χρυσῶι στεφάνωι ἀπὸ -]
[δ]ραχμῶν φιλ̣ο[τιμίας ἕνεκα----------πρὸς τὸν δῆμον -]
[..], ὅπως ἂν εἰδῶσ[ι πάντες--------ὅτι ὁ δῆμος ὁ Ἀθηναί]-
[ων] στεφανοῖ τ[οὺς------------------------------]
[-2–3-] πλεοντ[----------------------------------]
[-2–3-]ΒΓ̣Γ̣[--------------------------------------]

Textual notes

Restorations are those of *IG*¹ or Velsen's as printed in *IG* II² unless noted otherwise.

1. -]ωκρ̣[ατ-. I confirm the lower section of a vertical stroke read after the K in *IG* II¹. This, and the fact that the text is part of the prescript, suggests that we have to do with a name (Σωκρατ- Köhler), most likely the chairman.

5. ἐνπ̣[όριον. ἐμπ̣[όριον *IG* II¹. The nu is certain (for this orthography see Threatte I 601). I confirm the lower section of a vertical read
111 after it by *IG* II¹. |

6. [Μ]οιροκ̣[λ-. [.]ΟΙ⊢Ο-- *IG* II¹. ⊢ is in fact a rho, with rather high and thin loop, as in l. 4 (though damaged, almost the entire circuit is visible) and the second omicron is followed by the lower segment of a vertical stroke. I print the initial mu in square brackets, though what might be the upper left corner of it is visible.

8. τον Πειρ̣αεᾱ̣. τὸν Πει[ρ]αι[ᾶ] *IG* II¹. (The) Piraeus is unusual among Attic deme names in sometimes taking the article in inscriptions. Cf. my remarks at *ZPE* 130 (2000), 73 n. 19. The sequence of letters is not easy to make out, but on repeated examination at autopsy I read, after the iota, lower section of vertical stroke; lower half of alpha including cross-bar; E fully visible; Λ. For this orthography of the deme name (and the demotic) at this period see Threatte I 282–3.

The key to identifying the context of this decree is the new reading [M]-οιροκ̣[λ- in l. 6, for this is Moirokles of Eleusis[70] the well-known politician. See most recently S.B. Aleshire, *Asklepios at Athens* (Amsterdam, 1991), 244–6, with references to earlier bibliography, and *PAA* 658480. This creates a connection with [Dem.] LVIII. Shortly before its date of delivery, c. 340 (see M.H. Hansen, *Apagoge, Endeixis* [Odense, 1976], 137–8 no. 25), Moirokles had successfully proposed a decree aimed against those harming traders. He had persuaded not only the Athenians, but also the allies, to take measures:

> Μοιροκλῆς τοίνυν, ὦ ἄνδρες δικασταί, ὁ τὸ ψήφισμα γράψας κατὰ τῶν τοὺς ἐμπόρους ἀδικούντων, καὶ πείσας οὐ μόνον ὑμᾶς, ἀλλὰ καὶ τοὺς συμμάχους φυλακήν τινα τῶν κακουργούντων ποιήσασθαι... [Dem.] LVIII 53

From LVIII 56 it appears that a ten talent fine had recently been imposed, or was contemplated, against the Melians for providing a refuge for pirates (ὅτι τοὺς λῃστὰς ὑπεδέξαντο) against the terms of Moirokles' decree.[71]

The justification clause of our decree refers to men who had brought products (grain? cf. [Dem.] LVIII passim, the only traded product mentioned in Athenian decrees at this period) on to the (Athenian?) market (ll. 4–5); men who had voted a decree which had something to do with Moirokles (ἐψηφίσαντο, ll. 5–6); and men who had destroyed something, καὶ ἀφε̣ίλοντο τὸ π[-. Private individuals can bring products onto the market and destroy things, but they can not vote decrees. At this point at least we have to do with a public body, most likely a state. It might have been the Athenian state. In other words this might be a reference back to earlier honours which Athens had awarded the honorands, as e.g. no. 62, 6. But it is perhaps easier to take it as a foreign state (as e.g. *IG* II² 470b, 13, of Kolophonians), a state which might also have facilitated the bringing of products onto the Athenian market and have destroyed something. Köhler seems to have understood it in this way: "civitati cuidam, quae commeatu Athenienses adiuvisse videtur, decernebatur corona aurea". [Dem.] LVIII nicely supplies the context. The city would be among those allies whom

[70] The name is attested in Athens exclusively or almost exclusively for this man or members of his family. See *LGPN* II p. 319.

[71] For the historical context see most recently Bielman, 17; Dreher, *Hegemon* 277.

Moirokles persuaded φυλακήν τινα τῶν κακουργούντων ποιήσασθαι. Compliant allies were to be honoured, as states failing to take action, such as the Melians, were to be punished. In ll. 5–6 the sense might have been ἐψηφίσαντο Μοιροκ[λέους πείσαντος. If they are also the subject in l. 7, what they destroyed might perhaps have been a "pirate" facility. In l. 8 Hiller's suggestion, διατ[είχισμα, can not be ruled out, but we may rather have to do with the common verb in honorific decrees to denote a continuing pattern of behaviour, διατελέω, sc. in relation to (imports into?) the Piraeus. In ll. 11–13 the city proclaims that it will honour those who (help, encourage vel. sim.?) men who sail (Athenian traders or those bringing corn to Athens?) or perhaps those who take measures to prevent interference with those seeking to do so (cf. e.g. no. 43, no. 63).

It is notable that the proposer is from Moirokles' deme, Eleusis. If it is not Moirokles himself, this supplies a slight additional argument in favour of the identification of the well-known Moirokles as
112 M. Εὐθυδήμου | Ελευσ., who was prominent in the affairs of his deme (*PAA* 658490), rather than M. Καλλίππου Ἐλευσ., known only from the fun. monument, *IG* II^2 6043.

In a case such as this, where the honorand is a whole city and where the citation seems so closely linked to the circumstances of [Dem.] LVIII, the decree is unlikely to postdate the speech by very long (though no. 43 shows that some delay can not be ruled out in trade-related decrees). Moreover no city is honoured by an inscribed Athenian decree firmly datable between Chaironeia and the Lamian War. Probably, therefore, the decree pre-dates Chaironeia. This is one of only a handful of Athenian decree stelai inscribed non-stoichedon and dating to 352/1–322/1. The script (litt. volg. s. iv, Kirchner) is unusually rough and the line spacing unusually variable (vert. spacing 0.007–0.012).

81. IG *II^2 408*

Habicht ap. Tracy suggested that the decree "will be from the second prytany of 333/2, if in line 4 the name of the chairman is to be restored (from *IG* II^2 337, 29–30) as Φανόστρατος Φι]λαίδης". Certainty is impossible when only the chairman's demotic is preserved, but the space available for the chairman's name suits well as would the timing in relation to the history of the grain supply (there is known to have been a crisis in 335, [Dem.] XXXIV 38, cf. Tracy, *ADT* 33–4) and to the known movements of the general Diotimos (mentioned, ll. 7 and 9, cf. Davies). How might the full prescript be restored? I propose the following, with some hesitation given the uncommon features in the restoration of ll. 2–3 and the difficulty of the reading in l. 3:

333/2 [ἐπὶ Νικοκράτους ἄρχοντος ἐπὶ τῆς Πανδιο]- stoich. 34
[νίδος δευτέρας πρυτανέας ἧι Ἀρχέλας Χαι]-
[ρίου Παλληνεὺς ἐγραμμάτευε· Μετα]γε̣[ιτνι]-
[ῶνος..........22...........]ι̣ καὶ δεκ̣[ά]-
[τηι τῆς πρυτανείας· ἐκκλησ̣ία· τ]ῶ̣ν προέδρ[ω]-
[ν ἐπεψήφιζεν Φανόστρατος Φι]λαΐδης· ἔδο[ξ]-
[εν τῶι δήμωι·.......14.......]λου Ἐ̣ρχιεὺ[ς]
[εἶπεν·

2. The tribe is restored from *IG* II^2 337, 27. The secretary's name is fully preserved on *IG* II^2 338 = *Ath. State* I no. 15. For the orthography πρυτανέας for -είας cf. e.g. *IOrop* 296 (*Ath. State* I p. 107), 3 of 332/1; Threatte I 316. Alternatively one might restore πρυτανείας· Ἀρχέλας Χαιρ|ίου Παλληνεὺς ἐγραμμάτευεν (cf. *Ath. State* I p. 91).

3–4. Μετα]γε̣[ιτνι|ῶνος. We know from *IG* II^2 338 that 333/2 was an intercalary year in which 9 Metageitnion coincided with day 39 of pryt. 1. Any καὶ δεκάτηι date in the second prytany will accordingly have fallen into Metageitnion. In l. 3 Kirchner printed Ο̣Ε̣/ [...], more precisely the lower half of the O, the lower vertical and bottom horizontal of E and the lower section of the following diagonal. The reading goes back to Lolling ap. *IG* II 5, 196. I confirm that one also obtains an impression of Lolling's diagonal from squeezes. At autopsy, however (carried out before I considered the restoration) I could confirm the lower vertical and bottom horizontal of the E, but was doubtful whether any of the marks to the left and right of this could confidently be asserted to be inscribed traces. To the left of the E I received an impression of a lower left vertical, consistent with Γ (but not certainly an inscribed mark).

4. There is more than one way of completing the line, but the most attractive possibility would seem to be δευτέραι φθίνοντος ἐνάτηι καὶ δεκάτηι, [28 Metageitnion] = pryt. [II] 1[9], which would be four days later than the Assembly in no. 38, on the restoration of H. Usener, *Rh. Mus.* 34 (1879), 391–2, which, though not certain, is in my view the most attractive for that inscription (ἕκτηι φθίνοντος [Metageit.] = [pryt. II 15], consistent with a regular intercalary year in which a day before this one was omitted in a hollow Metageitnion).

If the year was not 333/2, the decree can be dated between 337 (no decree honouring grain traders certainly predates Chaironeia; for anx-
113 iety about the grain supply in the aftermath of the battle cf. *Ath.* | *State* IIIA n. 68. There is no explicit reference to a shortage or crisis in this decree) and 326 (the general Diotimos died before 325/4, when two naval debts were paid by his heir, *IG* II² 1629, 539–41, 622-9).

I note two further points relating to the names in this inscription. Πυρρίας has been suggested for the second honorand (ll. 6, 15 and 18, cf. Wilhelm, *Anz. Ak. Wien* 1942, 71 after H. Pope, *Non-Athenians in Attic Inscriptions* (New York, 1935), p. 282, 202; L. Robert, *BCH* Suppl. I, 1973, 440). The correct reading, however, is Καλλίας. The last three letters, -ιας are supplied in l. 6. The second letter can be read in line 18, where, under the mu of δῆμον in the previous line, an alpha is visible (cross bar very faint), printed correctly by *IG* II¹, but omitted in *IG* II². Of the names that will fit, Καλλίας is easily the most common, and is confirmed here by survival of what is perhaps a segment of the left diagonal of the Λ following the A in l. 18. It is attested for an official (?) of Herakleia Pontika (see Ameling, *IHeracl. Pont.* = *IK* 47, 1994, p. 145), probably the honorands' city of origin (cf. Wilhelm and *Ath. State* IIIA n. 89).

Kirchner restored the proposer as Βράχυλλος Βαθύλ]λου Ἐρχιεὺ[ς], attested as a decree proposer in 343/2 (*IG* II² 223C, 10 = *Ath. State* I no. 1; *LGPN* II Βράχυλλος 1). Since -λος is a common name-ending this is no more than possible. Another possibility: Θράσων Θρασυβού]λου Ἐρχιεὺς, cf. *LGPN* II Θρασύβουλος 11, Θράσων 19, *APF* 7303–4, 7384.

82. IG *II² 409*

The left side only is preserved. There have been three previous editions: *IG* II 197; *IG* II² 409 (includes restorations of Wilhelm); A. Wilhelm, *Attische Urkunden* V (1942), 150–2.

My text is:

337–320 ΣΙ. [-----------------------]
τὸ λ[οιπόν-------------------]
ιοις |//[--------ἐμπόρων καὶ? ναυ]-
κλήρων̣ [---------------δεδόχθ]-
αι τῶι δ̣ή[μωι ἐπαινέσαι?------κα]-
ὶ Ποτάμω̣ν[α----------------ἐν]
τῶι : πρόσ̣[θεν χρόνωι-------ὄν?]-
τες καὶ εὐν[----------------σῖ]-

τος ἐξάγετα[ι--------------τῶι]
δήμωι· χειρο[τονῆσαι δὲ------ἄν]-
δρας αὐτίκα μ̣[άλα---------οἴτι]-
νες ἀφικόμεν[οι---------------]-
ιν τὸν δῆμον τ[ὸν--------------]-
αι ὅπως ἂν σῖ[τος---------Ἀθήν]-
αζε καὶ ὅτι [-----------------ο]-
υσιν ὄντε[ς----------------Μι]-
λήσιοι α. [-------------------]-
ων καὶ ου[-----------τοῦ δήμου]
τοῦ Ἀθη[ναίων---------------]
δῆμον τ[ὸν------------------φ]-
ίλοι ὄ[ντες------------------]-
ν ἐπε[----------------------]-
ΛΙΤΙ[----------------------]
Ἀθη̣[ν----------------------]
ΟΤ[------------------------]

This very fragmentary decree apparently honoured Potamon and another (ll. 5–6), who had performed services in relation to the grain trade (ll. 3–4, 8–9). It also mentions [Mi]lesians (ll. 16–17) and made | pro- 114
vision for an embassy to be sent somewhere, with the apparent objective of facilitating Athenian grain imports (ll. 10 ff.). Köhler's text in *IG*[1], based on Velsen's transcript, included several modest, but important, restorations. *IG* II[2] incorporated a highly speculative continuous restoration of Wilhelm, yielding a 31 letter line (developed further in *Attische Urkunden* V), in which the city of Sinope, a colony of Miletus on the south shore of the Black Sea, features prominently. In a case such as this, where the text for the most part does not follow fixed formulae and where the right edge can not be determined, continuous restoration of the type attempted by Wilhelm is methodologically unsound, as is introduction of a place-name not mentioned in the surviving text (Hiller was also sceptical, cf. *RE* XV 1602 s.v. Miletos).[72] The embassy is no less likely to have been to secure an agreement with Miletos itself, or to conduct diplomacy with some other person or city (cf. Veligianni-Terzi, 91 n. 280). Note that we have at least one other decree honouring a Milesian grain-dealer from this period

---

[72] This type of overrestoration, which can be seriously misleading, is in my view the main flaw in the work of this great epigraphist (second only to the incomparable Köhler in the quality and quantity of his contributions to Attic epigraphy). No. 61 is a similar case. See especially the comments of Wilamowitz, cited above, n. 6.

(*IG* II[2] 407, perhaps dating to the oligarchy of 321–318, cf. M.B. Walbank, *ZPE* 67, 1987, 165–6) and it does not mention Sinope; and compare the embassy sent to treat with Dionysios of Heraklea about the confiscated sails of the grain trader, Herakleides of Salamis, at no. 43, 36–41. An embassy in this type of context does not necessarily imply a trade agreement. There are many ways that grain trade might be facilitated and obstructions to it removed (cf. also above, note on no. 73). Most of Wilhelm's restorations have been removed from the text printed above. A few specific points of note:

1. As Köhler's majuscule makes clear, the third letter is apparently a bottom vertical in the centre of the stoichos. Its central position perhaps explains why Wilhelm did not venture the otherwise, for his theory, attractive, Σιν̣[ωπ-. In fact the mark is very slight; I am not certain that it represents an inscribed stroke.

2–3. Αθηνα]|ίοις ? Wilhelm, or Μιλησ]|ίοις ?

11. The left, slightly sloping, stroke of the mu is fully visible. This confirms Köhler/Velsen's αὐτίκα [μάλα and undermines Wilhelm's αὐτίκα [ἐξ Ἀθηναίων ἁπάντων.

12–13. -ουσ]|ιν *IG* II, ἀξιώσουσ]|ιν Wilhelm, or perhaps an infinitive, e.g. ποιε]|ῖν, cf. *IG* II[2] 207, 4.

13–14. ἐπιμελεῖσθ]|αι Wilhelm.

17. ἀν̣[- or ἀκ̣[-. The top of a vertical to the left of the stoichos is visible, sloping very slightly backwards as commonly with nus (less markedly kappas) in this text (read also by Velsen). There is no sign of any adjoining horizontal or curved stroke at the top, indicating that Ε, Γ, Π etc. are unlikely. Eta would be possible from trace, but not in context. Kappa is possible, but more likely we can confirm Köhler/Velsen's ἀν̣[- (with diagonal starting slightly down from the top of the vertical, as elsewhere). Again this has the effect of undermining Wilhelm's ἄ[ποικοι.

23. After the tau the top two thirds of a vertical, slightly to left of centre in the stoichos, with no adjoining stroke (cf. Velsen). Epsilon can be ruled out, undermining Wilhelm's ἰσοπο]|λιτ[είαν. Most likely, the letter was iota, in which case perhaps αἰτι̣[-.

The lettering looks quite close to Tracy's "litt. volg. c. 345–320" (*ADT* 76–81). If the honorands are grain traders, the argument for a terminus post of c. 337 is the same as for no. 81 (see previous note). Marble and script look compatible with *IG* II[2] 436 (fig. 21a), which dates to after ca. 340 (specifies type of meeting, cf. n. 24), but there is no join. Tracy has not identified the hand and there are not enough grounds for a definite association.

84. IG *II² 363 + G. Malouchou,* Hόρος *14–16 (2000–2003), 58–9 no. 2*

For ease of reference I print my text in full, including the new fragment (c) recently published by Malouchou: | 115

\- -
[ἐπὶ τῆς.....10.....ἑβδόμ]η[ς πρυταν]- stoich. 29
[είας ἧι........15.......]ΑΓΟ[...5..]
[....8....ἐγραμμάτευεν· Ἀ]ν̣θ̣ε[στηρι]-
[ῶνος........15.......τῆ]ς πρ̣υ̣[τανε]-
[ίας· ἐκκλησία κυρία· τῶν π]ροέδρω[ν ἐπ]-
[εψήφιζεν...]Σ[.....9....]εύς· *vacat*
a [ἔδοξεν] τῶι δήμω[ι· Πολύευκ]τος Σωσ[τρ]-
[άτου Σφ]ήττιος ε[ἶπεν· ἐπει]δὴ Διον[ύσ]-
[ιος πρό]τερόν τε [ἐπηγγείλ]ατο τῶι [δή]-
[μωι ἐπι]δώσειν τ[ρισχιλίου]ς μεδίμ̣ν̣-
[ους εἴ τ]ι δέοιτ[ο.....10.....]. κεν ἐν
[...προ]τερ[........16........]ΑΣΤΙ
[...6...]ΟΡΙ[.........17........]ΛΓ[.]
[....7...].[..........21.........]
lacuna
[...5..καὶ σ]τρατ[εύεσθαι αὐτὸν τὰς σ]- *c*
[τρατιὰ]ς καὶ τὰς ε[ἰσφορὰς εἰσφέρει]-
[ν μ]ετὰ Ἀθηναίων· ἀ[ναγράψαι δὲ τόδε τ]-
[ὸ ψ]ήφισμα τὸν γραμ̣[ματέια τῆς βουλῆ]-
ς ἐν στήληι λιθίνη[ι καὶ στῆσαι ἐν ἀκ]-
ροπόλει· εἰς δὲ τὴν [ἀναγραφὴν τῆς στ]-
ήλης δοῦναι τὸν τα[μίαν τοῦ δήμου : v]
ΔΔΔ δραχμὰς ἐκ τῶν [εἰς τὰ κατὰ ψηφίσ]-
ματα ἀναλισκομένω[ν τῶι δήμωι. *vac.*]
in corona [*in corona*]
[ὁ δῆμος] [ἡ βουλή]

The only other significant conjecture is Wilhelm's plausible τῆι προ]τέρ[αι σπανοσιτίαι in l. 12. In l. 11 one might consider καὶ εὐεργέτ]η̣κεν (cf. *IG* II² 506, 4; before the K there is a segment of a right vertical).

Progress may be made on the date, on which the extensive bibliography between *IG* II² and 1980 may be traced via Schwenk 67 (add M.H. Hansen, *GRBS* 23, 1982, 344 no. 50).

A conservative text of the prescript is as follows:

[..........21..........]Η[....7...] b stoich. 29
[..........21..........]ΛΓΟ[...5..]
[..........21..........]//ΙΟ̣Ι//[..5..]
[.........19.........τῆ]ς̣ πρυ[τανε]-
[ίας· ἐκκλησία κυρία· τῶν π]ρ̣οέδρω[ν ἐπ]-
[εψήφιζεν...]Σ[.....9....]ε̣ύς· *vacat*
a [ἔδοξεν] τῶι δήμω[ι· Πολύευκ]τος Σωσ[τρ]-
[άτου Σφ]ήττιος ε[ἶπεν·

The readings in lines 1–3 were thoroughly reconsidered independently of partisan controversy by Schwenk and my judgement coincides in essentials with hers.[73] In 2 there is an apparent faint cross bar on the Λ, suggesting A, but it might be a casual mark. On the Γ there are two faint marks consistent with the lower two horizontals of E. It is possible that they are casual marks. Of Ο̣ the left portion is visible such that it might be Θ or O. It is very unlikely to be a casual mark or Ω or any
116 other letter. In 3 there are traces suggesting | that the first letter may be nu. The second is Θ or O. The third is a clear left vertical, eroded such that it dips below the normal bottom of the line. An iota more than usually displaced to the left can not be ruled out with certainty, but a casual mark is highly unlikely and the traces are inconsistent with Ψ or Y. The best reading, indeed apparently the only plausible reading in context, is Ἀ]ν̣θ̣ε̣[στηριῶνος, first proposed by Wilhelm ap. *IG* II². In what follows I discount proposed restorations that are inconsistent with these readings. Σ in 6 is a new reading from autopsy, but it does not impact on the central problem.

It is uncontroversial that the decree dates between Chaironeia and 318, the period of political activity of the proposer, Polyeuktos of Sphettos. A date a little before Chaironeia could not be ruled out, but is unlikely given that the principal service of the honorand related to the grain supply, which places the decree in a group honouring grain traders none of which must be dated to before Chaironeia, and the specification of the type of Assembly, which occurs only after 340.[74] If the prescript was regular in form (admittedly not quite certain) the letters in l. 2 belonged to the nomenclature of the secretary and that too has been uncontroversial. Most names of secretaries are known at

[73] The readings of the first editor, Lolling, *SB Ak. Berlin* 1887, 1073–4, are also substantially correct: -ΛΓΟ - Ι - ΝΟΙ// - (with the O after the gamma shown as lacking a segment to the right).

[74] Cf. n. 24.

this period such that there are four years that come into consideration: 336/5, 335/4, 331/0 and 326/5.[75] I print those restorations for each of these four years which, so far as I can see, minimise epigraphical and calendrical irregularities. As has been widely recognised in post-IG II^2 scholarship,[76] the eta in l. 1 does not seem consistent with that line's being the first and is most easily accounted for by assuming that the archon was separated off in a previous line at the top, an arrangement for which there are good parallels at this period.[77]

(a) 336/5 (intercalary)

[ἐπὶ Πυθοδήλου ἄρχοντος *vac.*]
[ἐπὶ της.....10.....ἑβδόμ]η[ς πρυταν]- stoich. 29
[είας ἧι........15.......]Α̣Γ̣Ο̣[...5..]
[....8....ἐγραμμάτευεν· Ἀ]ν̣θ̣ε̣[στηρι]-
[ῶνος........15.......τῆ]ς πρυ[τανε]-
[ίας·

336/5 has not previously been suggested for this decree. The secretary of this year, which was intercalary,[78] is unknown.[79]]Α̣Γ̣Ο̣[will be from his father's name. The missing numbers in 5 might be:[80]

(a) ὀγδόηι, δωδεκάτηι. 8 Anth. (4 × 30 + 4 × 29 + 8 = 244) = pryt. VII 12 (4 × 39 + 2 × 38 + 12 = 244). The eighth of a month was a so-called monthly festival day,[81] but meetings on this day are well attested at this period.[82] This is in sequence behind the meeting on 14 Mounichion,

[75] It will be noted that this list does not include 324/3, suggested by Kirchner in *IG* II^2. As Schwenk observes, this year was ruled out by the subsequent discovery that the secretary of 324/3 was Εὐφάνης Φρύνωνος Ῥαμνούσιος.

[76] First by B.D. Meritt, *Hesp.* 10 (1941), 42–9 no. 11.

[77] E.g. no. 97 of 331/0, no. 146 of 328/7.

[78] Implied by *IG* II^2 330 = *Ath. State* I no. 3, decrees 1 and 2.

[79] It has been thought that his name had 19 letters, but this was based only on no. 86, which can as easily be dated to 335/4 (see below).

[80] In *Hesp.* 41 Meritt originally proposed omission of the date in the month and a long date-in-prytany. However, there is no firmly attested case at this period of inclusion of a month name without a date in the month.

[81] Mikalson, *Calendar* 19–20, cf. 113 and 190. As noted above (*Ath. State* IIIA n. 65) in my view there is insufficient evidence to support a case that all these days were celebrated as major state festivals or that Assemblies were systematically avoided on them.

[82] See no. 104 with M.H. Hansen, *GRBS* 23, 1982, 336–7 (8 Elaphebolion 326/5); Aeschin. III 67 and no. 3 above (8 Elaphebolion 347/6); *Ath. State* I no. 15 = *IG* II^2 338, 32 (Council meeting, 8 Metageitnion 333/2).

pryt. IX 2 of this year, attested by *Ath. State* I no. 3 = *IG* II^2 330 decree 1, assuming that both Anthesterion and Elaphebolion were full;

(b) δευτέραι, ἑβδόμηι. 2 Anth. (5 × 30 + 3 × 29 + 2 = 239) = pryt. VII 7 (4 × 39 + 2 × 38 + 7 = 239). This would also be in sequence behind the meeting on 14 Mounichion, pryt. IX 2, assuming that one of Anthesterion and Elaphebolion was full and the other was hol-
117 low. A meeting on the second of a month | (Thargelion), another so-called monthly festival day, is attested on the stone by no. 34 decree 2 (322/1), q. v.

(b) 335/4 (ordinary)

[ἐπὶ Εὐαινέτου ἄρχοντος *vac.*]
[ἐπὶ τῆς.....[10].....ἑβδόμ]η[ς *vac.*] stoich. 29
[πρυτανείας· Πρόξενος Πυλ]αγό̣[ρου Ἀχ]-
[ερδούσιος ἐγραμμάτευε· Ἀ]ν̣θ̣ε̣[στηρι]-
[ῶνος ἐνδεκάτηι, τρίτηι τῆ]ς πρυ[τανε]-
[ίας

This year was first suggested by Meritt, *TAPA* 95 (1964), 213–7. There is no problem with accommodating the known secretary of the year in ll. 3–4, but the preceding text is impossible without substantial irregularity. Meritt's own solution was:

[..........[22]...........ἐπ' Εὐαιν]-
[έτου ἄρχοντος ἐπὶ τῆς...]η[ίδος πρυ]-
[τανείας ^{v} ἧι Πρόξενος κτλ.

The inclusion of a heading such as *name of honorand* προξενία before the archon is well paralleled at this period,[83] but the piling up of multiple irregularities in this solution is not attractive. In particular Meritt supplies no parallel for the inclusion of the name, but not the number, of the prytany.[84] It seems preferable to stick with the assumption of an archon separated off at the top. It is then a matter of arranging the prytany specification in a way which minimises irregularity. This is most easily done by assuming an irregularity in the stoichedon at line-end, in a sense already present if the archon was separated off at the top. Note also the minor line-end irregularities at l. 18, γραμ̣[ματέια or γραμ̣[ματέα + *vacat*, and l. 21 of the new fragment. The solution

[83] E.g. no. 13; no. 14; no. 27.

[84] There is no parallel for this in a prescript at this period, nor, so far as I know, in any other prescript before the Christian era.

I have printed above is one possibility. Another (unattractive) would be ἑβδόμ]η[ς πρ^vvv^υτανείας ἧι Πρόξενος κτλ.

For the date the possibilities would seem to be:

(a) ἐνδεκάτηι, τρίτηι, first suggested by Meritt, *Ath. Year* 88–9 (in relation to 331/0). 11 Anth. (3 × 30 + 4 × 29 + 11 = 217) = pryt. VII 3 (4 × 36 + 2 × 35 + 3 = 217). This coincides with the Pithogia, first day of the Anthesteria. Normally Assemblies on major festival days were avoided, but the rule was far from absolute and in any case it is possible that the pithos-opening took place in the evening, allowing time for an Assembly earlier in the day (suggested by Humphreys, *Strangeness* 226). Alternatively, with Hansen, one can assume a minor calendrical irregularity and restore the date in the month as δωδεκάτηι.

(b) δεκάτηι, δευτέραι. I.e. the day before (a). In decree prescripts δεκάτηι in a month is normally qualified ἱσταμένου, προτέραι or ὑστέραι (as at this period in no. 97 of 10th Skir. 331/0), but an unqualified appearance is not impossible (as apparently in the lost *IG* II^2 905 (archon Sonikos)).

(c) 331/0 (ordinary)

[ἐπὶ Ἀριστοφάνους ἄρχοντος *vac.*]
[ἐπὶ τῆς.....^{10}.....ἑβδόμ]η[ς πρυταν]- stoich. 29
[είας ἧι........^{15}.......]Α̣Γ̣Ο̣[...^{5}..]
[....^{8}....ἐγραμμάτευεν· Ἀ]ν̣θ̣ε̣[στηρι]-
[ῶνος ἐνδεκάτηι, τρίτηι (or δεκάτηι, δευτέραι, alternatives as (b)) τῆ]ς πρυ[τανε]-
[ίας· | 118

This year was first suggested by Meritt, *Ath. Year*. Meritt tried to accommodate in 2–3 the name on the moulding of no. 78, which at that time was thought to be the secretary of 331/0, but this is dubious (see note on no. 78). There is no other evidence for the secretary of this year.]Α̣Γ̣Ο̣[would be from his father's name. This solution entails assumption of no epigraphical irregularity beyond the separating off of the archon at the top, a feature already attested for this year by no. 97.

(d) 326/5 (ordinary)

[ἐπὶ Χρέμητος ἄρχοντος *vac.*]
[ἐπὶ τῆς Ἐρεχθηίδος ἑβδόμ]η[ς πρυταν]- stoich. 29
[είας ἧι Κηφ̣ισοκλῆς...^{5}..]Α̣Γ̣Ο̣[...^{5}..]
[....^{8}....ἐγραμμάτευεν· Ἀ]ν̣θ̣ε̣[στηρι]-

[ῶνος ἐνδεκάτηι, τρίτηι (or δεκάτηι, δευτέραι, alternatives as (b)) τῆ]ς πρυ[τανε]-
[ίας·

This year was first suggested by Meritt, *Hesp.* 10 (1941), 48–9. It was supported by Schwenk, whose opinion has since been accepted by others.[85] The secretary of this year, who is from tribe VII according to the secretary cycle, is known from *IG* II^2 800 = Schwenk 64 (year confirmed by *Ath. State* I no. 12 = *SEG* XXXV 74) to be Κηφισοκλῆς [-$^{c.\ 15-16}$-]. This could be made consistent with the space available in our decree by assuming a name such as Κηφισοκλῆς Ἀριστ]αγό[ρου Δαλιδαλίδης, though this would entail assumption of an abbreviated demotic in *IG* II^2 800 = Schwenk 64. Abbreviated demotics for secretaries are not common (and they do not appear elsewhere on *IG* II^2 800 = Schwenk 64), but do occasionally occur at this period.[86] A more serious problem is caused by the fact that a *kyria ekklesia* for this prytany of 326/5 is already attested by no. 104, which dates to 8 Elaph. = 30th of the 7th pryt. of Erechtheis.[87] Two assemblies of this description in a single prytany would be a serious irregularity.[88]

Grain shortages were doubtless a perennial cause of anxiety. However, in 336/5 or 335/4 the precise reference of the "previous grain shortage", if correctly restored, would be somewhat obscure. There is evidence for anxiety about the grain supply after Chaironeia, but not for a definite shortage (cf. *Ath. State* IIIA n. 68). In 331/0 the shortage would be the well-attested one in 335 (Dem. XXXIV 38 cf. Tracy, *ADT* 33). In 326/5 it would either be that one or an earlier phase of the shortage attested in 330–326 (Tracy, *ADT* 33).

On balance 331/0 seems to be the strongest possibility. 336/5 is possible. 335/4 and 326/5 can not be ruled out, but are much weaker options.

It would seem from fr. c, ll. 15–17, which bestows the privilege of paying taxes and doing military service on the same basis as Athenians, that the honorand of this decree was (or was to be) a metic and this accords well with the natural implication of the introductory

[85] E.g. Tracy, *ADT* 31.

[86] Certainly in no. 7 and no. 43. Cf. below on no. 86.

[87] No good case can be made for doubting this equation, which is partially restored. See Schwenk; Hansen, *GRBS* 23 (1982), 336–7.

[88] This problem was first noted by Pritchett–Neugebauer, 54–5. Cf. RO p. 509.

clauses that he was a grain trader. The inscription belongs in a series with the large group from this period which honour such grain traders (marked [G] in the list). The name Dionysios is extremely common and Meritt's suggested identification with the tyrant of Herakleia Pontika (*Hesp.* 1941, cf. no. 43), never more than remotely possible, now falls.

86. IG *II² 328 = Schwenk 15*

The left side of this decree, probouleumatic and proposed by Lykourgos, is not preserved. It is conventionally restored at stoich. 28, a length indicated by the formulaic lines 11–15, and dated to the intercalary year 336/5 (Maimakterion 27, discussion and earlier bibliography at Schwenk 15; or Metageitnion 27, Hansen). However, another year in the period 340/39–324/3 can also be restored, i.e. 335/4: | 119

335/4 [ἐπὶ Εὐαινέτου ἄρχοντος ἐπ]ὶ τῆς Ἀ[κ]- stoich. 28
[αμαντίδος τετάρτης πρυτ]ανείας ἧ-
[ι Πρόξενος Ἀχερδούσιος ἐ]γραμμάτ-
[ευεν· Μαιμακτηριῶνος τετ]ράδι φθί-
[νοντος, ἕκτει καὶ τριακοστ]εῖ τῆς πρ- 29 letters
[υτανείας· τῶν προέδρων ἐπ]εψήφιζε
[.........^{20}.........ἔ]δοξεν τῆ-
[ι βουλῆι καὶ τῶι δήμωι· Λυκο]ῦργος Λυ- 29 letters
[κόφρονος Βουτάδης εἶπε· περ]ὶ ὧν λέγ̣- 29 letters
[ει...^{5}..ς, δεδόχθαι τῆι βουλ]ῆι τοὺ-
[ς προέδρους οἳ ἂν λάχωσιν πρ]οεδρε-
[ύειν εἰς τὴν πρώτην ἐκκλησί]αν προ-
[σαγαγεῖν αὐτὸν εἰς τὸν δῆμ]ον καὶ [χ]-
[ρηματίσαι, γνώμην δὲ ξυμβ]άλλεσθα-
[ι τῆς βουλῆς εἰς τὸν δῆμον] ὅτι δοκε-
[ῖ τῆι βουλῆι, ἐπειδὴ...^{5}..]ς Εὔπορ[.]
[..........^{22}..........]ΙΠΓ̣[...]

1–2. The known prytanies in 335/4 are: pryt. 5 = Akamantis or Pandionis (no. 139);[89] pryt. 10 = Antiochis (e.g. no. 87).

[89] E. Schweigert, *Hesp.* 9 (1940), 327–8 no. 36 restored Ἀκαμαν]τ̣ίδος, but I agree with Schwenk in being unable to confirm the T (she also doubts the iota). In fact, the surface is not preserved at this point. There is a line of damage or erosion just where the vertical of a tau would be expected and this might give the impression of a vertical stroke on a squeeze. So Πανδιον]ίδος is possible.

3. Spacing suggests that the secretary's father's name was omitted (cf. e.g. no. 94; Henry, *Prescripts* 42–3). The secretary of 336/5 is unknown. The secretary of 335/4 was Πρόξενος Πυλαγόρου Ἀχερδούσιος (for whom see *Agora* XVI 76; no. 87 etc.), whose name + demotic suits exactly the space available.

4–6. In an ordinary year in which three of the first four months are hollow and one is full (or in which there is an irregularity of one day), 27 Maimakterion = 144th day ((1 × 30) + (3 × 29) + 27), 36th of pryt. 4 = 144th day (36 × 4). No datum for this year is inconsistent with these assumptions. The restoration of l. 5 yields a line length of 29 letters. There are two other lines where a case can be made for 29 letter restorations:

- L. 9, where the currently accepted restoration, printed above, also yields 29 letters. There can be no doubt that the proposer's name is correct. One might alternatively achieve a 28 letter line by restoring e.g. Λυκοῦργος Λυ|[κόφρονος Βουτάδ(ης) εἶπεν. Abbreviation of the proposer's demotic occurs at this period (e.g. no. 7 decree 1), but is uncommon.
- L. 8 has previously been restored with 28 letters and βολῆι for βουλῆι, but there was apparently no other case of -ο for -ου in this text. One might therefore restore βουλῆι for a 29-letter line.

No festivals or Assemblies are otherwise attested on Maimakterion 27 (Mikalson, *Calendar* 85).

The decree was probouleumatic, implying that Lykourgos was on the Council in the year it was passed (cf. Rhodes, *Boule* 108 n. 4, 250). *IG* II^2 1672, 302 refers to a decree of the Council proposed by Lykourgos about the sacrifice of an *aresterion* at Eleusis, apparently dating to a second period of office on the Council (329/8?).

I note that there is now no extant inscribed law or decree proposed by Lykourgos which certainly predates (a) the beginning of his first period of tenure ἐπὶ τῇ διοικήσει on Lewis' view (i.e. 336, cf. *Ath. State* II p. 138), (b) 335, Knoepfler's date for the acquisition of Oropos following the settlement with Alexander (*Eretria* XI 367–89, cf. *Ath. State* I p. 107). Including both self-standing laws and decrees and those referred to elsewhere in the epigraphical record, the
120 dates are: |

1. *Ath. State* III no. 37 = J. Camp, *Hesp.* 43 (1974) 322–4 no. 3: c. 337–325
2. This decree: 336/5 or 335/4
3. *IG* II² 1623, 276–85: 335/4 (joint proposal with Aristonikos of Marathon, cf. *Ath. State* I p. 108 n. 79)
4. *Ath. State* II no. 6 = *IG* II² 333: c. 335
5. *Ath. State* I no. 21 = *IG* II² 414 fr. a: 334/3?
6. *Ath. State* II no. 4 = *IG* II² 337 = RO 91: 333/2
7. *Ath. State* III no. 96 = *IG* II² 345: 332/1
8. *Ath. State* III no. 42 = *IG* II² 351 + 624: 330/29
9. *IG* II² 1672, 302: 329/8 or shortly before?
10. *IG* II² 1672, 303: 329/8 or shortly before?
11. *Ath. State* III no. 146 = *IG* II² 452: 328/7

B. *Decrees which possibly honoured foreigners or Athenians*

	Date	Reference	Honorand	Honour
113	mid-iv ? (K)[90]	*IG* II² 294.[91]	–	–
114	mid-iv ? (K)	*IG* II² 302.	Hegelochos or Hegeleos[92]	hosp. or dinner
115	mid-iv ? (K)	*IG* II² 296; Veligianni, A137.	–	gold c
116	mid-iv ? (K)	*IG* II² 323; P. Charneux, *BCH* 107 (1983), 266 (*SEG* XXXIII 284).	Kallias?[93]	–[94]

[90] "Litt. volg. s. iv" and "ante a. 336/5" (Kirchner).

[91] Not certainly a state decree. The chief officials of tribes were *epimeletai* (l. 7, cf. *IG* II² 1138, 8; 1139, 8 etc.).

[92] L. 6 may be restored, with Köhler, καλέσαι δὲ Ἡγέλ[οχον ἐπὶ ξένια, in which case Hegelochos will have been a foreigner, i.e. honorand of the decree, or possibly an envoy. Ἡγέλ[εω ἐπὶ δεῖπνον, however, is also possible, in which case he was probably an Athenian citizen (envoy?). Cf. e.g. no. 24; *Ath. State* I 86 n. 5.

[93] The left side is preserved. The only legible words are:
3 [Κ]αλλίαν Α[---]
ο πρ̣οξε[ν.....]
Kallias was a very common name and supplies insufficient basis to posit a connection with the Καλλίας Ἀ[- who was *proxenos* at Argos in iii BC (cf. Charneux).

[94] ο προξε[ν (perhaps ὁ πρόξε[νος) is not perhaps from an award of proxeny, but reference to an existing *proxenos* (cf. no. 107 b5).

Table (*cont.*)

		Date	Reference	Honorand	Honour
	117	mid-iv ? (K)	*IG* II² 320.[95]	–	c?[96]
	118	mid-iv ? (K)	*IG* II² 316.[97]	–	c
121	119	mid-iv ? (K)	*IG* II² 315.	–	c |
	120	mid-iv ? (K)	*IG* II² 314.	–	c
	121	mid-iv ? (K)	*IG* II² 313.	–	c[98]
	122	mid-iv ? (K)	*IG* II² 311.[99]	–[100]	–
	123	c. 350–340[101]	*IG* II² 257 + 300; M.B. Walbank, *ABSA* 85 (1990), 442–3 no. 12 (*SEG* XL 70); Veligianni, A138; Tracy, *ADT* 70.	–[102]	–

[95] The stone is now illegible, but there are good squeezes in Berlin. From them I read in ll. 5–8: φρατρι - | -ν τοὺς δ- | δο]ῦναι.. - | - ΣΤΩΝ ΕΠ -.

[96] If this was a decree of the Assembly, awarding a crown (στ]εφα[ν-, my reading of l. 1), one might restore ll. 5–8 to yield wording from a grant of Athenian citizenship, viz. γράψασθαι δὲ φυλῆς καὶ δήμου καὶ] φρατρί[ας--]ν τοὺς δ[ὲ πρυτάνεις -] δοῦναι [τὴν ψῆφον. The plural τὰ κοινά (l. 11), however, raises the alternative possibility that this was a decree of a corporate group, perhaps a phratry (l. 5, see e.g. *IG* II² 1237, 98). For phratries on the Athenian acropolis cf. e.g. *IG* II² 1238 = S.D. Lambert, *The Phratries of Attica*² (1998), T16; O. Palagia, *Hesp.* 64 (1995), 493–501. In that case l. 8,]ΣΤΩΝ ΕΠ[-, might be the name of the group (cf. Rationes, F11A, 5, Διπολιαστῶν ἐπιμεληταὶ), though there are clearly other possibilities.

[97] Decree of state or other group.

[98] Above remains of two crowns the very bottom of a text is preserved. Before the omega read by previous eds. in l. 1 is the lower section of a vertical stroke. The whole should perhaps be restored: ἐκ] τῶν ε[ἰς τὰ κατὰ ψηφίσματα ἀναλισκομένων τῶι δή]|μωι ⋮ Ͱ ⋮ διδόναι (stoich. 41). Compare the 1 drachma public subsidy paid to the exile Peisitheides of Delos (no. 8, 37–41). If the arrangement of the crowns was symmetrical one would expect 34 letters per line (if 2 crowns) or 51 letters (if 3 crowns), but symmetry in this matter was not always observed (e.g. the arrangement on no. 8 was not symmetrical).

[99] The stone is now illegible.

[100] The only preserved letters, on a moulding, are restored by Kirchner Θη]βαίω-. Alternatively one might think of a personal name such as Εὐβαίων (cf. *LGPN* II 163) or the month, Ἑκατομβαιών.

[101] Work of Tracy's "Cutter of *IG* II² 105", 368–339 BC. Inclusion of a hortatory intention clause suggests a date after c. 350. See A.S. Henry, *ZPE* 112 (1996), 105–19.

[102] Kirchner restored ὅπως [ἂν τὸ λοιπὸν ἅπαντ]ες φιλοτιμῶνται (ll. 7–8), which lacks a parallel. Preferable is [ἂν καὶ οἱ ἄλλοι ἄρχον]τες φιλοτιμῶνται, as at *IG* II² 488 =

Table (*cont.*)

	Date	Reference	Honorand	Honour	
124	c. 350–325[103]	*Agora* XVI 69 (ph.).	–[104]	–	
125	c. 350–325	O. Walter, *Öst. Jh.* 18 (1915), Beibl. 91–2 (ph.); P. Jacobsthal, *JHS* 58 (1938), 211 (ph.); Lawton no. 126 (ph.).	Two men (implicit in relief)	c	
126	c. 350–325	*IG* II^2 4630; Lawton no. 133 (ph.).	–[105]	–	
127	c. 350–325	Lawton no. 137 (ph.).	–	c	
128	c. 350–325	L. von Sybel, *Katalog der Sculpturen zu Athen* (1881) no. 5993; W. Peek, *AM* 67 (1942), 6 no. 2; Lawton no. 139 (ph.).	–	c	
129	c. 350–325	L.J. Roccos, *Hesp.* 60 (1991), 409 no. 4 (*SEG* XLI 134); Lawton no. 142 (ph.).	–	–	
130	c. 350–320[106]	Lawton no. 166 (ph.).	Two or three men	– |	122
131	c. 345–320 (T)	R. Stroud, *Hesp.* 40 (1971), 178–9 no. 26 (ph.); Osborne, *Nat.* X 32 (*SEG* XXXIII 101); Tracy, *ADT* 78.	Pant-	500 dr. gold c[107] + privilege in relation to eisphora?[108]	

SEG L 143, 19–20. In that case, as I noted at *Ath. State* I p. 111, the decree honoured one or more Athenian officials.

103 Tracy, per ep., on the basis of the lettering.

104 In l. 1 *Agora* XVI reads Π]αλληνεῖ Η[, taken by Woodhead to be the honorand. From autopsy and the Princeton squeeze I read Π]αλληνεὺ[ς, which will be the demotic of the proposer. Read (ll. 1–5): Π]αλληνεὺ[ς εἶπεν· ἐπειδή -|- πρότερόν] τε πρὸς τὸν δῆ[μον |-----]ππος ΤΟΥΣΤΕ[....|-----]ν ἐστεφάνωσ[εν..|---ἐψηφί]σατο ὁ δῆμος [-]. -ππος was the honorand or possibly an ancestor and there had been a previous crowning and decree in his favour.

105 The relief portrays three figures labelled [Δ]ημος (?) (seated) and Ἀθηνᾶ crowning Ἡρακλῆς. I doubt Lawton's reading, [θεο]ί above the names. This might be an honorific decree for a Herakleot (cf. no. 49, no. 143), but other interpretations are possible.

106 I read: [ἐπὶ Θεοφράστ]ου (340/39) ἄ[ρχ]οντο[ς ἐπὶ τῆς --|- πρυτανείας] ἧι [Ἄσπ]ε[τος or Εὐαινέτ]ου (335/4) ἄ[ρχ]οντο[ς ἐπὶ τῆς --|- πρυτανείας] ἧι [Πρό]ξ[ενος. Cf. no. 30.

107 Uncommon in state decrees at this period. It might suggest a decree of the Council (cf. no. 43 with footnote) or a non-state decree (see next note).

108 Cf. *IG* II^2 141, 29–36? It is uncertain whether the honorand was an Athenian (cf. *Ath. State* I p. 88) or a foreigner. A non-state decree is not impossible. Eisphora provisions (if that is what we have to do with in l. 8,]ι τῶν εἰσφ[-) occasionally occur

Table (*cont.*)

		Date	Reference	Honorand	Honour
	132[109]	c. 340–322/1[110]	*IG* II^2 293.	–	c
	133	c. 340–320 (T)	*IG* II^2 539; Osborne, *Nat.* PT150 (*SEG* XXXIII 83); Tracy, *ADT* 99.	[D?]elian[111]	[1000 dr.?] gold c[112]
	134	c. 340–320?	M.B. Walbank, *Hesp.* 58 (1989), 82–3 no. 8 (ph.) (*SEG* XXXIX 78); *Agora* XVI 81.	–[113]	–
123	134a	339/8[114]	E. Schweigert, *Hesp.* 7 (1938), 291–2 no. 18 (ph.) (*SEG* XVI 52); A.M. Woodward, *ABSA* 51 (1956), 2–3 no. V.	Theophantos?[115]	– |

in such decrees, mainly in leases, e.g. *IG* II^2 1241, 16; 2492, 24–7; *SEG* XXIV 151, 31. The verb in l. 7 might be εἶ]ναι or δοῦ]ναι.

[109] See note on no. 45.

[110] "Litt. volg. med. s. iv" (Kirchner). -ει for -ηι in the dative singular ending, λιθίνει, l. 4, is suggestive of a date after c. 340–330. Cf. Threatte I 378.

[111] Cf. *ID* 1507; above no. 8.

[112] On the crown value cf. footnote to no. 43. In l. 10 S.A. Koumanoudes, *Arch. Eph.* 1886, 110 no. 20 correctly read]ν ψηφι[, which rules out Köhler's δοῦναι τὴ]ν ψῆφ[ον τοὺς πρυτάνεις and a consequential identification of this as a citizenship decree. In light of the reference to the confirmation of previous grants in l. 5 we should perhaps read τὸ πρότερο]ν ψήφι[σμα (cf. e.g. *IG* II^2 182) and a requirement to inscribe the decree placed on τὸν κατὰ πρυ]ταν[είαν γραμματέα (l. 11).

[113] Walbank suggests that this was a decree bestowing honours for ransoming of captives, restoring [τῆ]ς ἐλευθ[ερίας in l. 3 (the theta, printed in square brackets by *Agora* XVI, is preserved) and τοὺ]ς μὲ[ν] λυτ[ρωσάμενος in ll. 8–9. Too little text survives for confidence. In l. 3 one might alternatively have to do with (a person from?) Ἐλευθεραί or Ἐλεύθερνα or even with Zeus Ἐλευθέριος or Dionysos Ἐλευθερεύς and ME[.]AYT[is a possible reading in l. 9 (alpha lacks cross-bar in l. 4).

[114] This is the only vacant year at this period for a secretary from Leontis (IV). He is attested only here and, with Schweigert, should be read [-$^{c.\ 12-13}$-]ωνος Χολλεί(δης)$^{(IV)}$ (Woodward suggested [Με]ιδῶνος, but the reading, based only on a photograph, is incorrect). *IG* II 221 has been thought to show that the name was Φαῖδρος, but the authenticity of this inscription is in doubt. See *Ath. State* I no. 8. The archon is absent from the prescript of this decree, as preserved. Was he omitted altogether or was he inscribed separately on the upper moulding (the spring of which is preserved on the left side of the fragment)? The same question arises with comparable fragments whose top is not fully preserved (most acutely with no. 7, q. v., but also e.g. with *SEG* XLVII 126). Unfortunately it can not be answered satisfactorily on current evidence. At this period there is no state law or decree heading an inscription with fully preserved top which lacks an archon date (on no. 43 decrees 2–5 lack archons, but decree 1 has one). On the other hand, while the archon was occasionally placed in a line to itself at the top of the main column of text (e.g. no. 146, no. 97), there is also no case certainly dating to this period in which the archon is inscribed on an upper moulding or in a heading

Table (*cont.*)

	Date	Reference	Honorand	Honour
135[116]	337/6	E. Schweigert, *Hesp.* 9 (1940), 325–7 no. 35 (ph.); M.H. Hansen, *GRBS* 23 (1982), 342 no. 21; Schwenk 5 (*SEG* XXXV 63); Tracy, *ADT* 78; *Agora* XVI 72; E. Arena, *ASAtene* 80 (2002), 309–25 (ph.); Brun, *Démade* 177 no. 2, cf. 149; Humphreys, *Strangeness* 82 n. 12 (*SEG* XXXVI 150), 123.	Mentions Lemnos[117]	c?
136	337–323 (T)	M.B. Walbank, *Hesp.* 51 (1982), 45–6 no. 4 (ph.) (*SEG* XXXII 74); *Agora* XVI 106F; Tracy, *ADT* 114 (*SEG* XLV 57); Veligianni, A176.	–	c?
137	c. 335 (T)	B.D. Meritt, *Hesp.* 29 (1960), 5 no. 4 (ph.) (*SEG* XIX 63); *Agora* XVI 152; Tracy, *ADT* 119.	-anias?	–

---

separated off from the main body of text. Placing the archon in a separate heading was fairly common in the earlier 4th century, but the practice seems to have died out about 350 (the latest securely dated case is *IG* II² 129 of 356/5, cf. Henry, *Prescripts* 23 n. 13, 34). The closest we have to exceptions on normal decree stelai (with dedications carrying decrees the archon may be included in a dedicatory formula at the top, e.g. *IG* II² 223 = *Ath. State* I no. 1) are no. 18 of c. 350?, where the archon is included in a heading with the honorand; and the unique no. 78 (q.v.), c. 337–323, where the whole prescript, possibly but not certainly including an archon date, is inscribed in the pedimental moulding at the top. In *SEG* XVI 55 = *Ath. State* II no. 8, which is sui generis, the secretary is in a separate heading, but it is uncertain whether he was preceded by an archon.

115 In ll. 5–6 read: περὶ ὧν | λέ]γει Θεόφαντος, the four letters ΕΟΦΑ occupying 3 stoichoi (Schweigert's Θ[..]ΑΝΙΟΣ was not far wrong; Woodward's Θ[...]ημος is incorrect). In ll. 8–9 restore προσ[αγαγεῖν Θεόφαντο|ν]. Theophantos was probably the honorand, an Athenian (as e.g. *IG* II² 243 = *Ath. State* I no. 20) or a foreigner (as e.g. *IG* II² 109). It is uncertain whether he is the same as the Theophantos honoured by no. 13 and no. 41.

116 The two fragments (fr. a from the beginning of a decree proposed by Demades and including the archon date) are compatible physically and as regards the script, but the line length in fr. b can not be established and a measure of caution about Schweigert's association is in place. The same mason might naturally inscribe more than one inscription in the same script and on the same type of stone (cf. *ZPE* 136, 2001, 65–70 = no. 106; no. 63 with note). In this case the only textual link is supplied by the readings περὶ ὧν οἱ θε|σμο]θέτα[ι λέγουσι in fr. a, 7 and θ]εσμοθετ- in fr. b, 27, but in fr. a there are other possibilities, e.g. a personal name, Πεισ]θέτα[ιρος.

117 Lemnos is mentioned twice in fr. b (ll. 10 and 19). The decree can be restored as honorific, but is so fragmentary that even that is uncertain. It can not be ruled out that it mentioned places other than Lemnos. e.g. in l. 19 one might think of Λ]ήμνωι κ[αὶ Ἴμβρωι καὶ Σκύρωι, cf. *SEG* XLVIII 96, 7.

Table (*cont.*)

	Date	Reference	Honorand	Honour
138*	335–322/1?	*IG* II² 171; J. Svoronos, *Das Athener Nationalmuseum* (Athens, 1908–37), 347–8 no. 93 (ph.); Lawton no. 153 (ph.).	Artikleides	c
139	335/4[118]	E. Schweigert, *Hesp.* 9 (1940), 327–8 no. 36 (ph.); Schwenk 19 (*SEG* XXXV 67); *Agora* XVI 76.	–[119]	
140	334/3–314/3 (T)	*IG* II² 601; Tracy, *ADT* 124.	–	c
141	334/3–314/3 (T)	E. Schweigert, *Hesp.* 8 (1939), 27–30 no. 7 fr. f (ph.); [as no. 106]; Lambert, *ZPE* 136 (2001), 68 no. 4b (*SEG* LI 87).	–[120]	–
124 142	334/3–314/3 (T)	*IG* II² 414 b; E. Schweigert, *Hesp.* 9 (1940), 335–9 no. 42 fr. k (ph.); [as no. 106]; Lambert, *ZPE* 136 (2001), 69 no. 4d (*SEG* LI 89).	–[121]	– |
143	330/29 or 329/8[122]	O. Walter, *Beschreibung der Reliefs im kleinen Akropolismuseum in Athen* (1923), 16–17 no. 17 (ph.); Lawton no. 129 (ph.).	Herakleot? (implicit in relief, cf. no. 49)	–
144	c. 330–300	W. Peek, *Kerameikos* III no. 1 (ph.); M.H. Hansen, *C&M* 38 (1987), 75–9 (*SEG* XXXVIII 68).	–	–[123]

[118] On the prytany (perhaps Pandionis rather than Akamantis) see n. 89.

[119] A possible reading of ll. 7–8 is:
[ᵛ Δημάδης] Δημέου Παιανιε[ὺς εἶπ]-
[εν· ἐπειδὴ Κ]α̣λ̣[λίξ]ενο̣[ς
However, the traces of the dotted letters are too slight for confidence.

[120] προγ[- (l. 5) might be a reference to ancestors in an honorific decree for a foreigner.

[121] δωρεὰς (l. 4) suggests an honorific decree. It may be for a foreigner (thus previous eds.) or perhaps an Athenian, if we restore along the lines: ὅπως ἂν καὶ οἱ ἄλλοι χ]ειροτο[νηθέντες - φιλοτιμῶνται περὶ τὸν δῆμον τὸν Ἀθηναί]ων εἰδό[τες ὅτι -] δωρεὰς [, cf. e.g. *IG* II² 330+445 = *Ath. State* I no. 3, 21; no. 43, 64–6.

[122] Walter noted that the archon is Ἀριστο]φῶν[τος (330/29) or Κηφισο]φῶν[τος (329/8). Traces in l. 2 suggest ἐπὶ τῆς -ίδο]ς τ[ρίτης or τ[ετάρτης πρυτανείας.

[123] For ll. 5–7 Peek suggested ὅτι ἀνὴρ ἀγαθός ἐστι περὶ τὸ]ν δῆμον τὸ[ν Ἀθηναίων καὶ τοῖς ἀεί πε]ριτυνχ[άνουσιν Ἀθηναίων χρήσιμος ὢν διατελεῖ. If this is on the right lines, the decree honoured a foreigner. ἐ]ι̣[πε]ιδὴ ἡ βο[υλὴ (l. 4), however, raises the possibility that it was a decree of the Assembly honouring the Council (cf. *IG* II²

'able (*cont.*)

	Date	Reference	Honorand	Honour
45	c. 330–300[124]	*IG* II² 548; S. Dow, *Hesp.* 32 (1963), 351 (*SEG* XXI 323).	–	–
46	328/7	*IG* II² 452; W.K. Pritchett, *Ancient Athenian Calendars on Stone* (Berkeley, 1963), 281–3; Schwenk 53; C. Habicht, *Chiron* 19 (1989), 4 (*SEG* XXXIX 89) (see above, notes on no. 56 and no. 86).	–[125]	
47	326/5[126]	*IG* II² 800; S. Dow, *Hesp.* 32 (1963), 358–63 (ph.) (*SEG* XXI 289); Schwenk 64.	-leos?	–
48[127]	324/3	B.D. Meritt, *Hesp.* 10 (1941), 50–2 no. 13 (ph.); Schwenk 72 (*SEG* XXXV 75); *Agora* XVI 92; Lawton no. 48; Tracy, *ADT* 124, 128; Veligianni, A177.	–	gold c | 125

223 = *Ath. State* I no. 1, B 7). The prescript is too fragmentary to restore with confidence. Hansen restored an "old-style" prescript structure, detecting in [Ἀχ]αρνε[ὺς (l. 1) the secretary of 347/6, known to be from that deme. However, as Lewis noted ap. Hansen 79 n. 12, the hand suggests a later date. A possible "new style" scheme is:

> -----------------
> [- ἐγραμμάτευεν *name + father's name*]
> [Ἀχ]αρνε[ὺς· τῶν προέδρων ἐπεψήφιζεν]
> [Δυ]σνίκη[τος *demotic. Name*]
> [..]ος Ἀρισ[τ- *demotic* εἶπεν· ἐ]-
> [πε]ιδὴ ἡ βο[υλὴ -

For the word order ἐγραμμάτευεν + name cf. e.g. no. 72, 4. Aside from 347/6 the secretary was from Acharnai in 337/6 and 327/6. Alternatively, as Lewis suggested, we may have to do with a list of *symproedroi*, in which case the date was probably not earlier than 333/2 (earliest case: no. 7, decree II).

124 The alpha of the demotic Ἀζην[ιεύς (l. 1) is legible on the Berlin squeeze (not legible now at autopsy or on the squeeze examined by Dow); as Wilhelm noted, it was probably the demotic of a *symproedros*. The earliest firmly dated decree with named *symproedroi* is no. 7 decree II, of 333/2. Since Azenia is now known to have been in Hippothontis before and after 307/6 and at both periods Hippothontis was the antepenultimate tribe in the official sequence (see J.S. Traill, *Hesp. Suppl.* 14, 1975, Table VIII), *pace IG* II² and Dow, no inference can any longer be drawn that the inscription dates to before 307/6. In fact the emphasis given to the proposer by the long vacat at the end of l. 3, though it occurs earlier, is especially common in the years 307–301 (Henry, *Prescripts* 63–6; S.V. Tracy, *Hesp.* 69, 2000, 227–33). Dow dates the lettering c. 330–300.

125 ἐπειδὴ --] ἐπιμε[λ- ? Dow. Or a name, Ἐπιμε[ν-?

126 Dow's dating of this inscription was confirmed by the publication of *SEG* XXXV 74 = *Ath. State* I no. 12 (same secretary).

127 The inscription as published by Meritt consists of three non-joining fragments. The relief on fr. a, with Athena to the left of a figure in smaller scale, indicates that

Table (*cont.*)

	Date	Reference	Honorand	Honour
149	323/2	*IG* II² 367 + Walter, *Öst. Jh.* 18 (1915) Beiblatt 91; C.J. Schwenk, *Antike Kunst* 19 (1976), 64–6 (ph.); S. Miller, *Hesp. Suppl.* 20 (1982), 103; A.N. Oikonomides, *AW* 5 (1982), 123–7 (*SEG* XXXII 91); Schwenk 81; Lawton no. 49 (ph.).	Mentions (honours?) Asklepiodoros in diplomatic context involving Phokians[128]	c [implicit in relief]
150	322/1	*IG* II² 372 + Add. p. 660; E. Schweigert, *Hesp.* 8 (1939), 173–5 no. 4 (ph.); J. Pečírka, *Listy fil.* 89 (1966), 262–6 (ph.); M.H. Hansen, *GRBS* 23 (1982), 345 no. 56; Schwenk 87; *Agora* XVI 95; Tracy, *ADT* 152; Brun, *Démade* 177 no. 13; Lambert, *Polis and Theatre.*	L]yk- or E]uk-?[129] [Theat.]	–

it probably honoured a foreigner (reliefs are not normally found on decrees honouring Athenians at this period). The line length is stoich. 31. Fr. c, broken on all sides, preserves 10 letters from a crowning clause, restored by Meritt: χ[ρυσῶι στεφάνωι | απο:.: δραχμῶν ἀ]ρετῆ[ς ἕνεκα καὶ δικαlιοσύνης τῆς εἰς] τὸν δῆ[μον. However, as Veligianni-Terzi points out, δικαιοσύνη is normally mentioned in decrees honouring Athenians, not foreigners (no. 40 is an exception). If, as she suggests, we replace it with εὐνοίας, the effect is to disturb Meritt's restoration of the fragment to the same line length as fr. a and to raise doubts about whether the two fragments are from the same inscription. The fragments otherwise appear compatible and were found together in the Agora, albeit in a Turkish context (grave XXXI in north peristyle of Hephaisteion, Agora grid E7), which might be accounted for by secondary use. Fr. b, a small fragment preserving no complete word, was found in grid F6. It may belong with the other two, but again certainty is impossible. These three fragments belong in a group cut by Tracy's "Cutter of EM 12807" with letter heights c. 0.007–0.008 and roughly square stoichedon grids c. 0.016–0.018. I separated some other incorrectly associated fragments in the group at *ZPE* 136 (2001), 65–70 (cf. no. 106). See also no. 90.

[128] The context may be diplomacy following the death of Alexander. (cf. H.H. Schmitt, *Die Staatsverträge des Altertums* III 24–5 no. 413). It is not very likely that the honorand was an Athenian envoy to Phokis (suggested by Oikonomides), since there would be no parallel at this period for a decree the main purpose of which was to honour an Athenian envoy (cf. *Ath. State* I) or for a decree with relief honouring an Athenian. More likely it honours Asklepiodoros and another, envoys from Phokis to Athens; or the reference may be to a Macedonian embassy to Phokis (cf. Diod. XVIII 11, 1).

[129] Like no. 95, this was a decree proposed by Demades at the Assembly in the theatre after the City Dionysia. As such, one would expect it to have related to the festival. Cf. note on no. 39. The date was apparently 18, 19 or possibly 13 Elaphebolion. See further, *Polis and Theatre.*

Table (*cont.*)

	Date	Reference	Honorand	Honour	
51	322/1[130]	*IG* II² 375; Schwenk 89; *I Orop* 300.	–[131]	–	
52	c. 350–300[132]	*IG* II² 269;[133] Lambrechts 156 no. 103; Veligianni, A128.	–	–[134]	126
53	c. 350–300?	M.B. Walbank, *Hesp.* 54 (1985), 313–4 no. 3 (ph.) (*SEG* XXXV 76); *Agora* XVI 135.	–	–[135]	
54	c. 350–300?[136]	*IG* II² 444.	Mytileneans ?[137]	c	

[130] This inscription, found in Oropos, but unfortunately lost, has a claim to be the last decree of the classical Athenian democracy. More precisely it is the latest before the establishment of the oligarchic regime becomes apparent in 321/0 with the mention of the ἀναγραφεὺς in decree prescripts (cf. A.S. Henry, *Hesp.* 71, 2002, 107–8). The date apparently preserved on the stone, ἕνηι καὶ νέαι Thargelion = pryt. X 3[?] is anomalous. The text is stoichedon, which effectively rules out a modern transcribing error. Either there was a gross calendrical disturbance on the transition to oligarchy (cf. a little earlier no. 34 decree II, also irregular, though only by 4 days) or, as has been generally assumed, Thargelion is an error on the stone for Skirophorion. In the latter case if, as is likely, 322/1 was intercalary, and assuming there were no calendrical irregularities, the decree was either passed on the very last day of the year, pryt. X 3[8] (restoring ὀγδο|ίηι κ]αὶ τριακοστῆι, with G.F. Unger, *Philol.* 38 [1879], 427, for the orthography cf. e.g. no. 40, 2) or the penultimate day, pryt. X 3[7] (restoring [ἑβδό|μηι κ]αὶ τριακοστῆι with Meritt, *Ath. Year* 111–2, who assumes that, as not infrequently at year-end, there was a one-day calendrical adjustment achieved by insertion of a second ἕνηι καὶ νέαι).

[131] πρ]άττων (14) in Attic decrees is usually from the common formula used of an honorand, λέγειν καὶ πράττειν τὰ ἄριστα vel sim. (Veligianni, 282–3). Note also that all the other decrees set up in Oropos at this period were honorific, cf. *Ath. State* I 107. C. Habicht, *Athens from Alexander to Antony* (1997), 46 raises the possibility of a connection with the transfer of Oropos out of Athenian control in the aftermath of the Lamian War. See also Habicht, *Studien zur Geschichte Athens* (1982) 198 no. 1 (*SEG* XXXII 158), drawing attention to *IG* II² 1469B, 120–2 (321/0?): τάδ᾽ ἐκ τῆς (σ)τοᾶς [--μετηνλέ]χθη? κατὰ τὸ ψ[ήφισμα τοῦ δήμου] | ὃ Ἡγήμων εἶπε (the proposer of this decree?, cf. *LGPN* II Ἡγήμων 4, *PAA* 480795).

[132] The hortatory intention clause indicates a date after c. 350, cf. n. 10 (in ll. 9–10 read perhaps εἰδῶσιν πάντες [ο|ἱ ἄλλοι ὅτι ἐπίστατα]ι ὁ δῆμος κτλ.). Kirchner dates the lettering "volg. med. s. iv" at *IG* II² 269, "fin. s. iv" at *IG* II² 515.

[133] *IG* II² 515 is a duplicate text of the same inscription (cf. *IG* II² Add. p. 661).

[134] πρόξε]νον εἶν[αι is a possible reading of l. 1. I confirm the reading of S.A. Koumanoudes, *Arch. Eph.* 1886, 105 no. 12 in l. 2,]ει εἶναι Ἀθ[. Wilhelm's πρόξενον καὶ εὐεργέτ]ην εἶναι Ἀθ[- is incorrect.

[135] It is uncertain whether this tiny fragment is from a decree. Walbank thinks in l. 1 of εὐεργ]έτης but]ε τῆς is as likely.

[136] Cf. "litt. volg. s. IV" and "post a. 336/5" Kirchner.

[137] Μυτιληναιο- in a crown on a fragment (top and ? left side preserved). If there was only one crown (which is uncertain), the width of the monument would be c. 0.28.

Table (*cont.*)

		Date	Reference	Honorand	Honour
	155	c. 350–300?[138]	*IG* II^2 439.	Mentions -okrates[139]	–
	156	c. 350–300?[140]	*IG* II^2 432.	–[141]	c?
	157	c. 350–300?[142]	*IG* II^2 431; Veligianni, A174.	–[143]	c?
	158	c. 350–300?[144]	*IG* II^2 427.	-aris[145] [G?]	hosp. or dinner
	159	c. 350–300?[146]	*IG* II^2 544.	Theo- and another?[147]	500 dr. gold c[14
	160[149]	c. 350–300	Lawton no. 167 (ph.).	One male	c
127	161	c. 350–300	Lawton no. 168 (ph.).	One male?[150]	–
	162	c. 350–300	Lawton no. 174 (ph.).	One male?	–

The fragment might be from a monument (stele?, base?) commemorating a crown awarded by the Mytileneans (and others?), cf. *SEG* XIX 204, or from an Athenian decree (or other monument?) commemorating a crown awarded to the Mytileneans.

138 "S. iv" Koumanoudes. "Litt. volg. s. IV" and "post a. 336/5" Kirchner.

139 The decree mentions envoys (πρεσβε- l. 10) and might have been honorific or e.g. from a treaty (cf. *Ath. State* IV).

140 "Post a. 336/5" (Kirchner); somewhat arbitrary, as not uncommonly with Kirchner's use of that chronological indicator.

141 Might be Athenian or foreigner.

142 This small fragment was lost before *IG* II^2. "Post a. 336/5" (Kirchner).

143 The restorations printed in *IG* II^2 are speculative. As Köhler saw, the final letter of 2 was not necessarily the initial letter of the honorand's name (καλέσ]αι δὲ Δ[- Pittakis, ἐπαινέσ]αι δὲ Δ[- Rangabé and Velsen followed by Kirchner). E.g. δεδ|[όχθαι τῶι δήμωι ἐπαινέσαι τ]ον δῆμ|[ον τον - (or name + father's name, -ον Δημ[ο-) καὶ στεφανῶσαι κτλ. is also possible (for the preceding -αι cf. *IG* II^2 649, 37, παρέσχηται· δε[δόχθαι).

144 "Litt. volg. s. iv" and "post-336/5" (Kirchner).

145 καλέσαι -]αριν ἐπὶ [-- εἰς τὸ πρυτανεῖον εἰς αὔ]ριον (ll. 7–9). E.g. Δημόχ]αριν, cf. *IG* II^2 172. L. 4 might be articulated σίτο Τ[(]σι τὸ τ[Velsen, is also possible).

146 "Litt. volg. s. iv" and "fin. s. IV" (Kirchner). The damaged state of the stone and the small number of surviving letters precludes confident dating.

147 In ll. 2–4 read perhaps ἐπαινέσ]α[ι] Θεο[-- καὶ --]αι//[..] ἀρε⟦σ⟧τῆ[ς ἕνεκα καὶ φιλοτιμίας καὶ] στεφανῶσαι κτλ. It is uncertain whether this is a decree of the state or other body and, if the former, whether the honorands were Athenians or foreigners.

148 Unexpected in a state decree, unless of the Council. See *Ath. State* IIIA n. 75.

149 Apart from the heading θε[οί] some letters are legible in the first 6 lines of the body of the decree, including δεδό]χθ[αι ? (l. 5) and]ι ἐπα[ινέσαι ? (l. 6).

150 There is lettering on the moulding under the relief. It is difficult to read. One might consider Ἡρ]ακλέαν, but the accusative would be unexpected if this is an honorific decree of the state (which is not certain).

138. IG *II*^{2} *171*

The date is not without interest in connection with the history of the cult of Amphiaraos in Attica and Athens' acquistion of Oropos and the Amphiaraion in the 330s. Some progress may be made. Fundamental now is Lawton's stylistic dating of the relief to around the last quarter of the fourth century. One may add that the appearance on this state decree of Amphiaraos will be most comfortable in the period of Athenian control over the Amphiaraion, between, probably, 335 (cf. Knoepfler, *Eretria* XI 367–89) and 322/1 (*Ath. State* I 107–8; *Ath. State* II no. 9; no. 151).[151] Köhler (*IG* II 5, 83c), followed by Kirchner, inferred a date in the first half of the century from the letter forms, but neither had seen the stone or a squeeze and the judgement was apparently based only on Lolling's transcript. The relatively few preserved letters are in a plain style and are difficult to date precisely, but in spacing, size (note especially the relatively small omicron)[152] and form are consistent with a date in the second half of the fourth century. I calculate the original width of the inscribed part of the stele at 0.43 m., indicating a line length of about 32 letters. The best fit in the period 340/39–322/1 appears to be the year 328/7, for which the restorations would be:

	Ἀμφιάραος Ἀρτικλείδης Ὑγίεια	*on moulding above relief*
	[θ ε ο] ί	
328/7	[ἐπὶ Εὐθυκρίτου ἄρχο]ντος ἐπὶ τῆς Ἀντι[ο]-	stoich. 32
	[χίδος ὀγδόης πρυτανείας ἧι Πυθ]ọ́[δηλ]ος	last 2 letters in 1 stoichos
	[Πυθοδήλου Ἁγνούσιος ἐγραμμάτευεν . .]	

Notes

1. The names label figures in the relief.

2. Inscribed on the body of the stele immediately above l. 3.

3–5. It is known from *IG* II^{2} 354 = *Ath. State* I no. 11 that Antiochis held the eighth prytany in 328/7. That decree honoured a priest of Asklepios (raising the possibility of a thematic link with our text,

[151] Lawton, p. 49, notes the similarity between the Amphiaraos on this relief and reliefs and statues from the Amphiaraion.

[152] Letter heights are mostly 0.006–0.007, Σ 0.008, O 0.0035–0.004. Stoich. horiz. 0.0132, vert. about the same.

cf. the reference to "other gods" in l. 35 of *IG* II^{2} 354). Previous eds. printed Ἀντι[οχ|ίδος, but the observation that the sigma at the end of l. 4 was an additional letter squeezed in at line-end (next note) implies that O was probably the last letter of l. 3.

4. -]ος previous eds. I read the upper segment of a curve, consistent with the first omicron of Πυθ]ο̣[δηλ]ος. It has not previously been observed that the last two letters of l. 4 have been squeezed in at the end of the line (spacing 0.011 rather than the usual 0.013 and margin after the sigma only 2 mm.). This type of irregularity to avoid breaking a name at line-end is quite common at this period.

Less attractive possibilities are the years 336/5 and 331/0, whose secretaries are not known. A somewhat stronger one is 335/4,[153] which entails restoration of a (less comfortable, but not impossible) 31 letter line, i.e.

335/4 [ἐπὶ Εὐαινέτου ἄρχο]ν̣τος ἐπὶ τῆς Ἀντι[ο]- stoich. 31
[χίδος δεκάτης πρυτα̣νείας ἧι Πρ]ό̣[ξεν]ος
[Πυλαγόρου Ἀχερδούσιος ἐγραμμάτευε]

It is known from no. 87 and *IG* II^{2} 331 that Antiochis held the tenth
128 prytany in 335/4. |

In the relief Artikleides is crowned by Hygieia, with Amphiaraos standing by. Clearly the decree was honorific, but it is difficult to advance its interpretation further. The name Artikleides appears to be a hapax.[154] One might think of an error for ΑΡΓΙΚΛΕΙΔΗΣ (cf. *LGPN* IIIB 49, Boeotia, ΑΡΓΙΚΛΙΔΑΣ), but the letter is clearly tau on the stone and the Ἀρτι- name element is well attested (e.g. Ἀρτίπους *LGPN* I 83, Αρτιξίδας *LGPN* IIIB 68), albeit not certainly for an Athenian (cf. *LGPN* II 67 s.v. Ἀρτίμας). Perhaps, therefore, the honorand was a foreigner. That would also be consistent with the presence of a relief on this decree. Decrees honouring Athenians at this period do not normally have relief (see further below). The honorand is depicted behind a low altar towards which he extended his right arm. It is now broken, but perhaps originally held something (Lawton suggests a phiale). Lawton sees in this some support for Kutsch's

[153] This year was originally suggested to me tentatively by John Morgan per ep., without knowledge of the measurements which determine line length.

[154] Noted by S.N. Koumanoudes, *Horos* 4 (1986), 16 and by E. Matthews and P. Gauthier, per epp.

suggestion[155] that he was a priest, but, as preserved, the iconography seems inconclusive (the inconographic symbol for a priest was a sacrificial knife, cf. e.g. Lawton no. 145) and an Athenian decree honouring a foreign priest would be unparalleled at this period (albeit not perhaps impossible if he was a priest or other religious functionary in office at the Amphiaraion when it was transferred to Athenian control?). There are clearly other possibilities (e.g. a doctor, cf. no. 34, or a donor to a building project, cf. no. 42, *IG* II^2 338 = *Ath. State* I no. 15). The decree was found together with a fragmentary votive for Hygieia near the Hephaisteion during the construction of the Athens-Piraeus railway in 1891, but the fragments might easily have wandered together from an original location on the acropolis (the commonest location for honorific decrees and location of a cult of Athena Hygieia, cf. *IG* II^2 334 = RO 81 B 9) or the Asklepieion (also an attested location of state decrees, see *IG* II^2 354 = *Ath. State* I no. 11, 28–29, cf. P. Liddel, *ZPE* 143, 2003, 91), or conceivably another central Athenian shrine of a healing deity.[156] For the association of Amphiaraos and Hygieia cf. *IG* II^2 4441. The extent of any direct connection with Oropos and the Amphiaraion remains obscure.

For completeness I note below reliefs listed by Lawton on which no inscribed letter is preserved, but where it can be inferred from physical features and the design of the relief that they are or may be from Athenian state decrees.[157] Most, but not all (cf. e.g. RO 79), state decrees with relief were honorific. No decree with relief at this period certainly honoured an Athenian (cf. *Ath. State* I and see further below).

1. Lawton no. 123. State or non-state? Male approaching Zeus and Hera (?). From honorific? decree perhaps connected with their cult. c. 350–325.

---

155 F. Kutsch, *Attische Heilgötter und Heilheroen* (1913), 39–41, 121 no. 248, 135 no. 13.

156 M. Meyer, *Die griechischen Urkundenreliefs* (*AM Beiheft* 13, 1989), 24, speculates that it was set up by the statue of Amphiaraos in the Agora (Paus. I 8, 2).

157 I exclude the following items in Lawton (some of which have letters on) as non-state or possibly dating before the period 352/1–322/1 or more comfortably dated after it: no. 139 (non-state?), no. 146 (non-state), no. 178, no. 179 = *AM* 37 (1912), 197 (second quarter of 4th cent.?), no. 180, no. 181 = *Hesp.* 3 (1934) 1 no. 2 (non-state, cf. *SEG* LI 101), no. 182 = *AM* 67 (1942), 5 no. 1 (post 321?); no. 185.

2. Lawton no. 124. Crowning of a male by Athena and another. c. 350–325.
3. Lawton no. 131. Crowning of a male by Athena. c. 350–325.
4. Lawton no. 134. Crowning of a male by Athena and another. c. 350–325.
5. Lawton no. 135. Athena. I doubt from autopsy Lawton's tentative reading on the moulding above the relief, [θεο]ί̣.
6. Lawton no. 136. Crowning? by Athena. c. 350–325.
7. Lawton no. 140. Crowning of a male by Athena, with another female (personification of city of honorand?) standing by. c. 350–325.
8. Lawton no. 141. Crowning by Athena. c. 350–325.
9. Lawton no. 149. Crowning of male military figure by ?Demos, with Athena standing by. c. 350–300.
10. Lawton no. 162. Fragment of stele and relief above depicting Athena. c. 350–300.
11. Lawton no. 163. Crowning by a female figure (not Athena).
129 c. 350–300. |
12. Lawton no. 165. Crowning of a male by a female with another female standing by (Demeter and Kore?). c. 350–300.
13. Lawton no. 170. Crowning of beardless male by ?Athena. c. 350–300.
14. Lawton no. 171. Crowning of a male by Athena. c. 350–300.
15. Lawton no. 172. Crowning of a male by ?Demos and Athena. c. 350–300.
16. Lawton no. 173. Crowning of three men by a male military figure (Oineus?, Ares?). May be non-state. c. 350–300.
17. Lawton no. 175. Two men (honorands?). c. 350–300.

There is, in addition, one relief with no letters which Lawton suggests was from a decree which honoured a priestess:[158]

Lawton no. 164 = *LIMC* II 977 no. 213 s.v. Athena. Depicts crowning of a priestess (presumably of Athena Nike) by a Nike held by Athena, c. 350–300. Since this priestess of Athena was appointed from all Athenians rather than from a genos (cf. *IG* I^3 35–6), it is not especially

[158] Cf. Lawton 125 no. 91, which Lawton suggests is from a decree honouring a priestess of Athena of the first quarter of the 4th century (cf. *Ath. State* II p. 125, where I should have noted the possibility that it was from a non-state decree, perhaps tribal, or a dedication without inscribed decree).

likely that the relief is from a non-state decree. This would, however, be a unique example at this period of an inscribed decree with relief honouring an Athenian. There appears to be no trace of a stele below the relief, raising the alternative possibility that it was a dedication by a priestess commemorating a decree of the People honouring her, but not actually inscribed with the decree.[159] | 130

[159] On the distinction between inscribed state decrees honouring Athenians and dedications made by Athenians who had been so honoured (which might from the 340s, but did not necessarily, include the text of the decree), see *Ath. State* I 86 with n. 8, II pp. 128–9.

CHAPTER FIVE

ATHENIAN STATE LAWS AND DECREES, 352/1–322/1: IV TREATIES AND OTHER TEXTS*

This is the fourth in a series of articles intended as prolegomena to fascicle 2 of *IG* II[3] and completes my list of the inscriptions planned for inclusion in that fascicle.[1] The article comprises: A Treaties and other diplomatic decrees; B Other laws and decrees (i.e. those which are not honorific, religious regulations or treaties/diplomatic); C Fragments unassignable to a specific category; D Inscriptions excluded; E Select addenda and corrigenda to *Ath. State* I–III; F Chronological table.

---

* This chapter was previously published in *Zeitschrift für Papyrologie und Epigraphik* 161 (2007), 67–100.

[1] I reiterate the many acknowledgements expressed in previous articles in the series and add here my thanks to Michael Walbank, including for showing me parts of *Hesperia Supplement* 38 in advance of publication. To abbreviations used in previous articles in this series add:

Ath. State I, II, IIIA, IIIB: S.D. Lambert, Athenian State Laws and Decrees, 352/1–322/1. I Decrees Honouring Athenians, *ZPE* 150 (2004), 85–120;
II Religious Regulations, *ZPE* 154 (2005), 125–59;
III Decrees Honouring Foreigners. A. Citizenship, Proxeny and Euergesy, *ZPE* 158 (2006), 115–58;
B. Other Awards, *ZPE* 159 (2007), 101–54;
Dinsmoor, *Archons:* W.B. Dinsmoor, *The Archons of Athens in the Hellenistic Age* (Harvard, 1931);
Heisserer, *Alexander:* A.J. Heisserer, *Alexander the Great and the Greeks: the epigraphic evidence* (Oklahoma, 1980);
Moretti, *ISE*: L. Moretti, *Iscrizioni storiche ellenistiche* (Florence, 1967);
Staatsvertr. II: H. Bengtson, R. Werner, *Die Staatsverträge des Altertums. II Die Verträge der griechisch-römischen Welt von 700 bis 338 v. Chr.* (2nd edn., Munich, 1975);
Staatsvertr. III: H.H. Schmitt, *Die Staatsverträge des Altertums. III Die Verträge der griechisch-römischen Welt von 338 bis 200 v. Chr.* (Munich, 1969);
Wilhelm, *Attische Urkunden* VI: A. Wilhelm, *Kleine Schriften. Abteilung III. Schriften aus Adolf Wilhelms Nachlass* (Vienna, 2006). *Teil II. Attische Urkunden* VI (ed. H. Taeuber);
Tracy, *Athens and Macedon:* S.V. Tracy, *Athens and Macedon. Attic Letter-Cutters of 300 to 229 BC* (California, 2003).
(K) – date determined principally by letter forms (Kirchner in *IG* II[2]);
(T) – date determined principally by letter forms (Tracy in *ADT*).
* against an inscription number indicates that there is a longer note on it following the table.

A *Treaties and other diplomatic decrees*[2]

	Date	Reference	State	
1	mid-iv (K)[3]	*IG* II^2 281; Dreher, *Hegemon* 150–1 (*SEG* XLVI 125).	?	
2	mid-iv	*IG* II^2 258 + 617; E. Schweigert, *Hesp.* 6 (1937), 327–9 no. 5 (ph.).	Chalkis or cities of Chalkidike[4]	
3	mid-iv (c. 349/ 8?)[5]	*IG* II^2 210 + 259; E. Schweigert, *Hesp.* 6 (1937), 329–32 no. 6 (ph.); A. Wilhelm, *Attische Urkunden* V (1942), 132–3; J. Pečírka, *Listy fil.* 89 (1966), 266–9 (ph. *b*) (*SEG* XXIII 52).	Akanthos and Dion (cf. M. Zahrnt, *Olynth und die Chalkidier*, 1971, 108, 146–50, 182–5; Hansen-Nielsen, *Inventory* no. 559, no. 569)[6]	
4	349/8	*IG* II^2 208; *Staatsvertr.* II no. 325; Lambert, *ZPE* 140 (2002), 78 (ph.).	(Akarnanian) Echinaioi (Hansen-Nielsen, *Inventory* no. 118)[7] |	67
5	347/6	*IG* II^2 213; *Syll.*^{3} 205; Tod II 168; *Staatsvertr.* II no. 328.	Mytilene[8]	
6	348 or 343?	*IG* II^2 125 + Add. p. 658; *Syll.*^{3} 191; D. Knoepfler, *Mus. Helv.* 41 (1984), 152–61; idem, *Praktika 8th Congress of Greek and Latin*	Decree against attackers of Eretria and other cities	

[2] I discuss some historical aspects of this group in edd. G. Reger, F.X. Ryan, and T. Winters, *Studies in Greek Epigraphy in Honor of Stephen V. Tracy* (forthcoming) [= this volume, chapter 17].

[3] Walbank's suggestion (*Hesp.* 58, 1989, 79–81 = *SEG* XXXIX 76) that the cutter was the same as *IG* II^2 278 (see section D) and no. 18, below, is doubted by Angelos Matthaiou per ep. In l. 11 read perhaps ἐξώ]λ[ε]ιαν εἶναι ἑαυτῶι κ[αὶ παισί (πανώ]λ[ε]ιαν (…) κ[αὶ τῶι γένει dub. Köhler). Cf. e.g. *IG* I^3 14̣, 17; 15̣, 39; *SEG* XXXIII 147, A62.

[4] The text is not obviously formulaic and the line length can not be determined. It can not be restored with confidence beyond obvious completions.

[5] If Köhler was right to identify the context as the Olynthian War.

[6] Other than obvious completions, one can begin to restore with confidence only from l. 13 (ἐπ[αινέσαι κτλ.).

[7] The decree was, or related to, a *symbola* agreement (l. 14). Cf. *Ath. State* IIIA p. 126 with n. 30.

[8] Renewal of alliance which had apparently lapsed after the Social War (oligarchy in power late 351/0, Dem. XIII 8, XV 19, later a tyrant, Kammys, Dem. XL 37). Cf. P. Brun, *REA* 90 (1988), 381–3; Dreher, *Hegemon* 28, 124, 177. Given the reference to the treasurer of the swift ship Paralos in ll. 7–8, one might think in l. 20 of the Paralos' sister ship Ammonias, reading τῆ]|ς Ἀμμ[ων-, but this would apparently be the earliest reference to it, cf. *Ath. Pol.* LXI 7 with Rhodes ad loc. and p. 53.

Table (*cont.*)

	Date	Reference	State
		Epigraphy 2 (1987) 312–19; idem in: edd. E. Frézouls and A. Jacquemin, *Les relations internationales* (1995), 309–64; Dreher, *Hegemon* 154–80 (*SEG* XLVI 123); RO 69.	
7	343/2	*IG* II^2 225 + Add. p. 659; *Staatsvertr.* II no. 337.	Messenians (and others?)[9]
8	341?[10]	*IG* II^2 230 + Add. p. 659; *IG* XII 9, 162; *Staatsvertr.* II no. 340, a only; W. Wallace, *Hesp.* 16 (1947), 145 (b only); D. Knoepfler, *BCH* 95 (1971), 223–44 (b only) (ph. ab) (*SEG* XXXII 77); idem, *REG* 98 (1985), 243–59 (a) (*SEG* XXXV 59); idem in: edd. E. Frézouls and A. Jacquemin, *Les relations internationales* (1995), 346; P. Gauthier, *Bull. ép.* 1987, 274; 1996, 168 (*SEG* XLV 1210); Tracy, *ADT* 84; Dreher, *Hegemon* 45–56 (*SEG* XLVI 119).	Eretria

[9] In 343/2 Athens sent ambassadors through Greece seeking alliance... ἐγένοντο μὲν οὖν αὐτοῖς τότε σύμμαχοι Ἀχαιοί, Ἀρκάδες οἱ μετὰ Μαντινέων, Ἀργεῖοι, Μεγαπολῖται, Μεσσήνιοι (Σ Aeschin. III 83; see further *Staatsvertr.*). *IG* II^2 225 has invariably been interpreted as the text of a multilateral alliance concluded on this occasion and ll. 5–6 restored, following Köhler, συμμαχία τοῦ [δήμ|ου τοῦ Ἀθηναίων καὶ—ων καὶ] Μεσσηνίω[ν -]. For multiple states in an Athenian alliance heading cf. e.g. *IG* II^2 112, 2–3 (362/1): συμμαχία Ἀθηναίων καὶ Ἀρκάδων καὶ Ἀχαιῶν καὶ Ἠλείων καὶ Φλειασίων, which, as was normal in this context, uses simple ethnics. τοῦ δήμου τοῦ in our text is unusual. It is not clear, however, that in 343/2 Athens concluded a single multilateral alliance rather than bilateral alliances with individual states. In the latter case, consistent with the space available in l. 6 of this non-stoich. text, one might restore συμμαχία τοῦ [δήμ|ου τοῦ Ἀθηναίων καὶ τοῦ δήμου τοῦ] Μεσσηνίω[ν.

[10] Work of Tracy's "Cutter of *IG* II^2 334", c. 345–320. The occasion was perhaps Phokion's ejection of the tyrant Kleitarchos and the establishment of democracy in Eretria in 341 (Σ Aeschin. III 103, cf. Knoepfler 1985, 243 n. 2).

Table (*cont.*)

<table>
<tr><th></th><th>Date</th><th>Reference</th><th>State</th><th></th></tr>
<tr><td>9</td><td>338/7</td><td>IG II² 236 + Add. p. 659; U. Wilcken, SB Ak. Berlin 1929, 291–318; Staatsvertr. III no. 403; Heisserer, Alexander 8–12 (ph.); RO 76.</td><td>Treaty establishing League of Corinth[11] [stands in close relation to SEG XVI 55 (cf. Ath. State II no. 8 pp. 147–8) and no. 10 (below)]</td><td></td></tr>
<tr><td>10</td><td>336?</td><td>IG II² 329; Tod II 183; Staatsvertr. III no. 403 II; Heisserer, Alexander 3–8, 12–24 (ph.); U. Wilcken SB Ak. München 1917, 10, 39–40; K. Rosen, Gnomon 54 (1982), 354–5; A. Tronson, AW 12 (1985), 15–19 (SEG XXXV 66).</td><td>Agreement between Macedon (Alexander, l. 8) and Athens [and other members of Hellenic League?] about payment and supply of troops on campaign[12] |</td><td>68</td></tr>
<tr><td>11</td><td>c. 325–300?</td><td>R.S. Stroud, Hesp. 40 (1971), 187–9 no. 34 (ph.).</td><td>Tenos[13]</td><td></td></tr>
</table>

[11] Athenian copy of a multilateral treaty. For excellent photographs see A. Wilhelm, *SB Ak. Wien* 1911 = *Attische Urkunden* I 1–31. In ll. 19–21 Wilcken's καὶ πολεμήσω…καθότι | [ἂν δοκῆι τῶι κοινῶι συνεδ]ρίωι καὶ ὁ ἡγεμὼ|[ν παραγγέλληι has seemed to make excellent sense and has been generally accepted, but the reading of the initial preserved letters of l. 21 is problematic. Köhler read ΤΩΙ and Wilhelm detected a trace before the tau and restored ἂν ἦι συντεταγμένον ἐμα]υτῶι. The sense is unexpectedly vague and seemingly inferior to Wilcken's, but Wilcken's PI was based only on a photograph and is doubtful. I agree from autopsy that the second letter might be I or T, but in first place I agree with Wilhelm in reading an upper right diagonal, as of Y or K, apparently inconsistent with P.

[12] Like no. 9, this seems to be the Athenian copy of a multilateral agreement between Macedon and her allies. The stone is now abraded such that rather more can be read from Wilhelm's excellent photograph, *SB Ak. Wien* 1911 = *Att. Urkunden* I 44–50, than currently with ease at autopsy. The script is very similar to no. 9 and the letter heights and stoichedon grids are identical, suggesting that this inscription may have been intended to complement no. 9 physically as well as in content. This (and indeed the style of lettering in general) goes against the suggestion of Tronson that no. 10 might date to the reign of Alexander II of Macedon (early 360s). In l. 4 read ε]χειν σῖτο[ν το]ὺς -. δόντας σῖτον in l. 12 raises the possibility]ε ὁπόσοι ἂν [δῶ]σιν in l. 6, though Wilhelm's [ἴω]σιν yields perhaps easier sense in context. For the rest, except for obvious completions, none of the restorations that have been proposed for this non-formulaic text is compelling.

[13] This fragment includes a decree (ll. 1–11) and a rider (ll. 12–14). The text is probably non-stoich. with syllabification at line ends. It is difficult to read. In l. 8 I read Τηνίων καὶ Ἀ̣θ̣η̣[ναίων], l. 4 perhaps Χα]ι̣ρέου, cf. *LGPN* I 478, II 469, l. 6 δ̣ούλ̣ους

Table (*cont.*)

	Date	Reference	State
12	323/2?	*IG* II² 370; F. Mitchel, *Phoenix* 18 (1964), 13–17 (*SEG* XXI 299); Moretti, *ISE* no. 1; *Staatsvertr.* III no. 413; I. Worthington, *ZPE* 57 (1984), 139–44 (*SEG* XXXIV 69).	Aetolians (and others?)[14]

B *Other laws and decrees*

	Date	Reference	Subject
13	c. 337–325?[15]	*IG* II² 411; A. Wilhelm, *Archiv Pap.* 11 (1935), 206–15; E. 69 Schönbauer, *Zeitschr. Sav.*	Decree about agreement with Sokles to exploit a resource[16] |

(νουλουσ[Stroud). As Stroud saw, in ll. 10–11 there is an invitation (to Tenian envoys?) to hospitality in the prytaneion. I propose the following text for the rider:

12 [ἔδοξεν τῶι δήμωι·----c. 14----]ους ἐκ Κεραμέεω[ν εἶπεν·v?] non-stoich.
[τὰ μὲν ἄλλα καθάπερ τῆι βουλῆι, ἐπει]δὴ δὲ αἱ συνθῆ[και --c. 5--]
[----------c. 30 ------------]χ[.]το[-----c. 14-----]

For diplomacy with Tenos Stroud compares *IG* II² 279; 660 (*Ath. State* III no. 110); 466 (similar script). Note also 2378. Κεραμέεων· cf. Threatte I 304–9.

[14] On the death of Alexander in 323 the Aetolians were first to join the Athenian alliance against Macedon (Diod. XVII 111, 3; XVIII 9, 5; 11, 1). As revised by Mitchel (who was first to identify the left margin correctly) the current text is:

323/2? Αἰτωλ[ῶν καὶ Ἀθηναίων]
φιλία [καὶ συμμαχία]

This is on a moulding above a patch of relief ground with anta. Above the first line is space enough for another line of text. Above the first alpha is apparent trace of an iota, not certainly an inscribed mark. It is followed by very uncertain traces of ΛΛ, raising the possibility Ἰλλ[υριῶν (who were parties to the Athenian alliance of 323, Diod. XVIII 11, 1). If not, the possibility raised by Moretti, that this relates to the Athenian-Aetolian detente of 307/6 (Paus. I 26, 3, *IG* II² 358 with Tracy, *ADT* 152) rather than the anti-Macedonian alliance of 323, remains open.

[15] From the lettering (Köhler, Kirchner, cf. no. 15) and the "Lykourgan" character of the measure. A slightly earlier date can not be ruled out.

[16] The character of the resource is nowhere specified in the surviving text, which, as Thür has recently emphasised, is sui generis (the closest comparandum is *IG* XII 9, 191). Since Wilhelm and Schönbauer it has been taken by most scholars, including Palme in his thorough re-edition, to be silver, but Thür, 180, has recently pointed up some apparent inconsistencies with the regular Attic system of silver mine administration.

Table (*cont.*)

	Date	Reference	Subject
		Stift. 55 (1935), 185–90; R. Hopper, *ABSA* 48 (1953), 207–9; D. Behrend, *Attische Pachturkunden* (1970) no. 18; D. Peppas-Delmousou, Ἀρχ. Δελτ. 30, 1975 [1983], B, 7; B. Palme, *Tyche* 2 (1987), 113–39 (ph.) (*SEG* XXXVII 77); A. Maffi, *Rev. hist. droit* 68 (1990), 109–10 (*SEG* XL 73); G. Thür, in: *Prakt. Wilhelm*, 175–84.	
14	337/6	B.D. Meritt, *Hesp.* 21 (1952), 355–9 no. 5 (ph.) (*SEG* XII 87); Schwenk 6; Lawton no. 38 (ph.); *Agora* XVI 73; RO 79 (ph.).	Law against tyranny
15*	337?[17]	*IG* II² 244; Kirchner, *Imagines* no. 62; F.G. Maier, *Griechische Mauerbauinschriften* (1959–1961), 36–48 no. 10 (ph., Tafel 7); Schwenk 3; G. Thür, *Lebendige*	Law providing for repair of walls and contract specifications (*syngraphai*) for the work at Mounichia

The alternative is not necessarily agricultural land. It might, for example, be a mineral other than silver ore, or a wild plant or animal product. εἶναι δ]|ὲ τὴν συλλογὴν Σωκ[λ]εῖ [καὶ τῆι πόλει πα]|νταχόθεν ὁπόθεν ἂ[ν] καρ[πεῖαι ὦσιν (ll. 16–18) seems to suggest that it might be found anywhere, not in any specific location, and the provisions preventing Athenians from trying to stop the work (ll. 24–33) perhaps indicate a roving brief (did it entail going onto other people's land?). The attempt to increase the city's revenue by imaginative schemes of resource exploitation was of course wholly characteristic of Lykourgan Athens (cf. *Rationes* 280–91; J.K. Davies, *Mediterraneo Antico* VII, 2, 2004, 509). It has been assumed, reasonably enough, that the text is a decree of the Assembly. In that case, however, we should expect δεδόχθαι [τῆι βουλῆι καὶ τῶι δήμωι in l. 5, whereas Palme read and I confirm an apparent delta following the word δεδόχθαι. As he points out (121–2), δεδόχθαι δ[ὲ would be unexpected. For a board of officials one would expect the definite article. A name, e.g. of a deme or other group (cf. *IG* II² 1241, 1, δεδόχθαι Δυα[λεῦσι, a phratry), would be possible epigraphically, but does not seem easy to reconcile with provision that the resource, whatever it was, be exploited "everywhere that it is to be had". The sharing of the profit of the enterprise with the city (ll. 10–15) would also *prima facie* imply an Assembly decree, though polis subgroups are found acting as agents of the city in this period: e.g. Hyp. *Eux.* 16–17, Paus. I 34, 1, *Agora* XIX L8 (tribes responsible for management of newly acquired land in Oropos); *Rationes* 238–9 (demes etc. responsible for selling surplus land on behalf of the city). Solutions to the puzzles remain elusive. [See this vol. ch. 16]

[17] Cut by Tracy's "Cutter of *IG* II² 244", c. 340/39–c. 320, the inscription perhaps relates to the programme of defensive works undertaken after the battle of Chaironeia (Dem. XVIII 248, 299–300; Aeschin. III 27, 236; Lyk. I 44).

Table (*cont.*)

	Date	Reference	Subject
		Altertumswissenschaft. Festgabe Hermann Vetters (1985), 66–9 (*SEG* XXXV 62); P. Gauthier, *Bull. ép.* 1988, 403 (*SEG* XXXVIII 64); Tracy, *ADT* 98; M.B. Richardson, in: edd. P. Flensted-Jensen et al., *Polis and Politics. Studies… Hansen* (2000), 601–15 (*SEG* L 141).	
16	333/2 or 332/1?	*IG* II² 417; D.M. Lewis, *Hesp.* 37 (1968), 374–80 no. 51; Lambert, *ZPE* 135 (2001), 52–60 (ph.); idem, *ZPE* 141 (2002), 122–3 (*SEG* LI 80); Humphreys, *Strangeness* 115–16 n. 17.	List of dedications by liturgists preceded by regulatory text (law?)

C *Fragments certainly or possibly from state laws or decrees, unassignable to a specific category*[18]

	Date	Reference	Description
17	c. mid-iv?[19]	*IG* II² 299.	Inscribing clause
18	c. mid-iv?	M.B. Walbank, *Hesp.* 58 (1989), 79–81 no. 6 (ph.) (*SEG* XXXIX 76); *Agora* XVI 58.	–[20]
19	c. mid-iv? (K)	*IG* II² 325.	–[21]
20	c. mid-iv? (K)	*IG* II² 322.	–

[18] I pass over here most of my fairly numerous, but largely inconsequential, improvements to readings of very small fragments.

[19] For the wording of ll. 1–2 cf. *Ath. State* IIIA no. 32 = *IG* II² 238 b 17–18; for ll. 2–3 cf. *Ath. State* IIIA no. 5 = *IG* II² 237, 36–37. Both date to 338/7.

[20] This fragment contains only a few letters (I was unable to confirm the reading of any whole word). Walbank suggested that the hand was the same as *IG* II² 278 (see below sect. D) and no. 1, but there seems too little to go on.

[21] In l. 2 read ΚΑΝΤΑΣ (πάντας Kirchner).

Table (*cont.*)

	Date	Reference	Description
21	c. mid-iv? (K)	*IG* II² 256.	Inscribing clause
22	c. mid-iv?	*IG* II² 255.	Presentation of envoys to the Assembly | 70
23	c. mid-iv? (K)	*IG* II² 263; M. H. Hansen, *GRBS* 25 (1984), 136 n. 33 (*SEG* XXXIV 65); Lawton no. 119 (ph.).	Prescript[22]
24	c. mid-iv?[23]	E. Schweigert, *Hesp.* 9 (1940), 335–9 no. 42 g (ph.) (*SEG* XXI 298); Osborne, *Nat.* D25 g; Schwenk 85 g; *Agora* XVI 94 g; Tracy, *ADT* 122; Lambert, *ZPE* 136 (2001), 66.	–
25	c. mid-iv?	M. B. Walbank, *Hesp.* 54 (1985), 312–3 no. 2 b (ph.) (*SEG* XXXV 65); idem, *Hesp.* 58 (1989), 75–8 no. 4 a–c (ph.) (*SEG* XXXIX 67); *Agora* XVI 45 a-c; Tracy, *ADT* 70 (*SEG* XLV 45).	–[24]

[22] Only the right side is preserved. The text (now largely illegible) is too fragmentary to support substantive restoration. For the prescript Kirchner suggested [ἐπὶ Θεμιστοκλέους (347/6) ἄρ]χο[ντος· ἔδοξε|ν τῶι δήμωι·...⁶...ἐπρυ]τάν[ευεν· τῶν | προέδρων ἐπεψήφιζεν Κλ]έαρ[χος - | -] ἐγραμμ[άτε|υεν· | -- ἐκ Κηδ]ῶν or ἐκ Κεραμέ]ων or Ξυπεται]ών εἶπεν. Hansen pointed out that one might bring the decree back to the period before 354/3, when proposers were introduced by name only, and read -ων as from the proposer's name, i.e. ἐπεστάτει· -]ων εἶπεν (cf. *IG* II² 110; 112) or ἔδοξεν τῶι δήμωι· -]ων εἶπεν (cf. *IG* II² 96). There are other possible schemes, e.g.:

[ἐπὶ ------- ἄρ]χο[ντος ἐπὶ τῆ]- stoich.
[ς ---ιδος---πρυ]ταν[είας· τῶν]
[προέδρων ἐπεψήφιζεν Κλ]έαρ[χος...]
[*demotic. Name demotic*] ἐγραμμ[άτε]-
[υεν· -----------]ων εἶπεν·
[περὶ ὧν -----------]νιων λέ-
[γ--

For the scheme of ll. 1–3 cf. *IG* II² 337 = *Ath. State* II no. 4 (333/2). For secretary with demotic only and placed after the chairman cf. *IG* II² 228 = *Ath. State* IIIB no. 70 (341/0). The context will be diplomatic if Kirchner's plausible suggestion for ll. 6–7, περὶ ὧν οἱ πρέσβεις τῶν -]νίων λέ|[γουσι, is correct.

[23] Style similar to "Cutter of *IG* II² 105", 368–339 (Tracy).

[24] 3 very small fragments associated by Walbank with *Ath. State* IIIA no. 52 = *IG* II² 272+274. Association rejected by Tracy.

Table (*cont.*)

		Date	Reference	Description
	26	After c. 350	E. Schweigert, *Hesp.* 7 (1938), 289–91 no. 17 c (ph.) (*SEG* XVI 51); *Ath. State* IIIB p. 102 n. 11.	Inscribing clause
	27	347/6	B.D. Meritt, *Hesp.* 29 (1960), 51 no. 65 (ph.) (*SEG* XIX 52); *Agora* XVI 70.	Prescript
	28	c. 345–c. 320 (T)	*IG* II^2 307 (= *IG* II^2 600); Tracy, *ADT* 84; *SEG* LI 74.	Inscribing clause[25]
	29	c. 345–c. 320 (T)	B.D. Meritt, *Hesp.* 32 (1963), 39–40 no. 40 (ph.) (*SEG* XXI 345); *Agora* XVI 90; Tracy, *ADT* 87.	Inscribing clause[26]
	30	340/39	*IG* II^2 451; S. Dow, *Hesp.* 32 (1963), 348; M.H. Hansen, *GRBS* 23 (1982), 347 no. 75; Tracy, *ADT* 70, 73–4, 78 n. 2 (*SEG* XLV 63); M.B. Walbank, *Phoenix* 51 (1997), 80 (*SEG* XLVIII 98).	Prescript[27]
71	31	c. 340–320 (T)	*IG* II^2 437; Tracy, *ADT* 98. |	–

[25] At 3 fin. I read δήμο]ụ : ΔΔΔ ^{v} δρα̲|χμὰς.

[26] The extent of erasure with no reinscription (whole of first three preserved lines) is unusual at this period.

[27] Above the inscription is preserved the lower left corner of a rectangular ground framed by antae, comparable to that found on decree stelai with a crowning relief. In this case the ground was occupied not by relief, but presumably by a painting (not now visible). The extensive vacat at the top of the main body of the stele was probably also painted. For paintings as substitutes for relief sculpture see *Ath. State* IIIA p. 119. The inscription dates to a period when the format of prescripts was in flux and is too fragmentary for substantive restoration. The line length can not be determined. πρυτα[νείας· ἐκκλησία· τῶν] is the generally accepted restoration of l. 3 and yields the earliest case of this type of meeting specification in a prescript (cf. RO 98 with note; the next dated case is *IG* II^2 330 = *Ath. State* I no. 3, 30 and 49, of 336/5). This is likely, but not quite certain. Köhler's tentative ἔδοξεν τῶι δήμωι would be unexpected in this position (as Reusch saw), but a date in the month is not perhaps impossible (for date in the month with no month name see e.g. *IG* II^2 229 = *Ath. State* IIIA no. 54, 341/0). Tracy noted that]ος Δ[in l. 5 could be restored to yield the secretary of 340/39, i.e. [...^{6}... Ἄσπετ]ος Δ[ημοστράτου Κυθήρριος ἐγραμμάτευεν. This is attractive. The naming of the secretary after the chairman (ll. 4–5) is unusual, but occurs in the same year in *IG* II^2 233 = *Ath. State* III no. 72. Tracy raises the alternative possibility that]ος Δ[was the proposer. That would imply that the secretary was omitted altogether, which is unusual, but does occasionally occur at this period (cf. Henry, *Prescripts* 43).

Table (*cont.*)

	Date	Reference	Description
32	After c. 340[28]	*IG* II² 436; *Ath. State* IIIB p. 115 (ph.).	Prescript
33	337/6	*IG* II² 241; Schwenk 8; Tracy, *ADT* 106; Brun, *Démade* 177 no. 4.	Prescript
34	c. 337–325[29]	*IG* II² 412; M.H. Hansen, *C & M* 33 (1981/2), 119–23 (ph.); *Ath. State* II pp. 129–30.	*Phasis* provisions from a law[30]
35	c. 337–325	*IG* XII 3, 1018; *IG* II² 447.	Oath formula[31]
36	336/5?[32]	B.D. Meritt, *Hesp.* 26 (1957), 207–8 no. 54 (ph.) (*SEG* XVII 27); Schwenk 16; *Agora* XVI 74.	Prescript

[28] Implied by ἐκκλησία in the prescript. Cf. previous note.

[29] Cf. Kirchner, "Litterae sunt aetatis Lycurgi".

[30] Hansen compares the *phasis* provisions in the Athenian law on silver coinage, *SEG* XXVI 72, 24–9. The stone is opisthographic. The entire "reverse" face has been subject to superficial reworking in the same fashion as the left part of the "front" face. The lettering on the "back" is in the same general style, but slightly smaller (h. 0.004–0.005 m., compared with 0.005–0.006 on the front), and the stoichedon grid is rather tighter (0.007–0.009, compared with 0.013 on the front). Letters are legible here and there, including ME upper right, PA lower left (no complete word). Some other laws at this period have smooth backs, but this is the only one preserving text on both sides, cf. *Ath. State* II pp. 129–30. For stones inscribed with multiple texts including laws cf. *IG* II² 333 = *Ath. State* II no. 6 (two laws); *SEG* XVIII 13 = *Ath. State* II no. 7 (law and decree); *IG* II² 244 = above no. 15 (law and *syngraphai*).

[31] This stone was found on Thera in 1860, moved to Strasbourg by Michaelis and apparently seen in Berlin by Hiller and Köhler. I have been unable to trace it, but have examined the squeeze in Berlin. Marble type ("Pentelicum esse videtur") and lettering appear to be Attic of the Lykourgan period (Köhler). It is unclear whether this is an Athenian pierre errante or a genuinely "Attic" inscription set up on Thera. Kirchner's restorations, insofar as they go beyond those in *IG* XII (γνώ]μην l. 5, ἀποδ̣[έκται l. 7 and τριάκοντ]α l. 8) seem arbitrary. The key ll. 4–6 read:...⁶...]ψω (γρά]ψω̣ Keil) ἀληθῆ -- | -- μην καὶ ἐπ-- | -- ἐὰν δέ μ]ὴ ὀμόσηι τὸ[ν ὅρκον --]. I have been unable to find precise parallels for this formula in Attic epigraphy, albeit that the restoration of l. 6 (apparently due to Hiller, *IG* XII) is attractive. It is possible that the inscription recorded a treaty of some sort. Thera may have been a member of the Second Athenian League (RO p. 104). Note also *IG* II² 179 (regulating legal arrangements with Naxos, but mentioning Thera).

[32] The lettering is non-stoichedon, poor and spidery, suggestive in these respects of a very late-4th or 3rd cent. hand, though not impossible in 336/5. A further oddity is that there appears to be the lower section of a vertical stroke after the eta of [ἐπὶ Πυ]-

Table (*cont.*)

		Date	Reference	Description
	37	335/4	*IG* II² 331 (= *IG* II² 882); Schwenk 22; Meritt, *Ath. Year* 80 (*SEG* XXI 270); M.H. Hansen, *GRBS* 23 (1982), 343 no. 27; S.V. Tracy, *Hesp.* 67 (1998), 220 n. 5 (*SEG* XLVIII 102).	Prescript[33]
	38*	334/3	*IG* II² 335 + Add. p. 659; E. Schweigert, *Hesp.* 9 (1940), 339–40 (ph.) (*SEG* XXI 274); Schwenk 23; M.B. Walbank, *ABSA* 85 (1990), 443 no. 14 (*SEG* XL 76); Tracy, *ADT* 122, 126–7.	Prescript
72	39	334/3–314/3 (T)	E. Schweigert, *Hesp.* 9 (1940), 334–5 no. 41 (ph.); *Agora* XVI 89; Tracy, *ADT* 124.	Clause providing for presentation to Assembly[34] |
	40	334/3–314/3 (T)	E. Schweigert, *Hesp.* 8 (1939), 27–30 no. 7 e (ph.); E. Schweigert, *Hesp.* 9 (1940), 335–9 no. 42 e (ph.) (*SEG* XXI 298); Osborne, *Nat.* D25 e; Schwenk 85 e; *Agora* XVI 94 e; Tracy, *ADT* 122, 127; Lambert, *ZPE* 136 (2001), 68 no. 4a (*SEG* LI 86).	–

θοδή[λου ἄρχοντος in l. 1. It does not look like a casual mark, but nor is it consistent with Πυ]θοδή[λου or Πυ]θοδή[μου (the mu in l. 3 has sloping outer bars). The latter is in any case not an attested name of an Athenian archon. *Pace* previous eds. *IG* II² 328 does not certainly supply the length of the name of the secretary of 336/5, since it may date rather to 335/4 *(Ath. State* IIIB pp. 119–21). The line length in our text is accordingly uncertain. The naming of the secretary *prima facie* goes against the suggestion of Schwenk that the decree was erected privately.

[33] L. 4 (end)-5 should read πρυταν]είας· | [τῶν προέδρων ἐπεψήφιζεν --c. 8–9--]χ̣ος v. The name of the chairman was e.g. Ἀριστόμα]χος. There is no room for the word ἐκκλησία, printed by previous eds. before τῶν προέδρων.

[34] This fragment belongs in a group with a number of others cut by Tracy's "Cutter of EM 12807", with letter heights c. 0.007–0.008 m. and roughly square stoichedon grids, c. 0.016–0.018 m. Cf. *Ath. State* IIIB n. 127. It may go with *Ath. State* IIIB no. 92 = *SEG* LI 84, for men from the Bosporan kingdom. In that case ll. 5–7, [προσαγαγεῖν…5..|…6…]τ̣ους (I agree with Woodhead that this reading is preferable to Schweigert's ν̣ους) [.̣……13……πρὸ|ς τὸν δῆμ]ον will conceal a reference to them. Given, however, that fragments with this lettering demonstrably belonged to several different inscriptions, caution is in order in the absence of a physical join.

Table (*cont.*)

	Date	Reference	Description
41	333/2	*IG* II^2 340; Schwenk 30.	Prescript
42	c. 340–320 (T) (333/2–320?)[35]	*IG* II^2 449 + R.S. Stroud, *Hesp.* 40 (1971), 183–6 no. 32 (ph.); D.M. Lewis, *ABSA* 50 (1955), 34 n. 26a; S. Dow, *Hesp.* 32 (1963), 348; Tracy, *ADT* 99, 103; J. Morgan ap. C. Kritzas, Ἀρχ. Δελτ. 49, 1994, B [1999], 17 (ph.) (*SEG* XLVII 126); G. Touchais et al., *BCH* 123 (1999), 640 (ph.).	Prescript
43	332/1	B.D. Meritt, *Hesp.* 5 (1936), 413–4 no. 11 (ph.) (*SEG* XXXII 84); Schwenk 34; M.H. Hansen, *GRBS* 23 (1982), 349 no. 85; *Agora* XVI 78; Lambert, *ZPE* 141 (2002), 119–20 (*SEG* LII 96).	Prescript
44	330/29	*IG* II^2 352; Schwenk 49.	Prescript
45	After c. 330[36]	B.D. Meritt, *Hesp.* 10 (1941), 41 no. 9 (ph.); *Agora* XVI 83.	Inscribing clause
46	c. 325?	E. Schweigert, *Hesp.* 9 (1940), 333–4 no. 40 (ph.); *Agora* XVI 88.	Inscribing clause

[35] I am grateful to John Morgan for discussion of the improved text of this prescript arising from his join. The top is not preserved, but there is a vacat above l. 1 and no archon or secretary is named in the prescript. ὀγδόηι καὶ τριακοστῆι (l. 2) shows that the year was intercalary. ἐκκλησία (l. 3) occurs for the first time in a prescript no earlier than 340/39 (see above, no. 30). συνπρόεδροι (ll. 5–11) are first listed in *Ath. State* III no. 7, of 333/2. The cutter is Tracy's "Cutter of *IG* II^2 244", 340–c. 320. 336/5 seems excluded by *Agora* XV 42 (different councillors). The earliest year consistent with these parameters is 333/2. 330/29 is also possible as are several years in the 320s.

[36] The lettering suggested to Meritt a date c. 330? (cf. *Agora* XVI), restoring ll. 2–3 δ]οῦνα[ι τὸν ταμίαν τ]οῦ δήμου ^{v}ΔΔΔ ^{v} δραχμ]ὰς. However, there are very few letters to go on and an amount for inscribing greater than 30 dr. would tend to suggest a date after c. 330 (cf. Loomis, *Wages* 163–4, RO p. 103). Alternatively we might restore δ]οῦνα[ι τὸν ἐπὶ τῆι δ]ιοικήσει…^{5}.. and date to after 304, cf. *IG* II^2 496 + 507; A.S. Henry, *Chiron* 14 (1984), 55. For the expression εἰς δὲ τὴν] ἀνα[γραφὴν καὶ τὴν ποίησιν cf. *Ath. State* I no. 1 (*Agora* XV 34), of 343/2, though it does not seem to occur again until after 304.

Table (*cont.*)

		Date	Reference	Description
	47	325/4	*IG* II^2 361 + Add. p. 360; D.M. Lewis, *ABSA* 49 (1954), 50 (*SEG* XIV 57); Schwenk 69; M.B. Walbank, *Hesp.* 54 (1985), 316; B. Nagy, *Hist.* 43 (1994), 275–85 (*SEG* XLIX 102).	?[37]
	48	324/3?	*IG* II^2 454; S. Dow, *Hesp.* 32 (1963), 350 (*SEG* XXI 293); Schwenk 75.	Prescript
	49	324/3[38]	B.D. Meritt, *Hesp.* 10 (1941), 49–50 no. 12 (ph.) (*SEG* XXI 290); Schwenk 71; *Agora* XVI 91.	Prescript
73	50	324/3	*IG* II^2 362; B.D. Meritt, *Hesp.* 10 (1941), 46–7 (ph.) (*SEG* XXI 291); Schwenk 73; Tracy, *ADT* 149.	Prescript |
	51	322/1	*IG* II^2 376; Meritt, *Ath. Year* 110; Schwenk 90; Lawton no. 51 (ph.).	Prescript
	52	c. 350–300?	B.D. Meritt, *Hesp.* 29 (1960), 51–2 no. 67 (ph.) (*SEG* XIX 56).	–
	53	c. 350–300?	B.D. Meritt, *Hesp.* 29 (1960), 51 no. 64 (ph.) (*SEG* XIX 62); *Agora* XVI 133.	–[39]

[37] Note πρε]σβε- in l. 9. Honorific? Treaty?

[38] Since they are reproduced by *SEG*, Schwenk and *Agora* XVI I should point out that the restorations of ll. 2, 4 and 5, presented by Meritt, *Ath. Year* 105, to yield the calendar equation [Pos. 28] = pryt. [V] 3[1], are uncertain. Other possibilities include, as John Morgan points out to me, Pyan. 18 = pryt. III 35. Meritt's 1941 text was better. ἐγραμμάτευε without ephelkystic nu occurs in this year in no. 50.

[39] Apart from Ἀ]θηναίων in l. 3 the only complete word on this very small fragment is the name Φορμίωνο[ς (l. 2). It was common (*LGPN* II 465 lists 33 cases, *FRA* 473 4 cases) and the bearer can not be identified. Where previous eds. read]ιων in l. 1 (Πασ]ίων Oikonomides), I read]γων. Cf. A.N. Oikonomides, *The Two Agoras in Ancient Athens* (1964), 98–9 no. 94; *AW* 23 (1992), 107–8; J. Trevett, *Apollodoros the Son of Pasion* (1992), 49 n. 31 (*SEG* XLII 93).

Table (*cont.*)

	Date	Reference	Description
54	c. 350–300?	M.B. Walbank, *Hesp.* 58 (1989), 84–5 no. 10 (ph.) (*SEG* XXXIX 92); *Agora* XVI 132.	–
55	c. 350–300?	M.B. Walbank, *Hesp.* 58 (1989), 84 no. 9 (ph.) (*SEG* XXXIX 87); *Agora* XVI 98.	?
56	c. 350–300?[40]	*IG* II^2 705.	Prescript
57*	c. 350–290?	*IG* II^2 738 + Add. p. 666.	Prescript
58	iv–iii	R.S. Stroud, *Hesp.* 40 (1971), 196 no. 48 (ph.).	–[41]
59	iv–iii	R.S. Stroud, *Hesp.* 40 (1971), 192 no. 41 (ph.).	–
60*	Mid-iv–iii	*IG* II^2 420; S. Dow, *Hesp.* 32 (1963), 347–8; B.D. Meritt, *AJP* 85 (1964), 304–6 (*SEG* XXII 93); M.H. Hansen, *GRBS* 23 (1982), 346 no. 68 (*SEG* XXXII 83); Schwenk 35.	Prescript

[40] Köhler and Reusch (*Hermes* 15, 1880, 340) dated this inscription to iv BC, Kirchner to early iii BC. There is very little to go on, but Sean Byrne points out to me that the orthography Αἰγηΐδος favours iv BC (cf. Threatte I 374–5, after 300 -ει- is the normal form and -ηι- is rare) and Tracy advises per ep. that, as regards the hand, he sees no objection to iv BC. As Reusch saw, the inclusion of a month name suggests a date after c. 350–340 (cf. RO p. 149 n. 1) and the equation 5th pryt. = Maimakterion 6 (or later date including ἕκτηι) would be consistent with an ordinary year in the period of 10 tribes. That would suit his suggested restoration (l. 1) ἐφ' Ἡγησίου (324/3) ἄρχο]ντος (cf. Meritt, *Ath. Year* 104–6), but too little text survives for certainty.

[41] In l. 1 Stroud thinks of τ]οὺς φίλο[υς τοὺς Ἀθηναίων or πρὸς τοὺς Ἀθηναί]ους φιλο[τιμίας. Alternatively perhaps a name Φιλο-. In l. 2 Stroud reads τ]ῆς ὁμον[οίας. If this is a reference in a decree to the abstract quality, the date would probably not be earlier than hellenistic, cf. *IG* II^2 687, 31; II^2 4985; *SEG* XXV 194, 495; XXVIII 364 etc. We might, however, have to do with the τετρήρης Ὁμόνοια, cf. *IG* II^2 1632 a 36, in which case this might be a naval document rather than a decree.

For completeness note also:

IOrop 291, 292, 293 (building specifications); 301 (encomium of Amphiaraos?).

IG II² 1128 = *IG* XII 5, 1277 = RO 40. Mid-iv BC. Regulation of ruddle export from Keos. Surviving text is of decrees passed by cities of Keos, but these were perhaps incorporated into the text of an Athenian decree (ll. 39–40).

IG II² 1629 = RO 100, 165–302. 325/4. Decree for a colony in the Adriatic. Cf. Wilhelm, *Attische Urkunden* VI no. 12.

15. IG *II² 244. Law on Repair of Walls*

The beginning of this law is printed in *IG* II² as follows:

[θ] ε̣ [ο ί]
[Κηφισοφῶν Κεφαλίωνος] Ἀ̣φιδναῖος εἶπεν· ἀγαθῆι τύχηι τοῦ [δήμου τοῦ Ἀθηναίων· ὅπως ἂν̣..........................42...................]
74 stoich. 111 |

Law prescripts can be briefer than decree prescripts (cf. *Ath. State* II pp. 139–40), but there is no 4th century parallel for a stone inscribed with a state law or decree beginning with the name of the proposer.[42] Richardson saw the problem and proposed the following solution for the beginning of line 2:

> [ἐπὶ Χαιρώνδου ἄρχοντος (338/7)]. Ἀφιδναῖος εἶπεν· or [ἐπὶ Φρυνίχου ἄρχοντος (337/6)]. Ἀφιδναῖος εἶπεν·

Κηφισοφῶν Κεφαλίωνος Ἀφιδναῖος is a well known individual (*LGPN* II Κηφισοφῶν 22, *APF* 8410), but, as Richardson notes, the restoration of this man (first proposed by A. Frickenhaus, *Athens Mauern im IV Jhdt.*, 1905, 14–29) or any other known person (she notes an alternative suggestion of Foucart, Δημήτριος Εὐκτήμονος of Aphidna = *LGPN* II Δημήτριος 183), when only demotic is preserved, is highly speculative. The solution she proposes is unsatisfactory, however, on two grounds: after 354/3 proposers are invariably given father's name and demotic (Henry, *Prescripts* 32) and no Athenian is attested as having a name equivalent to the form of a standard demotic before the

[42] The "unpublished" *SEG* LII 104 might supply such a parallel, but the date and precise character of this inscription are obscure. See below D no. 38.

late 3rd century (cf. Lambert in: *Prakt. Wilhelm*, 335).[43] My autopsy of the stone suggests a different solution. As Richardson notes (p. 601), it has been reused several times; for later purposes the bottom and the right side were cut down; and there are traces of mortar adhering to the right side and the top. In my view the stone has also been cut down at the top. The present top of this stele does not have the normal characteristics of the top of a stele intended for display: there is no moulding and no sign of a proper finish; and the cutting is very close to the first line of text. As I have noted elsewhere, secondary cuttings which run parallel with the text are quite common and can be deceptive (*ZPE* 139, 2002, 69–71). Sometimes newly created top or bottom surfaces may be reworked with care (e.g. if they are to be the external face of a wall, see *IG* II^2 488 with my remarks at *ABSA* 95, 2000, 492); often the newly created top or bottom is left rough and unfinished, typically with irregularities, chipping etc. at the top (or bottom) of the inscribed surface of the stone where it meets the new cutting. Here we have to do with the latter case. Indeed one wonders whether the trace of an epsilon recorded above the second alpha of ἀγαθῆι by the first editor, Dragatsis, Ἀρχ. Ἐφ. 1900, 91–102 (cf. P. Foucart, *Journ. des Sav.* 1902, 177–193 and 233–15), but not seen by any recent editor, may have been the product of an illusion created by damage at the current top of the inscribed surface where it meets the new cutting. The first line of the text, as now preserved, is so close to the preserved top that no trace of a line above could be genuinely visible. Maier notes (p. 40) damage to the top left corner of the stone since discovery, causing the loss of the first few letters of lines 2–5. It is unclear whether this process of damage might also have caused the loss of some stone at the top further to the right. Even if it is a true reading, however, the epsilon does not necessarily imply [θ]ε̣[οί]. It might have been from a previous line of ordinary prescript text.[44]

When secondary cuttings are made towards the top of a stone, this can be to remove a relief. That might have been the case here. For a law with relief cf. no. 14. Interestingly, there is a cutting in the top of that stele where someone has begun to sever the body of the stele

---

[43] I noted there that the only securely attested case BC appears to be the father of Δημοκράτης Σουνιέως Κολωνῆθεν, proposer of *IG* II^2 847 in 215/4 BC, cf. *SEG* XXI 684, and that Ἀφιδνα[-], attested as a name in 304/3 on *Agora* XV 61, 165, is better restored with an ending which would differentiate it from the demotic.

[44] In his minuscule text Dragatsis prints the epsilon larger than other letters, but in his majuscule transcript it is the same size.

from the relief, but not carried the job through. Compare the large number of reliefs, catalogued by Lawton, which preserve the top of the inscribed portion of the stele, with the first one or two lines of text.

Too few law prescripts are preserved on stone and those that are preserved vary too much for us to be able to reconstruct this prescript in its entirety. One would certainly expect a dating formula of some sort (probably including an archon, though *IG* II[2] 140 lacks one). Two
75 of the at least nine extant inscribed laws | also included a heading in the form νόμος περὶ -- (*Grain Tax Law*, 3–4; *Ath. State* II no. 6 at p. 140). In any case I suggest that the beginning of this inscription should be printed:

[........[19]........] Ạφιδναῖος εἶπεν· ἀγαθῆι τύχηι τοῦ [δήμου τοῦ Ἀθηναίων· ὅπως ἄν............................[42]........] stoich. 111?

The text is not sufficiently formulaic to permit very much more than obvious completions. What was the line length? Appended to the text of the law are *syngraphai* arranged in two columns of 27 letters each, in the same stoichedon grid as the text above and with one stoichos between the columns. It is impossible to restore the law text with a 55 letter line, i.e. on the assumption that there were only two columns of *syngraphai*. Three columns of *syngraphai* would yield a law text of 83 letters per line. This is not impossible; Foucart showed that, for most lines, 83 letter restorations are possible; but all more recent editors have followed Frickenhaus, 14–16 and Wilhelm[45] in assuming four columns and a 111 letter line for the law. There do not appear to be decisive arguments (cf. Maier, 40), but with Kirchner and other editors I continue to regard the 111 letter line hypothesis to be the more attractive, principally because it is difficult to arrive at persuasive 83 letter restorations of some lines (e.g. ll. 44–5).

The preserved dimensions of the stele are h. 0.80, w. 0.54, th. 0.125–0.13. The normal ratio of th., w. and h. (not of course an absolute rule) for decree stelai was 1:4.5:9. Only the thickness is original. The back is smooth, which is characteristic of inscribed Athenian laws, as I noted at *Ath. State* II pp. 129–30. The height seems unproblematic. There is a line or two missing from the top and some lines at the bottom. The width looks at first sight to be more of an issue. With a 111 letter line

[45] *Beiträge zur griechischen Inschriftenkunde* (Vienna, 1909), 232–3 and ap. *IG* II[2].

it will have been well over 1 metre. In other words this stele may have been about as wide as it was high. Two possibilities come to mind:

- (1) the monument consisted not of one stele, but two stelai clamped together, with the law text running across from one to another and two columns of *syngraphai* on each. This was the proposal of the first editor, Dragatsis, p. 95 (accepted by Frickenhaus). His positive case is not persuasive: certainly the current state of the right side, with mortar attaching, looks to be a consequence of subsequent use of the stele, not an original feature. Mortar from subsequent usages adheres to a large number of surviving stelai. It is not mortar, but clamp cuttings (in the top) and anathyrosis (of the sides) that indicate adjoining stelai. On the other hand, there is also nothing about this stone that would rule out such an arrangement. Since the original right side (and top, see above) are not preserved, any anathyrosis or clamp cuttings for joining this stele to another to the right would no longer be visible;
- (2) this stele was wider in relation to its height and thickness than was usual with decree stelai. This does not seem impossible.[46] The smooth back of this stele suggests that its mode of display was not the same as normal decree stelai, which had rough picked backs, not meant to be seen. Presumably it was set up in such a way that the back was visible and one could walk around it. It would seem possible, for example, that it was slotted into a monumental structure in which it was also supported at the sides.

Was this law about walls part of a "wall"? For a parallel cf. the sacrificial calendar of the polis, as revised at the end of the 5th century (*Sacrificial Calendar*). I note also that one other law text of this period has both a smooth back and a line length significantly longer than any decree, *IG* II^2 333 = *Ath. State* II no. 6, which contained at least two laws on religious subjects and was inscribed with an 82 letter line.

Richardson has made a good case that some inscribed laws (or inscribed laws generally—we do not have enough extant laws to tell which) were set up in places appropriate to their content and that this law, found in Mounichia, was placed there because it dealt

46 Another "stele" wider than it was high is discussed at *Ath. State* II pp. 125–7, but that was a rather different type of monument.

specifically with rebuilding of walls in Piraeus in general and Mounichia in particular. I am not, however, persuaded by her suggestion that it was set up in the quarry where the stone for the walls was to be
76 extracted. Laws and decrees were generally | displayed in central public locations, usually with some religious significance, not in workaday places remote from normal public view. Moreover, the smooth back does not immediately suggest that this stele was displayed in the type of niche in a rock face which Richardson illustrates at plate 2. If the back was up against a quarry wall, what would be the point of making it smooth? Finally, as Richardson herself notes in discussion with me, the particular slot on Prophetes Elias hill that she identifies as a possible base for this stele is unsuitable. It is 0.56 m. wide. That would suit the *preserved* width of our stele (0.54 m), but on any account the actual width of this monument was significantly greater than that. She comments that the stele was discovered "face down in the entranceway to a subterranean tunnel…today the tunnel…is covered by buildings which also overlie remains of the 5th century BC theatre in Mounichia in the city block framed by the streets Θεάτρου, Καραολή-Δημητρίου, Νεορίων and Τσαμάδου." Theatres were of course public places used for the erection of public inscriptions. I suspect that this inscription was originally set up in the theatre adjacent to its findspot. For an Athenian state decree of this period (possibly even of the same year) intended (I have argued) for erection in the Piraeus theatre cf. *IG* II² 410 = *Ath. State* I no. 10.

38. IG *II² 335 + Add. p. 659*

This is the key member of a group of three inscriptions which were dated by Schweigert to the same day. It was restored by him as follows:

[θε]οί *vac.*
334/3 [ἐ]π̣ὶ Κτησικ[λέους ἄρχοντο]- stoich. 21
[ς] ἐπὶ τῆς Ἀκα[μαντίδος ἐνά]-
[τ]ης πρυτανε[ίας, ἧι Μνησίφ]-
[ι]λος Μνήσ[ω]ν[ος Φαληρεὺς ἐ]-
[γ]ραμμάτευε[ν· Μουνιχιῶνο]-
[ς] ἕκτηι μετ' [εἰκάδας· ἐκκλη]-
[σ]ία· τῶν πρ[οέδρων ἐπεψήφι]-
[ζ]ε̣ν Δημο[κρ…ς Παιανιεύ]-
[ς· ἔ]δοξεν [τῶι δήμωι· Δημάδη]-
[ς Δ]η̣μ̣έο[υ Παιανιεὺς εἶπεν]·
- -

The prytany number and the month name were suggested to Schweigert by Meritt. Given the possibility of omitting ephelkystic nu on ἐγραμμάτευεν, there are in fact four month names which would fit the available space:

(i) Ποσειδεῶνος. For -ει- for -ι- in this month name see *Ath. State* IIIB no. 139. This, however, is ruled out by the fact that in 334/3, which was probably an ordinary year, ἕκτηι μετ' εἰκάδας of Posideon would have fallen in prytany 5 and πέμπτης does not suit the space in ll. 3–4;

(ii) Βοηδρομιῶνος, which in 334/3 would have fallen in the third prytany, i.e. τρί|τ]ης in ll. 3–4. This suits the space and was the restoration proposed by Köhler. The date is well attested as an Assembly day (*IG* II^2 665 and 837, cf. Mikalson, *Calendar* 61–2). It would not be consistent with the allocation of the ninth prytany of this year to Akamantis hypothesized in *IG* II^2 1493 + by F.W. Mitchel, *AJA* 70 (1966), 66, but Mitchel's theory is uncertain and the year of *IG* II^2 1493 + is wholly restored and is doubtful. Cf. *Ath. State* II p. 139 with n. 63. It seems that Mikalson was right, therefore, to retain this date as a possible alternative to (iii);

(iii) Meritt's restoration, printed above. Mounichion, ninth prytany. This also seems unproblematic. No festival is attested on this day (Mikalson, *Calendar* 148);

(iv) Θαργηλιῶνος. ἕκτηι μετ' εἰκάδας might have been the last day of the ninth prytany in this year and is therefore a possible restoration epigraphically and chronographically. However it was also the day of the Plynteria, the one day of the year for which we have explicit evidence that it was unsuitable for business | (Plut. 77
Alk. XXXIV 1, Xen. *Hell.* I 4, 12, cf. Mikalson, *Calendar* 160), so it would not be reasonable to restore it here.

The same restorations are possible in the two other inscriptions which Schweigert restored to this day:

IG II^2 414 a = *Ath. State* I no. 21 and *IG* II^2 405 = *Ath. State* IIIA no. 6.

57. IG *II^2 738 + Add. p. 666*

The calendar equation, 4th pryt. = early Pyanopsion, would normally imply the period of 12 tribes (cf. init. iii Köhler). As both John Morgan and Sean Byrne have pointed out to me, however, the relief (not in Lawton) and lettering style are perhaps suggestive rather of a (mid-?) 4th century date. The latest dated Attic decree reliefs pre-ii BC in Lawton's list are her no. 58 = *IG* II^2 503 of 302/1 and no. 59 = *IG* II^2 646 of 295/4. Morgan points out that the surviving letters of the name in l. 4 are consistent with the secretary of 338/7, Φίλιππος Ἀν]τ[ιφ]ή[μο]υ [Εἰ]ρεσίδης, and that, consistently with the 24 letter line length so derived, the archon of that year could be restored in l. 1: Χαιρώνδου. The details of the prytany in l. 3, however, would remain problematic. Morgan notes that they could be reconciled with this year by assuming that -ΡΤΗ̣Σ on the stone (unde τετά]ρτ[η]ς Köhler) is in error for Ἱπποθωντίδος τ]ρ⟨ί⟩τ[η]ς. The rest of the text can then be restored to yield 2 Pyanopsion = pryt. III 18 or 19, a regular equation for an ordinary year. The assumption of an inscribing error when so little text survives is rather drastic. This inscription probably dates to the period c. 350–290. The specific year, however, must remain undetermined on current evidence.

60. IG *II^2 420*

There has been no satisfactory attempt to reconstruct this prescript. There is not enough for certainty, but I set out below a possible scheme, exempli gratia. The line length I have chosen depends on my exempli gratia restorations of 3–4 and is arbitrary.

post 317 [ἐπὶ τῆς --ίδος ---]της πρυτανεία- stoich. 29
[ς ἧι......^{12}......ἐγρ]αμμάτευεν [..]
[ἕνηι καὶ νέαι· δωδεκάτ]ει τῆς πρυτ[αν]-
[είας· ἐκκλησία κυρία· τ]ῶμ προέδρ[ων ἐ]-
[πεψήφιζεν....^{8}....Εὐ]. υκράτ[ους.]-
[– *demotic* – συμπρόεδροι· Θ]ε̣ομνή[στος]
[----------------------]ΣΣ̣[...^{5}..]

The top survives, with pedimental moulding, uninscribed. For omission of the archon from a prescript, possible, but not certainly attested for a decree heading a stone in the period 352/1–322/1, cf. *Ath. State* IIIB p. 123 n. 114.

2. At the end I tentatively read ^{v}[^{v}].

3. As Hansen notes, omission of the month name is fairly common, especially with ἕνηι καὶ νέαι. The restored prytany date is arbitrary, simply chosen to suit the space.

4. Some other type of ἐκκλησία is also possible. I confirm Meritt's reading of the omega before the mu, ruling out Dow's suggested σ]-υμπρόεδρ[οι.

5–6. *IG* II² 450, 6–8, of 314/3, is the earliest example of the chairman being given father's name as well as demotic, so if the scheme here was the same, this inscription will not pre-date the regime of Demetrios of Phaleron. It can not be ruled out, however, that the date is earlier and the line length much longer, accommodating an archon at l. 1 in., a long secretary at l. 2 in., a month name in ll. 2–3 and a *vacat*, error or wordy description, e.g. of an Assembly meeting, at 4 in. (Hansen is probably right, however, to reject Meritt's ἐκκλησία στρατηγῶν παραγγειλάντων, a formula unattested before ii BC). In that case the scheme of ll. 4–6 would be: | 78

τ]ῶμ προέδρ[ων ἐ]-
[πεψήφιζεν *name—demotic* Εὐ]. υκράτ[ης..]-
[*fa.'s name—demotic*—εἶπεν· ἐπειδὴ Θ]ε̣ομνή[στος]

D *Inscriptions excluded*

Inscriptions which are not precisely datable have generally been included or excluded according to the highest date in the possible range, i.e. an inscription datable before or after 352/1 is normally excluded (except if dated "mid-iv BC" vel sim.), one datable before or after 322/1 is normally included. The following is a check-list of some inscriptions that were excluded after active consideration.[47]

1. *IG* II² 227. May date before introduction of annual secretaries in 365/4 or 364/3.[48] See *Ath. State* IIIA p. 126 n. 27.
2. *IG* II² 247. Part of *IRham* 3. See *SEG* LI 105.
3. *IG* II² 249. Develin, *AO* p. 313. May date before introduction of annual secretaries in 365/4 or 364/3.[49]
4. *IG* II² 250. May date before 352/1.

47 In several cases, and indeed in others not listed below, the judgement as to fascicle allocation is marginal and too much should not be read into it. I am grateful to Angelos Matthaiou, Graham Oliver, Sean Byrne and Stephen Tracy for discussion of these cases.

48 For the dating of the change to these years see A.S. Henry, *Hesp.* 71 (2002), 91–2.

49 Cf. Chronological Table, Section F, under 350/49.

5. *IG* II^2 253. J. Morgan joins *IG* II^2 332 and dates to 353/2.
6. *IG* II^2 268. After 322/1. See *Ath. State* IIIB p. 101 n. 1.
7. *IG* II^2 277 + 428. *SEG* XXXVII 86; XL 67. After 322/1.
8. *IG* II^2 278. Proposer (l. 5) has no father's name or demotic, indicating a date before 354/3 (cf. Henry, *Prescripts* 32).[50]
9. *IG* II^2 280. Develin, *AO* p. 352. "Cutter of *IG* II^2 105", 368–339 BC (Tracy, *ADT* 74–5). *SEG* XLV 68. May date before 352/1.
10. *IG* II^2 289. Goes with *IG* II^2 139, of 353/2 (M.B. Walbank, *AHB* 3.6 (1989), 119–22, *SEG* XXXIX 75).
11. *IG* II^2 291. Develin, *AO* p. 353. May date before 352/1.
12. *IG* II^2 317. Part of *IG* II^2 43. See *SEG* LI 68.
13. *IG* II^2 321 = 1001. Account or building specifications? See *SEG* LI 79.
14. *IG* II^2 324. Joins a fragment dating before 352/1.
    IG II^2 332: s.v. *IG* II^2 253.
15. *IG* II^2 350. Osborne, *Nat.* D39. After 322/1.
16. *IG* II^2 355. Schwenk 55. Dedication.
17. *IG* II^2 366. Schwenk 80. This is an abbreviated decree inscribed in a crown on a base. Though it is unclear whether normal prescript conventions strictly applied, a proposer with no father's name or demotic would normally indicate a date before 354/3 (cf. Henry, *Prescripts* 32) and the archon may therefore be the Kephisodoros of 366/5 rather than the Kephisodoros of 323/2. Angelos Matthaiou, who has examined the stone, reports that the lettering appears consistent with the earlier date.
18. *IG* II^2 401. Tracy, *ADT* 134; *SEG* XLVII 127; LI 90. After 322/1.
19. *IG* II^2 404. See most recently P. Brun, *ZPE* 147 (2004), 72–8. May date before 352/1.[51]
20. *IG* II^2 407 + *SEG* XXXII 94. *SEG* XXXVII 83; XL 79; Tracy, *ADT* p. 124; *Agora* XVI 106J. After 322/1.

79 21. *IG* II^2 413. Account. See *Ath. State* II pp. 143–4. |
    IG II^2 428: s.v. *IG* II^2 277.

22. *IG* II^2 438. Osborne, *Nat.* D40. *SEG* XXXIII 88; XL 78. After 322/1.

---

[50] Many changes in prescript formulation (e.g. as regards dating elements) happened gradually, but this one was unusually sudden and uniform. As Henry notes, the inclusion of father's names and demotics of proposers appears to have been invariable practice after it is first attested in 354/3.

[51] In which case, this is a very early instance of inclusion of month name and date in a decree prescript.

23. *IG* II^2 442 + 729. Dates c. 260–235. See Tracy, *Athens and Macedon* 134–7. *IG* II^2 524: s.v. *IG* II^2 580.
24. *IG* II^2 540a + *SEG* XXIV 117. *SEG* XL 68. After 322/1.
25. *IG* II^2 540b + *Agora* XVI 137. *SEG* XL 68. After 322/1.
26. *IG* II^2 542. After 322/1.
27. *IG* II^2 580. Goes with *IG* II^2 524 and dates after 322/1. Tracy, *Athens and Macedon* 150–1.
28. *IG* II^2 582. *SEG* XXIV 118. After 322/1.
29. *IG* II^2 727. S. Dow, *Hesp.* 32 (1963), 356–7 (*SEG* XXI 324); B.D. Meritt, *Hesp.* 32 (1963), 439; M.B. Walbank, *ABSA* 84 (1989), 402 (*SEG* XXXIX 108). John Morgan points out to me that the prescript can be restored to the same day as *Ath. State* IIIB no. 149, i.e. 18 [Pyanopsion] = pryt. [III 36] 323/2, assuming the archon was separated off at the top and reading Ἀρχίας Πυθοδώρο]υ̣ ἐ̣γ̣[ραμμά|τευεν in ll. 3–4.[52] This is possible, but can not be compelling with so little text preserved, and one hesitates solely on this basis to extend for a further three years the already long career of Tracy's "Cutter of *IG* II^2 1262", c. 320–c. 290 (Tracy, *ADT* 139, cf. *Athens and Macedon* 38–48).
    IG II^2 729: s.v. *IG* II^2 442.
30. *IG* II^2 1268/9. Account? See *SEG* LI 100.
31. *IG* II^2 4594. *SEG* XXXVII 78. Dedication. See *Ath. State* II p. 150 n. 83.
32. *SEG* XIX 51. Dedication. Includes apparently decree-like language (citation of a decree?), but unlike that of state decrees inscribed on dedications at this period.
33. *SEG* XXIV 114. *Agora* XVI 131. After 322/1.
    SEG XXIV 117: s.v. *IG* II^2 540a.
    SEG XXXII 94: s.v. *IG* II^2 407.
34. *SEG* XXXV 79. *Agora* XVI 143. After 322/1.
35. *SEG* XXXIX 113. *Agora* XVI 146. Non-state.
36. *SEG* XLV 206. Lease record? See *SEG* LI 140.
37. *SEG* XLV 207. There seems no case for identification as a law or decree.

[52] Graham Oliver and I confirm from autopsy that this is a better reading than -ε]υ̣ς̣ ἐ̣[γραμμάτευεν (Walbank, hesitantly followed by Tracy on the basis of a "not very good squeeze"). Lower half of epsilon is legible in second place. The impression of Σ seems to be caused by damage.

38. *SEG* LII 104. As Peter Rhodes points out to me, a case might be made from content for identifying this "unpublished" law from Brauron as 4th century in date, possibly Lykourgan (cf. *Ath. State* II section IV). There is also a rumour that it might be the work of Tracy's "Cutter of *IG* II^2 1262", c. 320–c. 290 (Tracy, *ADT* 139, cf. *Athens and Macedon* 38–48). However, Tracy himself advises per ep.: "I can definitively say that it is not the work of the Cutter of *IG* II^2 1262. Based on the lettering I would put the date close to 200 or even a bit later." One may wonder about the possibility of later re-inscription of a 4th century law; but for a definitive view we must await full publication, including fragments of this inscription which are known to exist but have not yet been "published" in any form.
39. *Agora* XVI 71. Lawton no. 120. See *SEG* LI 73. Non-state (genos Salaminioi?).
    Agora XVI 131: s.v. *SEG* XXIV 114.
40. *Agora* XVI 134. After 322/1.
    Agora XVI 137: s.v. *IG* II^2 540b.
    Agora XVI 143: s.v. *SEG* XXXV 79.
    Agora XVI 146: s.v. *SEG* XXXIX 113.
41. *Agora* XVI 147. Lawton no. 181. Non-state (tribal?). See *SEG* LI 101.
42. *Hesp.* 2 (1933), 397–8 no. 17. Dates c. 286/5–239. See Tracy, *Athens and Macedon* 88.

80 43. *Hesp.* 40 (1971), 197 no. 50. After 322/1. |

E *Select addenda and corrigenda to* Ath. State *I–III*

M.B. Walbank, *Hesperia Suppl.* 38 will publish the *editio princeps* of a number of small fragments from laws and decrees of this period. Where these join already published inscriptions they are noted below. Wilhelm, *Attische Urkunden* VI, unpublished on his death in 1950, has now been issued by the Vienna Academy. It includes discussions of several inscriptions in this series. Some, but by no means all, have been overtaken by subsequent scholarship.

Ath. State I: for further discussion of these decrees see *Ath. State* II pp. 125–9.

Ath. State I no. 1: see *Ath. State* II pp. 127–8.

Ath. State I no. 3. *IG* II^2 330 + 445. New fragment: Walbank, *Hesperia Suppl.* 38 no. 14.

Ath. State I sect. A or B. Sean Byrne, in the forthcoming volume commemorating Michael Jameson, joins *IG* II^2 824 and *SEG* XXXII 113 (first published by M.B. Walbank) to yield a block (self-standing?, top of a multi-block monument? Walbank) inscribed on both its surviving sides: on the front with an Assembly decree (decree I), headed by a dedication formula, --N-- | ἀνέθεσαν, and awarding foliage crowns to a group of officials who held office in 341/0; on the left side with another decree (decree II) praising and crowning (presumably the same) officials, ἐπειδὴ -- καλῶς καὶ δικαιῶ]ς ἐπεμελήθησαν -. In decree II the demotics of two men, apparently honorands, appear at the end of successive lines (11–12), ἐκ Κερ]ạμέων^{V} and Φα]ληρέα^{IX}. This suggests that we have to do with a group of officials arranged in tribal order, such as *hieropoioi* (cf. *Ath. State* I no. 13 with *Ath. State* II pp. 125–9), and that the names of the others would have filled the earlier parts of these lines. Decree I was passed by the Assembly and is introduced by ἔδοξεν τῶι δήμωι, so not probouleumatic in formulation. Decree II was probably a Council decree (cf. *Ath. State* I no. 1, decrees II–V). An alternative would be a decree of the officials themselves, honouring one of their own number (for such decrees see *Ath. State* I pp. 106–7), but the plural, ἐπεμελήθησαν, and the arrangement of the names in ll. 11–12 indicate that the decree honoured the whole board. As such it is also unlikely to be a decree of a single deme or tribe. As we saw at *Ath. State* I p. 88, the Assembly did not at this time normally take the initiative to inscribe its own decrees honouring officials where these entailed the award of foliage crowns and one would not therefore expect a clause providing for money for inscribing at the end of decree I. The Council also does not seem to have set up monuments commemorating the award of foliage crowns to Athenians, but at *IG* II^2 1156, 36–44, it provides for its decree awarding foliage crowns to the ephebes of Kekropis of 334/3 to be inscribed on the dedication set up by the ephebes themselves. It is very likely that the present dedication was also set up by the honorands. The money provided for in ll. 7–8 of decree I was not, if the above argument is correct, for inscribing and can not be for the crowns, which were foliage and cost nothing. I am inclined to think that it was for sacrifice and a dedication by the honorands (restoring along the lines [δοῦναι δὲ εἰς θυσίαν καὶ ἀνάθημα -] | δραχμ[-). For clauses of this type see *Ath. State* II pp. 128–9. At the preserved end of decree II there appears to have been an inscribing clause (the last or penultimate line ends τὸ ψή]φισμα). It may be that, as at *IG* II^2 1156, 43–4, it provided for the

Council's decree to be inscribed on the officials' dedication. It is possible that a decree of the officials honouring one of their own number was inscribed elsewhere on this monument. Cf. *Ath. State* I no. 13, text at *Ath. State* II p. 126 ll. 13–16 with following remarks.

Ath. State I no. 13. New text at *Ath. State* II p. 126.

Ath. State I no. 23. See also *Ath. State* II p. 128.

Ath. State II p. 125 I (a) (ii). This relief may not be from a state decree. Cf. *Ath. State* IIIB p. 130 n. 158.

Ath. State II no. 6. *IG* II^2 333. New fragment: Walbank, *Hesperia Suppl.* 38 no. 15.

Ath. State II no. 7 (*IG* II^2 334 +), p. 146. The comments of P. Gauthier, *Bull. ép.* 2006, 181 draw my attention to an unclarity in my discussion. To clarify: in my view the "Little" or "Annual Panathenaia" took place every year (not three years in four) at the end of Hekatombaion. It included the sacrifices etc. provided for in *Ath. State* II no. 7, which were managed by the "annual" *hieropoioi* referred to by *Ath.*
81 *Pol.* | LIV 7. Every fourth year the celebration was enhanced by additional elements (competitions etc.) known as the "Great Panathenaia" and managed by the *athlothetai.*

Ath. State II no. 12, pp. 149–50. In a fragmentary context the inventory of Artemis Brauronia, *IG* II^2 1526, 6 reads ἐφ' ἱερέως Πε- (cf. 1527, 1). Kirchner ad loc. is puzzled, "nam Dianae Brauroniae sacerdos est mulier", pointing to the reference to her *kyrios* in l. 27 of the same inscription and raising the possibility that this was a priest in a different cult; but it may be that, as with some other cults of Artemis and related deities,[53] Artemis Brauronia was served by both a priest and a priestess. In that case it would be possible that the priest of *IG* II^2 326 = *Ath. State* II no. 12 was priest of Artemis Brauronia.

Ath. State III no. 12. On *IG* II^2 448 see Wilhelm, *Attische Urkunden* VI 200 no. 21.

Ath. State III no. 49. *IG* II^2 419. The new fragment is Walbank, *Hesperia Suppl.* 38 no. 25.

Ath. State III no. 50. *IG* II^2 343. Wilhelm, *Attische Urkunden* VI 175–6 no. 2 (largely overtaken). Note also *SEG* LI 284, a funerary monument from Piraeus initially erected in c. 400 and inscribed in

[53] Priest and priestess of Artemis Kolainis: *IG* II^2 4817 (2nd–3rd cent. AD, cf. *IG* II^2 5057 with M. Maass, *Die Prohedrie des Dionysostheaters in Athen*, 1972, p. 126); priest and priestess of Bendis: *IG* II^2 1283, 21 (3rd cent. BC).

Phoenician, reused perhaps c. 50 years later to commemorate, in Greek, a Demetrios son of Demetrios of Sidon.

Ath. State III no. 56. *IG* II² 399. In reference to my remarks at p. 141 n. 115, Kallimachos might be a 3rd cent. archon of the Athenian cleruchy on Lemnos rather than the Athenian archon of 349/8. See below sect. F, table under 349/8.

Ath. State III no. 58. *IG* II² 254. Wilhelm, *Attische Urkunden* VI 198.

Ath. State III no. 68. *IG* II² 435. Wilhelm, *Attische Urkunden* VI 194–8 no. 19, which develops further his theory that the decree provided for exiles from Neapolis[54] and offers a complete restoration of ll. 2 (end)–16. He would date the inscription to the mid-340s, comparing *IG* II² 218 = *Ath. State* IIIB no. 64, for exiles from Abdera. The new restorations are brilliant, but largely unconvincing. At ll. 2–4 he restores:

> [.....τὸ]ν στρατηγὸ[ν......ἀποδοῦναι δὲ τοῖς ἥκουσι τ]- stoich. 45
> [ῶν Νεο]πολιτῶν ἐφόδι[α τὸν ταμίαν τοῦ δήμου ἑκάσστωι (sic) εἴ]-
> [κοσι] δραχμὰς ἐκ τῶν κ[ατὰ κτλ.

But the parallels he supplies for travel expenses (*IG* II² 124; 149 etc.) all relate to payments to Athenians (envoys, generals etc.) rather than foreigners. It is no less likely that an Athenian general was required to take some action in respect of (sc. Athenian) citizens, with travel expenses to be paid to the general and/or the citizens, articulating] πολιτῶν· ἐφόδι[α δὲ δοῦναι κτλ., or that travel expenses were to be paid to a group of (Athenian) citizens, i.e. δοῦναι δὲ τοῖς -- τῶν] πολιτῶν ἐφόδι[α κτλ. Expressions of this type to define a group of Athenian citizens are common, e.g. τοῖς τεταγμένοις τῶν πολιτῶν (*IG* II² 1299, 20), τοῖς ἀφικνουμένοις τῶν πολιτῶν (*IG* II² 888, 6–7), τοῖς παραγιγνομένοις τῶν πολιτῶν (*IG* II² 908, 2–3). At ll. 13–16 Wilhelm presents an imaginative restoration whereby Neapolitans at Athens (completely restored) are to receive a subsidy of 3 obols a day, ἐκ τῶν κατὰ] ψηφίσματα [ἀναλισκομένων ἑκάστωι ἡμέρης | ἑκάστης, ἕως ἂν ὁ χρ]όνος ἐ[ξέλθηι αὐτοῖς τῆς φυγῆς? Public subsidies for exiles can be paralleled at this period (e.g. *Ath. State* III no. 8 and no. 121, both

[54] Hansen-Nielsen, *Inventory* lists three cities of this name in the area of Thrace, no. 586, no. 634 and no. 677. Cf. the Athenian-Neapolitan alliance of 355, *IG* II² 128, probably directed against Philip, with Hansen-Nielsen, *Inventory* p. 863 (on no. 634).

a drachma a day), but the expression ἕως ἂν ὁ χρόνος ἐξέλθηι appears to be unexampled in Attic epigraphy (there are examples in other contexts from Asia Minor, e.g. IK *Rhodian Peraia* 353) and its use to refer to the "expiry" of exile is probably inappropriate. Such men, escaping in the wake of the advance of Philip or other adverse political circumstances, were not exiles for a fixed term; their return depended on unpredictable changes in political circumstances in their home cities. The language used in such cases at this period is both more prosaic and more formulaic, e.g. ἕως ἂν κατέλθωσιν (*IG* II^2 237, 24–5, Akarnanians), [ἕως ἂν κατέλθωσι|ν εἰς τ]ὴ̣ν αὑτῶν (*IG* II^2 218, 32–3, Abderites), ἕως ἂν κατέλθη[ι εἰς Δ]ῆ̱λον (*IG* II^2 222, 36–7, Peisitheides of Delos. In the case of Arybbas, former king of Molossia, the generals
82 are commissioned to restore him and his children to his ancestral | realm, *IG* II^2 226 = *Ath. State* IIIA no. 4 = RO 70, 42–7). As noted at *Ath. State* III p. 103 n. 20 I suspect that in]. ονος Ε[in l. 16 we have to do with a name or names listed at the end of the decree, perhaps of Athenian envoys vel sim. (identical with the "citizen(s)" referred to in l. 3?), cf. *IG* II^2 360, 44–5.

Ath. State III no. 84. *IG* II^2 363. Wilhelm, *Attische Urkunden* VI 189 no. 13 (largely overtaken). The reconstruction of ll. 8–12 proposed at *Ath. State* IIIB p. 116 is possible. For the structure, with multiple clauses following πρότερόν τε before the καὶ νῦν clause, cf. *IG* II^2 374. A single πρότερόν τε clause, however, is also possible (cf. *IG* II^2 351 = RO 94 = *Ath. State* IIIA no. 42, 11–15), in which case:

ἐπει]δὴ Διον[ύσ]-
[ιος πρό]τερόν τε [ἐπηγγείλ]ατο τῶι [δή]-
[μωι ἐπι]δώσειν τ[ρισχιλίου]ς μεδίμν-
[ους εἴ τ]ι δέοιτ[ο, καὶ νῦν..^{4}..]ηκεν ἐν
[...^{6}...]ΤΕΡ[........^{16}........]Α̣ΣΤΙ̇

For the structure cf. *IG* II^2 661, 19–23: ἐπει|[δὴ δ]ὲ οἱ ἐπιμεληταὶ [τ]ῶν μυστηρίων πρότερόν | [τε] (...) ἐπεμ|[ελή]θ[η]σαν τῆς θυσίας καὶ νῦν τεθύκασιν τὰ σω|[τήρ]ια... The most likely circumstance in which Dionysios might have offered to donate grain, if needed—the implication apparently being that it was not (cf. the offer of a financial contribution "for the war" at *IG* II^2 351 = *Ath. State* IIIA no. 42 = RO 94, 11–15)—seems to me the anxiety surrounding the grain supply which followed the defeat at Chaironeia (cf. *Ath. State* IIIA n. 68) and this confirms my preference (IIIB p. 119) for dating this inscription to 336/5, 331/0, or (less likely on other grounds) 335/4, rather than 326/5.

Ath. State III no. 85. *IG* II[2] 283. Wilhelm, *Attische Urkunden* VI 198–200 no. 20, offers the following restoration of ll. 2–12:

[.....[10].....ἐσιτ]ήγησεν ἐξ Αἰγύπτου τ[ῶν ἐ]- stoich. 34
[κεῖθεν σίτων καὶ κυ⟨άμ⟩ων εὐωνοτέρων ὑπη[ντ]- (sic, with no closure of first square bracket)
[ηκότων, χαρίζεσθ]αι προαιρούμενος τῶι δ-
[ήμωι τῶι Ἀθηναίων· κ]αὶ ἐν τοῖς ἄλλοις τοῖς
[τῆς πόλεως ἀγῶσι χρ]ήσιμον ἑαυτὸν παρασ[κ]-
[ευάζων διατετέλεκ]εν ἐμ παντὶ καιρῶι, καὶ
[πολλοὺς τῶν πολιτῶν] λυτρωσάμενος ἐξ Σικ-
[ελίας ἀπέστειλε Ἀθ]ήναζε τοῖς αὑτοῦ ἀναλ-
[ώμασιν καὶ ἰδίαι κα]ὶ κοινῆι πρὸς τὸν δῆμο-
[ν ἐνδεικνύμενος τ]ὴν εὔνοιαν ἣν ἔχων διατ-
[ελεῖ ἐκ προγόνων, κ]αὶ νῦν κτλ.

The crux is [.......[13]......]ΛΥΛΛΩΝ (l. 3) stone. In 2002 Walbank suggested μ̣ύλλων. In the same year I replied with ν]α̣ύλλων. Gauthier, *Bull. ép.* 2003, 245, remarked that the sense of my solution might perhaps be more satisfactory, but noted the absence of parallel for the expression ναύλλων εὐωνοτέρων. Wilhelm's καὶ κυ⟨άμ⟩ων is very weak (one wonders if he would ever have published it), entailing stoichedon irregularity and the (usually very dubious) assumption of gross inscribing errors next to a square bracket. Moreover, a reference to cheap imports of beans would be unparalleled in Athenian decrees of this type and period, which refer invariably and exclusively to grain (cf. my remarks on Humphreys' suggestion about rope, *Ath. State* III p. 105 n. 37), and scarcely seems consistent with the sense of ἐσιτήγησεν. Apart from this, however, Wilhelm's scheme is an improvement. Angelos Matthaiou, who kindly wrote to me about this inscription before the publication of *Attische Urkunden* VI, also thought of a reference to grain at l. 3 in., suggesting τ[υχὼ|ν ἐκεῖ σίτο καὶ ν]α̣ύλλων, which has the advantage of supplying a concrete noun to soften the strangeness (if strangeness there be) of εὐωνοτέρων with ναύλλων, though I have some hesitation about the linguistic register of τυχὼν ἐκεῖ in Athenian decree language of this period. He saw, with Wilhelm, the need to replace the previous editors' κ]αὶ προαιρούμενος in l. 4 with an infinitive, and hit on the same verb, suggesting ὑπηρ̣[ε|τεῖν καὶ χαρίζεσθ]αι. ὑπηρ̣[ε|τεῖν picks up on a proposal of mine, but Wilhelm's ὑπην̣[τ|ηκότων would account equally well for the vertical after the eta and is perhaps preferable to what would be a rather vacuous duplication of present infinitives, unexpected | in the generally tight 83
drafting of Athenian decrees at this period. At 6 in. Matthaiou suggests

τῆς πόλεως πᾶσιν in place of Velsen's τῆς πόλεως αγῶσι, comparing, for example, *IG* II^2 252, 4–5. Like Wilhelm, he saw that Velsen's ἀποδέδεικται at 11 in. should be replaced by ἐνδεικνύμενος. Wilhelm and Matthaiou have brought improvements to the linguistic structure of the restorations, but a wholly convincing solution to the problem of restoration in l. 3 in. remains elusive. In terms of historical substance Matthaiou and I are in agreement: only grain was at issue; it was imported by the honorand from Egypt; and he was perhaps able to make it available to Athenians relatively cheaply (that is surely the implication) wholly or in part because the freight charges were relatively low. I agree with Wilhelm's dating to the period after Chaironeia (p. 200): "Die Spende Z. 12 f.: καὶ νῦν εἰς τὴν φυλακήν weist auf die Zeit nach der Schlacht bei Chaironeia, vgl. A. Schaeffer, *Demosthenes*^{2} III S. 12 ff. und A. Kuenzi, Ἐπίδοσις S. 2."

Ath. State IIIB no. 92. May go with *Ath. State* IV no. 39, q.v.

F *Chronological table*[55]

Year	Archon[56]	Secretary[57] (tribe)	Year type[58]	Metonic cycle[59]
352/1	Ἀριστόδημος	Not known (I)	–	I [Cycle V, year 5]
351/0	Θέελλος	Χρέμης Φ[ιλοιτίο 'Ιων]|[ί]δης? (II)[60]	O?[61]	O [6]

[55] I discuss the chronology of this period more fully in the forthcoming volume in honour of Michael Osborne [= this vol., chapter 18]. I am very grateful to John Morgan (a strong advocate of the Metonic cycle) for discussion and for kindly showing me parts of his important "work in progress" on Athenian chronology.

[56] The archons of this period are well established. See Develin, *AO*.

[57] At this period the secretaries held office for a year, apparently in rotation by tribes (the "secretary cycle"). Explanatory footnotes are included where the secretary is not firmly attested, or not firmly dated (e.g. where allocation to a year depends only on the secretary cycle). For some part-names which may be from otherwise unattested secretaries of this period see *Ath. State* IIIA p. 130 n. 54, *Ath. State* IIIB pp. 115–19. See also IIIB p. 104 n. 31.

[58] This column shows the years for which there is direct evidence as to whether it was ordinary (O) or intercalary (I). Such evidence includes, for example, a fully preserved calendar equation clearly indicating one or other year type or, for an intercalary year, an inscription passed on 37th, 38th or 39th of a prytany (in ordinary years at this period prytanies had [34—possible at year-end], 35 or 36 days, cf. *Ath. Pol.* XLIII 2). With O? and I?, where the determination depends on epigraphic restoration or other forms of editorial intervention, that must be driven primarily by factors other than preconceptions about the quality of the year (e.g. in simple cases, number of letter

Table (*cont.*)

Year	Archon	Secretary (tribe)	Year type	Metonic cycle	
350/49	Ἀπολλόδωρος	Not known (III)[62]	–	O [7]	
349/8	Καλλίμαχος	Διεύχης Δημάρχου Φρεάρριος (IV)	–[63]	I [8]	
348/7	Θεόφιλος	Not known (cf. on 351/0) (V)	–	O [9]	
347/6	Θεμιστοκλῆς	Λυσίμαχος Σωσιδήμου Ἀχαρνεύς (VI)	I?[64]	I [10] |	84
346/5	Ἀρχίας	Κηφισόδωρος Ἀθηνοφάνους Φλυεύς (VII)	O?[65]	O [11]	
345/4	Εὔβουλος	[.. ^{5} ..]ενος I[.... ^{7} ...] ἐξ Οἴο[υ] (VIII)[66]	O?[67]	O [12]	

spaces). The evidence from prescripts of inscriptions in this series generally becomes relevant for these purposes from 338/7, the earliest year for which we have a prescript from Athens with all four dating elements: month, date in month, prytany and date in prytany. However, there is also enough information in *IG* II^2 228 = *Ath. State* IIIB no. 70 and *IG* II^2 229 = *Ath. State* IIIA no. 54 to indicate that 341/0 was intercalary (cf. Meritt, *Ath. Year* 10).

59 This column shows the quality of the year according to the theoretical scheme of 19 year cycles set out by Dinsmoor, *Archons* p. 423. 352/1 is the 5th year of Dinsmoor's Cycle V, 337/6 the first year of Cycle VI.

60 Attested only by *IG* II^2 205 = *Ath. State* III no. 14. See my remarks at *Ath. State* IIIA n. 38, where I note that 348/7 is a possible alternative. The style of lettering and form of the prescript argue against a date before the introduction of annual secretaries in the 360s.

61 The cost calculations at Dem. IV 28 are based on a year of 12 months.

62 In *IG* II^2 249 the secretary was from Paiania (III), but there is no indication that this inscription dates to this year. See sect. D no. 3.

63 S. Accame, *ASAA* 3–5 (1941–3), 81–2 no. 4, is a decree from Lemnos passed at an ἐκκλησία τῶν τετελεσμένων and dated to the archonship of Kallimachos, the first prytany, of Hippothontis, the seventh of intercalary Hekatombaion (Ἑκατομβαιῶνος ὑστέρου). If Kallimachos was the Athenian archon of 349/8, this would indicate that the year was intercalary, but Accame suggested a date for this inscription in the second half of the third century, which looks more consistent with the style of lettering. In that case Kallimachos was probably archon of the Athenian cleruchy on Lemnos.

64 Cf. D.M. Lewis, *ABSA* 50 (1955), 25–6.

65 The equation Posid. 27 (τετράδι φθίνοντος) = pryt. V 31 in *IG* XII 6, 261, 56–7 shows that this was an ordinary year (for Samian cleruchy).

66 The name occurs in part at *Ath. State* IIIB no. 65 = *IG* II^2 219, in part at *Ath. State* IIIB no. 66 = *IG* II^2 220, 23–6.

67 *ID* 104–24, 8 shows that this year contained 355 days and was therefore ordinary (for Athenian official at Delos).

Table (*cont.*)

Year	Archon	Secretary (tribe)	Year type	Metonic cycle
344/3	Λυκίσκος	Not known (IX)	–	I [13]
343/2	Πυθόδοτος	Κλεόστρατος Τιμοσθένους Αἰγιλιεύς (X)	–	O [14]
342/1	Σωσιγένης	Not known[68] (I)	–	O [15]
341/0	Νικόμαχος	Ὀνήσιππος Σμικύθου Ἀραφήνιος (II)	I?	I [16]
340/39	Θεόφραστος	Ἄσπετος Δημοστράτου Κυθήρριος (III)	–	O [17]
339/8	Λυσιμαχίδης	-]ωνος Χολλείδης (IV)[69]	–	I [18]
338/7	Χαιρώνδης	Φίλιππος Ἀντιφήμου Εἰρεσίδης (V)[70]	–	O [19]
337/6	Φρύνιχος	Χαιρέστρατος Ἀμεινίου Ἀχαρνεύς (VI)	–	O [Cycle VI, year 1]
336/5	Πυθόδηλος	Not known (VII)[71]	I?	I [2]
335/4	Εὐαίνετος	Πρόξενος Πυλαγόρου Ἀχερδούσιος (VIII)	O	O [3]

[68] In *IG* II^2 227 the secretary was from Euonymon (I), but there is no indication that this inscription dates to this year. See sect. D no. 1.

[69] Firmly attested only by *SEG* XVI 52 = *Ath. State* IIIB no. 134a. See my discussion there, p. 123 n. 114. The archon is not preserved. The period is indicated by lettering and prescript style and prosopography, the year by the secretary cycle.

[70] The name and beginning of the father's name are attested by *IG* II^2 237 = *Ath. State* IIIA no. 5 and *IG* II^2 238 = *Ath. State* IIIA no. 32. For the completion of the father's name and the demotic see *Agora* XV 39, 18 and *IG* II^2 2753 = M.I. Finley, *Studies in Land and Credit* (1952), 145 no. 97 + *SEG* XVII 61, 4.

[71] *IG* II^2 328 = *Ath. State* IIIB no. 86 has 19 letter spaces for the secretary. It may date to 336/5 or 335/4. See also *Ath. State* IIIB p. 104 n. 31.

Table (*cont.*)

Year	Archon	Secretary (tribe)	Year type	Metonic cycle
334/3	Κτησικλῆς	Μνησίφιλος Μνήσωνος [Φαληρεύς][72] (IX)	O?	O [4]
333/2	Νικοκράτης	Αρχέλας Χαιρίου Παλληνεύς (X)	I	I [5]
332/1	Νικήτης	Ἀριστόνους Ἀριστόνου Ἀναγυράσιος (I)	O	O [6]
331/0	Ἀριστοφάνης	Not known[73] (II)	O?	O [7]
330/29	Ἀριστοφῶν	Ἀντίδωρος Ἀντίνου Παιανιεύς (III)	I?	I [8]
329/8	Κηφισοφῶν	Σωστρατίδης Ἐκφάντου Εὐπυρίδης (IV)	O[74]	O [9]
328/7	Εὐθύκριτος	Πυθόδηλος Πυθοδήλου Ἁγνούσιος (V)[75]	I?	I [10]
327/6	Ἡγήμων	Αὐτοκλῆς Αὐτίου Ἀχαρνεύς (VI)	–	O [11]
326/5	Χρέμης	Κηφισοκλῆς [- - - c. 15–16 - - -] (VII)[76]	O?	O [12]
325/4	Ἀντικλῆς	Ἀντιφῶν Κοροίβου Ἐλευσίνιος (VIII)	I?	I [13]
324/3	Ἡγησίας	Εὐφάνης[77] Φρύνωνος ‘Ραμνούσιος (IX)	–	O [14]

[72] The only demotic of Aiantis that fits the space in *IG* II² 335 = *Ath. State* IV no. 38.

[73] Cf. *Ath. State* IIIB p. 104 n. 31.

[74] *IG* II² 1672 shows that the 1st and 2nd prytanies had 36 days, the 5th and 6th prytanies 35 days, indicating an ordinary year.

[75] Cf. *Ath. State* I p. 101.

[76] Attested by *IG* II² 800 = *Ath. State* IIIB no. 147 and *SEG* XXXV 74 = *Ath. State* I no. 12.

[77] For the name cf. *Agora* XV 53, 17–18.

Table (*cont.*)

	Year	Archon	Secretary (tribe)	Year type	Metonic cycle
	323/2	Κηφισόδωρος	Αρχίας[78] Πυθοδώρου Ἀλωπεκῆθεν (X)	O?[79]	O [15]
85	322/1	Φιλοκλῆς	Εὐθυγένης Ἡφαιστοδήμου Κηφισιεύς (I)	I?[80]	I [16] |

[78] For the name cf. *IG* II^2 448 = Osborne, *Nat.* D38, 3 with *SEG* LI 83 = *Ath. State* IIIB no. 106.

[79] On the Metonic system the 15th year of a cycle should normally be ordinary, the 16th intercalary (as e.g. in cycle V and in this cycle according to six of the seven predecessors of Dinsmoor tabulated in his *Archons* p. 370). Dinsmoor, *Archons* 373–4 with table, p. 423, believed that, in fact, 323/2 was intercalary and 322/1 was ordinary, but the calendrical data for these years are more easily reconcilable with an ordinary 323/2 and an intercalary 322/1.

[80] See previous note.

PART B

OTHER PROLEGOMENA

CHAPTER SIX

TEN NOTES ON ATTIC INSCRIPTIONS[1]*

The focus is mainly on persons, the order chronological.

1. IG *i³ 752* (Acropolis dedication by a son of -]etalos)*

IG i³ prints: c. 500–480? [Π]αλλάδ̣[ι ---]οστ̣ --- τοσ[-- Π]ετάλο παῖς ⁝ εὐχσ[άμ]ενος κτλ.

I do not repeat other reconstructions of the dedicator's father's name and surrounding text, correctly rejected by *IG* i³ (see *IG* i³ *app. crit.)*; but Raubitschek's Π]ετάλο may not be right either. Despite the *kome* Petalidai in Aphidna (*Rationes,* 194) and the occurrence of Πέταλος as a personal name elsewhere (see *LGPN* I, IIIA and B), it is not securely attested in Attica.[2] Θέταλος, on the other hand, is, and in

* This chapter was previously published in *Zeitschrift für Papyrologie und Epigraphik* 135 (2000), 51–62.

[1] Notes 1, 2 and 5–10 treat some of the 76 amendments presented in a paper on the restoration of partially preserved names in inscriptions delivered at a conference in memory of Adolf Wilhelm held in Athens, Autumn 2000, in more detail than will be possible in the published proceedings of that conference. Notes 3 and 4 are the first prolegomena to an edition of Athenian State Laws and Decrees, 353–322, with commentary in English and select translation (provisionally *IG* ii³ 2). I have examined inscriptions marked * at autopsy. Warm thanks are due to the Epigraphical Museum under Charalambos Kritzas and to the American School Agora Excavations under John Camp for facilitating access to the stones; and to Sean Byrne for helpful discussion. I use the following abbreviations:
APF: J.K. Davies, *Athenian Propertied Families* (1971);
Davies, *Wealth:* J.K. Davies, *Wealth and the Power of Wealth in Classical Athens* (1984);
LGPN: Lexicon of Greek Personal Names (II Attica, edd. M.J. Osborne and S.G. Byrne, 1994; *I, IIIA and B,* edd. P.M. Fraser and E. Matthews, 1987, 1997, 2000);
Parker: R. Parker, *Athenian Religion. A History* (1996);
Rationes: S.D. Lambert, *Rationes Centesimarum* (1997);
Schwenk: C.J. Schwenk, *Athens in the Age of Alexander* (1985);
Tracy, *ADT:* S.V. Tracy, *Athenian Democracy in Transition* (1995).

[2] [Πέ]ταλος at *IG* i³ 1153, 31 of c. 450 might alternatively be [Φύ]ταλος ([Θέ]ταλος is less likely in this later text, which otherwise shows gemination; i.e. one might expect Θέττ-). On Phytalos as eponym of a historical Attic *genos* see Parker, 318. For genos eponyms as personal names in v BC cf. Ἀμύνανδρος, Πραξίεργος etc. The woman's name Πετάλη, however, is attested in Attica (see *LGPN* II).

the right period and class, namely for sons of the tyrant Peisistratos and of Kimon.[3] Davies has already plausibly inferred from *FGH* 373 Heliodoros Περὶ Ἀκροπόλεως F5[4] that it occurred on an Acropolis dedication. Ours might be the dedication in question; and it is not out of the question that the dedicator was the tyrant's grandson.

2. IG *ii^2 2420 (List of men from Troizen)*

Kirchner published *IG* ii^2 2420 in 1931 as a iv BC list from the Piraeus of non-Athenian Greeks. In fact the inscription was found in Troizen. It had first been published by A.N. Meletopoulos, Παρνασσός 7 (1883), 79, and appears also as *IG* iv (1) 825. Presumably some time after 1883 it had been transported by sea across the saronic Gulf; a reminder, if such be needed, that we must be ready to be sceptical about alleged Piraeus findspots when firm evidence supporting them is lacking; that it is not only very close neighbours such as Salamis and Aegina that come into question as the origin of *pierres errantes* apparently discovered there;[5] and that it is not only in the distant past that stones could wander. The nine men on this list should accordingly be deleted from
51 *LGPN* II (three of them had names otherwise | unattested in Attica, i.e. Πραξιδάμας, Τιμόδαμος, Χοραγίων); and since Kirchner's readings are (convincingly) fuller than those of *IG* iv, adjustment is also needed to *LGPN* IIIA (addition of Ἀρχέλ[α]ς, l. 13, and Τιμ[όδα]μ[ος], l. 17).

3. IG *ii^2 410* (Honours for priests and hieropoioi)*

The key to understanding the context of this decree, remarkably defensive in tone, is not so much directly the people it honours, four priests and ten *hieropoioi*, but the place with which they were associated, the Piraeus. The four priesthoods, of Dionysos, Zeus Soter, Ammon and Poseidon Pelagios are all locatable in the Piraeus area. Two of the priests, Pausiades priest of Ammon, and Himeraios priest

---

[3] *APF* pp. 307, cf. 448–49.

[4] εἷς τῶν Κίμωνος παίδων Θετταλὸς ἐκαλεῖτο.

[5] On stones moving between Attica, Aegina and Salamis see recently J. Cargill, *Athenian Settlements of the Fourth Century BC* (1995), 123–24.

of Poseidon Pelagios, were from Phaleron.[6] This Piraeus connection is one of several indications, which I explore more fully elsewhere,[7] that this decree dates to the immediate aftermath of Athens' defeat by Philip of Macedon at the battle of Chaironeia in 338 BC, at which time the Piraeus briefly became a focus of attention as a safe haven.[8] Indeed it seems that it was originally intended that the decree be set up there. At 39–40 I read [σ]τῆσαι ἐν τῶι θεάτρωι τοῦ Διονύσου ⟦τ̣..³.] | ⟦μ....⁷...],[9] and restore ⟦τ[ῶι ἐ]|μ [Πειραεῖ]].[10] I should imagine that the erasure reflects the dying down of the panic which followed the battle. Instead of the Piraeus theatre, the decree was eventually set up more conventionally in the theatre of Dionysos at Athens (close to which it was found in the 19th century).

Other corrections from autopsy: at the end of 25 read τ̣ῶ̣ν ἡρ[ώ]-ων καὶ (cf. *IG* i³ 1079?). In 36, [ε]ἰς θυσίαν καὶ ἀνάθ̣η̣μα̣ : . [: δρ] αχμὰς. In Crown VII discount Koumanoudes' omicron (probably an illusion caused by damage) and read Εὐκ̣λ̣[είδου] or Εὐκ̣λ̣[έους], cf. *IG* ii² 1926, 105 and 107; *Syll.*² 606 n. 15.

In more ways than one this can be seen as the first "Hellenistic" Athenian decree.[11]

---

[6] Himeraios was brother of Demetrios of Phaleron. His priesthood suggests that the demotic by which Demetrios came to be known not only inside, but unusually also outside Athens (and by posterity), was not a mere formality, i.e. that the family had real connections with the Piraeus-Phaleron area.

[7] Proceedings of a conference at the Canadian Institute at Athens in Spring, 2000, due to be published shortly [= this volume, chapter 12].

[8] In the emergency Hypereides proposed ἱερὰ δὲ καὶ παῖδας καὶ γυναῖκας εἰς τὸν Πειραιᾶ ἀποθέσθαι. [Plut.] *Mor.* 849a. Cf. Hyp. F 27–39 Jensen. This finds an echo in the wording of our 14–16, where the honorands had sacrificed ἐφ' ὑγιείαι καὶ σωτηρίαι τῆς βουλῆς καὶ τοῦ δήμου τõ | Ἀθηναίων καὶ παίδων καὶ γυναικῶν καὶ τῶν ἄλλων κτημάτ|ων τῶν Ἀθηναίων. Note also Lyk. 1.17; [Plut.] *Mor.* 851a with R. Garland, *The Piraeus* (1987), 44.

[9] Of the erased letters, a vertical stroke is detectable at autopsy immediately after Διονύσου and a clear mu at the start of 40 (entirely visible at autopsy, less clear on Oxford squeeze). There may also be extremely faint trace of some of the other erased letters in 40.

[10] A. Wilhelm, *Wiener Studien* 51–52 (1943–47), 162–66, proposed ⟦τοῦ Ἐλ|ευθερέως⟧, but this was based on *IG* ii²'s incorrect Διονύσο[υ...⁵..] (editors before Kirchner, i.e. Köhler and Koumanoudes, correctly show [υ..⁴..]).

[11] Cf. P.J. Rhodes with D.M. Lewis, *The Decrees of the Greek States* (1997), 29 n. 89; J.D. Mikalson, *Religion in Hellenistic Athens* (1998), 42–44.

4. IG *ii*^{2} *417* (Law? and list of dedications by liturgists)*

A number of features make reading this inscription more than usually problematic: erratically inscribed letters,[12] damage of various sorts, including low ridges and shallow valleys running vertically from top to bottom and not easily assessed other than at autopsy, uncertain indications (possible extraneous letter traces) that the stone may previously have carried another text, ordinary abrasion, irregular non-stoichedon letter-spacing (from l. 5 onwards). It is clear that the stone has not deteriorated significantly since early editions. A full and thorough
52 autopsy is essential to a good reading; it has not been attempted | since Köhler.[13] I make no apology, therefore, for presenting a fresh edition of the whole, based primarily on such an autopsy carried out in 2001, secondarily on study of numerous digital photographs.

EM 7166. Fragment of white ("Pentelic") marble, left side preserved. Whether the original back survives at any point is difficult to say. Certainly it has been reworked; there is a cutting, roughly a quarter cylindrical segment max. 0.03 deep (like a basin or wide socket), at the back of the upper left corner of the inscribed face. Its radius is 0.175 along the top edge, 0.13 down the side. Acropolis, west of the Parthenon, 1839.

H. 0.42 (c. 0.39 inscribed), w. 0.335, th. 0.165.

Height of letters: ll. 1–5, 0.006–7 (some, e.g. Ο, Δ, 0.005); from l. 6, 0.004–6 (some larger, e.g. Φ 0.008, Σ, Υ 0.007–0.0075). Stoich. c. 0.0118 (square) (ll. 1–4). Space occupied by 10 letters (ll. 6–33): variable 0.082–0.101 (horizontal); c. 0.10 (vertical).

Edd. K.S. Pittakis, *Eph. Arch.* 1842, no. 959; A.R. Rangabé, *Antiquités Helléniques* II (1855) no. 1241; *IG* ii 172 (Köhler); *IG* ii^{2} 417 (Kirchner).

Other contributions to the text: S. Dow, *Studies…Robinson* II (1953), 360–62 (col. 1, l. 11); D.M. Lewis, *Hesp.* 37 (1968) 374–80,

[12] The hand is not identified by Tracy, *ADT*.

[13] Lewis unfortunately did not state the basis for his amendments. I suspect fairly quick autopsy supplemented by squeezes and/or photographs. His contributions were very acute and represented significant progress, but not so thorough that a few mistakes were not made and some improvements were not overlooked. This accords with the general impression I have of Lewis' work on difficult stones that had been edited previously (e.g. the *Rationes Centesimarum*).

no. 51 (col. 1 ll. 11, 15, 27, 29, col. 2 ll. 25, 28, 31, 32); *APF* p. 7 (col. 1 l. 26).

Cf. O. Palagia, *JHS* 95 (1975) 180–82; C. Lawton, *Attic Document Reliefs* (1995) no. 150 (ph.).

Epigraphical Notes

I note below points where the above text diverges significantly from *IG* ii[2] (which mostly follows *IG* ii). My line numbers are one higher than earlier eds. I do not normally note minor adjustments (e.g. removing letters from square brackets).

Lines 1–4 (end of text of law?)

The monument was probably quite wide (see discussion below) and the lines may have extended a good way further to the right.

1 fin. Rest. SDL. Permission (as opposed to obligation) to do things is usually granted to honorands *vel sim.*, and it is difficult to imagine who might be in question here except the liturgists themselves.

2 After γράψαι I read: bottom vertical to left of stoichos; illegible letter (cf. *IG*); bottom horizontal (as *IG*) and possible other traces consistent with E or Ξ; illegible letter (*IG* prints O, but this may be an illusion caused by damage); bottom right diagonal tending to vertical, as of M (bottom vertical *IG*); E (as *IG*). One might hazard a guess that what was to be permitted to be inscribed was the liturgists' names (on the stele? on the *phialai*?).

3 As Rangabé noted, the article in κατὰ τὸν ἄνδρα is surprising, but it is difficult to see how the phrase could mean here anything other than "per man". Cf. *IG* xii (5) 647, 12–13. The one drachma might be the cost of the writing referred to in the previous line. fin. rest. SDL. In this context εἰς δὲ is perhaps from the formulaic wording relating to payment for the stele.

4 καθότι ἂν τῶι δήμωι δοκῆι *vel sim.* occurs fairly frequently in the formulaic language of decrees (e.g. in this period *IG* ii[2] 149, 18–19, *SEG* xxxvii 77, 4), but I have been unable to trace a parallel for it at the very end of a text; perhaps it relates to (place of?) erection of the stele.

Line 5 (Heading) The letters are more spaced than in the above text. ἐληιρτού[ργ]-ησαν. On the spelling see L. Threatte, *The Grammar of Attic Inscriptions* I, 479. | 53

333/2 -- stoich.
or [....⁷...]Ọ[..⁴..]Ọ[--------------------------------τοῖς δὲ ληιτουργοῦ?]-
332/1? σιν ἐξεῖναι γράψαι ̣|[.]_..E [---------------------------------------]-
ου καὶ : ⊢ : κατὰ τὸν ἄνδρα· εἰς δὲ [τὴν ἀναγραφὴν τῆς στήλης ? -]
τῶι δήμωι δοκῆι.

οἵδε ἐληιρτού[ργ]ησαν ἐπὶ [------ἄρχοντος]· non stoich.

col. 1
[ε]ὐταξίας
Ἐρεχθηΐδος
Κηφισόδωρος Μειδίου Ἀ[να]γυράσιος : 𐅄 *vac.?*
Ἀρχέβιος Ἀρχεβιάδου Λ̣α̣μπ⟨τ⟩ρεύς : 𐅄 *vac.?*
Αἰγηΐδος
Θεόπομπος Πυρρίνου Γα̣[ργ]ή̣ττιος : 𐅄 *vac.?*
Νικοκλῆς *vacat* Κυ̣[δα]ν̣τίδης : 𐅄 *vac.?*
Πανδιονίδος
Διόφαντος Διοπείθου[ς Μυ]ρ̣ρινού(σιος) : 𐅄̣[-?]

col. 2
Θε[--
Δ . [--
Νι̣[κ? --
Λι̣[--
Λ̣ε̣ω̣ν[τίδος Σουνιεῖς?]
Ἡγ[--
Πύ[θ?--
. Λ[--
Λ̣[--

Πάμφιλος [Χ]αιρεφίλου Π[αια]νιεύς : 𐅄[-?]	ΞΕ[--
Λεωντίδος	Ἰπ̣[π--
Λεύκιος Θεοκλέους Σ[ου]νιεύς : 𐅄[-?]	Α̣Ι . [-
Πύθων Πυθο[κ]λέους̣ Σ[ου]νιεύς : 𐅄[.¹?].[-?]	. Α̣[--
Ἀκαμαντίδος	.. /[--
Ἀνδ[ρ]οκλῆς Ξείνιδος Σ[φήτ]τιος : . [.²?.].[-?]	Α̣υ[--
Ἐ̣πιτέλης *vacat* [Θορί]κιος : . [-?]	. Ο̣ . [--
[Ο]ἰνῃ̣ΐδος	. Υ[--
Σμῖκρος *vacat* [Ἀχ]αρνεύς : 𐅄. [-?]	ΦΙ[--
Μέ[ν]ιππος Δημοκράτου[ς Ἀχ]αρνεύς : 𐅄. [-?]	ΦΙ[--
Κεκροπίδος	Κολ̣[ωνεῖς]
Χαρίδημος Αἰσχύλου Ἀθ[μο]νεύς : 𐅄 *vac. ?*	Φα[ίν- ?
Χά[ρ]ης..[.ᶜ· ²⁻³.]. ου Αἰξων[εύς] : ΔΔΔΓ⊢⊢⊢⊢ *v.*	Κλ̣ε[--
Ἱπποθωντίδος	Λευκ̣[ονοεῖς]
Χαιρέδ[ημ]ος *vacat* ἐξ Οἴου̣ : 𐅄 *vac. ?*	...[--
Αἰαντίδος	Νι[κ? --
Θεόμνηστος *vacat* [ʽΡαμ]νούσιος : 𐅄⊢ *vac.*	. Ο⊢[-
[..]μοσθένης *vacat* [ʽΡα]μ̣νούσιος : 𐅄 *vac.*	Πα[ιονίδαι
[Ἀντιο]χίδος	--------

Epigraphical Notes (continued)

Col. 1 (*Eutaxia* liturgists).

There is an area of severe abrasion (water wear?) running up and down the stone to the right of most of the preserved numbers. 𐅄 *vac.?* means that, while the reading 50 drachmas is likely, it is not quite certain; 𐅄[-?] indicates a higher degree of uncertainty.

8, 9, 11, 12 𐅄 *vac.?* SDL, 𐅄 Kirchner. 8 Apparently the cutter inscribed ΛΑΜΠΞΕΥΣ.

11 Πυρρίνου Dow, Lewis, correctly; Πυρρίχου *IG*. Of the nu only the two verticals are clear.

14 Διοπείθου[ς Μυ]ρρινού : 𐅄̣[-?] SDL. Διοπείθου [Μυρ]ρινού : /// *IG*. The inclusion of the sigma at the end of the father's name is indicated by spacing. There are traces of the number; they are very difficult to read, but can be interpreted as from 𐅄.

15 𐅄[-?] SDL, H *IG* (doubted by Lewis).

17 𐅄[-?] SDL, 𐅄 *IG*.

18 𐅄[.].[-?] SDL, 𐅄 *IG*. There is a faint mark like the right diagonal and upper left diagonal of delta in about the second space to the right of the 𐅄. It may be a casual
54 mark, but it is difficult to rule out a number, 𐅄[Δ]Δ[-?]. |

20 Ἀνδ[ρ]οκλῆς SDL, Δη[μ]οκλῆς *IG*. The new reading is certain (it was almost deducible from Köhler's majuscule). I read the first four letters as: Α/Δ/Λ (A Pittakis and Rangabé); N completely visible including clear, rather low, diagonal; Δ (left diagonal and left section of horizontal clear, otherwise outline, damaged within); damaged area (very uncertain trace of left side of rho). fin..[..].[-?] SDL, H *IG*. The reading of the number is very difficult. Both H and 𐅄 are possible epigraphically. Further to the right there is a further mark (casual?, ⊢?, Δ?).

21 Ἐπιτέλης SDL, Σκ[ί]π[ω]ν previous eds. The new reading is sure. I read: E (part of every stroke visible); pi (completely visible); damaged area including uncertain trace of iota; right side of T; E with forward leaning vertical; Λ/A; H (cross bar faint);

Σ. fin. H *IG*. The currently visible mark does indeed appear to be H, but it can not be ruled out that, as with some other 50-signs in this text, the horizontal of the Γ is positioned low such that the verticals extend upwards beyond it; and there may also be very faint trace of an internal diagonal suggesting the pendent delta. 𐅄 can not be ruled out.

23 and 24 𐅄. [-?] SDL, 𐅄 Kirchner. In both lines there are faint marks like the left corner of delta after the 𐅄. They might be casual.

26 Ἀθ[μο]νεύς SDL, Ἀ[θμον]εύς *IG*. Davies noted that, on the then current reading, Α[ἰξων]εύς was also possible. I detect very faint (probable, but not 100% sure) trace of the upper and left section of Θ/Ο after the Α. Note also that the name Αἰσχύλος is now attested in Athmonon (*SEG* xxxvi 217, 90).

27 Λ[..⁴..]ου *IG*, Ω[..³.]ου Lewis. The father's name remains enigmatic. The first letter is difficult. Omega is perhaps possible from (damaged) trace, but citizen names in omega at this period are extremely rare and the legible trace is also (more?) consistent with *IG*'s Α/Δ/Λ (the apparent tails of omega might be caused by thickening of letter ends and on repeated viewing I tend to think the side of the letter consists of diagonals). Followed by: 2 verticals close together (as N, possibly damage) or upper tip of Α/Δ/Λ; space marginally less than is occupied in the previous line by the letters ΟΣΑΙ, towards the end of which, aligned between A and I in previous line, is possible trace of T/E/Ξ, and before that vague impression of Σ; ΟΥ. Ἀδ[εί]στου?

29 ἐξ Οἴου Lewis, correctly. For earlier attempts to decipher these letters see note to *IG* ii² 417. The following number might, from trace, as easily be Π or 𐅃.

31 𐅄⊢ SDL, 𐅄 previous eds. The drachma sign is clearly visible in its entirety.

Col. 2 (Liturgists of Pandionis and Leontis)

The surviving letters must, it seems, come from a list of another liturgy, which started in the lost lower section of col. 1. Lewis correctly identified deme-names of Leontis in 25, 28 and 32 (beginning one space to left of normal column edge) and this is confirmed by my reading of the tribe name in 10. There will be some other deme-names lurking in 14–22, their initial letters obscured by the area of wear which, as noted above, runs to the right of the numbers in col. 1. Here and there possible (but uncertain, cf. 31) traces of such initial letters are detectable. Not all the adjustments made to the readings of earlier eds. are noted below.

7 ΔΙ[- or Δω[-. 9 Λυ[-?

10 Λεων[τίδος Σουνιεῖς?] SDL, ΛΙΙ *IG* (aligned one space to left of column edge). The letters are slightly larger/more spaced than usual and the first three are to the left of the normal column edge. I read: left and upper right diagonals of Λ, bottom left corner of E (both traces might be casual marks and are uncertain), Ω or Α/Δ (*IG*'s Λ); N clear. Παν[διονίδος might also be read (lit from right), but would be difficult to reconcile with what follows. The deme (Sounion) follows from the tentative identifications in 11 and 12.

11 The only family in Leontis in *APF* with names in Ἡγ- is that of Hegias, Hegesippos and Hegesandros, sons of Hegesias of Sounion (*PA/APF* 6351).

12 One suspects membership of the family of Python son of Pythokles of Sounion, *PA/APF* 12478 (cf. col. 1, 18).

13 First letter: K (*IG*) or X.

15 No letter traces were shown in this line by *IG*. There are in fact very faint traces: Ξ (but note confusion of Ξ/E/T elsewhere in this text) followed by vertical (lower left corner of E?). Personal name Ξε[ν- ?

17 ΛΙ⊢ Kirchner (*IG* prints the final letter to look like vertical and lower curve of rho). The last letter is difficult; it might also be e.g. nu. Second letter might have bottom horizontal, i.e. epsilon.

18 Κα[- or Σα[- or Χα[-? ΛΛ *IG*.

19 Κ/ or Χ/ The letters are squat. Possibly Ἑκα[λεῖς] or Σκα[μβωνίδαι].

21 There are uncertain traces to the left of the O/Θ (A/Δ/Λ) and to the right (N?), but these do not suit any Leontis deme. Perhaps the trace to the left is illusory (cf. 31).

22 ΣY *IG*. The first letter is difficult. Σ should not be ruled out; but one occasionally gains an impression rather like rho. Of the second letter, probable bottom vertical and upper left diagonal of upsilon are apparent.

25, 28, 32 Deme names identified by Lewis.

26 Φα̣[ίν- ? SDL, Φ/ Köhler. Φαίνιππος is the only name attested in the liturgical class from Kolonai that suits the traces of the first two letters (*APF* 14734).

27 or perhaps Και.

29 Πιθ̣[- ? SDL, Κ̈[- *IG*.

31 ȮṖ̇ preceded by top horizontal, *IG*, but before a deme name in 32 it seems that Lewis must be right that the trace to the left of the column is to be discounted. So,

55 probably a personal name Θρ-, Θε- or Ὀρ-. |

Lewis persuasively interpreted this text in the light of his no. 51 (= *SEG* xxv 177), which records dedications by the liturgists of (probably) 331/0 of *phialai* weighing, in all cases where the number is preserved, 50 dr. Since our inscription apparently also listed the liturgists of a single year, followed by (in most cases) the 50 dr. symbol, the list apparently preceded by regulatory text, he inferred that the latter was the "founding law"[14] requiring liturgists to dedicate *phialai* on the Acropolis and that our inscription should accordingly date "a year or two earlier" than 331/0.

The left column lists those who performed the *Eutaxia* liturgy (presumably in the first year of the new dedication requirements), two per tribe (but only one from Hippothontis).[15] We do not have sure evidence as to what this liturgy was.[16] *Eutaxia* denoted good order, often (but not invariably) in a military context, and a quality especially appreciated in ephebes.[17] As a liturgy it was agonistic. We have a relief

[14] "Law" rather than "decree" because it was a law which introduced the compulsory dedication of *phialai exeleutherikai* at this period (*IG* ii[2] 1560). Lewis, 376.

[15] The tribe perhaps failed to find two liturgists (for parallels see Lewis, 378).

[16] Rangabé thought it was a liturgy concerned with the organisation of the other liturgies: "fonctionnaires employés…pour régler (τάξασθαι) l'ordre, la grandeur et les échéances des liturgies". The suggestion has dropped out of more recent bibliography and does not now look the most plausible, but it is symptomatic of how little we know about the detail of the liturgical organisation in the Lykourgan period that we can not, I think, certainly rule out something along these lines.

[17] See e.g. in this period O.W. Reinmuth, *The Ephebic Inscriptions of the Fourth Century BC* (1971), no. 2, ll. 31, 40, 58 and no. 9, ll. 7–8. Other references in an ephebic context are listed by Palagia, 181 n. 18, updatable via *SEG* indices s.v. εὐταξία. See also the notes of Jüthner and Waser, *RE* 1907 col. 1491–2 s.v. Eutaxia. For εὐταξία as "good order" in a festal context see *SEG* xxxiii 115, 28 (at a *pannychis*), probably xxxii 86, 38, and further below.

from an inscription which apparently honoured a victor in it,[18] datable stylistically to the last quarter of the 4th century and depicting the (lower half of the) honorand with shield, being crowned by the *Demos* (?), with a personification of *Eutaxia* standing by.

There is also a reference to *eutaxia* in the decree of 329/8 honouring the *epimeletai* of the Amphiareia (Schwenk no. 50 = *IOrop* 298), where it is provided that, at the next meeting of the *nomothetai*, it be proposed that the treasurer of the People give τοῖς αἱρεθεῖσιν ἐπὶ τὸν ἀγῶνα the 30 drachmas which are specified in the law for τῶι αἱρεθέντι ἐπὶ τὴν εὐταξίαν (39–45). We know too little to understand the background with confidence,[19] but probably the latter official was responsible not for the *Eutaxia* competition, but simply for "good order" (sc. at the festival), as for example at *SEG* xxxiii 115, 28.[20]

The shield held by the honorand on Lawton no. 150, the association of the quality of *eutaxia* with ephebes, as well as chronological coincidence (further below), suggest that the *Eutaxia* competition, funded by our liturgists, may have involved military exercises staged by the ephebes. A possible context for these is suggested by Ath. Pol.'s description of ephebic training: τὸν δεύτερον (sc. ἐνιαυτὸν) ἐκκλησίας ἐν τῶι θεάτρῳ γενομένης ἀποδειξάμενοι τῷ δήμωι τὰ περὶ τὰς τάξεις καὶ λαβόντες ἀσπίδα καὶ δόρυ παρὰ τῆς πόλεως περιπολοῦσι κτλ. Ath. Pol. xlii 4. In this case, the competition will have been founded together with, or very shortly after, the reorganised ephebate, for which evidence | first appears in 334/3.[21] It will presumably have been 56
abolished with other liturgies by Demetrios of Phaleron, its short life

[18] Lawton, no. 150. As Lewis noted, this relief will not, as earlier assumed, be from our inscription, which related to all liturgies, not only *Eutaxia*. The dimensions of the relief and its date are probably also incompatible with our inscription.

[19] Cf. Schwenk, 247. I doubt, however, if Schwenk is right to bring this 30 dr. into connection with the preceding text in which 100 dr. is to be advanced by the treasurer of the People to the *epimeletai* for a sacrifice (35–39). The 30 dr. was not, I should imagine, part payment for this sacrifice (which begs the question, where the other 70 dr. are to come from), but to meet a separate expense concerned with *eutaxia*.

[20] That the *Eutaxia* was a military competition was suggested by Palagia, but Petrakos *ad IOrop* 298 is perhaps right to be sceptical about inferring a link with the Amphiareia. The Amphiareia included gymnastic/military events (Schwenk no. 50, 16–18) and apparently involved the ephebes (e.g. Reinmuth no. 15, with D.M. Lewis, *CR* 87 (1973), 255 and Tracy, *ADT* 93; A. Chaniotis, *Kernos* 13 (2000), 205–6) but there is no secure reference to a *Eutaxia* competition in the documentation of the festival (e.g. the victor list, *IG* vii 414 = *IOrop* 520). Other recent discussion of this festival can be traced via Parker, 149, 247, 250 and Tracy, *ADT* 92–93.

[21] See most recently Tracy, *ADT* 10–11 n. 21.

explaining the paucity of our evidence for it. There are clearly some uncertain inferences here, but an ephebic *Eutaxia* competition and Lewis' posited chronological relation between our text and his no. 51 would both be consistent with a date for our text of 333/2 or 332/1.[22] Like the similar contemporary law imposing the dedication of *phialai exeleutherikai*, the measure is patently Lykourgan in spirit, and quite possibly in fact.[23]

Our new reading of the stone adds a little on the weight of the dedications. In addition to the 49 dr. *phiale*, we now also certainly have one at 51 dr. The minor variations from the 50 dr. norm tend to confirm (as John Davies points out to me) that we have to do with *phialai* rather than the liturgical contribution itself, as well as that the weight was carefully checked (by the treasurers of Athena with an eye to their accounts?). For the rest, there seems little doubt that 50 dr. was the norm, but the reading of the numbers is very difficult in many cases and it is possible (to put it no more strongly) that some of the weights were higher.[24] In any case, Lewis' restoration of all the weights in his no. 51 at 50 dr., where only three or four can be securely read, now seems overconfident.

The major gain, however, is prosopographical. It is not necessary here to go over the *Eutaxia* liturgists unaffected by significant new readings. What is known about them can conveniently be traced via *APF* (updatable via *LGPN* II). Most are from prominent families; in fact, only three of the seventeen men whose names are preserved are now otherwise unknown in person or by family: Smikros of Acharnai, Chairedemos of Oion and -mosthenes of Rhamnous; a striking indication of the depth of our evidence for the Athenian liturgical class at this period.[25] We now also have useful confirmation that the deme of Aischylos in [Dem.] lviii was very probably Athmonon, not Aixone

[22] Köhler's dating, 340–333, "propter litterarum speciem" was acute; Kirchner's "post 330" was based on overly speculative inferences that had been made about the appearance of Pamphilos of Paiania in col. 1 (l. 15; cf. *APF* pp. 566–68).

[23] See Lewis, 376. Whatever the "one drachma per man" of l. 3 refers to, the fine financial detail is typically Lykourgan.

[24] Liturgical supererogation? Cf. Davies, *Wealth* 26 and ch. 6; *Rationes*, 245 n. 111.

[25] Identification of these three might have been possible if their fathers' names had been included. The statistics can not be pursued in detail here, but while the number of performances of a liturgy for which we have evidence is relatively slight (cf. *APF* pp. xxix–xxx) this evidence for the *Eutaxia* liturgists is consonant with other indications that, if we suddenly acquired full information about every performance of every liturgy at this period, to a very large extent the liturgists would turn out to be identifi-

(l. 26, cf. *APF* p. 7); and the ranks of known contributors are swelled by two men whose identities were previously obscured by incorrect readings. Epiteles of Thorikos (l. 21) was already known as a trierarch c. 323/2, and his father (?), Smikythos, as a landowner in the mining area and councillor c. 340 *(APF* 4959).[26]

Most notable, however, is the new reading of 20. Xenokles son of Xeinis of Sphettos was among the most distinguished Athenians of the second half of the fourth century, holding the important office ἐπὶ τῇ διοικήσει between the two periods of Lykourgos' tenure and variously attested as liturgist and public benefactor *(APF* 11234).[27] Our new reading shows that he had a brother who was a substantial figure in his own right, Androkles of Sphettos. The two brothers[28] can now be seen as multiple "buyers", listed consecutively, at *IG* ii² 1593, 13–23, a fragment of accounts of uncertain type, now ascribed by Tracy to a cutter of the Lykourgan period.[29] Androkles of Sphettos, however,
57 is best known as the speaker of | [Dem.] xxxv (delivered 355–338),

able in person or by family. In other words, multiple liturgical burdens were borne by a relatively small number of (by and large known) families.

[26] The evidence for the name Σκίπων in published volumes of *LGPN* (I–IIIB) is now reduced to Σκείπων son of Ἀμέθυστος, ephebic *epengraphos* in 184/5 AD on *IG* ii² 2128, 186.

[27] See also D.M. Lewis, *Selected Papers* (ed. P.J. Rhodes, 1997), 227–29; C. Habicht, *Hesp.* 57 (1988), 323–27.

[28] There was apparently a third brother, Krates, named on a curse tablet with Xenokles in the 320s. See E. Ziebarth, *SBAB* 1934, 1023 no. 1 A, 22–23; *APF* p. 415.

[29] Androkles of Sphettos is listed (and should be restored as ὠνητής) in 19, 21 and 23, his guarantors being Charias of Potamos (20), Kephisodoros of Potamos (22) and Xenophon of Poros (24). Xenokles of Sphettos (various parts of his name survive, in some cases more than is printed in *IG* ii²) should be restored as ὠνητὴς in 13–14 (guarantor from Anagyrous), 15–16 (guarantor, Leostratos) and 17–18 (guarantor, Lysiades of Oion). Probably, the rest of the text should be restored similarly to yield alternate buyers and guarantors. In 1, read ἐγ[γυητὴ]ς (or possibly [ἐ]γγ[υητὴ] ς) Θε[οπε]ίθης Ἀλ[αιεύς]. A full new study of this neglected fragment is required and can not be attempted here. Ascribed by Tracy, *ADT* 107, to his Cutter of *IG* ii² 354, active 337–324, it is sandwiched in the Corpus between poletai records (*IG* ii² 1579 and 1581–89 = *Ag.* xix P), public leases (*IG* ii² 1590–1592 = *Ag.* xix L) and accounts of the Lykourgan public land sale programme (*IG* ii² 1580, 1594–1603 = *Rationes),* with all of which it has differences and points in common. Brief autopsy in 2001 revealed fragmentary text above, below and substantially to the left (another column?) of that printed in *IG* ii². Among notable features are the apparent absence of prices and item-by-item specification of properties and the inclusion of guarantors with "ὠνηταί" (normally a feature of lease documents; on the possible range of meaning of ὠνητής, however, see *Rationes,* 258). Nearly all the ὠνηταί (but fewer of the guarantors) are from known/prominent families. For another fragment of a financial document cut by the Cutter of *IG* ii² 354, see the Postscript to this Note.

and it is of considerable interest that this speaker is now identified as Xenokles' brother.[30] Together with a Nausikrates of Karystos, he had lent money to brothers from Phaselis to fund a commercial sea voyage and is suing for its return. There is no mention of family or connections, except at one place. Androkles had been introduced to the Phaselites by Thrasymedes, ὁ Διοφάντου υἱός, ἐκείνου τοῦ Σφηττίου, καὶ Μελάνωπος ὁ ἀδελφὸς αὐτοῦ, with whom, he says, he had close relations (6).[31] Diophantos of Sphettos, together with Euboulos, had been the leading financial officials of the generation before Lykourgos. The identification of the brother of Lykourgos' friend and stand-in as speaker of [Dem.] xxxv and as someone who enjoyed close relations with the family of Diophantos confirms that there were personal connections underlying the apparent policy continuities between Diophantos-Euboulos and Lykourgos.[32]

Gomme-Sandbach's tentative identification of the energetic old man Androkles at Men. *Samia* 606 (τρέχει, πηδᾷ, πολὺ πράττεται, μέλας περιπατεῖ), perhaps produced c. 314, with the speaker of [Dem.] xxxv, can not be more than speculative;[33] apart from Sphettos the name occurs in propertied circles in several demes (Aphidna, Acharnai, Euonymon, Poros). Xenokles certainly was prominent as an elderly man, however, i.e. in the early years of the restored democracy after 307 (see *APF*, p. 415). Androkles of Sphettos, priest of the eponymous at *Ag.* xv 131, 14f. (c. 220) will have been a descendant of one or other

[30] I follow more recent scholarly opinion (e.g. Gernet's 1954 edition, pp. 170–71) in accepting the authenticity of the documents at [Dem.] xxxv 10–13 and 14, in which the speaker's name and demotic are given. Other men named in these documents (but not elsewhere in the speech) are independently attested in (and their demotics confirmed by) the epigraphical record. E.g. Demokrateia, sister of the custodian of the loan agreement at 14, Archenomides son of Archedamas of Anagyrous, is on the funerary monument, *IG* ii^2 7277. See further next note.

[31] ἐκείνου τοῦ Σφηττίου is slightly odd language from someone who was himself a Sphettian and the sceptical might be inclined to suspect an interpolated gloss, or indeed that Androkles of Sphettos was not after all the speaker. More likely, consonant with the speech in general, it is simply slightly maladroit (cf. Gernet, 178: "le discours est faible, mal composé, peu convaincant").

[32] Cf. *Rationes*, 289 (on participation of Diophantos in Lykourgan land sale programme). I noted there that Sphettos seems to have been one of Lykourgos' power bases, and the links of Lykourgos' circle with the banker Pasion. A Phormio son of Ktesiphon of Piraeus appears as one of the witnesses to the loan agreement at [Dem.] xxxv 13 and 14; Davies' tentative identification of him with the well-known associate of Pasion, *APF* p. 436, now looks very likely.

[33] For Arnott (2000 Loeb edition) this Androkles is simply "an otherwise unidentified Athenian".

of the brothers (now clearly identifiable, with Pritchett, as the Ξείνι]δος Σφήττιον at *Ag.* xv 128, 39–41 and 55), as will Xenokles of Sphettos, subscriber in *SEG* xxxii 118, 57, and attractively identified by Habicht (op. *cit.* at n. 27) as honorand of *IG* ii^2 749 (unless that was Androkles, or Xenokles and Androkles jointly).

The new study of the stone, especially the identification of the tribe name in 10, enables us to build on Lewis' identification of demes of Leontis in the lower section of column two. The number of men from Kolonai and Leukonoion was equivalent to those demes' bouleutic quotas; but there is no known liturgy whose numbers and organisation corresponded to the Council in this way, and while the interpretation of lines 10–24 is far from sure, I have not yet found a way to read deme names followed | by numbers of personal names corresponding 58
to bouleutic representation.[34] Caution is appropriate, but I take it to be a good possibility that this list has something to do with the panel(s?) of 300 who were liable to the *proeisphora* and the trierarchy.[35] In any case the number of men seems too high for festival liturgies to be in question.[36]

Here too we have new prosopographical data, albeit necessarily tentative (details above, epigraphical notes). Line 11 may yield our first direct evidence of a liturgy performed by a member of the prominent Sounian family of the genos Salaminioi to which the brothers Hegesandros (associate of Timarchos in Aeschin. 1) and Hegesippos (probable author of [Dem.] 7) belonged (*APF* 6351; see also *ZPE* 125 (1999), 111–12). In l. 26 we probably have to do with the family of Phainippos of Kolonai, familiar in a liturgical context from [Dem.] xlii, though whether this was Phainippos himself or a relation whose name was the same or began with the same syllable, is impossible to say.

A monument inscribed both with the law introducing compulsory dedication of *phialai leitourgikai* and the liturgists of its first year of

---

[34] For example, if the names in 11 ff. are of Sounians (boul. quota 4), 15 ought to contain a deme name rather than, as the traces seem to suggest, a personal name beginning Ξε[ν-.

[35] Davies, *Wealth* 19. Cf. *APF* p. xxix. V. Gabrielsen, *Financing the Athenian Fleet* (1994), 211, however, argues that 1200 men were officially liable for trierarchies at this period.

[36] There appear to have been about 100 festival liturgies a year (*APF* pp. xxix–xxx); and in any case we would expect each of these to be listed separately (as in *SEG* xxv 177).

operation[37] will have been very substantial, consistent with the considerable preserved thickness of our fragment (16.5 cm., possibly not original). There are too many uncertainties about the monument (e.g. whether it was opisthographic, number of years listed) and about how many liturgists there were in a single year at this period to enable precise calculations; but for possible order of magnitude one might compare for example the great Council list of 304/3, c. 21–24 cm. thick, about two metres high and just over one metre wide, with a heading and names of 600 councillors and officers in 6 columns.[38]

Postscript: SEG *xlv 206 (Fragment of a financial document)*

I briefly discussed above the financial document, *IG* ii^2 1593, now ascribed by Tracy to his Cutter of *IG* ii^2 354, whose attested period of activity, 337–324, nicely coincides with that of Lykourgos. Not surprisingly for a cutter working at this time, he was responsible for several other financial texts, including the *poletai* records *IG* ii^2 1583 (*Ag.* xix P14), 1584 (P15), *Ag.* xix P16, P28 and P29 fr. b. At *ADT*, 108–10 (*SEG* xlv 206), Tracy presents the *editio princeps* (with ph.) of another small fragment of this cutter's work *(Ag.* I 4355), which I examined in 2000 and which should be added to his dossier of financial documents (a lease record?). The only lines yielding whole words are 7–11. Tracy suggests [εἰ]|ς Χίον [--] in 8–9, but can find no plausible explanation for ΩΤΤΗ at the beginning of 11. Abbreviation, I think, is the key. I would restore:

δέκα[-------------]-
ς τούς [------------]-
ς Χιον[----------πέμ]-
πτηΝ[----------μισθ]-
ωτ(ής) Τη[----------]

9 The personal name Χίονις, in nom. or gen. (i.e. father's name), i.e. lessee, guarantor, property owner *vel sim.*
10 πέμ]|πτη sc. οἰκία *vel sim.* or πέμ]|πτην. Cf. *Ag.* xix L6, 17, L9, 64 etc.
11 Cf. *Ag.* xix L9, 74, 79 etc. Less likely, abbreviated demotic in -ω (of a buyer or
59 lessee), followed by a number (price?), 2 tal., 100 dr. |

[37] The year heading in l. 5 tends to suggest that this list was intended to be the first of an annual series.

[38] See J.S. Traill, *Hesp.* 35 (1966), 222–23; *Ag.* xv 61.

Again we have a new prosopographical datum, for since the man named in 9 will on any account probably have been propertied, identity with Χίονις Δημοστράτου (I) Παιανιεύς, councillor c. 330 and member of a known propertied family *(Ag.* xv 47, 12; *PA/APF* 15550), is a distinct possibility.

5. SEG *xxxiii 115 (Timokrite's father)*

Τιμοκρίτη Πολυνίκου Ἀφιδναίου θυγάτηρ was honoured by the polis as priestess of Aglauros in 250/49? (*SEG* xxxiii 115, archon Polyeuktos).[39] Her paternal family is of some interest. A satisfactory socio-economic analysis of the Athenian priesthood is long overdue; and Timokrite may have been chosen from the genos Salaminioi (unfortunately the situation is not quite clear).[40] Her father is identifiable as councillor for Aphidna in 304/3. Read, at *Ag.* xv 59, 15,* [Πολύνι]κος Ἐπικ[ούρου] and at 61, 267,* [Π]ολῠ́[νι]κος Ἐπικούρο̣υ̣. Even without the attractive identification with Timokrite's father, Πολύνικος was the more likely restoration here than the current Πολύδικος, for it is a very much commoner name.[41] Polynikos' tenure of office as councillor is not an indication of socio-economic prominence. Neither he nor his father are as yet otherwise attested. They lived at a time when our evidence for the liturgical class is very solid (see above, Note 4). The probability is that the family did not belong to that class. This rather confirms, I think, the impression conveyed by her decree that Timokrite came to this priesthood, as it were, from nowhere (selected by lot?). That would not in itself be grounds for supposing that her family did not belong to the genos Salaminioi.[42]

---

[39] Discussion of this inscription up to 1996, mainly topographical, can conveniently be traced via *SEG* xlvi 137. For the date see M.J. Osborne in edd. P. Flensted-Jensen et al., *Polis and Politics…, Studies…Hansen* (Copenhagen, 2000).

[40] See *ZPE* 125 (1999) 114–15, where other members of her family are also discussed.

[41] *LGPN* II identifies 14 Athenians named Πολύνικος, from at least 10 demes. The only other Πολύδικος is the proposer of the Hellenistic decree, *SEG* xxvii 518, [Πο]λύδικος Στρατοκλ[έους….9–10….]. This man's deme, tentatively identified as Aphidna on the basis of the Councillor of 304/3 by C. Habicht, *Hypomnemata* 73 (1982), 203 (*SEG* xxxii 127), now reverts to obscurity. Ἐπικράτης, given as the name of the councillor of 304/3's father in *Ag.* xv, is a slip; OY is clearly legible on the stone after the kappa at 61, 267 and there are also traces of the the POY which inevitably follow.

[42] Cf. *CQ* 49 (1999), 484–89.

6. FD *iii (2) 25, 28 (Theoxenides the mint magistrate)*

The ephebe on the Pythais of 106/5 BC at *FD* iii (2) 25, 28, son of Μενοίτης, is currently restored as [Προ]ξενίδης. He should rather be identified as Θεοξενίδης, mint magistrate in or around the 70s BC.[43] We thereby dispose of the only post-iii BC Athenian case of the classical-sounding name Proxenides. Theoxenides, on the other hand, occurs five or six times post-200 BC. The mint magistracy tended to run in families and Μενοίτης was not a common name (*LGPN* II lists 6 cases, one v BC, the others, some or all of them probably identifiable or related, around or after 100 BC). The ephebe's father was undoubtedly Μενοίτης the mint magistrate of c. 117/6.[44]

7. IG *ii^2 4035 (Wife or daughter of Dios of Melite)*

Kirchner restored the i BC dedication *IG* ii^2 4035 to read [- Λ]εωνίδο[υ | - τ]ὴν ἑαυ[τοῦ | θυγατέρα, Πα]νδίου Μ[- | - γυναῖκα ἀ]νέθ[ηκεν]. As we can now see from *LGPN* II, however, Πάνδιος and the alternative Ἔνδιος are both characteristically classical names, neither attested after iii BC. Δῖος on the other hand, a very rare name in classical and
60 early hellenistic Athens, never at that period certainly | borne by a citizen, became more fashionable from mid-ii BC. Preferable, therefore, is Köhler's articulation (*IG* ii 1416), *Female name in accusative*]ν Δίου Μ[-.[45] θυγατέρα in 3 and γυναῖκα in 4 are both very dubious; Δίου might be a husband's or a father's name. Köhler thought Μ[- was the demotic of Marathon, but Μ[ελιτέως is the correct restoration, for the names Δῖος and Λεωνίδης occur in two well-known families of this period from Melite (*LGPN* II Δῖος (10)–(11), Λεωνίδης (23)–(34)). This dedication provides us with the valuable information that the families were connected.

---

[43] M. Thompson, *The New Style Coinage of Athens* (1961), p. 569. The date of C. Habicht, *Chiron* 21 (1991), 6 (after D.M. Lewis, *NC* 1962) requires slight adjustment. See J.H. Kroll, *Ag.* xxvi 81–82.

[44] M. Thompson, *op. cit.*, 574; Habicht, *op. cit.*, 21. The precise date and the possible identity of this man with the eponymous archon of 117/6 require further attention.

[45] The length of lines 2 and 3 in *IG* ii^2 4035 flows only from Kirchner's restoration and is not independently determinable.

8. Ag. *xvii 83* (Gravestone of Hades?)*

Curious as it may seem, one may find in the current standard epigraphical and onomastic works of reference an Athenian from Aphidna, son of Aristokritos, named Ἅδης,[46] commemorated on a gravestone from the Agora, *Ag.* xvii 83 (= *IG* ii^2 5718a): Ἅδης Ἀρι[σ]|τοκρίτου Ἀφ̣[ι]|δναῖος. With a tiny number of late exceptions, Athenian citizens were not given the names of gods; and even with the common theophoric names (Apollodoros, Dionysios etc.) deities of ill-omen were avoided.[47] ΑΔΗΣ are the first surviving letters on this funerary monument, the top of which is broken away (see ph., *Ag.* xvii pl. 10). *LGPN* II lists over 120 names with the termination -αδης. Undoubtedly we have to do with such a name here (note the word breaks at other preserved line ends).[48] [Ἀσκληπι]άδης is attractive from the point of view of popularity of the name and suitable length;[49] but in light of the large number of possibilities certainty is impossible. It is not clear to me that this gravestone must be as late as the ii AD date currently assigned to it.

9. IG *ii^2 7495* (An Athenian named S(e)idonios?)*

One of the many phenomena more readily amenable to analysis now that we have both *LGPN* II and its companion volume, edd. M.J. Osborne and S.G. Byrne, *The Foreign Residents of Athens* (1996), is the use of ethnics as personal names. Which ones occur (and which do not), when and why? Unique occurrences will encourage us to go back to the stone to check that the epigraphy has been got right. One such case is *IG* ii^2 7495, a very poorly inscribed gravestone of i AD (?), which currently supplies the Attic onomasticon with its only case

---

[46] Listed as such by both *LGPN* II and J.S. Traill, *The Persons of Ancient Athens* (1994–) no. 108010.

[47] On this most recently R. Parker, *Proc. Brit. Acad.* 104 (2000), 53–79; J. Curbera, *GRBS* 38 (1997) [2000], 405–6.

[48] This is an interesting case of rediscovery of a lost stone causing scholarship to go backwards. The stone had been transcribed by Fourmont and a correct text of it, based ultimately on Fourmont's transcript as published by Boeckh, *CIG* 601, may be found at *IG* ii^2 5727.

[49] As both Sean Byrne and John Morgan have pointed out to me.

of Σ(ε)ιδώνιος as a personal name, and the text of which is given by Kirchner as:

Κάλλων
Σειδωνί[ου]
[Σ]υπαλήτ[τ]ιος

Examination of the stone suggests that the letters in square brackets are not, as one might reasonably suppose, abraded; they seem never to have been inscribed (perhaps they were painted in). Moreover, if we may supply a sigma at the start of line 3, as we clearly must, we may also supply letters at the start of line 2. There is, I think, no doubt that what should have been inscribed is:

Κάλλων
Ποσειδωνίου
61 Συπαλήττιος |

This yields the common name Ποσειδώνιος in place of the unique Σειδώνιος and an approximately aligned left margin. Following normal epigraphical conventions, the text can be rendered, Κ^v^άλλ^v^ων | ⟨Πο⟩σειδωνί⟨ου⟩ | ⟨Σ⟩υπαλήτ⟨τ⟩ιος. Interestingly, given the quality of this monument, it would appear that the family may be traceable back to at least iv BC. See *LGPN* II s.v. Ἀντίπατρος (56)–(58), Λυσικλῆς (41)–(43) etc.

10. Ag. *xv 369, 63* (Citizen Citizen?)*

In the text of the prytany document of Pandionis of 166/7 AD (archon M. Valerius Mamertinus) given by *Ag.* xv 369,[50] one may read, in line 63, ἀντιγραφεὺς [Πολί(?)]τ̣ης. The restoration of the name is due to E. Kapetanopoulos, *Arch. Eph.* 1968, 178–79, no. 2, who was prudently tentative. Thanks to *LGPN* II, we can now see that it should be rejected, and not only because Πολίτης is one of over twenty names [..⁴..]της attested at Athens,[51] but because, before this date, it is not known to

[50] This text was first edited in the 15th century by Cyriacus of Ancona (ed. Moroni no. 96), whose edition did not, however, include this portion of it. Cf. E.W. Bodnar, *Cyriacus of Ancona and Athens* (1960), 150–52. The monument is now in the entrance hall of the Epigraphical Museum (EM 10316).

[51] In fact, the possibilities are wider than this, for comparison with the alignment of letters in ll. 61, 62 and 65, suggests that the correct text is [..c. 4-5..]τ̣ης. Enough

have been borne by an Athenian for 500 years. Indeed it is an interesting fact that the last Athenian citizen called "Citizen" is attested in the very last decade of the classical democracy (father of [-]τος on *IG* ii^2 1566, 24, c. 330–320 BC). | 62

---

remains of the tau (of both the vertical and the horizontal) for that letter to be probable.

CHAPTER SEVEN

FRAGMENTE ATHENISCHER EHRENDEKRETE AUS DER ZEIT DES LAMISCHEN KRIEGES (ZU *AG.* XVI 94 UND *IG* II^2 292)*

Es werden die folgenden Fragmente diskutiert, die ich in den Jahren 1999–2001 einer Autopsie unterziehen konnte:

(A) *Ag.* xvi 94. Elf Fragmente aus weißem Marmor, die meisten am oder nahe des Nordabhangs der Akropolis gefunden[1] und von Schweigert einer einzigen Inschrift zugewiesen.

Ursprüngliche (unbeschriebene) Rückseite nur auf fr. h erhalten (0,145 dick).

Buchstabenhöhe: 0,007–0,0085. Durchschnittliches Stoichedonraster: horiz. c. 0,0165–0,018, vert. c. 0,017–0,019. Alle (außer fr. g—siehe unten) vom „Cutter of EM 12807" gehauen, dessen Tätigkeit auf c. 334/3–314/3 v. Chr. datierbar ist (Tracy, *ADT* 122).

Wichtigste/neuere Literatur: *IG* ii^2 369 (fr. b); *IG* ii^2 414b (fr. k) und c (fr. j); E. Schweigert, *Hesp.* 8 (1939), 27–30 no. 7; ders., *Hesp.* 9 (1940) 335–39, no. 42; *SEG* xxi 298 und xxiv 102; Osborne D25; Schwenk no. 85; *Ag.* xvi 94; Tracy, *ADT* 122, 127 (*SEG* xlv 80).

Relief: C. Lawton, *Attic Document Reliefs* (1995) no. 50 (mit Photo).

Photos aller Fragmente bei Schweigert. Weitere Details und Literatur bei *Ag.* xvi.

---

* This chapter was previously published in *Zeitschrift für Papyrologie und Epigraphik* 136 (2001), 65–70. Mein herzlicher Dank gilt in Athen den Behörden des Epigraphischen Museums sowie denen der Agora für die Erlaubnis, die relevanten Fragmente zu studieren, dem Epigraphischen Museum auch für das Photo in Taf. III. Der Aufsatz ist zum Teil an der Universität Heidelberg geschrieben worden. Ich danke der Humboldt-Stiftung und Angelos Chaniotis dafür, daß sie meinen dortigen Aufenthalt ermöglicht haben, und Werner Rieß für die (deutsch-)sprachliche Verbesserung meines Textes.

Ag. xvi = ed. A.G. Woodhead, *Agora xvi. Inscriptions: the Decrees* (1997);
Henry, *Honours* = A.S. Henry, *Honours and Privileges in Athenian Decrees* (1983);
Henry, *Prescripts* = A.S. Henry, *The Prescripts of Athenian Decrees* (1977);
Osborne = M.J. Osborne, *Naturalization in Athens* (1981–3);
Schwenk = C.J. Schwenk, *Athens in the Age of Alexander* (1985);
Tracy, *ADT* = S.V. Tracy, *Athenian Democracy in Transition* (1995).

[1] Fr. h und fr. i sind in späteren Gebäuden der naheliegenden Agora wiederverwendet worden.

(B) EM 7140. Fragment aus weißem Marmor, rechte Seite erhalten.[2] Auf der Akropolis gefunden, „εἰς τὸ βόρειον τῶν Προπυλαίων, εἰς τὸν ἐκεῖ καταστραφέντα θόλον“ (Pittakis), 1859.

0,45 hoch, 0,22 breit, 0,108 dick.

Buchstabenhöhe: 0,007–8. Stoichedonraster: horiz. c. 0,0168, vert. c. 0,0168–0,0170. „Cutter of EM 12807“, 334/3–314/3 (Tracy, *ADT* 122).

Edd. Pittakis *Eph.* 1859, 3589; *IG* ii 151 (Köhler); *IG* ii^2 292 (Kirchner). Photo: Taf. III.

Unter den datierbaren athenischen Staatsdekreten befindet sich nur eines, das, strikt gesehen, nach dem jetzigen Stand der Forschung, aus der Mitte des Lamischen Krieges zu stammen scheint: *Ag.* xvi 94 (Schwenk 85). Schwenks Sammlung enthält zwar sieben Dekrete des Jahres 323/2, aber drei davon (Schwenk 79–81)[3] gehören in die Kriegsvorbereitungsphase;[4] eines ist nicht sicher in dieses Jahr zu datieren (84); zwei (82, 83) stammen zwar aus der fünften Prytanie des Jahres, sind aber in einem Fall sicher (83, für Euphron von Sikyon), in dem anderen wahrscheinlich (82, für Theophantos),[5] am Ende | des 65
Krieges zerstört und in ihrer erhaltenen Form erst einige Jahre danach zusammen mit späteren Ehrendekreten für dieselben Männer wieder-aufgestellt worden. Daher soll die in die achte Prytanie von 323/2 (d.h. Frühjahr 322) datierte, aus elf Fragmenten bestehende Inschrift, Schwenk 85, ein einmaliger zeitgenössischer Beweis athenischen Handelns während dieses epochalen Krieges sein. Schweigerts Zuweisung dieser elf Fragmente zu einer einzigen Inschrift aber ist nicht mehr haltbar. Eines (das sehr kleine fr. g) fällt sicher weg, da es nicht die Arbeit desselben Steinmetzen (des „Cutter of EM 12807“) ist wie die anderen Fragmente.[6] Dagegen darf *IG* ii^2 292 in Zusammenhang mit den restlichen 10 gebracht werden. Marmor, „Cutter“, Buchstabenhöhe und Stoichedonraster dieses Fragments sind mit denen von *Ag.* xvi 94 gleich bzw. vergleichbar.[7]

---

[2] Der Stein ist viel später zu einem anderen Zweck wiederverwendet worden; er zeigt (mittelalterliche?) Dekorationen auf der Rückseite.

[3] Zu 79, für Lapyris von Kleonai siehe auch P. Perlman, *Athenaeum* 67 (1989), 74–76 (*SEG* xxxix 93).

[4] I. Worthington, *ZPE* 57 (1984), 139–44 (*SEG* xxxiv 69), würde *IG* ii^2 370 (Bündnis zwischen Athen und Aitolien) auch in diese Zeit datieren.

[5] So Schwenk.

[6] So (meines Erachtens zu Recht) Tracy. Zudem hat Tracy, *ADT* 122 n. 1, bemerkt: “I am not completely confident that fragments e, h and k could not be from one or more other inscriptions.” Zu e, h und k siehe unten, Fragmentengruppe 4.

[7] Der aufmerksame Leser wird feststellen, daß sich nach meinen Meßergebnissen das Stoichedonraster von *IG* ii^2 292 von dem von *Ag.* xvi 94 um bis zu 0,2 mm

Diese 11 Fragmente (*Ag.* xvi 94—fr. g + *IG* ii^2 292) gehören aber auf keinen Fall derselben Inschrift an. Meiner Meinung nach haben wir es mit mindestens drei Inschriften zu tun (unten, 1–3), mit entsprechend 28, 26 und 36 Buchstaben pro Zeile, und einer Gruppe von Fragmenten, die keiner dieser drei Inschriften mit Sicherheit zugewiesen werden können (4).

1. *Ein Sohn von Demetrios wird geehrt (stoich. 28)*

Fr. a, b, c, d = *Ag.* xvi 94 fr. a, b, i, d.

fr. b
fr. a Θ ε [ο] ί fr. c
323/2 ἐπὶ Κη[φισοδ]ώρου [ἄρχοντος ἐπὶ] τῆς stoich. 28
[Ο]ἰνεῖ[δος ὀγ]δόης [πρυτανείας ἧ]ι Ἀρ-
[χίας Πυθοδώρου Ἀλωπεκῆθεν ἐγρ]α[μ]-
[μάτευεν..........21.........]
lacuna
[-----ἐπειδὴ-------------] fr. d
[.....9....]κεν τῶ[ι δήμωι....8....]
[.....9....] καὶ νῦν [.......13......]
[.....10.....]τῶι δή[μωι.....10.....]
[δεδόχθαι τῶι] δήμω[ι ἐπαινέσαι..3.]
[....7...Δημη?]τρίο[υ εὐνοίας ἕνεκα]
[καὶ φιλοτιμί]ας τ[ῆς εἰς τὸν δῆμον τ]-
[ὸν Ἀθηναίων κ]αὶ στ[εφανῶσαι αὐτὸν]
[χρυσῶι στεφά]νωι [ἀπὸ -- δραχμῶν]

Schweigerts Zusammenstellung von fr. a–c ist sicher. Oben war ein Relief angebracht (Lawton no. 50), von dem nur ein gut gehauener Fuß erhalten ist (auf fr. b). Fr. d hat Schweigert überzeugend auch mit 28 Buchstaben ergänzt (vgl. z.B. *IG* ii^2 304, 3–8) und mit Wahrscheinlichkeit derselben Inschrift wie a–c zugewiesen.

In folgenden Punkten unterscheidet sich mein Text von *Ag.* xvi 94:

4. ἐγρ]α[μ Frühere Herausgeber, Schweigert folgend. Ich konnte von dem Alpha bei der Autopsie keine sichere Spur erkennen (oberer Punkt zur linken Seite des Stoichos?).
6–7. πρότερόν | τε ἐπιδέδω]κεν *Ag.* xvi, oder ἐπέδω]κεν (vgl. z.B. *IG* ii^2 360, 8) oder ἐπέσταλ]κεν (vgl. *IG* ii^2 587) Lambert.

---

unterscheidet. In diesem Fall, in dem die Fragmente alle klein sind und das Stoichedonraster von einer Zeile zur nächsten eher variabel ist, fällt dieser Unterschied nicht ins Gewicht. Das durchschnittliche Stoichedonraster der einzelnen Fragmente von *Ag.* xvi 94 unterscheidet sich öfters um mehr als 0,2 mm.

7–8. καὶ νῦν [ἐπιδέδωκεν εἰς τὸν πόλεμον] Frühere Herausgeber, Schweigert folgend. Die Ergänzung ist möglich (vgl. z.B. *IG* ii^2 351, 13–16), aber unsicher. | 66

2. *Fünf Botschafter aus dem Bosporanischen Reich werden geehrt (stoich. 26)*

Ag. xvi 94 fr. c+j ergänzte Schweigert ebenfalls mit 28 Buchstaben. Von Osborne etwas verbessert sieht der geläufige Text (*Ag.* xvi) folgendermaßen aus:

[.....10..... 'Αθ]ην[αί]ων κα[....8....] fr. j stoich. 28
fr. c [......11.....] ὅτι δ[ύ]ναντ[αι ἀγαθὸν]
[δημοσίαι τε κ]αὶ ἰδ[ί]αι τ[οῖς τε ἀφικ]-
[νουμένοις εἰ]ς Βόσπορο[ν, ἐπαινέσα]-
[ι δὲ καὶ...5..κ]αὶ 'Αστυμ[.....9....]
[καὶ...6...καὶ] Πολ[υ]σθέν[ην...6...]
[....7..., καὶ στ]εφ[αν]ῶ[σαι ἑκάστους]
[τούτων χρυσῶι] σ[τεφάνωι....8....]

Diese Ergänzungen sind aus sprachlichen Gründen abzuweisen, sowohl hinsichtlich des zweiten (unmöglichen) τε in Z. 30 (tatsächlich ist das erste auch überflüssig, vgl. Denniston, 512) als auch des Ausdrucks στ]εφ[αν]ῶ[σαι ἑκάστους] | [τούτων in 34–35. An Stelle von ἑκάστους stand sicher ἕκαστον, und, obwohl τούτων an sich nicht mit Sicherheit auszuschließen ist, kommt αὐτῶν in diesem Zusammenhang viel häufiger vor.[8] Die Lösung besteht darin, mit 26 Buchstaben zu ergänzen (im folgenden wird das frühere fr. c zu meinem fr. 2a, fr. j zu fr. 2b):

[- ἐπειδὴ ---------]. [....7...] fr. b stoich. 26
fr. a [.....9....'Αθ]ην[αί]ων κα[ὶ?...6...]
[......10....] ὅτι δ[ύ]ναντ[αι ἀγαθὸ]-
[ν δημοσίαι κ]αὶ ἰδ[ί]αι τ[οῖς ἀφικν]-
[ουμένοις εἰ]ς Βόσπορο[ν, ἐπαινέσ]-
[αι....8....κ]αὶ 'Αστυμ[..4..καὶ.]
[....8....καὶ] Πολ[υ]σθέν[ην καὶ..]
[...6..., καὶ στ]εφ[αν]ῶ[σαι ἕκαστον]
[αὐτῶν χρυσῶι] σ[τεφάνωι -----]
[------------------------]

1. Bei der Autopsie erkannte ich den unteren Teil eines vertikalen Strichs in der Mitte von stoichos 19. 6. z. B. 'Αστυμ[ήδην.

[8] Vgl. Henry, *Honours* 46 n. 7.

Die Formulierung war anscheinend ἐπειδὴ + Beschreibung der Verdienste + ἐπαινέσαι (mit Nennung der Geehrten) καὶ στεφανῶσαι ἕκαστον αὐτῶν κτλ. Vgl. z.B. *IG* ii^2 338.[9] Die Wörter δὲ καὶ werden daher in Z. 6 nicht gebraucht.

Osborne hat als erster richtig bemerkt, daß 2a und b nicht zum selben Dekret gehörten wie die Fragmente meiner Inschrift 1, obwohl nach ihm beide Dekrete auf derselben Inschrift standen. Jetzt können wir sehen, daß 2a und b nicht nur zu einem anderen Dekret, sondern höchstwahrscheinlich zu einer anderen Inschrift gehörten, die, wie Inschrift 3, die Arbeit desselben „Cutter" war, dieselbe Buchstabenhöhe und dasselbe Stoichedonraster zeigt, aber eine andere Zei-
67 lenlänge hatte als Inschrift 1.[10] |

3. *Ende eines Ehrendekrets (stoich. 36)—Taf. III*

[.........^{17}........καὶ ἐπιμελεῖσθαι αὐτο?]- stoich. 36
[ῦ τὴν βουλὴν τὴν ἀεὶ βουλεύουσαν καὶ τοὺς στ?]-
[ρατηγοὺς τοὺς ἀεὶ στρατηγοῦντα?]ς, ὅπως ἄν μ[η]-
[δ' ὑφ' ἑνὸς ἀδικῆται. ἀναγράψαι] δὲ τόδε τὸ ψήφι-
[σμα ἐν στήληι λιθίνηι καὶ στῆ]σαι ἐν ἀκροπόλ-
[ει. εἰς δὲ τὴν ἀναγραφὴν τῆς στ]ήλης δοῦναι το-
[ν ταμίαν τοῦ δήμου ΔΔ δραχμὰς] ἐκ τῶν κατὰ ψηφ-
[ίσματα ἀναλισκομένων τῶι δή]μωι.
[*in corona*] *in corona*
[ἡ Βουλή] [ὁ] Δῆμος

Die Lesungen in *IG* ii^2 sind richtig. Die Ergänzungen (Köhlers, außer 7 med. ΔΔ Kirchner, 9 in. Wilhelm) sind auch im wesentlichen überzeugend. Die genauen Worte der „allgemeinen Schutz-" Bestimmung in 1–3 sind unsicher, aber der Sinn ging zweifellos in diese Richtung (vgl. Henry, *Honours* 176–81; die Ergänzung des Anfangs von Z. 4 ist

[9] Henry, *Honours* 8–9.

[10] Es ist theoretisch möglich, daß zwei Dekrete mit ungleichen Zeilenlängen auf derselben Inschrift standen. Zu dieser Zeit kommt dies aber selten vor, und wenn, dann waren die Buchstaben kleiner (c. 0,005 hoch) bzw. das Stoichedonraster enger, als es hier der Fall ist, oder der Übergang war mit einer Veränderung des Stoichedonrasters/der Buchstabengröße verbunden. Vgl. *IG* ii^2 330 (= Schwenk 18), Ende von 360 (= Schwenk 68), 365, 373 (siehe Majusc., *IG* ii 186).

wahrscheinlich wörtlich richtig, vgl. Henry, *Honours* 180). 4–8 entsprechen den gängigen Formularen.[11]

4. *Fragmenta sedis incertae*

Es bleiben noch die Fragmente *Ag.* xvi fr. e, f, h und k (die ich 4 a, b, c und d nenne). Keines der vier läßt sich mit Sicherheit den Inschriften 1, 2 oder 3 zuweisen.

[--------] H [----------] fr. a
[--------]ĖΠ[---------]
[--------]TE [---------]
[--------]ΛE [---------]

1. Cf. Tracy, *ADT* 127.

Dieses kleine Fragment könnte zu Inschrift 1 gehören, da es an genau demselben Ort wie fr. a gefunden worden ist: „in a probable early Roman context over paved court below Klepsydra, Agora T26–27“. Vgl. aber Tracy, oben n. 6.

Schweigert hat gezeigt (vgl. Osborne I, p. 84), daß fr. 4b mit 28 Buchstaben pro Zeile als letzte Bestimmung einer Bürgerrechtsverleihung ergänzt werden kann; es läßt sich aber genausogut als Präskript ergänzen:

[..⁵..]Λ[------------------]
[πρυτ]α̇νεί[ας, ἧι -------- ἐγραμμάτ]-
[ευεν·] ἐκκλ[ησία· τῶν προέδρων ἐπεψήφιζεν -]
[..³.]αιος ı[-------- συμπρόεδροι· ? ---]
[..³.]Π̇ΡΟΓ[------------------]
[..⁴..]ΟΝΑ[------------------]

4. ı[- Lambert. E Schweigert. Ḳ oder Ḥ Tracy.
6. [..³.] *Ag.* xvi, irrtümlich.

Vgl. *IG* ii² 336 (= Osborne, D23) III mit Henry, *Prescripts* 40–41. Die Buchstaben in Z. 5 und Z. 6 könnten zu Namen der *Symproedroi* gehören oder, da Namen, die ΠΡΟΓ enthalten, sehr selten sind, mögen die

[11] Es wäre üblicher gewesen, in 4–6 den Titel des Sekretärs zu geben, der für das Aufschreiben des Dekrets verantwortlich war. Dieses fehlt aber z. B. in *IG* ii² 125, Osborne D53, D54, D69 usw. Vgl. A.S. Henry, *Hesperia* (im Druck).

Symproedroi fehlen (s. Henry, *Prescripts* 40–41 n. 39), und wir könnten
68 etwa -- εἶπεν· ἐπειδὴ οἱ] πρόγ[ονοι--] (vgl. *IG* ii² 110, 21; 399, 6) ergänzen. |

Fr. 4c könnte zu einer „allgemeinen Schutz-" Bestimmung (vgl. Henry, *Honours* 176–81) gehören, etwa:

[------------------------------]Η[..³.]
[----------------------------]ΛΙΕΙ[..]
[-----------ἐπιμελεῖσθαι α]ὐ̣τῶν [.]
[------------------------------σ]τρατ-
[ηγ-------------------------ὅ]πως ἄ-
[ν μηδ' ὑφ' ἑνὸς ἀδικῶνται.---]ΗΝΕ
[-----------------------------------]Ο̣Λ̣

6–7 τ]ὴν ἐ[κκλησίαν Schweigert.

Es ist mir aber bisher nicht gelungen, den Text nach den üblichen Formulierungen in diesem Sinn vollständig zu ergänzen. Auf diesem Fragment sind, wie bei Inschrift 3, die Spuren des Zahneisens noch besonders klar zu erkennen, was ein (allerdings nicht entscheidendes) Argument dafür darstellt, daß die Fragmente zur selben Stele gehörten.

Die Reste von fr. 4d lassen sich mit keinem Text einer anderen attischen Inschrift unmittelbar vergleichen:

[---'Α]θηναι[----------]
[--- κεχ]ειροτο[νημέν ---]
[-----]ων εἰδό[τες ὅτι ---]
[-----] δωρεὰς κ[-------]
[-----]ου ἐκ τῶν [-------]
[-----]αι αὐτοῖ[ς--------]
[--- δημ]όσιον ἀν[------]
[--- γρα]φομένας /[------]
[-----]α καὶ το[--------]
[-----]ΑΣΤΗΣ [---------]
[--- τῶ]ι δή[μωι --------]
[-------------------------]

8. / Lambert, cf. *IG* ii 290.

κεχ]ειροτο[νημέν- (2) wird sich wahrscheinlich auf athenische Beamte beziehen; es ist aber nicht sicher, ob sie in diesem Fall die Geehrten sind.

Epigraphisch gesehen ist dieser Fall ein gutes Beispiel dafür, wie vorsichtig man mit der Zuweisung ähnlicher Fragmente zur selben Inschrift umgehen sollte. Schrift und Stein können in fast jeder Hinsicht übereinstimmen, die Fragmente müssen aber dennoch nicht zur selben Inschrift gehören. Dies sollte uns nicht überraschen. Es ist an sich nicht verwunderlich, daß ein Steinmetz sich entscheidet, auf mehreren Inschriften dieselbe Buchstabenhöhe und dasselbe Stoichedonraster zu verwenden.[12]

Historisch gesehen finden wir in diesen Fragmenten folgende Informationen:

Inschrift 1, aus dem Frühjahr 322, mitten im Lamischen Krieg, ehrt den Sohn eines gewissen Deme?]trios, einen Nicht-Athener, von dessen Verdienst wir nur wissen, was aus Z. 7 erschlossen werden kann, nämlich, daß er in der Vergangenheit etwas dem athenischen Volk geschickt oder gestiftet hat (Z. 7) und in der Gegenwart noch gute Werke vollbringt (Z. 8). Daß es sich um Getreide handelt, ist zu dieser Zeit nicht unwahrscheinlich (vgl. die von Tracy, *ADT* 32–33, erwähnten Inschriften); selbstverständlich aber sind in Kriegszeiten auch andere Arten von Hilfe möglich (vgl. Tracy, *ADT* 29). Wir wissen weder, woher er kommt, noch welche Ehren (außer dem goldenen Kranz) ihm verliehen wurden. | 69

Es ist möglich, daß diese Fragmente, wie die zwei anderen Ehrendekrete aus der Mitte des Krieges (Schwenk 82 und 83), zu einem später wiederaufgestellten Dekret gehörten, das in seiner ursprünglichen Form sofort nach dem Krieg zerstört worden war, und daß ein oder mehrere andere, spätere Dekrete für den Sohn von Demetrios bzw. Familienmitglieder o. ä. auf demselben Stein standen. Es mag aber auch sein, daß wir Fragmente des ursprünglichen, vielleicht kurz nach seiner Aufstellung zerstörten Dekrets besitzen. Auf alle Fälle sind Buchstaben, Oberfläche und Relief auf diesen Fragmenten ungewöhnlich gut erhalten. Sie machen den Eindruck, der Stein sei gestern gehauen worden, was für ein kurzes Leben der Inschrift sprechen könnte.[13]

Inschrift 2 wurde für 5 Männer aus dem Bosporanischen Reich gesetzt. Daß es sich bei dieser Inschrift um Getreide handelt, wie üblich in Bezug auf diese Region, und daß die Geehrten etwas mit der von

---

[12] Das Phänomen bedarf systematischer Untersuchungen bei mehreren Steinmetzen, was hier nicht versucht werden kann.

[13] Wie viele andere am Nordabhang der Akropolis gefundene Inschriftenfragmente gehören sie zu Inschriften, die ursprünglich mit mehr oder weniger hoher Wahrscheinlichkeit auf der Akropolis gesetzt worden waren (vgl. die Bemerkung von R. Stroud, *Hesperia* 40 (1971), 146). Man fragt sich, ob diese Inschrift nach Athens Niederlage im Lamischen Krieg von der Akropolis den Abhang hinuntergekippt worden sein könnte.

den Athenern oft geehrten dortigen Königsfamilie zu tun hatten,[14] sind sehr wahrscheinliche Vermutungen. Die Geehrten waren in der Lage gewesen, δημοσίαι κ]αὶ ἰδ[ί]αι τ[οῖς ἀφικν]|[ουμένοις εἰ]ς Βόσπρορον zu helfen. Von den Namen her, und da sie fünf sind, werden sie aber nicht der Königsfamilie selbst angehört haben.[15] Osborne dachte, sie könnten „...local citizens and merchants who facilitate matters for the Athenians at the business level“ sein, was nahezu richtig zu sein scheint. Wahrscheinlich aber waren sie nicht Privatmänner (n.b. δημοσίαι). Ich vermute, sie waren Beamte bzw. Botschafter des Königs Pairisades, die sich Athen gegenüber im Getreidehandel nützlich gemacht hatten. Vgl. *IG* ii^2 212 (aus 347/6, die hauptsächlich Mitglieder der Königsfamilie, aber auch deren Botschafter ehrt), 49–51: ἐπαινέσαι δὲ τοὺς πρέσβει[ς] | Σῶσιν καὶ Θεοδόσιον, ὅτι ἐπιμελοῦνται τ[ῶ]|ν ἀφικ[ν]ουμένων Ἀθήνηθεν εἰς Βόσπορον. Unsere Inschrift wurde während der Tätigkeit des „Cutter of EM 12807“, d. h. 334/3–314/3, angefertigt. Wie andere Inschriften dieser Periode, die mit Getreide zu tun haben, bezieht sie sich wahrscheinlich auf die Zeiten des Getreidemangels in den Jahren 335, c. 330–326 oder c. 323–20 (vgl. Tracy, *ADT* 30–35). Meiner Meinung nach gibt es keinen hinreichenden Grund mehr, die Inschrift historisch in Verbindung mit Inschrift 1 zu bringen.

Inschrift 3 und Fragmentengruppe 4: aus diesen Fragmenten erge-
70 ben sich keine nützlichen historischen Informationen. |

[14] Zu dieser Familie siehe Osborne T21.

[15] So zu Recht z.B. Osborne D25. Die Äußerungen von J.B. Brashinsky, *Acta of the Fifth Congress of Greek and Latin Epigraphy, Cambridge 1967* (1971), 119–23 (und in früheren Publikationen auf Russisch, siehe *Ag.* xvi) zu diesem und manch anderem Punkt in Bezug auf diese Inschrift waren nicht überzeugend (vgl. Osborne zu D25 und Woodhead zu *Ag.* xvi 94). Zutreffend aber ist Brashinskys Bemerkung (119): „...in the 4th cent. BC, there is not a single Attic decree in honour of a private Bosporan merchant...only the kings and a narrow circle of persons closely connected with them conducted this trade on the Bosporan side.“

CHAPTER EIGHT

THE ONLY EXTANT DECREE OF DEMOSTHENES*

> Παραυτίκα μὲν οὖν ἐπὶ τῇ νίκῃ (sc. at Chaironeia) διὰ τὴν χαρὰν ὁ Φίλιππος ἐξυβρίσας καὶ κωμάσας ἐπὶ τοὺς νεκροὺς μεθύων ᾖδε τὴν ἀρχὴν τοῦ Δημοσθένους ψηφίσματος, πρὸς πόδα διαιρῶν καὶ ὑποκρούων·
> "Δημοσθένης Δημοσθένους Παιανιεὺς τάδ' εἶπεν·"
>
> Plutarch *Dem.* xx. 3

The only extant decree of Demosthenes, *IG* ii² 231, has not attracted very much attention since, in the last year of the 19th century, Theodore Reinach published the lucid study, based on autopsy of the stone, which identified it as such. Historians have doubtless been deterred by the extremely fragmentary nature of the text,[1] which Reinach printed as five lines of prescript, concluding with Hamlet's last words:

---

* This chapter was previously published in *Zeitschrift für Papyrologie und Epigraphik* 137 (2001), 55–68. I am very grateful to Odile Cavalier and to Charalambos Kritzas for their courtesy in facilitating study of the two fragments of Demosthenes' decree, fr. a in the Musée Calvet, Avignon, fr. b in the Epigraphical Museum, Athens. For the photograph of fr. a at pl. VII I thank Odile Cavalier and Joël Antoine (Centre Camille Jullian, Aix-en-Provence, negative no. 120878, CNRS, R. Reveillac). For the photograph of fr. b at pl. VIII I thank the Epigraphical Museum, Athens. After I had provided him with the vital statistics of fr. a Michael Walbank realised independently that fr. b might potentially be part of the same decree and kindly shared with me his initial thoughts about it. Pierre Juhel generously advised me on military iconography; Jaime Curbera supplied helpful bibliographical indications, Elaine Matthews valuable information about volumes of *LGPN* in preparation. This article was prepared in part at the University of Heidelberg, where I was privileged to enjoy the financial support of the Humboldt Foundation. I use the following abbreviations:

Demosthenes: Ed. I Worthington, *Demosthenes, Statesman and Orator* (London, 2000);
Henry: A.S. Henry, *Honours and Privileges in Athenian Decrees* (Hildesheim, 1983);
Reinach: Th. Reinach, Pierres qui roulent, *REG* 13 (1900), 157–69;
Schwenk: C.J. Schwenk, *Athens in the Age of Alexander* (Chicago, 1985);
Silence et Fureur: Ed. O. Cavalier, *Silence et Fureur: La femme et le mariage en Grèce. Les antiquités grecques du Musée Calvet* (Avignon, 1996).
Other works referred to by author's name only are listed in the bibliography preceding the Greek text in sect. 1.

[1] I could find no reference to the inscription in the two most recent book-length studies of Demosthenes in English, *Demosthenes*, and R. Sealey, *Demosthenes and His Time* (Oxford, 1993). P. Carlier, *Démosthène* (Paris, 1990), 325, overlooks it.

5 Δημοσθένης] Δη[μ]ο[σθ]έ[νους Παια]ν[ιεὺς εἶπ]εν...
l. 7...συμ]μ[α]χο..
The rest is silence.

The image of the great talker cut off at the point of utterance may indeed seem a suitably poignant or, according to taste, amusing one. Kirchner in *IG* ii², however, was not wholly convinced by Reinach's text ("sunt sane, quae dubitationem moveant"), and this has set the tone for sporadic expressions of scepticism ever since, including even about whether the proposer can securely be identified as the great orator.[2] Epigraphists, it seems, have been deterred by the unusual location of the decree, which was removed from Athens to Venice as early as 1760 and, since 1841, has been in the collection of the Musée Calvet, Avignon.[3] My main purpose is to report that, in the first year of the 21st century, Demosthenes has broken his epigraphical silence. Close study of the Avignon fragment over two days in August 2001 yielded some modest textual progress (including confirmation of the
55 proposer's identity) | and, more substantially, enabled the identification of the last nine lines of Demosthenes' motion in a fragment found by James Oliver on the south slope of the acropolis, published by him in 1936 and now in the Epigraphical Museum, Athens.[4]

1. *Text*

Fr. a, Musée Calvet, Avignon, Inv. E 28. Fr. b, EM 12823. Two fragments of white marble. Fr. a, left and right sides and back preserved (see further sects. 2–3). Above the main text a relief. Above the relief a single moulding (inscribed) supporting a pediment (inscribed, mostly lost). Fr. b, left side and bottom preserved. Horizontal ground line for setting into base c. 0.072 from bottom. Fr. a, findspot not recorded. Transported in 1760 from Athens to Venice, where the stone formed part of the Nani collection. Purchased from G.D. Almorò Tiepolo by

[2] E.g. Meyer, 252.

[3] A valuable contribution, however, was recently made by the edition, with commentary (helpful especially on the relief) and excellent photograph, published by the current curator of antiquities of the Musée Calvet, Odile Cavalier, in *Silence et Fureur*.

[4] It is a pleasure to acknowledge that the association of these two fragments, like scores of other associations and joins made in recent years, was facilitated by Stephen Tracy's ground-breaking work on epigraphical hands.

A.L. de Sivry in 1820. Acquired by Musée Calvet, 1841.[5] Fr. b, south slope of acropolis, 1935.

Height (fr. a) 0.41 (of which relief, 0.195), (fr. b) 0.58; width (fr. a) 0.41 without moulding (relief, 0.35 towards top, 0.345 further down), (fr. b) 0.28; thickness of finished edge c. 0.06 (upper right of fr. a)—c. 0.07 (lower left of fr. b); thickness including rough back, (fr. a) upper (i.e. including moulding) 0.098 (left), 0.092 (right), lower 0.087 (left), 0.083 (right), (fr. b) 0.10.

L.h. l. 1 c. 0.028;[6] l. 2, mostly 0.008, P 0.011, O, Δ 0.007; l. 3ff. mostly 0.005 (Y, Σ up to 0.0065, Δ, O 0.004–0.005, X 0.0035–0.005). Stoich. (3ff.) square, 0.00975–0.0098. Lettering: "perhaps work of Cutter of *IG* ii^2 334" (S.V. Tracy, *Athenian Democracy in Transition* [Berkeley, 1995], 78, on fr. b; see further sect. 5).

Major editions, fr. a: P.M. Paciaudi, *Monumenta Peloponnesia* (Rome, 1761) II, 153–75 (drawing, 155); (*CIG* 475 [Boeckh]; *IG* ii 198 [Köhler];) T. Reinach, *REG* xiii (1900), 157–69 (photograph); (*IG* ii^2 231 [Kirchner]);[7] O. Cavalier, *Silence et Fureur*, 139–11 (phot.) (*SEG* xlvii 124); fr. b: J.H. Oliver, *AJA* xl (1936), 464 (phot.).

Other contribution to text: K.B. Stark, *Städteleben, Kunst und Alterthum in Frankreich* (Jena, 1855), 582 (l. 2).

Cf. (on Phokinos): M. Osborne, *Naturalization in Athens* (Brussels, 1981–83) T92; C. Habicht, in ed. H.-U. Cain et al., *Festschrift… Himmelmann* (*Bonner Jahrbücher*, Beiheft 47, Bonn, 1989), 321–22; (on relief): M. Meyer, *Die griechischen Urkundenreliefs* (*AM* Beiheft 13, Berlin, 1989), A91; J.Y. Marc, *REA* 95 (1993), 143–56; C. Lawton, *Attic Document Reliefs* (Oxford, 1995), no. 36. | 56

[5] On the origins of the Musée Calvet's antiquities collection see O. Cavalier, in *Silence et Fureur*, 20–22; on the Nani Collection, I. Favaretto, ibid. 27–36 (this inscription, 34); on this inscription, O. Cavalier, ibid. 140.

[6] The top of the single letter in this line, an alpha, does not survive. Its height is derived by projecting the left and right diagonals of the letter to the point where they meet.

[7] Based on Reinach's text. Kirchner also had a squeeze of Vohsen, "in quo tamen pauca dispiciuntur".

In pediment: A

On moulding: [π]ρ̣οξενία Φωκίνωι καὶ Νικάνδρωι καὶ Δεξι. [..$^{3-4}$.] fr.

Relief

340/39 [ἐπὶ Θεοφρά]στ[ου] ἄρχ[οντ]ο[ς] ἐπὶ τῆ̣ς [Ἱ]πποθωντ[ί]δο[ς] ἐνά- stoich. 42
[της πρυτανε]ία̣ς̣ ἧι Ἄσ[π]ε[το]ς Δ̣[ημ?]οστ̣ρά[το]υ [Κ]υθήρριος
[ἐγραμμάτευ]εν, ἑνδεκάτη[ι τ]ῆ[ς] πρ̣[υτ]α̣νεί[ας·] τῶν προέδ-
[ρων ἐπεψήφιζε]ν Ἀνδ̣ροκλῆς Ἁγ[νού]σιο̣ς̣· ἔδ[οξ]ε[ν τῶ]ι [δή]-
[μωι· Δημοσθένη]ς Δημοσθέ[νους Παια]νιε[ὺς εἶπ]εν· [..^{4}..]
[......^{12}......]δ̣ημο̣ς ΕΠΑ[...^{6}...]Ν[....^{9}....]Ο[...^{5}..]
[......^{12}...... συ]μμ[α]χο[..]. [.]....[..]..[......^{11}......]
[..........^{22}..........]ΚΛ̣ . [.........^{17}.........]
[....................^{42}....................]
[....................^{42}....................]
[...........^{24}...........]ΛΡ̣[........^{16}........]

c. 1–4 lines missing

[.......^{15}.......]..[............^{25}............] fr.
[- εἶναι - - π]ρο[ξένους τοῦ δήμου τοῦ Ἀθηναίων? α]-
[ὐτοὺς καὶ ἐκγό]νους καὶ̣ [ἐπιμελεῖσθαι αὐτῶν τὴν βου]-
[λὴν καὶ τοὺ]ς στρατηγοὺς [ὅπως ἂν μηδ' ὑφ' ἑνός ἀδικῶντ]-
[αι. ἀναγράψα]ι δὲ τήνδε τὴν [προξενίαν τὸν γραμματέα]
[τῆς βουλῆς] ἐν στήληι λιθί̣[νηι καὶ στῆσαι ἐν ἀκροπόλ]-
[ει· εἰς δὲ τ]ὴν ἀναγραφὴν τῆ[ς στήλης δοῦναι τὸν ταμία]-
[ν τοῦ δήμ]ο̣υ εἴκοσι δραχμ[ὰς ἐκ τῶν κατὰ ψηφίσματα ἀν]-
[αλισκο]μ̣ένων τῶι [δ]ήμωι. καλ[έσαι δὲ αὐτοὺς καὶ ἐπὶ ξέ]-
[νια εἰ]ς̣ τὸ πρυτανεῖον ε̣ἰ̣ς̣ α̣[ὔριον].

crown *[crown]*

crown

Translation

A. Proxeny for Phokinos, Nikandros and Dexi-. In the archonship of Theophrastos (340/39), in the ninth prytany, of Hippothontis, for which Aspetos son of [Dem?]ostratos of Kytherros (5) was secretary, on the eleventh of the prytany. Of the *proedroi* Androkles of Hagnous put the matter to the vote. It was decided by the People. Demosthenes son of Demosthenes of Paiania proposed: …*c. 8–11 lines, naming the honorands, stating the reason for their honours (including a reference to "ally" or "allies") and proposing to praise and crown them*… (15) [and that they be *p*]*ro*[*xenoi* of the Athenian People?] themselves and their descendants, and that the Council and the generals have a care for them so that they not be harmed by anyone. And that the secretary of the Council inscribe this proxeny on a stone stele and set it up on the acropolis. (20) And that the treasurer of the People give twenty drachmas for the inscription of the stele from the People's fund relating to decrees. And to invite them to hospitality in the *prytaneion* tomorrow.

2. *The association of fr. a and fr. b*

Both fragments are of the same white marble type commonly known as "Pentelic". The hand is compatible (see further below). Letter heights, stoichedon grid dimensions and line lengths are the same. Both fragments are from decrees awarding proxenies to three men (three names on upper moulding and three figures in the relief on fr. a, three crowns and text for plural honorands on fr. b). The sides and back are finished in the same rather unusual way: finished sides thickening from c. 0.06 (top) to c. | 0.07 (bottom); the back rough picked but flattened 57
in a central plateau at a thickness of c. 0.085 (top) to 0.10 (bottom). This plateau covers approximately the central area of the back, but towards the edges slopes down to meet the back edges of the thinner finished sides. The break at the upper right of fr. b continues the break to the lower left of fr. a. The top point of the inscribed face on fr. b (i.e. upper right) aligns approximately with the bottom point of the inscribed surface on fr. a (i.e. lower left). It is possible that the two fragments would physically join. I calculate that there are about 1–4 lines missing between fr. a, l. 13 and the first preserved line on fr. b, which, for ease of reference I number l. 16.

3. *The state of the stone: evidence of re-use and deliberate damage*

Like many surviving inscriptions originally set up on the acropolis, this one was later cut down for use as architectural blocks. On fr. a the original protrusion of the moulding to the right was removed to create a straight right edge, the top of the pediment cut back to create a roughly horizontal edge at the top. The breaks to the lower left and lower right were cut straight, but the resulting sides were not finished. The resulting block was square in its longest dimensions. There are slight traces of mortar on the front face, mainly around the top and the lower right edges. There is heavy wear of the front face below and to the right of a line running diagonally from the left edge at about the start of l. 10 to the top of the moulding at a point towards the end of l. 2 (above Ξ in Δεξι-). It affects not only the inscribed surface, but also the relief in the area between Athena and the first soldier, the lower part of Athena herself and the right end of the moulding; the area to the right of Athena is unaffected, probably because the surface at this point is sunken and "protected" by the higher figure of Athena to the left. The damage looks natural, and is of a sort frequently observable on Attic inscriptions; heavy footwear is perhaps the most likely cause. I am not persuaded by Reinach's suggestion (169) that this damage was deliberate, i.e. that the stone was "martelé ou gratté à dessin" in the context of a *damnatio memoriae* of Demosthenes, "soit après la condamnation de Démosthène dans l'affaire d'Harpalos, soit après sa proscription définitive", which resulted in the total destruction of his other decrees. However, there is one area of damage which does look deliberate. There has been an attempt to obliterate the faces and legs of the soldiers. This will not be due to Byzantine iconoclasm, since Athena's face, and the hands of the soldiers, are unaffected. It must have resulted from deliberate vandalism. That this took place shortly after the erection of the stele and was politically motivated is possible, but not demonstrable. There has been no attempt to erase Demosthenes' name, nor any other part of the text.

The back of both fragments with its central "plateau" may be original, arising presumably from an intention to place the stele flat against another surface at the back (e.g. a wall or other stele); or it may possibly have been reworked in this fashion in connection with the subsequent use of the stones as architectural blocks. There has been no deliberate erasure of the surface of fr. b, but it is also damaged to the right, somewhat more profoundly than on fr. a. The border of the damage traces a curve running from the top of the fragment to a point below the top of the central crown (consistent with the swinging of a door?). There are mortar traces adhering to the bottom, the inscribed surface and the back. The vertical break to the lower right of fr. b is similar to the angular break above it and the breaks on fr. a, i.e. straight but leaving an unfinished side. The breaks to the upper and lower left of fr. b are less clean.

4. *The Relief*[8]

The relief is cut in a shallow panel above the text, rather short in proportion to its width. To the right stands Athena wearing a *peplos* and

[8] This section takes as its starting point the recent treatments of the relief by Meyer, Lawton and Cavalier, who all include bibliographies of earlier discussions.

Corinthian helmet, her left hand resting on a shield to the right, her right hand extended to crown the first of three smaller figures to the left. In accordance with convention, | the divine figure is larger than 58
the humans; in this relatively short relief, the effect is emphasised by the incision of the top of Athena's helmet into the upper frame.[9] The three figures to the left all approach Athena with their right arms raised in a gesture of respect (cf. Lawton, 60). All wear short tunics. The first and tallest wears a muscle-cuirass with *pteryges* ("groin-flaps") and a plumed helmet and his extended left hand probably originally held a painted-in shield (not preserved). The second and (less clearly) third figures also appear to wear muscle-cuirasses, but without the clearly delineated *pteryges*. The second, smaller, figure wears a simple helmet without crest and in his left hand holds a long spear, filling the entire height of the relief.[10] His left arm and the incised line representing the spear (which may have been painted in) are cut into the relief ground. The third, smallest, figure, wears headgear which comes to a point at the top,[11] and carries in his left hand what is apparently a bow.

The quality of the work is not very high. The closest stylistic parallel is the fragmentary relief from a decree of an Attic non-state body recently published by Marc, only the left side of which is preserved, with part of the pediment, relief frame, figure of Athena and beginning of the text. The Athena, though portrayed with spear and shield, is very close to ours and Marc's suggestion that they are the product of the same workshop is very plausible. Marc also discusses other parallels, including the relief on the anti-tyranny law of 337/6 (*SEG* xii 87, Lawton no. 38).

In composition the relief is unremarkable. Since v BC *proxenoi* had been depicted as "small and relatively nondescript" figures "reverent in the presence of Athena" (Lawton, 32); by the later fourth century, however, when honours were increasingly awarded for specific

[9] Cf. the indentation of the upper frame caused by the top of the helmet of Athena on the relief published by Marc (below).

[10] For this feature of spears on Attic document reliefs cf. e.g. Lawton nos. 24 and 142 (Athena).

[11] Lawton, who did not examine the relief, describes this as a "spike". At autopsy it can be discerned that the impression of a long spike is probably partly illusion caused by damage. However, the headgear does seem to have a raised element on top, though it is not clear whether this is supposed to represent a metallic helmet moulded to a point (cf. the helmet of the first figure), or a (non-metallic?) cap with a central boss or point.

services, the iconography of the relief often reflected the nature of those services, in our case military (cf. Lawton, 32–33). The well-known resemblance between votive and document reliefs is apparent in our case in the worshipping gesture of the honorands. Lawton, 29, notes that this resemblance is partly to be accounted for by the fact that most document reliefs were set up in sanctuaries. As with nearly all inscriptions originating from the acropolis, we do not know exactly at what location on it our monument was erected, but it is not inappropriate in this context to envisage the whole outcrop as a vast sanctuary, with Athena as presiding goddess. For an argument that the honorands would have had a say in their portrayal on the relief see below, sect. 6, on ll. 20–24.

It seems clear that the three figures correspond with the three honorands whose names are on the upper moulding. The first represented Phokinos, his leading position and plumed helmet consistent with his likely identification as a Megarian general (see below). The second, slightly smaller, figure would be Nikandros, the third, smaller again, Dexi-. One suspects that Nikandros and Dexi- were (Megarian?) army commanders subordinate to Phokinos (perhaps related to him?),[12] Dexi- perhaps a commander of light-armed troops of a sort which generally played an auxiliary (sometimes a mercenary) role in Greek warfare.[13]

5. *The Hand*

"During the period from approximately 345 to 320 BC there flourished in Athens a number of cutters who inscribed letters that are very
59 similar in shape... many small or worn fragments cannot be | assigned
accurately to... known workmen" (Tracy, 76–80). Within what may be described as this "Common Style, c. 345–320 BC", Tracy found it possible to identify three distinct cutters, those of *IG* ii^2 334, 244 and 354. He lists our fr. a among his "Decrees Not Studied" (175); fr. b he attributes to the Common Style, noting that "it is perhaps the work of the Cutter of *IG* ii^2 334, but there are not quite enough clearly pre-

[12] Triple proxenies were rare (see further sect. 7). One is reminded of the honorific decree with relief of 347/6, *IG* ii^2 212 = Lawton no. 35, where the three honorands, Spartokos, Pairisades and Apollonios, were brothers.

[13] Cf. V.D. Hanson, *Hoplites* (London, 1991), index s.v. "missile-weapons".

served letters to enable attribution" (78, n. 3). Fr. a also belongs to the "Common Style". Two or three (not all) of the alphas on it are of the type Tracy identifies as characteristic of the Cutter of *IG* ii² 334: "fairly wide, turned slightly to the left (81)...often shorter than the other [letters]...crossbar...usually at the middle or above (82)". Of the other two letters that he designates as specially diagnostic of this Cutter, however, the two omegas on fr. a are too poorly preserved to be informative and the sigmas do not appear to "lean back" or to "have the bottom stroke nearly horizontal" (though Tracy also stresses the variability of this Cutter's sigmas). In short, fr. a provides some, but not perhaps quite enough, additional evidence to confirm attribution of this inscription to the Cutter of *IG* ii² 334. Of the other two "Common Style" cutters, the script has more in common with the Cutter of *IG* ii² 354. While the larger letters in the pediment and on the moulding are in the same general style, I find it difficult to tell if they are certainly by the same cutter as the main text.

6. *Commentary*

Fr. a is a typical example of an inscribed surface showing complex damage where squeezes and photographs are useful, but where the richer optical data available at autopsy (combining colour, variable light, three-dimensionality, texture), preferably carried out over more than one day, are essential to a good reading. Thanks to the kindness of the staff of the Musée Calvet, the stone was removed from its normal fixed position against a wall and I was able to examine it intensively over two days (17th and 18th August, 2001) placed flat on a table, using both natural light (through an open door) and a strong, mobile, artificial light source. My readings are based on this autopsy, on two squeezes which I made then, and on several photographs, conventional and digital. The good photographs published by R(einach) and Cavalier are also a useful control. It is clear from a comparison with R's text and photograph that the stone has not deteriorated significantly since his edition. Fr. b is much more straightforward; my readings of it are from autopsy, with photographs as control.

I do not normally discuss below insignificant changes to R's text of fr. a and O(liver)'s of fr. b (e.g. removal of letters from square brackets). I indicate a stoichos by a number in round brackets.

1. "On...distingue le bas d'un A ('Αθηνᾶ? 'Αθηναῖοι?)" R, n. 5; noted also by Cavalier ('Αθηνᾶ?), but overlooked by Kirchner, and other commentators since. The letter, larger than normal size (c. 0.028 full height) is complete except for its apex. It appears to be original, not an architectural mark connected with a later use. It stands roughly in the centre (in fact, c. 0.005–0.01 to left of centre) of the bottom of the tympanum of the pediment above the upper moulding. There are no other letters to the right or left and it does not seem likely that there were letter(s) above it. Its diagonals are deeply inscribed, the horizontal more shallowly. It is a wide letter and its horizontal slopes down slightly from left to right, both features that can be observed on alphas in the text below. There would seem to be four possible interpretations: (a) Ἀ(θηνᾶ). While decrees are often headed ΘΕΟΙ, I know of no Attic parallel for a decree headed with the name of an individual deity abbreviated to a single letter; (b) Ἀ(θηναῖοι). Again, no parallel comes to mind. The significance would also seem obscure. The honorands are being made *proxenoi*, not Athenian citizens; the Athenians award the honours, but that is also the case with countless other honorific decrees which do not carry this symbol; (c) this is the initial letter of the ethnic of the honorands. It was not unusual for honorific decrees to include symbolic references to the city of the honorands, often influenced by the city's coinage (see T. Ritti, *Sigle*
60 *ed emblemi sui decreti onorari | greci* [Rome, 1969]; Lawton, 62–63),[14]
and there are examples of individual letters being used in this way on decrees of other states (see the table, Ritti, 351–58; e.g. A[I] on a iii BC proxeny from Delphi for Timomachos of Aegina, Ritti no. 16 = *FD* iii 1 p. 109 no. 195 = *Syll.*³ 440; very close to our case, ΠΕ ligature in tympanum of pediment of iii BC proxeny from Delphi for citizens of Pellene, Ritti nos. 13 and 14 with pl. iv fig. 1= *FD* iii 1 p. 255 nos. 426, 427). There appears, however, as yet to be no Attic case of use of a single letter in this way. Moreover, although the ethnic of the honorands is not explicitly stated in the surviving text, a case can be made on onomastic and prosopographical grounds that the leading figure, at least, was from Megara (see below);[15] (d) the letter signifies

[14] Attic cases include *IG* ii² 2a = Lawton no. 79, a bull on a proxeny for a Boiotian; *IG* ii² 339a = Lawton no. 42, a sphinx and Chian amphora on a proxeny for a Chian.

[15] There is perhaps a possibility that the men were from Aigosthena, the at this period Megarian (?) outpost at the eastern end of the Corinthian Gulf, where the Spar-

"1". Again, there seems to be no close Attic parallel, though there are broadly comparable phenomena, e.g. the headings of the five columns of the sacrificial calendar from Erchia (*SEG* xxi 541), A, B, Γ, Δ, E. The implication would probably be that this inscription is the first of a series, e.g. that there were other stelai for other men (from other allied states?) honoured in the same context; or that other copies of this decree were set up at other locations. (c) or (d) seem the stronger possibilities [see now postscript].

2. Stark was first to make the crucial observation that the first word was προξενία (Ὀξίνια Paciaudi). On superscripts of this type cf. A.S. Henry, *The Prescripts of Athenian Decrees* (Leiden, 1977), 35; on the implication of the absence of εὐεργεσία from the heading see below, note to ll. 17–20. The three men honoured were:

A. Φωκῖνος. The vast quantity of epigraphical evidence that has accrued since Reinach wrote has not undermined his observation that this name is attested only for members of an identifiable family from Megara.[16] In summary, the other evidence for the family, discussed most recently by Habicht (cf. *LGPN* IIIB, p. 438, which adds the text published by R.M. Heath, *BSA* 19 [1912–13], 85 no. III) is:

(a) *IG* vii 1–7; Heath, *loc. cit.*; *SEG* ii 255. Φωκῖνος Εὐάλκου was one of 6 Megarian generals who held office for at least four years sometime between 306 and 301 or 295 and 288; and one of 6 arbitrators at Delphi (Φωκῖν[ος Εὐάλκου]) c. 300–290;

(b) *IG* ii^2 766 + *SEG* xxi 392, 36 with Osborne T92 (a). [Εὔα]λκος Φωκίνου Δ̣[ιομειεύς?], Athenian ephebe 246/5? (archon Philoneos, date M.J. Osborne, conference, 2001);

Habicht follows Osborne's suggestion that, in enrolling among the Athenian ephebes, (b) may have been giving effect to an honorific naturalization grant to his ancestor, (a), proposed by Stratokles of Diomeia, in whose deme he was accordingly enrolled.

tans defeated at Leuktra met with a relief force (Xen. *Hell.* vi 4.26, cf. below on l. 8); the ethnic Αἰγοσθενεύς, however, occurs once only in Attic epigraphy, on the late hell. funerary monument, *Ag.* xvii 395. Another possibility would perhaps be Ἀκαρνάν, cf. *IG* ii^2 237 and below n. 20.

16 At the time of writing *LGPN* I-IIIB were published. I am grateful to Elaine Matthews for confirming that, as yet, no cases of this name have come to light in preparatory work for later volumes of *LGPN*.

The case for identifying our Phokinos as a member of this family (grandfather, or possibly uncle, of (a)), while not perhaps conclusive, seems persuasive on onomastic grounds and gains some confirmation from the manner of Phokinos' portrayal on our relief.

B. Νίκανδρος. This common name is not otherwise attested at Megara (LGPN IIIB, p. 299).

C. Δεξι. [..$^{3-4}$.] Lambert, Δεξί[ππωι Paciaudi (majuscule: ΔΕΞΙΙ), Δεξί[ππωι?] (majusc. ΔΕΞΙΙΧ ..) R, Δεξιθ̣[έωι] Cavalier. What Paciaudi and Reinach read as a vertical after the iota is an apparently slightly curving diagonal stroke to the left of the stoichos. It is not consistent with pi (of which one would expect to detect also the horizontal); it is consistent with theta, but that letter would dip unexpectedly low. Moreover the stone seems uninscribed where one would expect the lower right of the letter. In the rest of the stoichos there is a faint impression of all the strokes of mu (of which the mark to the left would in that case be the lower left diagonal, the lower curving sec-
61 tion perhaps an extension | caused by erosion). I could not rule out that they are an illusion caused by casual marks. Following this there is a mark which could certainly be casual, but which might also be the lower-central left diagonal (and perhaps the spring of the horizontal) of alpha. Assuming that the last letter is dative iota, occupying less than normal letter-width, and that the moulding originally extended beyond the normal right edge, as it did to the left, we should have Δεξι[...$^{max.\ 5}$..]. I conclude that Cavalier's Δεξιθ̣[έωι],[17] Δεξιμ̣[ένηι][18] and Δεξιμ̣[άχωι][19] are all possibilities, the last perhaps the strongest. None of these names is attested for Megara; two other Δεξι- names are, Δεξικράτης and Δεξίλας (*LGPN* IIIB, p. 109).

3–7. Rest. R, except 6 'Α̣γ[νού]σ̣ι̣ος Lambert ([....^{7}...]ο[ς] R). R's treatment of the prescript is convincing. The archon is implied by the secretary, who is attested on another decree of 340/39 (see further below). The form of the prescript is precisely the same as *IG* ii² 237 of 338/7,

---

[17] Well attested across a wide geographical and chronological range.

[18] Not a common name, in *LGPN* I–IIIB only in Eretria, iv/iii BC; Megalopolis, ii BC.

[19] In *LGPN* I–IIIB this name occurs in late Hellenistic and early imperial Sparta, probably in Dodona in iv–iii BC, and in female form, Δεξιμάχα, in iii BC Akarnania. The single Attic case listed by *LGPN* II, on the red-figure vase, *ARV*² p. 1045 no. 8, c. 440–430 BC would also be the only certain v BC case; it should rather be restored as ['Αλ]εξίμαχος (13 in *LGPN* II, several v BC).

except that the latter also includes lunar month and date (the first decree to do so). I detect some additional letter traces, consistent with R's restorations. Two points invite comment:

4. Δ̣[ημ?]οστ̣ρά[το]υ. Δημ]οσ[τ]ρ[άτου R, who detected the apex of delta in first place (majuscule, 163); my photographs also appear to show a clear left diagonal of Δ. At autopsy, however, I recorded in third place a possible upper left corner of a letter, consistent with epsilon in Κλεόστρατος or pi in Ἱππόστρατος; my squeezes show traces that could be interpreted as consistent with ΔΗΜ or ΚΛΕ, but so faint that all could be illusory. The names Demostratos and Aspetos occur in father-son pairs in a propertied family in Kytherros at this period (*APF* 3623; *LGPN* II, pp. 76 and 111), but it would accord with patterns of Attic nomenclature if other names in—ostratos also occurred in the family. The father's name on the other decree of this year preserving the secretary's name, *IG* ii[2] 233, 4, is wholly restored.[20] With some hesitation I retain the current restoration.

6. The crucial letter of the demotic of Androkles is the second. The surface is well preserved in this stoichos. It was not inscribed in its centre or lower right. To the left there is a clear vertical adjoining a horizontal at the top. There appears to be a vertical in the upper right of the stoichos, but this is a casual discolouration of the stone. Gamma seems certain therefore (the letter is also visible on R's photograph); Ἁγνούσιος is the only demotic [.]γ[....7...]. Of the other letters I detect lower right diagonal of alpha; very faint/uncertain impressions of nu and omicron, nothing of upsilon, faint impression of upper and lower two strokes of sigma, vertical area of damage covering iota, omicron clear, top stroke of sigma. Hagnous was in Akamantis, which accords with the rule that the chairman be from a tribe other than that in prytany (Hippothontis). This is the first attestation of this common name in this deme.

7. Δημοσθένη]ς̣ Δημ̣οσθέ[νους Παια]ν̣ι̣ε̣[ὺς εἶπ]εν· [..4..] Lambert, Δημοσθένης] Δη[μ]ο̣σθέν̣[ους Παια]ν[ιεὺς εἶπ]εν R (majuscule), Δημοσθένης] Δημ̣ο̣σ̣θ̣έ̣[νους Παια]ν[ιεὺς εἶπ]εν Cavalier. At autopsy I detected the following traces additional to those reported by R.: extreme top and bottom tips of the sigma at the end of the name;

[20] *IG* ii[2] 451, ascribed to this year by Tracy, is also of no help. If Tracy is right, the secretary was omitted from this prescript.

lower left and right outer diagonals of mu and possible trace of part of the left inner diagonal. ΣΔΗΜΟΣΘΕ is also fairly easily legible on R's photograph. After the nu in the demotic, I detected a central vertical (i.e. of iota); a left vertical (i.e. of epsilon). No other father's name and no other demotic are consistent with these traces. Demosthenes the orator had no brother, let alone a politically active one with the same number of letters in his name as his own. It is certain that, as R
62 first | recognised, he was the proposer of this decree. In his majuscule R records faint trace of a sigma, εἶπ]εν· [.]Σ[..]. He does not include the letter in his minuscule text; I can not confirm it.

8.]δ̣ημ̣ος ΕΠΑ[...⁶...]Ν[.....⁹....]Ο[Lambert, ⊢Ρ̣ΟΣΕΠ[...⁶...]Ν R (majuscule). I read: of delta the bottom right corner (uncertain), of eta probable trace of R's ⊢ and possible slight trace of right vertical. My mu is shown by R as a rho with a section missing under the top stroke (in other words, like the horizontal and lower left vertical of H and a top vertical as Γ or Γ). I read (autopsy) a left upright, close to vertical (consistent with this cutter's mus) and (faint and uncertain) impression of the rest of the strokes of mu. My squeezes show a full and clear, if damaged, outline of mu. I agree with R's reading of the following four letters, ΟΣΕΠ (visible both at autopsy and on my squeezes). The surface of the following stoichos is uneven, but I detect (tentatively from squeezes, somewhat clearer at autopsy and on photographs, including Cavalier's) right and lower left diagonals and downward sloping cross-bar of a small alpha (the slope of the bar, up or down, is fairly common in this text). There is a mark to the left like a lower vertical, which, together with the sloping bar, can give the impression of nu, but that mark is probably casual/misleading. In context after ἐπ a vowel is in any case more comfortable than nu. The nu in (27) is clear (R placed it one space too far to the left), as is the omicron in (37). In (34) one gains a vague impression of eta, probably a casual mark. There is something to be said for ὁ] δ̣ῆ̣μ̣ος ἐπ' 'Α[λκισθέ]ν[ους ἄρχοντ]ο[ς. I have occasionally thought that traces consistent with ΘΕ might be detectable before the nu. For phrases of this type cf. e.g. *IG* ii² 330, 7; 2798; 3261. There is only one candidate in the period 403/2–339/8 whose name in the genitive is Α[...⁶...]Ν[-], 'Αλκισθένης, archon in 372/1, the year leading up to Leuktra, and before that suitably active on the diplomatic front (see R. Seager, *CAH²* vol. vi (1994), 179–181). We know of no developments in Athenian-Megarian relations in this context; but it was not unusual for

proxeny decrees to begin with references to past events involving the honorands or their ancestors/countrymen (e.g. *IG* ii^2 110, 21; 399, 6). A close parallel to a phrase of this type in this sort of decree is lacking, however, and in any case there is not enough to rule out obvious alternatives, such as name in -δημος, followed by father's name, 'Επα-, or a verb ἐπα[-.

9. [......^{12}......συ]μμ[α]χο[..]. [.]....[..]..[......^{11}.....] Lambert, συμ] μ[α]χο[- R, σ]υ̣μ̣μ̣αχο[- Cavalier. Other readings from autopsy (none sure): (22) A/K/X?; (24–27) vertical, slightly to left; Ξ/E?; Ξ/E?; left half of M?; (30–31) Ξ/E?; H? συ]μμ[ά]χο[υς] κ̣[α]ὶ̣ ξ̣έ̣ν̣[ου]ς̣ is perhaps possible.

10–16. The readings in 10 and 13 are new. 10 (23–25) perhaps κα̣ί̣ or (22–23) ΠΠ (though the left vertical on the first pi would be rather low). I can not confirm R's N in 10(20) or his P in 11(24), though in the latter case I can see a (possibly casual) mark consistent with a left vertical. 16(16)–(17) a lower upright to right of stoichos, sloping slightly inwards, consistent with M, N or possibly H (O printed a lower vertical), followed by very slight impression of Θ. On the space between fr. a and fr. b see sect. 2.

From the surviving text and the evidence of other Athenian proxeny decrees, of which about 42 are extant from 353–322, it is possible to infer that:

(a) as Rhodes has already deduced from the absence of the Council from the enactment formula in 6–7, this decree was non-probouleumatic, i.e. Demosthenes' motion did not follow or explicitly amend a proposal of the Council. For probouleumatic proxeny decrees at this period cf. e.g. *Hesp.* 43 (1974), 322 no. 3, *IG* ii^2 206 and 235. On the probouleumatic/non-probouleumatic distinction see P.J. Rhodes, *The Athenian Boule* (Oxford, 1972), 68, this decree, 260;

(b) the missing text will have named the honorands, justified their honours (with reference possibly to earlier honours/services, honours/services of ancestors etc.) and praised and crowned them. The last can be inferred from the crowns engraved at the bottom of the decree. Crowning was a common, but not invariable, element of proxeny decrees, occurring at this period e.g. on *IG* ii^2 238 = Schwenk 2; *IG* ii^2 347 = Schwenk 38. The precise wording varies. On *IG* ii^2 343 = Schwenk 84 it is: [ἐ]παινέσαι Ἀπολλωνίδην [Δημ]ητρίου Σι[δώνιον | κ]
63 αὶ στεφανῶσαι αὐτὸν $^{v.}$ χρυ[σ]ῶι στεφάνω[ι ἀπὸ | χ]ιλίων | δραχμῶν

ἀρετῆς ἕνεκα καὶ εὐνοία[ς τῆ|ς] εἰς τὸν δῆμον τὸν Ἀθηναίω[ν]· καὶ εἶναι αὐ[τὸν | π]ρόξενον κτλ.[21]

With the exception of my tentative restoration of 17 to yield a grant of proxeny without euergesy, all the elements of this grant occur frequently at this period.

17–20. Lambert. O(liver) read and restored:

> [......12......αὐ]τὸ[ν εἶναι πρόξενον καὶ εὐεργέτην]
> [αὐτὸν καὶ ἐκγό]νους κα[τὰ τὸν νόμον καὶ ἐπιμελεῖσθα]-
> [ι αὐτοῦ τοὺς] στρατηγοὺ[ς καὶ τὴμ βουλὴν ὅτου ἂν δέητ]-
> [αι·

O's perception that we have a proxeny grant (to ἐκγόνους) followed by the "general protection" formula (common in proxeny decrees) seems sound, but his wording is not consistent with the legible letters, the plural honorands, or the attested formulae at this period.[22] For my restoration of the "general protection" formula cf. Henry, 176–81; for co-ordination with καί, less common than δέ at this period, but not at all rare, 178 sect. 2(a); τὴν βουλὴν καὶ τοὺς στρατηγούς as subject, 179 sect. 2(e); purpose clause, 180 sect. 2(f). The preceding proxeny formula is less easy. Henry, 133, cites as a typical example *IG* ii² 106, 13–15: εἶναι αὐτὸ]|ν πρόξενον καὶ εὐ[εργέ]την [τ]ô [δήμο τô 'Αθηναίων κα]|ὶ αὐτὸν καὶ ἐγγόνο[ς], but neither this nor anything very close to it can be reconciled with the remains of l. 17, i.e. a fully visible rho in (15) (very clear on O's photograph, despite his printed tau), followed by certain omicron. I restore, therefore, a grant of proxeny only, without euergesy. Such grants (discussed by Henry, 140–41) are much more unusual than proxeny+euergesy grants. Henry counts around a dozen secure examples between mid-iv BC and early ii BC (e.g. close to our period, *IG* ii² 130 + *SEG* xix 49, 12–14; *IG* ii² 132, 7–9; 540, 11–13?). None precisely matches the wording I restore here (whether singular or plural). The typical formulation is: εἶναι αὐτὸν πρόξενον τοῦ δήμου τοῦ 'Αθηναίων καὶ αὐτὸν καὶ ἐκγόνους. Though syntactically unnecessary, the καὶ before αὐτὸν/-οὺς seems to have been an ingrained element of this formula in both proxeny and proxeny+euergesy grants and it is with some reluctance that one finds oneself required by the

[21] Michael Walbank attractively suggests that, given the military context of our decree, the justification may have been in terms of the honorands' ἀνδραγαθία.

[22] For example, Henry, 135, notes only one very late (ii BC) example of a proxeny grant qualified by κατὰ τοὺς νόμους (*IG* ii² 1024, 29–31; cf. also his p. 141).

line length to omit it[23] (for a more radically shortened formulation, cf. *SEG* xix 80, 25–26, later iii BC, εἶναι δ'αὐτὸν πρόξενον [αὐτὸν καὶ ἐκ]|[γόν]ους). The heading of our decree (l. 2), however, perhaps lends some support to an award of proxeny only: *IG* ii^2 133 and 406 are headed προξενία καὶ εὐεργεσία + name(s) of honorands; *IG* ii^2 130, an award of proxeny only, has, like ours, the heading προξενία + name(s) of honorands (*IG* ii^2 339a = Schwenk 29 is also headed προξενία only, but the text of the decree is not preserved beyond the prescript).

20–24. Rest. O. O's restoration of these lines corresponds with contemporary formulae and is convincing. For προξενίαν in place of the usual ψήφισμα in the inscription formula cf. e.g. *IG* ii^2 240, 20. Though the information that Demosthenes' decree was placed on the acropolis, on the south slope of which fr. b was found, is formally new, it is no surprise. It was the normal place for decrees honouring foreigners.

When the state contributed to funding inscriptions in the period 386–332, the amount seems invariably to have been 20 or 30 drachmas. It has not yet proved possible to clarify the rationale behind the difference; a variety of factors may have been relevant. What is clear, however, is that stelai varied enormously in their overall size, size of lettering, quality of marble etc., and that the inclusion of a more or less costly extra such as relief sculpture was fairly infrequent. Lawton notes that, where the amount allocated is preserved on laws and decrees with reliefs before 332/1, there is a fairly even split between | 20 and 30 dr. 64
Though not demonstrable with certainty on current evidence, it seems highly likely that honorands (or their sponsors) had the option of contributing to the expense of stelai honouring them; and that this was the major, perhaps the only, circumstance, in which honorific decrees came to be adorned by reliefs. This would be consistent with the likelihood that, in some cases, stelai were wholly privately funded;[24] with the appearance of extravagant reliefs on decrees for wealthy foreign potentates;[25] and with the absence of any reference to relief

[23] One wonders whether a possible motive for omission here might have been a desire to avoid the slight awkwardness of καὶ three times in succession in a 2+1 arrangement: καὶ αὐτοὺς καὶ ἐκγόνους καὶ ἐπιμελεῖσθαι...

[24] This inference is commonly made where the payment clause is lacking, e.g. *IG* ii^2 450 (cf. S.D. Lambert, *BSA* 95 (2000), 486–9); *IG* ii^2 337; 228.

[25] E.g. for *IG* ii^2 226 = Lawton no. 122, the stele for Arybbas, ex-king of the Molossians, the state paid 30 dr., but it is not only much bigger than most 30 dr. stelai, it also has two elaborate high-quality reliefs (cf. Meyer, 156); the monumental *IG* ii^2

sculpture in any inscribed payment clause. It would also be consistent with the possibility that εἰς in the formula εἰς δὲ τὴν ἀναγραφὴν τῆς στήλης δοῦναι κτλ. has the connotation, "the treasurer shall give *towards* the inscription of the stelai..." In cases such as ours there is also an argument in the content of the relief. With the votives which underlie the iconography of a relief composition such as ours, the figures portrayed as reverently approaching Athena would normally themselves have been responsible for the relief; *they would have chosen to portray themselves in this way*. It might seem diplomatically inappropriate, however, for the Athenian state, at its own initiative, to portray foreign honorands as suppliants to Athena. It is attractive to suppose that where document reliefs take this form it is because the honorands had a say in the way they were portrayed; and that they had such a say because they (or their sponsors, i.e. in this case Demosthenes) also paid for them.[26]

24–25. Reading and rest. Lambert. [καλέσαι δὲ ἐπὶ ξένια εἰς αὔριον εἰς] τὸ πρυτανεῖον O, which, however, is inconsistent with the letter traces after πρυτανεῖον. My text corresponds with the normal structure of this formula, for which see Henry, 262–271; for the precise wording cf. *IG* ii^2 466b, 46. From this formula accrues the small gain in knowledge that Phokinos, Nikandros and Dexi- were (almost certainly) in Athens when this decree was passed.

Crowns

Under the text there are inscribed crowns, one complete, to the left, one below it to the right, in the centre of the stele; it is obvious from this arrangement that there will have been a third crown to the right, on a level with the one on the left. They do not, as was common, have the honorands' names inscribed within them (it is possible that, as with features of the relief, they were painted in), but they can naturally be taken to represent crowns awarded to the three honorands.

212 = Lawton no. 35, for the rulers of the Bosporos, also equipped with high quality sculpture, also cost the Athenian state just 30 dr.

[26] On payment clauses see B.T. Nolan, *Inscribing Costs at Athens in iv BC*, PhD., Ohio, 1981. On payment for reliefs cf. Meyer, 19–21; Marc, 152; Lawton, 25–26, is more hesitant.

7. *Discussion*

As we saw above (note on l. 1), the large alpha in the pediment of this decree generates a measure of doubt about Reinach's identification of the honorands as from Megara, rather than from a state with ethnic in A-; but, as we also saw (note on l. 2), Reinach's case for identifying the leading honorand Phokinos as a Megarian general from a known family, while not conclusive, remains strong. If it is correct, the circumstances of the decree must lie, as Reinach saw, in the unusually good relations that subsisted between Megara and Athens from, it appears, 343 (when Athens had apparently intervened against pro-Macedonian politicians there), until the defeat of the allies at Chaironeia in 338.[27] Up to 341 Demosthenes frequently refers to threats, both vague and specific, that Megara, as ever a strategically | crucial 65
neighbour to Athens in the build-up to a major conflict between Greek states, might come under Macedonian control;[28] in that year Megara was apparently included in an Athenian-Chalcidian expedition to free another strategically important city, Oreos in Euboea, from the pro-Macedonian tyrant Philistides,[29] an expedition which, in 330, Demosthenes claimed credit for proposing (Dem. xviii 79); and apparently shortly afterwards (winter, 341/0?) Aeschines (iii 94–98) seems to suggest that Kallias of Chalcis, acting in concert with Demosthenes in and around the Peloponnese, had obtained promises of financial support *inter alia* from Megara. In 330 (Dem. xviii 237) Demosthenes includes Megara in a list of states with whom he claims credit for securing alliance in the pre-Chaironeia period. The literary sources do not give us the names of leading pro-Athenian politicians in Megara at this time; as Reinach suggested, our decree can probably be taken to imply that they included Phokinos. Reinach's suggestion that Phokinos may have been the Megarian general in the Oreos campaign is also attractive, though by the time of this decree, spring 339, that campaign lay two years back. Our sources are silent about Megarian activities between the winter of 341/0 and 338; but it seems very possible that there were

[27] See E. Meyer, *RE* xv 1 (1931) s.v. Megara, col. 193; R.P. Legon, *Megara* (Cornell, 1981), 290–94. Athenian intervention: Plut. *Phoc.* 15; Dem. x 8, xviii 295, xix 294–96, 334 etc. apparently relate to the same circumstances.

[28] See e.g. Dem. viii 18; ix 17–18 (both early 341); cf. xix 87.

[29] Steph. Byz. s.v. 'Ωρεός = *FGH* 103 Charax F19. Cf. *FGH* 328 Philochoros F159 with Jacoby's note; Σ Aeschin. iii 85.

other joint actions in this period of strenuous diplomatic and military activity directed against Philip,[30] and while the relief makes linkage to specific allied action(s) attractive, it should also be borne in mind that the college of (normally five) generals seems to have been the "eigentliche Regierungsbehörde" in Megara (cf. E. Meyer, [n. 27] col. 199) and the relief may also allude more generally to Phokinos' prestige in that capacity.

Historically we learn disappointingly little from the new text of Demosthenes' motion. Aside from the tantalising remains of its first two lines,[31] the decree is wholly formulaic and its specific provisions can all be found among the 40 or so other extant Athenian proxenies of the period 353–322. The apparent omission to designate the honorands *euergetai* as well as *proxenoi* is unusual, but its significance (if any) is unclear.[32] Though to an extent an honour recognising past services, there was also an expectation that *proxenoi* would continue to act in the Athenian interest at home; and the award carried with it some privileges at Athens, albeit at a rather lower level than the rarer honour of naturalization.[33] The obligation on the Athenian Council and generals to "look after" the honorands was perhaps not wholly a formality in the factional conditions in Greek states in the year before Chaironeia; the invitation to an official dinner the following day suggests that the honorands were in Athens when the decree was passed. It is no surprise that the decree was non-probouleumatic; inevitably that was common with decrees proposed by leading politicians, other than in the maximum of two years in their lives when they served on the Council.[34] A triple proxeny, as Michael Walbank points out to me, was rare; but in the absence of more precise information about the

[30] A recent summary of these from Demosthenes' point of view is given by T.T.B. Ryder in *Demosthenes*, 79–82.

[31] See sect. 6, on ll. 8–9.

[32] A possibility is that they or their ancestors had been nominated *euergetai* on a previous occasion. Relevant in this connection may be Dem. xx 131, which, if the text is not corrupt and the rhetoric not exaggerated, appears to imply that, in 355, large numbers of Megarians and Messenians enjoyed *ateleia* at Athens.

[33] There is no satisfactory up-to-date study of iv BC Athenian proxenies. C. Marek, *Die Proxenie* (Frankfurt, 1984) focuses mainly on non-Athenian evidence; A. Gerolymatos, *Espionage and Treason* (Amsterdam, 1986) believes *proxenoi* played an important role in intelligence gathering, cf. F.S. Russell, *Information Gathering in Classical Greece* (Ann Arbor, 1999), 76–83. See also A. Lambrechts, *Tekst en Uitzicht van de Atheense Proxeniedecreten tot 323 v. C.* (Brussels, 1958), M. Walbank, *Athenian Proxenies of the 5th century BC* (Toronto, 1978).

[34] See P.J. Rhodes, *The Athenian Boule* (Oxford, 1972), 70.

honorands (e.g. if they were related, even whether they were all from the same city) and the circumstances of the award, speculation on the reasons for it in this case is fruitless.[35] | 66

A final intriguing issue raised by this decree, however, is perhaps worth comment. Broadly speaking the total numbers of decrees successfully proposed by individual Athenian politicians should be a good indicator of their relative influence.[36] In the period 355–322 we know of more decrees proposed by Demosthenes than by any other Athenian. Including literary sources, in 1984 Hansen counted 39, as against 21 for Demades, Lykourgos being the only other politician to achieve double figures (11).[37] If we consider inscriptions alone, however, the picture is very different: of the 85 epigraphically attested decrees counted by Hansen, 11 were proposed by Demades, 10 by Lykourgos; no other politician exceeds 3; and we have just one proposed by Demosthenes. What is the explanation for this disparity between the literary and epigraphical record? Reinach's suggestion that Demosthenes' decrees were destroyed in an act of *damnatio memoriae* does not, as he thought, find support in such evidence as there is for deliberate damage to our decree (see sect. 3 above). In fact, the survival of two fragments of the same decree, in a state wholly typical of Athenian decrees originally erected on the acropolis, argues positively against such a theory. Hansen's data show that it is possible that the explanation is statistical, i.e. that the relative numbers indicated by our "sample", namely the extant decrees, do not reflect the relative numbers among those actually passed in this period (at least 13,000 in Hansen's view), but not that this is probable.[38] In any case statistical quirk is unlikely to be the whole explanation. It should be relevant that, between the failure of his policy at Chaironeia and the Harpalos affair, Demosthenes

---

[35] It would seem that this is the only extant Athenian proxeny decree for Megarian(s); see Marek, *op. cit.*, 8. Of c. 42 extant proxeny decrees of 353–322, c. 4 may be for single or plural honorands, c. 28 are for single honorands, c. 10 for plural honorands, mostly two, but in some cases the number is unknown; *IG* ii^2 278 may have been for three. For the possibility that the honorands were related see n. 13.

[36] "Broadly speaking" because there are, of course, potential distorting factors. E.g. the extent to which minor political figures might have put their names to proposals actually initiated by major ones may have differed. I doubt if this would, in general, have made a significant difference to the totals (cf. Hansen, [next note], 142); but see further below.

[37] M.H. Hansen, *GRBS* 25 (1984), 123–55; table at 132–34. The figures have not changed significantly for our purposes since Hansen wrote.

[38] Hansen 144 with n. 39.

was patently a less active politician than he had been since 355.[39] Even to the extent that he continued to be active, if there is anything in a well-known jibe of Aeschines, at least in the immediate aftermath of Chaironeia Demosthenes may have lacked the confidence and support to propose his own decrees, getting others to put their names to them on his behalf.[40] In any case, one reason why Demosthenes is poorly represented among proposers of surviving decrees of 355–322 is probably that, for the second half of that period, he was, in fact, not an active decree-proposer.[41] There are two other points, however, of which the poor representation of Demosthenes among preserved decrees reminds us. In general, as Hansen persuasively argued (and as *prima facie* the decree-proposer statistics suggest), the traditional tendency to view Athenian politics at this period as dominated by a small number of very active politicians (including, of course, Demosthenes) is probably mistaken. Influence seems rather to have been thinly spread, with a very wide range of individuals involved in active politics, many of them, given the relative poverty of our sources, probably completely unknown to us. More specifically, though it is clear enough that Demosthenes was influential in one area of policy in the lead-up to Chaironeia, precisely the period of our decree, across his career as a whole he was probably a great deal less politically significant than one
67 would gather from literary sources, which, to an overwhelming extent, | are speeches authored by Demosthenes himself, by other orators but relating to Demosthenes, or, in the case of later writings, reflect this Demosthenic bias of the surviving contemporary literary record. Ultimately the reason for this bias has to do not with the political status of Demosthenes during his lifetime, but with the respect accorded to

[39] On Demosthenes during this period see most recently I. Worthington in *Demosthenes*, 90–113.

[40] ὑμεῖς δὲ (i.e. the Athenians) κατὰ μὲν τοὺς πρώτους χρόνους οὐδ᾽ ἐπὶ τὰ ψηφίσματα εἰᾶτε τὸ Δημοσθένους ἐπιγράφειν ὄνομα, ἀλλὰ Ναυσικλεῖ τοῦτο προσετάττετε. Aeschin. iii 159. This might imply, however, no more than that there was a single well-known case where Nausikles was alleged to be acting as a front for Demosthenes, or perhaps simply where the Assembly preferred Nausikles' proposal to Demosthenes'. Aeschines' spin evolved into the more specific claim of Plutarch (of course of no independent historical value), *Dem.* xxi, that, between Chaironeia and Philip's death, τοῖς δὲ ψηφίσμασιν οὐχ ἑαυτόν, ἀλλ᾽ ἐν μέρει τῶν φίλων ἕκαστον ἐπέγραφεν…ἕως αὖθις ἀνεθάρρησε Φιλίππου τελευτήσαντος.

[41] The distribution of preserved decrees over time at this period exaggerates this effect, since disproportionately somewhat more decrees are preserved dating to 337/6–322/1 than to 355/4–338/7.

his oratory after his death.[42] The Demosthenes of Plutarch's Philip was a prolific decree proposer; but the small difference between Plutarch's wording of the proposer-clause of an Athenian decree by Demosthenes chanted by a drunken Philip after Chaironeia, and the reality of such a clause as witnessed by our decree, is significant: the insertion, *for the sake of the metre*, of the word τάδ'. Plutarch's image tells us more about the essentially literary quality of the posthumous "Demosthenes myth" than it does about the prosaic realities of political influence at Athens in the third quarter of the fourth century.

Demosthenes may have broken his epigraphical silence, but it can not be said that, with the words published here, he has become a noisy figure on the epigraphical stage. Their oratory may have been less admired by later generations, but their outstanding record as successful proposers of extant laws and decrees points to the most influential Athenian politicians of the generation between the Social War and the end of the classical democracy: Lykourgos and Demades.

Postscript

While correcting the proofs it occurred to me that I should mention another possible solution to the problem of the alpha in the pediment of this decree, namely that it represents the final alpha of ΜΕΓΑ. Symbols on proxeny decrees are frequently based on symbols or letters used on the coinage of the honorands' state (see above, sect. 6, commentary on l. 1). ΜΕΓ or ΜΕΓΑ occurs commonly on the coinage of Megara (see e.g. J.H. Kroll, *Agora* xxvi [Princeton, 1993], 216–19). This solution would nicely reconcile the pedimental lettering on this inscription with the likelihood that its honorands were Megarians. The difficulty is that of envisaging where the rest of the letters might be. In the tympanum they could only be in the missing top section. However, the pitch of the pediment is very shallow; there would not have been room for any more letters of comparable size above the alpha. They might, however, have been smaller and squeezed in, e.g. along the lines:

[42] On this see most recently C. Cooper in *Demosthenes*, 224–245.

MEΓ
A

Or, perhaps they were arranged on the pedimental moulding (of which a small section is preserved to the lower left). I am not sure that this is
68 the correct solution; but it would seem to be a serious possibility. |

CHAPTER NINE

FISH, LOW FARES AND *IG* II^2 283*

In her collection of inscriptions relating to the ransoming of captives, *Retour à la liberté. Libération et sauvetage des prisonniers en Grèce ancienne* (Paris, 1994), no. 4,[1] Anne Bielman gave us a welcome re-edition of an Athenian decree fragment of considerable interest, *IG* ii^2 283; and in this journal Michael Walbank has now independently proposed stimulating solutions to some of its outstanding problems. Since there is, I believe, a little more that can usefully be said, it may be helpful to print my provisional text of the fragment, prepared in the context of my work on a new edition of the ca. 270 Athenian state laws and decrees datable to 352/1–322/1. It is based primarily on autopsy carried out in 2002. As can be seen from the photograph at plate I, the surface of the stone is in fairly good condition and, except for letters on the edge of a break, readings are not problematic.

* This chapter was previously published in *Zeitschrift für Papyrologie und Epigraphik* 140 (2002), 73–79.

I am very grateful to Charalambos Kritzas and the staff of the Epigraphical Museum for facilitating study of the stone and for the photographs at plates I–II; to Michael Walbank for kindly showing me a draft of his note in advance of publication; and to Graham Oliver for helpful discussion of food-supply aspects. Schwenk = C.J. Schwenk, *Athens in the Age of Alexander* (Chicago, 1985). Tracy = S.V. Tracy, *Athenian Democracy in Transition* (Berkeley, 1995).

[1] This otherwise very valuable work is slightly marred from an epigraphical point of view (including in this case) by more or less minor mistakes in the texts and statements that letter-traces noted by previous editors are not legible, although they are, in fact, visible at autopsy. Squeezes and photographs are useful, but for a large proportion at any rate of Attic inscriptions fully satisfactory texts can not be achieved without careful autopsy of the stones. Even the best photographs often fail to reveal letter-traces, or produce illusions of trace where there is none (two-dimensionality is part of the problem); and for example traces caused by discolouration of the stone as a result of oxidisation along the path of a letter, a frequent phenomenon especially on "Pentelic" marble, and often also "edge traces", i.e. those slightly below the surface plane as the stone breaks away, do not appear on squeezes.

EM 7127. Plate I. Fragment of greyish white marble, right side and possibly back preserved. Acropolis, excavations at Erechtheum, 1839.

Height 0.20, width 0.245, thickness 0.07–0.08 (finished side survives to thickness of 0.056).

Letter heights: 0.004–0.005 (Ω 0.002–0.004, O 0.003–0.004, E, Σ, X 0.005–0.006). Stoich. (square?) horiz. c. 0.0105, vert. c. 0.0108.

Edd. K. Pittakis, *Arch. Eph.* 1839, 220, no. 234; A.R. Rangabé, *Antiquités Helléniques* II (Athens, 1855), 62–63, no. 390; *IG* ii 143 (Köhler and Velsen, both autopsy); *IG* ii^2 283 (Kirchner squeeze, Velsen, Wilhelm); Bielman no. 4 (with ph. of squeeze, pl. II, 2, rather dark).

Other contributions to text: A. Wilhelm *per ep. ad* B.D. Meritt, reported by A.M. Woodward, *BSA* 51 (1956) 7, n. 2 (l. 14); D. Knoepfler, *ap.* Bielman (l. 14); M. Walbank, *ZPE* 139 (2002), 61–65, no. 5 (l. 3, autopsy).

Cf. A. Kuenzi, *Epidosis* (Bern, 1923, reprinted New York, 1979), 41 and 52; A. Lambrechts, *Tekst en Uitzicht van de Atheense Proxeniedecreten tot 323 v. C.* (Brussels, 1958), 57–58 and 134; P. Garnsey, *Famine and Food Supply in the Graeco-Roman World* (Cambridge, 1988), 150–54; W.K. Pritchett, *The Greek State at War. Part V* (Berkeley etc., 1991), 272, n. 386, and 274; C. Veligianni-Terzi, *Wertbegriffe in den attischen Ehrendekreten der klassischen Zeit* (Stuttgart, 1997), 83–84 no. A135.

c. 337? stoich. 34

\-----------------------------------
[........16........]E. I//[........15.......]
[.....10.....ἐσιτ]ήγησεν ἐξ Αἰγύπτου τ[..3.]
[......12......ν]αύλλων εὐωνοτέρων ὑπηρ̣[ε]-
[.......14.......κ̣]αὶ προαιρούμενος τῶι δ-
73 [ήμωι τῶι Ἀθηναίων κ]αὶ ἐν τοῖς ἄ̣λλοις τοῖς̣ |
[.......14.......χρ]ήσιμον ἑαυτὸν παρασκ-
[ευάζων.....10.....]εν ἐμ παντὶ καιρῶι, κα[ὶ]
[πολλοὺς τῶν πολιτῶν] λυτρωσάμ̣ενος ἐξ Σικ̣-
[ελίας ἀπέστειλε Ἀθ]ήναζε τοῖς αὐτοῦ ἀναλ-
[ώμασιν, καὶ ἰδίαι κα]ὶ κοιν⟨ῆ⟩ι πρὸς̣ τὸν δῆμο-
[ν ἀποδέδεικται? τ]ὴν εὔνοιαν ἣν ἔχων διατ-
[ελεῖ ἐκ προγόνων? κ]αὶ νῦν εἰς τὴν φυλακὴν v. 1
[ἐπέδωκε τάλαντον] ἀργυρίου· ἀγα[θ]ῆ̣[ι τ]ύχη[ι]
[δεδόχθαι τῶι δήμ]ωι ἐπαινέσαι Φ[...5..]. ο[ν?]
[.......13......Σ]αλαμίνιον καὶ [στεφανῶσ]-
[αι...6...στεφάνωι] εὐ̣ν̣[οία]ς ἕ̣[νεκα...6...]
\--------------------------------

Epigraphical Notes

The line length of 34 letters was established by Köhler. 11 (and possibly 7) as restored and 12 have 33 letters. The cutter does not always place the cross-bars of N and H with care and in 10 inscribed KOINNI for KOINHI. His cross-bars on alphas are frequently faint, or sometimes not apparent at all (indicated with subscript dots where the letter could be mistaken for Λ). I register below the first scholar to have proposed the more significant readings and restorations.

1 I confirm the epsilon first read by Rangabé (lower vertical and bottom horizontal survive, the horizontal slightly detached from the bottom of the vertical, like the first epsilon in 2). After this, in a damaged area at slightly subsurface level, one obtains an impression of Δ (cf. Rangabé). Finally, there is a left vertical, first read by Köhler.

2 in. Köhler after Rangabé.

3 in. ν]α̣ύλλων Lambert, ΛΥΛΛΩΝ Pittakis, Δ̣ΥΛΛΩΝ Wilhelm in *IG* ii², μ̣ύλλων Walbank. I confirm that there is trace, somewhat fainter than other letters, but quite clear, of an inscribed Λ before the upsilon as the stone breaks away to the left. This might, in this hand, be the right half of M, but the distance from the following upsilon,[2] the absence of definite trace of the left half of the letter and, particularly, the obliqueness of the angle of the right diagonal, make Λ in my judgement the preferable reading. There is no trace of either bottom or central cross-bar. Deltas on this stone have clear crossbars[3] (and in any case no plausible restoration in -]δυλλων is apparent); those on alphas, on the other hand, are quite often very lightly inscribed or undetectable (l. 5, ΑΛΛΟΙΣ). See further below.

3 fin. ὑπηρ̣[ε]- Lambert, ὑπηǀ//[.] Kirchner, ΥΠΗ[- other eds. I confirm Kirchner's reading of the left vertical after the eta. For the supplement see below.

5 in. Köhler.

6 in. [τῆς πόλεως ἀγῶσι Kirchner. No doubt 6 in. expressed circumstances in which the honorand had made himself useful, but, as Bielman saw, Kirchner's specific wording lacks adequate parallel; in fact it

[2] I measure the distance from what would be the apex of the mu to the centre of the upsilon at 0.0125. The distance between the centres of letters in the rest of the line is in the range 0.009–0.012.

[3] Any impression of such a bottom bar which may be given by the phot. at pl. I is illusory. It is possible, but unlikely, that a bottom bar has been entirely eroded.

suggests an entirely different, and inappropriate, meaning, i.e. festival contests staged by the city at which an honorand might be awarded *proedria* (cf. *IG* ii[2] 385, b, 17–18; 450, b, 5–6 etc.).

6 fin.-7 in. The vertical and what is probably the spring of the upper diagonal of the K are clear, confirming Kirchner's παρασκ̣[ευάζων. His διατετέλεκ]εν is a plausible main verb (cf. e.g. *IG* ii[2] 682, 20), though
74 its postponement | with respect to the participle in this construction is slightly odd (normal word order, *IG* ii[2] 229, 8; 682, 20; 1281, 10; 1310, 4; *SEG* xl 141, 8 etc.; somewhat similar postponement however at 448, 41–42) and another verb can not be ruled out, perhaps εὐεργέτηκ]εν (cf. *IG* ii[2] 506, 4). For the restoration one letter short cf. 11.

8 in., 9 ἀπέστειλε Kirchner. Σι[κελίας Pittakis. Of the final kappa of 8 the left vertical and the spring of the diagonals are clear (cf. Köhler's majuscule for the vertical; Velsen *ap.* Köhler read ⊢; Kirchner printed the kappa undotted).

10 in Rangabé.

11 ἀποδέδεικται Velsen *ap.* Kirchner (yielding a 33 letter line). Veligianni-Terzi, 84, notes that this verb would be a hapax in this context in classical inscriptions, but it was to be very common in early Hellenistic decrees, e.g. *IG* ii[2] 374, 5; 470b, 16; 588, 2; 641, 17.

12 in. ἐκ προγόνων Kirchner.

13–16 Köhler, except where noted.

14 fin. ^O Velsen, ˈO Kirchner. At autopsy what is probably the top of a vertical or, less likely, an apex, ^, is detectable. The mark is too central in the stoichos for it to be likely that ^ is the right half of mu or ˈ a right vertical, e.g. of N. The possibilities are too wide for a confident attempt at restoration. However, there is no name currently attested on Cyprus that will fit Velsen's reading, and just two that fit Kirchner's: Φ[ιλούν]ι̣ο[ν] or Φ[ιλοίτ]ι̣ο[ν] (see *LGPN* I; the latter was suggested here by Wilhelm *ap* Woodward). Φιλούνιος was father of Onasagoras, who apparently held the Phoenician office of "temple-barber" in the Nymphaeum of Kafizin in late-iii BC; Φιλοίτιος was a potter, attested at the same site in the same period.[4] Φ[ιλότιμ]ο[ν], suggested to Bielman by Knoepfler *exempli gratia* and attested on a syllabic inscription on an archaic pot from the necropolis of Salamis,[5] is also among the possibilities.

---

[4] T.B. Mitford, *The Nymphaeum of Kafizin* (Berlin, 1980), 259, 261–63.

[5] V. Karageorghis, *Salamis* 4, *Excavations in the Necropolis of Salamis* II (Text) [Cyprus, 1970] p. 273. Correct the reference in *LGPN* I.

16 θαλλοῦ Pittakis, followed by Köhler and later eds., or χρυσῶι Lambert. Bielman supported restoration of a "green" (i.e. olive) crown on the grounds that a golden crown should be followed by specification of its price. While such price specifications are normal, however, there are several occasions in the second half of the fourth century when they are omitted (e.g. *IG* ii^2 237, 14–15, 337 BC, possibly same year as our text, cf. A.S. Henry, *Honours and Privileges in Athenian Decrees* (Hildesheim, 1983), 25). The issue must be left open.[6]

Discussion

We are probably not missing much more than the prescript from the top of the decree. At the bottom the text breaks off in the middle of the description of the honours. We can not be sure what, if anything besides the crown, was awarded, though nomination as *proxenos* and *euergetes* is a strong possibility. As Lambrechts pointed out, the wording about services rendered "privately and publicly" (l. 10) is common in proxeny decrees; and the three other major inscriptions honouring Cypriot and Phoenician traders from the 330s and 320s (see below) all awarded these honours.

The honorand was from Salamis (15). As Bielman notes this will have been the city on Cyprus rather than the island off Attica; one may add to her argument about the use of the ethnic in 15 (p. 14, n. 5) that the reference at 4–5 to the honorand's giving preference (sc. to Athens)[7] suggests that he was not an inhabitant of Athenian territory, especially if, as I suspect, the implication is that he had chosen
to | import to Athens rather than elsewhere. Traders of grain who 75
inhabited Athenian territory and others assisted by Athenian maritime finance were under legal obligation to import to Athens (see Garnsey, 139–10). For the same reason, despite the impression to the contrary created by his actions, our honorand is *prima facie* unlikely to have been an Athenian metic at the time this decree was passed. His name

[6] Bielman correctly notes that the whole crowning clause is restored and therefore not quite certain. The only other likely wording in this position, however, would be the naming of a second honorand. It seems fairly clear from the preceding text that only one honorand was involved.

[7] I agree with Bielman that this is the effect of προαιρούμενος in 4, though strictly the construction is probably "and giving preference, he *perfect or aorist main verb in 7* at every opportunity, showing himself useful to the Athenian People also in the other *circumstances specified at start of 6*."

was probably Greek, but there is a strong possibility that he was a Phoenician. It was common practice for Phoenicians to "translate" their names into Greek when operating in the Greek world.[8] In any case, this inscription belongs in a group of decrees which bear witness to Athenian encouragement of Cypriot and Phoenician traders in or around the 30s and 20s, notably the extensive series awarding proxeny and other honours to Herakleides son of Charikleides of Salamis (*IG* ii^2 360 = Schwenk no. 68, 330/29–325/4); the proxeny for Apses son of Hieron and Hieron son of Apses of Tyre (M. Walbank, *ZPE* 59 (1985), 107–11 = *SEG* xxxv 70 = *IG* ii^2 342+, c. 333?); the proxeny for Apollonides son of Demetrios of Sidon (*IG* ii^2 343 = Schwenk no. 84, 323/2); and the permission granted the Kitians in 333/2, on the motion of Lykourgos, to found a temple of Aphrodite, located in the Piraeus (*IG* ii^2 337 = Schwenk no. 27).[9]

Four specific services rendered by the honorand are mentioned in the surviving text:

1. He had imported grain from Egypt (2)

On this important evidence for Egypt as a source of Athenian grain see Garnsey, 150–53. As he notes, it is not easy to establish the extent to which it was a common source or an occasional one at this time; the explicit mention of the origin might, but does not necessarily, hint at the latter; and there is a possible (but again, not necessary) suggestion of a context in which the traditional Black Sea source had become less easy because of the Macedonian presence in the north and the war with Philip. On problems with the Egyptian source of supply a little later, in the 320s, see Garnsey, 152.

[8] On "translated" Phoenician names see e.g. O. Masson, *BCH* 93 (1969), 679–700; P.M. Fraser, *BSA* 65 (1970), 31–36; and note e.g. the iv BC bilingual Greek-Phoenician Attic tombstones for Cypriots from Kition, *IG* ii^2 9031–36.

[9] Herakleides is a common translation of a Phoenician theophoric Melqart-name (cf. e.g. Fraser, *op. cit.* 31). For Phoenician theophoric Mikl-names rendered as Greek Apollo-names cf. Fraser, 34; for an example of a Phoenician named "Demetrios", Masson, op. cit. 698. On the names of the Tyrians, Walbank, op. cit. 108, n. 4; O. Masson, *BCH* 92 (1968), 398–99. I confirm from autopsy that Walbank's new reading, [Ἱ]ἐ̣ρωνα in 10, is very probably correct (what are probably the extreme top and bottom points of the epsilon are visible on the break of the stone) and that [Θή]ρωνα, suggested by Clermont-Ganneau, *Rec. Arch. Or.* I (1888), 190–92, is undermined by the absence of inscribed trace, where one would expect to see it in the right half of the stoichos, of the right vertical of eta. On the ethnicity of the Kitians who founded the temple of Aphrodite cf. R. Parker, *Athenian Religion* (Oxford, 1996), 160, n. 29.

2. Something in the genitive plural at a rather low price (3)

Walbank makes the interesting suggestion that this was μ̣ύλλων, a type of fish imported salted from the Black Sea. This, if correct, might suggest that our honorand was, after all, also trading actively in the north, as well as the south, east and west (Sicily, see further below), and would be important new evidence for the iv BC fish trade. Epigraphically, however (see above), I prefer to read the letter before the upsilon as alpha and to restore ν]α̣ύλλων, "freight-charges" or "fares". Unlike μύλλος, which, so far as I know, would be a new word to both Attic and non-Attic epigraphy, ναῦλ(λ)ος is well attested at this period in this type of context, whether with one lambda or two (cf. Threatte ii, 22), both in relation to freight (e.g. *IG* ii² 1128, 13, c. mid-iv BC, fixing the freight charge to be paid by ruddle producers on Keos to Athenian ruddle shippers at 1 obol per [talent?]),[10] and persons (*SEG* iii 92, 18, iii BC, where the honorand is praised for transporting some children and requiring οὔτε ναῦλον, οὔτε ἀνάλωμα). Cf. *IG* ii² 1672, 126, 159; 1674, 6; *SEG* xxxiv 14, 75. The construction will be a genitive absolute, "the | fares being rather low", or a genitive of price, "for 76
rather low fares". The plural will imply multiple cargoes or passengers, or possibly multiple voyages.[11]

At the end of the line a restoration from the root ὑπηρε(τ)- seems all but compulsory. My initial thought was:

(a) καὶ ν]α̣ύλλων εὐωνοτέρων ὑπηρ̣[έ]τας *verb such as* ἀπέστειλεν κ]αὶ κτλ. with ὑπηρ̣[έτας understood as military servants or batmen (as e.g. Thuc. 3.17), perhaps even accompanying soldiers ransomed by the honorand in Sicily (8–10). The honorand would have allowed free passage to captives travelling alone, but levied a small charge on accompanying servants. In that case, however, one might expect this service to have been mentioned in 10; and there are perhaps more attractive possibilities, including transport of Athenian naval personnel (in the context of the war with Philip?), cf. the decree for the rulers of the Bosporan kingdom of 347/6, *IG* ii² 212, 59–60, where the Athenians resolve, δοῦναι δ[ὲ τὰ]ς ὑπη[ρεσί]α]ς ἃς αἰτοῦσι. (On the likely meaning of ὑπηρεσίαι here, "ships' officers" rather than "crew",

[10] ...ναῦλλον δὲ τελεῖν ὀβολὸν τοῦ [ταλάντου.

[11] This is apparently the first instance of the word in the plural in an Attic inscription, but plural usage is well enough attested elsewhere, e.g. *SEG* xxxiv 558, 41 (ii BC Thessaly). Cf. also Hesych. s.v. ναῦλα.

see K. Dover in A. Gomme et al., *Hist. Comm. Thuc.* (OUP, 1970), on 6.31, 3; J. Morrison, *JHS* 104 (1984), 48–59). So perhaps:

(b) καὶ ν]α̣ύλλων εὐωνοτέρων ὑπηρ̣[ε|σίας ἀπέστειλεν κ]αὶ κτλ.

Or, as Graham Oliver suggests to me, we might have to do with ὑπηρετέω, "render service". This verb also occurs in *IG* ii² 212, where the Bosporan rulers have announced their intention, ὑ[π]ηρετήσειν π|ροθύμως ὅτου ἂν ὁ δῆμ[ος] δ[έη]τα[ι] (16–17). So perhaps:

(c) καὶ -- ν]α̣ύλλων εὐωνοτέρων ὑπηρ̣[έ|τησεν φιλοτίμως κ]αί κτλ. In this case the low fares might have been charged on carriage of freight (grain?) rather than persons.

3. He had ransomed many Athenian citizens from Sicily and despatched them to Athens at his own expense (8–10).

Garnsey, 153, notes that the reference to Sicily probably implies that our trader was also active on the western trade route, which seems to have become a regular source of grain for Athens at this period. The commonest view is that these Athenians had been captured by "pirates" on that trade route (thus e.g. Garnsey, 153; Bielman, 15; also P. McKechnie, *Outsiders in the Greek Cities in the fourth century BC* (London, 1989), 119; C. Ferone, *Lesteia* (Naples, 1997), 144). Two serious alternatives have been suggested. Pritchett links this text with the reference to Chairestratos' trierarchy in Sicily at Isae. 6.1 and supposes that they were soldiers captured on an (otherwise unattested) Athenian military expedition to Sicily before 364; and Walbank has now also suggested that they were soldiers, captured (as mercenaries?) in the context of Timoleon's activities in Sicily in the 340s. The possibilities are clearly wide, though Pritchett's suggestion would distance our honorand's service chronologically rather far from the likely date of the decree (see further below);[12] and if the context was piracy this, together with the decree for Kleomis of Methymna (*IG* ii² 284 = Bielman no. 5), would be the earliest epigraphical reference to a mode

[12] The suggestion that has been raised from time to time that the reference might be to the Sicilian expedition in the Peloponnesian War, is impossible from this point of view. An honorand who had rendered service "now" (12) at the time of our decree, could not also have rendered service two generations previously. Cf. Bielman. There is nothing to support McKechnie's suggestion that our decree might have been a re-inscribed version of a late 5th cent. one (such a re-inscription is in any case not likely at this period) and, as this paper will demonstrate, several aspects of our decree argue against it.

of capture that occurs much more commonly in iii and early ii BC inscriptions.[13]

4. Privately and publicly he had continued to show the good will displayed by his ancestors towards the *demos* and had now given one talent "for the guarding" εἰς τὴν φυλακὴν (10–13). | 77

I agree with those scholars who have sought a context for this inscription in the 40s or early 30s (Kirchner: ante 336/5; Bielman: mid-iv BC or a little later;[14] Garnsey: 30s or late 40s; Kuenzi, 41 and 52: c. 337; Walbank: shortly before Chaironeia, c. 340?). The lettering, ascribed by Kirchner to his broad category, "volg. med. s. IV", is tending markedly towards Tracy's more narrowly defined "Common Style, c. 345–320", and indeed shares several of the features that he notes as characteristic of this style on pp. 76–77.[15] Especially striking is the chi. It is untypical of the very small chis of Tracy's "Common Style" in that it is as large as, or larger than, the average letter height, but its most striking feature is that, in l. 11 (less markedly in the more damaged case in 13) it tilts far to the left so that it is halfway between X and +. Moreover, in 11 at least, the upper right part of the letter is not, as usually the case, made in a single cut with the lower left, but is a separate stroke displaced very slightly to the right. I have not made a systematic study of the cutters of the 340s, but I have noticed this precise feature on one other inscription, *IG* ii^2 208, the treaty of 349/8 between Athens and the Echinaioi (pl. II). The larger chi in the heading on the moulding of this inscription is exactly the same, both as regards the tilt and the placing of the separate upper right and lower left strokes. The chis in the body of *IG* ii^2 208 also have the tilt, though not the separate upper right and lower left strokes. The lettering of the two inscriptions also has other features in common.[16] While there is

---

[13] Cf. Bielman, 232. Bielman, 231, notes that a military context is more common in iv BC inscriptions.

[14] Bielman's chronological argument from the award of an olive crown in 16, however, is not persuasive. The crown may have been of gold (see epigraphical notes).

[15] Tracy, 76–81. Tracy also names his style, "Litterae Volgares Saec. IV", but to avoid confusion with Kirchner's broader category I use the English term when referring to Tracy's style.

[16] Some alphas with left diagonal raised higher off the bottom of the stoichos than the right; kappa with long diagonals; mu with centre point tending to extend to, or nearly to, bottom of letter; nu with diagonal sometimes beginning at the top, sometimes slightly down from the top of the left vertical; omicron/theta cut in two separate upper and lower sections; tendency for sigma to sit rather low in the stoichos;

insufficient text on either of these inscriptions to establish a "hand" by the rigorous methodology applied by Tracy, the similarities are such as to create a *prima facie* case that the cutter of both inscriptions was the same.

In terms of a specific date, Kuenzi's suggestion that this inscription belongs in the immediate aftermath of the battle of Chaironeia, i.e. c. 337, remains very attractive. Both anxiety about the food supply and measures for strengthening defences at this critical time are well attested (e.g. Lyk. 1.18, 42 etc.; Din. 1.80; Dem. 18.171 and 248, which uses the term *phylake* more than once; the petition of Demochares reproduced at Plut. *Mor.* 851a–b mentions explicitly the donation of a talent by Demosthenes after the battle);[17] and the wording of our decree, with its vague reference to *phylake* as the purpose of the honorand's donation, is suggestive that the present moment (νῦν, 12) was, or had recently been, one of crisis for the *demos* (10, the last mentioned appropriate noun), which was the case immediately after Chaironeia, but not obviously in the decade or so before.[18] The decree probably represents one of the earliest recorded foreign contributions to an Athenian *epidosis,* a phenomenon that was to recur occasionally in the Hellenistic record (see the table, Kuenzi, 51–56, cf. 29–30; Migeotte, *Souscriptions,* 9–46; the only earlier example appears to be that of
78 Kleonymos of Crete, mentioned at | Isae. 5.38, of 391, Migeotte 12–14 no. 2, cf. 358–68). Moreover, as Garnsey points out, Chaironeia was a

---

tau sometimes with gap between top of vertical and horizontal, and with horizontal sloping down from left to right; upsilon sometimes three separate strokes, sometimes with left "diagonal" cut in same stroke, or nearly same, stroke, as bottom "vertical"; some omegas very flat (2–3 mm), some with left tail shorter than right. Letter heights on the two inscriptions are 0.004–0.005, with bigger letters such as Σ slightly higher and smaller ones, such as O, slightly shorter. Stoichedon grid dimensions are also very similar (av. c. 0.01 square on *IG* ii^2 208, c. 0.0105 horiz., c. 0.0108 vert. on 283; such slight differences in average grid dimensions are normally insignificant, especially with small fragments such as these).

[17] Cf. Garnsey, 154–55. As Tracy notes, however (p. 32), the donation of a further talent mentioned in this context, εἰς τὴν σιτωνίαν ἐν τῇ σιτοδείᾳ, perhaps belongs to the later food supply crisis of 328/7. For the likelihood that there was a formal *epidosis* after Chaironeia cf. Din. 1.80 and see L. Migeotte, *Les souscriptions publiques dans les cités grecques* (Quebec and Geneva, 1992), 18–19 no. 6.

[18] Bielman correctly notes that it is possible that the *phylake* had been more precisely specified earlier in the decree, but it is not common in these decrees for the context of a service to be alluded to more than once. For a more sceptical view than mine about the dating of our decree to the context of the post-Chaironeia *epidosis*, see L. Migeotte, *Hist.* 32 (1983), 145.

long-term watershed in relation to Athens' food supply, her reduced international standing after the battle, including the dissolution of the second Athenian League, making her more vulnerable to supply problems and requiring her to curry favour, in a way that she had not done before, with important traders: "the honorific decree to the trader-benefactor was born... in the post-Chaironeia period" (Garnsey, 162).[19] Honorific decrees were part of a reciprocal continuum which extended backwards in time certainly, but also into the future, with the intention of encouraging further acts of goodwill by the honorand and emulation of him by others, who, as the decree sometimes explicitly states, might expect to be honoured for comparable future services. Our decree belongs at the head of the long series honouring traders as Athens exerted itself to secure food supplies in the two decades after Chaironeia and on through the Hellenistic period.[20]

---

[19] The decree of 346 for the rulers of the Bosporos, *IG* ii² 212, certainly also belongs in a food-supply context, but the honorands were of higher socio-political status than the later "trader-benefactors" and the decree is part of a broad nexus of diplomatic relations between Athens and the Bosporan kingdom. Cf. P. Brun, *L'orateur Démade* (Bordeaux, 2000), 146. Similarly, the naturalisation decree of 407? for King Euagoras of Salamis and his sons, *IG* i³ 113, and the honours awarded this self-conscious "Hellene" in 393 (*Ag.* xvi 106B = *IG* ii² 20 + D. Lewis and R. Stroud, *Hesp.* 48 (1979), 180–93) belong to a wholly different level and context of diplomatic relations from those for our Salaminian trader-benefactor. A similar contrast in socio-political level is notable between the decree for the trader, Apollonides of Sidon (above) and the previous surviving decree for a Sidonian, that of c. 370s for king Straton, *IG* ii² 141 (on the date, *SEG* xlv 1210), albeit that the latter also had a commercial context.

[20] For a recent summary of the epigraphical evidence relating to the food supply from the two subsequent decades and down into the third century see Tracy, 30–35. I shall discuss some of these decrees further elsewhere. In the meantime note that the decree honouring Bosporans (probably ambassadors), *IG* ii² 414c+ = *Ag.* xvi 94 fr. c+j (Tracy, 32, under *IG* ii² 369+) is no longer dated to early 322, see *ZPE* 136 (2001), 65–70. The reading is very difficult, but I tentatively suggest, from autopsy, that the proposer of the decree for Apollonides of Sidon, *IG* ii² 343 = Schwenk no. 84 (Tracy, 33), may have been Πολυκ]λῆς Πο[λυκράτους] Ἀναγυράσιο[ς]. *Inter alia* this suits in terms of spacing Schweigert's attractive restoration of the prescript to yield the date in the fifth prytany of 323/2 on which the chairmanship of the *proedroi* was held by Epameinon of Erchia (same Assembly as the first decree for Euphron of Sikyon, *IG* ii² 448). Polykles was the opponent of Apollodoros in the dispute over a hierarchy which is the subject of Dem. 50. Since Apollonides was doubtless a Phoenician (see above n. 9), this identification, if correct, would cast an interesting sidelight on the prejudice which Apollodoros, an Athenian citizen of great wealth but foreign origin, alleges that Polykles displayed towards him, expressed in the latter's famous quip, ἄρτι μῦς πίττης γεύεται· ἐβούλετο γὰρ Ἀθηναῖος εἶναι (Dem. 50. 26).

It is this pivotal character which is our decree's particular significance in the broader perspective. It may or may not be one of the earliest honouring the ransoming of men captured by "pirates"; but it has a good claim to be the earliest honouring a "trader-benefactor" and the earliest honouring a foreign contribution to an Athenian *epidosis.* In these ways the decree presages Hellenistic conditions and practices; and in this respect it takes its place alongside *IG* ii^{2} 410, the important decree honouring priests in Piraeus cults and *hieropoioi,* which, as I have argued elsewhere, should probably also be dated to the aftermath of the battle of Chaironeia, and which also displays features that were to be characteristically Hellenistic: an increased focus, in bestowing honours, on those proposed by and for domestic officials, and a
79 greater defensiveness in public religious attitudes.[21] |

[21] Cf. *ZPE* 135 (2001), 52, no. 3; P.J. Rhodes with D.M. Lewis, *The Decrees of the Greek States* (Oxford, 1997), 29 with n. 89; J.D. Mikalson, *Religion in Hellenistic Athens* (Berkeley, 1998), 42–44.

CHAPTER TEN

ON *IG* II^2 546*

IG ii^2 546, a fragment from the top of an Athenian honorific decree, broken on all sides except the back, and crowned by a small, uninformative, patch of relief, is currently ascribed to the period of the oligarchy following Athens' defeat in the Lamian War.[1] This is problematic because the decree does not, as one would expect in the years from 321/0, include a heading naming the *anagrapheus*. Dow, following a suggestion of Pritchett and Meritt (p. 5), tentatively proposed that the *anagrapheus* might have been inscribed on the lost moulding above the relief, but there is no parallel for such an arrangement among the inscriptions of the oligarchy.[2] In fact, the current dating of this

---

* This chapter was previously published in *Zeitschrift für Papyrologie und Epigraphik* 141 (2002), 117–122.

Many thanks are due to Charalambos Kritzas and the staff of the Epigraphical Museum for facilitating the study of this decree (EM 7258), and for the photograph at plate III; and to Graham Oliver and Peter Thonemann for helpful discussion and suggestions. I alone am responsible for views expressed and for any errors. The following abbreviations are used:

Dow: S. Dow, The Preambles of Athenian Decrees Containing Lists of Symproedroi, *Hesp.* 32 (1963), 335–365;

Henry: A. S. Henry, *The Prescripts of Athenian Decrees* (Leiden, 1977);

Lawton: C. Lawton, *Attic Document Reliefs* (Oxford, 1995);

Pritchett and Meritt: W.K. Pritchett and B.D. Meritt, *The Chronology of Hellenistic Athens* (Cambridge Mass., 1940);

Schwenk: C.J. Schwenk, *Athens in the Age of Alexander* (Chicago, 1985).

[1] See Dow, 351, where relevant earlier bibliography can also be traced (cf. *SEG* xxi 304). On the relief see Lawton no. 151 with pl. 80; M. Meyer, *Die griechischen Urkundenreliefs (AM Beiheft* 13, Berlin, 1989), 301 A 128. Preserved are the lower portions of two clad figures, one to the left facing left, one to the right facing right, and, at the extreme right, a foot of an apparently smaller figure, perhaps an honorand, facing to the left. Lawton comments that "there should have been something to the left side of the relief engaging the attention of the figure who has turned in that direction". That "something" was perhaps the second honorand (for the two honorands, see note on 11–12 below). If my restorations are correct the composition was not symmetrical. The centre point will have been the letter Σ of ΑΡΧΟΝΤΟΣ, which is aligned under the front (left) foot of the rightward of the two larger figures.

[2] State decrees with relief from the oligarchic period are altogether rather few; the only securely dated example appears to be *Ag.* xvi 97 = *SEG* xxi 303. There are occasional instances from other periods of superscription of a magistrate over a relief, e.g. *IG* ii^2 128 = Lawton no. 28 (archon of 356/5). The parallel cited in this connection

inscription is a hangover from *IG* ii², at which time it was believed that named *symproedroi* did not occur in inscriptions earlier than 318/7. Since it has been known that named *symproedroi* occur sporadically from 333/2 onwards,[3] such a late dating has been unnecessary. The true date, I suggest, is indicated by the letters in l. 2, Ἀριστ[-, for these are the initial letters of the name of the secretary of 332/1, Ἀριστόνους Ἀριστόνου Ἀναγυράσιος.[4] Both this man's name and the name of the archon of this year, Niketes, can comfortably be accommodated in ll. 1–3. Since the first editor, Köhler (*IG* ii. 5. 245b), a 36 letter line has been posited. In fact the line length may have been 35 or 36 letters; in either case there will have been occasional additional letters, or spaces, or other minor irregularities, a common feature of decrees of this period.[5] The text printed below assumes 35 letters per line, as
117 this requires the smaller number of | irregularities. This line length also

by Pritchett and Meritt, 5, however, *Ag.* xvi 71 (archon of 346/5), is unlikely to be a state document. Probably it is a decree of the *genos* Salaminioi (cf. *SEG* xlvii 146bis; I discuss it further in *Horos,* forthcoming). In any case it is methodologically unsatisfactory to ascribe decrees with normal democratic prescripts to the period of the oligarchy, based on a posited superscript over a relief. By that reasoning many fragmentary decrees of the last decades of democracy might be assigned to the oligarchic period.

[3] See Dow; Henry, 40–41. The earliest example is Schwenk 31 (= *IG* ii² 336) B 6ff. of 333/2.

[4] This date was considered and rejected by Pritchett and Meritt, 4, n. 19, on the grounds of "difficulties with the calendar equations, and various technical objections". For two possible calendar equations, see below. Unspecified "technical objections" supply no basis for an argument.

[5] To take just two examples from this year (both of which I have examined at autopsy):

(a) *IG* ii² 346 = Schwenk 37, a stoich. 25 text with only 24 letters in the first line of the prescript, achieved probably by a *vacat* after the tribe name at the end of the line (5) and possibly 26 in the second (6, though here one might alternatively restore πρυτα[ν]έ[ας] for πρυτα[ν]ε[ίας], also a possibility in our decree, see below);

(b) *IG* ii² 347 = Schwenk 38, a stoich. 22 text with 27 (sic) letters in fr a+b, 11, ΤΩ for ΤΩΙ in 14 (not noted accurately by Schwenk), 23 letters in 15 caused by inscription of ΑΙ of δεδόχθαι in one stoichos. Since an accurate text of fr. c of this inscription (= EM 5119), first correctly associated with fr. a + b by Wilhelm, has never been published, I take the opportunity of supplying one here. It follows fr. a + b after a *lacuna* of uncertain length:

[---------- εἰς δὲ τὴν] stoich. 22
[ἀναγραφὴν τῆς στήλης δοῦν]-
[αι] τ[ὸν ταμία]ν τοῦ [δήμου ΔΔΔ]
δραχμ[ὰ]ς ἐκ τῶν κατ[ὰ ψηφίσμ]-
ατα ἀναλισκομέν[ω]ν τῶ[ι δήμω]- 23 letters
ι. *vacat*
vacat 0.515 *to original bottom*

The second and third alphas in 5 are inscribed in a single stoichos.

produces a text in which it is apparent that some attention has been given to minimising the breaking of syllables, words, and at least in one case (the chairman) names, at line ends. For clarity of presentation the text incorporates my suggested calendar equation, "equation a"; for another possible restoration, based on an alternative "equation b", see the notes.

332/1 [ἐπὶ Νικήτ]ου ἄρχοντος ἐπὶ τῆ[ς Αἰαντίδος^{IX} ἐβ?]- stoich. 35
[δόμης? πρυτ]ανείας, ἧι Ἀριστ̣[όνους Ἀναγυράσ]-
[ιος ἐγραμμ]άτευε· δεκάτει ὑ[στέραι Ἀνθεστηρ?]- 36 letters
[ιῶνος, ἕκτει?] καὶ δεκάτει τῆ[ς πρυτανέας· τῶν]
[προέδρων ἐπ]εψήφιζεν Φανο[.......^{14}.......^{I}]
[συμπρόεδροι·] Δι[ό]γνητος Ἐρ[...^{II}....^{13}......]
[....^{8}....^{III} Χαι]ρέδ̣ημος Σουν[ιεύς^{IV}.....^{9}....]
[......$^{12\mathrm{V}}$......]θά̣λ̣ης Λακιά[δης^{VI}.....^{10}.....]
[......^{11}..^{VII}....]α̣χος ἐκ Κοίλη[ς^{VIII}......^{12}......]
[..^{4}..^{X}. ἔδοξεν τ]ῶι δήμωι· Δημο[.......^{13}......]
[......^{11}.....]ς εἶπεν· ἐπειδ̣ὴ [......^{12}......]
[....^{8}....Δόλο?]πες δια̣τε̣λοῦ[σι εὖνοι ὄντες]
[τῶι δήμωι τῶι Ἀ]θηναίων καὶ π̣[οιοῦσιν ὅτι δύ]-
[νανται ἀγαθὸν κ]αὶ νῦν καὶ ἐν̣ [τῶι ἔμπροσθεν]
[χρόνωι τοῖς στρ]ατευομένοι[ς......^{11}.....]
[.....^{9}....χρησ]ίμους αὐτο̣ὺ[ς......^{11}.....]
[.....^{10}.....ἀπο]φαίνουσ[ι̣.......^{14}.......]
[.......^{14}.......] πρόθυ[μ........^{15}.......]
----

1 in.–3 in. Lambert || 3 med-5 in. Köhler, Ἀνθεστηρ|ιῶνος, ἕκτει]? Lambert || 6–18 Köhler, with minor adjustments; 7 in. Lolling in *IG* ii^{2} 546, 13 π̣[οιοῦσιν Lambert, 14 fin.—15 in. G. Oliver.

Notes

Little of importance in this text hangs on difficult or controversial readings (see l. 12 for the only significant point). The placement of square brackets and dots accords with Graham Oliver's and my reading of the stone at autopsy. The stoichedon grid is 0.012 m. square. The somewhat spidery hand is not identified by S.V. Tracy, *Athenian Democracy in Transition* (Berkeley, 1995).

1. The *symproedroi* were eight in number, one from each tribe except the tribe in prytany and that of their chairman (cf. Dow). From the list of *symproedroi* in 6–9 it can accordingly be inferred that the tribe in prytany was I Erechtheis, IX Aiantis or X Antiochis. In 332/1 Erechtheis held the ninth (Schwenk 40 = *I Orop.* 296 = *IG* vii 4252)

and Antiochis the eighth (e.g. Schwenk 38 = *IG* ii^2 347) prytany, but in neither of those prytanies does it seem that the 21st of a month coincided with a καὶ δεκάτει date of the prytany.[6] The tribe in prytany
118 should accordingly have been IX Aiantis. If one | restored with a 36 letter line, it would be necessary to posit a *vacat* or equivalent irregularity at or towards the end of line 1.

1–2. The number of the prytany flows from my suggested calendar equation, 21st Anthesterion = 16th day of pryt. 7 ("equation a"). This equation would seem to require the minimum of stoichedon and calendrical irregularity, but see below for another possibility, "equation b". There is general agreement that 332/1 was an ordinary, not an intercalary, year (see *Ag.* xvi p. 119; also the discussions of Schwenk, under the inscriptions of this year). The calendrical data for this year available hitherto[7] were consistent with the following arrangement of number of days per month and prytany, as set out by B.D. Meritt, *The Athenian Year* (Berkeley, 1961), 85–88:

Months:

Hek	*Met*	*Boe*	*Pya*	*Mai*	*Pos*	*Gam*	*Anth*	*Ela*	*Mou*	*Tha*	*Ski*
29	30	29	30	29	30	29	30	29	30	29	30

Prytanies:

1	2	3	4	5	6	7	8	9	10
36	36	36	35	35	35	35	35	35	36

Pritchett and Neugebauer's scheme[8] differed in that the first four prytanies were given 36 days, in accordance with the "rule" of *Ath. Pol.*

[6] On the scheme for this year implicit in "equation a" and "equation b", 21st Elaph. = 9th day of pryt. 8 (two days after the passage of several extant decrees, at the Assembly on 19th Elaph., see Schwenk 36–39); 21st Moun. = 3rd day of pryt. 9; 21st Tharg. = 33rd day of pryt. 9.

[7] The following calendar equations for this year are reasonably firmly attested: (a) 9th Boed. = 32nd day of pryt. 2 (*IG* ii^2 368 = Schwenk 82, cf. Schwenk 33); (b) 19th Elaph. = 7th day of pryt. 8 (the four decrees, Schwenk 36 = *IG* ii^2 345—Schwenk 39); (c) 11th Tharg. = 23rd day of pryt. 9 (Schwenk 40–41). Although not controversial, the calendar equation in (a) is heavily restored and is not quite sure. Alternative possible restorations, however, will make little difference for our purposes. In a regular ordinary year in which the first two months have 59 days between them and the first two prytanies 36 days, 9th Boed. will in any case coincide with the 32nd day of pryt. 2, and this equation is consistent with both the alternative new schemes for the year 332/1 proposed below.

[8] W.K. Pritchett and O. Neugebauer, *The Calendars of Athens* (Cambridge Mass., 1947), 48–49.

xliii 2, and this was compensated for by assuming a succession of two full months early in the year.

The new calendrical data for 332/1 implicit in "equation a" could be accommodated by adjusting Meritt's scheme as follows:

Months:

Hek	*Met*	*Boe*	*Pya*	*Mai*	*Pos*	*Gam*	*Anth*	*Ela*	*Mou*	*Tha*	*Ski*
29	30	29	30	30	30	30	29	29	30	29	29

Prytanies:

1	2	3	4	5	6	7	8	9	10
36	36	36	35	35	35	36	35	35	35

It will be noted that, for consistency with this scheme, 11th Posideon will have fallen on the 16th day of pryt. 5. Accordingly if the basic approach (Meritt's) to restoring the highly fragmentary Schwenk 34 = *Hesp.* 5 (1936), 413–14 no. 11, were maintained, it would be necessary to change the number in l. 5 from πέμπ]τει καὶ δεκάτει to ἕκ]τει καὶ δεκάτει and to posit two *vacats* or equivalent irregularity earlier in the line (note that there is a *vacat* on the stone in l. 7 of this decree), as follows (alternative I):

[ἐπὶ Νικήτου ἄρχοντος ἐπὶ τῆς] Κεκροπί- stoich. 31
[δος πέμπτης πρυτανείας ἧι Ἀρ]ιστόνου-
[ς Ἀριστόνου Ἀναγυράσιος ἐγρ]αμμάτε[υ]-
[εν· *v* Ποσιδεῶνος ἐνδεκάτει, *v* ἕκ]τει καὶ
[δεκάτει τῆς πρυτανείας· τῶν πρ]οέδρων
[ἐπεψήφιζεν--[16] *name + demotic*--] *v* ἔδ[οξ]-
[εν κτλ.

Alternatively, avoiding the posited *vacats* and adapting a line of restoration suggested by M.H. Hansen, *GRBS* 23 (1982), 349 no. 85, one could restore the prytany as the tenth, the 13th or 15th days, and the month as Skirophorion, the 7th or 9th days (alternative II): | 119

[ἐπὶ Νικήτου ἄρχοντος ἐπὶ τῆς] Κεκροπί- stoich. 31
[δος δεκάτης πρυτανείας ἧι Ἀρ]ιστόνου-
[ς Ἀριστόνου Ἀναγυράσιος ἐγρ]αμμάτε[υ]-
[εν· Σκιροφοριῶνος ἑβδόμει, τρί]τει καὶ
or: [εν· Σκιροφοριῶνος ἐνάτει, πέμπ]τει καὶ
[δεκάτει τῆς πρυτανείας· τῶν πρ]οέδρων
[ἐπεψήφιζεν--[16] *name + demotic*--] *v* ἔδ[οξ]-
[εν κτλ.

IG ii^2 546 can be accommodated to the "rule" of *Ath. Pol.* that the first four prytanies were of 36 days by "equation b", 21st Gamelion = 19th day of pryt. 6, as follows:[9]

332/1	[ἐπὶ Νικήτ]ου ἄρχοντος ἐπὶ τῆ[ς Αἰαντίδος^{IX} ᵛᵛ] [ἕκτης πρυτ]ανείας, ἧι Ἀριστ[όνους Ἀναγυράσ]- [ιος ἐγραμμ]άτευε· δεκάτει ὑ[στέραι Γαμηλιῶ]- [νος, ᵛ ἐνάτει] καὶ δεκάτει τῆ[ς πρυτανέας·	stoich. 35

This is consistent with the following scheme for the year as a whole:

Months:

Hek	*Met*	*Boe*	*Pya*	*Mai*	*Pos*	*Gam*	*Anth*	*Ela*	*Mou*	*Tha*	*Ski*
29	30	29	30	29	30	30	30	29	30	29	29

Prytanies:

1	2	3	4	5	6	7	8	9	10
36	36	36	36	35	35	35	35	35	35

In this case Schwenk 34 would most comfortably be restored according to alternative II.

It will be clear that equation b is best accommodated to a 35 letter line. For the *vacat* after the tribe name in l. 1 cf. n. 5 (a). A *vacat* (or punctuation) after the month name in 4 could be accounted for by a perceived need, in this unusual word order (see note on 3–4, below), to clarify that the following number relates to the prytany and not to the month.[10]

2–3. There are several cases of the omission of the secretary's father's name at this period, e.g. Schwenk 31, 7–8 = *IG* ii^2 336 B, of 333/2 (cf. Henry, 42–43). If one restored with 36 letters it would be necessary, on equation a, to posit a single *vacat* or equivalent irregularity at or towards the end of l. 2.

[9] Alternatively it would be possible to reconcile "equation a" with the rule of *Ath. Pol.* by assuming that days were inserted into/subtracted from the "lunar" calendar to secure a regular succession of prytanies (see recently W.K. Pritchett, *ZPE* 128 (1999), 89–91).

[10] If one took δεκάτει ὑστέραι, like δεκάτει μετ' εἰκάδας (cf. Hesych. s.v. δεκάτη προτέρα), to mean literally "the tenth day counting backwards from the end of the month" one could construct an argument that it would be more appropriate to a full month and hence to the scheme of equation b. Apparently, however, the meaning of this term (very rare in extant state decrees until well into the hellenistic period) was purely conventional, i.e. it could be used to designate 21st in either type of month (as, it seems, in the sacrificial calendar from Erchia, *SEG* xxi 541). Cf. most recently W.K. Pritchett, *Athenian Calendars and Ekklesias* (Amsterdam, 2001), 41–87.

3 med.–4 in. On the very rare placement of the date in the month before the month name see Henry, 56. For the month name see the note on 1–2. On the basis of a 35 letter line, there will, on equation a, have been an additional letter inserted at some point in the square brackets at the end of the line, e.g. AI might have been inscribed in one stoichos (cf. n. 5 (b)). There would be no irregularity if a 36 letter line were assumed.

4 (prytany date). See note on 1–2. Under equation a, on the assumption of a 36 letter line the normal spelling πρυτανείας could be restored. If the line had 35 letters, one might restore, as shown, πρυτανέας (for parallels at this period cf. Threatte I, 316), or assume e.g. EI inscribed in a single stoichos. Cf. n. 5 (a). | 120

5–6. If the restoration of Aiantis is correct in l. 1, the only tribe available for the chairman is I Erechtheis. His deme, however, is not identifiable. As has long been recognised, since there is no deme in Ἐρ- in Erechtheis, the first listed *symproedros* must have come from tribe II Aegeis, in which there are two demes in Ἐρ-, Erchia and Erikeia.

10–11. Names in Δημο- are common and the statistics for decree proposers indicate that many men are attested as proposers of only one decree at this period, see M.H. Hansen, *GRBS* 25 (1984), 123–55 = *The Athenian Ecclesia* (Copenhagen, 1989), II, 93–127 (for known politicians, not attested as decree proposers, with names in Δημο- that would fit the space here, see Hansen, 145–47). Among known decree proposers, however, the following could be restored:

(a) assuming that l. 10 had 35 letters, Δημο[σθένης Δημοκλέ|ους Λαμπτρεύ]ς, proposer of *IOrop* 298 = Schwenk 50, honouring the *epimeletai* of the Amphiareia in 329/8, and of *IG* ii² 360, 5 = Schwenk 68, honouring Herakleides of Salamis in 325/4;

(b) assuming that l. 10 had 36 letters, Δημο[σθένης Δημοσθέν|ους Παιανιεύ]ς, the great orator, attested as proposer of many decrees in the literary record, but of only one in the epigraphical, *IG* ii² 231+, of 340/39.[11]

[11] See *ZPE* 137 (2001), 55–68. Angelos Matthaiou kindly points out to me that, strictly speaking, it would be epigraphically possible to restore the proposer of this decree as Δημαίνετο]ς Δημοσθέ[νους Παια]νιε[ύς, a man attested only by his mid-iv BC funerary monument, *IG* ii² 7033, and member of a family active in deme and tribal affairs, but not at national level (cf. J. K. Davies, *Athenian Propertied Families* (Oxford, 1971), no. 3276). Given, however, the obscurity of this man and the known activity of Demosthenes the orator in the diplomatic context to which this inscription belongs (i.e. alliance-building in the lead-up to Chaironeia), the possibility that Demainetos

11–12. I agree with *IG* ii[2] in printing the first surviving letter of 12 as π̣. All three strokes of the letter are visible, easily interpretable as a pi with rather low horizontal and rather long right vertical, as normally on this stone, and with left vertical projecting somewhat above its point of juncture with the horizontal stroke. There is a slight possibility that the letter intended was H. The other etas in this text are regular in shape, with the exception, however, of the one in l. 13, which quite closely resembles this letter. Since Köhler's first edition, the name has been restored as Δόλο]πες. This is likely enough (the Dolopes were neighbours of the Thessalians and were to be Athenian allies in the Lamian War, see Diod. xviii 11.1), but not quite sure. There is no other extant Athenian decree honouring a Dolopian, and no Dolopian is listed by M.J. Osborne and S.G. Byrne, *The Foreign Residents of Athens* (Leuven, 1996). None of the other ethnics in -οψ listed by F. Dornseiff and B. Hansen, *Rückläufiges Wörterbuch der griechischen Eigennamen* (Ares reprint, Chicago, 1978), 317, e.g. Αἰθίοψ etc., is especially plausible at this period in this context. However, the redating of the decree takes it back to a period when -ες for the nominative plural of an ethnic, demotic etc. in -ευς, though very rare, can not be ruled out (see Threatte I, 189). E.g. Σινω]π̂ες is a remote possibility (for persons from Sinope resident at Athens in iv BC see Osborne and Byrne, 289–93).[12] Alternatively, reading eta instead of pi, one might have an ethnic in -ηες; such a form is very rare, but not wholly unparalleled, cf. Παλῆες (apparently from Παλεύς) at *IG* i[2] 1070 (? iv BC, fun. mon.), Κολωνῆες for the demesmen of Kolonai at *Ag.* xv 43, 94 (335/4). In any case, probably there were two honorands, ἐπειδὴ *name* καί *name* Δόλο?]π̣ες. If the names were all very short and the men were brothers, as frequently in decrees for plural honorands, there would also be room for a short father's name before the ethnic. The honorands had rendered service in a military context (cf. note on 14–15), possibly the war with Philip before 338 or allied operations under Macedonian leadership after that date. Beyond that, we do not have enough information for worthwhile speculation on the circumstances of the decree.

---

of Paiania and not Demosthenes of Paiania was in fact proposer of this decree would seem on current evidence to be very remote.

[12] A. Wilhelm's restoration of *IG* ii[2] 409 as relating to Sinope, however (cf. *SBAW* 220.5 (1942) = *Attische Urkunden* V, 150–52 no. lv) is speculative (the name does not occur in the unrestored part of the text). I shall discuss this decree further elsewhere.

12–13 in. Rest. Köhler. If 12 had 36 letters, διατελοῦ[σιν, if 35, -σι (cf. ἐγραμμ]άτευε in 3). | 121

13–14. π̣[ράττουσι ὅτι δύνανται ἀγαθόν Kirchner after Köhler. From trace, the Π might be Γ. Kirchner's restoration creates a 36 letter line (as would π̣[οιοῦντες). Preferably, for a 35 letter line, π̣[οιοῦσιν (cf. *IG* ii² 206, 9; 360, 7, etc.).

14–15. ἐν [τῶι Ἑλληνικῶι πολέμωι Köhler. This restored reference to the Lamian War, questioned already by N.G. Ashton, *JHS* 104 (1984), 153 n. 16, must fall in consequence of the new dating. Instead, Graham Oliver persuasively suggests ἐν [τῶι ἔμπροσθεν ǀ χρόνωι (35 letters, or, for a 36 letter line, ἔμπροσσθεν, cf. *IG* ii² 132, 6; *Ag.* xvi 102, 11–12 and 104, 11–12 etc.). Though the drift of the sense in 15–18 is clear enough, the syntax is not precisely recoverable. Nevertheless, as usual with the "making themselves useful" formula, the pronoun in 16 was probably not *IG*'s αὐτοὺς, but the reflexive αὑτọὺς followed by παρασκευάζω or παρέχω; and ἀποφαίνουσι (subject probably Athenians, e.g. generals, reporting on the honorands)…πρόθυμ- (sc. the honorands) perhaps belonged to a separate main clause, linked to what preceded by καί or δέ (cf. e.g. *IG* ii² 401, 10; 408, 7 with Wilhelm, [n. 12], 152–54; 428, 5; *SEG* xxiv 119, 3 etc.). | 122

CHAPTER ELEVEN

AFTERWORDS*

1. IG *ii² 417, the Eutaxia Liturgy and the Relief, Lawton no. 150*

At *ZPE* 135 (2001), 56–57 (with ph., Tafel I), I made a case that the *Eutaxia* liturgy, attested for Athens by *IG* ii² 417, involved the funding of competitions between ephebes, introduced together with the reformed ephebic system in or shortly before 334/3 and abolished as a liturgy after 317 by Demetrios of Phaleron. Nigel Kennell has kindly drawn my attention to the evidence for a competition in *eutaxia* for youths or ephebes in a number of hellenistic cities. With no claim to completeness, the following is a list of examples attested BC:

1. Beroia, 175–167: P. Gauthier and M.B. Hatzopoulos, *La Loi Gymnasiarque de Beroia* (Athens, 1993), p. 21 B 45 and B 54 (those under 30);
2. Chalcis, 130–90: D. Knoepfler, *BCH* 103 (1979), 170 (ephebes, *neoteroi*);
3. Cnidus, late hell.: W. Blümel, *EA* 25 (1995), 62–63, no. 33 (*SEG* xliv 902) (youths);
4. Erythrai, 110–85: *I Erythrai* (*IK* 1) 81 (*paides*);
5. Massalia, 200–1: *IG* xiv 2445 (ephebes);
6. Mylasa, Hydai, hell.: *I Mylasa* II (*IK* 35) 909, 6–7 (*paides*);
7. Samos, 210–100: *IG* xii. 6. 179, 182 and 183 (*paides?*, *neoi* etc.);
8. Sestos, 133–120: *I Sestos* (IK 19) 1, 83 (age not specified);
9. Tanagra, 100–80: *IG* vii 557 (age not specified).

The geographical and temporal distance between our case and these will clearly make inferences as to detail hazardous, but they do seem

---

* This chapter was previously published in *Zeitschrift für Papyrologie und Epigraphik* 141 (2002), 122–124.

Many thanks are due to Charalambos Kritzas and the staff of the Epigraphical Museum, Athens, for facilitating the study of EM 381 (*IG* ii² 1593) and for the photograph of it reproduced at plate IV, and to Elene Kourinou and the staff of the National Museum, Athens, for facilitating the study of NM 2958 (Lawton no. 150). Lawton = C. Lawton, *Attic Document Reliefs* (Oxford, 1995).

to strengthen the argument that the Athenian *Eutaxia* was also an ephebic competition.

I have now had the opportunity to examine, in the National Museum at Athens, the relief, Lawton 150 (ph. at her pl. 79),[1] which is our only other firm evidence for the Athenian *Eutaxia* liturgy. The (high-quality) relief consists of a full-size female figure to the right, labelled
ΕΥΤΑΞΙΑ, pointing to a | male figure in similar scale centre-left, lean- 122
ing on a crutch (*Demos* ? or just possibly, as suggested by U. Kron, *Die zehn attischen Phylenheroen* (*AM Beiheft* 5, Berlin, 1976), 237–38, 281 (9) a tribal hero),[2] who stands next to (extreme left) a smaller male figure wearing a short chiton, his left arm draped with a mantle and his hand resting on the rim of a shield. On my interpretation this figure was an ephebe, i.e. probably representing the ephebes of a single tribe, or the ephebate in general. The upper parts of both male figures are broken away. In the background is a tripod mounted on a column, clearly a reference to an agonistic event. Both *IG* ii^2 417 and the relief are of white, "Pentelic", marble and both stones are broken such that it is difficult strictly to rule out on physical grounds that they might have come from the same stele.[3] The top section of the text is missing from *IG* ii^2 417, so on any account there would have been an extent of stone between it and any relief. Both stones are, or may be, broken at the back, so thickness can not be used as a criterion. Width is a more promising one, though even here absolute certainty is not achievable, since the original left side of the relief and the original right side of *IG* ii^2 417 are missing. Preserved widths are fairly close (inscription, 0.335; relief, 0.355), but the right side of the inscription cuts through the beginning of a second column of names. Even if there were only two columns of names (in fact unlikely, cf. my remarks, p. 59), the original width of *IG* ii^2 417 will have been substantially greater than the preserved width of the relief. This could only be accommodated by assuming that the composition extended substantially further to the left, with figures etc. additional to those preserved. A comparison with

[1] M. Meyer, *Die griechischen Urkundenreliefs* (*AM Beiheft* 13, Berlin, 1989), A 142. On the relief see most recently M.I. Pologiorgi, in O. Palagia and W. Coulson eds., *Regional Schools in Hellenistic Sculpture* (Oxford, 1998), 41 with ph., pl. 14 (*SEG* xlviii 106).

[2] It is possible that, like *Eutaxia*, this figure was labelled on the architrave above its head.

[3] That relief and inscription belonged together was first doubted by D.M. Lewis, *Hesp.* 37 (1968), 376 with n. 25; Lawton left open the possibility that they did so.

the width and composition of other Attic document reliefs (compare Lawton's plates) shows this to be unlikely. Unless, remotely, there was a row of ephebes (cf. Lawton no. 138), the composition as preserved is probably complete. If so, the argument for dissociating relief and inscription is not only physical, but thematic. The relief relates specifically to *Eutaxia*, the inscription lists the performers of other liturgies as well. The relief has to do with a competition; the inscription with the dedication of *phialai* by performers of liturgies.

If, however, this relief does not belong with *IG* ii² 417, what will have been the content of the inscription to which it did relate? There would seem to be two obvious possibilities:

(a) it honoured the victorious tribal contingent of ephebes in one year's *Eutaxia* competition (that the latter was organised on a tribal basis can be inferred from *IG* ii² 417). In that case the inscription might perhaps have been a decree of the relevant tribe, though some more complicated arrangement can not be ruled out. Cf. the ephebic inscriptions collected by O.W. Reinmuth, *The Ephebic Inscriptions of the Fourth Century BC* (Leiden, 1971) (note e.g. his no. 1, with decree of the relevant tribe, of the Boule and of two demes, all honouring the tribal contingent of ephebes, in some cases together with their *sophronistes*). This would be consistent with the large male figure being either *Demos* (which awarded the prize) or the tribal hero of the victorious ephebic contingent, being singled out, as it were, by *Eutaxia*;

(b) it was from the state decree, or more likely law, which instituted the *Eutaxia* liturgy and competition, c. 334/3. In that case one will interpret *Eutaxia* as, so to speak, imposing herself on or inspiring the *Demos*, by means of a competition (the tripod) for the ephebes (the figure extreme left), the *Demos* and its ephebes being closely linked on the left side of the composition.

2. IG *ii² 1593 and Xenokles and Androkles of Sphettos*

In my note on *IG* ii² 1593 at *ZPE* 135 (2001), 57–58 n. 29, I overlooked the helpful discussion of M.B. Walbank, *ZPE* 107 (1995), 69–72. Since no photograph of the stone, inscribed in extremely small lettering,[4]

[4] The normal letter height is 0.003–0.004 m., with letters such as Β, Σ, Υ, Φ, up to about 0.005.

has yet been published, I take this opportunity to supply one (pl. IV). Walbank's text represents | a major advance on that in the Corpus. 123
My own autopsy of the stone and the identification of the "buyers" of col. 2, ll. 20–31, as the brothers Xenokles and Androkles of Sphettos, necessitate some slight adjustments, as follows:[5]

ω̣[νητής ᵛ] non-stoich.
[Ξενοκλῆς] Σφήττ : ἐγγυ[ητ]ής ᵛ
[....c. 7...Ἀν]α̣γυ : ὠν[η]τ̣ : Ξ[ε]ν̣ο- ᵛ
[κλῆς Σφητ] ⁝ ἐγ : Λεώστ̣ρατ[ος] ᵛ
[....c. 7...] ὠ̣νητὴς Ξενοκλῆ[ς ᵛ] ᵛ
[Σφή]ττ̣[ιο]ς̣ : ἐγγ : Λυσιάδης ἐξ [Οἴου]
[ὠνητ]ή[ς : Ἀνδ]ροκλῆς Σφήττ[ιος ᵛ]
[ἐγγυητή]ς̣ [: Χα?]ιρίας Ποτάμιος ᵛ
[ὠνητής :] Ἀνδροκλῆς Σφήττιος ᵛ
[ἐγγυητή]ς̣ : Κηφισόδωρος Ποτάμ̣[ι]
[ὠνητής : Ἀνδ]ροκλῆς Σφήττιος ᵛ
[ἐγγυητής : Ξ]ενοφῶν Πόριος ᵛ

Spacing between letters varies considerably and precise calculation of numbers of letters to be restored in square brackets is not possible. The extent of vacats at line-ends varies from 1 to about 4 or 5 spaces.

The only significant divergence here in terms of readings is at l. 25, where Walbank prints the demotic as [..c. 4..]Λ̣ι[..]ς̣. His Λ̣ represents the trace which I read as the right horizontal and upper section of the vertical of a tau. I agree with him that it is followed by a vertical stroke, but across the top of this vertical runs a horizontal, of which the left tip and most of the right side are clear, i.e. a certain tau. Otherwise, my text differs substantively only in the restorations at 21 in. and 23 in.

In the next edition of *Horos* I shall show *inter alia* that it was very probably Androkles of Sphettos and not, as believed hitherto, his brother Xenokles, who was *agonothetes* on *IG* ii² 3073 in 307/6.[6]

As for the context of the transactions recorded by *IG* ii² 1593, there is little, on current evidence, that can be added to what Walbank and I have said. From the hand the period is certainly Lykourgan. The type of the account, listing "buyers" and guarantors with no specifications of

[5] The only other significant improvement I can offer for the time being is the reading of the guarantor in col. II, l. 8 as Theopeithes of Halai. For my text of this line see my note in *ZPE* 135 (not quite accurately reproduced at *SEG* xlviii 155).

[6] I shall also note that, as David Jordan kindly informs me, the third brother, Krates, supposedly on the curse tablet *SBAB* 1934, 1023 no. 1A, 22–23 (cf. J.K. Davies, *Athenian Propertied Families* (Oxford, 1971), p. 415), is a ghost.

price or of the items transacted, is unique. As Walbank notes, it would seem to imply that the items were in some way equal, with some men "buying" multiple shares (3 each in the case of our brothers). Walbank raises the possibility that the "buyers" contracted for provision of stone quarried for a public monument. Something along these lines is quite possible; though it is also possible that we have to do with some more grandiose Lykourgan scheme designed to profit the public finances, religious or secular, comparable in these ways to the public land sales recorded in the *Rationes Centesimarum*. If so, as with those sales, the relative prominence of the "buyers"[7] would illustrate rather well the dictum of Humphreys, that Lykourgos' programme was "carried through by the energetic co-operation of an appreciable segment
124 of the upper class".[8] |

[7] In addition to our brothers note e.g. Aristomachos of Halai, "buyer" of two "shares" (cols. 2, 9 and 11) and also among the wealthy demesmen of Halai who subscribed to a new statue of Aphrodite, *IG* ii^{2} 2820, 10, with *SEG* xlvii 211.

[8] S.C. Humphreys, Lycurgus of Butadae, in J.W. Eadie and J. Ober eds., *The Craft of the Ancient Historian: Essays…C.G. Starr* (Lanham Md, 1985), 204; cf. S.D. Lambert, *Rationes Centesimarum* (Amsterdam, 1997), 289.

CHAPTER TWELVE

IG II^2 410: AN ERASURE RECONSIDERED*

IG II^2 410 is an Athenian state decree honouring priests and *hieropoioi*, which, I shall suggest, probably dates to the immediate aftermath of Philip of Macedon's epoch-making victory over Athens and her allies at the battle of Chaironeia in 338 BCE. It was to be set up in the theatre of Dionysos (line 39); and indeed it was next to this theatre in Athens that the inscription was discovered, nearly complete, with no sign of subsequent re-use, in the 19th century. Immediately after the words "theatre of Dionysos" some text was erased. This paper will argue for a new interpretation of this erasure. I begin, however, by presenting a revised text of the whole inscription.[1]

Honours for Priests and Hieropoioi

EM 7239. Stele of white marble (at one time broken in two fragments, lower left) preserving original sides, bottom and back. Found with *IG* II^2 190 (fragment of early 4th century inscription honouring a Pelagonian king) near theatre of Dionysos, "πρὸς νότον τῆς σκηνῆς...παρὰ τὴν δενδρόφυτον λεωφόρον" (Koumanoudes), date unspecified. H. 1.15 (1.01 inscribed, including crowns), w. 0.458 (top), 0.510 (bottom), th. 0.12. L.h. 0.005 (a few letters 0.006, omicron 0.004). Stoichedon (square) 0.010. "Litt. volg. s. IV" (Kirchner), fairly carefully cut towards top, but deteriorating further down.

Main editions: Koumanoudes 1877; *IG* II (5) 184b (Köhler, from transcript of Lolling); [*Syll.*^{2} 606 (Dittenberger)]; *IG* II^2 410 (Kirchner); [*Syll.*^{3} 289].

---

* This chapter was previously published in D. Jordan and J. Traill (eds.), *Lettered Attica, Proceedings of the Athens Symposium*, March 2000 (Canadian Archaeological Institute at Athens, 2003), 59–67.

I am most grateful to Charalambos Kritzas and the staff of the Epigraphical Museum for enabling me to study the stone, and to Graham Oliver, Sean Byrne, Peter Liddel and an anonymous reader for comment and assistance.

[1] This is based primarily on autopsy in 1999. Thanks are also due, however, to Charles Crowther for enabling me to check readings against the (pre-World War II) squeeze of this inscription held at the Centre for the Study of Ancient Documents, Oxford.

Other contributions to the text: Wilhelm 1943–47; Oikonomides 1958:
58 39–40. Both summarised at *SEG* XXII 94. |

338/7? ΣΤΟΙΧ. 45

[------------------------]κτο Σκ[αμβωνίδ?]-
[ης εἶπεν· περὶ ὧν ἀπαγγέλλουσι ὁ ἱερεὺ]ς τοῦ Διο[νύσ]ο[υ..]
[.........19........καὶ οἱ? ἱεροποι]οὶ οἱ αἱρε[θ]έντε[ς]
[ὑπὸ τῆς βουλῆς περὶ τῶν ἱερῶν ὧν? ἔ]θυον τῶι Διονύσωι καὶ
[τοῖς ἄλλοις θεοῖς οἷς προ]σῆκε θύειν ὑπὲρ τῆς βουλῆς κα-
[ὶ τοῦ δήμου τοῦ Ἀθηναί]ων· ἀγαθῆι τύχηι· ἐψηφίσθαι τῆι βο-
[υλῆι τοὺς προέδρο]ς̣ οἳ ἂν λάχω[σ]ι̣ προεδρεύειν ἐν τῶι δήμ-
[ωι εἰς τὴ]ν̣ πρώτην ἐκκλησίαν προ̣σαγαγεῖν τὸν ἱερέα
[τ]οὺς ἱεροποιοὺς πρὸς τὸν δῆμον καὶ χρηματίσαι περὶ ὧν
λέγουσιν, γνώμην δὲ ξυμβάλλεσθαι τῆς βουλῆς εἰς τὸν δῆ-
[μ]ον ὅτι δοκεῖ τῆι βουλῆι, τὰ μὲν ἀγαθὰ δέχεσθαι τὸν δῆμο-
ν̣, ἃ ἀπαγγέλλουσι ὁ ἱερεὺς καὶ οἱ ἱεροποιοὶ γεγονέναι ἐ-
ν τοῖς ἱεροῖς οἷς ἔθυον τῶι Διονύσωι καὶ τοῖς ἄλλοις θε-
οῖς ἐφ' ὑγιείαι καὶ σωτηρίαι τῆς βουλῆς καὶ τοῦ δήμου τõ
Ἀθηναίων καὶ παίδων καὶ γυναικῶν καὶ τῶν ἄλλων κτημάτ-
ων τῶν Ἀθηναίων· ἐπαινέσαι δὲ τὸν ἱερέα τοῦ Διονύσου Με-
ιξιγένην Χολλείδην καὶ τὸν τοῦ Ποσειδῶνος τοῦ Πελαγί-
ου Ἱμεραῖον Φαληρέα καὶ τὸν τοῦ Διὸς τοῦ Σωτῆρος Νικοκ-
λέα Ἁγνούσιον καὶ τὸν τοῦ Ἄμμωνος Παυσιάδην Φαληρέα
φιλοτιμίας ἕνεκα τῆς πρὸς τὴν βουλὴν καὶ εὐσεβείας τῆ-
ς πρὸς τοὺς θεοὺς καὶ στεφανῶσαι [ἕκ]αστον αὐτῶν χρυσῶι
στεφάνωι ἀπὸ : 𐅅 : δραχμῶν ἐπειδὰν τ[ὰς] εὐ[θ]ύνας δ[ῶ]σ[ι]· ἐπε̣-
ιδὴ δὲ οἱ ἱεροποιοὶ οἱ αἱρεθέντες ὑπὸ τῆς βουλῆς καλῶς̣
καὶ φιλοτίμως ἐπεμελήθησαν τ[ῆ]ς παρασ[τάσ]εως τῶν ἱερέ-
ων καὶ τῶν θυσίων [.......traces 20.......] τῶν ἡρ[ώ]ων καὶ
τἆλλα τὰ περὶ τὴν Ι[.........traces 22.........]ΙΛ[.] ἐπιμε-
μ̣έλ̣ηνται δικαίως καὶ φι[λ]οτ[ίμ]ως, [ἐπαι]νέ[σ]αι τοὺς ἱεροπ-
οιοὺς Εὔνομον Εὐωνυμέα, [Σ]υ[β]α[ρ]ίτην [Γ]αρ[γήττι]ον, Γνωσία-
ν Κυδαθηναιέα, Φιλέαν Παιονίδην, [Χα]ι[ρεφάνην Σφήτ]τιον,
Ἀπολλόδωρον Πτελεάσιον, [Α]ὐ̣τ̣ο̣[σθ]έ̣νην [Ξυπεταιόν]α, Ἀμία-
ντον Αὐρίδην, Ἐπικράτην Ἀφιδ̣ν̣α̣ῖ[ο]ν̣, Φ̣ιλ̣[όστρατ]ον Παλλη-
νέα ἀρετῆς ἕνεκα καὶ δικαιοσύνης τῆς εἰς τὴν βουλὴν κα-
ὶ τὸν δῆμον τὸν Ἀθηναίων καὶ ἐπιμελεία[ς] τῆς περὶ τὰ ἱερ-
[ὰ] καὶ στεφανῶσαι ἕκαστον αὐτῶν χρυσῶι στεφάνωι ἀπὸ : [𐅅]
δραχμῶν, ἐ[π]ειδὰν τὰς εὐθύνας δῶσ[ι]. δοῦναι δὲ αὐτοῖς καὶ
[ε]ἰς θυσίαν καὶ ἀνάθημα̣ :̣ . [: δρ]αχμὰς τὸν ταμίαν τοῦ δήμο
[ἐ]κ τῶν κατὰ ψηφίσματα ἀναλισκομένων τῶι δήμωι· ἀναγρά-
ψαι δὲ τόδε τὸ ψήφισμα τὸν γραμματέα τῆς βουλῆς ἐν στήλ-
ηι λιθίνηι καὶ [σ]τῆσαι ἐν τῶι θεάτρωι τοῦ Διονύσου ⟦τ..3..⟧
⟦μ...7...⟧ εἰ[ς] δὲ τὴν ἀναγραφὴν τῆς στήλης δοῦναι τὸν τα-
μίαν τοῦ δήμου : Δ Δ Δ [Δ] : δραχμὰς ἐκ τῶν κατὰ ψηφίσματα [ἀ]ν-
59 αλισκομένων τῶι δήμωι. |

in crowns:

(I) Φιλέαν Ἀντιγένου[ς] Παιονίδην	(II) Ἀπολλόδωρον Εὐκτήμονος Πτελεάσιον	(III) Χαιρεφάνην *vacat* Σφήττιον
(IV) Ἐπικράτην Γλαύκων[ος] Ἀφιδναῖον	(V) Εὔνομον *vacat* Εὐωνυμέα	(VI) Συβαρίτην *vacat* Γαργήττιον
(VII) Αὐτο[σ]θένην Εὐκλ[–] Ξυπετ̣α̣ιόν[α]	(VIII) Ἀμίαντον *vacat* Αὐρίδην	(IX) Φιλόστρατον *vacat* Παλληνέα
	(X) Γνωσίαν Χαιρήμονος Κυδαθηναιέα	

vacat 0.14

Epigraphical Commentary

I do not generally note below differences from previous editions in the status of a letter, i.e. between dotted, bracketed or unbracketed. On the occasional use of ο for ου (1?, 7?, 14, 36), uncommon in state decrees by this period, see Threatte 1980, 256.

1–8 As restored by Koumanoudes except where indicated.
1–2 (proposer) Oikonomides.
2–3 καὶ οἱ τῶν ἄλλων θεῶν καὶ οἱ δέκα ἱεροποι]οὶ Wilhelm. Possibly correct, but cf. 8–9, 12, which lack reference to the other priests.
4 περὶ τῶν ἱερῶν Lambert; ὑπὲρ τῶν ἱερῶν Koumanoudes; but ὑπὲρ in the sense of περὶ, common later in such a context (e.g., *Ag.* XV 76.7–9, 279/8 BCE; 78.5, 273/2 BCE), is less easy to parallel at our period. Cf. *IG* II² 354.34 (328/7 BCE).
7 Kirchner, προέδρους Koumanoudes.
24 τ[ῆ]ς παρασ[τάσ]εως Lambert; [τῆς παραστάσεως] Dittenberger, cf. *Syll.*² 554. See further below, n. 20.
24–25 For ἱερέων = ἱερείων cf. Threatte 1980: 315.
25 Lambert (perhaps τῶν θεῶν καὶ] τῶν ἡρ[ώ]ων, cf. *SEG* XXVI 121.13); [..4..]O[..] καὶ [-10-]ΗΡΙΩΝ Koumanoudes; [-8-]ΤΌ̣[..]Ι[-10-]ηρίων Köhler/Lolling.
26 Ι[..4..]Μ[..3..]ΙΩΙΩ[-10-]ΙΤΑΙ Koumanoudes; Ι[..3..]μ[.]ιο[..]ε[-12-]ΙΛ[.] Köhler/Lolling.
27–end Except in 33 and 36–37, most letters in stoichoi 9–45 and in the crowns are now very difficult to read (both at autopsy and from the Oxford squeeze); I reproduce the text of *IG* II² except where indicated. | 60
34 (end) : [𐅄] Köhler; :Ι Koumanoudes (trace of this stroke is perhaps still detectable); :Χ Lolling.
36 Lambert; κατ' ἄνδ[ρ]α [..5..δρ]αχμάς Köhler (similar Koumanoudes; Köhler's majuscule: ΑΝΔ[.]Α.).

39–40 Erased text: ⟦τ[ῶι ἐ]/μ [Πειραεῖ]⟧ Lambert (slight traces of Πειραεῖ are perhaps visible); ⟦τοῦ Ἐλ/ευθερέως⟧ Wilhelm, based on Kirchner's Διονύσο[υ..⁵..] ([υ..⁴..] Koumanoudes and Köhler, correctly). Discussed further below.
Crown V father's name, T[..⁵..]O[.] Koumanoudes, but no later ed.
Crown VII Εὐκλ[είδου] or Εὐκλ[έους] Lambert, cf. *IG* II² 1926.105, and 107; *Syll.*² 606 n. 15. Εὐ[....]ο[.] Koumanoudes (the O perhaps arises from a casual mark in this shape on the join of the two fragments); ΕΥΙΛ Köhler (but what is probably the upper diagonal of the K is visible).

The top has been broken away (perhaps it included a relief), depriving us of the prescript, but otherwise we have nearly all the text. It records a resolution of the Council (6) that the Assembly should honour four priests (named 16–22) and ten *hieropoioi* (23ff., one from each tribe). The occasion was a report to the Council by the honorands themselves, led by the priest of Dionysos, about the sacrifices they had performed for the Health and Safety of the Athenian Council and People, their children, wives and other possessions (13–16). The Council refers the report to the Assembly, recommending that it honour the priests for their zeal for honour (*philotimia*) towards the Council and their piety (*eusebeia*) towards the gods, and that each be awarded a golden crown after rendering his accounts (to 22). In 23–35 we learn that the *hieropoioi* had also performed their functions well and that they also were rewarded with golden crowns. Money was allocated to them for sacrifice and a dedication (35–37); and the secretary of the Council was required to inscribe the decree on a stele in the theatre of Dionysos (37–39). Finally, the treasurer of the People was to allocate 40 drachmas for the inscription of the decree from the People's fund for matters relating to decrees (40–42). The names of the ten *hieropoioi* are inscribed within depictions of crowns under the text of the decree.

The loss of the prescript has deprived us of most of the proposer's name, rendering him unidentifiable,[2] and, crucially, of the date of the decree. It must have been before the death of one of the honorands, Himeraios of Phaleron, in 322/1,[3] and occasional use of the orthography -ο for -ου probably pushes us back into the third quarter of the century.[4] Two of the *hieropoioi*, Philostratos of Pallene (31–32) and Phileas of Paionidai (29), served on the Council, in 335/4 and 336/5 respectively;[5] our *hieropoioi* were appointed by the Council (23), with

[2] Cf. Hansen 1984: 139.
[3] Plut. *Dem.* 28 etc. (*PA* 7578).
[4] Cf. above, textual notes.
[5] *Ag.* XV 43.210 and 42.244.

which body they patently found favour; it may be that each of the two men's terms as *hieropoioi* was in the event a prelude to service on that body.[6] | 61

The decree breaks new ground in setting a Hellenistic tone. Rhodes has noted that, in the 4th century, honorific decrees based on reports from the honorands are almost exclusively foreign-policy related, either for foreigners or Athenian envoys who have been engaged in diplomacy.[7] In the Hellenistic period it became more common for such decrees to honour domestic officials; and ours is a notably early example of this inward focus. Similarly, Mikalson would see in the decree's concern with the "health and safety" of the Athenian People, their families and other possessions, signs of a rather defensive religious attitude that was to be characteristically Hellenistic: "Athens," he writes, "no longer is militarily and economically pre-eminent, threatening others. Under the power of Macedon she is now the one threatened and will remain threatened throughout the Hellenistic period."[8]

The defeat of Athens by Philip at the battle of Chaironeia in 338 in many respects marked the dawn of Hellenistic Athens; after it, she was never to be a fully independent power again. The defensive anxiety apparent in our decree would be particularly suitable in the immediate aftermath of the defeat, when Athenians feared that Philip would follow up his victory with an invasion of Attica; and the gratitude and relief, which are also apparent, would be appropriate in light of Philip's decision not to do so. The decree may well date to this time; it may, rather literally, be the first "Hellenistic" Athenian decree; and here another important aspect of the document is relevant: its connection with the Piraeus.

The leading honorand was Meixigenes of Cholleidai, priest of Dionysos. We know his father, Mikon, from [Dem.] 58 as a full time merchant who spent most of his time at sea and became embroiled in a legal dispute relating to the handling of one of his cargoes. Meixigenes himself was honoured on *IG* II² 1254 by the Paraloi, the Piraeus-based

[6] If our *hieropoioi* were a committee of the Council (i.e. all Council members), dates of 336/5 and 335/4 could almost certainly be ruled out for our document, since either Philostratos or Phileas would in that case have served on the Council in two consecutive years, which is not likely. See Rhodes 1984, 201. However, our text states that the *hieropoioi* were appointed by the Council (ὑπὸ τῆς βουλῆς, 23), not from it. Develin 1989: 375 is misleading.

[7] Rhodes with Lewis 1997: 29 n. 89.

[8] Mikalson 1998: esp. 42–4.

corporation which manned the sacred ship Paralos; probably he had served as the group's treasurer.[9] Of the other three priests mentioned, only one is identifiable in person, Himeraios, brother of Demetrios of Phaleron, himself a well-known politician, prosecutor in the Harpalos affair in 323 and executed in the aftermath of the Lamian War in 322/1.[10] Another of them, however, Pausiades of Phaleron, bore the same demotic; probably the families of both men had real connections with the port area. The fourth honorand, Nikokles of Hagnous, was priest of Zeus Soter, priest, that is, in the large temple of Zeus Soter and Athena Soteira in the Piraeus, which, in Pausanias' day was "the
62 thing most worth seeing" in the port[11] and whose cult, as | we know both from Aristophanes' *Wealth* and from the Lykourgan records of sales of skins from animals sacrificed at major festivals, was one of the most popular in 4th century Athens.[12] The connection of this cult with the decree's major theme, the Safety of the People, is obvious; and there is a striking passage in Lykourgos' speech against Leokrates which, in associating the cult with the circumstances of Chaironeia, is again suggestive that our decree belongs in the same context. In it Lykourgos accuses Leokrates of abandoning the city in its hour of need, shamelessly slipping out of the Piraeus in view of the Acropolis and the sanctuary of Zeus Soter and Athena Soteira.[13]

Pausiades' priesthood was that of Ammon, undoubtedly also located in the Piraeus, where a 3rd century decree bestowing honours in connection with construction of an annexe to Ammon's temple (a προσοικοδομία) was found.[14] The cult served by Himeraios, that of Poseidon Pelagios, is not otherwise attested; but deity, epithet and context point to a Piraeus location.[15]

---

[9] Davies 1971: 57—58. Cholleidai was not a large deme (bouleutic quota 2, location unknown; just three members of liturgical class listed in Davies 1971, see p. 621. Cf. Lambert 1997: 186). The common Piraeus link perhaps suggests a connection between Meixigenes' family and Kallidamas son of Kallimedon of Cholleidai, honoured by the deme Piraeus on *IG* II^2 1214 (early 3rd cent.; his father is named on the dedication, Meritt 1946, as member of a board of officials of unknown nature).

[10] Davies 1971: 108.

[11] Paus. 1.1.3.

[12] Ar. *Wealth* 1171 ff.; *IG* II^2 1496.88–89 and 118–119. Cf. Parker 1996: 238–241.

[13] Lykourgos 1.17. Cf. Garland 1987: 44.

[14] *IG* II^2 1282. Cf. Parker 1996: 195–196; Woodward 1962.

[15] Thus Mikalson 1998: 42–43, who attractively suggests (n. 93) that this was the Poseidon for whom Lykourgos established dithyrambic competitions in the Piraeus ([Plut.] *Mor.* 842a). Cf. *SEG* XXVI 72.42 and 46–47 ("stele of Poseidon" in Piraeus).

We know rather less about the 10 *hieropoioi*. In our context, however, it is notable that Phileas son of Antigenes of Paionidai (29 and crown I) also proposed, in 331/0, a state decree honouring an actor, probably an actor at the City Dionysia;[16] and perhaps it is not coincidental that the father of Philostratos of Pallene (31–32 and crown IX), Nikostratos son of Philostratos of Pallene, was secretary in 363/2, when a state decree was passed relating to an inventory of offerings, amongst others to Ammon and Paralos, and apparently set up in the Piraeus.[17]

It may have been in the context of Philip's threat at the time of Chaironeia that a defensive ditch was dug in the Piraeus;[18] and in the general anxiety after the battle, Hypereides proposed that metics and slaves be granted citizenship and, in a striking echo of the wording of our decree (13–16), that "sacred objects, women and children, should be conveyed to the Piraeus for safekeeping."[19] It is not difficult to imagine that, in this atmosphere, the Council might also have requested the priests of the four major Piraeus cults to sacrifice for the Health and Safety *inter alia* of the "children, women and the other possessions of the Athenians" and have appointed a body of *ad hoc hieropoioi* to assist;[20] nor that, when Philip did not in the event follow up his victory
with an invasion | of Attica, the Council and Assembly might have 63
been sufficiently relieved and grateful to award generous honours; for in these circumstances especially, it was to the favour of the gods, more than to her army, that Athens owed her safety.

We have honorands and cults with a strong Piraeus connection, therefore, at a time (I suggest) when Piraeus was a special focus of attention. It is against this background that we may turn to consider

---

16 *IG* II^2 348 = Schwenk 1985 no. 44.

17 *SEG* XXI 241; Woodward 1962.

18 [Plut.] *Mor.* 851a, cf. 847d. Garland 1987: 44.

19 ἱερὰ δὲ καὶ παῖδας καὶ γυναῖκας εἰς τὸν Πειραιᾶ ἀποθέσθαι. [Plut.] *Mor.* 849a. Cf. Hyp. F 27–39 Jensen; Garland 1987: 44. On the mood of near panic in Athens after Chaironeia see Lykourgos 1.39–42. Probably, as the anonymous reader of this paper suggests, the Piraeus was thought relatively safe as under the protection of Athens fleet, which remained a significant force after Chaironeia.

20 Mainly it seems with the acquisition (παράστασις, *LSJ* sense 6) of sacrificial animals and such like and, as the text can now be read, something to do with heroes (lines 24–25; Piraeus heroes included Eetion, Eurymedon and Paralos; a Piraeus heroon is attested by *IG* I^3 1079. Cf. Garland 1987: 111–138 and 159). One suspects that the *hieropoioi* contributed personally to the cost and that this may be the reason why their names rather than those of the more senior priests are inscribed in the crowns.

the erasure in lines 39–40. The sense of the text comes to a natural stop after Διονύσου, and begins again in line 40 with the conventional clause providing for the inscription of the decree at public expense. As Wilhelm saw, this should imply that the text that originally stood in the erasure in some way completed or qualified the sentence ending ἐν τῶι θεάτρωι τοῦ Διονύσου, the qualification or completion having been deliberately removed after the rest of the decree had been inscribed.[21] Wilhelm's own suggestion, τοῦ Ἐλευθερέως, cannot be right, since it is based on Kirchner's indication in *IG* II^2 that 13 letters are missing, whereas in fact there are only 12.[22]

Erasures are not always absolutely thorough; and traces of the earlier text sometimes remain visible. This is such a case, for, on careful examination, some faint traces are indeed apparent in the erased area.[23] Most clearly, the original first letter of 40 was a *mu*. It is easier to read towards the left, but is in fact detectable in its entirety; patently the erasure was not carried right up to the left edge of the stone. Similarly there is a faint trace of the very first letter to be erased, a vertical stroke after the upsilon of Διονύσου.

Once these traces have been detected, and against the background discussed above, the solution becomes, I think, fairly clear. In addition to the theatre of Dionysos in Athens, there was also a well-known theatre of Dionysos in the Piraeus. Famously site of political rallies in 411 and 404,[24] as well as of regularly constituted meetings of the Assembly,[25] in 324/3 it was leased out to a syndicate who agreed to pay 330 dr. per annum rent and to maintain it in good repair.[26] It was located about halfway up the north-west flank of Mounychia hill.[27] I suggest that it was originally intended that this decree should be set up
64 in the theatre of Dionysos in the Piraeus, ἐν τῶι θεάτρωι τοῦ | Διονύσου

[21] Wilhelm 1943–47.

[22] The mistake seems to have been Kirchner's. Both Koumanoudes in his *editio princeps* and Köhler in the first edition of *IG* II show the correct number of missing letters.

[23] I am grateful to Sean Byrne for his second opinion on the reading of these traces at autopsy. They are clearer at autopsy than on the Oxford squeeze.

[24] E.g., Thuc. 8.93.1; cf. Xen. *Hell.* 2.4.32; Lys. 13.32.

[25] E.g., Dem. 19.60. Cf. McDonald 1943: 51–56.

[26] Stroud 1974 no. Ill = *Ag.* XVI 93.

[27] Some remains were excavated in the 19th century. The extensive bibliography on the theatre can be traced *via* von Eickstedt 1991: 115; Garland 1987: 161 with 221; *Ag.* XVI p. 138.

τῶι ἐμ Πειραεῖ.[28] This both fits the visible traces[29] and has the correct number of letters. Later, the prescribed location was changed (presumably before erection), by simple erasure, to the theatre of Dionysos unspecified, i.e., implicitly the one in Athens.

No other Athenian state decree preserves a clause stating that it was set up in the theatre of Dionysos in the Piraeus, though we should not rule out the possibility that some were. As already noted, the Assembly met there on occasion, and state laws and decrees were certainly sometimes erected elsewhere in the Piraeus.[30] That we do not have any examples may simply be one instance of the phenomenon that, thanks to continuous habitation and development of the port, the antiquities of Piraeus are less well preserved than those of the city. It is notable, however, that theatres were fairly common locations for deme decrees.[31] We do not know if any deme decree of Piraeus was set up in the local theatre of Dionysos or the associated *Dionysion*;[32] but both at local and state levels it was common to erect decrees honouring priests and other religious functionaries in the relevant cult location.[33]

The theatre of Dionysos at Athens was certainly a location of public events and display beyond the theatrical, narrowly defined. Honorific statues were erected there,[34] the Assembly met there on occasion,[35] and

---

[28] For the spelling Πειραεῖ instead of Πειραιεῖ at this period see Threatte 1980: 282–284 (e.g., *IG* II² 380.9, of 320/19; *Ag.* XVI 93, of 324/3).

[29] Both Byrne and I think that it may be possible to detect very slight traces of some of the other letters, in particular in line 40.

[30] Those preserving the relevant clause specifying a Piraeus location are *SEG* XXVI 72.46–47; Dem. 20.36; *IG* II² 125.18–19; 1035a.15. Others, e.g. *IG* II² 244 (= Schwenk 1985 no. 3), were also patently set up in this area.

[31] See Whitehead 1986: 96 with n. 51.

[32] Decrees of the deme Piraeus were set up in various locations. See *IG* II² 1177.23–24, 1214.37–38, *Ag.* XVI 93.27. Interestingly the last, concerning the lease of the Piraeus theatre, was not set up in the theatre itself, but the Piraeus agora. It was not uncommon for inscriptions recording leases to be set up on the land to which the lease related, cf. e.g. the lease of the Dyaleis, Lambert 1998a: T5.55–57. However, while the Dyaleis inscription *was* the lease, the Piraeus inscription merely records a copy of the lease (the lease itself was in the keeping of an individual, lines 27–28) and also includes honours for those involved. One can see that, for this, the local agora might have seemed the more appropriate place of display.

[33] The state decree of 328/7 honouring Androkles, priest of Asklepios, for example, was set up in the sanctuary (*hieron*) of Asklepios (*IG* II² 354 = Schwenk 1985 no. 54.28–29). An example at deme level is *IG* II² 1199, a decree of Aixone honouring *hieropoioi* of Hebe and set up in the *hieron* of Hebe.

[34] See e.g., *IG* II² 648.6–7 (= Osborne 1981: D69).

[35] Thuc. 8.93–94; law at Dem. 21.9; McDonald 1943: 47–51; *Ag.* XVI 79 with Woodhead's note.

honours might be awarded there (or their award prohibited).[36] There are earlier state decrees which seem to have been set up there;[37] but ours is apparently the earliest surviving in which this location is speci-
65 fied in | the text as preserved. In fact, it is the only inscription which expresses the location in exactly this way. The other decrees, all dating from the 3rd or 2nd centuries, all speak of the precinct (*temenos*) or the temple (*naos*) of Dionysos, or in one case of the *Dionysion*, never specifically of the theatre.[38] The difference, one suspects, is due simply to the fact that the originally intended location was the Piraeus theatre and the wording still reflects that. If, from the start, it had been intended to set this decree up in Athens, the reference would perhaps have been rather to the *temenos* or *naos* or the *Dionysion*, as in these later decrees.[39] In any case it is clear enough that the later decrees set up in this area honoured men who had performed some official service in, or were otherwise connected with, the cult of Dionysos or the theatre.[40]

Our case suits the pattern: the priest of Dionysos is the leading honorand and, as we have seen, at least one of his fellow honorands seems also to have had theatrical links.

How then should we explain the change in our text? The originally inscribed location is unique among surviving decrees. The Piraeus connections of the honorands and the cults they served were clearly a

[36] Aeschin. 3.33–35. The development of these uses at this period may connect with the Euboulan-Lykourgan reconstruction of the theatre, on which see most recently Hintzen-Bohlen 1997: 21–29.

[37] *IG* II^2 18 (394/3 BCE), for example, the honorific decree for Dionysios of Syracuse, proposed by the poet Kinesias. Perhaps also *IG* II^2 190, found with our inscription. There are lists of inscriptions found in this location taken from some early publications at Bardane and Malouchou 1992 etc., vol. 1, pp. 56–59 and 184–189; vol. 2, pp. 62–64 and vol. 3, see index p. 152.

[38] *IG* II^2 657.70 (παρὰ τὸν νεὼ τοῦ Διονύσου); *IG* II^2 668.35–36; 780.23; 896.19 and 55 (all ἐν τῶι τεμένει τοῦ Διονύσου); *IG* II^2 648.11–12 = Osborne 1981: D69 (ἐν τῶι Διον]υσίωι). There may not have been a significant difference of meaning between these three designations of location. The precinct of Dionysos, with its two temples, was located behind the stage of the theatre. See Travlos 1971: 537–541.

[39] Is there perhaps an implication that, in the Piraeus, the relative situations (or at least uses) of theatre and associated *Dionysion* did not precisely mirror those of their equivalents in the city? Cf. Garland 1987: 161.

[40] Patently in *IG* II^2 668, 780, and 896. *IG* II^2 657 awards honours for political services, but the honorand is the poet Philippides. The circumstances of the fragmentary *IG* II^2 648 (= Osborne 1981: D69) were probably comparable.

factor;[41] but if my suggested dating of this decree is correct, it may well be that the original intention also reflects the same confidence about the relative safety of the Piraeus and the same anxiety about the fate of the city after Chaironeia that is apparent in Hypereides' proposal and in Lykourgos' speech. The change to the more usual (and more prominent) Athens location would reflect the dying away of this initial panic, as it became apparent that Philip would not invade Attica, consonant with the communal sigh of relief of which our whole decree is an echo.[42] | 66

Bibliography

Bardane, B.N. and G.E. Malouchou. 1992, 1993, and 1998. *Αρχείον των μνημείων των Αθηνών και της Αττικής*, vols 1–3 (vols 2–3, Malouchou only). Athens.

Davies, J.K. 1971. *Athenian Propertied Families*. Oxford.

Develin, R. 1989. *Athenian Officials 684–321 BC*. Cambridge.

Eickstedt, K.-V. von. 1991. *Beiträge zur Topographie des antiken Piräus*. Athens.

Garland, R. 1987. *The Piraeus From the Fifth to the First Century B.C.* New York.

Hansen, M.H. 1984. "The Number of *Rhetores* in the Athenian *Ecclesia*, 355–322 B.C.," *GRBS* 25: 123–155.

Hintzen-Bohlen, B. 1997. *Die Kulturpolitik des Euboulos und des Lykurg*. Berlin.

Koumanoudes, S.A. 1877. "Επιγραφαί εκ του Ασκληπιείου και των πέριξ τόπων," *Ἀθήναιον* 6: 482–486 no. 3.

Lambert, S.D. 1997. *Rationes Centesimarum*. Amsterdam.

——. 1998a. *The Phratries of Attica* (2nd ed.) Ann Arbor.

——. 1998b. "The Attic Genos Bakchiadai and the City Dionysia," *Historia* 42: 394–403.

McDonald, W.A. 1943. *The Political Meeting Places of the Greeks*. Baltimore.

Meritt, B.D. 1946. "Greek Inscriptions," *Hesperia* 15: 177–178 no. 25.

Mikalson, J.D. 1998. *Religion in Hellenistic Athens*. Berkeley.

Oikonomides, A.N. 1958. *Υπερείδου λόγοι*. Athens.

Osborne, M.J. 1981. *Naturalization in Athens*. I. Brussels.

Parker, R. 1996. *Athenian Religion: a History*. Oxford.

[41] It is a possible, though not necessary, implication that there were one or more sessions of the Assembly held in the Piraeus theatre in the aftermath of Chaironeia. Cf. n. 26.

[42] One can only speculate on the mechanics of the amendment, but one will guess that Meixigenes himself was involved. Priests had a measure of control over what was done in their precincts. Meixigenes was probably priest in the Piraeus (cf. Lambert 1998b: especially 399 n. 29). Is it possible that he was also priest of the Athens cult? (If so, he may have been a member of the genos Bakchiadai, cf. Lambert 1998b). That would perhaps have facilitated the switch of intended locations. The priest of Zeus Soter may have had joint tenure of the city and Piraeus cults at this time; at least, the Piraeus priest only starts being specified explicitly as such in the 3rd century (*IG* II^2 783. Parker 1996: 240 n. 79, interprets this as implying rather that the city cult acquired a priest for the first time in the 3rd century).

Rhodes, P.J. 1984. "Members Serving Twice in the Athenian Boule and the Population of Athens Again," *ZPE* 57: 200–202.
Rhodes, P.J. with D.M. Lewis. 1997. *The Decrees of the Greek States*. Oxford.
Schwenk, C.J. 1985. *Athens in the Age of Alexander*. Chicago.
Stroud, R.S. 1974. "Three Attic Decrees," *CSCA* 7: 279–298.
Threatte, L. 1980. *The Grammar of Attic Inscriptions*. 1. Berlin.
Travlos, J. 1971. *Bildlexikon zur Topographie des antiken Athen*. Tübingen.
Whitehead, D. 1986. *The Demes of Attica*. Princeton.
Wilhelm, A. 1943–47. "Διόνυσος Ἐλευθερεύς," *Wiener Studien* 51–52: 162–166.
67 Woodward, A.M. 1962. "Athens and the Oracle of Ammon," *BSA* 57: 5–13. |

CHAPTER THIRTEEN

GREEK INSCRIPTIONS IN THE UNIVERSITY MUSEUM, OXFORD, MISSISSIPPI*

The University Museum at Oxford, Mississippi, holds a number of Greek inscriptions belonging to the David M. Robinson Memorial Collection of Greek and Roman Antiquities. All but one of them have been published, mostly by Robinson himself or more recently by R.A. Moysey.[1] The purpose of this note is to make available the unpublished text and to contribute some comments on the Attic items in the collection.

What follows is based primarily on my autopsy of the stones in 2003 and on squeezes and photographs made then.

1. *Monument commemorating an Olympic victory. iii AD. UM. G. 77.3.573*

Fragment of a stele of white marble. Left side preserved. Back reworked (trough, with oil stains). Moulded border to inscribed face. Findspot unknown.

H. 0.40, w. 0.197, th. 0.10 (finished side, 0.085). L.h. 0.016–0.019. Lunate epsilon and sigma. ω. Z. Vertical line spacing 0.026. Unpublished. Listed by Bodel–Tracy, p. 138.

---

* This chapter was previously published in *Zeitschrift für Payrologie und Epigraphik* 148 (2004), 181–186.

I am very grateful to William Griffith and other staff of the University Museum at Oxford for their courtesy in facilitating access to the stones. I use the following abbreviations:

Bodel–Tracy: J. Bodel and S.V. Tracy, *Greek and Latin Inscriptions in the USA, a Checklist* (Rome, 1997).

Henry: A.S. Henry, *Honours and Privileges in Athenian Decrees* (Hildesheim, 1983).

Rhodes–Osborne: P.J. Rhodes and R. Osborne, *Greek Historical Inscriptions 404–323 BC* (Oxford [England], 2003).

Sacrificial Calendar: S.D. Lambert, The Sacrificial Calendar of Athens, *ABSA* 97 (2002), 353–399.

Schwenk: C. Schwenk, *Athens in the Age of Alexander* (Chicago, 1985).

Tracy, *ADT*: S.V. Tracy, *Athenian Democracy in Transition* (Berkeley, 1995).

[1] All the Greek and Latin inscriptions in the museum are listed by Bodel–Tracy, 138–9.

I offer a tentative text and some provisional remarks.[2]

iii AD -----------
[.]Ϲ̣Ϲ̣ΕΜϹ̣//------
ΚΛΕΙΝΟΜϹ̣-----
ΩΜΟΥΛ-------
ἀλ̣λ̣’ ετε.------
καὶ ΟΙΚΛ------
χάλκεον------
εζομεν--------
cτορνυ|//------
τον μεν-------
Ἤλιδος |//------
ἀμφοτερ-------
εζεcθαι-------
η καὶ μη------
ὅπωc Ε-------
νείκηc Η-------
181 ----------- |

Notes

The style of the lettering and orthography suggest a date around the early third century AD.

1. First Ϲ̣, sigma or epsilon. Second Ϲ̣, sigma or epsilon. Final Ϲ̣, sigma, epsilon, omicron or less likely theta.

2. Ϲ̣, the lower left segment of a round letter. There is a mark suggestive of the spring of the central horizontal of epsilon, but this may be damage. From the trace, omicron, epsilon, theta, sigma and omega are all possible. κλείν’ ομϹ̣-?

3. Possibilities would seem to include ’P]|ωμουλ[-, ὤμου λ- (ὦμος, shoulder), ὠμοῦ λ- (ὠμός, raw).

4. Λ̣Λ̣, might be A or Λ from trace. fin. /?

5. οἰκα̣[δ(ε) ? οἱ κα̣- or οἱ κλ̣-?

7. See 12.

8. fin. slightly forward sloping upright stroke. N or possibly M.

9. τὸν μέν?

12. -έζεcθαι or ἕζεσθαι. Perhaps the same verb as in 7, εζομεν-

[2] In both I am much indebted to Jaime Curbera of the Berlin Academy (*Inscriptiones Graecae*) and Benjamin Millis of the American School of Classical Studies at Athens, who are not, however, responsible for remaining flaws.

14. ὅππωϲ· artificial gemination of pi for the sake of the metre. Cf. *IG* II^2 4514, 10; L. Threatte, *The Grammar of Attic Inscriptions* I (Berlin, 1980), 534.

This appears to be a metrical inscription commemorating a victory at the Olympic Games. "Elis", location of Olympia, is mentioned in 10 and "victory" in 15. For victory inscriptions from Olympia see W. Dittenberger and K. Purgold, *Die Inschriften von Olympia* (Berlin, 1896), section IV, nos. 142–243 (cf. sections V and VI). It is not clear whether this monument was set up there or elsewhere. It is also unclear whether the beginnings of lines on the stone all coincide with the beginnings of verses. χάλκεον (6) probably refers to a bronze statue of the victor (cf. *Inschr. von Olymp.* no. 352). In 8 we have part of the verb στόρνυμι, to strew, in verse to "calm" or "soothe" or in this agonistic context perhaps rather to "lay low", "defeat" or "destroy". Compare the Marathon epigram, Lyk. 1. 109:

Ἑλλήνων προμαχοῦντες Ἀθηναῖοι Μαραθῶνι
χρυσοφόρων Μήδων ἐστόρεσαν δύναμιν

and note the comments of D.L. Page, *Further Greek Epigrams* (Cambridge, 1981) p. 231. "The one" τὸν μέν (9) may have been answered by "the other" τὸν δέ (competitors, competitions?). Cf. "both" (of them?), ἀμφοτερ[-, in 11.

2. *Fragment of Athenian law code. 410–404 BC. UM. G. 77.3.668*

Edd. *IG* I^3 236b (Lewis, from a phot. and detailed description of L. Turnbull, and noting that there is a squeeze in Princeton); R.A. Moysey, *ZPE* 78 (1989), 201–4 no. 2 (from autopsy, squeezes, phot.) (ph.) (*SEG* XXXIX 18).

Lewis identified *IG* I^3 236b as a non-joining fragment of *IG* I^3 236a, which is inscribed in Attic script with law relating to the trierarchy. (The reverse of 236a contains part of the sacrificial calendar of Athens in Ionic script = *Sacrificial Calendar*, Fragment 3). The left side of 236b is preserved, but it is otherwise broken all round. It has been cut down in modern times at the back (cf. *Sacrificial Calendar*, 355 n. 12).[3]

[3] Moysey inverts the stoichedon grid dimensions. They are horiz. 0.0105, vert. 0.0138, compatible with 236a.

On this monument see most recently *Sacrificial Calendar*, 353–7. The Attic side of it probably belonged to the earlier phase of the revision of the Athenian law code, 410–404, the Ionic side to the later phase, 403/2–400/399. The text was inscribed on one or more series of stelai which, at least in the Ionic phase, were joined by clamps in the top, with the text running across from one stele to another. The situation in the Attic phase in this respect is obscure (*Sacrificial Calendar*, 355 with n. 16). If our fragment does belong to the trierarchic
182 law, there is a question whether it would be from the same stele | as the larger fragment, from an adjoining stele or a non-adjoining but neighbouring one. Moysey notes minor differences from 236a in the script, marble and weathering and inclines to the view that the fragments were from different stelai. One might add that, while it is clear from the remains of the bottom of a post-hole on the preserved back of 236b that it was from a block later used as a threshhold, the pristine state of the lettering on the Ionic face of 236a (= *Sacrificial Calendar* F3 with phot. pl. 33) indicates that it never formed part of the upper face of a threshhold block. The text of our fragment is indeed so fragmentary that there is room for scepticism as to whether it belonged to the same law as 236a. The identification depends crucially on two restorations:

(a) τριεράǀǀρχο χσυνεγορ̣[in 9–10. In a legal context this might alternatively be one of the other officials in -αρχος, e.g. πολεμάǀǀρχο.
(b) δρǀǀαχμὰς ἒ χσύλ̣[ινα vel sim. in 12,[4] where Lewis suggested that the reference might be to payment for timber for shipbuilding. However, as Moysey notes, the only definitely legible stroke of the last letter is the upper part of a left vertical. This does not necessarily imply lambda. In fact, to the right, I detect what may be very faint trace of the top of the right vertical of N (visible on Moysey's photograph). Most likely therefore, δρǀǀαχμὰς ἒ χσυν̣[-. Cf. χσυνεγορ̣[in 10.

The cutting down of the back of the fragment is very unfortunate since it prevents determination of whether there was anathyrosis of the left side. On the anathyrosis bands for joining the stelai of the law code see briefly, *Sacrificial Calendar*, 361–2; in more detail, S. Dow, *Hesp.*

[4] The rough breathing, ἓ, in Moysey's text on p. 201 is a misprint.

30 (1961), 58–73. On 236a there are bands at both the Attic and Ionic faces. The surviving thickness of the finished side of 236b, 0.029, is comparable with the thickness of the bands on 236a and related fragments (see Dow, pp. 60, 64, 66, all ca. 0.025–0.030), but this may be coincidental. There is no physical indication that the current back edge of the finished side was the back edge of an anathyrosis band. It is also notable that our fragment preserves the left edge of the text, with margin. If, as seems likely, the fragment does belong to the law code, it was from the left side of a stele (or stele-series) in the Attic phase (cf. *Sacrificial Calendar* F8 with note on F8, pp. 361–2).

3. *Attic inventory. iv BC. UM. G. 77.3.579*

D.M. Robinson, *AJP* 58 (1937), 38–44 (ph.). In col. 1, above Robinson's line 1 are traces of a further line, as follows:

(371/0) [ἐπὶ Φρασικλείδο]υ φ̣[ιάλη] non-stoich.

The Y is aligned above the Y of Λυσισ]τράτου (archon of 369/8) in Robinson's l. 2. For the restoration of the archon of 371/0 rather than of 370/1, as the sequence would otherwise suggest, see D. Harris, *The Treasures of the Parthenon and Erechtheion* (Oxford, 1995), 59 nos. 87–88.

In col. 2, ll. 2–10 should read:

[σταθμὸν Χ?]
δ[ευτέρα *vac.*]
στα[θμὸν Χ?]
τρίτη *v* [*vac.*]
σταθμὸν̣ [ΧΓΙ-?]
τετάρτη̇ στ̣[αθμὸν Χ?]
κε<φά>λα̇ιο[ν]
σταθμοῦ *v* [*vac.*]
ὑδριῶν <Χ>ΧΧΧΓΙ[-?]

8 <φά> = ΙΛ 10 <Χ> = / lap.
ΓΙ-?] at 6 fin. might belong alternatively in 2, 4 or less likely 7. | 183

4. *Athenian decree. c. 330 BC. UM. G. 77.3.665*

Fragment of white marble, broken on all sides. H. 0.168 (0.135 inscribed), w. 0.110 (0.097 inscribed), th. 0.034. L.h. 0.005–0.006.

Stoich. horiz. 0.0106, vert. 0.011 (sic; the measurements in *ed. princ.* are incorrect). Lettering: "Cutter of *IG* II^2 334", c. 345–c. 320 (Tracy, *ADT* 87). There is marked reddish discoloration of the marble along the path of the letters, caused by oxidisation (and/or paint remnants?).

Edd. A.J. Heisserer and R.A. Moysey, *Hesp.* 55 (1986), 177–82 (ph.) (*SEG* XXXVI 149). Cf. R.A. Moysey, *AJA* 90 (1986), 212; P. Gauthier, *Bull. Ép.* 1988, no. 370.

Heisserer and Moysey printed both a conservative text without determination of the line length and minimal restorations and, with reservations, a fuller reconstruction at a rather long stoich. 44, tentatively suggested to them by Woodhead and reproduced in *SEG*. The fuller reconstruction is unsatisfactory (cf. the critical remark of Gauthier) and may be set aside. The only identifiably formulaic passage is at 11–13 and it is best restored with a 31 letter line (see below). My text is:

c. 330

[.......13......]ΟΣ[........16........] stoich. 31
[......12......]ΙΣ̣ΙΟΣ[........15.......] ΙΟ occupy 1 stoichos
[.....10.....τὴ]ν̣ σκην[ὴν......12......]
[....8....δωρ]εάς· διδ[όναι δὲ....8....]
[.....10.....ἐ]παγωγη[.......14.......]
[......11.....]ι χρῆσθ[αι......12......]
[....8....το]ῦ μετοικ[ίου......11.....]
[ἐπιμελείσθ]ω̣ δὲ ἡ βου[λὴ τῶν.....9....]
[....8....ω]ν οἷς ὁ δῆμ[ος......12......]
[..4..τὴν δω]ρεὰν, ὅπως ἂ[ν......12......]
[....7...μὴ] ἀδικῶντα[ι· ἀναγράψαι δὲ τό]-
[δε τὸ ψήφισ]μ̣α τὸν γρ̣[αμματέα τῆς βουλῆ]-
[ς καὶ στῆσαι ἐν ἀ]κ̣[ροπόλει·.....10.....]

Notes

The position of the left and right margins is arbitrary. Unless noted otherwise, the restorations are those in Heisserer and Moysey's more conservative text (p. 177), referred to below as "*ed. princ.*"

3. τὴ]ν σκη⟦ν⟧[ὴν *ed. princ.*, who comment that "the cutter seems to have corrected a mistake in the final preserved letter. He apparently had inscribed epsilon rather than nu. The middle and bottom horizontals are visible." These "middle and bottom horizontals" are in fact casual marks (the bottom one is too low to be a letter stroke). The letter is a straightforward, but damaged, nu.

4. Heisserer and Moysey persuasively identify διδ[όναι in 4 as the beginning of the clauses awarding privileges, running to the middle of 11. The present tense, διδόναι, rather than the more common aorist, δοῦναι, suggests a permanent or recurring privilege (cf. e.g. *IG* II^2 212 = Rhodes-Osborne no. 64, 39, τὸ δὲ ἀργύριον διδόναι τοῖ|ς ἀθλοθέταις...for crowns to be awarded recurrently at every Great Panathenaia). On any account 4–6 are not formulaic.

5. Gauthier, reading only from the phot. in *ed. princ.*, identified the first preserved letter as dotted Ξ. *Ed. princ.* printed an undotted pi. The letter is a certain pi, clearly legible in its entirety. ἐ]παγωγή would apparently be a hapax in Athenian decrees. It might be a reference to circumstances of invasion or attack, *LSJ* sense 3; or Heisserer and Moysey may be right that the meaning is equivalent, or close, to εἰσαγωγή (they compare the sense "bringing in" at Th. VII 24. 3, οὐδ' οἱ ἔσπλοι ἀσφαλεῖς ἦσαν τῆς ἐπαγωγῆς τῶν ἐπιτηδείων) and that we have to do with a privilege in relation to import(/export?). Cf. e.g. *IG* I^3 174, 14–15, ἐξεῖναι αὐτῶι πλεῖν καὶ χρήματα εἰσάγειν (see also *SEG* XL 72); *IK Erythrai* 6 | = Rhodes–Osborne no. 8, 6–11, καὶ ἀτέλειαν 184
| [π]άντων χρημάτων καὶ | [ἐ]σαγωγῆς καὶ ἐξαγωγῆς | [κ]αὶ πολέμο καὶ εἰρήνης. As they note, however, ἐ]π' ἀγωγή[ν is also possible.

6.]ι χρῆσθ[αι is obscure. Apart from the usage of this verb in relation to building noted by Heisserer and Moysey (*SEG* XXXIII 143, 3, *IG* II^2 244, 91), one might think of the provisions in decrees about laws to be applied in the honorand's case, νόμοις...χρῆσθαι, e.g. *IG* II^2 10 = Rhodes–Osborne no. 4, 6.

7. As Heisserer and Moysey note, this will probably have been a grant of exemption from the metic tax (ἀτέλειαν τοῦ μετοικίου) (cf. Henry, 244–5).

8–10 med. Lam. ἐπιμελείσθ]ω δὲ ἡ βου[λὴ ὅπως--|--]ΝΟΙΣ ὁ δῆμ-[ος --|-- δω]ρεάν· *ed. princ.* Heisserer and Moysey were undoubtedly correct to identify 8–11 as a version of the common "general protection" clause (cf. Henry, 171–81), though the wording does not correspond precisely with the attested formulae and can not be restored fully. The key to the structure of the clause is]νοις in 9. It is difficult to find a good parallel in this type of context at this period for προξέ]-νοις (suggested to Heisserer and Moysey by Lewis), and the plural in Woodhead's ἐν τοῖς προτέροις χρό]νοις would also be unexpected (the usual phrase has time in the singular, e.g. ἐν τῶι ἔμπροσθεν χρόνωι). My initial thought was προγό]νοις or ἐκγό]νοις, but it is difficult to see that any dative plural noun is in place here. δω]ρεὰν in the following line suggests that it is preferable to articulate, ω]ν οἷς, i.e. "let the Council take care of the X to whom the People...made/make the grant, so that...they come to no harm." "made/make the grant" will be a version of the familiar phrase in honorific decrees, ὁ δῆμος ἔδωκε...τὴν δωρεὰν (e.g. *IG* II[2] 212 = Rhodes-Osborne no. 64, 20–24). The tense of the verb might have been aorist, present or perfect. X will be a noun-phrase in the genitive. Compare e.g. *IG* II[2] 245, 8–9, ἐπιμελέσ]θων δὲ αὐτῶ[ν] οἱ στ[ρατηγ|οὶ ὅπως μηδ' ὑφ' ἑνὸς] ἀδικῶνται; *SEG* XXVIII 75, 26–8, ἐπιμελείσθω δὲ καὶ ἡ βουλὴ...τῶν ἐπιδημούντων Ἀντιοχέων ὅπως ὑπὸ μηθενὸς ἀδικῶνται; *IG* I[3] 178, 4–6, where it is provided that the Council take care (hε βολ]ὲ ἐπιμελέσθο) that neither Dorkis, nor his wife nor his descendants come to any harm (καθhόπος δ'ἂν | [μὲ ἀδικε͂ται Δόρκις κτλ.).

10. ὅπως ἄ[ν Lam. ὅπως δ̣' [ἂν *ed. princ.* / is legible. The stroke thickens towards the bottom, giving at first sight an impression of Δ, but, in fact, to the right of the thickened end there is uninscribed stone where one would expect the bottom horizontal of a Δ. The letter was accordingly Λ or A. The context indicates A. What may be the spring of the cross-bar is visible on one of my squeezes.

11 fin.–13 Lam. ἀδικῶντα[ι --- ἀναγράl|ψαι δὲ τόδε τὸ ψήφισ]μ̣α τὸν γρ̣[αμματέα --|--]κ̣[--- *ed princ.* ὅπως δ' [ἂν *nomen* καὶ οἱ ἔγγονοι α|ὐτοῦ μηδ' ὑφ' ἑνὸς] ἀδικῶντα[ι ἐπιμελείσθω ἡ βουλή· ἀναγρ|άψαι δὲ τόδε τὸ ψήφισ]μ̣α τὸν γρ̣[αμματέα τῆς βουλῆς ἐστήληι λ|ιθίνηι καὶ στῆσαι ἐν ἀ]κ̣[ροπόλει· Woodhead ap. *ed. princ.* (with two letters in one stoichos restored at 13 in.). In 13 the upper section of the vertical and both diagonals of the kappa are legible on my squeeze. Woodhead envisages an awkward repetition of the clause, ἐπιμελείσθω ἡ βουλή, after ἀδικῶντα[ι (cf. 8). With the new reading ἄ̣[ν for δ̣' [ἂν in 10, however, the need to make space for a main clause after ἀδικῶνται evaporates. Moreover, the normal structure of the protection clause in the 4th century is ἐπιμελείσθω (or, more commonly, -αι)...ὅπως ἂν..., not ὅπως ἂν...ἐπιμελείσθω...(cf. Henry, 176–8). For the inscription clause following immediately μηδ' ὑφ' ἑνὸς ἀδικῶνται, cf. *IG* II[2] 237, 31; 252, 16; 287, 13. The wording of the inscription clause at this period varies considerably in detail. I print the version which best suits the preserved letters. It yields a line length of 31 letters, comfortably within the normal range for honorific decrees at this period. A precise equivalent may be found in the decree of 330/29 for Eudemos of Plataia, *IG* II[2] 351 (= Rhodes–Osborne no. 94), 33–5.

While there was more than one *skene* in Attica,[5] since this is a decree of the polis and not of a deme or other subgroup, Heisserer and Moysey's suggestion that the reference is to the Lykourgan rebuilding of the theatre of Dionysos, which is known to have been completed at this period, and to which the honorands can be presumed to have made a contribution (δωρ]εάς, 4), is persuasive (cf. Tracy, *ADT* 10 | 185
n. 18; on the *skene* and the archaeology of the rebuilding see B. Hintzen-Bohlen, *Die Kulturpolitik des Euboulos und des Lykurg* [Berlin, 1997], 28). As Heisserer and Moysey note, there is an attractive parallel with the famous decree of 330/29 for Eudemos of Plataia, proposed by Lykourgos, *IG* II^2 351 = Rhodes–Osborne no. 94, in which Eudemos is honoured for supplying oxen for the building of the "stadium and the Panathenaic theatre" (usually held to be an error for "Panathenaic stadium and theatre of Dionysos", cf. Rhodes–Osborne p. 477).[6] It may not be coincidental that the inscription clause of our decree is restorable with the precise wording used in the decree for Eudemos, raising the possibility that proposer and/or secretary (i.e. year) were the same.

5. *Eleusinian (?) inventory. c. late–iv BC? UM. G. 77.3.681*

R.A. Moysey, *Hesp.* 54 (1985), 141–3 (*SEG* XXXV 1731).

For the identification of the text as Attic rather than Delian see J. Tréheux, *Bull. Ép.* 1989 no. 376 = *SEG* XXXIX 169. The marble is "Hymettian".

1 fin. While I can see from my squeezes what induced the reading of the last letter as K, at autopsy I inclined strongly to ⊢, i.e. we should probably read a noun in the genitive plural followed by a weight,]ριων Δ̣⊢[--.

6. *Attic funerary epigram. Late hell.–early imp. UM. G. 77.3.670*

R.A. Moysey and E.F. Dolin, *ZPE* 69 (1987), 90–2 (*SEG* XXXVII 198).

---

[5] The *skene* in the theatre in the Piraeus is referred to in connection with building works in the deme decree of Piraeus, *SEG* XXXIII 143 = Schwenk no. 76, of 324/3; cf. Gauthier.

[6] I shall argue elsewhere that another decree proposed by Lykourgos and honouring a Plataian, *IG* II^2 345 = Schwenk no. 36, of 332/1, also relates to this building programme.

The first letter in 1 is a certain H, confirming Moysey and Dolin's σ]ῆμ' and ruling out Bousquet's σ]ῶ̣μ'.

Curbera will make some adjustments to the text of the dedication, UM. G. 77.3.663 = *ZPE* 78 (1989), 204–7 (*SEG* XXXIX 204), in his edition for *IG* II^3. I have nothing new on UM. G. 77.3.661 = *IG* I^3 499 (naval catalogue), .664 = *IG* I^3 925 (votive), .580 = *Hesp.* 13 (1944), 16–21 (mortgage horos), or .566 = *ZPE* 72 (1988), 88–9 (*SEG* XXXVIII
186 251) = *IG* II^2 12926 (fun. mon.). |

CHAPTER FOURTEEN

RESTORING ATHENIAN NAMES*

Of the 63,000 men and women listed in the Attica volume of the *Lexicon of Greek Personal Names*, well over 90% are known from inscriptions; eloquent testimony, if such be needed, to the importance of epigraphy for the study of ancient Athens.[1] The statistic is also a product of the centrality of people in ancient Athenian epigraphic practice. Whether as officials, honorands, dedicators, the deceased on funerary monuments, or in the proliferation of name-lists, it is individual human beings that took the centre of the epigraphic stage. One result is that the disciplines of epigraphy, onomastics and prosopography are inextricably linked; it is no accident that epigraphists have made many of the most important contributions to our knowledge of Athenian people and names, including all four distinguished editors of the comprehensive Attic onomastic corpora: Johannes Kirchner (*PA*, 1901–3), Michael Osborne and Sean Byrne (*LGPN* II, 1994, *FRA*,
327 1996) and John Traill (*POAA*, in progress). | A crucial aspect of this work for the practising editor of inscriptions—one where no scholar's

---

* This chapter was previously published in A.P. Matthaiou and G. Malouchou (eds.), *Attikai Epigraphai, Praktika Symposiou eis mnemen Adolf Wilhelm* (Athens, 2004), 327–341.

[1] I am very grateful to all who commented on earlier versions of this paper, both at the conference and privately, especially to Sean Byrne and Jaime Curbera; to Alan Henry for reading a final draft; and to the authorities in the British School at Athens, the Agora and above all the Epigraphical Museum, for their courtesy in facilitating access to the stones. I adopt the abbreviations used in *LGPN* II in addition to the following:

FRA: *The Foreign Residents of Athens*. Edd. M.J. Osborne and S.G. Byrne, Leuven 1996;

LGPN II: *A Lexicon of Greek Personal Names, II Attica*. Edd. M.J. Osborne and S.G. Byrne, Oxford 1994 (Addenda and Corrigenda on *LGPN* website);

POAA: *The Persons of Ancient Athens*. Ed. J. Traill, Toronto 1994–. This has not yet reached the letters pi and tau. Accordingly most references in this study are to *LGPN* II.

In the table I^3 = *IG* I^3, II^2 = *IG* II^2 etc. *Ath. Rel.* = R. Parker, *Athenian Religion, A History*, Oxford 1996. *Beiträge* = A. Wilhelm, *Beiträge zur griechischen Inschriftenkunde*, Vienna 1909.

contributions surpass those of Adolf Wilhelm—is the restoration of partially preserved names. I shall approach this subject today with the help of 76 new suggestions, most of them relating to such names, set out in the table at the end of the paper. The majority arise from a fairly systematic study I have carried out of restored names beginning in pi and tau (which together account for about 10% of the Attic onomasticon).

Three considerations account for the large majority of my suggested revisions;[2] they can be expressed in terms of three principles: "go back to the roots"; "avoid overrestoration"; and "follow the trend".

By "go back to the roots" I mean in part that (of course) the starting point for any restoration must be an accurate reading of what is preserved on the stone, preferably including autopsy, and an accurate assessment of the number of missing letters. In those cases in the list marked with an asterisk I have been able to verify readings at autopsy and in 14 of these the results are significant for the restoration of the name.[3] It also, however, means tracing the bibliographical record through to its origin; not always a straightforward task. Since Kirchner saw it in the Piraeus museum and published it in 1931, apparently for the first time, *IG* II^2 2420 has been thought to be a iv BC list of non-Athenian Greeks from the Piraeus. Kirchner was unaware, however,
328 that the inscription | had actually been found in Troizen. It had been published first by Meletopoulos in 1883[4] and appears also as *IG* IV

[2] As I have sought to make clear in the table, while some in my view are certain, others are merely probable or good alternative possibilities. Also, I do not purport to give here a full description of the factors which need to be taken into account when the epigraphist is restoring names. Very little will be said, for example, on strictly linguistic questions. 47 relates to restoration of Roman names in Attica, a subject not discussed here; it requires a systematic study of its own.

[3] 4, 5, 16, 23, 28, 31, 32, 13/35, 38 (spacing), 43, 46, 52, 59 (spacing), 71. Lest this should seem implicitly critical of earlier editors, I should perhaps emphasise that most of these readings are difficult and several remain uncertain. Also, for every revised reading proposed, numerous others which I examined turned out not to require revision and are therefore not listed in this study. Readings of course take precedence over other arguments such as the preference for restoring a more common name. **5** was hitherto the common Ἀμεινο[κλῆς], but there is a certain phi after the omicron, yielding our first case, in Attica or elsewhere, of a name in Ἀμεινοφ- (cf. the names in Καλλιφ- and Ἀριστοφ-). On a stone where there are frequent errors, however, e.g. **3**, we may amend away unlikely name segments where a plausible alternative is apparent. (No Attic name in AEl- is attested).

[4] *Παρνασσὸς* 7 (1883) 79, found ὑπό τινος ἐργάτου ἐπὶ τῆς ἀκροπόλεως τῶν Τροιζηνίων πλησίον τῶν ἐρειπίων τοῦ ναοῦ τῆς Σθενιάδος καλουμένης Ἀθηνᾶς κατὰ τὸν Πausανίαν (II 187, 4).

(1) 825. We may probably assume that, at some time before Kirchner saw it, the stone was transported across the Saronic gulf from Troizen to Piraeus, and that the latter was then mistakenly taken to be its original findspot. One of the results of the repatriation of this inscription is that three names should be altogether deleted from *LGPN* II: Πραξιδάμας, Τιμόδαμος and Χοραγίων.[5]

Where the stone is lost the importance of the early bibliography becomes even greater. With 69 for example, an athletic victor from Hippothontis in a ii BC catalogue, the restoration [Τ?]ι[μ?]όμαχος has not been challenged since proposed by Köhler; but our text derives ultimately from Fourmont, whose apparently fairly accurate transcription as reproduced by Boeckh showed the first letter as illegible, but the third as a clear lambda. Since there is an attested Athenian name with these letters (albeit fairly rare), [Φ]ιλόμαχος, and since it is attested in the same period (once in the same period and tribe), it is the preferable restoration here.

It can be helpful to extend the bibliographical trail into unpublished papers, even if there have been reliable autopsies. Since it was first published by Koumanoudes in 1871, *IG* II^2 10453, a funerary monument broken on the right, once built into the wall of George Finlay's house in Athens and showing the beginning of a name and an ethnic, has been thought to be the gravestone of a man from Torone (1). Köhler read the same letters as Koumanoudes, and the same letters can still be read from the stone in its current home in the British School. It is only when we turn to Finlay's unpublished notebooks that we see that he read two more letters on both lines, suggesting, if Finlay's drawing is correct, that the stone was broken at some point after he made it, but before publication by Koumanoudes. From the ending of the ethnic as preserved by Finlay it appears that the monument was for a woman, not a man, perhaps named Ἀγλωκράτ[η], only the second Toronean woman known at Athens. This case incidentally illustrates
another point. Epigraphists (most of | whom, it must be said, have 329
been men) may unthinkingly restore men's names. That is reasonable in public inscriptions, where women are rarely named. It is less so in private funerary monuments and dedications, where women are more strongly represented.

[5] 45, 68, 76. See also 8, 9, 10, 14, 15, 49.

A common pitfall into which the epigraphist may be tempted is over-restoration; in this context, the unequivocal restoration of one name where others are at least equally possible. Perhaps the most strikingly overrestored name in the list is Πολί?]της (33), a council official of ii AD (albeit that the scholar responsible prudently inserted a "?"). There are around 200 Athenian names ending -της. Admittedly only some of these would fit the space, but Πολίτης is among the least likely, for the name is not known to have been borne by any Athenian for five centuries before this date. Significantly perhaps, the last citizen to be called "Citizen" is attested in the last decade of the classical democracy. Another case is **30**, where a ii BC ephebe from Themakos ending -χος has been restored [Πλούταρ]χος. Admittedly only some of the 200 possibilities will fit the space and [Πλούταρ]χος is the only one attested in the deme Themakos (on the gravestones *IG* II^{2} 6207–8). With such a small deme, however, this fact is not statistically significant. We know the names of only 45 members of Themakos from the whole of antiquity;[6] that, among these, only one name in -χος occurs is more likely to be a product of the smallness of this sample than of the realities of naming patterns in the deme.[7]

This leads us nicely onto the third principle, "follow the trend". By this I mean that restorations which accord with known patterns of nomenclature are more likely to be right, other things being equal, than those which run counter to them. Occasionally, as the Πλούταρχος case illustrates, we do not have enough evidence for a pattern to be established. This will usually be a problem with small demes; it is also an issue e.g. with women's names; but fortunately, for most purposes, the sample of onomastic data that we possess for Attica (we probably know the names of very roughly 10% of all Athenian citizen males who lived between v BC and iii AD) is large enough to bear rational inference based on detectable patterns.

The need to "follow the trend", a factor with the majority of the
330 revisions | in the list, is well illustrated by 2. An Athenian named Hades would breach two clear rules of Greek mainland citizen naming practice: with a tiny number of exceptions, almost all in the Christian era, humans were not given the names of gods; and even with names

[6] Source: *LGPN* on-line search.

[7] Other cases of overrestoration: 51, 67, 74.

deriving from gods, which were very common (Apollodoros, Dionysios etc.), deities of ill-omen were avoided.[8] *LGPN* II, however, lists over 120 names with the *termination* -αδης. These are the first surviving letters on a funerary columella, the top of which is broken away (see phot., *Ag.* xvii pl. 10). It is clear, I think, that the initial letters of this man's name were in a previous line, now lost (note the word breaks at other preserved line-ends). As both Sean Byrne and John Morgan have pointed out to me, [Ἀσκληπι]|άδης was the most common name at this period of suitable length, but there are too many possibilities for certainty.

This is also an example of another fairly common phenomenon of which the epigraphist must be wary, sequences of letters which can form names in their own right, but might also be parts of other names.[9] An example is 59, again on a funerary monument, very poorly inscribed and thought until now to yield our only Attic instance of the use of Σειδώνιος, otherwise attested only as an ethnic, as a personal name, in line 2. The start of that line would in that case be indented with respect to lines 1 and 3. On any account there are letters missing at the end of line 2 and the start of 3. It seems that they were never inscribed (perhaps they were painted in). It is preferable to restore additional letters also at the start of 2, yielding the common Ποσειδώνιος in place of the unique Σειδώνιος, and an approximately aligned left margin, i.e.:

Κ^{v}άλλ^{v}ων
[Πο]σειδωνί[ου] *or* <Πο>σειδωνί<ου>
[Σ]υπαλήτ[τ]ιος *or* <Σ>υπαλήτ<τ>ιος

4, a father's name on a list of councillors, is another case where the
letters read | hitherto probably do not form the entire name. On any 331
account we have to do with a name otherwise unattested in Attica.
The current suggestion, Αἰτω[λ]ίδης, seems acceptable in itself,
but at autopsy I thought that the extreme bottom right corner of

---

[8] See most recently R. Parker, *Proc. Brit. Acad.* 104 (2000) 53–79; J. Curbera, *GRBS* 38 (1997) [2000] 405–6.

[9] This was a point, incidentally, to which Wilhelm was sensitive; it was he for example who realised that the victorious *choregos* on the dedication, *IG* II^2 3047, was not, as earlier thought, E]riphos, a name not securely attested for an Athenian, but Phile]riphos, a name known to occur in a prominent Athenian family. A. Wilhelm, *Attische Urkunden* V 143–44. Cf. *APF* p. 535.

a delta was probably detectable before it. If the reading is correct, this must, I think, be the first example, in Attica or apparently elsewhere, of the name Δαιτωνίδης. It is well attested outside Attica in its non-patronymic form, Δαίτων (*LGPN* I and IIIB) and in its dialect equivalent, Δαιτώνδας (*LGPN* IIIA and B).[10] One result is to remove from the Attic onomasticon the only personal name derived from "Aetolia".

At its most basic, "follow the trend" means that, other things being equal, it is preferable to avoid restorations which yield names not otherwise attested where there are alternatives yielding attested names;[11] and that a more common name is preferable to a significantly less common one.[12] This is at issue with 26 and 27, the only two Attic cases of the name Πέταλος, both with initial letter(s) restored. We can not be confident that the restoration is wrong, because the name is well enough attested outside Attica, and there was a *kome* in Aphidna called Petalidai.[13] But in the archaic case especially, 26, a father's name on an Acropolis dedication, there is the very tempting alternative, [Θ]έταλος, attested in this period and class for sons of Peisistratos and Kimon. "εἷς τῶν Κίμωνος παίδων Θετταλὸς ἐκαλεῖτο" states Heliodoros in F5 of his work on the Acropolis. As John Davies has noted, this may imply that the name Θέταλος occurred on an Acropolis dedication; perhaps ours is the dedication in question.

In order to "follow the trend" we of course have to know what the trend is; and here there is much work still to be done to analyse the data which thanks to *LGPN* are becoming readily accessible for the first time. For the purposes of this paper I have generally treated Attica as an onomastic unit, but how far this is justifiable and how far we should think rather in terms of wider, supra-Attic, onomastic patterns and
332 trends is one of many questions awaiting | systematic study.[14] Similarly
there is much to be done to identify and explain regional patterns

[10] Δαιτώνδας was discussed by A. Wilhelm, *Bull. int. Acad. Polonaise* 1930, 139–45 = *Akademieschriften* II, 293–99.

[11] A factor with 2, 3, 17, 21, 26 and 27, 39, 43, 57 and 58, 59, 75.

[12] A factor with 6–7/72, 18, 25, 35, 36, 46, 61, 65, 71.

[13] Eponyms of patronymic-type group names used as toponyms sometimes occur as personal names, e.g. Φίλαιος, Δημοτίων etc.

[14] For many cities the sort of statistical analysis possible for Athens is hindered by more limited data. On hellenistic Rhodes see A. Bresson, *Dialogues d'Histoire Ancienne* 7 (1981) 345–62.

within Attica.[15] Wilhelm was very sensitive to the potential existence of such patterns. He noted for example the tendency for names with the element -μηλο, referring to sheep or goats, to occur in suitably pastoral demes.[16] One of these demes was Paiania, where the name Φιλόμηλος was borne by members of a prominent family of the classical period (*APF* 1466970); it may be that we have another example in this deme on a funerary monument, albeit centuries later, at 39. The current restoration, Πολύμ[αχ]ος, is a name not otherwise known in Attica;[17] Πολύμ[ηλ]ος, an attested post-classical Athenian name, is an attractive alternative.

Naming and social class is another subject that awaits more systematic investigation. It is generally recognised that names of patronymic form, i.e. in -ίδης, were characteristic of the Athenian upper classes in the classical period, but we should not lose sight of the fact that, where a name of this form and the equivalent basic, non-patronymic, form are both attested, the basic form is significantly, about 4 or 5 times on average, more common. Other things being equal, therefore, the basic form is the more likely restoration.[18]

As well as synchronic patterns, there are diachronic ones to be taken into account. At the simplest level, names could go in or out of fashion.[19] We have already noted Πολίτης, not attested after 320 BC. Another example is provided by a i BC dedication (19), restored since Kirchner to read: [- Λ]εωνίδο[υ | -τ]ὴν ἑαυ[τοῦ | θυγατέρα, Πα]νδίου
333 Μ[- | - γυναῖκα ἀ]νέθ[ηκεν]. In fact, | however, Πάνδιος and the alternative Ἔνδιος are both characteristically classical names, neither of them attested after iii BC. Δῖος, on the other hand, an extremely rare name in classical Athens, seems to have become more fashionable at precisely the period of this dedication and Kirchner would have done better to adhere to Köhler's articulation (*IG* II 1416), yielding a female name

---

[15] E.g. how far theophoric names might be derived from local cults. Cf. Parker, *op. cit.* (n. 8). Interestingly, 44 seems to be our first pre-hellenistic Poseidon-derived name from Sounion.

[16] A. Wilhelm, *Attische Urkunden* V 144.

[17] In fact there is only one other case in *LGPN* I–IIIB, Π̣ολύμ̣αχος c. 245–220 BC at *IG* VII 2717, 9.

[18] See 16, 21, 66? (basic form preferable), 28, 37, 66? (high status, classical period, patronymic form preferable/possible). A rather different argument from social context is a factor at 65.

[19] Other cases where this is a factor: 22, 29, 33, 37 (Πολύκλειτος), 38, 47, 48, 50, 54, 56, 62.

in the accusative ending in nu followed by a husband's (or father's)[20] name Δίου. Köhler, following earlier editors, guessed that the deme was Marathon, but in fact the names Δῖος and Λεωνίδης occur in a well known family of this period from Melite,[21] to which deme the Leonides and Dios on this dedication should also be assigned.

Another example of this sort of reasoning is 23, where a metic worker on the Erechtheum account, *IG* II^2 1654, has until now been restored as [Πάτρο]κλος. My suspicions were aroused by the fact that this name is not otherwise attested in Attica for seven centuries after the completion of the Erechtheum; and indeed it turns out that a trace of the right side of an omega is detectable before the kappa. The restoration [Σ]ῶ̣κλος is assured, as is identification with the worker of this name attested on other Erechtheum accounts. This and other considerations enable us to see that this account, the only one currently dated to iv BC, and thought to belong to a period when the building was under repair, in fact belongs in a sequence with the other extant Erechtheum accounts of the last decade of v BC.

I have investigated two naming patterns of particular interest to editors in a little more detail. First, the occurrence of demotics as names. We are quite frequently faced with a sequence of letters that looks as if it comes from a demotic; but sometimes the question arises, could it be a name? My finding here is that names which are broadly similar to demotics are fairly common, but names precisely equivalent to standard demotic forms are almost always avoided, at least before the Christian
334 era (when Ἐλευσίνιος became a common name).[22] | Κηφίσιος and Κηφισίων, for example, are well attested, and there is even a Κηφισῆς of Kephisia at the end of v BC. But Κηφισιεύς, the standard demotic, never occurs as a personal name. The only fairly secure exception to this rule that I have been able to find for an Athenian citizen BC is Σουνιεύς, father of Δημοκράτης Σουνιέως Κολωνῆθεν, proposer of

[20] The restorations θυγατέρα in 3 and γυναῖκα in 4 are very doubtful.

[21] *LGPN* II Δῖος (**10**)–(**11**), Λεωνίδης (**23–34**). Cf. E. Rawson, *Athenaeum* 73 (1985) 49–50.

[22] Given the international popularity of the Mysteries in this period, Ἐλευσίνιος probably connoted more than a simple demotic (cf. Ἀθήναιος, which had become a popular name a little earlier). Apart from this case, use of demotics as names remains very rare in the Christian era.

IG II[2] 847 in 215/4 BC.[23] This shows that such a name was possible for a citizen, at least in the Hellenistic period; but statistically the chances are tens of thousands to one against, and as a general rule the epigraphist should therefore avoid interpreting demotics as personal names when there are other possible explanations to hand. He should also where possible avoid restoring a name to yield a demotic form. 11, for example, a iv BC councillor Ἀφιδνα[-, is less likely to have been called Ἀφιδνα[ῖος] than by another name from the same root, not identical to the demotic of Aphidna.

17, the father's name of the secretary of 369/8, involves the same issue. In 1893 Wilhelm restored Παι[ωνίδ]ῃς,[24] but this was based on the then current view that Παιονίδης occurred as a personal name at *IG* II[2] 1666, 3, where it has now long been recognised as the demotic of Paionidai. Some alternatives are noted at 17; but in the circumstances it is probably more prudent, with Kirchner, to leave this name unrestored.

A very important pattern for the editor to be aware of is how fathers' names tended to relate to their sons'. The general picture has long been clear: early a tendency to name sons after their grandfathers; later for them to share name components with their fathers (Polyxenos son of Polykrates, Polykrates son of Epikrates, Dorotheos son of Polydoros etc.), with a second or third son possibly having the father's name; later still, commoner for sons to be named after their fathers.[25] What seems not previously to have been established is the chronology | of these developments and the relative probabilities.[26] 335
Analysis of names beginning with pi and tau shows that, in Attica, the crucial turning point is c. 200 BC and that the change took place

[23] Possibly also a name at *SEG* XXI 684, 4. Even here it is perhaps just possible that the nominative was e.g. Σουνιῆς and that the genitive in *IG* II[2] 847 has been assimilated to the demotic. The suspicion arises that he might have been of servile or foreign origin. Cf. Anaxandrides *PCG* F4, 3–4: πολλοὶ δὲ νῦν μέν εἰσιν οὐκ ἐλεύθεροι, εἰς αὔριον δὲ Σουνιεῖς. On unique names as indicators of foreign origin see C. Habicht, *Proc. Brit. Acad.* 104 (2000) 119–27.

[24] A. Wilhelm, *Eranos Vindobonensis* (1893), 245 n. 3. The stone has long been illegible at this point and earlier witnesses are unsure. Cf. Osborne's note, *Naturalization* I, D10, p. 48.

[25] See M. Runes, *Wiener Studien* 44 (1924/5) 170–78. For an analysis of naming patterns within families on hellenistic Rhodes and modern Karpathos see A. Bresson, *op. cit.* (n. 14).

[26] I am most grateful to Sean Byrne for help in compiling the following statistics.

not gradually, but quite suddenly over the space of a generation or two, c. 200–150 BC. Among persons listed under pi and tau in *LGPN* II, in evidence dating before 200 there are c. 140 cases of fathers and sons sharing name components, only c. 25 where they have the same name. In other words before then it is 5–6 times more common in inscriptions for a father and son to share name components than it was for them to have the same name. After 200 the reverse is the case. Fathers and sons with the same name become common, while especially after c. 150 the sharing of name components becomes rare. The figures are, c. 27 cases of shared name components later than 200, only c. 18 of them after mid-ii BC, compared with c. 192 cases of shared names. In other words, after 150 BC shared names are about 10 times more common than shared name components. In fact, after 150 BC shared name components (rather like late cases of patronymic-type names) are sufficiently unusual to justify suspicion of deliberate onomastic archaism. The explanation for this sudden change in naming practice requires careful consideration, and lies beyond the scope of this paper; it would be interesting if, so early, there was imitation of Roman practice. But for the epigraphist the fact of the change is itself important: other things being equal, we are more likely to be right if we restore shared name components rather than shared names before 200, and we are much more likely to be right if we adopt precisely the opposite policy after 150. This observation is a factor influencing a number of the amendments in the list.[27]

It can help persuade us that a restoration is right if it yields identity, or a family link, with a known individual.[28] With 50, for example, an
336 ephebe on the | Pythais of 106/5 BC currently [Προ]ξενίδης, several things fall nicely into place if we instead restore [Θεο]ξενίδης to yield identity with a mint magistrate of this name of c. 70s BC.[29] The career chronology patently suits very well; we dispose of the latest, by a cen-

---

[27] Pre-200: 16, 20 (where the question is, which component(s)?), 21, 31, 38 and 40, 42, 53, 60, 63, 70; Post-150: 24. Transition: 41. Cf. **5**. From these results it would seem that editors have been rather too ready to restore fathers and sons with the same name pre-ii BC, but that they have less commonly restored shared name components inappropriately post-iii BC.

[28] There are pitfalls. E.g. as C. Habicht has pointed out, the same father-son name pair may occur in different demes. See *ZPE* 103 (1994) 117–27.

[29] Date: *Ag.* XXVI 81–82.

tury, of the attested cases of the classical-sounding name Προξενίδης; and we may comfortably identify the ephebe's father, whose name, Μενοίτης, was not very common, with the Μενοίτης who was mint magistrate in about 117/6, for we know that the mint magistracy was a post which tended to run in families. I note explicitly in the list other cases where a restoration is supported by such identifications or family links.

In general, restorations are more convincing when supported by more than one line of argument. I finish with a case where a new reading and a new identification flowing from restoration of a common name in place of a rare one yield new information about a priestly family (35). The decree of the 240s BC honouring Τιμοκρίτη, priestess of Aglauros, first published in 1983, has hitherto attracted most attention from topographers interested in locating the Aglaurion;[30] but it is no less significant for what it tells us about this important cult and priesthood, possibly identical with the state priesthood of Aglauros supplied by the genos Salaminioi. Hitherto Timokrite's paternal family has proved unidentifiable; it is a modest step forward that we can, I think, now identify her father, Polynikos of Aphidna, with a councillor of 304/3 from Aphidna currently restored as [Π]ολύ̣[δι]κος. Even without this identification, [Π]ολύ̣[νι]κος would be the better restoration, for it is much the commoner name. A fresh reading of *Ag.* xv 61 indicates that Polynikos' father's, i.e. Timokrite's grandfather's, name was Ἐπίκουρος rather than, as currently thought, Ἐπικράτης. Polynikos' tenure of office as councillor is not an indicator of high social status and Epikouros is otherwise unknown. As ever, it is difficult to distinguish apparent obscurity (i.e. lack of evidence) from genuine (i.e. lack of prominence at the time); but current indications do not suggest distinction. We may hope that, in the future, we shall learn more about this family, which, whether distinguished or not, offers potential insight into the status and character of the Athenian priesthood. | 337

[30] See the summary of discussion up to 1996, *SEG* XLVI 137. Also *ZPE* 125 (1999) 114–15.

Name Revisions

LGPN II/*FRA*	REVISION
***1**. Ἀγλώκρ[ιτος] (*FRA* **7138**) Torone f. iv BC II^2 10453	Ἀγλωκρά̲τ̲[η?] | Τορωναί̲α̲. See *BSA* 95 (2000) 499, E9[1]
***2**. Ἄδης (1, unique) Aphidna i BC–ii AD (date: SDL) *Ag.* XVII 83	[Ἀσκληπι??|]άδης Ἀρι[σ]|τοκρίτου Ἀφ[ι]|δναῖος (cf. II^2 5727, same insc.)
3. Ἀείστρ[ατος] (1, unique) Kytheros 155/4 BC *Ag.* XV 225, 91	A<ρ>ιστο[-]. Cf. Tracy, *ALC* pp. 165–66, who reads AEIΣTO[-
***4**. Αἰτω[λ]ίδη(ς)? (1, unique) f. [-] Skamb. c. 333 BC *SEG* XXVIII 52, 32	Δ̣αιτω[ν]ἰδο̣?
***5**. Ἀμεινο[κλῆς] (6) Kettos c. 333 BC *SEG* XXVIII 52, 76	Ἀμεινοφ[άνης??]. Cf. Ἀμεινοκλῆς (**7**) s. Anti*phanes* Kettos 266/5 BC
***6**. Ἀρεσίας and *7. Ἀρέσιππος	See **72**
8. Ἀριστόλας (3) ATHENS* iv BC II^2 2420, 14	Delete from *LGPN* II. Not an Attic inscription (= *IG* IV (1) 825)
9. Ἀρχέλ[α]ς (5) ATHENS* iv BC ib., 13	As **8**. Add to *LGPN* IIIA
10. Ἀρχικράτης (5) ATHENS* iv BC ib., 11	As **8**
11. Ἀφιδνα[ῖος] (1, unique) Euonymon 304/3 BC *Ag.* XV 61, 165	Ἀφιδνα[- (Ἀφιδνα[ιεύς] *vel sim.*)
***12**. Ἐξήκε[στος] (17)	See **17**
***13**. Ἐπικρά[της] (42)	See **35**
14. Καλλίμαχος (105) ATHENS* iv BC II^2 2420, 10	As **8**
15. Λακράτης (8) ATHENS* iv BC ib., 16	As **8**
***16**. Μνησωνί̣[δης] (2, of two) Phrearrhioi c. 333 BC *SEG* XXVIII 52, 60	Μνήσων Μ̣[νησ-] Cf. Μνησίστρατος (**21**), Μνησίφιλος (**12**)
***17**. Παι[ωνίδ]ης̣ (1, unique) f. Ἐξήκε[στος] Azenia 369/8 BC II^2 103 = Osborne, *Naturalization* D 10, 3	No restoration (thus II^2). Possibilities include Ἐξ̣ή[κεστος] Παυ[σανί]ο̣ (cf. II^2 1569, 36–37 and II^2 5312) and Ἐξ̣η[κίας Ἐ]παν̣[δρίδ]ο̣
18. [Παμμ]ένης (4) s. Διότιμος ATHENS 98/7 BC *Hesp.* Suppl. 15 (1975) p. 54 no. 7 c, 59	Or [Εὐμ]ένης. For number of letters restored cf. l. 63 (phot., *Hesp.* Suppl. 15, pl. 25b). Perhaps father of Διότιμος (**31**) s. Εὐμένης Azenia m. i BC

[1] I am not persuaded by A. Henry and J. Traill, *BSA* 96 (2001), 321–25, that the normally accurate Finlay was probably mistaken in this case. The ease with which an already broken inscription may come to be broken again will be familiar to any epigraphist who is experienced at working with stones, especially where the inscription is in re-use (in this case in a garden wall).

Table (*cont.*)

LGPN II/*FRA*	REVISION
19. [Πά]νδιος (3) s. Μ[-] ATHENS i BC II^2 4035, 3	*Female name in acc.*]ν Δίου Μ[ελιτέως]
20. [Παντα?]λέων (5) s. Παντα[-] ATHENS 273/2 BC II^2 676, 24	Or Λέων Παντα[λέοντος]. Cf. M. Runes, *Wien.Stud.* 44 (1924/5) 172
***21**. Πασικλεί(δης) (1, unique) f. Ἀγακλῆς Pergase 333/2 BC II^2 2401 = *SEG* XXXIX 184, 15	Or Πασικλεί(ου) (cf. II^2 2401, 13). The stone is now near-illegible
338 ***22**. Π[α]τρο[κλῆς] (20, unique after c. 175 BC, except II^2 7260, i AD Kirchner, date doubtful) f. -]ώτιον wife of a Κηφισεύς imp. *Ag.* XVII 180	Or Π[α]τρο[βίου] or Π[α]τρο[φίλου]. Cf. Πατρόβιος (**1**) and Π̣ατρόφιλος (**1**)–(**2**), all Kephisia i–ii AD |
***23**. [Πάτρο]κλος (4) ATHENS* 406/5 BC? (date: SDL) II^2 1654, 7 f.	[Σ]ῶ̣κλος. See *ZPE* 132 (2000), 157–60
***24**. [Πειθ?]όδημος (2) s. Πείθων Cholleidai 39/8 BC II^2 1043, 96	Or [Κριτ]όδημος [Πιστ]όδημος
25. [Π]εισίθε[ος] (2, of two) Phrearrhioi 371/0 BC *SEG* XXVIII 148, 8	Or [Δ]ε̣ισίθε[ος]
***26**. [Π]έταλος (1, of two) f. -]όστ[ρα]τος ATHENS c. 500 BC I^3 752	Or [Θ]ετάλο. Cf. *FGH* 373 Heliodoros F5; *APF* pp. 307 and 448–49
***27**. [Πέ]ταλος (2, of two) ATHENS c. 450 BC *Ag.* XVII 6, 31 = I^3 1153, 31	Or e.g. [Φύ]ταλος (cf. *Ath. Rel.*, 318. For genos eponyms as personal names in v BC cf. Ἀμύνανδρος, Πραξίεργος etc.)
***28**. Πιστί[δης] (2) Kekropis 374/3 BC II^2 1421, 2 (with add. p. 799) (treasurer of Athena)	Πιστίδ[ης] (left diagonal of delta visible at autopsy. J. Curbera reports that the Berlin squeeze slightly favours Πιστίδ̣[ης] over Πιστία̣[ς])
29. Πίστος (1, unique pre-ii AD) ATHENS m. iv BC II^2 1621, 119 (genitive)	Other name Πιστο[-
30. [Πλούταρ]χος (16) Themakos 119/8 BC *SEG* XXI 477 I, 124	No restoration. 200+ names in -χος in *LGPN* II. Cf. II^2 1566, 24
***31**. [Πολ]έ[μ]αρχος (6) s. Τελέσων Halai 304/3 BC II^2 488, 12	Τ[ελ]έ[σ]αρχος. See *BSA* 95 (2000) 492–95, E6
***32**. Π[ολί?]οχος (3) f. [-]ίδης ATHENS? 332/1 BC Aleshire, *Asklep.* Inv. III, 79 (Aleshire: Π[ολι]όχου or Π[ασι]όχου or Π[ρολ]όχου)	Π̣α̣σ̣ι̣όχου? (tentative new reading, autopsy). For the name cf. *LGPN* I
***33**. [Πολί?]τ̣ης (4, unique post-320) ATHENS 166/7 AD *Ag.* XV 369, 63	No restoration, c. 200 names in -της in *LGPN* II

Table (*cont.*)

LGPN II/*FRA*	REVISION
34. Πολ[ύαι]νος (6) Marathon i BC/i AD II^2 3177, 1 (stone lost; text corrupt. Cf. *Ath. Rel.*, 287)	Or Πολ[ύξε]νος. Possible descendant of Πολύξενος **(14)** Marathon ii BC. Deme and context suggest connected with Bouzygai/Gephyraioi (cf. *SEG* XXX 85, 20–21) rather than archon epon. (thus Graindor)
***35**. [Π]ολύ̣[δι]κος (1, of two) s. Ἐπικρά[της] Aphidna 304/3 BC *Ag.* XV̇ 59, 15; 61, 267	[Π]ολύ̣[νι]κος Ἐπικούρο̣υ̣ (61, 267), [Πολύνι]κος Ἐπικ[ούρου] (59, 15). = father of Τιμοκρίτη̣ priestess of Aglauros on *SEG* XXXIII 115. Deme of [Πο]λύδικος **(2)** reverts to obscurity (C. Habicht, *Hypomnemata* 73 (1982) 203 = *SEG* XXXII 127 had suggested Aphidna)
36. [Πολ]ύκαρπος (3) s. Ἡρακλείδης Marathon ii AD *SEG* XXXV 176	[Ε]ὔκαρπος. Probably = one of Εὔκαρπος **(30)–(32)**, all Marathon ii AD
37. Πολυκλ[ῆς]? (9) (or Πολύκλ[ειτος]?, not common pre-ii AD) ATHENS c. 250 BC *AM* 85 (1970) 227 no. 440 (cavalryman)	Or Πολυκλ[είδης] (also a more likely alternative than Πολύκλειτος for Πολυκλῆς **(5)*** and **(23)**). Cf. *AM loc. cit.* no. 441 with p. 238 and 239
***38**. [Πολυκ]τήμων (3, of three) s. Πολύξενος f. Πολυκράτης Kerameis f. iv BC II^2 6335, 1	[Εὐκ?]τήμων. Slightly preferable on grounds of alignment. =, or relation of, Εὐκτήμων **(30)** Kerameis 336/5 BC. Cf. **40**
39. Πολύμ[αχ]ος (1, unique) f. Ἀρίστυλλα Paiania imp. ii^2 7026/7 + add. p. 881	Πολυμ[ήλ?]ου. Πολυμάχου Fourmont (*CIG* 922), Πολυμ[άχ]ου Stamires ap. II^2 add. Note that Fourmont's transcript was slightly faulty in 1. 3 and AX and HΛ can appear very similar if roughly inscribed/abraded
***40**. [Πολ]ύξενος (12) f. [Εὐκ?]τήμων Kerameis f. iv BC II^2 6335, 2	Or [Ε]ὔξενος. Cf. **38**
339 **41**. [Πολύξ]ενος (21) s. [Πολ]ύξενος Sphettos c. 180 BC II^2 2333, 53	Or [Φιλόξ]ενος. ?Family link with Φιλόξενος **(57)–(58)** Sphettos hell. |
42. Πολυ̣[στράτος] (33) f. Πολύστρατος (34) Phlya c. 332/1 BC *Ag.* XV̇ 73 = *SEG* XXXVI 155, 77	Πολυ̣[κλῆς]?, Πολυ̣[μήδης]?, Πολύ̣[μνηστος]? All attested in Phlya s. iv BC
***43**. Πολυ[φά]ης (1, unique) Phlya 117/6 BC II^2 1009 II, 81	Πολυκ[λ]ῆς. Πολυκλῆς **(34)** of Phlya perhaps a iv BC ancestor
***44**. Ποσ[-. f. Χαρίας Sounion c. 333 BC *SEG* XXVIII 52, 69 (councillor)	Ποσ[ειδίππου. ?= -]ιππος s. Χαρίας Sounion c. 346/5 BC *ID* 104–22a, 2*
45. Πραξιδάμας (1, unique) ATHENS* iv BC II^2 2420, 12	As **8**
***46**. [Π]ρα[ξ]ικλέης (4) Euony. 367/6 BC *Ag.* XV 14, 11 (cf. *APF* 12164)	Or Φ̣ρασ̣ικλέης. New reading (autopsy) consistent with either name

Table (*cont.*)

	LGPN II/*FRA*	REVISION
***47.**	[Π]ρόκλος (1, unique pre-c. 100 AD) ATHENS s. i BC II² 3539, 3	ATHENS*. = cognomen Proculus. See *BSA* 95 (2000) 501–2, E11
***48.**	[Πρ]όμαχος (8, latest) s. [Ἀγ?]ροίτης Phrearrhioi ii BC II² 7730	Or [Ἰσ]όμαχος. Perhaps [Ἰ]σόμαχος. Name attested 108/7 BC
49.	Πρόνοος (1, unique) ATHENS* iv BC II² 2420, 15	As **8**
50.	[Προ]ξενίδης (3, unique post-iii BC) s. Μενοίτης ATHENS 106/5 BC *FD* III (2) 25, 28	[Θεο]ξενίδης. = Θεοξενίδης **(2)** and son of Μενοίτης **(2)**
51.	[Πρ]όξενος (1) ATHENS v BC I³ 1047, 2	No restoration. 19 -όξενος names in *LGPN* II. [Πρ]όχσενος **(18)** also doubtful
***52.**	[Π]ρ[οφ]αντίδε[ς] (1, unique) ATHENS c. 410 BC *Ag.* XVII 22, 97 = I³ 1192, 97	Ἐπιφαντίδε[ς]? (SDL, autopsy and J. Curbera, Berlin squeeze). N.B. the Πρόφαντος in *LGPN* II is probably Προφάν[ης], see *SEG* XLI 81
53.	Πρωτό(μαχος) (12) f. Πρωτόμαχος Kephisia c. 259–255 BC *Ag.* XV 86, 51	Or Πρωτο(κλῆς) (or Πρῶτος?). ?=, or same family as, Πρωτοκλῆς **(4)** Kephisia 328/7 BC *Ag.* XV 49, 16
54.	[Πυ]θαγόρας (1, unique pre-hell.) ATHENS 480–450 BC I³ 581	[Πει]θαγόρας, [Ὀρ]θαγόρας, or even [Θεμισ]θαγόρας
55.	Π[υθέ]ας (stone: Π[..³.]ο) (31) f. Ἀνδρά<ρ>η[ς] Teithras m. iv BC *SEG* XXIV 152, 1 (renter of property from deme Teithras)	Π[ύρρ?]ο. ?Related to Πύρρος **(42)** s. Δημοκλείδης Teithras 128/7 BC and Δημοκλῆς **(61)** and **(62)** Teithras s. iv BC Cf. *APF* 3509 and 3510
56.	[Πυρ?]γίων (14, unique post-iii BC) ATHENS? imp. II² 12020, 5, cf. *AM* 67 (1942) 187, n. 1 (genitive)	[Εὐα]γίωνος (or rarer [Γορ]γίωνος)
57.	Πυρρί(ων) (1) ATHENS 113/2 BC Thompson, *New Style Coinage* p. 580; and *58. [Π]υρρί[ων] (2, of two) ATHENS? f. iii BC II² 2352, 12	Πυρρίας (suggested by *LGPN* II as alternative)
***59.**	Σειδώνι[ος] (*LGPN* s.v. Σιδώνιος) (1, unique) f. Κάλλων Sypalettos i AD II² 7495	[Πο]σειδωνί[ου] or <Πο>σειδωνί<ου>. ?Family traceable back to iv BC; see Κάλλων **(21)**, Ἀντίπατρος **(56)–(58)**, Λυσικλῆς **(41)–(43)**, etc.
60.	Τει[σικλῆ]ς (2) s. Τεισικλῆς (3, who was also f. Εὐκτήμων) Aphidna iv BC II² 1927, 119; *Hesperia* 9 (1940) 58, no. 7	Or Τεί[σαρχο]ς, Τεί[σιάδη]ς, Τεί[σιππο]ς. If Euktemon was eldest son, however, our man might be a second (or later) son named for his father
61.	[Τ]εισικράτεια (3, of three) d. Ἀλκίμαχος Angele s. iv BC *AD* 18 (1963) Chron. p. 45, 4	[Π?]εισικράτεια. Cf. S. Lambert, *Rationes Centesimarum*, Amsterdam 1997, 152. [Τε]ισικράτεια **(2)** may also be [Πε]ισικράτεια
***62.**	[Τελεσ?]ήγορος (2, unique hell.) ATHENS 183/2? BC *Ag.* XV 182, 8	Or [Εὐ]ήγορος, [Ἰσ]ήγορος |

Table (*cont.*)

LGPN II/*FRA*	REVISION
63. [Τελεσῖ]νος (4) s. Τελεσῖνος Acharnai 267/6? BC *SEG* XXI 671, 10	Or [Λυσῖ]νος. ?Family link with Λυσῖ[νος] **(3)** Acharnai 203/2 BC
***64.** [Τελε]σφόρος (6) Gargettos 165/6 AD II² 2090, 52 (father of ephebe)	[Ἀνθε]σφόρου. = f. Εὐφράνωρ **(15)** Gargettos, ephebe 163/4 AD
65. [Τ]ηρεύς (2. Only other case on II² 2478a, 5, a Verzeichnis von Männern und Frauen geringeren Standes, *Beiträge,* 76, no. 63) ATHENS* c. 175 AD *SEG* XXIX 152 V, 86 (father of *epengraphos*)	[Ν?]ηρεύς. Name attested in this period for seven citizens and three times on ephebic lists, for an *epengraphos* and two fathers of *epengraphoi*
66. Τιμαρχ[ίδης] (8) f. Κηφίσιος Ikarion s iv BC II² 4605 (dedication)	Or Τιμάρχ[ου]
67. Τίμ[αρχος] (12) ATHENS? i BC–i AD (date, *IOrop)* II² 4857 (= *IOrop* 462), 3. Text of 1–5: Ἀρίστω[ν καὶ] | Ἀσκληπ[ιάδης] | και Τίμ[αρχος οἱ] | Τιμάρχ[ου τὴν ἑαυ]|τῶν μητ[έρα Φιλί]|ππαν Τι[- κτλ.	No restoration. Many possible names. Alternative text: Τίμ[- καὶ] | Τιμάρχ[ος]. (The restoration of lines 1–2 is also uncertain. Cf. *I Orop* 554 and II² 7746)
68. Τιμ[όδα]μ[ος]? (1, unique) ATHENS* iv BC II² 2420, 17	As **8.** Add to *LGPN* IIIA
69. [Τ?]ι[μ?]όμαχος (6) f. -ς Hippothontis c. 130 BC II² 964, 4	[Φ]ιλομάχου (reading, *CIG* 232; restoration cf. Φιλόμαχος **(1)–(3)**)
70. [Τιμ]ο[σθέ]νης (9) s.Τιμ[οσ]θ[έν]ης Phyle c. 323 BC XII (9) 1242, 27	[Δημ?]ο[σθέ]νης. ?Family link with Δημοσθένης **(44)** s. -λος Phyle
***71.** [Τι]μόστρατ[ος] (2) ATHENS m. iv BC II² 2325, 246 (*TrGF* I p. 250 no. 83)	Τ̣[ι]μόστρατ[ος] (new reading, autopsy, uncertain) or [Δη]μόστρατ[ος] (more common name)
***72.** [Τλημπό?]λεμος (7) f. Ἀρε[- Euonymon 402/1 BC *Ag.* XIX P 2 g, [10], cf. *APF* 12888. Spacing suggests Ἀρέ[σιππος (2 only in *LGPN* II)	Or Ἀρε[σίας Μνησιπτο]λ̣έμου. ?Family link with Ἀρεσίας **(7)** s. Φ[-] Euonymon iv BC
73. [Τλή]σων (4) s. Τλησιμένης Athmonon m. iv BC II² 2385, 8	Or [Κτή]σων. ?Family link with Κτήσων **(11)** and **(12)** Athmonon
74. [Τρ?]όφ(ιμος?) (24) Paionidai ?ii AD II² 2211, 11	No restoration. Very many possibilities
75. [Τυ]χωνίδης (1, unique) ATHENS? ?iv BC *CIA* App. 9, 10	[Ἀρ?]χωνίδης, [Κι?]χωνίδης, both attested.
341 **76.** Χοραγίων (1, unique) ATHENS* iv BC II² 2420, 9	As **8** |

CHAPTER FIFTEEN

POLIS AND THEATRE IN LYKOURGAN ATHENS: THE HONORIFIC DECREES*

Despite their potential for illuminating relations between polis and theatre, inscribed decrees of the Assembly honouring foreigners for services relating to Athenian drama have attracted little recent attention from either epigraphists or historians.[1] My purpose here is to take a step towards rectifying the situation by presenting fresh texts and translations of the ten inscriptions of this type which are intended for inclusion in fascicle 2 of *IG* II^3 (352/1–322/1).

Demosthenes 21, against Meidias, delivered in 347/6, is our principal literary source for the special Assembly which regularly took place in the theatre of Dionysos after the City Dionysia in Elaphebolion. It contains the texts of two laws, both mainly about the bringing of formal legal complaints (*probolai*) at this Assembly for offences committed during the festival.[2] The second law seems to | envisage special 53

* This chapter was previously published in A.P. Matthaiou and I. Polinskaya (eds.), *Mikros Hieromnemon. Meletes eis mnemen Michael H. Jameson* (Athens, 2008), 53–85. It is a privilege to present this paper on honorific decrees for theatrical people in a volume in honour of Michael Jameson, though, as I knew him, he was neither histrionic nor much troubled by *philotimia*. I found in him rather a generous spirit and a profound scholarly mind of great range (the lemmata he prepared for *IG* I^3 are outstanding in my view). For helping me to improve earlier drafts of this paper I am grateful to Josine Blok, Nick Fisher and Peter Wilson. None of them is responsible for remaining flaws.

[1] There is no mention of them, for example, in the appendix to chapter II of A. Pickard Cambridge, *The Dramatic Festivals of Athens*, Oxford ^{2}1968, introduced, somewhat misleadingly (p. 101), "this appendix contains a transcript of practically all the inscriptions bearing on the Dionysia and Lenaia".

[2] Dem. 21.8 (providing for the special Assembly, that it should deal first with sacred matters and then *probolai* relating to the festival) and 21.10 (preventing distraint during the festivals and providing for *probolai* at the special Assembly in cases of attempted distraint). Discussed by MacDowell, 226–36 and most recently by A. Scafuro, *Dike* 7 (2004) 113–33. Dem. 21 arises from Demosthenes' formal complaint, lodged at the special meeting after the City Dionysia of 349/8, that, while performing his duties as *choregos,* he had been physically assaulted by Meidias. The text of the first law in Dem. 21 is corrupt, but as conventionally amended it specifies, somewhat obscurely, that the Assembly is to take place on the day after the Pandia (cf. Parker, *Polytheism* 477–8). Other evidence suggests that the date of the Assembly and the length of the City Dionysia (which apparently began on 10 Elaphebolion) were

Assemblies after other performance festivals, the Dionysia in Piraeus, the Lenaia[3] and the Thargelia, and in *IG* II^2 350 = Osborne, *Nat.* D39 an Assembly which apparently took place in Anthesterion[4] of an uncertain year (318/7?) is designated ἐν Διονύσου,[5] but elsewhere in inscriptions ἐν Διονύσου refers to the special meeting after the City Dionysia (or possibly, in very fragmentary cases where the date is not preserved, meetings after other performance festivals). *IG* II^2 212 = Rhodes-Osborne 94, of 347/6, appears to confirm the implication of the laws in Dem. 21 that the Assembly was devoted to matters arising from the festival.[6] The rest of the epigraphic record bears this out. It
54 seems | that all decrees passed at this special Assembly dealt, or can be interpreted as having dealt, with matters connected with the City Dionysia.

From *IG* II^2 223 = *Ath. State* I no. 1 (cf. *Ath. State* II 127–8) we learn that, at the Assembly ἐν Διονύσου in 342, the People honoured the Council for its successful management of public order, τῆς εὐκοσμίας

---

not always the same. *IG* II^2 212 appears to imply that the Assembly took place before 18 Elaphebolion in 347/6 (see below); no. 1–no. 4 show that it was on 19 Elaphebolion in 332/1; *IG* II^2 780, 781, 896 and perhaps 929, on 21 Elaphebolion in years of the 3rd and 2nd centuries. See also notes to no. 7 and no. 9 (below). Cf. D.M. Lewis, *CR* 91 (1977) 216. MacDowell, 227–8, based on Aeschin. 2.61 and 3.68, argues for 17 Elaphebolion in 347/6. This may be right (a slightly earlier date is not impossible), but we can not infer a general rule from the date attested in a single year. Cf. C. Pélékidis, *Histoire de l'éphébie attique*, Paris 1962, 301–6.

[3] Cf. perhaps *IG* II^2 18 = Rhodes-Osborne 10.

[4] Ἀνθεστ]ηριῶνος Ε[- (l. 4). The crucial rho in the month name is dotted in *IG* II^2, undotted by Osborne, who adds a dotted eta before it. I could not confirm the H from the stone but the trace following does give the impression of P and does not look consistent with Λ.

[5] This decree does not obviously relate to theatrical matters and none of the festivals listed in the law at Dem. 21.10 took place in Anthesterion. It is conceivable that we have to do with the Anthesteria, at which there were rites performed in the Dionysion ἐν Λίμναις on 12 Anthesterion, Thuc. 2.15, cf. most recently Humphreys, *Strangeness* 223–75, especially 226–7 and 254, below n. 18 and Parker, *Polytheism* chapter 14, but Assemblies took place "in the theatre" on other occasions, e.g. at the beginning of the ephebes' second year of service (*Ath. Pol.* 42.4, the location, of course, has a suitably paideutic resonance), and *IG* II^2 350 may be a unique instance of an Assembly there unrelated to a dramatic festival being termed ἐν Διονύσου. In decree prescripts from iii BC onwards such Assemblies were encompassed by the designation, ἐν τῶι θεάτρωι (but as correctly noted by J. Dillery, *CQ*^{2} 52 [2002] 46, there is no well founded earlier instance).

[6] At ll. 56–7 an item of business is to be taken not, as the usual formula has it, "at the next Assembly", but at the Assembly "on the eighteenth", the "next Assembly" being avoided because it was the special Assembly after the Dionysia and so unavailable for other business. For this interpretation see Reusch, 41; D.M. Lewis, *ABSA* 50 (1955) 25–6 ("always for business arising out of the festival").

τοῦ θεάτρου, at the festival and that, on the motion of Phanodemos of Thymaitadai (the Atthidographer, *FGH* 325, cf. *Ath. State* I 87), the Council provided for that decree to be inscribed.[7] After about 340 prescripts of decrees tended to become more detailed, sometimes including specifications of the type of meeting at which a decree was passed, and ἐκκλησία ἐν Διονύσου appears for the first time in a prescript in no. 1 and no. 4 of 332/1. On no. 2 and no. 3 this designation does not appear but the date in the prescript is the same. In other words all four decrees were passed at the same Assembly.[8] No. 1 honours a son of Onoma-, perhaps an actor, no. 2 Amphis of Andros, apparently the comic poet of that name. In no. 3, for a son of Aristeides and no. 4, for a son of -emos of Plataia, the character of the honorands' services is not recoverable, but the fact that the decrees were passed at the Assembly ἐν Διονύσου ought to imply that they related to the festival. Moreover a connection may be made between no. 4 and no. 5, which, two years later, honoured Eudemos son of Philourgos of Plataia inter alia (ll. 15–18) because he had donated 1,000 oxen towards the construction "of the stadium and the Panathenaic theatre" (see note on no. 5). In no. 6 the honorands had apparently contributed towards the construction of a *skene*, which may well be that of the new theatre of Dionysos. In no. 7, passed at the Assembly ἐν Διονύσου in the last year of the classical democracy, 322/1, the honorands' services are again not recoverable. No. 8 of the 330s or 320s honoured an actor, as did no. 9, passed apparently at an Assembly | ἐν Διονύσου in the period 337–323. 55
The honorand of the latter may have been Nikostratos. No. 10, which perhaps dates to the 320s, also honoured a Nikostratos, possibly the same man, possibly another actor of the same name, possibly the performer of some other function which justified honours for "rendering good service to a succession of *choregoi* at the City Dionysia".

---

[7] Cf. *IG* II^2 354 = *Ath. State* I no. 11, which honoured a priest of Asklepios inter alia for making himself useful to the superintendents of good order in the theatre (οἱ λαχόντες ἐπιμελητ[α]ὶ τῆς εὐκοσμίας τῆς περ[ὶ] τὸ θέατρον, ll. 15–17). The Asklepieion neighboured the theatre on the south slope of the acropolis. This decree was not, however, passed at the special Assembly, but at a regular Assembly on the last day of Elaphebolion, 328/7. It is possible that *IG* II^2 2827 = *Ath. State* I no. 23 also honoured officials in connection with the City Dionysia (cf. *Ath. State* II 128). The concern of these decrees with order and restraint is characteristic of this period. Cf. N. Fisher, *Aeschines: Against Timarchos*, Oxford 2001, 65–6.

[8] This is the only Assembly in the period 352/1– 322/1 which produced four extant inscribed decrees.

The awards are significant, but not extravagant (none of the decrees bestows the highest honour, citizenship).[9] As usual in honorific decrees, crowns are bestowed, a gold one for the actor (?) in no. 1 and a foliage one for Eudemos of Plataia, both unremarkable. Amphis the poet, however, receives a more unusual ivy crown, suitable to services to Dionysos, the first such award in an inscribed state decree.[10] No. 1 and no. 2 both bestow the status most commonly awarded a foreign honorand at this period, *proxenos* and benefactor. More unusually Eudemos is designated a benefactor without receiving the proxeny. The character of the other awards he receives suggest that he may have been a metic, as apparently were the honorands of no. 6 and no. 10.[11]

The erection clauses of no. 1, no. 5 and no. 6 are preserved, showing that they were set up on the acropolis, and the findspots of the other fragments would be consistent with original placement there. On the other hand decrees were occasionally set up in the area of the theatre of Dionysos, including, to judge from its discovery there, *IG* II^2 18 = Rhodes-Osborne 10, in 393 for Dionysios of Syracuse, proposed by the poet Kinesias, and at this period (ca. 340–330) *IG* II^2 410, honouring priests (including a priest of Dionysos) and *hieropoioi*, also found close to the theatre.[12] The findspots of no. 2 and no. 9 in particular would also be consistent with original placement in the theatre; and in the hellenistic period *IG* II^2 780 and 896, carrying decrees passed at the special Assembly, were set up in the precinct (*temenos*) of Dionysos, as apparently was *IG* II^2 657, not passed at that Assembly, but honouring the poet Philippides and found in the same area. The general pattern
56 is that before 321 the large majority of Athenian decrees | were set up on the acropolis, with some dispersal to "specialist" sites observable in the hellenistic period;[13] but the theatre of Dionysos seems to have been available and in at least occasional use at our period as a site for erecting decrees. If my interpretation of no. 4, no. 5 and no. 6 is correct,

[9] For the types of honour awarded in Athenian decrees see Henry, *Honours; Ath. State* III A 115–9.

[10] Cf. Henry, *Honours* 40.

[11] Cf. Whitehead, *Ath. Metic* 29–30.

[12] The erection clause of this decree specifies that it is to be set up in the theatre of Dionysos. I suggested in D. Jordan and J. Traill eds., *Lettered Attica*, Athens 2003, 57–67 (*SEG* LI 76), that after this clause the words "in the Piraeus" were originally inscribed and then erased and that the priests honoured all served Piraeus cults. Cf. *ZPE* 135 (2001) 52 no. 3; *Ath. State* I no. 10.

[13] Cf. P. Liddel, *ZPE* 143 (2003) 79–93 (theatre/sanctuary of Dionysos, pp. 91–2).

building work on the theatre may have been underway in the late 30s. In addition at this period a new temple and stoa were apparently built in the adjoining precinct.[14] It is possible that, while in progress, this work adversely affected the attractiveness or practicability of this area as a place for erection of decrees, but it is uncertain whether this was a factor influencing the placement of at least some of our group on the acropolis.

Except for no. 5 these inscriptions are mostly too fragmentary to be very informative individually. They acquire significance mainly as a group. Apart from one or two early outliers honouring poets (no actor seems to have been honoured on an extant inscribed Athenian state decree before the 330s), they are the first inscribed decrees to honour foreigners for their services to Athenian theatre and, while there continue to be occasional decrees of this type in the hellenistic period (though none explicitly for an actor)[15] such decrees never again occur with such frequency. As often with the emergence of genres of decree, there is some uncertainty about how far the novelty consisted in the passing of the decrees, how far in inscribing them. Epigraphic activity at Athens reached a peak of intensity in the Lykourgan period and, for example, while some Athenians had been honoured by decree at least since the 5th century, such decrees only began to be inscribed regularly in the 340s.[16] On the other hand it is clear enough that the inscribing of an honorific decree represented an enhancement of the honour bestowed and the efflorescence of this "theatrical" genre around the 330s should undoubtedly also be connected with the promotion of the City Dionysia and other aspects of Athenian theatre, and of festal and cultural life more broadly, which is a well-known | 57
feature of Lykourgan Athens and which is apparent, for example, in the establishment of the tragic canon as symbolised by the erection in the theatre of bronze statues of Aeschylus, Sophocles and Euripides and

[14] Cf. J. Travlos, *Pictorial Dictionary of Ancient Athens*, London 1971, 537–9; Hintzen-Bohlen, 21–9.

[15] In *IG* II^2 713 (early iii BC) the honorand [Arist]on son of Echthatios of Thebes was restored by Wilhelm as a pipe-player at the Dionysia (see Add. p. 666). In a non-dramatic context, from the later 3rd cent. pipe-players were also honoured with other Council officials in prytany inscriptions (*Agora* XV, pp. 11–12). In the classical period their epigraphical appearances in festival contexts are otherwise on monuments celebrating or recording victories, *IG* II^2 3042 etc., *IG* II^2 2311; cf. I.E. Stephanis, Διονυσιακοί Τεχνῖται, Herakleion 1988.

[16] Cf. *Ath. State* I, *Ath. State* II section I; *Ath. State* III B, note 158.

by the fixing of authoritative texts of their works, and in the rebuilding of the theatre of Dionysos to which two or three of our decrees may relate.[17] Lykourgos is associated in our sources with these and other theatre-related projects and it is no surprise that he is the proposer of two of the decrees in our group.[18] More striking is the fact that the other outstandingly prominent politician of the 30s and 20s, Demades, was also responsible for two. It is frustrating that both are so poorly preserved, for if their theatrical subject matter could be confirmed it might enhance Brun's recent attempt to give us a more rounded and balanced portrait of this politician than has conventionally been conveyed by the negative "spin" of the literary record. There seems to be no other firm evidence for his engagement with the theatre, though it is interesting to consider these two inscriptions alongside the 3rd century decree proposed by his homonymous grandson, *IG* II^2 713 + Add. p. 666, which honoured a Theban (pipe-player?) in a theatrical context and, as Peter Wilson points out to me, alongside the anecdote in Plut. *Phok.* 30 about allegations of Demades' illegal display of wealth in a *choregia* involving a large chorus of foreigners.[19] There may have been not only a greater rivalry between these two political giants of the 30s and 20s, but also a greater coincidence of purpose across a wider range of policy spheres than is sometimes recognised.[20] The other three

[17] [Plut.] *Mor.* 841f., 851f–852e; *IG* II^2 457. Cf. R. Parker, *Athenian Religion*, Oxford 1996, 242–55; Humphreys, *Strangeness* 77–129; Hintzen-Bohlen, 21–31. This spirit is also evident in non-state contexts, e.g. in building works in the Piraeus theatre (*SEG* XXXIII 143 = Schwenk 76, of 324/3) and in decrees of demes (e.g. *IG* II^2 1198 = Schwenk 66, Aixone, 326/5) and tribes (e.g. *IG* II^2 1157 = Schwenk 65) honouring *choregoi* (cf. Tracy, *ADT* 12).

[18] Other projects: e.g. he proposed that *komoidoi* compete in the theatre at the Chytroi (last day of the Anthesteria, cf. above n. 5), the winner to qualify automatically as an actor at the City Dionysia. [Plut.] *Mor.* 841f; Humphreys, *Strangeness* 254; Parker, *Polytheism* 297.

[19] On this passage see also Brun, *Démade* 151–3. For another anecdote about Demades which might have a theatrical context see Humphreys, *Strangeness* 255.

[20] Coincidence of purpose: e.g. service together on a Pythais, *Syll.*^{3} 296 = *FD* III 1 no. 511, and on the board of *epimeletai* of the Amphiaraia, 329/8, Schwenk no. 50 = *Ath. State* I no. 17. Rivalry: e.g. Lykourgos apparently opposed the proposal to grant Demades the *megistai timai*, Athen. 11.476d, Lyk. fr. IX (ed. Conomis), fragments 57–60 (ed. Blass). Apart from the Assembly after the City Dionysia in 332/1 they both proposed decrees at the same Assembly in 334/3 (Schwenk 23–25, cf. *Ath. State* I 108 no. 21) and 328/7 (*IG* II^2 399 and 452, cf. *Ath. State* III no. 56). Cf. C. Habicht, *Chiron* 19 (1989) 1–5. To an extent at least the reputations of Lykourgos as "anti-Macedonian" and Demades as "pro-Macedonian" are a product of rhetorical posturing of opponents (of Demades) and supporters (of Lykourgos and Demosthenes), at the time and subsequently. See most recently Brun, *Démade* 79–81, 139–42.

proposers whose | names are partially preserved (no. 1, no. 2, no. 9) 58
are all different men, consistent with the general impression conveyed by the epigraphical record that, while a few politicians may have been particularly prominent, at this period policy was made and carried forward by a reasonably broad base of politically active citizens. That policy in this case was to give expression to the Periclean idea that Athens should be the *paideia* of Greece,[21] not precisely in the overbearing imperial manner of the 5th century, but rather to an extent by redeploying the cultural products of that age, above all Athenian drama, and by exploiting the symbolic capital associated with them, to bolster the city's status at a time when political and military power were ebbing away.[22]

As Humphreys puts it, "attention was paid to the face which Athens turned to visitors from the rest of Greece".[23] Demosthenes has Meidias caricature the Assembly after the City Dionysia as a meeting at which he was condemned "by those who left the *phrouria*, chorus-members, foreigners and all that sort" (Dem. 21. 193). Making due allowance for rhetorical distortion and exaggeration, it is not implausible that this Assembly was commonly attended by an unusually large number of people, perhaps including foreigners.[24] It is striking that the impression given by this speech is that the meeting was occupied with a negative agenda, *probole* actions and the pursuit of malefactors; but it is also wholly characteristic that it is the epigraphical record of the the late 40s, 30s and 20s that turns to us the meeting's positive face as a forum in which wide exposure could be given to honours awarded in the context of one of the city's leading cultural institutions.[25]

It is illuminating to consider our group in the context of the full
corpus of | inscribed Athenian decrees honouring foreigners at this 59

[21] Cf. Humphreys, *Strangeness* 120.

[22] The conscious appropriation of the glories of 5th cent. Athens was a notable feature of the "Lykourgan" agenda. Another epigraphical example: *Ath. State* II no. 3.

[23] *Strangeness* 87.

[24] Cf. Wilson, *Khoregia* 167 with note 55, on the possibility that non-Athenians might have been eligible to lodge formal complaints (*probolai*) at this Assembly.

[25] Of course it is possible that there was some change in the legal arrangements for this meeting between the time the laws cited in Dem. 21 were passed and the 330s. However, the scope of business at this special Assembly does not, I think, have any direct connection with the issue between Demosthenes and Aeschines in the *De Corona* case, whether crowns awarded by the People (i.e. at a regular Assembly meeting) could be announced (not at the special meeting after the festival but) during the Dionysia itself (Aeschin. III 47 etc.).

period.[26] Such decrees, potent levers in the honour-driven world of Greek diplomacy,[27] are by far the most numerous type of inscribed decree. 150 survive from the period 352/1–322/1 (from a total of about 270 laws and decrees of all types). 60 or so are sufficiently fully worded and well preserved to be informative about their context. About 30 of these, i.e. around half, are concerned directly or indirectly with military-political diplomacy directed for or against Macedon, roughly two thirds of them relating to the period before Chaironeia (including decrees honouring Athenian supporters in exile at Athens after the battle), a third after (some "pro-Macedonian", some "anti-Macedonian" from the Lamian war period). 12 honour grain traders and represent an attempt by Athens to counteract the damaging effects of her loss of power after Chaironeia (including dissolution of the Second Athenian League) on the security of her food supply at a time of widespread shortages. Our 10 connected with the theatre form the third main subcategory, similar in size and roughly coincident in time of origin, with the decrees honouring grain traders.

In a world where the city's political and military capacity to secure its food supplies was much diminished, it was obliged to rely to an extent on the good will of grain traders, to be secured in part by the prospect of honours. There was undoubtedly a comparable dynamic operating in the theatrical sphere. By the Lykourgan period the Greek theatre had many of the attributes of an entertainment "industry", with fierce competition to attract international "star" poets and actors, by financial or other incentives. Alexander is said to have paid off a fine imposed on the actor Athenodoros for failing to appear at the City Dionysia in order to appear instead at one of his own festivals; and to have given 10 talents to the comic actor Lykon. In 306 Samos

[26] For an annotated list of these see *Ath. State* III. The sample of decrees we possess is probably sufficiently large and random to be broadly representative of the major diplomatic preoccupations of the Assembly at this time.

[27] This may be illustrated by the wording of a decree such as *IG* II² 402 + *SEG* XLII 91: "...in order that as many as possible of the friends of the king and of Antipater, having been honoured by the Athenian People, may benefit the city of the Athenians...". The honour is expected to have an influence on the behaviour of the honorand with respect to the city that grants it. Note also the "hortatory intention" clauses, which appear in honorific decrees from about 350 and which state that the honour is granted to encourage emulation of the honorand by others in the expectation that they too will be honoured (A.S. Henry, *ZPE* 112 [1996] 105–19). *Philotimia* becomes an explicitly recognised virtue in honorific decrees of the state at about the same time, cf. D. Whitehead, *C & M* 34 (1983) 55–74; Rhodes-Osborne pp. 232–3.

honoured the actor Polos for reducing his fee and | accepting deferred 60
payment in exchange for the entire box-office proceeds. Lykourgos himself proposed a decree offering large cash prizes (600 to 1,000 drachmas, say roughly twice a normal annual wage) for dithyrambic poets in the Piraeus; and it is clear that, like modern celebrities, "star" performers could acquire "elite" levels of wealth.[28] There appears to be no decree of this period honouring a contemporary *Athenian* poet or dramatist. If Athens wished to showcase itself as the leading city of Greek drama, there was patently a realisation that this was to be achieved not only by building splendid theatres and putting up statues of the best Athenian dramatists of the past. The city also needed to exert itself to attract international "star" performers, and she did so by offering both financial incentives and, as our decrees indicate, the less tangible, but no less real, incentive of honour. Like grain traders, star poets, actors and theatrical benefactors were to be admitted to the same "hall of fame" as the military and political figures who had traditionally been the major recipients of state honours.

The way decrees honouring theatrical people jostled (both metaphorically and, one may imagine, literally on the acropolis) with those motivated by political and military diplomacy directed at Macedon and by food supply concerns also illustrates nicely the interpenetration of theatrical and "real" political and economic life in 4th century Athens.[29] The same phenomenon is observable in an institution such as liturgies, in which the trierarchy and *choregia* competed, as it were in the same arena, for the attention of wealthy benefactors; by legal cases with both theatrical and "real" life dimensions, such as that in which Demosthenes delivered his speech against Meidias;[30] and in the use of the theatre of Dionysos as a meeting place of the Assembly and as one of the few locations other than the acropolis itself where state decrees were sometimes erected. The special Assembly in the theatre

---

[28] On this aspect of the 4th century Greek theatre see especially E. Csapo in C. Hugoniot, F. Hurlet and S. Milanezi eds., *Le statut de l'acteur dans l'antiquité grecque et romaine*, Tours 2004, 53–75. Athenodoros and Lykon: Plut. *Alexander* 29; Polos: *IG* XII 6, 56; Lykourgos: [Plut.] *Mor*. 842a. Foreign dramatists at Athens: e.g. Anaxandrides of Rhodes or Kolophon, *PCG* II 236; Apollodoros of Karystos, *PCG* II 485–501, perhaps, like Amphis (see below), made an Athenian citizen (Sud. a 3404, *PCG* II 486). Foreign actors: Csapo, *op. cit.*, 68–9.

[29] On the reverse aspect of this interpenetration, i.e. the prevalence of political themes in Athenian drama, see most recently P.J. Rhodes, *JHS* 123 (2003) 104–19.

[30] This point is well brought out in the context of the *choregia* and court cases by Wilson, *Khoregia*.

was located right on the intersection between the theatrical and the political and the overlapping of these spheres of human activity seems
61 to have | been a feature of some of the individual decrees passed at it. It is evident in one of the few honorific decrees from before the 330s with theatrical connections, *IG* II² 18 = Rhodes-Osborne 10, set up in the theatre of Dionysos in 393 and proposed by the dithyrambic poet Kinesias. It honoured a fellow poet, but he was no ordinary theatrical professional, but Dionysios of Syracuse, archon of Sicily as the decree describes him, whose political support Athens was doubtless eager to acquire. A political agenda also patently informs some later decrees of this type. Philippides, for example, poet and honorand of *IG* II² 657 in the early 3rd century, was an influential figure at the court of Lysimachos.[31] Previous to his donations to building projects Eudemos of Plataia (no. 5) had promised a financial contribution "to the war" and one might suspect that Athens' famous and traditionally close political relationship with Plataia was relevant to the circumstances of this decree and no. 4.[32] Otherwise the fragmentary state of our group of decrees makes it difficult to tell how far they also had a "real world" political subtext. One might suspect it of the two proposed by the great diplomatist Demades, but the circumstances of these decrees are wholly obscure (note also no. 8). In connection with Amphis one might recall that Athens had sought help from Andros after Chaironeia (cf. Lyk. 1.42) and that among those forced into exile at Athens after the battle were two Andrians, whose courage, ἀνδραγαθία (during the battle?), was recognised by *IG* II² 238 = Schwenk 2 = *Ath. State* III A no. 32. According to the Suda Amphis was an Athenian.[33] If this can be taken reliably to imply that he subsequently obtained Athenian citizenship (cf. Osborne, *Nat.* III–IV PT 138) his accumulated services must have been substantial. Our decree awards him the lesser (but still considerable) honour of proxeny, but it is notable that he is praised in it for his "justice", δικαιοσύνη, a quality normally attributed in the formulaic language of honorific decrees to Athenian officials, not foreigners.[34] May we infer that Amphis had fulfilled an office normally

[31] Plut. *Demetr.* 12.

[32] Though resident at Athens (ll. 28–30), however, Eudemos was patently not entitled to Athenian citizenship, i.e. apparently was not a descendant of those Plataians to whom citizenship had been granted in 427. See [Dem.] LIX 104; Osborne, *Nat.* D1; Whitehead, *Ath. Metic* 24 note 74, 29–30.

[33] Ἄμφις, κωμικός, Ἀθηναῖος, Sud. a 1760; *PCG* II 214.

[34] Veligianni-Terzi, *Wertbegriffe* p. 105; D. Whitehead, *C&M* 44 (1993), 67–8.

associated with citizen status? Had he produced a comedy at the City Dionysia of 331? Unfortunately we do not know. | 62

Texts[35]

1. FOR A SON OF ONOMA- (ACTOR?). Found in Agora. E. Schweigert, *Hesp.* 8 (1939) 26–7 no. 6 (ph.); Schwenk 39 (*SEG* XXXV 71); *Agora* XVI 79; *Ath. State* III no. 39. "Cutter of *IG* II^2 354", 337–324 (Tracy, *ADT* 107).

332/1 stoich. 29

[ἐπὶ Νικήτου ἄρχοντος ἐπὶ τῆς Ἀντιο]-
[χίδος ὀγδόης πρυτανείας ἧι Ἀριστό]-
[νο]υ[ς Ἀριστόνου Ἀναγυράσιος ἐγραμ]-
[μά]τευ[ε]ν· Ἐ[λαφηβολιῶνος ἐνάτηι ἐπὶ]
[δέ]κα, ἑβδό[μηι τῆς πρυτανείας· ἐκκλη]-
[σία] ἐν Διο[νύσου· τῶν προέδρων ἐπεψή]-
[φιζ]εν Ν[ι]κ[όστρατος Κόπρειος· ἔδοξεν]
[τῶι δ]ήμωι· Ε[..........^{20}..........]
[...]ασιος εἶ[πεν· ἐπειδὴ.....^{9}.....ὁ ὑ]-
[ποκ?]ριτὴς[..........^{21}..........]
[...]ε προα[..........^{21}..........]
[...]τῶι Δ[.........^{19}........., δεδ]-
[όχθαι] τῶ[ι δήμωι ἐπαινέσαι....^{7}...]
[.]ν Ὀν[ο]μα[.......^{13}......καὶ στεφαν]-
[ῶ]σαι χρυσ[ῶι στεφάνωι· εἶναι δ' αὐτὸν]
[κ]αὶ πρόξε[νον καὶ εὐεργέτην τοῦ δήμ]-
[ο]υ τοῦ Ἀθη[ναίων αὐτὸν καὶ ἐκγόνους]
[α]ὐτοῦ· ἀνα[γράψαι δὲ τόδε τὸ ψήφισμα]
[ἐ]ν στήληι [λιθίνηι καὶ στῆσαι ἐν ἀκρ]-
[ο]πόλει· εἰ[ς δὲ τὴν ἀναγραφὴν τῆς στή]-
[λη]ς δοῦνα[ι τὸν ταμίαν τοῦ δήμου...]
[δρ]αχμὰς ἐκ [τῶν κατὰ ψηφίσματα ἀναλ]-
[ισ]κομένων [τῶι δήμωι].
vacat 0.055

Translation

In the archonship of Niketes (332/1), in the eighth prytany, of Antiochis, when Aristonous son of Aristonous of Anagyrous was secretary. On the nineteenth of | Elaphebolion, (5) the seventh of the prytany. 63

[35] I have examined all the inscriptions at autopsy. See also *Ath. State* III.

Assembly in the theatre of Dionysos. Of the presiding committee Nikostratos of Kopros was putting to the vote. The People decided. E- son of—of—proposed: since—(10) the actor (?)....the People shall decide, to praise—son of Onoma- [of -?] and (15) crown him with a gold crown; and he shall be *proxenos* and benefactor of the Athenian People, himself and his descendants; and to inscribe this decree on a stone stele and stand it on the acropolis; (20) and the treasurer of the People shall pay [20 or 30] drachmas for inscribing the stele from the People's fund for expenditure on decrees.

Note

Lines 7 and 9 (where the letters ΣΙΟ are inscribed in two stoichoi) apparently had 30 letters. The restorations are due mostly to Schweigert. || 9–10 ὁ ὑ|ποκ]ριτὴς is my suggestion, based on no. 8 and no. 9 and the fact that the decree was passed ἐν Διονύσου (ὁ Ἀ|βδη]ρίτης Meritt ap. Schweigert). || 11–12 One might think of προά[γωνι and τῶι Δ[ιονυσίων (cf. no. 10, 3–4), but there are other possibilities, e.g. προαι[ιρούμενος and Schweigert's τῶι δ[ήμωι.

2. FOR AMPHIS OF ANDROS (POET). *b* was found in the area of the Asklepieion. *b* S.A. Koumanoudes, Ἀθήναιον 6 (1877) 131–2 no. 6; *ab* A. Wilhelm, *AM* 15 (1890) 219–22; *IG* II 5, 173b (Köhler); *abc IG* II² 347; Schwenk 38; *Ath. State* III A no. 40. See also W.K. Pritchett, *CSCA* 5 (1972) 176; S.D. Lambert, *ZPE* 141 (2002) 117–8 note 5. "Cutter of *IG* II² 337", 337–323 (Tracy, *ADT* 114). The crowning relief probably depicted Amphis being crowned by Demos (Lawton 103 no. 45 (ph.)).

332/1 *a* [ἐπὶ Ν]ικήτου ἄρχοντος [ἐπὶ τ]- *b* stoich. 22
[ῆς Ἀν]τιοχίδος ὀγδοίη[ς πρυ]-
[τανεί]ας, ἧι Ἀριστόνου[ς Ἀρι]-
[στόν]ου Ἀναγυράσιος ἐ[γραμ]-
[μάτε]υεν· Ἐλαφηβολιῶν[ος ἐν]-
[άτει] ἐπὶ δέκα, ἑβδόμει τ[ῆς π]-
[ρυτα]νείας· τῶν προέδρω[ν ἐπ]-
[εψήφ]ιζεν [Ν]ικόστρατος [Κόπ]-
[ρειο]ς· ἔδο[ξ]εν τῶι δήμωι· [Ἀρι]-
[στόξ]ενος Κ̣[η]φισοδότου [...]
64 [...ε]ὺς εἶπεν· [ἐ]πειδὴ Ἄνφις Δι[...] |
[...Ἄ]νδριος διατελεῖ ἐ[...]-
[....] ὢ̣ν τῶι δήμωι τῶι Ἀθ[ηνα]-

[ίων κα]ὶ νῦν καὶ ἐν τῶ(ι) παρ[εληι]-
[λυθό]τι χρόνωι, δεδόχθαι [τῶι]
[δήμωι] ἐπαινέσαι Ἄνφιν [Δι .]-
[...⁵..] Ἄνδριον καὶ στεφ[ανῶ]-
[σαι κι]τ̣τοῦ [στε]φάνωι ἀρ[ετῆ]-
[ς ἕνεκα̣ καὶ δικ]αιοσύν[ης· εἶ]-
[ναι δὲ αὐτὸν πρ]όξενον [καὶ ε]-
[ὐεργέτην τοῦ] δήμου τ[οῦ Ἀθη]-
[ναίων καὶ ἐκγό]νο[υς...⁶...]
[-------------------------]

lacuna

[-------------- εἰς δὲ τὴν]
[ἀναγραφὴν τῆς στήλης δοῦν]-
[αι] τ̣[ὸν ταμία]ν τ̣οῦ [δήμου...]
δραχ̣μ̣[ὰ]ς ἐκ τῶν κ̣ατ[ὰ ψηφίσμ]-
ατα ἀ̣ναλισκομέν[ω]ν τ̣ῶ̣[ι δήμω]-
ι. *vac.*

vacat 0.515

Translation

In the archonship of Niketes (332/1), in the eighth prytany, of Antiochis, when Aristonous son of Aristonous of Anagyrous (5) was secretary. On the nineteenth of Elaphebolion, the seventh of the prytany. Of the presiding committee Nikostratos of Kopros was putting to the vote. The People decided. Aristoxenos (10) son of Kephisodotos of [Kephisia or Piraeus] proposed: since Amphis son of Di- of Andros has continued to be [well disposed?] towards the Athenian People, both now and (15) previously, the People shall decide: to praise Amphis son of Di- of Andros and crown him with an ivy crown for his excellence and justice; (20) and he shall be *proxenos* and benefactor of the Athenian People, himself and his descendants... [*text missing*]... and (25) the treasurer of the People shall give [30 *or* 20] drachmas for inscribing the stele from the People's fund for expenditure on decrees. | 66

Note

There are stoichedon irregularities in 11, 15 and 28 (crowding) and in 14 an iota is omitted. Restorations are due to Koumanoudes and Wilhelm (9–10 [Ἀρι|στόξ]ενος Köhler). The name Amphis is rare (not otherwise attested for an Athenian, *LGPN* II 28) and the identification of the honorand as the comic poet, *PCG* II pp. 213–35, first suggested by Koumanoudes, was argued convincingly by Wilhelm (cf. *Berl. phil. Wochenschr.* 1902, 1098). || 12–3 Though it does not suit the space, given the stoichedon irregularities elsewhere on this stone Wilhelm's ε[ὔ|νους] is possible. Cf. Veligianni-Terzi, *Wertbegriffe* 88 A147; D. Whitehead, *C & M* 44 (1993) 69 note 118 (*SEG* XLIX 101); ἐ[πιε|ικὴς] D.M. Lewis, *ABSA* 49 (1954) 37.

3. FOR A SON OF ARISTEIDES. Found on acropolis. *IG* II 174 (Köhler); *IG* II² 346; Schwenk 37; *Ath. State* III B no. 95. See also Henry, *Honours* 263. "Litt. volg. c. 345–c. 320" (Tracy, *ADT* 77).

I [---------------------------- ἐκ]
[τῶν κατὰ ψηφίσματ]α ἀν[αλισκομ]- stoich. 25
[ένων τῶι δήμωι· κα]λέσαι δ[ὲ αὐτὸ]-
[ν καὶ ἐπὶ ξένια] ε[ἰ]ς τὸ πρυ[τανεῖ]-
[ον εἰς αὔριον]. *vac.*
332/1 *II* [ἐπὶ Νικήτου] ἄρχοντος ἐπ[ὶ τῆς ᵛ]
[Ἀντιοχίδος] ὀγδόης πρυτα[ν]έ[ας],
[ἧι Ἀριστό]νους Ἀριστόνου Ἀν[αγ]-
[υράσιος ἐ]γραμμάτευεν· Ἐλαφ[ηβ]-
[ολιῶνος ἐν]άτηι ἐπὶ δέκα, ἑ[β]δόμ-
[ηι τῆς πρυτ]ανείας· τῶν προ[έ]δ[ρω]-
[ν ἐπεψήφιζε]ν Νικόστρατος Κό[π]-
[ρειος· ἔδοξε]ν τῶι δ[ήμ]ωι· Δημά[δη]-
[ς Δημέου Παια]νιεὺς εἶπεν· [ἐπει]-
[δὴ.....⁹....]ο[ς] Ἀρι[σ]τήιδ[ου..]
[....⁷... διατε]λεῖ εὔνους [ὢ]ν τ[ῶ]-
[ι δήμωι τῶι Ἀθηνα]ίω[ν] καὶ ὑ[....]
[.........¹⁷........]|καὶ [..]Ε[.]
[..........¹⁹.........]ΣΤ[..]Τ[.]
68 -------------------------------- |

Translation

I...from the People's fund for expenditure on decrees; and to invite him to hospitality in the *prytaneion* tomorrow.

II In the archonship of Niketes, in the eighth prytany, of Antiochis, when Aristonous son of Aristonous of Anagyrous was secretary. On the nineteenth of Elaphebolion, the seventh of the prytany. Of the presiding committee Nikostratos of Kopros was putting to the vote. Demades son of Demeas of Paiania proposed: since -os son of

Aristeides of—continues to be well-disposed towards the Athenian People and…

Note

I was perhaps a decree honouring (the same?) man in a different year. The invitation to hospitality (ξένια) rather than dinner (δεῖπνον) shows he was a foreigner. Restorations are due to Köhler (3–4 Henry, *Honours* 263, καὶ αὐτὸν Köhler). || 17 My tentative new readings might indicate ὑπ̣ε̣[κρίνατο (cf. no. 9) or more likely ὑπ̣ὲ̣ρ̣ (Y[previous editors).

4. FOR A SON OF [EUD?]EMOS OF PLATAIA. Both fragments found on acropolis. *IG* II 173 (Köhler); *IG* II^2 345 + Add. p. 659; Schwenk 36; *Ath. State* III B no. 96. "Cutter of *IG* II^2 334", c. 345–c. 320 (Tracy, *ADT* 84). There is a partially preserved crowning relief showing parts of a male (the honorand?) and female (Athena?) (Lawton 103 no. 44 (ph.)).

a θεοί. *vac.* stoich. 30

332/1 ἐπὶ Νικήτου ἄρ[χοντος ἐ]πὶ τῆς Ἀντιοχ- *b*
ίδος ὀγδόης π[ρυτανεία]ς ἧι Ἀριστόνο-
υς Ἀριστόνο[υ Ἀναγυράσι]ος ἐγραμ[μά]τ-
ευεν· Ἐλαφη[βολιῶνος ἐν]άτηι ἐπὶ δέκα,
ἑβδόμ[ηι τῆς πρυτανείας]· ἐκκλησία ἐν
[Διονύσου· τῶν προέδρων ἐ]πεψήφιζεν̣ Ν-
[ικόστρατος Κόπρειος· ἔδ]οξεν τῶι δήμ-
[ωι· Λυκοῦργος Λυκόφρονο]ς Βουτάδης ε-
[ἶπεν· ἐπειδὴ....^{7}...Εὐδ?]ήμου Πλα[τ]αι-
[εὺς πρότερόν τε ἐπηγγεί]λατο τ[ῶ]ι [δ]ήμ- | 70
[ωι.........^{18}.........]ς γίγνητ[α]ι τ̣-
[..........^{20}..........]αι ἀργυ[ρί]ου̣
[..........^{20}..........]ο̣ παρέ[σχε]ν τ-
[..........^{20}..........]ν καὶ ν̣[ῦ]ν̣ [ἐ]πι-
[δέδωκεν.......^{13}......]ΥΣΤ̣[....]ΓΟΥ
[...........^{21}..........]ΑΣ̣ΣΑ[...]ΗΚ
[...........^{21}..........]ΙΣ[...]ΝΤΟ
[..........^{19}.........ἐστ]εφ[άνωσ]αν?
[............^{23}...........]ΟΣ[..]υ̣ ἐπ-
[............^{24}............]αθ[η]ν̣αι-
[......^{12}......δεδόχθαι τῶι] δήμωι ἐπ-
[αίνεσαι......^{11}.....ήμου Πλατα]ιέα̣
- -

Translation

Gods. In the archonship of Niketes, in the eighth prytany, of Antiochis, when Aristonous son of Aristonous of Anagyrous was secretary. (5) On the nineteenth of Elaphebolion, the seventh of the prytany. Assembly in the theatre of Dionysos. Of the presiding committee Nikostratos of Kopros was putting to the vote. The People decided. Lykourgos son of Lykophron of Boutadai proposed:

(10) since—son of -emos of Plataia both previously announced to the People... so that there should be... money... provided.... (15) and has now donated... crowned him?... (20)... Athenians *(or* Panathenaia)... the People shall decide to praise—son of -emos of Plataia...

Note

The restorations are mainly Köhler's (7 in. was first restored by Reusch). In 15–23 the readings and restorations are mine. The most significant feature of this inscription is the parallels with no. 5:

(a) both were inscribed on unusually thick blocks;[36] (b) letter
71 sizes (c. 0.006) | and stoichedon grid (c. 0.0135) are the same. The script is very similar, though Tracy advises per ep. that the cutter may be different; (c) both were proposed by Lykourgos; (d) both honorands were Plataians, in no. 5 Eudemos son of Philourgos, in no. 4.....^{10}.....]ήμου. Εὔδημος is the only name in -ημος attested in Plataia (*LGPN* IIIB p. 152). H. Pope, *Non-Athenians in Attic Inscriptions* (New York 1935), 229, may be right that the honorand of no. 4 was Εὐδ]ήμου and related to the honorand of no. 5; (e) both texts begin with a reference to a previous benefaction and continue with a reference to a current one, in identical phraseology, ἐπειδὴ *honorand* πρότερόν τε ἐπηγγείλατο τῶι δήμωι.... καὶ νῦν ἐπιδέδωκεν. ἀργυ[ρί]ου at no. 4, 13, suggests that we have to do with a financial contribution; the honorand of no. 5 had offered to donate a sum of money towards a war fund. There may also be a connection between no. 4,

[36] The preserved thickness of no. 5 (the back of which has been reworked) is 0.21 (top)-0.24 m. (bottom). No. 4 (original back not preserved) is 0.35 thick. Compare the massive decree for Arybbas of Molossia (*IG* II^2 226 = Rhodes-Osborne 70), the largest extant Athenian honorific decree stele, which is just 0.25 thick. Cf. *Ath. State* II 129; III A 118. It seems possible that no. 4, in particular, was not inscribed on a normal stele.

ll. 20–22 and no. 5, ll. 18–21; in fact the precise wording of no. 5, πρὸ Παναθη|ναίων καθὰ ὑπέσχετο, δεδόχθαι τῶι δήμωι ἐπαινέσαι, could be accommodated at no. 4, 21–23.

In l. 16 earlier eds. restored a reference to a general (το]ῦ στ[ρατη]γοῦ). This is possible, but at autopsy I tentatively read Υ̣ΣΤΑ̣Σ̣[..] Ε̣ΟΥ.

5. FOR EUDEMOS SON OF PHILOURGOS OF PLATAIA. Both fragments found on the acropolis (b on north slope). *IG* II 176 (Köhler); *IG* II² 351 + 624 (Add. p. 660); Schwenk 48; Rhodes-Osborne 94; *Ath. State* III A no. 42. Lettering similar to no. 4 (but Tracy, per ep., advises that the cutter may be different).

a

[Ε ὐ δ ή μ] ο υ Π λ α τ α ι [έ ω ς]
330/29 [ἐπὶ Ἀρισ]τοφῶντος ἄρχοντο[ς *v*] stoich. 24
b [ἐ]π[ὶ τῆς] Λεωντίδος ἐνάτη[ς] π[ρυ]-
ταν[εία]ς, ἧι Ἀντίδωρος Ἀντίν[ου]
Παι[ανι]εὺς ἐγραμμάτευεν : ἐ[ν]-
[δ]εκά[τ]ηι Θαργηλιῶνος, ἐνάτη[ι]
[κ]αὶ δ[ε]κάτηι τῆς πρυτανείας· [*v*]
[τ]ῶν π[ρ]οέδρων ἐπεψήφιζεν Ἀντ[ι]-
φάνη[ς] Εὐωνυμεύς· ἔδοξεν τῶι [*v*]
[δήμωι]· Λυκοῦργος Λυκόφρονος
[Βουτά]δης εἶπεν· ἐπειδὴ *vac.*
[Εὔδημ]ος πρότερόν τε ἐπηγγ[εί]- | 73
[λατο τ]ῶι δήμωι ἐπιδώσειν [εἰ]ς
[τὸν π]όλεμον εἴ τ[ι] δέ[οι]το [XXX]X
[δ]ραχμὰς καὶ νῦν [ἐπ]ι[δέδ]ωκ[εν *v*]
εἰς τὴν ποίησιν τοῦ σταδ[ί]ου [*v*]
καὶ τοῦ θεάτρου τοῦ Παναθην[αϊ]-
κοῦ χίλια ζεύγη καὶ ταῦτα *vac.*
πέπομφεν ἅπαντα π[ρὸ Π]αναθη[*v*]-
ναίων καθὰ ὑπέσ[χετο, δ]εδόχθ[αι]
τῶι δήμωι ἐπαι[νέσαι Ε]ὔδημ[ον]
[Φι]λούργου Πλατα[ιέα] καὶ στ[ε*v*]-
φανῶσαι αὐτὸν θαλλõ στεφ[άνωι]
εὐνοίας ἕνεκα τῆς εἰς τὸν *vac.*
δῆμον τὸν Ἀθηναίων· καὶ εἶνα[ι]
αὐτὸν ἐν τοῖς εὐεργέταις το[ῦ]
δήμου τοῦ Ἀθηναίων, [α]ὐτὸν κα[ὶ]
ἐκγόνους, καὶ εἶ[ν]α[ι] αὐτῶι *vac.*
ἔνκτησιν γῆς καὶ οἰκίας, καὶ *v*
στρατεύεσθαι αὐτὸν τὰς *vac.*
στρατιὰς καὶ τὰς εἰσφορὰς*vv*

εἰσφέρειν μετὰ Ἀθηναίων· *vac.*
ἀναγράψαι δὲ τόδε τὸ ψήφισμα
τὸν γραμματέα τῆς βουλῆς καὶ
στῆσαι ἐν ἀκρ[ο]πόλει· εἰ[ς] δ̣[ὲ] τὴν
ἀναγραφὴν τῆς στήλη[ς δοῦ]ν̣αι
τὸν ταμίαν τοῦ δήμ[ο]υ̣ [- - -]
δραχμὰς ἐκ τῶν εἰς τὰ κα[τὰ ψη^{v}]-
φίσματα ἀναλισκομέν[ων τῶ]ι [^{v}]
δήμωι. *vac.*
vacat 0.40

Translation

Eudemos of Plataea
In the archonship of Aristophanes (330/29), in the ninth prytany, of Leontis, when Antidoros son of Antinous (5) of Paiania was secretary. On the eleventh of Thargelion, the nineteenth of the prytany; of the presiding committee Antiphanes of Euonymon was putting to
74 the vote. The People decided. (10) Lykourgos son of | Lykophron of Boutadai proposed: since Eudemos both announced previously to the People that he would donate for the war, should it be needed, [4,000] (15) drachmas, and now has donated for construction of the stadium and the Panathenaic theatre a thousand yoke of oxen and has sent them all before the Panathenaia, (20) as he promised, the People shall decide to praise Eudemos son of Philourgos of Plataia and crown him with a foliage crown for his good will towards the (25) Athenian People; and he shall be among the benefactors of the Athenian People, himself and his descendants, and shall have right of ownership of land and house and (30) to perform military service and pay capital taxes (*eisphorai*) on the same basis as Athenians; and the secretary of the Council shall inscribe this decree and (35) stand it on the acropolis; and the treasurer of the People shall give [20 or 30?] drachmas for inscribing the stele from the People's fund for expenditure on decrees.

Note

Underlined pairs of letters were inscribed in a single stoichos. The text was mostly established by A. von Velsen, *Arch. Zeit.* 17 (1859) *Anz.* 69–74. The top and back were reworked in the 1st cent. BC, when *IG* II^{2} 4233 was inscribed on the back. Either there was an unusually drastic ca. 10 day dislocation of the calendar in Thargelion of 330/29 or

there is an error in the prescript (perhaps, as suggested by G.F. Unger, *Philol.* 38, 1879, 426 and Suppl. V 1889, 672, the prytany date in ll. 6–7 should have been inscribed as 29th, ἐνάτηι καὶ εἰκοστῆι, rather than 19th, ἐνάτηι καὶ δεκάτηι). The Panathenaic stadium and the theatre of Dionysos were both building projects associated with Lykourgos ([Plut.] *Mor.* 841d. 852; *IG* II^2 457, *b* 5–7) and in the expression "stadium and Panathenaic theatre" in ll. 16–17 there may be another error, viz. "Panathenaic" may have been attached to the wrong noun.[37] In addition the text on this stone is arranged in an unusual fashion for this period, stoichedon but with systematic use of crowding and vacats at line-ends, some of them extensive, to achieve syllabified breaks.[38] The
apparent errors and | the unusual layout raise the possibility that this 76
decree might belong to a reinscription of decrees proposed by Lykourgos provided for in the decree honouring him in 307/6, as preserved at [Plut.] *Mor.* 852e (the inscribed version of this decree, *IG* II^2 457, breaks off before this passage),[39] but the physical similarities to no. 4 (see above), attributed by Tracy to a cutter whose latest firmly dated work belongs c. 320, argue against this, and the text in [Plut.], which appears to be corrupt at this point, may have provided for the erection of decrees relating to Lykourgos rather than decrees proposed by him.[40]

---

[37] Cf. Rhodes-Osborne p. 477. Alternatively "theatre" might mean the spectators' seats at the Panathenaic stadium (cf. A.P. Matthaiou, Τὸ θέατρον καὶ τὸ Λύκειον, in *Ἀμύμονα Ἔργα.* Τιμητικὸς τόμος γιὰ τὸν καθ. Βασ. Κ. Λαμπρινουδάκη, E. Simantoni-Bournia et al. (eds.), Athens 2007, 501–508.

[38] There is an increasing sporadic tendency towards syllabification in the period 352/1–322/1, achieved in stoichedon texts by occasional use of vacats and crowding (observable for example in *IG* II^2 354 = Schwenk 54, of 328/7) and in a handful of decrees by abandonment of stoichedon altogether, but the multiple extensive vacats and crowding in this case are unusual.

[39] ἀναθεῖναι δ' αὐτοῦ, καὶ εἶναι κύρια, πάντα τὰ ψηφίσματα τὸν γραμματέα τοῦ δήμου ἐν στήλαις λιθίναις καὶ στῆσαι ἐν ἀκροπόλει πλησίον τῶν ἀναθημάτων (ed. J. Mau, Teubner 1971). I am grateful to Peter Liddel for drawing my attention to this passage.

[40] There have been attempts to amend or reorder the wording (see the app. crit. of Mau's edition), but none has addressed the key point that decrees were not normally conceived of as being "of" their proposers ("that all his decrees be valid and that the secretary of the People inscribe them…" in Fowler's Loeb translation), but of the Athenian Council and People. In Athenian decrees the language used here usually expresses the thought that decrees voted *for* or *about* someone should be valid. Thus e.g. at *IG* II^2 275, 5–7, in Wilhelm's restoration, εἶνα|ι δὲ] κύρια [τ]ὰ ψηφίσμα[τα ὅσα Ἀθηναῖοι ἐψηφίσαντο | π]ερὶ αὐτ[οῦ, cf. K. Clinton, *The Sacred Officials of the Eleusinian Mysteries* (Philadelphia 1974), p. 18, ll. 9–11; *IG* II^2 1128, 11; *SEG* XVI 42, 17. One might therefore consider amending αὐτοῦ to περί αὐτοῦ or perhaps simply to αὐτῶι (cf. de Meziriac's amendment at 852d of MSS πράττοντος αὐτοῦ to πράττοντα αὐτῶι, accepted in Mau's text).

6. Findspot unknown. A.J. Heisserer and R.A. Moysey, *Hesp.* 55 (1986) 177–82 (ph.) [*SEG* XXXVI 149]; S.D. Lambert, *ZPE* 148 (2004) 184–6 no. 4; *Ath. State* III B no. 98. "Cutter of *IG* II² 334", c. 345–c. 320 (Tracy, *ADT* 87).

- - - - - - - - - - - - - - - - -

c. 330 [......13......]ΟΣ[........16........] stoich. 31
[......12......]ΙΣ̣ΙΟΣ[........15.......]
[.....10.....τὴ]ν σκην[ὴν......12......]
[.....10.....δωρ]εὰς διδ[......12......]
[.....10.....ἐ]παγωγη[.......14.......]
[......11.....]ι χρῆσθ[αι......12......]
[ἀτέλ-? το]ῦ μετοικ[ίου......11.....]
[ἐπιμελείσθ]ω δὲ ἡ βου[λὴ τῶν.....9....]
77 [....8....ω]ν οἷς ὁ δῆμ[ος......12......] |
[....τὴν δω]ρεάν, ὅπως ἂ[ν......12......]
[μηδ' ὑφ' ἑνὸς] ἀδικῶντα[ι· ἀναγράψαι δὲ τό]-
[δε τὸ ψήφισ]μα τὸν γρ[αμματέα τῆς βουλῆ]-
[ς καὶ στῆσαι ἐν ἀ]κ[ροπόλει·.....10.....]

- -

Translation

...[since *the honorand(s?)*..are making?] a donation...[towards] the stage building..., they (*or* he) shall be granted...(5) import (?)...use...exemption (?) from metic tax...and the Council shall take care of the—to whom the People...[has made] (10) the grant, so that...(*plural*) suffer no wrong; and the secretary of the Council shall inscribe this decree and stand it on the acropolis...

Note

In l. 2 the letters IO occupy one stoichos. The restorations in ll. 3–8 are those of Heisserer and Moysey. The line length and the text of 8 fin.-13 are mine (2004). A connection with no. 5 is created by the reference to the *skene* (l. 3) and by the identical inscribing clause (ll. 11–13), which might suggest that the secretary (i.e. year) or proposer (i.e. Lykourgos) were the same. On the *skene* of the theatre of Dionysos in the context of the rebuilding see Hintzen-Bohlen 28.

7. Found in Athens (τῆς κάτω πόλεως). S.A. Koumanoudes, Ἀρχ. Ἐφ. 1886, 101 no. 8 (A. Wilhelm, *Hermes* 24 [1889] 144–6); *IG* II² 372 + Add. p. 660; E. Schweigert, *Hesp.* 8 (1939), 173–5 no. 4 (ph.); Schwenk 87; *Agora* XVI 95. See also M.H. Hansen, *GRBS* 23 (1982) 345 no. 56; Tracy, *ADT* 152 note 2 (*SEG* XLV 81); *Ath. State* III B no. 150. "Cutter of *IG* II² 498", 321–302 (Tracy, *ADT* 152).

322/1 [ἐπὶ Φιλοκλέους ἄρχοντος ἐπὶ τῆς] stoich. 27
[...⁵..ίδος ὀγ]δό[ης πρυτανείας ἧι]
[Εὐθυγένης Ἡφ]αισ[τοδήμου Κηφισι]-
[εὺς ἐγραμμάτ]ευε[ν· Ἐλαφηβολιῶνο]-
[ς...⁶...ἐπ]ὶ δέκα, [...⁵..τῆς πρυτα]-
[νείας· ἐκκ]λησία ἐ[ν Διονύσου· τῶν π]-
[ροέδρων ἐ]πεψήφ[ιζεν.....¹⁰.....]
[....⁷...]ς· ἔδοξ[εν τῶι δήμωι· *vac.*] | 78
[Δημάδη]ς Δημέ[ου Παιανιεὺς εἶπεν]·
[ἐπειδὴ .]υκΟ[.........¹⁷........]

Translation

In the archonship of Philokles (322/1), in the eighth prytany, of—, when Euthygenes son of Hephaistodemos of Kephisia was secretary. (5) On the -teenth of Elaphebolion, the—of the prytany. Assembly in the theatre of Dionysos. Of the presiding committee—of—was putting to the vote. The People decided. Demades son of Demeas of Paiania proposed: (10) [since *or* about what] *name?...*

Note

The restorations are mostly due to Wilhelm. The date (l. 5) was perhaps 13, 18 or 19 Elaphebolion (τρίτηι, ἐνάτηι or ὀγδόηι at 5 in.).[41] The honorand (l. 10) was perhaps Ε]ὐκο- or Λ]υκο- or Ε]ὐκρ-.

[41] Cf. Schwenk, Hansen. *IG* II² 350 might induce one to consider the seventh prytany (ἑβ]δό[μης πρυτανείας in l. 2) and the month Anthesterion (ll. 4–5), but *IG* II² 371 shows that the name of the tribe which held the seventh prytany in 322/1 had 11 letters in the genitive. There is only space for nine letters in l. 2. Moreover, unless one assumes a gross calendrical or epigraphical irregularity, it seems impossible to find restorations to suit the space available in l. 5.

8. FOR AN ACTOR. Found on acropolis. Wilhelm, *UdA* 221; *IG* II^2 429; Ghiron-Bistagne, *Acteurs* 80–1 (ph.) [*SEG* XXVI 77]; *Ath. State* III B no. 75. See also Veligianni-Terzi, *Wertbegriffe* 104 A172. "Cutter of *IG* II^2 244", 340/39–ca. 320 (Tracy, *ADT* 98).

----
c. 340–320 --....^{7}...]ΑΡΕ[...] stoich.
--...^{5}..]ις αυτοι[.]
--....] ὑποκρινο[μ]-
--....]α καὶ οὐδει//
--...] ἀγῶνα τὸν [..]
-- ποι]εῖ ἀγαθὸ[ν..]
79 --....] κοινῆι [...] |
--....] Ἀθ[η]να[ι...]

The text is from the part of the decree which describes the honorand's services, which included "acting" (l. 3) and "nothing (or never) *verb*...the competition at the [Dionysia?]" and "doing what good he could...publicly [and privately?] for [the] Athenian [People]". Veligianni-Terzi notes that the language used implies that the honorand was a foreigner.

Note

1 π]αρε[χ- Wilhelm. || 4–5 οὐδέν A.R. Rangabé, *Antiquités helléniques* II (1855) no. 991, δράματ]α καὶ οὐδέπ̣|[οτε παραλείπων ? τὸν] ἀγῶνα τὸν Δ[ι|ονυσίων Wilhelm comparing *IG* XIV 1102.14 (μήτε ἀγῶνα παραλιπών). No-one else has read the delta in l. 5. || 6 ἀγαθὸ[ν ὅ τι δύναται vel sim. Veligianni-Terzi. || 7–8 καὶ] κοινῆι [καὶ | ἰδίαι τόν τε δῆμον τὸν] Ἀθη[ν]α[ίων (sic) καὶ Wilh.

9. FOR AN ACTOR. Found between theatres of Dionysos and Herodes Atticus. S.A. Koumanoudes, Ἀθήναιον 5 (1876) 184–5; Wilhelm, *UdA* 218–20; *IG* II^2 348; Ghiron-Bistagne, *Acteurs* 79 (ph.) (*SEG* XXVI 76); Schwenk 44; *Ath. State* III B no. 78. "Cutter of *IG* II^2 254", 337–323 (Tracy, *ADT* 114).

-------------- *in tympanum of pediment*
337–323 Μ/----------- non-stoich.
ἐπὶ δέ[κα----------]
ἐκκλησί[α ἐν Διονύσου· τῶν προέδρων]
ἐπεψήφιζ[εν------------------------------]

ΝικόστρατοΣ/------------------------------------ *on moulding*
Φιλέας Ἀντ̣[--------------εἶπεν·] stoich.
ἐπειδὴ Π|-------------------------
ὁ ὑποκρ[ιτὴς------------------ ὑπεκ]-
[ρ]ίνατ[ο---------------------------]
[.]ΣΤΙ--------------------------------
ἐψη̣[φίσθαι-------------------------]
--- | 81

Like no. 8 the text of ll. 7–11 is from the wording describing the honorand's services. He was apparently an actor (ll. 8–9).

Note

The arrangement whereby the beginning of the decree is inscribed in the pedimental moulding at the top of the stele is very unusual. *IG* II² 113 (*SEG* XXXIX 91) = *Ath. State* III B no. 102 is somewhat similar. Given that the decree appears to have honoured an actor and was passed between 13th and 19th of the month, which would suit the special Assembly after the City Dionysia (cf. footnote 3, above), Wilhelm's restoration of l. 3 is persuasive. However, since the text in the pediment is non-stoich and there is line-end syllabification throughout and since on any account the prescript was abbreviated, it is not possible either to determine the line length precisely or to restore any other line fully and I pass over here the speculative restorations of the prescript proposed by Wilhelm and others. Among the possibilities for l. 1 are Ἀκα]|μα[ντίδος (Wilh.), ἐγραμ]|μά̣[τευεν or a name. If Nikostratos, inscribed on the moulding at the bottom of the pediment, was the secretary (so Wilhelm) the year was probably 336/5 or 331/0 (the only two years during the known career of the cutter of this inscription whose secretaries are not attested). However, after about 350 honorands were commonly inscribed on mouldings, secretaries scarcely ever, while secretaries were occasionally omitted from prescripts altogether (cf. Henry, *Prescripts* 43–4).[42] As Koumanoudes recognised, the name can be articulated Νικοστράτο Σα̣[- or Νικόστρατος /. No. 10 also honoured a man named Nikostratos in a theatrical

[42] It would theoretically be possible to restore the prescript on the basis that the decree dates to the Assembly in the theatre of Dionysos in 332/1, when a Νικόστρατος Κόπρειος was chairman (cf. no. 1–no. 4), reading ἐπεψήφιζ[εν *vac*] | Νικόστρατος / [- *father's name* _ _ *demotic* _ _ _ _]. However, the chairman was normally a nescioquis. He is never inscribed separately on a moulding and never given a father's name at this period.

context. || 6 Α Φιλέας Ἀντιγένους Παιονίδης (*IG* II^2 410) and a Φιλέας Ἀντιφῶντος of unknown deme (*IG* II^2 1251) are attested at this period. The proposer of this decree might be either of these men, or neither. || 7 ΠΙ was taken by Wilhelm to be the honorand's name. Koumanoudes considered π[ρόσοδον ποιησάμενος. If Nikostratos was the honorand, one might consider πρ̣[ότερόν τε (cf. e.g. *IG* II^2 399), though Klaus Hallof reports that the Berlin squeeze is more suggestive of ΠΕ̣[- -. || 8–10 ὁ ὑποκρ[ιτὴς τοῖς τε Διονυσίοις ὑπεκ|ρ]ίνατ[ο φιλοτίμως ἔν τε τοῖς ἄλλοις
82 | ἐ]στί[ν ἀνὴρ ἀγαθὸς περί | Ἀθηναίους Wilhelm, καλῶς καὶ φιλοτίμως καὶ ἐ]στὶ[ν Veligianni-Terzi, *Wertbegriffe* 89 A148. Or perhaps καὶ νῦν | ἐ]στὶ[ν (answering to πρ̣[ότερόν τε, cf. above no. 4 and no. 5).

10. FOR NIKOSTRATOS. Found in Athens (τῆς κάτω πόλεως). S.A. Koumanoudes, Ἀρχ. Ἐφ. 1886, 106–7 no. 14 (A. Wilhelm, *Hermes* 24 [1889] 329–31); *IG* II 5, 245e; *IG* II^2 551; *Ath. State* III B no. 101. See also J. Pecírka, *The Formula for the Grant of Enktesis in Attic Inscriptions*, Prague 1966, 84–5 (*SEG* XXIV 109).

329/8–322/1? stoich. 29

- -
[...] Νικοστρατ[.........^{17}........]
[..] δεδόχθαι τῶι δήμ[ωι, ἐπειδὴ Νικόσ]-
[τρ]ατος διατελεῖ περ[ὶ τὸν ἀγῶνα τὸν]
[Δι]ονυσίων φιλοτιμο[ύμενος καὶ περ]-
[ί τ]ὴν αὐτοῦ ἐπιμέλεια[ν καὶ τοῖς χορη]-
[γο]ῖς τοῖς αἰεὶ χορηγο[ῦσιν προθύμως]
[ὑ]πηρετῶν τὰ περὶ τοὺ[ς...^{6}..., ἐπαινέ]-
[σ]αι Νικόστρατον Κη[.......^{13}......]
[.]την καὶ στεφανῶ[σαι αὐτὸν...^{6}...σ]-
[τ]εφάνωι· εἶναι [δὲ........^{15}.......]
[κα]ὶ ἐγγόνοι[ς καὶ γῆς καὶ οἰκίας ἔγκ]-
[τ]ησιν κατ[ὰ τὸν νόμον· ἀναγράψαι δὲ τ]-
[όδε] τὸ ψ[ήφισμα ἐν στήληι λιθίνηι τὸ]-
[ν κα]τὰ [πρυτανείαν γραμματέα ---]
- -

Translation

...Nikostratos...that the People shall decide, since Nikostratos continues to be ambitious for honour as regards [the competition at the] Dionysia and (5) his responsibilities at it (?), and to serve enthusiastically a succession of *choregoi* as regards the [pipes? choruses?], to praise Nikostratos son of Ke- of—(*or* of Ke-, the pipe-player *or* actor *or* poet) and crown him with a—(10) crown; and he and his descendants shall enjoy [equality of taxation (sc. with Athenians)?] and right of ownership of land and house according to the law; and the prytany secretary shall inscribe this decree on a stone stele… | 83

Note

In l. 6 the letters ΙΣ in τοῖς are inscribed in one stoichos. In l. 7 the last preserved letter, Υ, is to the left of its stoichos. The restorations are due to Koumanoudes (4 fin.-5 in. Köhler, 5 fin.-6 in. and 10–14 Wilhelm). || 1–2 ἀγαθεῖ τύχ|ει] Köhler. || 3 περ[ὶ τὸν ἀγῶνα τὸν Wilamowitz ap. Wilh. (ἀγῶνα τῶν Koum.). For the singular cf. *IG* II^2 680.7; no. 8, l. 5. || 7 τοὺ[ς θεοὺς Koumanoudes, αὐλούς Wilhelm. I suggest χορούς. The honorand's father's name or ethnic began Κη- (l. 8). -την in l. 9 is his ethnic or profession. Wilhelm 1889 and *UdA* 221, suggested τὸν αὐ|λη]τὴν (cf. his restoration of *IG* II^2 713 + Add. p. 666, but there is no unrestored state decree honouring a pipe-player until the prytany decrees of late-iii BC, cf. n. 15) or ὑποκρι]τὴν. ποιη]τὴν is perhaps unlikely. In l. 10 the privilege awarded was perhaps *isoteleia* (αὐτῶι ἰσοτέλειαν, cf. Henry, *Honours* 246 with n. 51). In 12 the iota of ἐγκ|τ]ησιν is placed to the left of its stoichos (as e.g. the final iota of 11).

In grants of *enktesis* the qualification κατὰ τὸν νόμον (l. 12) is absent in 330/29 (no. 5, above) and occurs for the first time in 325/4 (*IG* II^2 360, 20). The decree should date before the abolition of the *choregia* by Demetrios of Phaleron (ll. 5–6; no | state decree inscribed at public 84
initiative certainly dates to the period of his rule, cf. S.D. Lambert, *ABSA* 95 [2000] 488). Inscribing by the prytany secretary (ll. 13–14) argues against a date during the oligarchy of 321/0–318 (A.S. Henry, *Hesp.* 71 [2002] 107–8), but the short-lived democracy of 318/7 can not be ruled out.

The name Nikostratos was common. Poets: *IG* II^2 3094; *PCG* VII p. 93 Nicostratus II. Actors: no. 9 above?; *IG* II^2 2318, 332; 2320, 32.

Bibliography

Ath. State: S.D. Lambert, Athenian State Laws and Decrees, 352/1–322/1. I Decrees Honouring Athenians, II Religious Regulations, III Decrees Honouring Foreigners, *ZPE* 150 (2004) 85–120, 154 (2005) 125–159, 158 (2006) 115–158 (= III A), 159 (2007) 101–154 (= III B).

Brun, *Démade*: P. Brun, *L'orateur Démade*, Bordeaux 2000.

Ghiron-Bistagne, *Acteurs*: P. Ghiron-Bistagne, *Recherches sur les acteurs dans la Grèce antique*, Paris 1976.

Henry, *Honours*: A.S. Henry, *Honours and Privileges in Athenian Decrees*, Hildesheim 1983.

Henry, *Prescripts*: A.S. Henry, *The Prescripts of Athenian Decrees*, Leiden 1977.

Hintzen-Bohlen: B. Hintzen-Bohlen, *Die Kulturpolitik des Eubulos und des Lykurg*, Berlin 1997.

Humphreys, *Strangeness*: S.C. Humphreys, *The Strangeness of Gods*, Oxford 2004.

Lawton: C.L. Lawton, *Attic Document Reliefs*, Oxford 1995.

MacDowell: D.M. MacDowell, *Demosthenes. Against Meidias*, Oxford 1990.

Osborne, *Nat.*: M.J. Osborne, *Naturalization in Athens*, Brussels 1981–3.

Parker, *Poytheism*: R. Parker, *Polytheism and Society at Athens*, Oxford 2005.

Reusch: A. Reusch, *De diebus contionum ordinarium apud Athenienses*, Strasburg 1879.

Rhodes-Osborne: P.J. Rhodes and R. Osborne edd., *Greek Historical Inscriptions* 404–323 BC, Oxford 2003.

Schwenk: C.J. Schwenk, *Athens in the Age of Alexander*, Chicago 1985.

Tracy, *ADT*: S.V. Tracy, *Athenian Democracy in Transition*, Berkeley 1995.

Veligianni-Terzi, *Wertbegriffe*: C. Veligianni-Terzi, *Wertbegriffe in den attischen Ehrendekreten der klassischen Zeit*, Stuttgart 1997.

Whitehead, *Ath. Metic*: D. Whitehead, *The Ideology of the Athenian Metic*, Cambridge 1977.

Wilhelm, *UdA*: A. Wilhelm, *Urkunden dramatischer Aufführungen in Athen*, Vienna 1906.

Wilson, *Khoregia*: P. Wilson, *The Athenian Institution of the Khoregia*, Cambridge
85 2000. |

CHAPTER SIXTEEN

ATHENS, SOKLES, AND THE EXPLOITATION OF AN ATTIC RESOURCE (*IG* II² 411)[1]

Inscriptions make an immense contribution to our understanding of the operation of the Attic silver-mines. Above all a wealth of information is yielded by the detailed lists of mine leases, dating from 367/6 to ca. 300 BC, which form part of the inscribed records of the officials responsible for letting Athenian state contracts, the *poletai* (conveniently collected, with brief but useful introduction, by Langdon (1991); for the list of 367/6, with translation and helpful commentary, see Rhodes and Osborne 2003: no. 36). Among other relevant inscriptions are inscribed markers (*horoi*), many of which show mining property, including not only plots of land, but e.g. workshops with associated slaves and smelting ovens, being used as security for loans under the procedure known as πρᾶσις ἐπὶ λύσει. A few years ago I had the pleasure of collaborating with Ellis Jones in the publication of two such markers, which he had discovered while directing cleaning operations at a silver ore-washery, part of an ore-treatment works on the north side of the upper Agrileza valley, and which probably recorded loans raised on the security of the works (Ellis Jones and Lambert 1999 = *SEG* XLVIII 172–3; for a vivid depiction of the complex world of silver-mine finance see Demosthenes 37).

In this paper I shall present and discuss another inscription that has been thought to relate to silver mining, though, as we shall see, it is doubtful whether it does so. It is (apparently) a decree of the Athenian Assembly of the 'Lykourgan' period (ca. 337–325 BC) in which the city grants to an (unidentifiable) man named Sokles the right to exploit a

---

[1] This chapter was previously published in N. Sekunda (ed.), *Ergasteria. Works Presented to John Ellis Jones on his 80th Birthday* (Danzig, 2010), 115–125.

It is a pleasure and an honour to offer this paper in celebration of someone who has not only made an immense contribution to the archaeology of the Attic silver-mines (and of much else besides), but is also one of the most humane and good-humoured people that it has been my good fortune to know. I am very grateful to the honorand himself for communicating his views on this inscription to me *per ep.* and to Robin Osborne for reading a draft.

resource, usually taken to be silver. It has not been wholly neglected by scholars, but it is not to be found in the index of one important treatment of Athenian economic and financial history at this period (Faraguna 1992), and is given the briefest footnote reference in the most recent general survey of the life and times of Lykourgos (Humphreys 2004: 100 n. 58). The principal work on the inscription has been published in German, and the two most important recent contributions (by Palme and Thür) have been driven primarily by an interest in legal issues. The inscription is of considerable interest not only from this point of view, and for the puzzles it presents, but as a significant document of Athenian attitudes to the development of the economic resources of Attica in this period. I examined the stone a few years ago in the context of work on *IG* II³. Presented below is a text and an English translation, followed by some observations which develop points I have made briefly elsewhere (Lambert 2007: 69 no. 13 with n. 16).

Text and Translation

Two joining fragments of a stele of white marble, left side preserved.
115 Found on the Acropolis in excavations east of the Propylaia, 1838. |

Principal editions: *IG* II 203 (Köhler, based on transcripts of his own and of A. von Velsen); *IG* II² 411 (Kirchner, incorporating restorations of Wilhelm); Wilhelm 1935; Palme 1987 (ph.) (*SEG* XXXVII 77); Thür 2004 (*SEG* LIII 91).

See also: Schönbauer 1935: 185–90; Hopper 1953: 207–9; Behrend 1970: 71–2 no. 18; Peppas-Delmousou 1975; Maffi 1990 (*SEG* XL 73); Lambert 2007: 69 no. 13 (ph.).

Stoichedon 31 (32 in ll. 7, 9 and 24 on Wilhelm's restorations)

----

c. 337–325?

[.]Ι̣ΣΕ[.]Ν γένηται [.........18.........]
Ν̣ εἰσηγεῖται Σωκλ[........16........]
Λ̣Θ̣Η ποίησεσθαι Τ[.........17........]
Ν̣ καθ[ό]τι ἂν τῶι δήμ[ωι.......14.......]
[.]Α̣Θ̣[.]Ι δεδόχθαι Δ[........15.......εἶ]-
[ν]αι μὲν Σωκλέα [κ]ύρ̣[ιον.......13......]
[.]ν ὅθεν φησὶν τὴμ πρό̣σ̣[οδον ἔσεσθαι τῶι]
δήμωι· ἐπειδὰν δὲ̣ εἰσ[.......14.......]
εραν καταστήσηι τὴ[ν ....8.... εἶναι τ]-
ὴν κάρπωσιν Σωκλεῖ κ[αὶ τῆι πόλει πέντ]-
ε καὶ εἴκοσι ἔτη· καρπ[οῦσθαι δὲ τὸ μὲν ἕ]-
τερον ἔτος τὴμ πόλιν, τ[ὸ δὲ ἕτερον ἔτος]

Σωκλέα ἐναλλάξ, ἕως [ἂ]ν [ἐξίηι ἀμφοτέρο]-
ις τὰ πέ[ντ]ε καὶ εἴκο[σι] ἔ[τη, ἐν δὲ τῶι πρώ]-
[τ]ωι ἡ πόλις. κομίζεσθαι [δὲ τὴν καρπεία]-
[ν] τοῖς αὐτῶν τέλεσιν ἑκ[άτερον· εἶναι δ]-
ὲ τὴν συλλογὴν Σωκ[λ]εῖ [καὶ τῆι πόλει πα]-
νταχόθεν ὁπόθεν ἄ[ν] καρ[πεῖαι ὦσιν· ἐπα]-
νύτω δὲ Σωκλῆς τὴν συλλ[ογὴν τῆς καρπε]-
ίας ἐπὶ τοῦ ἄρχοντος το[ῦ ἀεὶ ὄντος· ὁ αὐ]-
τὸς δὲ τρόπος ἔστω τ[ῆ]ς συ[λλογῆς περὶ τ]-
ῆς πράσεως καὶ τῆς τ[ι]μή[σεως καὶ τῆς πρ]-
άξεως τῶγ χρημάτων Σωκλ[εῖ καθάπερ ἂν]
τῆι πόλει γίγνηται· ἐπει[δὰν δ' ἀναλάβηι]
Σωκλῆς τὴν ἐργασίαν [.......14.......]
ἐξέστω μηδεν[ὶ μ]ήτε εἰ[πεῖν μήτε ἐπιψη]-
φίσαι ὡς δεῖ ἀφ[ε]λέσθα[ι Σωκλεῖ τὴν ἐργ]-
ασίαν ἢ διακωλῦσαι ἐρ[γαζόμενον, πρὶν]
καρπώσηται τὸν γ[εγραμμένον χρόνον· ἐ]-
ὰν δέ τις εἴπηι [ἢ ἐπιψηφίσηι ὡς δεῖ ἀφε]-
[λ]έσθαι, ὀφειλέ[τ]ω [χιλίας δραχμὰς ἱερὰ]-
[ς] τῆι Ἀθηνᾶι κα[. .]Δ[........16........]
[..]λει τῆς βλάβη[ς]· τὴ[ν δὲ δίκην δικάζεσ]-
[θα]ι ἐν ταῖς ἐμπο[ρικαῖς· ἐὰν δέ τις ἢ αὐτ]-
[ὸς] κλέπτων ἢ ὑπο[πέμπων κλέπτας ἤ τι κα]-
[κοτ]εχνῶν ἁλίσκ[ηται ἢ διακωλύηι Σωκλ]-
[έα ἐ]ργαζόμενο[ν ....18.........] | 116
[...] καὶ Σωκλέα [.........19.........]
[...] Σωκλεῖ πα[.........20.........]
[...5..] ἡ πόλι[ς.........21.........]

The text is due mainly to Wilhelm, who followed Köhler in many places. Palme read more letters than previous editors and I was mostly able to confirm his new readings at autopsy ‖ 3 ΤΙ[Palme ‖ 4–5 δή[μωι δοκῆι· τύχηι τῆι ἀ|γ]αθ[ῆ]ι Wilh. Palme read ΑΘΑΙ, but at autopsy I thought the apparent A before I might be a distorted H ‖ 5 I confirm the Δ read by Palme after δεδόχθαι. δ[ήμωι τῶι Ἀθηναίων ? (see below) ‖ 6–7 πάντων τῶν ἐδαφ|ῶ]ν Wilh. ‖ 8 [βάθος ὀρύξας Wilh. ‖ 8–9 φαν]ερὰν Koe. There are numerous possibilities, including, as Robin Osborne suggests to me, ἱ]ερὰν ‖ 9 ἀργυρῖτιν Wilh., Schönbauer, πρόσοδον Palme ‖ 12 end ἔτος] Kirchner ‖ 15–16 Palme, τοὺς καρποὺ|ς] Wilh. ‖ 18 Palme, δεί[ξηι Σωκλῆς· Wilh. I confirm Palme's new reading ‖ 21 περὶ Palme, καὶ Wilh. ‖ 23 Palme, χρημάτω[ν ὁπόταν ἡ κάρπωσις] Wilh. ‖ 25 [μηκέτι Ἀθηναίων] Wilh. ‖ 29 τὸ[ν γεγραμμένον, 31–2 ἱερὰ] ς Kirchner ‖ 32–3 [κ]α[τά]δ[ικός τε γενέσθω τῆι πό]λει Wilh., κα[ὶ] ἠδ[ικηκὼς ἀποτινέτω Σ|ωκ]λεῖ ? Thür ap. Palme. I doubt whether the trace before Δ is an inscribed mark.

Translation

. . . shall be . . . introduce . . . Sokles . . . make . . . as the People . . . (5) shall decide . . . that Sokles be master of . . . from which he says there will be income for the People; and when . . . has established the . . ., (10) the profit shall be for Sokles and the city for twenty-five years; and the city shall have the profit in the one year and Sokles in the other year in alternation, until the twenty-five years have elapsed for both, and in the first year (15) the city shall have it; and each shall bring in the proceeds at their own expense; and the gathering shall be for Sokles and the city from everywhere that there may be proceeds; and Sokles shall complete the gathering of the proceeds (20) by the end of each archon year; and Sokles shall have the same means of gathering as regards sale and valuation and exaction of money as there would be for the city; and when Sokles has started (25) the working, it shall not be possible for anyone . . . to propose or put to the vote that Sokles should leave off the working, or to hinder him working, until the profit has been reaped for the prescribed time; (30) and if anyone proposes or puts to the vote that Sokles should leave off, he is to pay one thousand drachmas sacred to Athena and . . . the damage; and the matter shall be subject to litigation in the commercial courts; but if anyone is caught (35) stealing or causing theft or conspiring maliciously, or prevents Sokles from working . . . and Sokles . . . Sokles . . . (40) the city. . . .

Date and Summary

The date is determined by two factors: the letter forms, which indicate the 'Lykourgan' period (ca. 330 BC, Köhler, followed by Kirchner); and the content of the decree, which points in the same direction. The
117 340s cannot, however, be ruled out. |

Under the terms of the decree Sokles is to have charge or control of something (6) from which he claims that income will accrue to the People (7–8) and, once Sokles (or the city?) has established something (8–9, perhaps abstract, e.g. the profitability of the operation, or perhaps concrete and practical), he is to share the proceeds of its exploitation with the city for twenty-five years, Sokles and the city receiving the profit in alternate years, both parties bearing their own costs (11–16). Sokles and the city are to gather the profit from everywhere that it is to be had, Sokles completing his gathering of it by the end of the relevant archon-year (16–20).

Earlier scholars assumed that the vocabulary in καρπ- in ll. 15–24 referred to the literal fruit or product of the operation, and συλλογή to its 'gathering'. Palme, however (122–4), shows that the word for what is to be gathered, the beginning of which is preserved in l. 18 (καρ̣-) and the end in l. 20 (-ιας), ought to be καρπεία, which means financial proceeds or profit ('usufruct, enjoyment' LSJ, cf. *IG* XII 5 721.7 with *SEG* XVI 483, καρπεία τῶν κρεῶν = proceeds from sale of sacrificial meat), not fruit or product (= καρπός. For συλλογή = reaping of a profit, see Palme, 135). κάρπωσις in l. 10 similarly has a financial connotation ('use, profit' LSJ, cf. Xen. *Cyr*, 4.5.16). The focus in this part of the inscription is not, therefore, on the practical aspects of the operation, but on the financial arrangements. The 'alternate years' in which Sokles and the city are to reap their profit are not, it seems, to run from the point that profit begins to flow, but from archon-year to archon-year.

This financial focus is confirmed by what follows. Sokles is permitted (I would regard the provision as permissive rather than, with Palme, mandatory) to 'gather' the profit by 'sale' and by valuation and exaction of money (ll. 20–4). Palme argues that 'sale' (πρᾶσις) means, in effect, 'lease' (μίσθωσις) (cf. the vocabulary of buying, ὠνητής = 'buyer' of a mining lease, in the *poletai* lists). Sokles will not necessarily exploit the resource himself, but may lease or sub-contract the work (or his tenure of the land, if tenure is involved, though this is doubtful, see below). Perhaps this is also meant to include permission to raise cash by loans on the security of the resource (πρᾶσις ἐπὶ λύσει). If the lessee/sub-contractor defaults on the terms of his contract there is to be a legal process of valuation (i.e. of the amount owed by the lessee/contractor) and exaction of what is owed. In any case what is 'gathered' by these procedures is not, or not directly, a product, but money.

Whatever the resource is, the city patently regards itself as in control of it, and it could normally lease or sub-contract rights over it, as it did for example in relation to contracts for collecting taxes and to leases of mines, and could pursue in the courts those who defaulted on their contracts. In this case, however, the right to exploit the resource is being ceded by the city to an individual, and the city needs to clarify that he has the same rights to (sub-)contract as the city would enjoy. It may be relevant that he is mentioned by name only, not identified clearly as an Athenian citizen (i.e. with father's name and demotic) or a foreigner (with ethnic). We cannot be certain, but the impression is

of someone whose status is indeterminate or ambiguous; a freedman perhaps, or even a slave. (The name Sokles is attested in Attica both for citizens and non-citizens, including ca. 330–320 for a freedman in *IG* II^2 1569.22). Elsewhere in the text he seems to be treated as a foreigner (see below). The property rights of foreigners (still more so those of slaves) in Attica were very limited, e.g. they could not normally own
118 land or | houses, and hence, *a fortiori*, there were restrictions on their capacity for πρᾶσις. This may be an additional reason for this clause.

From the next clause it becomes apparent that Sokles is to undertake work (ἐργασία, 25) in relation to the resource; and the text finishes with extensive provisions designed to prevent interference. Anyone who proposes or puts to the vote (it seems in the Council or Assembly) a proposal that Sokles is to leave off the work, or interferes with his work before the prescribed time has elapsed (it is not quite clear whether this means the 25 years or the individual alternate years) is to pay a heavy fine, payable to Attica's patron goddess; then there is a clause about 'damage' which can not be reconstructed. Private cases (*dikai*, specifically for 'damage'?) are to be treated as commercial (*emporikai*), the significance of which is probably not that the exploitation of the resource involved trade, but that the commercial courts, unusually blind to the civic status of litigants, were suitable to function as a forum in which a (foreigner? freedman?) such as Sokles could pursue a suit against anyone who had damaged the legitimate pursuit of his 'business' (thus Palme, 138). Further provisions follow, including against theft, presumably of the resource over which Sokles is being given control, or its product.

It is a possible interpretation that Sokles is to carry out his work only in alternate years, and that the city will make its own arrangements for exploiting the resource in the other years; but it may be that the city envisages that Sokles will in practice carry out the necessary work of development and exploitation continuously throughout the 25-year period and it is simply that the profits will be reckoned to the city in alternate years. Perhaps the city was deliberating leaving its options open.

The arrangement is *sui generis* and there is no parallel in Attica, or very close parallel elsewhere. The closest is in an Eretrian inscription, *IG* XII 9, 191 (322–309/8 BC), in which one Chairephanes is commissioned to drain a marsh and reclaim the land for agricultural usage in exchange for rights to exploit the land.

What is the resource?

The central puzzle presented by this inscription is: what is the resource that is to be exploited? In early scholarship Sokles was taken to be a lessee of public land, generally assumed to be agricultural, but in 1935 Wilhelm and Schönbauer in collaboration made a case that the decree has to do with the mining of silver, and this has been widely accepted, though some have hesitated (e.g. Hopper, 208, and Behrend, 71, continued to regard an agrarian interpretation as possible). In 1987 Palme presented a thorough and important re-edition, arguing in favour of the silver-mining interpretation, but emphasising that this was not a straightforward mining concession, but that Sokles was a 'prospector' for new mines, granted a shared right to the profits of any that he succeeded in developing, to be exercised by leasing out their exploitation in alternate years.

While the text is not well enough preserved to rule out agriculture or silver, there are problems with both. Palme adduces several arguments against the agricultural interpretation. Not all are wholly convincing, but it does seem doubtful that what Sokles was given control over, or tenure of (ll. 6–7), was specific plots or areas of land. For that one would have expected more precise specification (compare the detailed descriptions of | locations in the mining leases, and indeed 119
generally in Attic leases), and the wording in l. 18 gives an impression that the resource might be found all over the place (πανταχόθεν), rather than in specific locations. Moreover, μίσθωσις is the term for leasing invariably used in ordinary land-leases; the right of πρᾶσις granted Sokles in l. 22 is therefore probably not a right to let agricultural land.

The silver-mining interpretation is also not compelling. There is nothing in the surviving text that implies it; and all Wilhelm's restorations in this sense have accordingly been noted above in the apparatus rather than included in the text. For example the term ἔδαφος was used in the mining area to designate land which was privately owned, but over which the city had sub-surface mineral rights (cf. Ellis Jones and Lambert 1999: 132 n. 6, Rhodes and Osborne 2003: 181), but the restoration of the term in ll. 6–7, [πάντων τῶν ἐδαφ|ῶ]ν, 'all the grounds', is gratuitous. Moreover Thür, while inclined to follow Palme in most respects, drew attention to some serious difficulties with his interpretation, including that the arrangement for exploiting the resource (25-year period, profit in alternate years) seems inconsistent with the system for mine leasing as described in the *Ath. Pol.* (47.2) and implied by the *poletai* records, in which new mines (referred to in some *poletai* records as καινοτομίαι) were leased for periods of (probably) seven years. Once a new mine had been identified by Sokles, it should have been a καινοτομία and ought to have come under these arrangements. Ellis Jones himself (per ep.) shares these doubts about silver, writing persuasively 'surely mine leases are for much shorter periods…it would be too easy without very close supervision for Sokles to hide/reserve a good "lode" towards the end of the "state's year" until he could "openly" "discover" it fairly early on in his "own" year of profit….by ca. 337–325 the silver areas of the Laureotike would be well explored, and rights of ownership of land etc. well established…was there by then any scope for some "geological expert" (???Sokles??) to prospect and find "veins" hitherto undiscovered? And could the state *in reality* seemingly sign away the traditional rights of land-owners (probably very aware of their rights and the possibilities of opening up new resources of wealth for themselves and their families) in that area to some "roving-eye expert" like Sokles?'

The solution, I suggest, may lie in looking to possibilities beyond agriculture and silver mining, and perhaps beyond any rights specifically in land.

Palme's point that, while there is plenty of evidence for enhanced mining activity, there is none for measures to open up new land for exploitation at this period, is one of his weaker arguments for the mining option. Certainly there is good evidence for intensified development of the silver mines from the 350s, if not before (Palme: 132–3, see also Faraguna 1992: chapter 5): for Xenophon in the *Poroi* in the mid-350s (4.28), 'development has only recently got underway again' and 'there are not as many *kainotomiai* now as previously', while improved exploitation of the mines was important if the city's financial situation was to be ameliorated. Though the interpretation of the *poletai* records is not straightforward, they show clearly enough that this was followed through in subsequent decades, with the re-opening of old mines (παλαιὸν ἀνασαξιμόν, first perhaps in Langdon 1991 P9, ? mid-century) and clear signs of intensified production (e.g. while 17 mines were leased in the complete list of 367/6, Langdon 1991 P5, over 80 are recorded in the fragmentary list of 342/1, Langdon 1991 P26). The literary record bears this out, with the intensified activity producing a
120 rash of mine litigation (e.g. Dem. 37, ca. 346 BC; [Plut.] | *X Orat.* 843d,

Lykourgos' prosecution of Diphilos for illegal mineworking yielding 160 talents; Hyp. *Eux.* 34–6, 330–324 BC, stating explicitly that more *kainotomiai* were being undertaken than previously. On the development of the mines to ca. 320 see Lauffer 1979: 159–63).

Such measures to improve the exploitation of the city's resources were not restricted to the mining sector, however. Beginning perhaps in the late-340s (the precise date is unclear), Athens conducted a major programme of sales of public land to private individuals, much of it apparently marginal in productive terms, intended no doubt in part to raise money for the city, but also, it seems, to maximise the exploitation of Attica's landed resources (see Lambert 1997, especially 283–5, with references to other evidence for pressure on land resources and responses to it at this period). An emphasis on careful management and exploiting resources to the maximum runs like a golden thread through the city's economic and financial policies at this period, it is not restricted to one or other economic sector.

Xenophon in his last work, the *Poroi,* written in 355/4, had set the tone. The Social War with Athens' allies had put an intolerable strain on the city's finances and Xenophon sets out a number of imaginative schemes to improve the revenues (the focus, as in our decree, is on the city's πρoσόδοι), including establishment of a state-owned merchant fleet and a workforce of state-owned mining slaves. Until the late 340s, the leading proponent of practical policies to improve the city's finances was Euboulos, but after the defeat at Chaironeia in 338/7, it was Lykourgos. In the words of a decree of 307/6 granting him posthumous honours, he was 'treasurer of the public revenue of the city for three periods of four years' ([Plut.] *X Orat.* 852b, cf. 841b) and is said to have increased the annual income of the city to 1,200 talents ([Plut.] *X Orat.* 842f). Some of Xenophon's proposals were impractical, but the approach adopted in reality also encompassed some ambitious and ingenious schemes: the major programme of public land sales all over Attica co-ordinated by demes, phratries etc. on behalf of the city was one. On a smaller scale a system for selling off the skins of sacrificial animals was another (*IG* II^2 1496, cf. Humphreys 2004: 85). Sokles' proposal was probably in this mould: a novel scheme designed to exploit some hitherto underexploited resource. The decree conveys somewhat of an impression that the profits from the operation are going to flow fairly effortlessly. If (what is admittedly not clear) the actual working of the resource is going to be organised by the city and by Sokles in alternate years, as Robin Osborne points out to me it doesn't look

as if any very skilled workforce can have been involved, or anything that required any very substantial continuous long-term investment of manpower or resources, and it is notable that no arrangements are made, at least in the surviving text, for the sale of the product. One might think in the modern world of something like bottling mineral water; in ancient Attica one might think perhaps of the gathering of salt (among the properties owned by the *genos* Salaminioi was a salt-pan, Rhodes and Osborne 2003: no. 37, l. 17), or some other mineral, or (to mention another topic in which our honorand has an interest) of wild honey, or the tapping of resin, or perhaps the trapping of some wild bird or animal. Ellis Jones himself attractively suggests (per ep.) 'medicinal herbs in some stated (traditionally reserved, holy?) areas to be tended/preserved and cropped…over the 25-year period…years ago in the 1970s in my *only* sabbatical term in a lifetime's teaching I spent April to June/July or so in Crete, and seem to remember vil-
121 lage women collecting wild flowers and herbs, and I don't think | they were restricted to collecting on their own family plots, if the farmer/farmer's own wife did not choose to collect such plants as grew along the fences or under and around their olive trees.' The resource, whatever it was, was apparently widespread (cf. πανταχόθεν in l. 18) and Sokles sought and obtained from the city a roving brief to exploit it, including a notably strong series of protections against interference. If the decree did not actually convey a right in land, one wonders if the operation might nevertheless have required access to other people's land. Particularly if the product was animal or vegetable, the arrangement of the annual periods by archon-year (beginning ca. July) might just have related to a seasonal cycle of some kind.

The issue in this text that has most interested legal historians is its implications for the character and extent of the mining rights claimed by the state (see Harrison 1968: 315, Appendix D, and most recently Thür 2004). The decree may be relevant to this issue if the resource in question was mineral; but especially if it was animal or vegetable, then what we have here is the city exercising right of ownership, or at least control, over what had previously been a publicly available resource in a way that seems to have asserted the public interest over that of individual citizens, who, the provisions against interference suggest, may be inconvenienced, if not worse. A similar dynamic can be observed in the public land sale programme: what had apparently been publicly available property (including such things as public threshing floors) was claimed by the city and sold off to private individuals to improve the city's 'revenue'. The proposals in Xenophon's *Poroi* had entailed the extension of state ownership of resources to a remarkable degree. Assertion of the collective interest over private economic interests seems to have been a feature of the city's real-life efforts at this period to improve the exploitation of the resources of Attica, that land which 'has the natural potential to produce the most ample revenues' (ἡ χώρα πέφυκεν οἵα πλείστας προσόδους παρέχεσθαι, Xen. *Poroi* 1.2. On attempts to strengthen the idea of the Athenian *koinon* at this period see now Azoulay forthcoming).

Postscript: is this a state decree?

There is an unresolved epigraphical puzzle about this decree. In a sense it is minor, and I cannot see an easy solution to it; but it needs to be addressed as it has the potential to affect our whole interpretation. How should we reconstruct the text in l. 5? Whether or not it was preceded by an invocation of 'good fortune' (and I suspect it was), it is clear that δεδόχθαι in l. 5 ought to be from the formulaic clause introducing the substance of the decision: '[X proposed….] for good fortune that it be decided by the People that Sokles be master of…'. There are countless examples of this formula in Athenian state decrees of this period, e.g. *IG* II^2 338.10–11 (333/2): τύχηι ἀγαθῆι δεδόχθαι τῶι δήμωι, ἐπειδὴ Πυθέας αἱρεθεὶς ἐπὶ τὰς κρήνας….In place of τῶι δήμωι we might have τῆι βουλῆι for a decree of the Council, or τοῖς νομοθέταις for a law, but that is about the limit of the possibilities indicated by parallels. Wilhelm suggested δεδόχθαι τῆι βουλῆι καὶ τῶι δήμωι, but as Palme notes (120–1), this can be ruled out on several grounds: it is four letters too long for the line, and the formula combining Council and People in one expression is not found in decrees of the Lykourgan period. Moreover Palme reads, and I confirm, a *delta* after the word δεδόχθαι (not likely, on this stone, to be a Α or Λ). | 122

Two lines of approach seem open. The first is to contemplate the possibility that this is not a decree of the Athenian state but of some other body with name in Δ-, cf. for example δεδόχθαι Δυαλεῦσιν (a phratry) μισθῶσαι τὸ χωρίον τὸ Μυρρινοῦντι, *IG* II^2 1241, 1–2. This, however, seems difficult to reconcile with the other provisions of the decree: the resource is one over which the city claims control, it is potentially everywhere, the profit of its exploitation is to be shared with the city. Subgroups of the *polis* are found acting as its agents in this period; for example land in Oropos, acquired from Philip II after Chaironeia or perhaps rather from Alexander in 335 (cf. Knoepfler 2001: 367–89; Rhodes and Osborne 2003: no. 75) was allocated to the tribes in pairs (Hyp. *Eux.* 16–17, Lalonde, Langdon. Walbank 1991: L8), and demes, phratries and other groups were made responsible for the public land sale programme referred to above (Lambert 1997: 238–9). There was no Attic tribe in Δ- at this time, but there were four in Α- and one in Λ-, so one might restore a pair of tribe names here in the dative and interpret the whole decree as relating to Oropos. This is very uncomfortable, however, and not only because of the rule that one should not assume an inscribing error, in this case Δ- for Α- or Λ-, next to a lacuna. One would not expect tribes to pass entrenchment clauses prohibiting *anyone* (i.e. surely any Athenian) from making a proposal in the Assembly to stop Sokles' work, or create new offences and specify the courts in which they were to be heard.

We might consider a less radical solution, retaining the People as the body passing this decree. In that case might Δ- be the initial letter of δήμωι? The omission of the definite article before δήμωι would be a severe irregularity, but might be alleviated to a degree (not entirely) by assuming postponement. In this formula 'the People' stands usually by itself. However, in other contexts 'the People' is frequently 'the *Athenian* People', τῶι δήμωι τῶι Ἀθηναίων, as e.g. anyone who kills Peisitheides of Delos is to be an enemy τῶι δήμωι τῶι Ἀθηναίων (*IG* II^2 222.33) or at the Little Panathenaia where meat is to be distributed τῶι δήμωι τῶι Ἀθηναίων (Rhodes and Osborne 2003: no. 81, B 24). 'Of the Athenians' normally occurs where there is an external perspective, e.g. in a treaty or a decree honouring a foreigner, or where foreigners are at least in the picture (e.g. those participating in the Panathenaia); but the phrase is so common that it could trip easily off a decree-drafter's pen or cutter's chisel, and this sometimes happened when it was not needed. In the Assembly decree of 330/29 or shortly after honouring Herakleides of Salamis (Rhodes and Osborne 2003: no. 95), Herakleides is praised for his *philotimia* εἰς τὸν δῆμον τὸν Ἀθηναίων (35–6) and an embassy is sent to Dionysios, tyrant of Herakleia, to recover the sails which he had confiscated from Herakleides and to ask him not to harm those sailing to Athens in future. If he does that Dionysios will be acting justly and will lack nothing that is just from the People, οὐθεν⟦ὸς ἀτυχ⟧ήσει τοῦ δήμου ⟦τ[ο]ῦ Ἀθηναίων⟧. In this inscription there were originally a number of inscribing errors and the cutter has gone back over them making corrections. The

letters ⟦ὸς ἀτυχ⟧ for example stand in an erasure: the letters originally inscribed there were erroneous and have been corrected to those that can now be read. At the end of the same sentence the letters τ[ο]ῦ Ἀθηναίων are not inscribed over an erasure; they are the letters that were originally inscribed; erased, but still faintly legible. The words were superfluous in this formula; but the drafter or cutter was so used to attaching them to references to 'the People' that he has done so inadvertently here and then gone back and removed them. If something similar has occurred in our text, what was inscribed might have
been: τύχηι |...ἀ]γαθῆι δεδόχθαι δ[ήμωι τῶι Ἀθηναίων εἶ]|[ν]αι μὲν 123
Σωκλέα, which suits the space precisely. The discomfort remains. I can find no parallel in Attic inscriptions for omission of the first article in τῶι δήμωι τῶι Ἀθηναίων. It is certainly not what one would expect in an Attic decree of this period, but I have not yet been able to find a better solution.

Bibliography

V. Azoulay, 'Lycurgue et l'invention d'un nouveau koinon', paper delivered at a conference in Paris in 2009, *Clisthène et Lycurgue d'Athènes. Autour du politique dans la cité classique.* Proceedings, V. Azoulay, P. Ismard (eds.), forthcoming, Paris, Publications de la Sorbonne, 2011.

D. Behrend, *Attische Pachturkunden* (Munich 1970).

J. Ellis Jones, S.D. Lambert, 'Two Security Horoi from an Ore-Washery at Agrileza, Southern Attica' *ZPE* 125 (1999) 131–6.

M. Faraguna, *Atene nell' età di Alessandro. Problemi Politici, Economici, Finanziari* (Rome 1992).

A.R.W. Harrison, *The Law of Athens. Vol. I. The Family and Property* (Oxford 1968. Revised edition, with Foreword and Bibliography by D.M. MacDowell, London 1998).

R.J. Hopper, 'The Attic Silver Mines in the Fourth Century BC' *BSA* 48 (1953) 200–54.

S.C. Humphreys, 'Lycurgus of Boutadai', originally published in J.W. Eadie and J. Ober (eds.), *The Craft of the Ancient Historian: essays in honour of Chester G. Starr* (Lanham Md. 1985), republished with Afterword as chapter 3 of *The Strangeness of Gods* (Oxford 2004).

D. Knoepfler, *Eretria XI. Décrets érétriens de proxénie et citoyenneté* (Lausanne 2001).

S.D. Lambert, *Rationes Centesimarum* (Amsterdam 1997).

——, 'Athenian State Laws and Decrees 352/1–322/1: IV Treaties and Other Texts' *ZPE* 161 (2007) 67–100.

M.K. Langdon, 'II Poletai Records' in Lalonde, Langdon, Walbank (1991) 53–143.

G.V. Lalonde, M.K. Langdon, M.B. Walbank, *The Athenian Agora XIX. Inscriptions,*
Horoi, | Poletai Records. Leases of Public Lands (Princeton 1991). 124

S. Lauffer, *Die Bergwerkssklaven von Laureion* (second edition. Wiesbaden 1979).

A. Maffi, Review of Palme 1987 in *Rev. hist. droit* 68 (1990) 109–10.

A.P. Matthaiou, G. Malouchou (edd.), Ἀττικαὶ ἐπιγραφαί. Πρακτικὰ Συμποσίου εἰς μνήμην *Adolf Wilhelm (1864–1950)* (Athens 2004).

B. Palme, 'Ein attischer Prospektorenvertrag? *IG* II^2 411' *Tyche* 2 (1987) 113–39.
D. Peppas-Delmousou, ''Επιγραφικό Μουσείο Αθηνών' *Arch. Delt.* 30 (1975) [1983], B, 7.
P.J. Rhodes and Robin Osborne, *Greek Historical Inscriptions 404–323 BC* (Oxford 2003, corrected paperback edition 2007).
E. Schönbauer, 'Vom Bodenrecht zum Bergrecht' *Zeitschrift der Savigny Stiftung* 55 (1935) 183–235.
G. Thür, 'Prospektion und Bergregal in *IG* II^2 411' in Matthaiou, Malouchou (2004) 175–84.
125 A. Wilhelm, 'Attische Pachturkunden' *Archiv für Papyrusforschung* 11 (1935) 206–15. |

CHAPTER SEVENTEEN

INSCRIBED TREATIES CA. 350–321: AN EPIGRAPHICAL PERSPECTIVE ON ATHENIAN FOREIGN POLICY[*][1]

It is a welcome feature of Tracy's *Athenian Democracy in Transition* (Tracy 1995) that he prefaces his meticulous analysis of letter cutters of 340–290 BC with a concise "Historical Overview" in which he embeds the inscriptions of the period into a historical narrative, "Chaironeia to Ipsos and Beyond" and specific studies of "The Lamian War", "The Inscriptions and the Food Supply" and "The Inscriptions and Demetrios of Phaleron". Nearly all inscribed Athenian state laws and decrees of this period fall into one of three categories.[2] By far the most numerous are the honorific decrees, including both decrees honouring foreigners and, a new genre in the 340s and fewer in number, decrees honouring Athenians.[3] Regulations concerning festivals and other religious matters, several of them laws, are a second category,[4] inter-state treaties a third. Nearly all the inscriptions referred to by Tracy in his Historical Overview are honorific decrees or religious regulations. Treaties, in contrast, are not much in evidence. He refers to two at the beginning of his Overview: the treaty establishing the League of Corinth, *IG*, II^{2}, 236 (Tracy 1995, n. 1) and the agreement with Alexander the Great about troop supply, *IG*, II^{2}, 329 (Tracy 1995, n. 2); and at p. 24 n. 11 he mentions *IG*, II^{2}, 370, the heading of an alliance between Athens and Aetolia, which may date to the Lamian War period. My purpose in this paper is not so much to fill the gap—it reflects a real hiatus in inscribed Athenian treaties between Chaironeia and the Lamian War—but to emphasise it by contrasting this period of treaty-silence with | the busier one that preceded it and to illumine it 153

* This chapter was previously published in G. Reger, F.X. Ryan and T.F. Winters (eds.), *Studies in Greek Epigraphy and History in Honor of Stephen V. Tracy* (Bordeaux, 2010), 153–160.

[1] I am very grateful to Peter Rhodes for reading a draft and for valuable suggestions.

[2] For the few which fall outside them see Lambert 2007b.

[3] See Lambert 2004, 2005, 125–9, 2006, and 2007a.

[4] Lambert 2005, 129–151.

with a glance at that other, much more numerous, genre of diplomatic decree, the honorific decree for foreigners.

The following inscribed treaties and other decrees dealing with interstate relations are extant from the period ca. 350–322/1:[5]

Before 338/7[6]

1. Mid-fourth cent. *IG*, II^2, 281; Dreher 1995, 150–1 (*SEG*, 46, 125). Oaths from a treaty, apparently relating to settlement of a dispute by arbitrators (l. 4).
2. Mid-fourth cent. *IG*, II^2, 258+617; Schweigert 1937, 327–329 (ph.). Decree about (alliance with?) Chalkis or cities of Chalkidike. Mentions allies, enemies, generals and oaths.
3. c. 349/8? *IG*, II^2, 210+259; Schweigert 1937, 329–332 (ph.); Wilhelm 1942, 132–133; Pečirka 1966a, 266–9 (*SEG*, 23, 52); Walbank 1989, 119–122 (*SEG*, 39, 75). Cf. Zahrnt 1971, 108, 146–150, 182–185. Decree about Akanthos and Dion (ll. 4 and 14), cities of eastern Chalkidike (Hansen and Nielsen (eds.) 2004, no. 559 and no. 569), whose envoys are praised ll. 13–15. Mentions allies (l. 3) and Philip (l. 13).[7] Decree followed by text in larger letters (names of envoys/ oathtakers?). Perhaps dates to Olynthian War.
4. 349/8. *IG*, II^2, 208; *Staatsverträge* II no. 325. Photograph at *ZPE*, 140 (2002), 78. Decree based on representations from envoys of the Echinaioi (from Akarnania, cf. Hansen and Nielsen (eds.) 2004, no. 118). The decree was, or related to, a judicial convention (*symbola*, l. 14).
5. 347/6. *IG*, II^2, 213; *Syll.*^{3}, 205; Accame 1941, 135; Tod 1948, 168; *Staatsverträge* II no. 328. Renews alliance between Athens and Mytilene which had apparently lapsed after the Social War. Cf. Brun 1988, 381–3; Dreher 1995, 28, 124, 177.

---

[5] For more detail, photographs and some new readings see Lambert 2007b.

[6] One might add to this list *IG*, II^2, 207, probably of 349/8, which awards Athenian citizenship and other honours to Orontes, satrap or former satrap of Mysia, and which goes on to deal with other aspects of relations, including a *symbola* agreement (Gauthier 1972, 82–83, 168–169 no. XIII) and supply of grain for Athenian troops on campaign. See Lambert 2006, no. 2.

[7] In Wilhelm's restoration of ll. 10–13 the decree establishes an alliance between Akanthos and Dion and Athens and provides for Akanthos and Dion to "[destroy] the stele [about the alliance] with Philip", [καθελεῖν δ' αὐ]τοὺς τὴν στή[λην τὴν περὶ τῆς συμμαχίας πρ]ὸς Φίλιππον, cf. *IG*, II^2, 116, 39.

6. 348 or 343? *IG*, II^2, 125; *Syll.*^{3}, 191; Knoepfler 1984, 152–161, 1987, 312–319, 1995, 309–64; Dreher 1995, 154–180 (*SEG*, 46, 123); Rhodes and Osborne 2003, 69. Not a treaty, but a decree discouraging attacks on Eretria and other allied cities. | 154
7. 343/2. *IG*, II^2, 225 + Add. p. 659; *Staatsverträge* II no. 337. Alliance with Messenians (and others?). One of several Peloponnesian states which made alliances with Athens at this time (Schol. Aeschin. 3, 83).
8. 341?. *IG*, II^2, 230 + Add. p. 659; *IG*, XII, 9, 162; *Staatsverträge* II no. 340; Wallace 1947, 145; Knoepfler 1971, 223–244, 1985, 243–259, 1995, 346; P. Gauthier, *Bull. ép.* 1987, 274; 1996, 168 (*SEG*, 45, 1210); Dreher 1995, 45–56 (*SEG*, 46, 119). "Cutter of *IG*, II^2, 334" (ca. 345–ca. 320), Tracy 1995, 84. Alliance with Eretria, followed by list of oath-takers. Perhaps on occasion of ejection of the tyrant Kleitarchos and the establishment of democracy there (Aeschin. III 103).

Between 338/7 and 322/1

9. 338/7. *IG*, II^2, 236; *Staatsverträge* III no. 403; Heisserer 1980, 8–12; Rhodes and Osborne 2003, 76. Athenian copy of multilateral treaty with Philip II establishing League of Corinth. Tracy 1995, 7 n. 1.
10. 336? *IG*, II^2, 329; Tod 1948, 183; *Staatsverträge* III no. 403 II; Heisserer 1980, 3–8, 12–24; Rosen 1982, 354–355; Tronson 1985, 15–19 (*SEG*, 35, 66); Worthington 2004, 2007. Fragment of Athenian copy of (multilateral?) agreement with Alexander (l. 8) about provision and supply of troops. Tracy 1995, 7 n. 2.
11. 323/2 (or 307/6?). *IG*, II^2, 370; Mitchel 1964, 13–17 (*SEG*, 21, 299); Moretti 1967, no. 1; *Staatsverträge* III no. 413; Worthington 1984, 139–44 (*SEG*, 34, 69). Heading of an alliance with Aetolians (and others?). Tracy 1995, 24 n. 11.

From mid-century through to the battle of Chaironeia, therefore, we have eight inscribed treaties or other decrees dealing with interstate relations. Fairly predictably they concern the maintenance and management of the Second Athenian League (Mytilene 5, Eretria and other allies 6, Eretria again 8) and alliance building aimed more or less directly against Philip, in northern Greece (Chalkidike? 2, Akanthos and Dion 3), Euboea (Chalkis? 2, cf. 6 and 8) and the Peloponnese (Messenians, 7). 1 appears to relate to an interstate arbitration, but

we know nothing of the context. 4 was or related to a judicial convention with the Echinaioi, one of a striking number of inscriptions documenting Athens' deliberate concern at this period to maintain
155 longstanding good relations with Akarnania.[8] |

The period between Chaironeia and the Lamian War shows a very different picture. At one end we have two treaties with the dominant power—one with Philip, one with Alexander. They differ from the other documents in the above list in important respects. While the others are bilateral treaties, or multilateral treaties in which Athens is the leading party, these are Athenian copies of multilateral agreements in which Macedon is the leading party. The treaty with Philip, *IG*, II^2, 236, includes a fragmentary list of the contracting parties in which Athens (her name is not preserved) apparently rubbed shoulders with the cities whose names we can read: Thessalians, Thasians, Thracians, Ambrakiots, Phokians and Lokrians, Oitaians and Malians etc. Uniquely, the surviving fragment of the inscribing clause of the treaty with Alexander, *IG*, II^2, 329, provided for it to be set up at Pydna (since our copy was found on the Athenian acropolis, the missing portion of the clause presumably provided for copies in allied cities). Very unusually, the back of the treaty with Philip was not rough-picked, like normal stelai, but smooth, as if to take another inscription. There are only seven stelai with smooth backs among the over 250 stones inscribed with Athenian state laws and decrees of this period (see Lambert 2005, 129–132). Most of them are laws rather than decrees. Does this signify that the treaty with Philip was "law-like" in its constitutional status, permanence and importance? Perhaps. But what determines this physical attribute may be another inscription which belongs in a pair with *IG*, II^2, 236, *SEG*, 16, 55 = Lambert 2005, no. 8. In the first line after the heading, *SEG*, 16, 55 refers directly to *IG*, II^2, 236 ("the stele about the peace"). It too has a smooth back. Moreover its thickness (0.132 m.) is precisely the same as *IG* II^2 236 and it is inscribed in a very similar style of lettering[9] and the same stoichedon grid. *SEG*, 16, 55 makes new arrangements for a festival;[10] and (apparently by virtue of their quality as laws) other stelai inscribed with fes-

[8] Cf. Lambert 2005, 136.

[9] Tracy 1995, 78 ascribes *SEG*, 16, 55 to his style, "litt. volg. 345–320".

[10] Athenian? Panhellenic, organised by the Macedonians? (Lambert 2005, 147–148).

tival and religious regulations of this period also have smooth backs.[11] The back of the treaty with Alexander, *IG*, II^{2}, 329, is not preserved, but its lettering is very similar to that on *IG*, II^{2}, 236 and *SEG*, 16, 55 and the stoichedon grid has the same dimensions. These three inscriptions belong in a group both thematically and physically.[12]

At the other end of this period we have what may be a fragment of the anti-Macedonian alliance system of the Lamian war, *IG*, II^{2}, 370
(unless it belongs rather | to the Aetolian-Athenian detente of 307/6).[13] 156
There is no inscribed Athenian treaty dating between the set of three inscriptions that inaugurate the post-Chaironeia world and the one which may mark Athens' attempt to escape from it.[14]

It would seem reasonable enough to interpret this silence as indicative of Athenian impotence on the international stage and of her lack of scope for manouevre as a subordinate ally of the Macedonians; but a more nuanced picture emerges if we bring into the frame that other diplomatic genre of inscribed decree, the decree honouring foreigners.[15] Most such decrees honoured individual foreigners, but a few honoured whole cities and, as such, are documents of interstate relations comparable to treaties. They are:

Pre-Chaironeia

1. Elaious?, 345/4, *IG*, II^{2}, 219; Schweigert 1939, 172–173; Lambert 2007a, no. 65. Elaious (in Chersonese, member of Second Athenian League) had honoured Athens the previous year, *IG*, II^{2}, 1443, 93–5; cf. no. 3.
2. Pellana, 345/4 and 344/3, *IG*, II^{2}, 220 = Rizakis 1995, 345–346 no. 615; Lambert 2007a, no. 66.

---

[11] *IG*, II^{2}, 333 = Lambert 2005, no. 6; *SEG*, 32, 86 = Lambert 2005, no. 9. The law fragment, *IG*, II^{2}, 412 (on which see Hansen 1981–2, 119–123 and Lambert 2007b, no. 34) is opisthographic.

[12] For this and other reasons Tronson's argument that *IG*, II^{2}, 329 relates not to Alexander the Great but to Alexander II of Macedon (early 360s) is unconvincing.

[13] A possibility raised by Moretti, cf. Paus. I 26, 3, *IG*, II^{2}, 358 with Tracy 1995, 152.

[14] A fragment published by Stroud 1971, 187–189 no. 34 (ph.) (revised Lambert 2007b, no. 11) concerns relations with Tenos. It might belong to the late 320s, but is as likely to date to the last two decades of the century (after 307/6?) Cf. *IG*, II^{2}, 279, 660 (see below), 466 (similar script). Note also *IG*, II^{2}, 2378.

[15] For a full list of the over 160 extant inscribed decrees of 352/1–322/1 which honoured foreigners and further discussion of individual texts see Lambert 2006, 2007a.

3. Elaious, 341/0, *IG*, II^2, 228 = Rhodes & Osborne 2003, 71; Lambert 2007a, no. 70. Elaious was consistently loyal to Athens (Dem. XXIII 158; cf. no. 1; *Agora* XVI 53).
4. Tenedos, 340/39, *IG*, II^2, 233 = Rhodes & Osborne 2003, 72 (and *IG*, II^2, 232, of 345–338, cf. Rhodes & Osborne 2003, p. 361); Lambert 2007a, no. 67 and no. 72.
5. An allied city?, ca. 340 or a little later, *IG*, II^2, 543. Apparently honoured a city which had taken measures against pirates in accordance with a policy sponsored by Moirokles (cf. Dem. LVIII 53,
157 56). See revised text and discussion, Lambert 2007a, no. 73. |

Between Chaironeia and Lamian War (or Lamian War?)

6. People of Kyth[nos], ca. 330–320, *IG*, II^2, 549 + 306, cf. Tracy 1995, 36 n. 2, 98, 99, 103; Lambert 2007a, no. 99. I confirm from autopsy Tracy's tentative association of the two fragments. A work of Tracy's "Cutter of *IG* II^2 244", 340/39–320. The allocation of 50 dr. for the inscribing costs indicates a date after c. 330 (Loomis 1998, 163–164).

Lamian War

7. People of Sikyon, honoured together with Euphron of Sikyon by a decree of 323/2, reinscribed in 318/7. *IG*, II^2, 448, 1–34. See most recently Oliver 2003, 94–110 (ph.). *IG*, II^2, 575 = Lambert 2006, no. 12 is apparently a fragment from the original version of the decree.

   Note also: 8. People of Tenos, ca. 350–300, *IG*, II^2, 660, decree 1; Lambert 2007a, no. 110. The date is uncertain (Reger 1992, 365–383, suggests ca. 306).

The pattern is strikingly similar to the treaties: before Chaironeia Athens is busy rewarding and encouraging loyal allies. 1 and 3, for Elaious, support a bulwark against Philip in the Chersonese; 4, the latest document of the Second Athenian League, rewards League member Tenedos for assistance, apparently in resisting Philip's attack on Perinthos and Byzantium. The city honoured by 5 had apparently participated in League measures against pirates, aimed principally at improving the grain supply. The context of 2, for Pellana, is obscure (anti-Macedonian alliance-building in the Peloponnese?).[16] After Alexander's death, she returns to the same mode, honouring a city which, under the influence of Euphron, was offering support to the rebellion against Macedon. In between there is little or nothing (the context of no. 6 is obscure. It mentions ?Kythnian general(s) and might date to the Lamian War period).

A rather different picture, however, emerges from the honorific decrees for individual foreigners (see Lambert 2006 and 2007a for a full catalogue). Such decrees may properly be regarded as diplomatic levers. After mid-century this becomes explicit in the wording, which, from then on, frequently emphasises the value of *philotimia* and incorporates 'hortatory intention' clauses, encouraging others to emulate the honorands in the expectation that they will be similarly honoured. Overt diplomatic intention is also apparent in the opening clause of a decree like Lambert 2007a no. 105 (late 320s): | 158

"In order that as many as possible of the friends of the king and of Antipater, having been honored by the Athenian People, may benefit the city of Athens…."

Decrees honouring individual foreigners do not let up in frequency after Chaironeia. The impression of diplomatic activity that emerges from them is not one of decreased intensity, but rather of a shift of emphasis and direction. Macedon is the dominant preoccupation, implicitly or explicitly, and they show Athens relating to it in, broadly, three ways: before (and briefly after) Chaironeia and again after the death of Alexander, the objective is to support and encourage individuals who were influential in their home cities on behalf of Athens and against Macedon;[17] both before and in the few years after Chaironeia and again during and after the Lamian War she honours opponents of Macedon seeking refuge at Athens;[18] and between Chaironeia and

[16] Cf. *SEG*, 3, 83; Rizakis 1995, 29–30.

[17] Certain or possible instances include: *IG*, II^2, 235 = Lambert 2006, no. 29, for Apelles of Byzantium (340/39?); *IG*, II^2, 231 + *SEG*, 51, 75 = Lambert 2006, no. 30, for Phokinos, Nikandros and Dexi- (of Megara?, 340/39); *IG*, II^2, 238 = Lambert 2006, no. 32, for Drakontides and Hegesias of Andros (338/7); *IG*, II^2, 276 = Lambert 2007a, no. 77, for Asklepiodoros son of Poly- (337/6?); *IG*, II^2, 575 = *IG*, II^2, 448 decree 1 = Lambert 2006, no. 12, for Euphron of Sikyon (323/2); *IG*, II^2, 368 decree 2 = Lambert 2006, no. 13, for Theophantos (323/2); *IG*, II^2, 365 = Lambert 2007a, no. 107, for Lapyris of Kleonai (323/2).

[18] E.g. *IG*, II^2, 218 = Lambert 2007a, no. 64, for Dioskourides and his brothers, of Abdera (346/5); *IG*, II^2, 226 = Rhodes & Osborne 2003, 70 = Lambert 2006, no. 4,

the Lamian War (and again after it) she can be seen exerting herself to maintain good relations with the newly dominant power and those who were influential there.[19] After Chaironeia, two new genres of decree emerge: decrees honouring grain traders, a response to Athens' sudden loss of international power and influence following the defeat and the consequent dissolution of the Second Athenian League, and to increased vulnerability to the acute supply problems of the 30s and 20s;[20] and, the third most numerous category, decrees for theatrical
159 benefactors and | celebrities aimed at maintaining Athens' status as the the most important centre of theatre in an increasingly competitive international environment.[21]

Apart from a few years after the Peloponnesian War, being a subordinate member of an alliance led by someone else was a new experience for Athens and required fundamental adjustments, not only in the direction of her foreign policy, but in her modes of operation on the international scene. If membership of the League of Corinth did not prohibit alliances, it certainly reduced the scope for making them and when Athens was not fighting any wars and had not got her own league to maintain, there was likewise little occasion to praise whole states. No inscribed Athenian alliance is extant after the Peloponnesian War until Athens' break from Sparta in the mid-90s; and after the Peace of Antalkidas in 386 she had also been obliged to show restraint. The terms of the alliance with Chios of 384/3 (*IG*, II^2, 34 = Rhodes and Osborne 2003, 20) are notably defensive, explicitly within the framework of the Peace and "on terms of freedom and autonomy". In fact the battle of Chaironeia represents a long term watershed. In the fifth century and the fourth century to 338 alliances are a fairly common component of the Athenian epigraphical corpus, after Chaironeia a very rare one.[22] In the immediate post-Chaironeia

---

for Arybbas, former king of Molossia (342?); *IG*, II^2, 237 = Rhodes & Osborne 2003, 77 = Lambert 2006, no. 5, for Akarnanian exiles (338/7); *IG*, II^2, 545 + 2406 = Tracy 1995, 87–88, for Thessalian exiles (321/0?); *IG*, II^2, 448 decree 2, for descendants of Euphron of Sikyon (318/7).

[19] E.g. *IG*, II^2, 240 = Lambert 2006, no. 33, for a son of Andromenes (337/6); perhaps *IG*, II^2, 239 = Lambert 2006, no. 55, for Alkimachos (337/6); *IG*, II^2, 402 + *SEG* XLII 91 = Lambert 2007a, no. 105, for "friend(s) of the king and Antipater" (late 320s).

[20] Decrees of this type were helpfully listed and discussed by Tracy 1995, 30–35. Some additions and adjustments to his list and further discussion at Lambert 2006, 2007a (inscriptions marked [G]).

[21] I discuss the ten decrees in this category and their historical context in Lambert 2008 (marked [Theat.] in Lambert 2006, 2007a).

[22] This may easily be seen from a perusal of the *Staatsverträge*.

period, however, what the epigraphical record shows is not so much a complete Athenian withdrawal from international diplomacy, but significant modifications in foreign policy objectives in response to the new circumstances and a marked shift of emphasis from the interstate level of operation to a focus on achieving those objectives through relations with individual foreigners. The overall impression is one of a radical diminution of Athens' role on the international stage, but not of a decrease in diplomatic energy.[23] | 160

Bibliography

Accame, S. (1941): *La lega ateniese*, Rome.

Brun, P. (1988): "Mytilène et Athènes au IVe siècle av. J.C.", *REA*, 90, 373–384.

Dreher, M. (1995): *Hegemon und Symmachoi. Untersuchungen zum zweiten athenischen Seebund*, Berlin.

Frézouls, E., and A. Jacquemin, eds. (1995): *Les relations internationales*, Paris.

Gauthier, Ph. (1972): *Symbola*, Nancy.

Gehrke, H.-J., N. Luraghi and L. Foxhall, eds. (forthcoming): *Intentional History. Spinning time in Ancient Greece.* [Stuttgart, 2010].

Hansen, M.H. (1981–2): "The Athenian *Heliaia* from Solon to Aristotle", *Classica & Mediaevalia*, 33, 9–47.

Hansen, M.H., and T.H. Nielsen, eds. (2004): *An Inventory of Archaic and Classical Poleis*, Oxford.

Heisserer, A.J. (1980): *Alexander the Great and the Greeks*, Norman, Oklahoma.

Humphreys, S. (2004): *The Strangeness of Gods*, Oxford.

Jordan, D., and J. Traill, eds. (2003): *Lettered Attica: A Day of Attic Epigraphy. Actes du Symposium d'Athènes/Proceedings of the Athens Symposium, 8 mars/March 2000*, Toronto (Publications of the Canadian Archaeological Institute at Athens, no. 3).

Knoepfler, D. (1971): "La date de l'annexion de Styra par Érétrie", *Bulletin de correspondance hellénique*, 95, 223–244.

——. (1984): "Le décret d'Hégésippe d'Athènes pour Érétrie", *Museum Helveticum*, 41, 152–161.

——. (1985): "Les Cinq-Cents à Érétrie", *REG*, 98, 243–259.

——. (1987): "Le décret d'Hégésippe d'Athènes pour Érétrie", in: *Praktika 8th Congress of Greek and Latin Epigraphy* 2 (1987), 312–319.

——. (1995): "Une paix de cent ans et un conflit en permanence: étude sur les relations diplomatiques d'Athènes avec Érétrie et les autres cités de l'Eubée au IVe siècle av. J.-C.", in: Frézouls & Jacquemin 1995, 309–364.

Lambert, S.D. (2003): "IG II^{2} 410: An Erasure Reconsidered", in: Jordan & Traill 2003, 56–67.

[23] There are also suggestions, in the epigraphical record of the post-Chaironeia period, of an aspiration to return to a world in which Athens is again capable of fighting wars and making alliances, consistent with the attention that was paid at this period to naval works and (re-)creation of the ephebeia (on these see most recently Humphreys 2004, chapter 3). For example, marked attention is paid to the cult of Athena Nike (*IG*, II^{2}, 403 = Lambert 2005, no. 3; [Plut.], *X Orat.*, 852b, cf. Paus. I, 29, 16; *IG*, II^{2}, 334 + = Rhodes & Osborne 2003, 81, 20–22 = Lambert 2005, no. 7; Lambert 2007a, 130). I explore this further in Lambert forthcoming.

——. (2004): "Athenian State Laws and Decrees 352/1–322/1: I Decrees Honouring Athenians", *Zeitschrift für Papyrologie und Epigraphik*, 150, 85–120.
——. (2005): "Athenian State Laws and Decrees 352/1–322/1: II Religious Regulations", *Zeitschrift für Papyrologie und Epigraphik*, 154, 125–159.
——. (2006): "Athenian State Laws and Decrees 352/1–322/1: III Decrees Honouring Foreigners. A. Citizenship, Proxeny and Euergesy", *Zeitschrift für Papyrologie und Epigraphik*, 158, 115–158. | 380
——. (2007a): "Athenian State Laws and Decrees 352/1–322/1: III Decrees Honouring Foreigners. B Other Awards", *Zeitschrift für Papyrologie und Epigraphik*, 159, 101–154.
——. (2007b): "Athenian State Laws and Decrees 352/351–322/321: IV. Treaties and Other Texts", *Zeitschrift für Papyrologie und Epigraphik*, 161, 67–100.
——. (2008): "Polis and Theatre in Lykourgan Athens. The Honorific Decrees", in: Matthaiou & Polinskaya 2008, 53–85.
——. (forthcoming): "Connecting with the Past in Lykourgan Athens. An Epigraphical Perspective", in: Gehrke *et al.* forthcoming, [225–38].
Loomis, W.T. (1998): *Wages, Welfare Costs and Inflation in Classical Athens*, Ann Arbor.
Matthaiou, A. and I. Polinskaya, eds. (2008): *Mikros Hieromnemon. Meletes eis mnemen Michael H. Jameson*, Athens.
Mitchel, F.W. (1964): "A Note on IG II^2 370", *Phoenix*, 18, 13–17.
Moretti, L. (1967): *Iscrizioni storiche ellenistiche*, I, Rome.
Oliver, G. (2003): "(Re-)locating Athenian Decrees in the Agora: *IG* II^2 448", in: Jordan & Traill 2003, 94–110.
Pečirka, J. (1966a): "Disiungenda", *Listy filologicke*, 89, 266–269.
Reger, G. (1992): "Athens and Tenos in the Early Hellenistic Age", *Classical Quarterly*, 42, 365–383.
Rhodes, P.J., and R. Osborne (2003): *Greek Historical Inscriptions 404–323 BC*, Oxford.
Rizakis, A.D. (1995): *Achaïe*, I, Athens.
Rosen, K. (1982): Review of Heisserer 1980, *Gnomon*, 54, 353–362.
Schweigert, E. (1937): "Inscriptions in the Epigraphical Museum", *Hesperia*, 6, 317–332.
——. (1938): "Inscriptions from the North Slope of the Acropolis", *Hesperia*, 8, 264–310.
——. (1939): "Greek Inscriptions (1–13)", *Hesperia*, 8, 1–47; "Epigraphical Notes", 170–176.
Stroud, R.S. (1971): "Inscriptions from the North Slope of the Acropolis, I", *Hesperia*, 40, 146–204.
Tod, M.N. (1948): *A Selection of Greek Historical Inscriptions. Vol. II. From 403 to 323 BC*, Oxford.
Tracy, S.V. (1995): *Athenian Democracy in Transition. Attic Letter-Cutters of 340 to 290 B.C.*, Berkeley.
Tronson, A. (1985): "The Relevance of IG II^2, 329 to the Hellenic League of Alexander the Great", *Ancient World*, 12, 15–19. | 390
Walbank, M. (1989): "A proxeny-decree of 353/2 B.C. (IG II^2 139)", *Ancient History Bulletin*, 3, 119–122.
Wallace, W.P. (1947): "The Demes of Eretria", *Hesperia*, 16, 115–146.
Wilhelm, A. (1942): *Attische Urkunden*, 5, Vienna.
Worthington, I. (1984): "*IG* II^2 370 and the Date of the Athenian Alliance with Aetolia", *Zeitschrift für Papyrologie und Epigraphik*, 57, 139–144.
——. (2004): "Alexander the Great and the Greeks in 336? Another Reading of *IG* II^2 329", *Zeitschrift für Papyrologie und Epigraphik*, 147, 59–71.
——. (2007): "Encore *IG* II^2 329", *Zeitschrift für Papyrologie und Epigraphik*, 162, 114–116.
Zahrnt, M. (1971): *Olynth und die Chalkidier*, Munich.

PART C

CHRONOLOGY

CHAPTER EIGHTEEN

ATHENIAN CHRONOLOGY 352/1–322/1 B.C.[*][1]

One of Michael Osborne's remarkable achievements in recent years has been to combine the administrative burdens of high university office with a continuing output of authoritative publications on one of the most complex and demanding topics in Ancient Greek History: the chronology of Athens in the 3rd century BC. The work is of fundamental importance since, in that century, the full sequence of Athenian archons has yet to be established. The 4th century is much better served by our sources and all the archons are securely dated. Other chronological issues, however, remain unresolved. In recent years I have been preparing a new edition of the ca. 270 inscribed Athenian state laws and decrees of the years 352/1–322/1 (*IG* II^3 fascicule 2), work which has necessarily entailed an engagement with these issues, for it is in this period that prescripts begin to contain all four dating elements: month and date in the month; prytany and date in the prytany. This generates so-called "calendar equations", which are fundamental to the study of Athenian chronology. I have noted improvements to readings and restorations of calendar equations and other chronological information in a series of articles preparatory to the new fascicule.[2] Based on this work I have compiled a table showing the key features of each year. This is presented below, followed by some remarks on points of interest. | 91

* This chapter was previously published in A. Tamis, C.J. Mackie and S. Byrne (eds.), *Philathenaios. Studies in Honour of Michael J. Osborne* (Athens, 2010), 91–102.

1 I am grateful to Peter Rhodes and Nick Fisher for reading a draft.

2 Lambert 2004, 2005, 2006, 2007a and b.

	Year	Archon[3]	Secretary (tribe)	Actual year type	Year type according to Metonic cycles
	352/1	Aristodemos	Not known (I)	–	I [Cycle V, year 5]
	351/0	Theellos	Chremes son of Ph[iloitios of Ioni]dai* ? (II)[4]	O?[5]	O [6]
	350/49	Apollodoros	Not known (III)		O [7]
	349/8	Kallimachos	Dieuches son of Demarchos of Phrearrhioi (IV)	–	I [8]
	348/7	Theophilos	Not known (see on 351/0) (V)	–	O [9]
	347/6	Themistokles	Lysimachos son of Sosidemos of Acharnai (VI)	I?[6]	I [10]
	346/5	Archias	Kephisodoros son of Atheno-phanes of Phlya (VII)	O?[7]	O [11]
	345/4	Euboulos	-enos son of I- of Oion (VIII)	O?[8]	O [12]
	344/3	Lykiskos	Not known (IX)	–	I [13]
	343/2	Pythodotos	Kleostratos son of Timos-thenes of Aigilia (X)	–	O [14]
92	342/1	Sosigenes	Not known (I)	–	O [15] |

[3] The evidence for the archons of this period is collected by Develin 1989.

[4] Might alternatively be restored,—son of Ph[- of Eiresi]dai (V), and dated to 348/7.

[5] The cost calculations at Dem. 4.28 are based on a year of 12 months.

[6] This can probably be inferred from Aeschin. 3.67 and *IG* II[2] 212 = Lambert 2006 no. 3 = Rhodes/Osborne, *GHI* 64. Cf. Lewis 1955.

[7] The equation Posideon 27 = pryt. V 31 at *IG* XII (6) 261, 56–7 (Athenian cleruchy on Samos) indicates that this was an ordinary year. The equation conforms to the Athenian system of months and prytanies (including use of the Athenian prytany name Pandionis) and, with Meritt 1961: 72–73, it seems reasonable to take it as evidence for the quality of the year at Athens (a different view at Pritchett 2001: 199 n. 10).

[8] *I. Délos* 104–24. 8 shows that the secretary of the Athenian shipbuilders at Delos was paid for 355 days work this year, which should therefore have been ordinary. Cf. Lewis 1955. The context probably implies that reckoning was by the Athenian calendar (a different view at Pritchett 2001: 199 n. 10).

Table (*cont.*)

Year	Archon	Secretary (tribe)	Actual year type	Year type according to Metonic cycles
341/0	Nikomachos	Onesippos son of Smikythos of Araphen (II)	I?[9]	I [16]
340/39	Theophrastos	Aspetos son of Demostratos of Kytherros (III)	–	O[17]
339/8	Lysimachides	- son of -on of Cholleidai* (IV)		I [18]
338/7	Chairondes	Philippos son of Antiphemos of Eiresidai (V)	–	O[19]
337/6	Phrynichos	Chairestratos son of Ameinias of Acharnai (VI)	–	O [Cycle VI, year 1]
336/5	Pythodelos	Not known (VII)	I?	I [2]
335/4	Euainetos	Proxenos son of Pylagoras of Acherdous (VIII)	O[10]	O [3]
334/3	Ktesikles	Mnesiphilos son of Mneson [of Phaleron] (IX)	O?	O [4]
333/2	Nikokrates	Archelas son of Chairias of Pallene (X)	I[11]	I [5]
332/1	Niketes	Aristonous son of Aristonous of Anagyrous (I)	O[12]	O [6]
331/0	Aristophanes	Not known (II)	O?	O [7]
330/29	Aristophon	Antidoros son of Antinous of Paiania (III)	I?	I [8]
329/8	Kephisophon	Sostratides son of Ekphantos of Eupyridai (IV)	O[13]	O [9]

[9] Probably implied by *IG* II^{2} 228 = Lambert 2007a no. 70 and *IG* II^{2} 229 = Lambert 2006 no. 54 (cf. Meritt 1961: 10).

[10] See below n. 25.

[11] See below n. 24.

[12] See below n. 25.

[13] *IG* II^{2} 1672 shows that the 1st and 2nd prytanies had 36 days, the 5th and 6th prytanies 35 days, indicating an ordinary year, consistent with the two extant prescripts, *IG* VII 4254 = Lambert 2004 no. 17 and *IG* II^{2} 353 = Lambert 2007a no. 100. Cf. Meritt 1961: 94–95.

Table (*cont.*)

Year	Archon	Secretary (tribe)	Actual year type	Year type according to Metonic cycles
328/7	Euthykritos	Pythodelos son of Pythodelos of Hagnous (V)	I?	I [10]
327/6	Hegemon	Autokles son of Autias of Acharnai (VI)	–	O [11]
326/5	Chremes	Kephisokles—(VII)	O?	O [12]
93 325/4	Antikles	Antiphon son of Koroibos of Eleusis (VIII)	I?	I [13] |
324/3	Hegesias	Euphanes son of Phrynon of Rhamnous (IX)	–	O [14]
323/2	Kephisodoros	Archias son of Pythodoros of Alopeke (X)	O?	O [15]
322/1	Philokles	Euthygenes son of Hephaisto-demos of Kephisia (I)	I?	I [16]

In addition to the archon, prescripts of Athenian decrees usually name the secretary of the Council. This office was also annual at this period, rotating among the ten tribes,[14] and is also important for the dating of inscriptions. How does the above list of annual secretaries compare with the most recent previous one, in Develin 1989? There are adjustments of detail, but no new secretary has been added. In fact "progress" has rather been in the other direction. Of the seven years in which the secretary is noted above as "not known", Develin left only four entirely blank. The other three depended on speculative reasoning, which has turned out to be questionable.[15]

[14] The tribal "secretary cycles" were discovered by Ferguson 1898. They were apparently suspended at some points between 261/0 and 239/8 (cf. Osborne 2003). There is no reason to doubt their operation at this period, but, as with the Metonic cycles (see below), a divergence from the cycle can not be ruled out in years for which we have no direct evidence. The two secretaries marked * are attested on inscriptions which lack an archon date and are allocated to specific years on the basis of the secretary cycle.

[15] Following earlier scholars, Develin tentatively allocated *IG* II^2 249, with secretary from Paiania (III), to 350/49, *IG* II^2 227, with secretary Kalliades of Euonymon (I), to 342/1, but in both cases the inscription may date before the introduction of annual

The changes help clarify the range of possible dates for some inscriptions.[16]

A similar story emerges with other aspects of dating. In addition to 43 inscriptions that were actively considered for inclusion in the fascicule, but were rejected, in some cases because of changes to previously accepted dates,[17] the | dating of around 50 inscriptions intended for 94
inclusion in the fascicule has been improved. There is only one, however, where I have proposed a new *single* solution to the identification of its year: *IG* II^2 546 = Lambert 2007a no. 94, honouring two men and previously dated after 322/1, but which perhaps belongs rather in 332/1. In general it has been a matter of widening, rather than narrowing down, the possibilities. For example, *IG* II^2 328 = Lambert 2007a no. 86, a decree proposed by Lykourgos, which fixes his first period of office as councillor and has conventionally been dated to 336/5, is as likely to belong in 335/4.

What implications do my results have for other outstanding issues in the chronology of this period? The topic that has attracted most attention in recent Athenian calendar studies relates to the pattern of ordinary and intercalary years. In order to reconcile the differing spans of time occupied by a solar year and 12 lunar months, Athens operated a system whereby an "intercalary" month was added to the year from time to time. According to Diodoros (12.36), in 433/2 the astronomer Meton presented a system of nineteen year cycles. Under this system certain years in a cycle were designated intercalary, namely the 2nd, 5th, 8th, 10th, 13th, 16th and 18th.[18] Over the duration of the cycle this would ensure the synchronisation of the solar and lunar calendars. According to Diodoros, most Greek cities continued to use the Metonic system to his day, but there has been no scholarly consensus on whether it was adopted in Athens. In recent years the cycles

---

secretaries in 365/4 or 364/3 (cf. Lambert 2007b, section D). He listed the secretary of 331/0 as Nikostratos, who is named on the moulding of the very fragmentary *IG* II^2 348 = Lambert 2007a no. 78, but the inscription preserves no archon date and Nikostratos may not have been secretary. If he was, the possible years are 336/5 and 331/0. Following the improved dating of *IG* II^2 328 (below), it can no longer be inferred from that inscription that the name of the secretary of 336/5 had 19 letters. On the secretary of 339/8 see Lambert 2007a no. 134a with n. 114.

[16] E.g. *IG* II^2 363 + *SEG* 51.72 = Lambert 2007a no. 84, honouring the grain trader Dionysios, which may date to 336/5, 331/0 or, less likely, 335/4 or 326/5.

[17] See Lambert 2007b, section D.

[18] See especially Dinsmoor 1931.

have found a champion in John Morgan.[19] For the Hellenistic period in general Christian Habicht has found Morgan's work persuasive,[20] and Michael Osborne has argued for the cycles in his studies of 3rd century chronology.[21] Before the mid-4th century there is insufficient evidence to corroborate the cycles. From then until the end of the classical Athenian democracy in 322/1 the flow of data improves considerably, thanks largely to an increase in the dating information supplied by the prescripts of inscribed Athenian decrees. An Athenian month normally contained either 30 days ("full") or 29 days ("hollow").[22] In
95 addition | to the 12 months, the year was divided for administrative purposes into ten prytanies. In any year the Councillors from each of the ten tribes served as the "prytany", or executive committee, of the Council in rotation. In ordinary years prytanies normally contained 35 or 36 days, in intercalary years 38 or 39 days (see further below). From 338/7 extant prescripts begin to include all four dating elements: month and date in the month; prytany and date in the prytany.

There are various ways in which the calendrical information in decree prescripts can show whether the year was ordinary or intercalary. The prescript may explicitly designate the month as intercalary.[23] Or, it may specify that a meeting took place on (37th? see below), 38th or 39th of a prytany, implying an intercalary year.[24] Or, the cal-

---

[19] He gives a brief summary of his findings at Morgan 1996. His work is as yet largely unpublished. I am grateful to him for discussion of this and other calendrical matters.

[20] Habicht 1997: v–vi.

[21] See Osborne 2003.

[22] The sequence of months was: Hekatombaion, Metageitnion, Boedromion, Pyanopsion, Maimakterion, Posideon, Gamelion, Anthesterion, Elaphebolion, Mounichion, Thargelion, Skirophorion. The year apparently began with the first new moon after the summer solstice. Cf. Plato, *Laws* 767c with Morgan 1996.

[23] E.g. Ποσιδεῶνος ἐμβολίμου ἐν[δεκάτει, *IG* II^2 785.4 (ii BC, archon Charikles). There is no instance of this in an Athenian decree prescript at this period. The one case where it appears that a meeting took place in an intercalary month is *IG* II^2 360 = Lambert 2006 no. 43 = Rhodes/Osborne, *GHI* 95. 4–5, passed in 325/4 on 34th of pryt. 5, 11th of a month which (not unusually at this period) is unspecified on the stone, but can probably be identified as intercalary Posideon, in sequence behind *IG* II^2 361 = Lambert 2007b no. 47, passed on 23 Thargelion = pryt. X 5.

[24] E.g. *IG* II^2 338 = Lambert 2004 no. 15, of 333/2, on which the Assembly decree was passed on 9 Metageitnion = pryt. I 39, the preceding Council decree (ll. 32–3) on the previous day, 38th of the prytany.

endar equation as a whole may show that the year was ordinary or intercalary.[25]

The last two columns in the table above set out the sequence of ordinary and intercalary years. The final column shows the quality of the year as predicted by the Metonic cycles.[26] The preceding column shows the quality of the year as implied by the empirical data. Except where noted in the footnotes, these data derive from the prescripts of Athenian laws and decrees.[27] "I" or "O" mean that the year is clearly attested as ordinary or intercalary. Where there is a degree of uncertainty this is indicated by "I?" or "O?". To qualify for designation as "I?" or "O?", any epigraphic | restoration or other editorial interven- 96
tion must be driven by considerations other than preconceptions about the quality of the year; for example, in a text arranged stoichedon[28] (as most are at this period), the number of letter spaces available for a restoration. Otherwise I leave the penultimate column blank. Three examples of "blank" years will help illustrate this policy. Two inscriptions have been attributed to the year 339/8. *IG* II 221 = Lambert 2004 no. 8 is under strong suspicion of being a forgery and can not, therefore, be used as evidence for the quality of this year. *SEG* 16.52 = Lambert 2007a no. 134a was passed on pryt. X 32, but neither month name nor date in the month is preserved. Since the tenth prytany would have more than 32 days in both an ordinary and an intercalary year, the inscription does not determine whether this year was ordinary or intercalary. 337/6 is a similar case. The key inscription is *IG* II^2 242 + 373 = Lambert 2006 no. 34 (decree I).[29] It was passed on ἕνηι καὶ νέαι (the "last day" of) [Skirophorion] = pryt. X [35]. The decree was honorific and, as was common with such decrees, was

[25] E.g. *SEG* 48.101 = Lambert 2007a no. 87, passed on 18 Skirophorion = pryt. X 23, 335/4, shows the year was ordinary. Similarly, the four extant decrees of 332/1 passed on 19 Elaphebolion = pryt. VIII 7 (Lambert 2006 no. 39 = *Agora* XVI 79, no. 40 = *IG* II^2 347, Lambert 2007a no. 95 = *IG* II^2 346 and no. 96 = *IG* II^2 345) and the two on 11 Thargelion = pryt. IX 23 (*IG* VII 4252 = Lambert 2004: 107 and *IG* VII 4253 = Lambert 2004 no. 16) show that year was ordinary. For an equation for an intercalary year see previous note.

[26] Cf. Dinsmoor 1931: 423.

[27] The detail for each inscription of every year can be traced via Lambert 2004, 2005, 2006, 2007a and b. Meritt 1961 tabulated the data then available (to be used with caution).

[28] I.e. in vertical columns such that each line has the same number of letters.

[29] *IG* II^2 243 = Lambert 2004 no. 20 was also passed on this day, as perhaps was *IG* II^2 276 = Lambert 2007a no. 77, but they do not supply independent evidence for the date.

apparently passed at the last Assembly of the year. "Skirophorion" suits precisely the number of letter spaces available, as does "35th" (πέμπτηι καὶ τριακοστῆι). However, if the year had been intercalary, ἕνηι καὶ νέαι Skirophorion would normally have coincided with pryt. X 38. On a possible spelling, ὀγδοίηι καὶ τριακοστῆι,[30] that would also suit the available space, as would pryt. X 37, ἑβδόμηι καὶ τριακοστῆι. That is also possible, since end-year adjustments could cause ἕνηι καὶ νέαι Skirophorion sometimes to fall on pryt. X 34 in an ordinary year, pryt. X 37 in an intercalary year.[31] No other inscription bears significantly on the quality of the year.[32] 324/3 is a third case of this type. The
97 key inscription for determining the | quality of the year is *IG* II^2 362 = Lambert 2007b no. 50. The archon's name, Hegesias, is preserved, dating the inscription firmly to 324/3. In more recent scholarship the prescript is restored to [18] Thargelion = pryt. IX 29, which is a regular equation for an ordinary year. However, the date in the month, ὀγδόηι ἐπὶ δέκα, is wholly restored and "13th", τρίτηι ἐπὶ δέκα (restored in *IG* II^2), would suit the space equally well and be consistent with an intercalary year.[33]

A straightforward example of my policy with "I?" and "O?" is 331/0, where the key inscription, *IG* II^2 349 = Lambert 2007a no. 97, was passed on 10 Skirophorion = pryt. X 1[6], a regular equation for an ordinary year. The "six" in "sixteen" ([ἕκτ]ει καὶ δεκάτει) is the only number that suits the space. However, it is restored and to that extent

---

[30] For the more usual ὀγδόηι. Cf. *IG* II^2 347 = Lambert 2006 no. 40.

[31] Cf. *IG* II^2 415 = Lambert 2004 no. 5 (ἕνηι καὶ νέαι Skir. = pryt. X 34).

[32] *IG* II^2 239 = Lambert 2006 no. 55 can be restored [5 Gamelion] = [pryt. VI 5] in an ordinary year. Spacing probably implies the 6th prytany, but *e.g.* 5 Gamelion = pryt. VI 18 would suit for an intercalary year. *Agora* XVI 72 = Lambert 2007a no. 135 can also be restored to 5 Gamelion = pryt. VI 5, but we know only that it was passed on 5th of a prytany and there is insufficient basis for confident restoration. *SEG* 35.64 = Lambert 2004 no. 2 was passed on pryt. X [2]2 and has been restored to 16 Skirophorion, which suits an ordinary year (and was tentatively accepted by me [2004: 91 n. 27]), but 13 Skir. = pryt. X 22 would suit an intercalary year. *Agora* XVI 73 = Lambert 2007b no. 14, was passed in pryt. IX, *IG* II^2 240 = Lambert 2006 no. 33 and *IG* II^2 241 = Lambert 2007b no. 33 on the same day of pryt. X (same chairman), but they preserve no other calendrical information.

[33] No other inscription bears on the quality of 324/3. *IG* II^2 547, previously dated to 324/3, might alternatively date to 326/5 or 325/4. See Lambert 2004 no. 7 with pp. 101–103. The only information preserved in *Agora* XVI 91 = Lambert 2007b no. 49, is that it was passed on a date in prytany later than the thirtieth, insufficient basis for restoration. *Agora* XVI 92 = Lambert 2007a no. 148 was passed in pryt. VI, but preserves no other calendrical information. *IG* II^2 454 = Lambert 2007b no. 48 dates to 26 Skirophorion, pryt. X, apparently of this year, but there is no date in the prytany.

uncertain. 336/5 is another example. The only decrees which bear on the quality of this year are in *IG* II^2 330 + 445 = Lambert 2004 no. 3. The Assembly decree of this year at ll. 47–8 was passed on the last day of a month, ἕνηι καὶ νέαι, [3]7th of a prytany. τριακοστῆι in the prytany date is wholly restored, but is implied by spacing. The reference to 37th day would usually imply an intercalary year. However, like other decrees honouring Athenian officials, it was probably passed at the last Assembly of the year, a time when we know that calendrical adjustments might be made by the addition or subtraction of days. Though there would be no secure parallel for a 37-day prytany in an ordinary year, such an irregularity can not be ruled out with certainty. That the year was intercalary gains some confirmation, however, from the dating of the preceding Council meeting at ll. 29–31, to 14th of an unknown month, 2nd of an unknown prytany. One would normally expect the preparatory Council meeting for an Assembly in the tenth prytany to have taken place in the ninth or tenth prytanies. The numbers do not suit the tenth prytany, in an ordinary or an intercalary year, but they suit the ninth prytany in an intercalary year, in which the second day could fall comfortably on 14 Mounichion. In an ordinary year, pryt. IX 2 would fall several days later in Mounichion. Some other cases of "O?" or "I?" are more complex, but in each case the evidence favours the quality of year as shown. | 98

What conclusions can we draw about the operation of the Metonic cycles at this period? First, and importantly, the empirical data are consistent with their operation. In other words, there is no year where they indicate a year-quality different from that predicted by the Metonic cycles. Of the 31 years under review, in four (on a conservative view) there is very good evidence that the quality of the year was that predicted by the cycles; in a further fourteen years there are strong indications that it was. In over half (18 of 31) of these years, therefore, it seems that the Metonic cycle was certainly or probably observed. It is a reasonable working hypothesis that, in the 13 other years of this period, the cycle was also in operation. However, there is also every indication that, in general, the Athenian calendar did not operate according to rigid rules, and that there was scope for flexibility to bend or suspend such rules as there were, when this was demanded by political or other circumstances. To take a notorious example, at the end of the 4th century Mounichion was renamed Anthesterion to accommodate Demetrios' wish to be initiated in the Lesser Mysteries and then Boedromion for his initiation in the Greater

Mysteries.[34] Moreover, the intercalation of days into the festival calendar was a fairly frequent occurrence. No Assembly certainly occurred on such a day at this period, but Assemblies on such days are well attested later in the 4th century;[35] and irregularities in calendar equations within the same year seem to imply that such intercalations happened in this period also.[36] For that reason, unless we have evidence for a particular year, we can not prove that it was ordinary or intercalary, simply because it was predicted to have the quality under the Metonic cycles. There are conceivable circumstances under which the archon (the Athenian official responsible for regulation of time), or the Assembly or *nomothetai* (if the matter was regulated by decree or law, as it probably was) might have decided to make a particular year ordinary or intercalary out of the normal cycle.

I conclude with brief remarks on two other outstanding issues. The first relates to the number of days in a prytany. *Ath. Pol.* 43.2, which was written during this period, states that the first four prytanies of a year had 36 days, the remaining six 35 days and, though he does not
99 state it, this has reasonably been extrapolated | to imply that, in an intercalary year, a comparable system operated, with 39 days in the first four prytanies, 38 days in the others. Did *Ath. Pol.'s* rule always apply? There is no reason, in any of the prescripts I have studied, to suppose that it was contravened. All are either definitely consistent with the rule or can be restored or interpreted in conformity with it. Where a calendar equation suggests an anomaly, this is more likely, on general grounds, to be the result of interference with the festival calendar than interference with the prytanies. In intercalary years whole months were inserted into the festival calendar. On other occasions, as we have seen, there is direct evidence for intercalations of individual days and even, in effect, for transposition of days and months to a completely different time of the year from usual. There is no direct evidence for this sort of tampering with the prytany calendar. As with other aspects of the calendar, it is possible that there was an undocu-

[34] Plut. *Dem.* 26, cf. 12; Diod. 20.110.

[35] E.g. *IG* II² 358. 3–4 with Tracy 1995: 152 (307/6?), 'Ε[λαφηβολιῶνος ἕνηι καὶ ν]-έαι ἐμβολίμωι. See also *IG* II² 458 (307/6). *IG* II² 368 decree 2, of 323/2, may have been passed on an intercalary day, but that depends on restoration (see Lambert 2006 no. 13).

[36] E.g. *IG* II² 242 + 373 = Lambert 2006 no. 34 (decree 2), of 322/1, where the fully preserved calendar equation, 2 Thargelion = pryt. IX 23, probably implies an intercalary year in which there was an additional intercalation of about 4 days.

mented irregularity, a possibility increased by the fact that information given us by *Ath. Pol.* is not always fully accurate or complete or, where rules are concerned, immutable.[37] But as it is a reasonable working hypothesis that the secretary cycles and the Metonic cycles applied at this period, it is a reasonable working hypothesis that the rule of *Ath. Pol.* also applied.

Much research remains to be done on the sequence of full and hollow months and the omitted day in the hollow month (was it the "second day from the end of the month", δευτέρα φθίνοντος, or an earlier one?).[38] The prescripts of this period are relevant,[39] but they do not supply conclusive evidence on these questions, which need examination across a much wider time span. John Morgan is making important progress, as yet unpublished. Exchanges with him[40] lead me to offer one observation. The lunar calendar was, first and foremost, a religious calendar, used to regulate the timing of sacrifices and festivals. The dates on which religious events took place were specified by law, in particular, at this period, by the sacrificial calendar of the polis, inscribed as part of the general revision of Athenian law at the end of
the 5th century, and amended from time to | time by new laws when 100
additions were made to the festival programme.[41] The calendar specified which sacrifices were to take place on which days in various cycles (annual, biennial, quadrennial etc.). If the specified date was δευτέρα φθίνοντος, or any other date, that date ought not to have been omitted in the relevant month of the relevant cycle. This raises the possibility that the omitted day was not, as commonly assumed, immutable, but varied depending on the requirements of the religious calendar.[42]

---

[37] Cf. the comments of Rhodes 1981: 518–520. He now writes to me: "I still believe what I said... except that I'd now say more positively that what *Ath. Pol.* states is probably what the law stated", but "we shouldn't regard a rule which happens to be stated in *Ath. Pol.* as immutable".

[38] Discussed by Pritchett most recently at 2001, chapters 2 and 3 (to be read with caution). He argues for δευτέρα φθίνοντος. Meritt had supported ἐνάτη φθίνοντος, the day on which the countdown to the end of the month began.

[39] See e.g. *IG* II² 339a = Lambert 2006 no. 38 with n. 70.

[40] See also Pritchett 2001: 65–66.

[41] Cf. Lambert 2005: 144.

[42] Sacrificial calendar: Lambert 2002 (add the new fragment, Gawlinski 2007). At F3A l. 5 an event probably in Thargelion, perhaps connected with the Plynteria, and possibly biennial, is dated [δευτέραι] φθίνοντος. In a private religious calendar, end of 1st cent. AD (?), *IG* II² 1367. 26, an offering is dated to the second day before the end of Mounichion. In the table of Athenian festivals at Parker 2005 no event is dated to "29th" of a month and only the continuation of the Eleusinian Mysteries in

Bibliography

Develin, R. 1989: *Athenian Officials 684–321 BC.* Cambridge.

Dinsmoor, W.B. 1931: *The Archons of Athens in the Hellenistic Age.* Cambridge Mass.

Ferguson, W.S. 1898: *The Athenian Secretaries.* Cornell University Press.

Gawlinski, L. 2007: "The Athenian Calendar of Sacrifices. A new fragment from the Athenian Agora", *Hesperia* 76: 37–55.

Habicht, Ch. 1997: *Athens from Alexander to Antony.* Cambridge, Mass.

Lambert, S.D. 2000: "Two notes on Attic leges sacrae", *Zeitschrift für Papyrologie und Epigraphik* 130: 71–80.

—— 2002: "The Sacrificial Calendar of Athens", *Annual of the British School at Athens* 97: 353–399.

—— 2004: "Athenian State Laws and Decrees, 352/1–322/1. I Decrees Honouring Athenians". *Zeitschrift für Papyrologie und Epigraphik* 150: 85–120.

—— 2005: "Athenian State Laws and Decrees, 352/1–322/1. II Religious Regulations". *Zeitschrift für Papyrologie und Epigraphik* 154: 125–159.

—— 2006: "Athenian State Laws and Decrees, 352/1–322/1. III Decrees Honouring Foreigners. A. Citizenship, Proxeny and Euergesy", *Zeitschrift für Papyrologie und*
101 *Epigraphik* 158: 115–158. |

—— 2007a: "Athenian State Laws and Decrees, 352/1–322/1. III Decrees Honouring Foreigners. B. Other Awards", *Zeitschrift für Papyrologie und Epigraphik* 159: 101–154.

—— 2007b: "Athenian State Laws and Decrees, 352/1–322/1. IV Treaties and Other Texts", *Zeitschrift für Papyrologie und Epigraphik* 161: 67–100.

Lewis, D.M. 1955: "Notes on Attic Inscriptions. XXVI", *Annual of the British School at Athens* 50: 25–26.

Meritt, B.D. 1961: *The Athenian Year.* Berkeley.

Morgan, J.D. 1996: "The Calendar and the Chronology of Athens", *American Journal of Archaeology* 100: 395.

Osborne, M.J. 2003: "The Athenian Archon Diomedon and his Successors", *Zeitschrift für Papyrologie und Epigraphik* 143: 95–100.

Parker, R. 2005: *Polytheism and Society at Athens.* Oxford.

Pritchett, W.K. 2001: *Athenian Calendars and Ekklesias.* Amsterdam.

Rhodes, P.J. 1981: *A Commentary on the Aristotelian Athenaion Politeia.* Oxford.

Tracy, S.V. 1995: *Athenian Democracy in Transition. Attic Letter-Cutters of 340 to 290*
102 *BC.* Berkeley. |

Boedromion is dated to "21st" or "22nd". The "deme" calendars may also be relevant. Note e.g. in the "Greater Demarchy" at Erchia sacrifices on δεκάτη ὑστέρα (= "21st") Hekatombaion (*SEG* 21.541 col. 3. 1–3, col. 4. 1–3) and Mounichion (col. 4. 41–43). This cycle may have been biennial (cf. Lambert 2000: 75).

APPENDIX

SELECT ADDENDA AND CORRIGENDA (2011)

In 2011 I published two papers, originally delivered at conferences in 2009, which discuss in broader contexts a number of the inscribed laws and decrees treated in this book:

"What was the point of honorific decrees in Classical Athens", in S.D. Lambert (ed.), *Sociable Man. Essays on Ancient Greek Social Behaviour in Honour of Nick Fisher* (Swansea, 2011), 193–214.

"Some Political Shifts in Lykourgan Athens", in V. Azoulay and P. Ismard (eds.), *Clisthène et Lycurgue d'Athènes. Autour du politique dans la cité classique* (Paris, 2011), 175–90.

p. 40. *I Orop* 296 [*IG* II^3 1, 349]. Decree honouring Amphiaraos. See now A. Scafuro, "The Crowning of Amphiaraos", in L. Mitchell and L. Rubinstein (eds.), *Greek History and Epigraphy. Essays in Honour of P.J. Rhodes* (Swansea, 2009), 59–86.

p. 46 no. 27. *IG* II^2 1155. The text requires revision. I have an article in preparation.

p. 65 no. 6. *IG* II^2 333 [*IG* II^3 1, 445]. Laws about cult objects. See article cited below, on p. 66, 230–31.

p. 66. *IG* II^2 403 [*IG* II^3 1, 444]. I discussed this inscription, and several others, in the context of the "past-connective" mentality of the Lykourgan period in "Connecting with the Past in Lykourgan Athens: an Epigraphical Perspective," in L. Foxhall, H.-J. Gehrke and N. Luraghi (eds.), *Intentional History. Spinning Time in Ancient Greece* (Stuttgart, 2010), 225–38.

p. 80 no. 7. *IG* II^2 334 + *SEG* XVIII 13 [*IG* II^3 1, 447]. Law and Decree about Little Panathenaia. Further progress with this text is registered in the *IG* apparatus, including valuable suggestions made to me per ep. by Simone Follet, the late Michael Jameson, Charalambos Kritzas and Angelos Matthaiou. See also the article cited above (on p. 66), 231–33.

p. 82 no. 10. *SEG* XXV 82 [*IG* II^3 1, 551]. About the Dipolieia. See the article cited above (on p. 66), 233.

p. 101 no. 2. *IG* II^2 207 [*IG* II^3 1, 295]. Decree honouring Orontes. See M.J. Osborne, "A Ghost Archon?", *ZPE* 164 (2008), 81–84. In my view 349/8 remains the most likely date for this decree.

p. 102 no. 5. *IG* II^2 237 [*IG* II^3 1, 316]. Decree honouring Phormio and Karphinas. See my article cited above (on p. 66), 234–35. On the proposer, Hegesippos of Sounion, see now J.K. Davies, "Hegesippos of Sounion. An Underrated Politician", in S.D. Lambert (ed.), *Sociable Man. Essays on Ancient Greek Social Behaviour in Honour of Nick Fisher* (Swansea, 2011), 11–24.

p. 114 no. 17. *IG* II^2 267 [*IG* II^3 1, 495]. William Mack per ep. plausibly identifies the tiny fragment of relief on this inscription as a crab's claw, which, since the crab is a symbol of Akragas (e.g. *Agora* XXVI 171 no. 421), supports the possibility I raised in *ZPE* 158 that the honorand might be restored as from that city, -τρωι Ἀκ[ραγαντίνωι. The fragment does not seem to be part of the same inscription as *IG* II^3 1, 432, the decree proposed by Lykourgos for the grain trader Sopatros of Akragas (e.g. the hand is different and perhaps also the marble), but restoration of the honorand of 495 as -πά]τρωι and a family connection with Sopatros are attractive. Note that Lykourgos, proposer of the decree for Sopatros, proposed decrees for two apparently related Plataians: *IG* II^3 1, 352 for Eudemos son of Philourgos of Plataia and *IG* II^3 1, 345 for [Eudemos son of Eud?]emos of Plataia.

p. 117 no. 27. *IG* II^2 357 [*IG* II^3 1, 420]. Proxeny for a man from Eretria. -]ιτοκλῆς .[- - - ἐγραμμάτε]υεν (ll. 3–5). In 2006 I expressed doubts about the restoration of the secretary of 327/6 Αὐ]ιτοκλῆς [Αὐτίου Ἀχαρνεὺς. These have been confirmed by Klaus Hallof's reading on the Berlin squeeze, and my subsequent confirmation at a further autopsy of the stone in Athens, of what appears to be the bottom of a central vertical after -τοκλῆς. Taking into account also the extent of uninscribed surface to the left of this apparent letter stroke, this would seem to rule out a father's name in A[. The inscription perhaps dates to a year after ca. 340 (indicated by ἐκκλ[ησία, l. 7) whose secretary is otherwise unknown.

p. 117 no. 30. *IG* II^2 231 + *SEG* LI 75 [*IG* II^3 1, 312]. Decree proposed by Demosthenes. J. Kroll suggests per ep. that the letter A in the pediment might signify the ethnic Ἀργεῖος. Cf. on coins *Agora* XXVI 241–42 nos. 781, 783.

p. 122 no. 44. *IG* II^2 342 + *SEG* XXXV 70 [*IG* II^3 1, 468]. Decree honouring Apses and Hieron of Tyre. Angelos Matthaiou attractively suggests per ep. reading ll. 3–5 e.g. ε|ὐωνότερο]ν (scil. σῖτον) ἢ ὁ ἐξ Ἰ[τα]λ̣ίας καθίστ[αται|ι. The honorand had imported grain at a cheaper price from Carthage (. ἐ]κ Καρχη̣[δόνος.....⁹....|....⁷...κ]εκόμικ[εν ll. 2–3) than was available from Italy.

p. 141 no. 66. *IG* II^2 220 [*IG* II^3 1, 304]. Decrees honouring the city of Pellana. Köhler thought no more than two lines were missing between fragments a and b. Angelos Matthaiou points out, per ep., that one can not rule out that the lacuna was slightly longer.

p. 141 no. 68. *IG* II^2 435 [*IG* II^3 1, 404]. Angelos Matthaiou per ep. defends Wilhelm's restoration of the honorands (l. 3) as Νεα]πολιτῶν.

p. 144 no. 81. *IG* II^2 408 [*IG* II^3 1, 339]. Decree honouring Mnemon and Kallias of Herakleia. R. Descat, in B. Marin and C. Virlouvet (eds.), *Nourrir les cités de Méditerranée,* 592, suggests (l. 12) πυρῶν Σι̣[νωπικῶν, comparing *IG* II^3, 1, 440, where, however, there is no reference to Sinope in the text preserved on the stone. The conventional restoration (Köhler's), Σι̣[κελικῶν (there is probable trace of the lower [Koe.] or upper [Lam.] section of a central vertical after the Σ), is preferable. Cf. Wilhelm, *Attische Urkunden* 5 (1942), 152–54 no. LVI; [Dem.] 56.9.

p. 145 no. 85. *IG* II^2 283 [*IG* II^3 1, 430]. Decree honouring Ph- of Salamis. See now D. Whitehead, "Athenians in Sicily in the Fourth Century BC", in C. Cooper (ed.), *Epigraphy and the Greek Historian* (Toronto, 2008), 57–67.

p. 151 no. 103. *IG* II^2 356 [*IG* II^3 1, 361]. Following exchanges with several correspondents I am now persuaded that Kirchner's restoration of the honorand as an otherwise unknown Memnon (...⁵.. ἐπειδ]ὴ Μ[έ]μνω[ν] l. 11) is incorrect. After ἔδοξ[ε]ν [τῶι] δήμωι[ι (ll. 10–11) one expects the name of a proposer (cf. e.g. *IG* II^3, 1, 352.9–11; 355.9–10; 356.8–10; 359.8–9; 362.6–7). From the Berlin squeeze Klaus Hallof tentatively suggests...⁵..]ν Ε̣[ὐ]μνή̣[σ]τ[ου] Ἀ-. The wording of ll. 23–34 (praising the ancestors and father of Thymondas) suggests that the honorand was Thymondas himself.

p. 171 no. 127. Lawton no. 137 [*IG* II^3 1, 395]. This relief from an honorific decree is in the British Museum (inv. no. 773). From autopsy in 2010 I read, above the relief, labelling the figure of Athena depicted below: Ἀ̣θ[ηνᾶ]. On the moulding below the relief: θ[εοί].

p. 185 no. 6. *IG* II^2 125 [*IG* II^3 1, 399]. Decree against attackers of Eretria. On the proposer, Hegesippos of Sounion, see the article by J.K. Davies cited above, note on p. 102 no. 5.

p. 209. *IG* II^2 824 + *SEG* XXXII 113 [*IG* II^3 1, 311]. Decrees honouring Athenian officials. See S.G. Byrne, "The Dedication of the Orgeones of Prospalta, *IG* II^2 2355", in A.P. Matthaiou and I. Polinskaya (eds.), *Mikros Hieromnemon. Meletes eis mnemen Michael H. Jameson* (Athens, 2008), 117–32, at 125–6 no. 1.

p. 210 no. 7. See note on p. 80 no. 7.

pp. 211–12 no. 68. See note on p. 141 no. 68.

pp. 213–14. See note on p. 145.

p. 232. In "The First Athenian Agonothetai", *Horos* 14–16 (2000–2003), 99–105, I argued that (a) the *agonothetes* on *IG* II^2 3073 was not Xenokles, but his brother Androkles of Sphettos, (b) *pace* my comment here, the lively old gentleman named Androkles alluded to by Menander at *Samia* 606–8 was indeed this same Androkles of Sphettos, σφάττοι (608) being a punning allusion to his deme.

pp. 249–72. See note on p. 117 no. 30.

pp. 273–84. See note on p. 145.

p. 297. On Androkles of Sphettos see note on p. 232.

pp. 321–336. I explored some of the themes of this paper further in "*LGPN* and the Epigraphy and History of Attica", in R.W.V. Catling and F. Marchand (eds.), *Onomatologos. Studies in Greek Personal Names presented to Elaine Matthews* (Oxford [Oxbow], 2010), 143–52.

p. 342. S.G. Byrne, "Some People in Third-Century Athenian Decrees", in R.W.V. Catling and F. Marchand (eds.), *Onomatologos. Studies in Greek Personal Names presented to Elaine Matthews* (Oxford [Oxbow], 2010), 122–31, at 127–28, attractively suggests that the second decree on *IG* II^2 713 + Add. p. 666 is a third-century re-inscription of one proposed by Demades the famous orator, not, as previously believed, one proposed by a homonymous grandson. In that case this was a third decree proposed by Demades in a theatrical context.

Inscriptions in IG *II^3 1, 2, published since the prolegomena collected in this volume*

Walbank = M.B. Walbank, *Fragmentary Decrees from the Athenian Agora, Hesperia Suppl.* 38 (2008).

1. *IG* II^3 1, 402. Honours Kephisophon of Paiania. Ca. 345–335. G.E. Malouchou, in *Attika Epigraphika. Meletes pros timen tou Ch. Habicht* (2009), 97–110, joining a new fragment with one first published by Walbank, 24–25 no. 22.

2. *IG* II^3 1, 407. Ca. 345–320. Walbank, 22–23 no. 20.

3. *IG* II^3 1, 410. Ca. 345–320. Walbank, 15–16 no. 12.

4. *IG* II^3 1, 425. Ca. 340–320? Walbank, 23–24 no. 21.

5. *IG* II^3 1, 451. Ca. 335–300? Walbank, 31–32 no. 29.

6. *IG* II^3 1, 465. Ca. 334–314. Walbank, 28 no. 26.

7. *IG* II^3 1, 486. Shortly before 321/0?. Walbank, 26 no. 24.

8. The following are included among the *Leges et Decreta generis dubii et Incerta*: *IG* II^3 1, 532 = Walbank, 16 no. 13; 537 = Walbank 20–21 no. 17; 538 = Walbank 21 no. 18; 541 = Walbank 21–22 no. 19; 545 = V.N. Bardani, *Horos* 17–21 (2004–2009), 39–44; 546 = Walbank 19 no. 16; 547 = Walbank 14–15 no. 11; 548 = Walbank 25–26 no. 23; 568 = Walbank 30 no. 28.

INDICES

1. *Inscriptions Discussed*

2. *IG II^3 Concordance*

3. *Names*

A. *Honorands (persons, cities etc.)*

B. *Other Persons*

4. *Subjects*

5. *Greek*
(*see also* Grammar [Index 4])